Teacher Guidebook
Level E

A Reason For Spelling® Teacher Guidebook - Level E

ISBN#: 0-936785-34-9
TL#: SPTGE2012

Published by The Concerned Group, Inc.
P.O. Box 1000, Siloam Springs, AR 72761

Publisher: Russ L. Potter, II • Project Director: Kristin Potter
Senior Editor: Bill Morelan • Layout and Design: Mark Decker
Copy Editor: Mary Alice Hill • Story Editor: Tricia Schnell
Proofreaders: Daniel Swatsenberg, Rachel Tucker

Created by MOE Studio, Inc.
Authors: Rebecca Burton, Eva Hill, Leah Knowlton, Kay Sutherland
Black and White Illustrations: James McCullough
Colorization for Student Edition: Mark Decker
Design and Layout: Greg Hauth • Project Leader: Greg Sutherland

Printed in the United States on recyclable paper

For more information about ***A Reason For Spelling***®, ***A Reason For Handwriting***®, ***A Reason For Science***® and ***A Reason For Guided Reading***® go to: ***www.AReasonFor.com***

Contents:

Acknowledgments:

Field Test Participants:

Virginia Allen, East Rockaway, New York • Mrs. Christine Baker, Belleville, Pennsylvania • Judy M. Banks, Carmichael, California • Darya Birch, San Clemente, California • Mari Anne Burns, Baton Rouge, Louisiana • Karen Dafflitto, St. Louis, Missouri • Kristen J. Dorsett, Prescott, Arizona • Ms. Laura Guerrera, East Rockaway, New York • Mrs. Anne Gutierrez, San Antonio, Texas • Jeanette O. Kappel, Winstead, Minnesota • Sharon K. Kobilka, San Antonio, Texas • Connie Kozitza, Winsted, Minnesota • Vivian I. Sawyer, Carmichael, California • Harold W. Souther, San Antonio, Texas • Cleo F. Staples, Auburn, California • Suezy Tucker, Auburn, California • Martha Woodbury, Los Angeles, California

Special thanks to:

Dr. Larry Burton, Dr. Carol Campbell, Dr. Lee Netherton, Melvin Northrup, Phyllis Paytee, Dr. Linda Romig

Placement Tests

In order to evaluate readiness and accurately meet individual student need, a simple placement test is recommended at the beginning of each school year.

***Step 1:** Administer the test*

Number your paper from one to twenty. I will say the word once, use the word in a sentence, then say the word again. Write a word beside each number on your paper.

(Allow ample time and carefully monitor progress.)

***Step 2:** Evaluate the corrected tests using the following criteria:*

If the student correctly spells 17 to 20 words:

- Assign the student to Level E program
- Encourage the student to work independently
- Select and assign several Other Word Forms to spell and test

If the student correctly spells 8 to 16 words:

- Assign the student to Level E program
- Allow opportunities to work independently
- Offer Other Word Forms activities

If the student correctly spells 0 to 7 words:

- Assign student to Level E, but use regular lessons without Other Word Forms
- Be sure student completes all regular activities
- May wish to administer Level D test

Placement Test Level E

1.	athlete	He is my favorite **athlete.**
2.	respect	I always show **respect** for God.
3.	launch	Come help me **launch** my rocket.
4.	museum	I like to visit this **museum.**
5.	piece	I need a **piece** of paper.
6.	gallon	He spilled a **gallon** of milk.
7.	deposit	I will **deposit** money in the bank.
8.	carton	This **carton** is sturdy.
9.	narrow	The cave had a **narrow** passage.
10.	dining	We will eat in the **dining** room.
11.	dolphin	I like the **dolphin** at the zoo.
12.	plunge	Watch her **plunge** into the pool!
13.	chorus	I just know the **chorus** of the song.
14.	design	My painting has a nice **design.**
15.	dribble	He learned to **dribble** the ball.
16.	version	Which game **version** do you like?
17.	citrus	**Citrus** fruits are good for you.
18.	formula	We mixed **formula** for the calves.
19.	account	I have an **account** at the bank.
20.	rhyme	What will **rhyme** with "skating?"

Placement Test Level D

1.	practice	I have to **practice** the piano.
2.	meant	I **meant** to finish my project.
3.	station	I painted at the art **station.**
4.	hollow	The log is **hollow.**
5.	rescue	We will **rescue** the kitten.
6.	dream	She had a funny **dream.**
7.	pretend	I **pretend** to be a gorilla.
8.	wreath	He put a **wreath** on the door.
9.	cough	His **cough** is getting better.
10.	decide	I can't **decide** what to buy.
11.	bounce	I shouldn't **bounce** on the bed.
12.	fault	It is my **fault** the books fell.
13.	garbage	The **garbage** truck came today.
14.	curious	She is **curious** about the package.
15.	choice	We made a **choice** to obey.
16.	rather	I'd **rather** play tag than swing.
17.	castle	I made a large cardboard **castle.**
18.	fountain	The **fountain** is lit up at night.
19.	cereal	That is my favorite **cereal.**
20.	herself	She made cookies by **herself.**

Introduction

Level **E**

Day One

Literature Connection - Each week begins with a Scripture verse, followed by a theme story that develops the principles found in that verse. Topic and description are provided to inform the teacher of story content. Some teachers may choose to use this theme story for the Monday morning devotional. (A dramatized CD version of the story is also available.)

Discussion Time *(optional)* - Discussion questions follow each story, giving the teacher the opportunity to evaluate student understanding, and to encourage students to apply the values found in the Scripture to their own lives.

1 Literature Connection
Topic: The mentally challenged
Theme Text: Psalm 127:1

Tony in Training

Tony painfully determines to learn more about the limitations of the mentally challenged and resolves to work on his prejudice.

2 Discussion Time
Check understanding of the story and development of personal values.

- Have you ever participated in a race to raise money for a good cause?
- When and what for?
- Why was Tony participating in the Turkey Trot?
- Why was he training so hard?
- Was that a good reason to train so diligently?
- What does it mean when someone says you just put your foot in your mouth?
- How did Tony put his foot in his mouth?
- How did he feel when he realized Mr. Canfield's son was mentally challenged?
- How did Tony's reason for running change?

Lesson 14 Day 1

133

134

Copyright ©2012 by The Concerned Group, Inc. All rights reserved.

Day One (cont.)

Preview - The test—study—test sequence begins with this pre-test which primarily uses sentences related to the story. Research has shown that immediate correction by the student—under teacher supervision—is one of the best ways to learn to spell.

Customize Your List *(notepaper graphic)* - An opportunity is provided to test additional words of the teacher's choice.

Say *(bubble graphic)* - Instructions to the students that are to be read aloud by the teacher are marked with the Say symbol for easy identification.

Progress Chart *(chart graphic)* - Students may record their Preview scores for later comparison against their Posttest scores. (Reproducible master provided in Appendix B.)

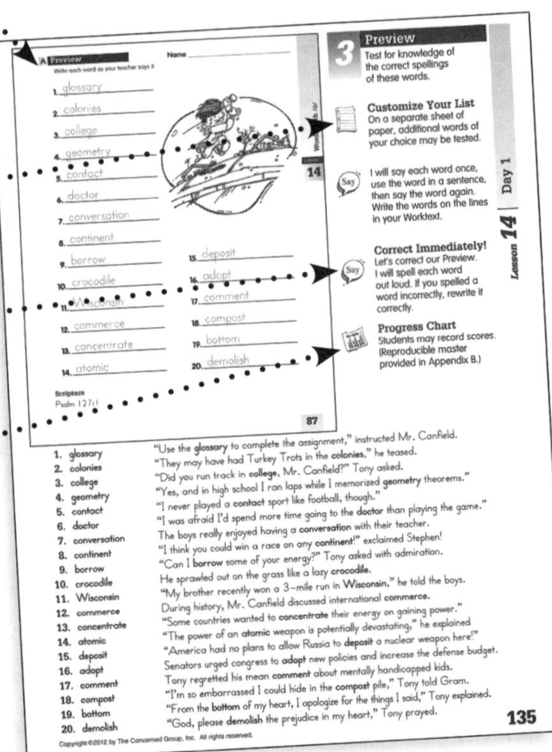

3 Preview
Test for knowledge of the correct spellings of these words.

Customize Your List
On a separate sheet of paper, additional words of your choice may be tested.

Say: I will say each word once, use the word in a sentence, then say the word again. Write the words on the lines in your Worktext.

Correct Immediately!
Say: Let's correct our Preview. I will spell each word out loud. If you spelled a word incorrectly, rewrite it correctly.

Progress Chart
Students may record scores. (Reproducible master provided in Appendix B.)

Lesson 14 Day 1

1. **glossary** — "Use the **glossary** to complete the assignment," instructed Mr. Canfield.
2. **colonies** — "They may have had Turkey Trots in the **colonies**," he teased.
3. **college** — "Did you run track in **college**, Mr. Canfield?" Tony asked.
4. **geometry** — "Yes, and in high school I ran laps while I memorized **geometry** theorems."
5. **contact** — "I never played a **contact** sport like football, though."
6. **doctor** — "I was afraid I'd spend more time going to the **doctor** than playing the game."
7. **conversation** — The boys really enjoyed having a **conversation** with their teacher.
8. **continent** — "I think you could win a race on any **continent**!" exclaimed Stephen!
9. **borrow** — "Can I **borrow** some of your energy?" Tony asked with admiration.
10. **crocodile** — He sprawled out on the grass like a lazy **crocodile**.
11. **Wisconsin** — "My brother recently won a 3-mile run in **Wisconsin**," he told the boys.
12. **commerce** — During history, Mr. Canfield discussed international **commerce**.
13. **concentrate** — "Some countries wanted to **concentrate** their energy on gaining power."
14. **atomic** — "The power of an **atomic** weapon is potentially devastating," he explained
15. **deposit** — "America had no plans to allow Russia to **deposit** a nuclear weapon here!"
16. **adopt** — Senators urged congress to **adopt** new policies and increase the defense budget.
17. **comment** — Tony regretted his mean **comment** about mentally handicapped kids.
18. **compost** — "I'm so embarrassed I could hide in the **compost** pile," Tony told Gram.
19. **bottom** — "From the **bottom** of my heart, I apologize for the things I said," Tony explained.
20. **demolish** — "God, please **demolish** the prejudice in my heart," Tony prayed.

135

Copyright ©2012 by The Concerned Group, Inc. All rights reserved.

Day One (cont.)

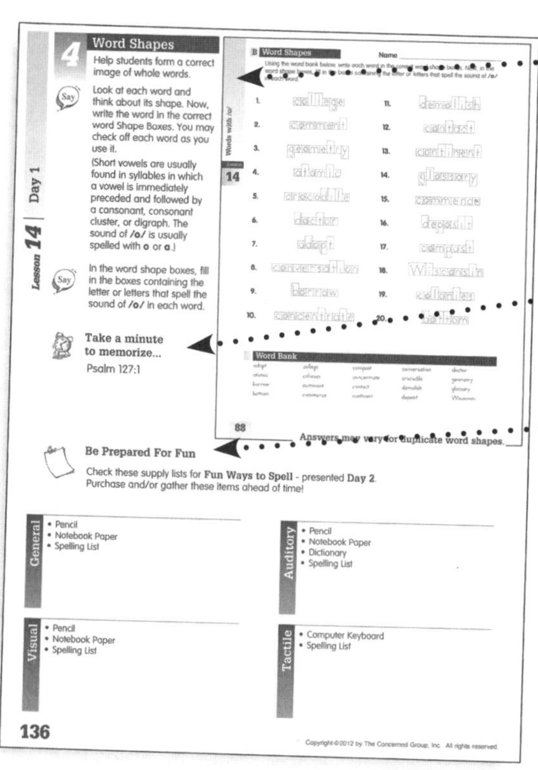
Lesson 14 | Day 1

4 Word Shapes

Help students form a correct image of whole words.

Look at each word and think about its shape. Now, write the word in the correct word Shape Boxes. You may check off each word as you use it.

(Short vowels are usually found in syllables in which a vowel is immediately preceded and followed by a consonant, consonant cluster, or digraph. The sound of /o/ is usually spelled with o or a.)

In the word shape boxes, fill in the boxes containing the letter or letters that spell the sound of /o/ in each word.

Take a minute to memorize... Psalm 127:1

Be Prepared For Fun

Check these supply lists for Fun Ways to Spell - presented Day 2. Purchase and/or gather these items ahead of time!

General: • Pencil • Notebook Paper • Spelling List

Auditory: • Pencil • Notebook Paper • Dictionary • Spelling List

Visual: • Pencil • Notebook Paper • Spelling List

Tactile: • Computer Keyboard • Spelling List

Answers may vary for duplicate word shapes.

136

Copyright ©2012 by The Concerned Group, Inc. All rights reserved.

Word Shapes - The use of "Shape Boxes" is a research-based method that helps students form a correct visual image of each spelling word. An additional exercise is provided to enhance student identification of spelling patterns and thus strengthen phonemic awareness.

Take a Minute *(clock graphic)* - Reminders are provided for committing to memory the Scripture verses upon which the stories are based.

Be Prepared for Fun *(list graphic)* - For teacher convenience, a weekly supply list is provided for "Fun Ways to Spell" on Day 1. Supplies for the "General" activity are readily available in most classrooms. Other categories may require minimal extra planning.

Day Two

Hide & Seek - This research-proven method of spelling instruction is highly effective for dealing with multiple intelligences and varying learning styles.

Other Word Forms *(optional)* - A variety of activities allow students to become familiar with other forms of the week's spelling words.

Fun Ways to Spell - Four options are offered each week. In addition to a "General" activity, "Auditory," "Tactile," and "Visual" options are provided for students with different learning styles. Suggestions are also given for adapting these activities to various classroom settings.

Day Three

Language Arts Activity - Research studies show that meaningful, practical use of spelling words helps students become more familiar with the words they are studying. The weekly "Working with Words" activity is designed to offer practice in this area.

Take a Minute - Reminders to commit Scripture verses to memory are provided periodically.

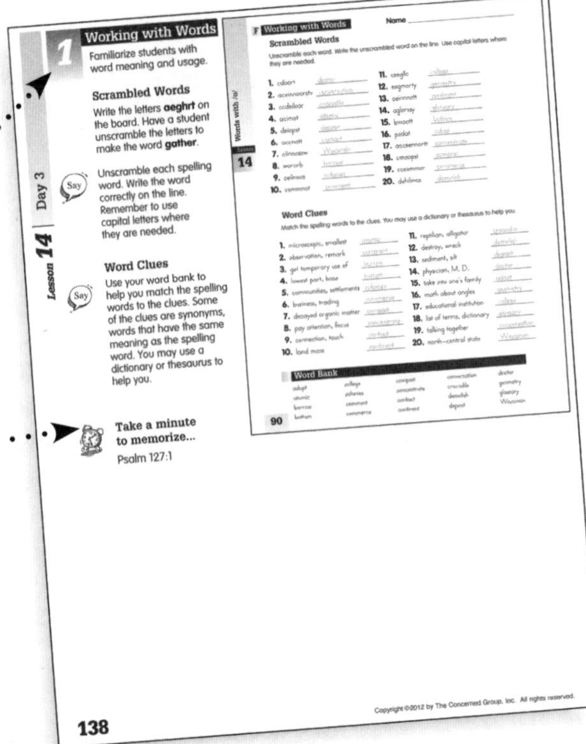

Lesson 14 Day 3

1 Working with Words

Familiarize students with word meaning and usage.

Scrambled Words

Write the letters **aeghrt** on the board. Have a student unscramble the letters to make the word **gather**.

Say: Unscramble each spelling word. Write the word correctly on the line. Remember to use capital letters where they are needed.

Word Clues

Say: Use your word bank to help you match the spelling words to the clues. Some of the clues are synonyms, words that have the same meaning as the spelling word. You may use a dictionary or thesaurus to help you.

Take a minute to memorize...

Psalm 127:1

F Working with Words

Scrambled Words

Word Clues

Word Bank

90

138

Day Four

Dictation - Students write dictated words to complete sentences. This strengthens their word usage and context skills. Previously taught spelling words are also included in this activity, providing maintenance of spelling skills.

Proofreading - Proofreading allows students to become familiar with the format of standardized tests as they mark misspelled words. Proofreading is also a critical skill that can be incorporated in students' own writing.

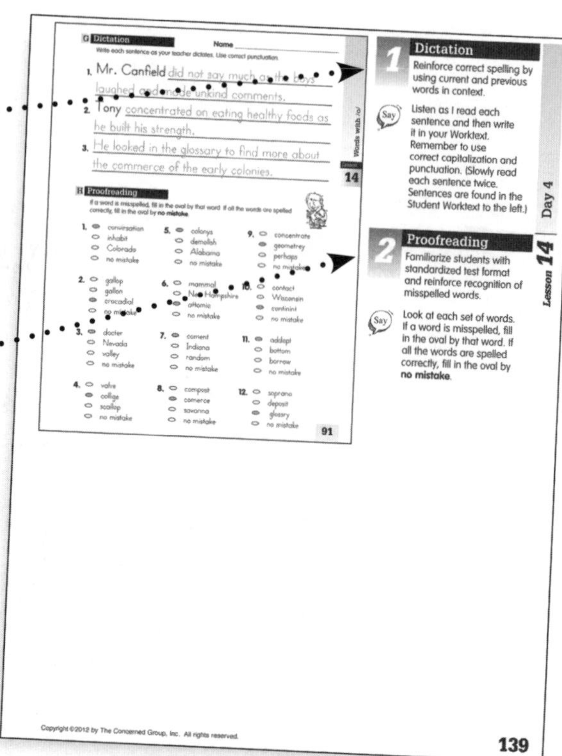

G Dictation

1. Mr. Canfield did not say much, as the boys laughed and made unkind comments.
2. Tony concentrated on eating healthy foods as he built his strength.
3. He looked in the glossary to find more about the commerce of the early colonies.

H Proofreading

91

1 Dictation

Reinforce correct spelling by using current and previous words in context.

Say: Listen as I read each sentence and then write it in your Worktext. Remember to use correct capitalization and punctuation. (Slowly read each sentence twice. Sentences are found in the Student Worktext to the left.)

2 Proofreading

Familiarize students with standardized test format and reinforce recognition of misspelled words.

Say: Look at each set of words. If a word is misspelled, fill in the oval by that word. If all the words are spelled correctly, fill in the oval by **no mistake**.

Lesson 14 Day 4

139

Day Four (cont.)

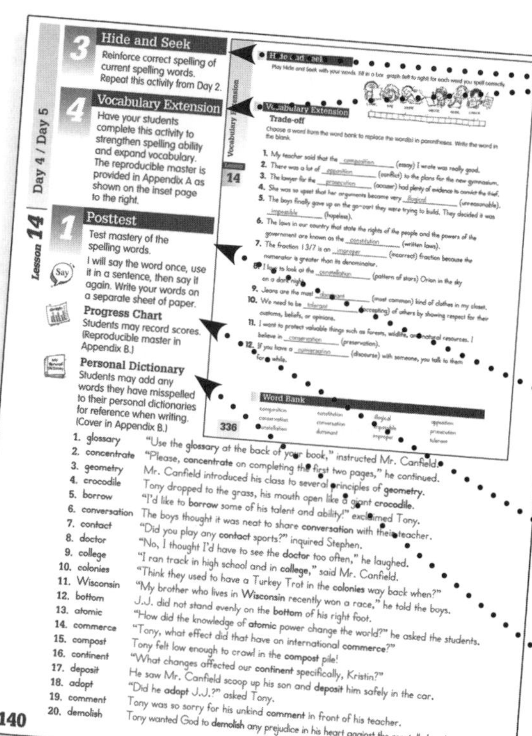

3 Hide and Seek
Reinforce correct spelling of current spelling words. Repeat this activity from Day 2.

4 Vocabulary Extension
Have your students complete this activity to strengthen spelling ability and expand vocabulary. The reproducible master is provided in Appendix A as shown on the inset page to the right.

1 Posttest
Test mastery of the spelling words.
I will say the word once, use it in a sentence, then say it again. Write your words on a separate sheet of paper.

Progress Chart
Students may record scores. (Reproducible master in Appendix B.)

Personal Dictionary
Students may add any words they have misspelled to their personal dictionaries for reference when writing. (Cover in Appendix B.)

1. glossary "Use the glossary at the back of your book," instructed Mr. Canfield.
2. concentrate "Please, concentrate on completing the first two pages," he continued.
3. geometry Mr. Canfield introduced his class to several principles of geometry.
4. crocodile Tony dropped to the grass, his mouth open like a giant crocodile.
5. borrow "I'd like to borrow some of his talent and ability!" exclaimed Tony.
6. conversation The boys thought it was neat to share conversation with their teacher.
7. contact "Did you play any contact sports?" inquired Stephen.
8. doctor "No, I thought I'd have to see the doctor too often," he laughed.
9. college "I ran track in high school and in college," said Mr. Canfield.
10. colonies "Think they used to have a Turkey Trot in the colonies way back when?"
11. Wisconsin "My brother who lives in Wisconsin recently won a race," he told the boys.
12. bottom J.J. did not stand evenly on the bottom of his right foot.
13. atomic "How did the knowledge of atomic power change the world?" he asked the students.
14. commerce "Tony, what effect did that have on international commerce?"
15. compost Tony felt low enough to crawl in the compost pile!
16. continent "What changes affected our continent specifically, Kristin?"
17. deposit He saw Mr. Canfield scoop up his son and deposit him safely in the car.
18. adopt "Did he adopt J.J.?" asked Tony.
19. comment Tony was so sorry for his unkind comment in front of his teacher.
20. demolish Tony wanted God to demolish any prejudice in his heart against the mentally handicapped.

140

Lesson 14 | Day 4 / Day 5

Copyright ©2012 by The Concerned Group, Inc. All rights reserved.

Hide & Seek/Vocabulary Extension *(optional)* - Through practice of additional words similar to the weekly spelling lists, students are provided with vocabulary extension opportunities. (Note: These pages are not in the Student Worktext. Reproducible masters are provided for each week in Appendix A.)

Day Five

Posttest - The test—study—test sequence of learning is completed with the posttest. Again, most sentences relate to the theme story.

Progress Chart *(chart graphic)* - Students may now record their posttest scores to evaluate their weekly progress.

Personal Dictionary *(dictionary graphic)* - Students may add any words they have misspelled to their personal dictionaries. Each student may refer to his/her custom dictionary while journaling or during other writing activities. (Reproducible cover in Appendix B.)

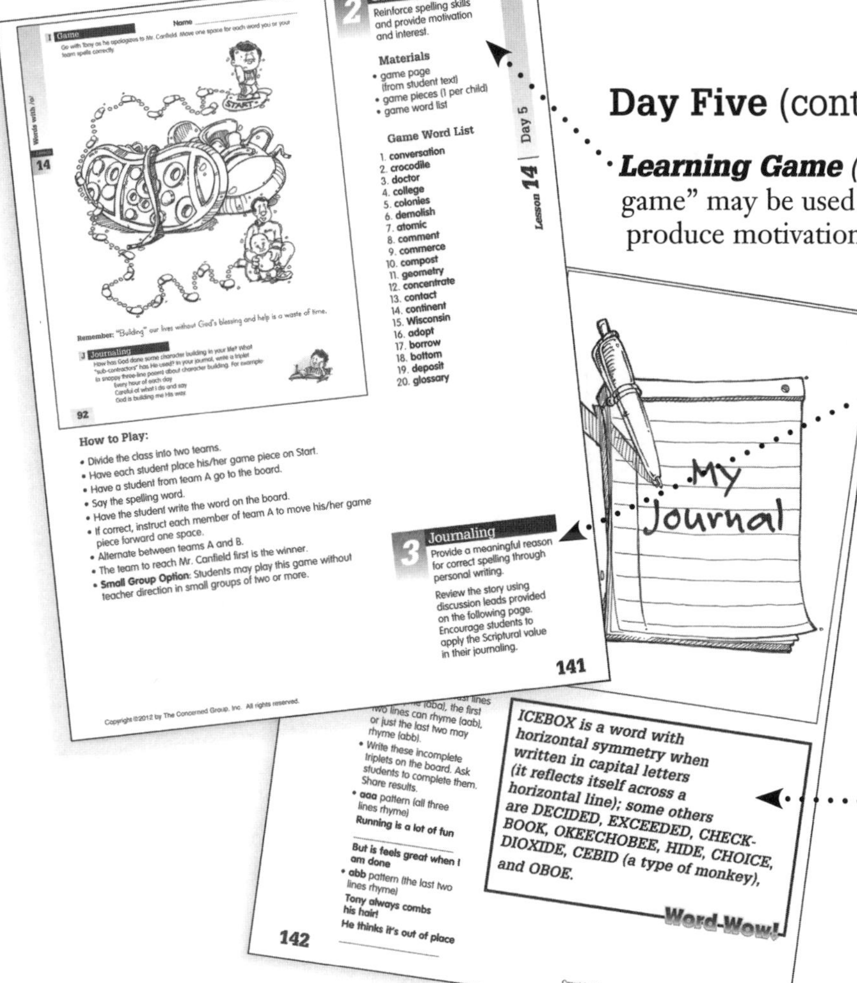

2 Game
Reinforce spelling skills and provide motivation and interest.

Materials
- game page (from student text)
- game pieces (1 per child)
- game word list

Game Word List
1. conversation
2. crocodile
3. doctor
4. college
5. colonies
6. demolish
7. atomic
8. comment
9. commerce
10. compost
11. geometry
12. concentrate
13. contact
14. continent
15. Wisconsin
16. adopt
17. borrow
18. bottom
19. deposit
20. glossary

How to Play:
- Divide the class into two teams.
- Have each student place his/her game piece on Start.
- Have a student from team A go to the board.
- Say the spelling word.
- Have the student write the word on the board.
- If correct, instruct each member of team A to move his/her game piece forward one space.
- Alternate between teams A and B.
- The team to reach Mr. Canfield first is the winner.
- **Small Group Option:** Students may play this game without teacher direction in small groups of two or more.

3 Journaling
Provide a meaningful reason for correct spelling through personal writing.
Review the story using discussion leads provided on the following page. Encourage students to apply the Scriptural value in their journaling.

Lesson 14 | Day 5

141

Copyright ©2012 by The Concerned Group, Inc. All rights reserved.

ICEBOX is a word with horizontal symmetry when written in capital letters (it reflects itself across a horizontal line); some others are DECIDED, EXCEEDED, CHECKBOOK, OKEECHOBEE, HIDE, CHOICE, DIOXIDE, CEBID (a type of monkey), and OBOE.

Word-Wow!

142

Day Five (cont.)

Learning Game *(optional)* - The weekly "board game" may be used to reinforce spelling skills and produce motivation and interest in good spelling. Most games can be played multiple times.

Journal Entry - The underlying goal of spelling instruction is to create better writers. This weekly journaling activity allows students to apply their spelling skills in a meaningful way, while encouraging them to make the featured value their own. Guided discussion questions are provided to assist in reviewing the value taught by the story.

Word Wow! - Interesting insights into words and their meanings are provided to capture student interest.

Research Basis

A Reason For Spelling® emphasizes a balance between spelling skills, application, and student enjoyment. In short, it is designed to be both meaningful and fun! Each level promotes successful classroom practices while incorporating the following research findings:

Research Findings: / *Application:*

Daily Practice. A daily period of teacher-directed spelling activities based on meaningful content greatly enhances student proficiency in spelling.

Daily lessons in ***A Reason For Spelling***® provide systematic development of spelling skills with a focus on Scripture verses and values.

Spelling Lists. The most productive spelling lists feature developmentally-appropriate words of highest frequency in writing.

Through daily lessons, challenge words, and other word forms, ***A Reason For Spelling***® focuses on the high frequency words children and adults use in daily writing.

Test—Study—Test. Effective educational programs are built on the learning model of "Test—Study—Test."

A Reason For Spelling® follows a weekly pretest/posttest format, and also includes a cumulative review for each unit.

Accurate Feedback. Pretest and proofreading results are crucial in helping students identify words that require their special attention.

Regular pretests and proofreading activities in ***A Reason For Spelling***® help students identify words requiring their special attention.

Visual Imaging. Learning to spell a word involves forming a correct visual image of the whole word, rather than visualizing syllables or parts.

Every lesson in ***A Reason For Spelling***® features word-shape grids to help students form a correct visual image of each spelling word.

Study Procedures. The most effective word-study procedures involve visual, auditory, and tactile modalities.

A Reason For Spelling® uses the "look, say, hide, write, seek, check" method as a primary teaching tool.

Learning Games. Well-designed games motivate student interest and lead to spelling independence.

A Reason For Spelling® includes a wide variety of spelling games at each instructional level.

Self-Correction. Student focus, accomplished through such activities as self-correction of pretests, is an essential strategy for spelling mastery at every grade and ability level.

Teacher directed self-correction of pretests and reviews is encouraged throughout ***A Reason For Spelling***®.

Regular Application. Frequent opportunities to use spelling words in everyday writing contribute significantly to the maintenance of spelling ability.

A Reason For Spelling® provides opportunities for journaling in each lesson to promote the use of assigned spelling words in personal writing.

Cohen, Leo A. 1969. *Evaluating Structural Analysis Methods Used in Spelling Books*. Doctoral Thesis, Boston University.

Davis, Zephaniah T. 1987. Upper Grades Spelling Instruction: What Difference Does It Make? *English Journal*, March: 100-101.

Dolch, E.W. 1936. A Basic Sight Vocabulary. *The Elementary School Journal*, Vol. 36: 456-460.

Downing, John, Robert M. Coughlin and Gene Rich. 1986. Children's Invented Spellings in the Classroom. *The Elementary School Journal*, Vol. 86, No. 3, January: 295-303.

Fiderer, Adele. 1995. *Practical Assessments for Literature-Based Reading Classrooms*. New York: Scholastic Professional Books.

Fitzsimmons, Robert J., and Bradley M. Loomer. 1980. *Spelling: The Research Basis*. Iowa City: The University of Iowa.

Gardner, Howard. 1993. *Multiple Intelligences: The Theory in Practice*. New York: Basic-Books.

Gentry, J. Richard. 1997. *My Kid Can't Spell*. Portsmouth, NH: Heinemann Educational Books.

Gentry, J. Richard and Jean Wallace Gillet. 1993. *Teaching Kids to Spell*. Portsmouth, NH:Heinemann Educational Books.

Gentry, J. Richard. 1985. You Can Analyze Developmental Spelling-And Here's How To Do It! *Early Years K-8*, May:1-4.

Goswami, Usha. 1991. Learning about Spelling Sequences: The Role of Onsets and Rimes in Analogies in Reading. *Child Development*, 62, 1110-1123.

Graves, Donald H. 1977. Research Update: Spelling Texts and Structural Analysis Methods. *Language Arts 54* January: 86-90.

Harp, Bill. 1988. When the Principal Asks, "Why Are Your Kids Giving Each Other Spelling Tests?" *Reading Teacher*, Vol. 41, No. 7, March: 702-704.

Hoffman, Stevie and Nancy Knipping. 1988. Spelling Revisited: The Child's Way. *Childhood Education*, June: 284-287.

Horn, Ernest. 1926. *A Basic Writing Vocabulary: 10,000 Frequently Used Words in Writing*. Monograph First Series, No. 4. Iowa City: The University of Iowa.

Horn, Thomas. 1946. *The Effect of the Corrected Test on Learning to Spell*. Master's Thesis, The University of Iowa.

Horsky, Gregory Alexander. 1974. *A Study of the Perception of Letters and Basic Sight Vocabulary Words of Fourth and Fifth Grade Children*. Doctoral Thesis, The University of Iowa.

Lacey, Cheryl. 1994. *Moving On In Spelling*. Jefferson City, Missouri: Scholastic.

Lutz, Elaine. 1986. ERIC/RCS Report: Invented Spelling and Spelling Development. *Language Arts*, Vol. 63, No. 7, November: 742-744.

Macmillan Dictionary for Children. 1997. New York: Simon and Schuster Books for Young Readers.

Marino, Jacqueline L. 1978. *Children's Use of Phonetic, Graphemic, and Morphophonemic Cues in a Spelling Task*. Doctoral Thesis, State University of New York at Albany.

Morris, Darrell, Laurie Nelson and Jan Perney. 1986. Exploring the Concept of 'Spelling Instructional Level' Through the Analysis of Error-Types. *The Elementary School Journal*, Vol. 87, No. 2, 195-197.

Nicholson, Tom and Sumner Schachter. 1979. Spelling Skill and Teaching Practice-Putting Them Back Together Again. *Language Arts*, Vol. 56, No. 7, October: 804-809.

Rothman, Barbara. 1997. *Practical Phonics Strategies to Build Beginning Reading and Writing Skills*. Medina, Washington: Institute for Educational Development.

Scott, Jill E. 1994. Spelling for Readers and Writers. *The Reading Teacher*, Vol. 48, No. 2, October: 188-190.

Simmons, Janice L. 1978. *The Relationship Between an Instructional Level in Spelling and the Instructional Level in Reading Among Elementary School Children*. Doctoral Thesis, University of Northern Colorado.

Templeton, Shane. 1986. Synthesis of Research on the Learning and Teaching of Spelling. *Educational Leadership*, March: 73-78.

Tireman, L.S. 1927. *The Value of Marking Hard Spots in Spelling*. Doctoral Thesis, University of Iowa.

Toch, Thomas. 1992. Nu Waz for Kidz tu Lern Rdn, Rtn. *U.S. News & World Report*, September 14: 75-76.

Wagstaff, Janiel M. *Phonics That Work! New Strategies for the Reading/Writing Classroom*. Jefferson City, Missouri: Scholastic.

Watson, Alan J. 1988. Developmental Spelling: A Word Categorizing Instructional Experiment. *Journal of Educational Research*, Vol. 82, No. 2, November/December: 82-88.

Wilde, Sandra. 1990. A Proposal for a New Spelling Curriculum. *The Elementary School Journal*, Vol. 90, No. 3, January: 275-289.

English as a Second Language (ESL)

Effective teachers are always sensitive to the special spelling challenges faced by ESL students. While it is not practical to provide specific guidelines for every situation where the teacher may encounter students with limited English proficiency, the following general guidelines for two of the most prominent cultural groups (Asian & Hispanic) may prove helpful.

alphabet Many Asian languages have a significantly different kind of alphabet and students may need considerable practice recognizing English letters and sounds.

vowels Some Asian languages do not have certain English vowel sounds. Speakers often substitute other sounds. Spanish vowels have a single sound: *a* as in *ball*, *e* as in *eight*, *i* as in *ski*, *o* as in *over*, *u* as in *rule*. The Spanish *a* is spelled *e*, *e* is spelled *i* or *y*, and *i* is often spelled *ai* or *ay*.

ô The variety of *ô* spellings may cause some problems for Spanish-speaking students.

ü, u̇ The *u̇* sound does not occur in Spanish, and may cause problems.

ou This sound is spelled *au* in Spanish.

r This sound does not exist in Spanish. Many Asian languages do not have words ending with *r*.

b, d, h, j Spanish and Asian speakers often confuse the sounds of *b* / *d* and *h* / *j*.

ge, gi, j In Spanish, *ge*, *gi*, and *j* most closely resemble the English *h*.

l, f Many Asian languages do not have these sounds.

k, q The letter *k* does not exist in Spanish, but the sound *k* is spelled with either *c* or *qu*. The letter *q* always occurs with *ue* or *ui*.

p, g In most Asian languages, the consonants *p* and *g* do not exist.

v In Spanish, the letter *v* is pronounced *b*.

w There are no Spanish-originated words with the letter *w*.

y In Spanish, *y* is spelled *ll*.

x, z In Spanish, *x* is never used in the final position. There is no letter or sound for *z*.

ch, sh The Spanish language does not have the sound *sh*. Spellers often substitute *ch*. Many Asian languages do not contain *sh* or *ch*.

wh, th The initial *wh* and *th* sounds do not exist in most Spanish and some Asian languages. The Spanish *d*, however, is sometimes pronounced almost like the *th*.

kn This sound may be difficult for both Spanish and Asian spellers.

s clusters Spanish clusters that begin with *s* are always preceded by the vowels *a* or *e*. The most common clusters that will cause problems are *sc*, *sk*, *sl*, *sm*, *sn*, *sp*, *sq*, *st*, and *sw*. Many of these do not occur in Asian languages.

pl, fl, tr, fr, dr These sounds are used in Spanish, but may not be present in some Asian languages.

ng, nk, nt, nd Many Asian languages don't have *ng*, *nk*, *nt*, or *nd*. Spanish doesn't include the *ng* ending.

silent letters The only silent letter in Spanish is *h*. Silent consonants such as those in *mb*, *lk*, and *gh* do not occur in Spanish or Asian languages.

double consonants The only double consonants in Spanish are *cc*, *ll*, and *rr*.

ed In Spanish, the suffix *ed* is pronounced aid. This can be very confusing, especially when the *ed* has the soft *t* sound as in *dropped*.

plurals Spanish rules for adding plurals are: For words ending in a vowel, add *s*. For words ending in a consonant, add *es*. This may cause confusion both in pronunciation and spelling of English words.

contractions Only two contractions are used in Spanish: *a el* becomes *al*, and *de el* becomes *del*. Apostrophes do not exist.

syllables Many Asian languages consist entirely of one and two syllable words. Thus, many longer English words are often confusing.

Spelling Generalizations

In the English language, spelling cannot be taught primarily by rules or generalizations. It's a complex language that has evolved from many other languages and therefore contains many irregularities. There are exceptions to almost all spelling rules.

Research, however, indicates that some generalizations are of value in teaching children to spell. These generalizations have few exceptions and apply to a large number of words. Familiarity with these spelling rules can be helpful to many learners. In addition, generalizations that deal with adding suffixes to words can be quite valuable in expanding a student's ability to spell other word forms.

The following generalizations may prove to be helpful:

- The letter *q* is always followed by *u*.
- Every syllable contains a vowel. *Y* can also serve as a vowel.
- Words that end in silent *e*:
  … drop the *e* when adding a suffix beginning with a vowel. (live, living)
  … keep the *e* when adding a suffix beginning with a consonant. (time, timely)
- Words that end in *y*:
  … are not changed when adding suffixes if the *y* is preceded by a vowel. (say, saying)
  … change the *y* to *i* when adding suffixes if the *y* is preceded by a consonant, unless the suffix begins with *i*. (try, tried, trying)
- When *ei* or *ie* are used in a word, the *i* usually comes before the *e* except when they make the */ā/* sound, or follow after a *c*. (believe, eight, ceiling)
- Words ending in one consonant preceded by a single vowel usually double the final consonant when adding a suffix beginning with a vowel. (begin, beginning)
- Words ending with the sounds made by *x*, *s*, *sh*, and *ch* add the suffix *es* to form plurals. (mix, mixes)
- Proper nouns and most proper adjectives begin with capital letters.

Multiple Intelligences

In recognition of the multiple intelligences theory, ***A Reason For Spelling***® provides activities to meet the varied needs of your students. (See "Fun Ways to Spell," and "Hide & Seek.")

Scripture Translation

Each weekly lesson in ***A Reason For Spelling***® begins with a Scripture verse. This is followed by a contemporary theme story designed to bring out key values found in the verse.

Teachers are strongly encouraged to introduce each lesson by reading the "Theme Text" aloud (or have a student read the verse aloud to the class). This helps set the stage for the principles and values students will be focusing on that week.

Scripture verses used in ***A Reason For Spelling***® are similar in most translations, allowing teachers to use the Scripture translation their school prefers, without affecting academic content.

Personal Spelling Dictionary

A great way to encourage students' spelling awareness is to help them develop and maintain their own Personal Spelling Dictionary at their desk to refer to when writing. This can be either a spiral-bound or loose-leaf notebook with a few pages designated for each letter of the alphabet. Throughout the school year, encourage students to constantly add words to their Personal Spelling Dictionary, not only from spelling class, but from other classes as well. These should include words a student finds difficult to spell, as well as words of particular interest. (Reproducible cover in Appendix B.)

Word Walls

Another excellent method of promoting spelling awareness in your classroom is to create a word wall. This wall (often a large bulletin board) contains commonly used words and words of special interest to your class. The classroom word wall becomes a permanent reference list that students may refer to as they read and write.

Words may be arranged in a variety of ways. Some examples include traditional alphabetical order; groups (such as math words, weather words, color words); or by the targeted vowel, for example:

A	E	I	O	U
April	cheese	listen	worry	judge
capture	leather	price	bought	curious
carpet	perfect	tonight	knock	pollute

Some words could even have picture or context clues added. Sample words from word families being studied, or interesting words students want to know how to spell are added throughout the year. Students should be reminded not to simply copy the words from the wall, but to look at the word needed, then write it from memory—or write the word they are having difficulty with, then check it against the word wall.

Games can be played using the word wall as well.

- Rhyming Words: Ask students to find a word that "rhymes with phone."
- Sentence Sense: Write the letter **w** on the board, then say "Look for a word that begins with a **w** and fits this sentence: I _ _ _ _ _ _ _ Jesus."
- Dictate & Write: Dictate a sentence for students to write using words found only on the wall.
- Read My Mind:

Say: I am thinking of one of the words on the wall. It has ______ letters. It begins with _____ . The vowel is ______. It fits in this sentence: ________________.

Flip Folders

The Flip Folder is a great way for students to use the research-based, time-tested "Look—Say—Hide—Write—Seek—Check" method to learn spelling words. They may do this activity on their own or with a partner.

On the front of a standard file folder, make two cuts to create three flaps (see diagram below). On a separate piece of paper, have students make three columns, then write the words they need to study in the first column. Now have students slide the paper into the folder so that the words are under the first flap.

- Open Flap 1 and ***Look*** at the first word.

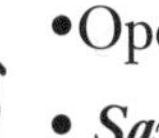

- ***Say*** the word out loud
- Now ***Hide*** the word by closing the flap.
- Open Flap 2 and ***Write*** the word in the middle column.
- Open Flaps 1 & 2 and ***Seek*** the word to ***Check*** your spelling. If the word is misspelled. . .
- Open Flap 3 and ***Write*** the word correctly in the third column.

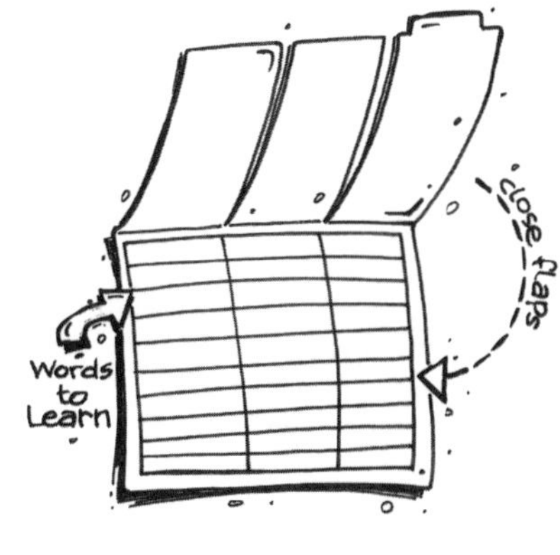

The goal of ***A Reason For Spelling***® is to create proficient and self-reliant spellers and writers. By combining inventive spelling (through journaling) with formal spelling instruction, an excellent environment is created for students to develop into expert spellers. (Reproducible Journal cover in Appendix B.)

Inventive Spelling/Journaling

As children learn to spell, they go through several stages. The move from one stage to another is gradual even though students may spell from more than one stage at one time. Just as a toddler who is talking in complete sentences doesn't suddenly regress to babbling, so students tend to remain relatively stable within and between stages. Recognized stages of spelling development include:

Precognitive Stage: Children use symbols from the alphabet for writing words, but letters are random and do not correspond to sound. (eagle = dfbrt; eighty = acbp)

Semiphonetic Stage: Children understand and consistently represent sounds with letters. Spellings are often abbreviated representing only the initial and/or final sounds. (eagle = e; eighty = a)

Phonetic Stage: Students in this stage spell words like they sound. The speller perceives and represents every sound in a word, though spellings may be unconventional. (eagle = egl; eighty = aty)

Transitional Stage: Students think about how words appear visually. Spelling patterns are apparent. Spellings exhibit customs of English spelling such as vowels in every syllable, correct e-marker and vowel digraph patterns, inflectional endings, and frequent English letter sequences. (eagle = egul; eighty = eightee)

Conventional Stage: This stage develops over years of word study and writing. Correct spelling has different instructional levels. Correct spelling for a group of words that can be spelled by the average third grader would be "third grade level correct" spelling. (eagle = eagle; eighty = eighty)

An effective way to help students transition through the stages is to edit their first drafts, then talk with them about corrections. Discuss why changes are necessary. Encourage students to rewrite journal entries so others can read them easily. Display student work whenever possible. Teach students that invented spelling makes it easier for the writer, but that revision to standard spelling is a courtesy to the reader.

Word Lists

Word lists in ***A Reason For Spelling***® are based on frequency of use in student and adult writing; frequency of use in reading materials; spelling difficulty; and grade level familiarity.

Studies used in the development of these lists include: *Dolch Basic Sight Vocabulary* (a list of 220 high frequency words); *The American Heritage Word Frequency Book* (a study of word frequency in print materials for grades three through nine); *Starter Words* (the 190 most frequently used words in children's writing, school materials, and adult print materials); and *A Basic Vocabulary of Elementary School Children.*

These standard references were extensively cross-checked with other respected studies (Gates; Horn; Greene & Loomer; Harris & Jacobson). It is significant to note that very few differences were found among these sources.

For teacher convenience, lesson numbers follow each word.

Level-D

accept-2
across-14
against-3
agree-4
ahead-3
alike-5
all right-16
almost-16
aloud-15
alphabet-13
already-16
although-11
among-10
annoy-21
anyway-29
anywhere-26
apartment-10
appear-27
applause-16
appointment-21
April Fools' Day-31
Arbor Day-31
arrest-2
arrow-2
attic-2
author-16
avenue-7
avoid-21
awful-16
backyard-29
bandage-2
barber-17
bare-26
barnyard-17
bathroom-29
bathtub-29
battle-23
beard-27
beast-14
beautiful-7
became-4
bedroom-29
bedspread-29
behave-4
believe-4
belt-10
bent-10
birth-19
blade-8
blank-10
blanket-8
blood-1
bloom-7
bluff-13
bomb-11
bounce-15
branch-1
brand-1
breakfast-3
bridge-8
broom-7
built-3
bulldozer-20
bulletin-20
burst-19
butcher-20
button-25
cabbage-2
cane-4
cape-4
capture-22
cardboard-17
carnival-17
carpet-17
cart-17
castle-23
cave-4
cellar-14
cereal-27
champion-25
chance-14
cheer-27
chef-13
chicken-25
chief-4
choice-21
chose-5
Christmas-31
citizen-14
clear-8
climb-11
clue-7
coach-5
collect-2
Columbus Day-31
comb-11
comfort-3
common-25
compare-26
cord-16
cotton-25
cough-13
couldn't-28
county-15
couple-3
cousin-3
crack-8
craft-13
cream-8
crooked-20
crow-5
crust-10
cure-20
curious-20
curl-19
curtain-25
curve-19
dairy-26
damage-2
danger-22
dare-26
dead-3
decide-14
deer-27
delight-11
depend-2
dessert-19
destroy-21
dew-7
didn't-28
disappear-27
disappoint-21
dive-5
dock-1
dollhouse-15
donor-22
dragon-25
dream-8
drift-13
drum-8
due-7
dumb-11
during-20
dust-1
Easter-31
either-22
elephant-13
else-14
employ-21
enjoyment-21
enough-13
enter-22
everybody-29
evil-23
except-2
exciting-14
fail-4
fair-26
false-16
famous-14
fare-26
farmer-17
farther-17
fault-16
favor-22
fear-27
feather-22
fence-14
festival-23
fierce-27
final-23
finger-22
fireplace-29
firm-19
fist-1
flock-1
flour-8
flow-8
flute-7
fog-16
folks-11
footprint-20
forest-16
forward-10
fountain-25
freight-4
frost-10
frown-15
fry-8
fully-20
furious-20
furniture-19
further-19
garbage-17
garden-17
gear-27
general-23
gentle-23
germ-19
glance-14
glare-26
glue-7
goodness-20
government-10
gown-15
graph-13
grave-8
groan-8
Groundhog Day-31
growl-15
guard-10
hadn't-28
hair-26
Halloween-31
handful-20
Hanukkah-31
hardly-17
hare-26
harm-17
harsh-17
haul-16
hawk-16
he'd-28
he'll-28
here's-28
herself-29
hollow-5
homemade-29
homework-29
honor-22
hospital-23
however-15
human-7
humor-22
hung-1
I'd-28
Independence Day-31
instead-3
iron-5
it'll-28
jelly-4
joint-21
jungle-23
kitchen-25
knife-11
knob-11
label-23
Labor Day-31
laid-4
laugh-13
lazy-4
lead-3
lean-4
least-4
leather-3
legend-10
lemon-25
level-23
limb-11
lion-25
listen-25

loaf-13
lonely-5
loyal-21
marbles-17
Martin Luther King Day-31
May Day-31
meant-3
measure-3
Memorial Day-31
merchant-10
mild-10
model-23
moist-21
moment-10
motor-22
movement-7
movie-7
mustard-2
nature-22
near-27
neither-22
New Year's Day-31
newspaper-29
nothing-2
notice-5
noun-15
nurse-19
oak-5
object-2
offer-16
office-13
oily-21
orphan-13
ought-11
outdoors-15
oven-25
overalls-29
overlook-20
owl-15
owner-22
package-2
Passover-31
past-1
pasture-22
pause-16
peace-14
pear-26
pebble-1
perfect-19
period-27
photograph-13
picture-22
pile-5
pine-5
plank-8
plastic-2
playground-29

pleasant-3
plural-20
point-21
police-14
pollute-7
possible-23
pound-15
powder-15
practice-2
Presidents' Day-31
press-14
pretend-10
public-2
puddle-23
pumpkin-2
pure-20
purpose-19
quarrel-16
railroad-29
rather-22
rear-27
reason-25
recess-14
reign-11
rejoice-21
remind-10
repair-26
reply-5
reptile-1
rescue-7
ribbon-25
ridge-1
robin-25
roof-7
rose-5
rough-13
royalty-21
ruin-25
sauce-16
scarce-26
scare-26
scarf-17
scene-14
science-14
scout-15
secret-4
self-1
several-23
share-26
she'll-28
she's-28
shove-1
simple-23
sincerely-27
sink-1
sir-19
siren-25
skirt-19

slippery-9
smash-9
smoke-8
snap-8
somewhere-29
son-14
soybean-21
spark-17
speak-8
spear-27
spill-9
spirit-9
split-9
spray-9
stare-26
starve-17
station-4
steady-9
steer-27
stew-8
stool-9
stout-15
stove-5
strap-9
stretch-9
strike-9
stroke-9
struck-9
stuff-13
style-9
sunshine-29
supply-5
sure-20
sweat-3
swept-1
swift-13
tear-27
Thanksgiving-31
there's-28
they'd-28
thorough-11
thoughtful-11
thread-9
thrill-9
throat-9
tied-5
tiger-5
topsoil-21
total-23
touch-1
tough-13
tourist-20
toward-16
tower-15
tray-4
trouble-3
trout-15
true-9

trust-1
tune-7
turkey-19
uncle-23
underground-15
understand-10
unknown-11
upstairs-26
usual-7
Valentine's Day-31
visitor-22
voyage-21
we've-28
wealth-3
wear-26
weary-27
weird-27
weren't-28
what's-28
where's-28
who's-28
whom -7
whose-11
within-29
wooden-20
worry-19
worst-19
worth-19
wouldn't -28
wreath-11
wren-11
wrong-10
yarn-17
yesterday-3

Level-E

accent-1
account-29
accuse-11
acid-1
adapt-1
admire-9
admit-3
adopt-14
adult-5
adverb-26
aerobics-16
Africa-19
afternoon-23
aimless-27
aisle-17
Alabama-13
Alaska-21
album-5
alcohol-4
alibi-9
Amazon-22

anchor-26
angle-25
announcer-29
Antarctica-15
appeal-8
area-16
argument-15
Arizona-16
Arkansas-15
arrive-9
artery-15
artichoke-15
Asia-7
aspect-1
aspire-17
assist-3
astronaut-4
athlete-1
atlas-1
atomic-14
attend-2
audience-4
Australia-4
autograph-19
automatic-4
automobile-4
average-20
aware-16
awkward-4
backup-21
badge-20
banana-1
banjo-10
banner-1
banquet-21
bargain-15
barracks-16
barren-16
barrier-16
basketball-23
batch-1
biceps-17
blaze-22
blizzard-22
boldly-10
border-28
borrow-14
bottom-14
boundary-29
brief-8
broadcast-23
brother-in-law-23
browse-29
bruise-22
buffalo-10
bundle-25
burden-26
burial-25

byte-9
California-1
camera-1
Canada-1
candlestick-23
canoe-11
caramel-16
cardiac-15
cargo-10
cartilage-15
carton-15
cavern-1
cavity-1
central-25
chaos-21
chapter-26
chart-15
charter-26
chase-7
chorus-21
circuit-5
cirrus-27
citizen-22
citrus-27
clause-4
clerk-26
clever-26
cliffs-3
climate-17
closeness-27
closet-22
clout-29
coffee-4
college-14
colonies-14
Colorado-13
combat-13
combine-17
comment-14
commerce-14
compare-16
compartment-15
compile-17
compost-14
compound-29
concentrate-14
confuse-11
congress-27
Connecticut-31
construct-5
contact-14
contain-7
continent-14
control-10
conversation-14
cornea-28
cornerstone-28
corridor-28

tense-2
Texas-2
tomb-11
trophy-19
truly-11
tulip-11
tundra-5
umbrella-2
umpire-5
useless-11
Utah-11
valley-13
valve-13
veil-7
vein-7
Vermont-4
version-26
vetoes-8
view-11
Virginia-3
virus-27
voltage-10
walrus-27
Washington-4
weapon-2
weather-2
West Virginia-26
wharves-31
whereabouts-29
wield-8
wife-9
willpower-29
Wisconsin-14
wisdom-5
witness-27
wreck-31
Wyoming-10

Level-F

abandon-1
abdomen-1
ability-3
abolish-4
absence-31
abundant-27
accelerator-21
accessory-21
accurate-21
achievement-31
acquaintance-15
acquire-15
acquittal-15
acreage-14
action-25
actual-1
adjective-19
admonish-4
adobe-10
advantage-14
advertise-16
advice-9
advise-16
advocate-28
aggressive-19
agreeable-5
alfalfa-1
alligator-1
altogether-21
amazement-27
amendment-27
analysis-1
ancestor-1
apology-14
appearance-31
approximately-26
apricot-4
archaeology-14
architecture-15
arrogance-31
ashamed-13
assembly-26
assistance-31
associate-28
assurance-31
astronomy-4
atmosphere-11
attempt-2
attention-25
attorney-21
attractive-19
automotive-19
bacteria-11
balance-1
barometer-20
bazaar-29
behavior-21
beliefs-8
bellow-2
benefit-2
betrayed-13
bewildered-13
beyond-4
bilingual-5
billion-25
binoculars-20
biography-4
biology-14
bizarre-29
boarder-29
boast-10
border-29
botanist-4
brackets-1
brakes-29
breaks-29
breathe-8
cafeteria-11
calcium-1
calculate-1
calendar-20
calorie-1
capital-29
capitol-29
capsule-1
captain-1
career-11
cashier-11
caution-25
cavalry-1
ceiling-8
centimeter-20
certificate-21
challenge-1
chameleon-15
chandelier-11
channel-1
character-15
chemical-15
cherish-2
chimney-3
chronic-15
cinema-3
civilize-16
classified-13
clenched-13
clockwise-16
coarse-29
coastal-10
coax-10
cocoa-10
coincidence-31
collision-25
colon-10
comfortable-5
commandment-27
community-26
compact-28
comparative-19
complain-7
complete-8
compress-28
compromise-16
computer-20
conceal-8
conceit-8
concerned-13
concert-28
condense-2
conflict-28
congratulations-17
connect-2
conscience-31
consequence-15
consumer-20
contaminated-1
content-28
contest-28
convertible-5
cooperate-21
correct-21
council-29
counsel-29
courage-14
creased-13
creation-25
crescent-31
criminology-14
criteria-11
critical-5
crucial-5
cruelty-26
cunning-13
current-27
cursive-19
cushion-25
customer-20
customize-16
cyclone-9
cylinder-3
decision-25
declarative-19
defeat-8
definitely-26
definition-25
degree-8
dehydrated-13
delete-8
deliberate-28
delicate-2
delightful-9
density-2
dentist-2
deodorant-27
dependence-31
depth-2
describe-9
desolate-28
detective-19
determination-17
develop-2
devotion-25
diagonal-5
diagram-9
diameter-1
diamond-9
diesel-8
digestive-19
dimensions-17
direction-25
disagree-22
disappearance-22
disappointment-22
disbelief-22
discard-22
discharge-22
disclose-22
discomfort-22
disconnect-22
discontinue-22
discount-22
discourage-22
discover-22
disengage-22
disgrace-22
disguised-13
disgust-22
dishonest-22
dislike-22
dismay-22
dismiss-22
disorder-22
displease-22
dispute-22
dissatisfy-22
distance-31
distrust-22
division-25
document-27
dreary-11
drenched-13
dripped-13
duplicate-7
durable-5
dyeing-29
dying-29
dynamite-9
eclipse-3
ecology-14
economy-4
edible-5
editorial-5
eerie-11
elective-19
electrical-5
electron-4
elementary-2
elevator-21
eligible-5
emotion-25
empathize-16
enable-7
encourage-14
endanger-20
endeavor-21
engrave-7
enterprise-16
entertain-7
entirely-9
entrance-28
environment-27
equality-15
equipment-15
equivalent-15
erode-10
erosion-25
especially-26
estimate-28
ethnic-2
evacuate-7
eventually-26
evidence-31
excellent-27
excessive-19
exchange-7
excitement-27
excursion-17
excuse-28
executive-19
exercise-16
expense-2
experience-11
explain-7
exploration-17
extent-27
extinct-3
familiar-20
fascinating-13
fashion-25
favorable-5
federal-5
fertilize-16
fiction-25
finalize-16
foliage-14
fraction-25
fragment-27
franchise-16
frontier-11
function-25
galaxy-1
gallery-1
gemology-14
gently-26
geology-14
geranium-7
glacier-20
gnarled-13
gorilla-3
graceful-7
graduation-17
grammar-20
gravity-26
greedy-8
growth-10
headache-15
headquarters-15
hemisphere-11

heredity-26
hibernate-7
hoarse-29
hopeful-10
humidity-26
hydrant-9
hypnotize-16
identify-9
illusion-17
illustration-7
imagine-1
imitate-3
immediately-26
imperative-19
impress-28
improvement-31
improvise-16
inactive-19
incident-27
incisor-9
indent-27
indestructible-5
influence-31
ingredient-27
inheritance-31
innocent-27
inspiration-17
instant-27
instinct-3
instruments-27
integration-7
interfere-11
interference-31
interior-11
interrogative-19
intersection-17
inventive-19
invitation-17
involve-4
island-9
italics-1
itemize-16
judgment-27
junction-25
juvenile-9
kilogram-3
kilometer-20
knight-29
language-14
league-8
leisure-8
leopard-2
license-9
lieutenant-31
limerick-3
linear-3
localize-16
locate-10
maintenance-31
majestic-2
majority-26
meanwhile-8
melancholy-15
memorize-16
merchandise-16
merely-11
Messiah-9
mileage-14
militia-3
milligram-3
millimeter-20
mineral-3
minority-26
mission-25
moderate-4
monitor-21
monopoly-4
morale-1
multiplied-13
murder-20
murmur-20
musician-17
mystery-3
myth-3
mythology-14
nationality-26
native-19
nebula-2
niece-8
notify-9
nuclear-20
nuisance-31
nutrition-25
oasis-7
oath-10
occasionally-26
occupation-17
octagon-4
opinion-25
opportunity-26
organize-16
original-14
otherwise-16
outright-9
outstanding-13
oval-10
ovation-10
overabundant-23
overanxious-23
overburden-23
overcharge-23
overemphasize-23
overestimate-23
overflow-23
overhear-11
overindulge-23
overload-23
overreact-23
overseas-23
overshadow-23
oversimplify-23
oversleep-23
overthrow-23
overtime-23
passenger-20
patience-29
patients-29
patriot-7
peaceful-8
peasant-27
percentage-14
perimeter-20
permission-17
personality-26
persuasive-19
petrified-13
piano-10
piercing-11
pioneer-11
poetry-10
politician-17
pollen-4
polygon-4
popularity-26
population-17
portable-5
possessive-19
postage-14
postdate-10
postponed-13
posttest-10
potatoes-7
poverty-26
practically-26
precise-9
predator-21
predict-3
prediction-17
preference-31
preferred-13
prefix-8
premiere-11
premonition-17
preposition-17
prerequisite-15
present-28
prevent-2
primitive-19
principal-29
principle-29
printer-20
prison-3
privilege-3
probable-5
probe-10
problem-4
procedure-21
processor-21
product-4
productive-19
professor-21
program-10
programmer-20
progress-28
project-28
prominence-31
promise-4
prompt-4
proofread-28
propeller-20
propose-10
prospect-4
protein-10
protest-28
proton-10
provide-9
quantity-15
question-15
quotation-15
radioactive-19
realize-16
reasonable-5
recognize-16
recycle-9
referee-8
reference-31
reflect-2
refund-28
refuse-28
region-25
reindeer-11
release-8
reliable-5
religion-25
remainder-20
remarkable-5
remedy-2
repeal-8
repeated-13
replace-7
represent-27
representative-19
requirement-15
rescind-3
reservation-17
respiration-7
response-4
responsible-5
restrictive-19
resume-28
revolution-17
rhythm-3
rivalry-9
robot-4
sacred-7
salvation-17
savage-14
Savior-21
scheme-15
scholarship-15
scientist-9
scrimmage-14
season-8
secede-8
secluded-13
segment-27
senator-21
server-20
session-25
severe-11
shadow-10
shallow-1
sheer-11
shoulder-20
siege-8
significance-31
similar-20
singular-3
skeleton-2
slalom-4
slavery-7
sneer-11
socialize-16
society-9
sociology-14
solution-17
special-2
speech-8
splendor-21
squander-15
steadily-26
storage-14
straight-29
strait-29
student-27
subject-28
sufficient-31
superintendent-31
superlative-19
survey-7
survive-9
suspect-28
syllable-5
symbol-3
symbolize-16
sympathize-16
synchronize-15
synonym-3
taught-29
taut-29
technique-15
technology-14
terminal-21
terrible-5
terrific-21
textile-2
theology-14
theory-21
thermostat-21
thesis-8
tomorrow-10
tradition-17
transfer-21
transmitted-13
transport-28
uncommon-4
underbid-23
underestimate-23
undergrowth-23
underline-23
underpass-23
underpay-23
understate-23
undertake-23
underwater-23
unearthly-26
uneducated-13
unfortunately-26
urgent-27
usually-26
uttered-13
vacant-27
vegetable-5
vegetarian-17
vegetation-7
vertebrate-7
vessel-2
veteran-2
veterinarian-17
victory-21
video-10
visible-5
vitamin-9
vocation-7
volcano-7
volunteer-11
waist-29
waste-29
watch-4
worshiped-13
yearling-11
zoology-14

Curriculum Objectives

Literature Connection
To increase comprehension and vocabulary development through a value-based story.

Discussion Time
To check understanding of the story and encourage personal value development.

Preview
To test for knowledge of correct spellings of current spelling words.

Word Shapes
To help students form a correct visual image of whole words and to help students recognize common spelling patterns.

Hide & Seek
To reinforce correct spelling of current spelling words.

Other Word Forms
To strengthen spelling ability and expand vocabulary.

Fun Ways to Spell
To reinforce correct spelling of current words with activities that appeal to varying learning styles.

Dictation
To reinforce using current and previous spelling words in context.

Proofreading
To reinforce recognition of misspelled words, and to familiarize students with standardized test format.

Language Arts Activity
To familiarize students with word meaning and usage.

Posttest
To test mastery of the current spelling words.

Learning Game
To reinforce correct spelling of test words.

Vocabulary Extension
To provide advanced spellers with the opportunity to enrich their vocabulary.

Journaling
To provide a meaningful reason for correct spelling through personal writing.

Unit Tests
To test mastery of the correct spelling of the words from each unit.

Action Game
To provide a fun way to review spelling words from the previous unit.

Certificate
To provide opportunity for parents or guardians to encourage and assess their child's progress.

Parent Letter
To provide the parent or guardian with the spelling word lists for the next unit.

***Phonics Units** (Levels A and B only)*
To provide a supplement for promoting phonemic awareness, and a review of basic phonic skills.

Common Spelling Patterns

The following list of sounds and spelling patterns will help you easily identify words with similar patterns.

Sounds	Sample Words	Sounds	Sample Words
a	**a**sk, h**a**t	ō	**o**ld, b**oa**t, h**oe**, gl**o**be, bl**ow**
ā	**a**pron, l**a**te, m**ai**l, pl**ay**	ô	t**a**lk, c**au**se, dr**aw**, s**o**ft, th**ough**t
ä	f**a**ther, p**a**rt, h**ea**rt	ôr	st**or**y, m**or**e, w**ar**d, f**our**
âr	aw**are**, f**air**, b**ear**, th**ere**	oi	p**oi**nt, b**oy**
b	**b**erry, a**b**le, scru**b**	ou	ab**ou**t, pl**ow**
ch	**ch**eese, bun**ch**, la**tch**, na**tu**re	p	**p**lan, re**p**ly, sna**p**, su**pp**ly
d	**d**og, la**dd**er	r	**r**an, me**rr**y, mo**r**e, **wr**ite
e	b**e**d, h**ea**vy, s**ai**d	s	**s**ay, gue**ss**, **sc**ent, pri**c**e, **c**ity
ē	sh**e**, h**ea**t, fr**ee**, n**ie**ce, k**ey**	sh	**sh**ip, ca**sh**, mi**ss**ion, ma**ch**ine, spe**ci**al, vaca**ti**on
f	**f**ish, loa**f**, o**ff**, enou**gh**, pro**ph**et	t	**t**en, pu**t**, bu**tt**er, crease**d**
g	**g**ive, for**g**ot, shru**g**	th	**th**in, e**th**nic, wi**th**
h	**h**as, any**h**ow, **wh**ole	th̲	**th**em, wor**th**y, smoo**th**
wh	**wh**ine, **wh**ich	u	c**u**p, d**o**ne, wh**a**t, y**ou**ng
i	d**i**g, g**y**m	ū	h**u**man, y**ou**, n**ew**, t**u**ne
ī	f**i**nd, p**ie**, m**i**ce, tr**y**	ü	cl**ue**, d**o**, s**oo**n, fr**ui**t
îr	cl**ear**, d**eer**, p**ier**ce, c**er**eal, h**ere**	u̇	t**oo**k, sh**ou**ld, p**u**sh
j	**j**ust, en**j**oy, **g**erm, hu**ge**, bu**dge**	ûr	**ear**n, st**er**n, f**ir**st, w**or**k, Th**ur**sday
k	**k**eep, hoo**k**, sti**ck**, s**ch**ool, **c**an	v	**v**isit, a**v**oid, arri**v**e
l	**l**eft, Ju**l**y, hau**l**, fu**ll**y, te**ll**	w	**w**ash, drive**w**ay
m	**m**eal, cal**m**, cli**mb**, co**mm**on, hy**mn**	y	**y**oung, famil**i**ar
n	**n**ice, fu**n**, tu**nn**el, **kn**ow	z	la**z**y, ja**zz**, pri**z**e, rai**s**e, rein**s**, e**x**ample
ng	alo**ng**, bri**nging**, thi**n**k	zh	mea**s**ure, ero**s**ion
o	n**o**t, p**o**nd, w**a**tch	ə	**a**bove, wat**er**, anim**a**l, gall**o**n, thankf**u**l

Daily Lesson Plans

Letter

Provide the parent or guardian with the spelling word lists for the first unit.

Give your parents or guardian this letter that lists your spelling words for the next unit. Put it where you will remember to practice the words together.

Dear Parent,

We are about to begin our first spelling unit containing five weekly lessons. A set of twenty words will be studied each week. All the words will be reviewed in the sixth week. Values based on the Scriptures listed below will be taught in each lesson.

Lesson 1	Lesson 2	Lesson 3	Lesson 4	Lesson 5
accent	attend	admit	alcohol	adult
acid	credit	assist	astronaut	album
adapt	delta	cliffs	audience	circuit
aspect	denim	discuss	Australia	construct
athlete	healthy	disk	automatic	crumb
atlas	heifer	England	automobile	District of Columbia
banana	lever	glisten	awkward	freedom
banner	Maryland	glitter	clause	gruffly
batch	method	history	coffee	hungry
California	New Mexico	hymn	crawl	minutes
camera	respect	income	exhaust	museum
Canada	selfish	index	launch	numb
cavern	shelter	infant	laundry	opossum
cavity	strength	insist	lawyers	pulse
gram	tennis	kidnap	on-line	shrug
latch	tense	limit	precaution	suffix
mass	Texas	lizard	somersault	summary
Montana	umbrella	Michigan	strawberry	tundra
panic	weapon	Mississippi	Vermont	umpire
planet	weather	Virginia	Washington	wisdom
Psalm 71:8	Psalm 25:6,7	Psalm 51:10,12	Psalm 92:2,4	Psalm 16:8,9

Have each student remove this letter from his or her Worktext prior to beginning Lesson 1.

Topic: God's protecting presence
Theme Text: Psalm 71:8

Home Alone? - NOT!

Katelynn becomes a latchkey kid and learns God is with her when she feels her need for Him and when she doesn't.

"I don't know what the big deal is. I've been home alone before." Katelynn Hatasaki fastened her house key to the shiny chain heaped on the kitchen counter.

"You have your key, Katie?" Mr. Hatasaki checked his watch as he opened the front door for his two daughters.

Katelynn lifted the key she had just hung around her neck. "Right here. Don't worry, Dad." She patted his arm as she followed her older sister, Jennifer, out the front door of the apartment.

"Now remember to turn the thermostat to 74° as soon as you come in—just like I showed you. It will take a while for the apartment to cool down, but don't keep adjusting the temperature." Mr. Hatasaki surveyed the room before he shut the door behind them.

"You can call Dad at the gas station or I'll just be in the next building at Krugers' apartment." Jennifer grabbed Katelynn's shoulder, "Do you have Krugers' number? You can always dial 911 if you have a bad asthma attack or something. They'll find you even if you can't talk."

"Don't be so dramatic, you guys. All the phone numbers are on the counter. I'll be fine. It's just until Mom's off work." Katelynn held her head high and sauntered down the stairs towards the family car.

Katelynn hummed to herself that afternoon as she climbed the stairs to her family's third-floor apartment. She pulled the shiny new chain from around her neck. The 10-year-old girl gripped the key tightly in her hand and twirled the chain as she marched past her neighbors' apartments. "I wonder how long Jennifer will be at the Krugers' baby-sitting?" She stopped in front of the red door marked 308-B.

A car door slammed in the parking lot. Katelynn looked over the railing and saw a tall, dark-haired man locking the door of a big black pickup. The back of the loaded truck was covered with a green tarp. The man glanced up at her as he started toward the stairs. Their eyes met for an instant before Katelynn turned back toward her apartment.

"I don't recognize him," she mumbled. "I wonder if he's coming up here?" Katelynn hurriedly slipped the key into the lock and pushed the door open. "I don't want him to know I'm by myself." She quickly stepped into the dark interior and slammed the door. She hastily locked the doorknob, turned the deadbolt and slid the chain into place. "He can't be a salesman," she said to herself. "I wonder what he's doing here?"

Katelynn leaned against the warm door and surveyed the room. She could feel her heart thumping loudly. She wiped away the sweat dripping into her eyes and reached over to open the blinds when she remembered her mom's warning, "Katelynn, leave the front blinds closed. Someone walking by may notice you're alone. Don't answer the phone or the door. I'll be home by 4:00."

Katelynn slung her backpack on the kitchen counter. She poured herself a glass of juice before she turned on the air conditioner. The baby next door cried. The refrigerator hummed. She froze when she heard footsteps outside the apartment—and relaxed when they continued on. "It's too quiet! I hear every little sound." Her own voice sounded loud in the empty apartment.

The phone jangled. She automatically reached for it, then jerked her hand back as if she'd been burned. "I'm not supposed to answer that thing; but maybe it's Beth. I could talk to her for a while," she reasoned. The caller didn't leave a message on the answering machine. Katelynn sighed and picked up the cordless phone. "Maybe I'll call Beth. Mom just said not to answer the phone."

"Whew! It's hot in here." She fanned herself with a magazine. "I'm going to change into something cooler." As she passed the bathroom she noticed her favorite shirt on the floor. "I think I'll do a load of wash." She talked to herself as she collected more dirty clothes. "This should be enough to do a small load." She dumped the clothes into the washer. "It's so hot in here. I wonder if I did that thermostat right?" She closed the lid of the machine and smiled. "That's good. Now, where did I put the phone?"

Katelynn wiped the moisture off her forehead with a towel and picked up the cordless phone. She checked the thermostat again. It was set right on 74°. She nudged the dial a little lower. Warm sunlight streamed in through the sliding-glass door beside her. She reached over to pull the heavy drapes closed when movement below caught her eye.

A young girl in front of the next apartment building was wildly waving her arms. When she paused, a woman started gesturing with her hands. A little blond-haired boy came running around the end of a U-Haul truck and tapped the girl on the shoulder. He pointed to a door on the second floor. Katelynn unlocked the sliding-glass door and stepped out onto the balcony to get a better view. She soon realized that none of the three was saying a word. The young girl seemed to be the most expressive. It looked as if she were angry about something. "They must be moving in today. I bet the girl is about my age."

Mr. Rippy roared by between the apartments on his big riding mower. The new girl didn't

Story (continued)

turn around—or even seem to notice the deafening noise right behind her. Suddenly it hit Katelynn—the girl was deaf! She was using sign language to talk to her family. Katelynn jumped when the phone in her hand rang. She remembered not to answer it though. "That girl can't hear anything! It's *always* quiet for her." Katelynn reached behind her and shut the screen door. It was actually cooler outside than it was in the apartment. She continued to watch the family. A teenage boy joined them. When he unlocked the door of apartment 205-B, she decided he must be the older brother.

"I wonder if they're all deaf? Maybe the girl will go to Knowlton Elementary." Katelynn was so busy watching the family that she ignored the spasms of her bronchial tubes until it was hard to force air into her lungs. Whee-heee. Whee-heee. She wheezed in the hot grassy-smelling air. It was so interesting watching the family talk to each other with their hands she hadn't stopped to use the inhaler at the first sign of her asthma attack.

She reluctantly walked back into the kitchen without shutting the door and picked up her backpack. She rummaged through it until she found the small aerosol dispenser. "What's triggering this episode, I wonder?" She walked back onto the balcony. As the asthma flared, it was getting harder and harder for her to breathe. She inhaled two puffs of the medication and held her breath. It helped, but the wheezing didn't stop. "I wonder…Whee-heee…when Mom…Whee-heee…will get here?"

She shuffled back into the apartment and flopped onto the couch. The apartment was unbearably hot. She started to get up to check the thermostat again, when she heard footsteps. They slowed as they approached and stopped right outside the door. Her eyes widened as she watched the doorknob turn. She heard the sound of a key in the deadbolt! She huddled on the couch and stuffed a fist into her mouth as the door opened—until it was stopped by the chain.

"Katelynn, open the door. I'm home." Mrs. Hatasaki peeked in through the crack in the door.

Katelynn let out the breath she had been holding. "Whee-hee. I'm…Whee-hee…coming…."

"Katie, have you taken your medication?" The girl nodded. "Why is the sliding-glass door open? You know that cut grass always triggers an episode. How come the air-conditioner isn't turned on? It's like an oven in here." Mrs. Hatasaki bustled around the apartment. She turned the switch on the thermostat to "cool"—and the air-conditioner cycled on immediately. She shut the sliding-glass door and the dryer door. "When did you take your last dose of medication?"

Katelynn looked at her watch. "About…Whee-hee…10 minutes ago."

"Take another dose at 4:00." Mrs. Hatasaki sat down beside her daughter and wiped her face with a cool cloth.

"I'm glad you're…Whee-hee…home, Mom." Katelynn smiled weekly. "I did remember not to answer the phone…Whee-hee…or open the blinds. I started the wash."

Mother and daughter sat quietly on the couch as the apartment cooled down. Mrs. Hatasaki rubbed Katelynn's back and wiped her face with a damp washcloth. Her breathing became less labored after she took the next dose of medication, so Mom got up and went into the kitchen to start supper.

"Katelynn, why don't you put that load of clothes into the dryer?" Mrs. Hatasaki closed the oven door and set the timer.

Katelynn stood up, stretched, and walked over to the sliding glass door. Mr. Rippy was almost finished mowing the lawn. She silently watched the new family carrying things up to their apartment. The dark-haired man from the black pickup was helping the teenage boy carry a dresser up the stairs. When he got to the door, he set his end of the dresser down and turned to sign something to the girl following them. They laughed and went together into the apartment. "He must be their Dad," Katelynn mused. "I was so worried about him I forgot to turn the thermostat to 'cool,' I stood on the balcony while the grass was being mowed, and I nearly forgot to start the washer."

She smiled and took a deep breath. As she relaxed, she knew who had been with her all day long—when she was confident and sure of herself AND when she was afraid and all alone. "Thanks, God," she breathed.

2 Discussion Time

Check understanding of the story and development of personal values.

- Tell about a time you stayed alone.
- How did you feel?
- How did Katelynn feel about staying home at the beginning of the story?
- How did she feel when she noticed the stranger from the black pickup coming up the stairs?
- What did Katelynn do when she heard footsteps stop outside the apartment and then saw the doorknob turn?
- Later as Katelynn stood at the sliding glass doors and watched the new family move in, why did she feel thankful?

A **Preview** Name ____________

Write each word as your teacher says it.

1. latch
2. aspect
3. accent
4. acid
5. adapt
6. camera
7. gram
8. mass
9. batch
10. banana
11. banner
12. atlas
13. Canada
14. athlete
15. Montana
16. planet
17. California
18. panic
19. cavern
20. cavity

Words with /a/

Lesson 1

Scripture
Psalm 71:8

5

3 Preview

Test for knowledge of the correct spellings of these words.

Customize Your List
On a separate sheet of paper, additional words of your choice may be tested.

I will say each word once, use the word in a sentence, then say the word again. Write the words on the lines in your Worktext.

Correct Immediately!
Let's correct our Preview. I will spell each word out loud. If you spelled a word incorrectly, rewrite it correctly.

Progress Chart
Students may record scores. (Reproducible master provided in Appendix B.)

1.	latch	Katelynn reached for the chain to **latch** the door.
2.	aspect	Mr. and Mrs. Hatasaki tried to teach Katelynn every **aspect** of safety.
3.	accent	Being alone seemed to **accent** every little sound.
4.	acid	The natural **acid** in the orange juice burned Katelynn's dry throat.
5.	adapt	It would be difficult to **adapt** to deafness.
6.	camera	She looked through the lens of her dad's **camera.**
7.	gram	Katelynn tried to remember Mr. Canfield's definition of **gram.**
8.	mass	She knew that **mass** meant a body of matter.
9.	batch	She saw a **batch** of cookies in the jar on the counter.
10.	banana	Katelynn peeled a **banana,** but felt too hot to eat.
11.	banner	Katelynn straightened the school **banner** she had hanging on her wall.
12.	atlas	Next, she aimlessly leafed through the giant **atlas** on the coffee table.
13.	Canada	She tried to memorize the provinces of **Canada.**
14.	athlete	A famous **athlete** was pictured beside the facts about the country.
15.	Montana	She also read about the thoroughbreds in **Montana.**
16.	planet	Katelynn felt as if she were alone on the **planet.**
17.	California	The pictures of the beaches of **California** made her feel more hot.
18.	panic	Katelynn knew **panic** would worsen her asthma attack.
19.	cavern	Noises in the hallway outside the apartment echoed like in a **cavern.**
20.	cavity	Her chest **cavity** ached as her bronchial tubes tightened.

4 Word Shapes

Help students form a correct image of whole words.

Look at each word and think about its shape. Now, write the word in the correct word Shape Boxes. You may check off each word as you use it.

(Short vowels are usually found in syllables in which a vowel is immediately preceded and followed by a consonant, consonant cluster, or digraph.)

In the word shape boxes, fill in the boxes containing the letter or letters that spell the sound of **/a/** in each word.

Take a minute to memorize...

Psalm 71:8

B Word Shapes Name ____________________

Using the word bank below, write each word in the correct word shape boxes. Next, in the word shape boxes, fill in the boxes containing the letter or letters that spell the sound of **/a/** in each word.

1.	Montana	11.	planet
2.	California	12.	Canada
3.	cavern	13.	cavity
4.	panic	14.	camera
5.	athlete	15.	mass
6.	banner	16.	acid
7.	aspect	17.	gram
8.	adapt	18.	batch
9.	atlas	19.	latch
10.	accent	20.	banana

Word Bank

accent	athlete	batch	cavern	mass
acid	atlas	California	cavity	Montana
adapt	banana	camera	gram	panic
aspect	banner	Canada	latch	planet

6

Answers may vary for duplicate word shapes.

Be Prepared For Fun

Check these supply lists for **Fun Ways to Spell** - presented **Day 2**. Purchase and/or gather these items ahead of time!

General
- Pencil
- Graph Paper (1 sheet per child)
- Spelling List

Auditory
- Voice Recorder
- Spelling List

Visual
- American Sign Language reproducible master (provided in Appendix B)
- Spelling List

Tactile
- Soccer Ball, Basketball, Tennis Ball, or 4-Square Ball
- Spelling List

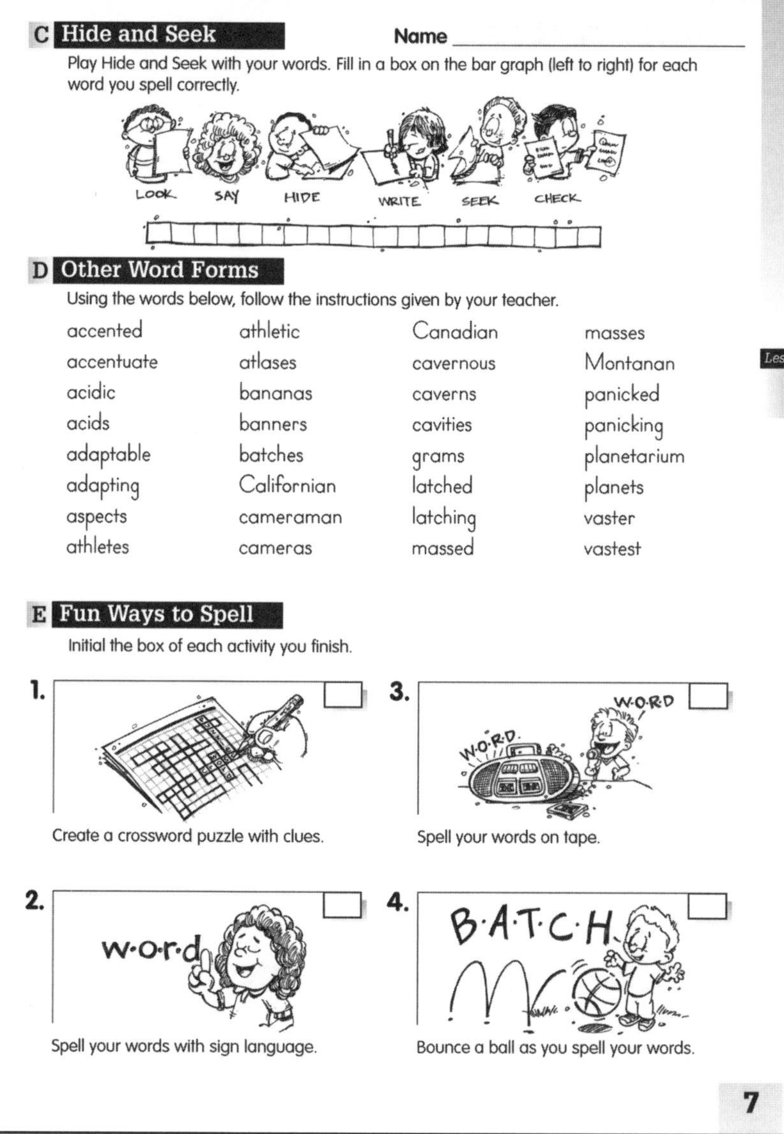

1 Hide and Seek

Reinforce spelling by using multiple styles of learning.

On a white board, Teacher writes each word — one at a time. **Have students:**

- **Look** at the word.
- **Say** the word out loud.
- **Spell** the word out loud.
- **Hide** (teacher erases word.)
- **Write** the word on paper.
- **Seek** (teacher rewrites word.)
- **Check** spelling. If incorrect, rewrite word correctly.

Day 2

Lesson 1

2 Other Word Forms

This activity is optional. Have students write original sentences using these Other Word Forms:

acidic
Montanan
massed
cavernous

3 Fun Ways to Spell

Four activities are provided. Use one, two, three, or all of the activities. Have students initial the box for each activity they complete.

Options:

- assign activities to students according to their learning styles
- set up the activities in learning centers for the students to do throughout the day
- divide students into four groups and assign one activity per group
- do one activity per day

General

To create a crossword puzzle...
- Use a pencil to arrange your words on graph paper.
- Overlap words where letters are shared.
- Don't create any new words.
- Outline each word with a marker and number it.
- Write a clue for each word.
- Erase your words.
- Trade with a classmate and work each other's puzzles.

Auditory

To spell your words using a voice recorder...
- Record yourself as you say and spell each word on your spelling list.
- Listen to your recording and check your spelling.

Visual

To spell your words with sign language...
- Have a classmate read a spelling word to you from the list.
- Spell the word using the American Sign Language alphabet.
- Do this with each word on your list.

Tactile

To bounce a ball as you spell your words...
- Look at the first word on your list.
- Bounce the ball as you say each letter of the word aloud.
- Do this with each word on your list.

Lesson 1 | Day 3

1 Working with Words

Familiarize students with word meaning and usage.

Scrambled Words

Write the letters **alst** on the board. Have a student unscramble the letters to make the word **last**.

Unscramble each spelling word. Write the word correctly on the line. Remember to use capital letters where they are needed.

Word Clues

Use your word bank to help you match the spelling words to the clues. Some of the clues are synonyms, words that have the same meaning as the spelling word. You may use a dictionary or thesaurus to help you.

Take a minute to memorize...

Psalm 71:8

Words with /a/ — Lesson 1

F Working with Words Name ______________________

Scrambled Words

Unscramble each word. Write the unscrambled word on the line. Use capital letters where they are needed.

1.	aeehltt	athlete	**13.**	aadpt	adapt
2.	aamnnot	Montana	**14.**	aaacdn	Canada
3.	aaabnn	banana	**15.**	acinp	panic
4.	acdi	acid	**16.**	acepst	aspect
5.	acitvy	cavity	**17.**	aelnpt	planet
6.	abcht	batch	**18.**	achlt	latch
7.	aacfiilnor	California	**19.**	acenrv	cavern
8.	agmr	gram	**20.**	aacemr	camera
9.	catcne	accent			
10.	aalst	atlas			
11.	amss	mass			
12.	abennr	banner			

Word Clues

Match the spelling words to the clues. You may use a dictionary or thesaurus to help you.

1.	emphasize, stress	accent	**10.**	Earth, Mars	planet
2.	void, depression	cavity	**11.**	pennant, flag	banner
3.	alarm, scare	panic	**12.**	tropical fruit	banana
4.	runner, swimmer	athlete	**13.**	unit of mass	gram
5.	cave, hollow	cavern	**14.**	photographic tool	camera
6.	appearance, condition	aspect	**15.**	charts, maps	atlas
7.	quantity, bulk	mass	**16.**	group, bunch	batch
8.	corrosive, erosive	acid	**17.**	coastal state	California
9.	adjust, accommodate	adapt	**18.**	fasten, secure	latch

Word Bank

accent	athlete	batch	cavern	mass
acid	atlas	California	cavity	Montana
adapt	banana	camera	gram	panic
aspect	banner	Canada	latch	planet

8

G Dictation

Name ______________________

Write each sentence as your teacher dictates. Use correct punctuation.

1. Katelynn began to panic when the tall man looked at her.
2. Mom made a batch of cookies after supper.
3. Katelynn got the atlas to find a map of Canada.

Words with /a/

Lesson 1

H Proofreading

If a word is misspelled, fill in the oval by that word. If all the words are spelled correctly, fill in the oval by **no mistake**.

1. ○ adapt ● acsent ○ gram ○ no mistake
2. ● camra ○ latch ○ banner ○ no mistake
3. ● asid ○ California ○ batch ○ no mistake
4. ○ athlete ○ mass ● canada ○ no mistake
5. ● panick ○ Canada ○ rake ○ no mistake
6. ○ cavity ○ planet ○ love ● no mistake
7. ○ banana ● aspekt ○ cavern ○ no mistake
8. ● planit ○ aspect ○ panic ○ no mistake
9. ● lacth ○ atlas ○ camera ○ no mistake
10. ○ acid ○ Montana ● atlus ○ no mistake
11. ○ broom ● cavirn ○ accent ○ no mistake
12. ○ flute ● Montanna ○ look ○ no mistake

9

1 Dictation

Reinforce correct spelling by using current and previous words in context.

Listen as I read each sentence and then write it in your Worktext. Remember to use correct capitalization and punctuation. (Slowly read each sentence twice. Sentences are found in the Student Worktext to the left.)

Day 4

Proofreading

Familiarize students with standardized test format and reinforce recognition of misspelled words.

Look at each set of words. If a word is misspelled, fill in the oval by that word. If all the words are spelled correctly, fill in the oval by **no mistake**.

Lesson 1

3 Hide and Seek

Reinforce correct spelling of current spelling words. Repeat this activity from Day 2.

4 Vocabulary Extension

Have your students complete this activity to strengthen spelling ability and expand vocabulary. The reproducible master is provided in Appendix A as shown on the inset page to the right.

1 Posttest

Test mastery of the spelling words.

I will say the word once, use it in a sentence, then say it again. Write your words on a separate sheet of paper.

Progress Chart

Students may record scores. (Reproducible master in Appendix B.)

Personal Dictionary

Students may add any words they have misspelled to their personal dictionaries for reference when writing. (Cover in Appendix B.)

Hide and Seek

Play Hide and Seek with your words. Fill in a bar graph (left to right) for each word you spell correctly.

Vocabulary Extension

Crossword Puzzle

Use the clues below to complete the puzzle.

Down

2. last book of the Old Testament
3. enormous
4. book of the Bible following Nahum
6. word meaning the opposite
8. book of the Bible before Hosea

Across

1. book of the Bible that follows Ruth
3. motor fuel
5. book of the Bible between Zephaniah and Zechariah
7. move forward
9. fifth book of the New Testament
10. occurring every year
11. one of the four gospels

Word Bank

Acts	antonym	gigantic	Malachi
advance	Daniel	Habakkuk	Matthew
annual	gasoline	Haggai	Samuel

---

1. **accent** — Katelynn tripped over the **accent** rug just inside the door.
2. **batch** — Katelynn thought about making a **batch** of muffins to go with dinner.
3. **gram** — Katelynn noticed the juice did not have a single **gram** of fat.
4. **cavity** — The cold juice made the **cavity** in her upper molar throb.
5. **acid** — The **acid** in the juice burned her throat as she drank.
6. **mass** — Mr. Canfield defined **mass** for his class that day.
7. **camera** — Katelynn put her dad's **camera** back in its case.
8. **adapt** — She wondered how a person could **adapt** to deafness.
9. **aspect** — She began to consider every possible **aspect** of being deaf.
10. **banner** — Her school **banner** is bright green with gold letters.
11. **atlas** — The giant picture **atlas** on the coffee table was very heavy.
12. **Montana** — There were photos of beautiful horses on the pages about **Montana.**
13. **Canada** — She imagined standing by the great Niagara Falls in **Canada.**
14. **athlete** — Katelynn does not plan to become a professional **athlete.**
15. **banana** — She put the uneaten **banana** on the top shelf of the refrigerator.
16. **panic** — Each noise increased Katelynn's feelings of **panic.**
17. **planet** — Katelynn felt like she was alone on the **planet.**
18. **cavern** — The empty apartment seemed to echo like a **cavern.**
19. **latch** — When her mom got home, Katelynn had to remove the chain from the **latch.**
20. **California** — The atlas lay open to pictures and information about **California.**

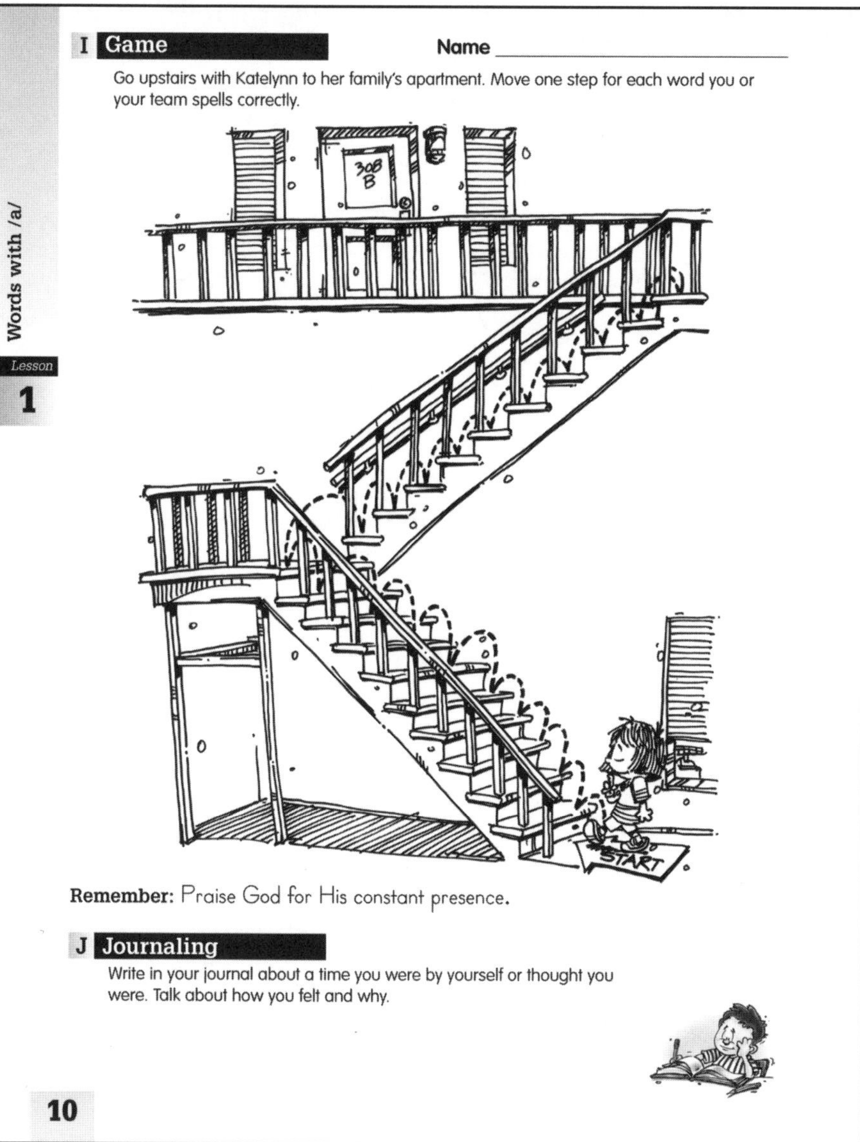

I **Game** Name ____________________

Go upstairs with Katelynn to her family's apartment. Move one step for each word you or your team spells correctly.

Remember: Praise God for His constant presence.

J **Journaling**

Write in your journal about a time you were by yourself or thought you were. Talk about how you felt and why.

Words with /a/

Lesson 1

10

2 Game

Reinforce spelling skills and provide motivation and interest.

Materials

- game page (from student text)
- game pieces (1 per child)
- game word list

Game Word List

1. **accent**
2. **acid**
3. **adapt**
4. **camera**
5. **gram**
6. **banana**
7. **banner**
8. **Canada**
9. **Montana**
10. **panic**
11. **planet**
12. **aspect**
13. **mass**
14. **California**
15. **batch**
16. **latch**
17. **athlete**
18. **atlas**
19. **cavern**
20. **cavity**

Day 5

How to Play:

- Divide the class into two teams.
- Have each student place his/her game piece on Start.
- Have a student from team A go to the board.
- Say the spelling word.
- Have the student write the word on the board.
- If correct, instruct each member of team A to move his/her game piece forward one space.
- Alternate between teams A and B.
- The team to reach the apartment first is the winner.
- **Small Group Option**: Students may play this game without teacher direction in small groups of two or more.

3 Journaling

Provide a meaningful reason for correct spelling through personal writing.

Review the story using discussion leads provided on the following page. Encourage students to apply the Scriptural value in their journaling.

Journaling (continued)

- As she left for school, how did Katelynn feel about being left alone later in the afternoon? (She was confident and sure of herself.)
- What did Katelynn see on her way up to the apartment that worried her? (A stranger in a black pickup truck.)
- After Katelynn locked the apartment door, why was she so aware of all the little noises? (She was scared.)
- Why was Katelynn fascinated by the new neighbors moving in? (There was a girl her age waving her arms around.)
- When Mr. Rippy roared by on the lawn mower what did Katelynn discover about the new girl? (She was deaf.)
- Later as she watched the family finish moving in what did she realize? (God was with her all the time.)

Some Common Abbreviations:

a.m. = Ante Meridiem or Before Noon

AWOL = Absent Without Offical Leave

rpm = Revolutions Per Minute

RSVP = Repondez S'il Vous Plait or Respond, please

Literature Connection

Topic: Judging friends' motives
Theme Text: Psalm 25:6, 7

"R.S.V.P. by ______"

When Beth doesn't get an invitation to Laney's slumber party, she learns things are not always as they appear.

Dear Megan,

We just got a modem for our computer today! Mom installed a program so we can use the Internet—now you can e-mail us. My address is: smalltowngirl@KOL.com. This will be fun writing back and forth! My stepdad says he needs access to the World Wide Web for his work. Mom wants e-mail so she can keep in touch with her family and friends back in New York City without having such a huge phone bill. Maybe my busy father in New York can write me once in a while too.

I finally get to have a slumber party! Mom said I could invite whoever I want, so I'm asking all the girls in my class. I wish you lived here. It's going to be this weekend. Rachel and Katelynn are helping me plan it. I've decided on a 50's theme. I want everyone to dress up in clothes like they wore back in the olden days. You know—those poodle skirts, blouses, white bobby socks, and saddle shoes—stuff like that. I've gotten cat-eye glasses and white scarves for everyone's hair. It should be funny. Mom's going to take lots of pictures. I'll send you some by snail mail later. Do you or Brittany have any ideas for a 50's party? Our school has already started. Has yours? Mr. Canfield is our teacher. He's African-American. The boys like him because he is so good at sports!

Laney

Dear Diary,

Laney, Rachel, and Katelynn have been talking about Laney's sleep-over all week. Laney asked Rachel and Katelynn to help her plan it. Laney missed my last sleep-over. She came to one a long time ago, though. It was the first week she moved here from New York City. I bet she'll do something really different. Maybe it's because she's from such a big city. She always comes up with ideas that nobody else ever thinks of. She draws really well too.

Beth

Dear Megan,

Got your e-mail last night. Thanks for the ideas. Tell Brittany hi for me. I wish you guys were here. No, I haven't been to the Skatepark here. Small towns don't have tracks for BMX bikes or skateboards. Mom and I went shopping again last night. We bought little Slinkys, yo-yos, and bouncy glitter balls for game prizes. The shopping here isn't like New York City. But we finally found the tissue paper stuff for everyone to make wrist corsages like you told me about. We even got some of those long, skinny, pink balloons. One of my books shows how to twist the balloons into the shape of a poodle. You know, poodles—to remind you of poodle skirts. This is going to be so much fun! Rachel and I made some neat invitations. I'm going to pass them out at school tomorrow.

Laney

Dear Diary,

Everyone is talking about Laney's sleep-over. Katelynn said it's going to be a 50s theme. I don't have any saddle shoes like they were talking about, but I have a white blouse and Mom is going to cut off a pair of my old pants to make pedal pushers. I told her about the poodle skirts, and she showed me a picture of Grandma in pedal pushers. Mom wasn't even born yet. Grandma didn't have any wrinkles and Grandpa was with her. Grandpa had his arm around Grandma and she was wearing a pair of pants that came just past her knees. They had little slits in the legs so she could move better. They were standing in front of two funny-looking bikes. I can borrow some of Mom's white socks. Mine never stay white very long.

Beth

Dear Megan,

I've finished the invitations. We've asked everybody to R.S.V.P. by tomorrow. Mom is taking me to school early this morning. I'm going to put one on every girl's desk. They'll see them when they first come in.

To answer your question. I skate and ride with two boys—Stephen and Tony. (Don't get any ideas, now.) We don't have a Skatepark, but a man named Mr. Sample lets us ride in an empty lot he owns. We've kind of made our own track with jumps and everything for the bikes. We skate on the sidewalks and a parking lot in Mason Springs Park.

I like your idea about a record-shaped cake. Getting some of those single-use cameras is a good idea, too. It would be fun if we took some pictures ourselves. Gotta go if I'm going to get to school early this morning.

Laney

Dear Diary,

Everyone got an invitation to Laney's slumber party—except for me. "R.S.V.P by Thursday," they say. That's French for "tell me if you're coming." Can you believe she expects everyone to write and tell her if they want to come? What's wrong with the phone? She even invited Sarah. I don't know what her problem is. Maybe I'm just not good enough for her New York tastes. She skipped my sleep-over. She told me she forgot all about it. I bet she just didn't want to come. She went skating with Tony or something. I can't remember now. It was last year during Spring Break. She was supposed to go back to New York and see her father. I wish Laney would just go back to New York—and stay. We don't need snobs like her here.

Beth

Story (continued)

Dear Megan,

Mom can't believe how much I write to you. I don't mind writing letters when I don't have to address or mail them. How is Brit doing? Has she gotten any new pets lately? The strangest thing happened today. I passed out the invitations this morning, you know. And everyone is excited about it except for this girl in my class named Beth. She doesn't say a word. She acts mad or something. I missed her party last spring but it was an accident. She was real nice about it. She ate with the boys at lunch today. She's good at sports and has been friends with Tony and Stephen since before first grade. She's acting so weird. We're not best friends but she didn't even talk with the girls at recess. She played catch with Tony. Who knows?

Laney

Dear Diary,

I wasn't planning on writing in here so often, but I am so mad! I would love to make Laney feel as left out as I do. I can't believe she didn't invite me to the slumber party!! I've never liked her very much. She always spends so much money on clothes. I don't like her hair either. It looks like a boy's hair cut. Katelynn asked me what I'm going to wear to the slumber party. I told her I wasn't in the mood to make a fool out of myself and dress up like my grandma. I don't like the goofy glasses they wore back then or the music or the white socks. I told her Luke and I were going to camp by our creek this weekend. I'd better go tell Luke.

Beth

Dear Megan,

Yes, I'm sure Beth got her invitation. Katelynn told me Beth doesn't like my 50's theme. She's going to camp out by their creek this weekend with her brother Luke. She told Katelynn she wouldn't be caught dead in cat-eye glasses and she doesn't like 50's music either. I wish she'd tell me instead of everyone else. Sarah told me she didn't think she would be able to come. Her mom is sick or something. Beth hasn't said a word—except to Katelynn. I guess I should go talk to her. Everyone else is coming.

Laney

Dear Diary,

I don't even want to go to school tomorrow. All everyone can talk about is Laney's party. I'm sick of Laney this and Laney that. I'm sick of hearing about the 50's. I'm sick of being sick of it!

Beth

Dear Megan,

It all makes sense now. Tony found Beth's invitation by the computer at the back of our classroom. I must have dropped it there. It wasn't opened. She thought I didn't want her to come to the party. I'll have to agree it sure looked that way. I wish she had just come and told me. She didn't even tell her best friend, Katelynn. I guess she was embarrassed that she was the only girl in the class who wasn't invited. What a mess! I told her I was sorry. I think she believes me.

Laney

Dear Diary,

Whew....What a mess. I just responded by mail to Laney's invitation. I know I could have used the phone, but I like writing. Laney found my invitation today. She'd dropped it. She told me she was sorry. I told her I was sorry. I don't know why I have such a hard time seeing the good in her. I didn't say very kind things about her. I think I'll tear out those pages in my diary. On second thought, I don't think I will. I need to leave them there to remind me to look for the good in people—like the Lord looks at me.

Beth

2 Discussion Time

Check understanding of the story and development of personal values.

- Why was Laney e-mailing Megan in New York?
- Have any of you ever kept a diary or journal?
- Raise your hand if you have sent e-mail.
- What did you like or dislike about putting your thoughts and ideas in print?
- What is Laney planning for all the girls in her class?
- How did Beth react when she didn't get an invitation?
- How did Laney respond when Beth didn't want to come to her party?
- What could they have done to solve the problem more quickly?
- How does the Lord look at us?

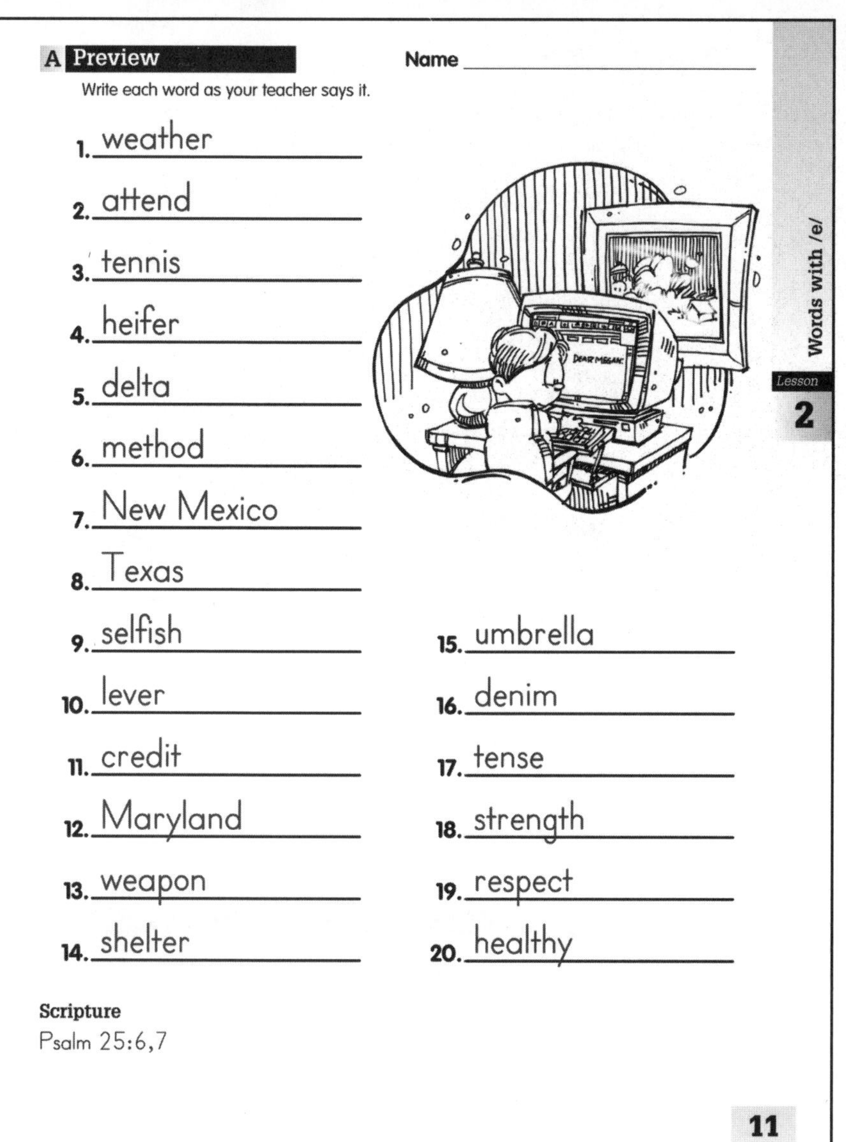

3 Preview

Test for knowledge of the correct spellings of these words.

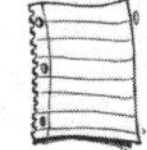

Customize Your List

On a separate sheet of paper, additional words of your choice may be tested.

I will say each word once, use the word in a sentence, then say the word again. Write the words on the lines in your Worktext.

Correct Immediately!

Let's correct our Preview. I will spell each word out loud. If you spelled a word incorrectly, rewrite it correctly.

Progress Chart

Students may record scores. (Reproducible master provided in Appendix B.)

1.	weather	Laney hoped the **weather** would be nice the day of her party.
2.	attend	She bought prizes and favors for everyone she'd asked to **attend.**
3.	tennis	Each glitter ball bounced high like a **tennis** ball.
4.	heifer	Beth was thinking of raising a **heifer** for her 4-H project.
5.	delta	Mr. Canfield taught his class that **delta** can describe anything triangular.
6.	method	Mr. Canfield's **method** of teaching is interesting and unique.
7.	New Mexico	He pointed out some interesting facts about **New Mexico.**
8.	Texas	**Texas** borders New Mexico.
9.	selfish	"I think Laney is so **selfish,**" wrote Beth.
10.	lever	Beth twisted the **lever** on the water fountain angrily.
11.	credit	Beth did not give Laney any **credit** for being thoughtful.
12.	Maryland	"I wish she'd move back to **Maryland,** or New York, or wherever!" Beth fumed.
13.	weapon	She used her anger as a **weapon** to defend her hurt feelings.
14.	shelter	Beth tried to **shelter** her feelings by acting uninterested in the party.
15.	umbrella	She grabbed her **umbrella** before walking grumpily to her family's truck.
16.	denim	Her **denim** jumper felt hot in the afternoon sun.
17.	tense	Beth felt **tense** and hurt as she wrote in her diary.
18.	strength	She asked God to give her the **strength** to treat Laney with kindness.
19.	respect	God wants us to **respect** each other's feelings.
20.	healthy	Beth prayed for a **healthy** attitude toward Laney.

Day 1

Lesson 2

4 Word Shapes

Help students form a correct image of whole words.

Look at each word and think about its shape. Now, write the word in the correct word Shape Boxes. You may check off each word as you use it.

(Short vowels are usually found in syllables in which a vowel is immediately preceded and followed by a consonant, consonant cluster, or digraph.)

Say

In the word shape boxes, fill in the boxes containing the letter or letters that spell the sound of **/e/** in each word.

Take a minute to memorize...

Psalm 25:6,7

Words with /e/

B Word Shapes **Name** ____________________

Using the word bank below, write each word in the correct word shape boxes. Next, in the word shape boxes, fill in the boxes containing the letter or letters that spell the sound of **/e/** in each word.

1. respect
2. denim
3. umbrella
4. Texas
5. delta
6. method
7. strength
8. credit
9. Maryland
10. selfish
11. shelter
12. healthy
13. New Mexico
14. heifer
15. lever
16. weather
17. weapon
18. tennis
19. tense
20. attend

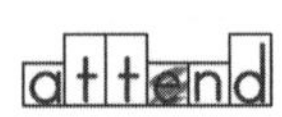

Word Bank

attend	healthy	method	shelter	Texas
credit	heifer	New Mexico	strength	umbrella
delta	lever	respect	tennis	weapon
denim	Maryland	selfish	tense	weather

12

Answers may vary for duplicate word shapes.

Be Prepared For Fun

Check these supply lists for **Fun Ways to Spell** - presented **Day 2**. Purchase and/or gather these items ahead of time!

General
- Pencil
- Notebook Paper
- Spelling List

Auditory
- Pencil
- Notebook Paper
- Dictionary
- Spelling List

Visual
- Pencil
- Notebook Paper
- Spelling List

Tactile
- Computer Keyboard
- Spelling List

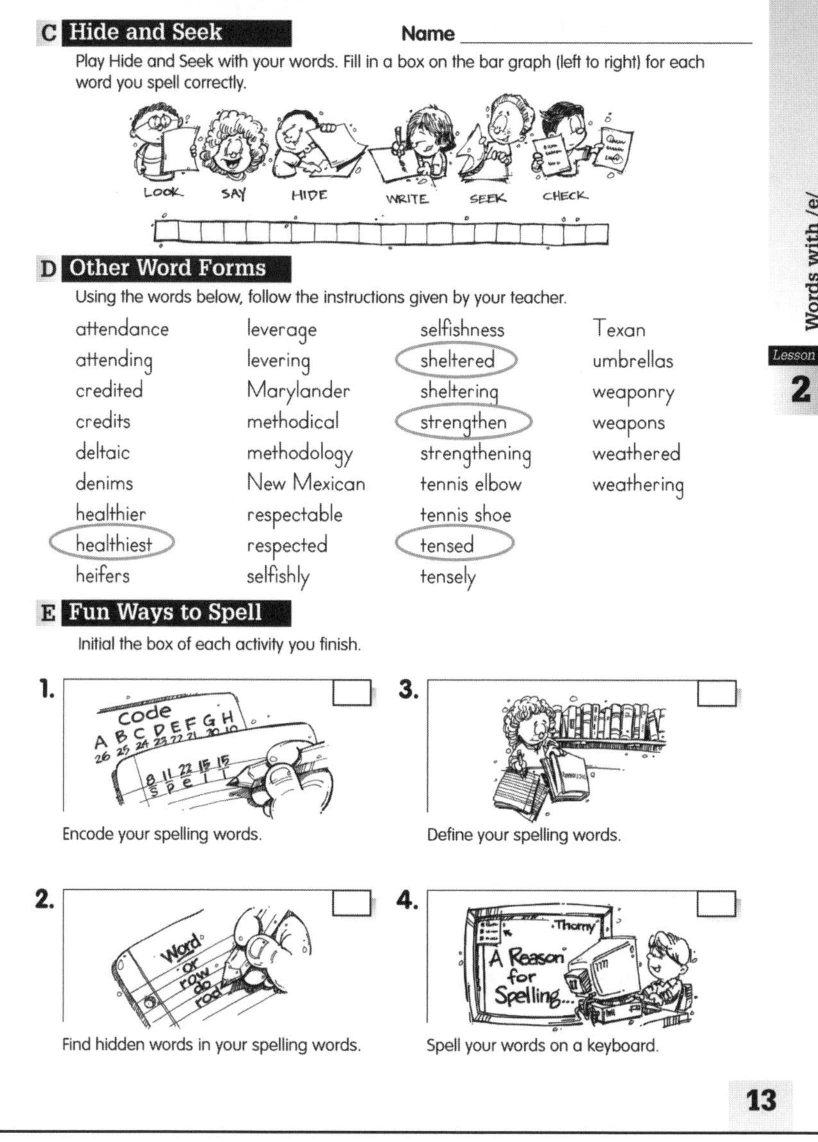

C Hide and Seek Name ____________________

Play Hide and Seek with your words. Fill in a box on the bar graph (left to right) for each word you spell correctly.

D Other Word Forms

Using the words below, follow the instructions given by your teacher.

attendance	leverage	selfishness	Texan
attending	levering	sheltered	umbrellas
credited	Marylander	sheltering	weaponry
credits	methodical	strengthen	weapons
deltaic	methodology	strengthening	weathered
denims	New Mexican	tennis elbow	weathering
healthier	respectable	tennis shoe	
healthiest	respected	tensed	
heifers	selfishly	tensely	

E Fun Ways to Spell

Initial the box of each activity you finish.

1. Encode your spelling words.

2. Find hidden words in your spelling words.

3. Define your spelling words.

4. Spell your words on a keyboard.

Words with /e/

Lesson 2

13

1 Hide and Seek

Reinforce spelling by using multiple styles of learning.

On a white board, Teacher writes each word — one at a time. **Have students:**

- **Look** at the word.
- **Say** the word out loud.
- **Spell** the word out loud.
- **Hide** (teacher erases word.)
- **Write** the word on paper.
- **Seek** (teacher rewrites word.)
- **Check** spelling. If incorrect, rewrite word correctly.

2 Other Word Forms

This activity is optional. Have students find and circle the Other Word Forms that are antonyms of the following:

relaxed
unprotected
weaken
sickliest

3 Fun Ways to Spell

Four activities are provided. Use one, two, three, or all of the activities. Have students initial the box for each activity they complete.

Options:

- assign activities to students according to their learning styles
- set up the activities in learning centers for the students to do throughout the day
- divide students into four groups and assign one activity per group
- do one activity per day

General

To encode your spelling words...

- Write the alphabet on your paper.
- Write your own code for each letter underneath it.
- Write your spelling words in your code.
- Trade papers with a classmate and decode the words.
- Check to make sure your classmate spelled the words correctly.

Auditory

To define your spelling words...

- Ask a classmate to look up a word from your spelling list in the dictionary and read the definition to you, but not the spelling word.
- Decide which word on your list matches this definition and write the word.
- Ask your classmate to check your spelling.
- Switch with a classmate and continue taking turns.

Visual

To find hidden words in your spelling words...

- Choose a word from your spelling list.
- Write it on your paper.
- Find and write as many smaller words as you can that are contained within your spelling word.
- Do this with each word.

Tactile

To spell your words on a keyboard...

- Type your spelling words on a keyboard.
- Check your spelling.

Working with Words

Familiarize students with word meaning and usage.

Hidden Words

Explain that the spelling words for this week are hidden in the puzzle. After finding each word, the student should write the word under the correct heading.

Use the word bank to help you find each of the words in the puzzle. Words may go across, down, or diagonally. Circle, then write the words.

Take a minute to memorize...

Psalm 25:6,7

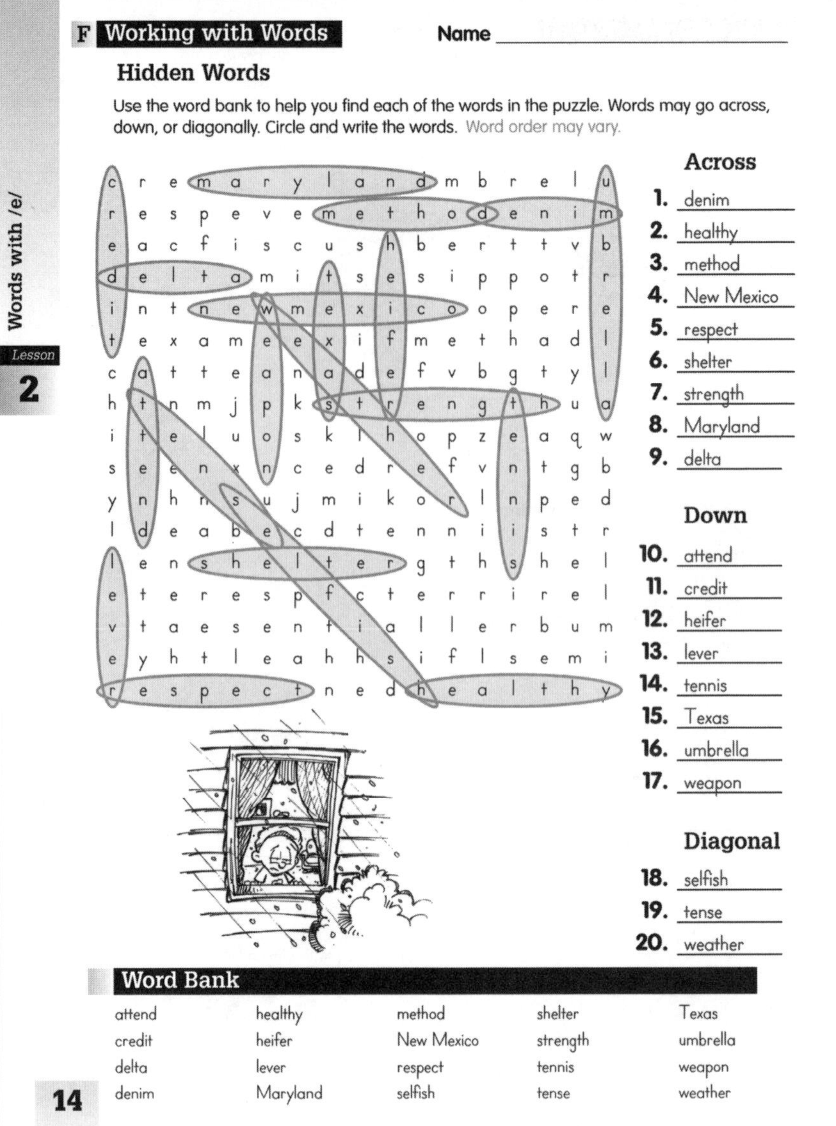

F Working with Words Name ____________

Words with /e/ — Lesson 2

Hidden Words

Use the word bank to help you find each of the words in the puzzle. Words may go across, down, or diagonally. Circle and write the words. Word order may vary.

c r e m a r y l a n d m b r e l u
r e s p e v e m e t h o d e n i m
e a c f i s c u s h b e r t t v b
d e l t a m i t s e s i p p o t r
i n t n e w m e x i c o o p e r e
t e x a m e e x i f m e t h a d l
c a t t e a n a d e f v b g t y l
h t n m j p k s t r e n g t h u a
i t e l u o s k l h o p z e a q w
s e e n x n c e d r e f v n t g b
y n h n s u j m i k o r l n p e d
l d e a b e c d t e n n i i s t r
l e n s h e l t e r g t h s h e l
e t e r e s p f c t e r r i r e l
v t a e s e n f i a l l e r b u m
e y h t l e a h h s i f l s e m i
r e s p e c t n e d h e a l t h y

Across

1. denim
2. healthy
3. method
4. New Mexico
5. respect
6. shelter
7. strength
8. Maryland
9. delta

Down

10. attend
11. credit
12. heifer
13. lever
14. tennis
15. Texas
16. umbrella
17. weapon

Diagonal

18. selfish
19. tense
20. weather

Word Bank

attend	healthy	method	shelter	Texas
credit	heifer	New Mexico	strength	umbrella
delta	lever	respect	tennis	weapon
denim	Maryland	selfish	tense	weather

14

G Dictation

Name ______________________

Write each sentence as your teacher dictates. Use correct punctuation.

1. Beth said, "I think she is just plain selfish not to ask me to her house!"
2. I would rather wear tennis shoes than dress like my grandmother.
3. The weather man is calling for rain, so I'm going to take my umbrella.

Words with /e/

Lesson **2**

H Proofreading

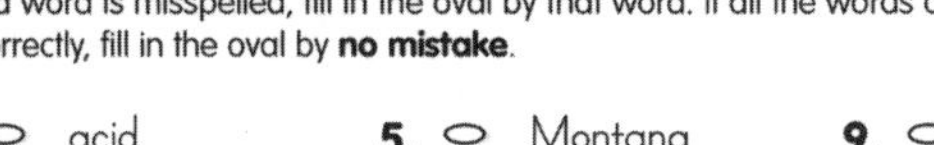

If a word is misspelled, fill in the oval by that word. If all the words are spelled correctly, fill in the oval by **no mistake**.

1.
- ○ acid
- ○ credit
- ● wepon
- ○ no mistake

2.
- ● heffer
- ○ latch
- ○ athlete
- ○ no mistake

3.
- ● helthy
- ○ batch
- ○ delta
- ○ no mistake

4.
- ○ mass
- ○ atlas
- ○ selfish
- ● no mistake

5.
- ○ Montana
- ● umbrela
- ○ shelter
- ○ no mistake

6.
- ● teniss
- ○ planet
- ○ cavern
- ○ no mistake

7.
- ● tinse
- ○ Canada
- ○ California
- ○ no mistake

8.
- ○ banner
- ● Mariland
- ○ respect
- ○ no mistake

9.
- ○ method
- ● wethar
- ○ camera
- ○ no mistake

10.
- ○ accent
- ○ lever
- ● new mexico
- ○ no mistake

11.
- ○ panic
- ○ adapt
- ○ Texas
- ● no mistake

12.
- ○ attend
- ○ denim
- ● strenth
- ○ no mistake

15

1 Dictation

Reinforce correct spelling by using current and previous words in context.

Listen as I read each sentence and then write it in your Worktext. Remember to use correct capitalization and punctuation. (Slowly read each sentence twice. Sentences are found in the Student Worktext to the left.)

Day 4

2 Proofreading

Familiarize students with standardized test format and reinforce recognition of misspelled words.

Look at each set of words. If a word is misspelled, fill in the oval by that word. If all the words are spelled correctly, fill in the oval by **no mistake**.

Lesson 2

3 Hide and Seek

Reinforce correct spelling of current spelling words. Repeat this activity from Day 2.

4 Vocabulary Extension

Have your students complete this activity to strengthen spelling ability and expand vocabulary. The reproducible master is provided in Appendix A as shown on the inset page to the right.

Lesson 2 — Vocabulary Extension

Hide and Seek

Play Hide and Seek with your words. Fill in a bar graph (left to right) for each word you spell correctly.

Vocabulary Extension

Trade-off

Choose a word from the word bank to replace the word(s) in parentheses. Write the word in the blank.

1. Genesis (book of the Bible meaning beginning) tells sacred history from the first day of creation to the death of Joseph.
2. I don't recommend (suggest) that you wait very long to begin your science project.
3. I have only a vague memory (recollection) of when I was very little.
4. It is essential (important) for you to understand how to work these math problems.
5. King Artaxerxes sent Ezra (a priest) to set up civil and religious laws in Jersalem.
6. Moses led the Israelites from Egypt in a grand Exodus (departure) after they had been held in slavery for a long time.
7. The king sent a messenger (courier) to tell the other armies the news of the battle.
8. There is an appendix (index) at the end of the book that tells the definitions of your words.
9. This beautiful woman, Esther, (Mordecai's cousin) became the Queen of Persia.
10. This table looks so old, I am sure it must be a genuine (authentic) antique.
11. We like to visit the cemetery (graveyard) to read the names and dates on the tombstones.
12. You can record this music on a cassette (tape) to listen to in your car.

Word Bank

appendix	essential	Ezra	memory
cassette	Esther	Genesis	messenger
cemetery	Exodus	genuine	recommend

326

1 Posttest

Test mastery of the spelling words.

I will say the word once, use it in a sentence, then say it again. Write your words on a separate sheet of paper.

Progress Chart
Students may record scores. (Reproducible master in Appendix B.)

Personal Dictionary
Students may add any words they have misspelled to their personal dictionaries for reference when writing. (Cover in Appendix B.)

1. weather	Laney watched the **weather** report to see the forecast for her birthday.
2. heifer	Beth has not decided whether she will raise a **heifer** or a lamb for 4-H.
3. New Mexico	Mr. Canfield gave the class a quiz about **New Mexico.**
4. Texas	He also asked several questions about the state of **Texas.**
5. credit	Laney got **credit** for the bonus question on the quiz.
6. delta	During math, Mr. Canfield drew a triangle and wrote **delta** under it.
7. Maryland	"She can move back to **Maryland**, or New York, or wherever," said Beth.
8. weapon	Disinterest was her **weapon** to defend her hurt feelings.
9. method	Laney wasn't sure of the best **method** to win Beth as a friend.
10. shelter	Beth tried to **shelter** her hurt feelings by acting like she didn't care.
11. attend	She acted as if she did not care to **attend** Laney's party.
12. lever	Angrily she twisted the **lever** on the water fountain.
13. strength	God can give us **strength** to be kind to someone who has hurt us.
14. tennis	Beth kicked off her school shoes and put on her **tennis** shoes.
15. tense	She felt **tense** and angry and wanted to relax.
16. denim	She plopped down on her **denim** floor pillow to write.
17. selfish	"I think Laney is **selfish** and spoiled," she wrote in her diary.
18. healthy	She knew she did not have a **healthy** attitude toward Laney.
19. respect	God says we should **respect** others and care about their feelings.
20. umbrella	After school, Beth offered to share her **umbrella** with Laney.

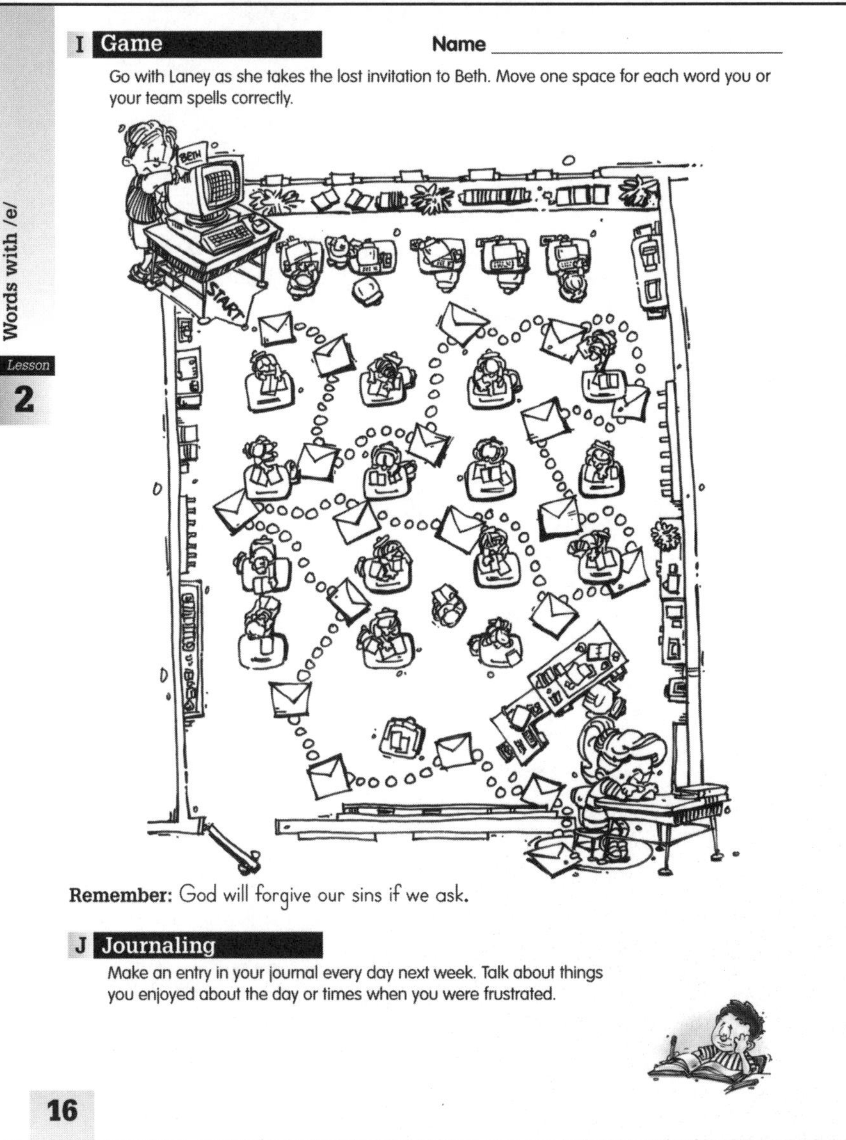

I Game Name ____________________

Go with Laney as she takes the lost invitation to Beth. Move one space for each word you or your team spells correctly.

Remember: God will forgive our sins if we ask.

J Journaling

Make an entry in your journal every day next week. Talk about things you enjoyed about the day or times when you were frustrated.

16

2 Game

Reinforce spelling skills and provide motivation and interest.

Materials

- game page (from student text)
- game pieces (1 per child)
- game word list

Game Word List

1. **weapon**
2. **weather**
3. **credit**
4. **heifer**
5. **healthy**
6. **delta**
7. **selfish**
8. **shelter**
9. **umbrella**
10. **attend**
11. **denim**
12. **strength**
13. **tennis**
14. **tense**
15. **Maryland**
16. **respect**
17. **method**
18. **lever**
19. **New Mexico**
20. **Texas**

How to Play:

- Divide the class into two teams.
- Have each student place his/her game piece on Start.
- Have a student from team A go to the board.
- Say the spelling word.
- Have the student write the word on the board.
- If correct, instruct each member of team A to move his/her game piece forward one space.
- Alternate between teams A and B.
- The team to reach Beth first is the winner.
- **Small Group Option**: Students may play this game without teacher direction in small groups of two or more.

3 Journaling

Provide a meaningful reason for correct spelling through personal writing.

Review the story using discussion leads provided on the following page. Encourage students to apply the Scriptural value in their journaling.

Journaling (continued)

- Why did Laney start e-mailing Megan? (They got a modem for their computer and a program to hook them up to the Internet.)
- Why do you think Beth and Laney seem to always misunderstand each other? (They have different backgrounds. Beth has grown up on a farm. Laney grew up in New York City. Beth may be jealous of Laney, too.)
- Why did Beth decide not to throw out her diary? (She wanted to remind herself to look for the good in people.)
- Has writing something down ever helped you discover something new or understand something better? Why or why not?

The word kayak is spelled the same forward and backward. It is a one-word palindrome.

1 **Literature Connection**
Topic: A clean heart
Theme Text: Psalm 51:10, 12

Jeans, Juice, and a Jerk

When Kristin wears expensive new jeans to a messy outdoor party, she finds that more than the jeans need cleaning.

"Hurry up, Kristin." Nine-year-old Cathy grabbed her shoes and sat on the side of her bed to put them on. "You're not even dressed yet and the party starts in 15 minutes!"

"Okay, okay!" Kristin grabbed a shirt off the pile on her bed and slipped it over her head. "I'll be ready in a second, and the Hugheses only live a couple blocks away. We won't be late."

Mom opened the door to the room Cathy and Kristin shared and stuck her head in. "Dad said to let you girls know the car is leaving for the Hugheses' house in five minutes." She stepped all the way into the room and looked at the older girl. "Kristin, it may not be a good idea to wear those jeans to Carol's party. Don't you have an older pair?"

"But, M-o-m! These jeans are the brand everyone's wearing now." Kristin plopped down onto her bed.

"It seems I've heard that particular argument before, especially at the store when you were begging me to buy them." Mrs. Wright shook her head and added, "Just remember, Kristin, if they get ruined you won't have 'the brand everyone's wearing' anymore. They were much too expensive to replace. The party's in the backyard because some of the activities and games will be too messy for indoors."

"Maggy!" Dad called from further down the hall.

Mom glanced at her watch. "Three minutes left, girls!" She closed the door gently as she left to see what Dad wanted.

Kristin jumped up and pulled some socks out of a drawer.

"The party invitation even said something about wearing old clothes," Cathy reminded her as she threaded a belt through the loops of her old jeans. "Aren't you going to change?"

"No." Kristin reached for a shoe, "I'll just be really careful and not do any of the things that might mess up my jeans." She glanced up and noticed the look on her little sister's face. "Well, Mom didn't say I had to change!" She grabbed the other shoe. "Since Carol's in high school now, there'll be lots of older kids at this party. I want to look good tonight."

Colored lights were strung everywhere. The Hugheses' backyard was transformed into a mini-carnival with activities for kids of all ages, including a water balloon toss, bobbing for apples, a dart throw and even a pie-eating contest. Kristin stood around most of the evening, avoiding all the things that could ruin her expensive new jeans.

"Hey, Kristin!" Cathy hurried by with Jared, Carol's ten-year-old brother. "C'mon! They're bringing out homemade ice cream!"

"M-m-m-m. Sounds good, doesn't it?" The girl Kristin had been talking to turned to follow Cathy and Jared toward the table on the patio.

"Yes, it sure does! I love homemade ice cream." Kristin walked beside her new friend. She couldn't remember her name, but she was a seventh-grader and seemed really nice.

The long table was covered with a bright plastic tablecloth. On one end, two large freezers of homemade ice cream were surrounded by bowls, spoons and napkins. The other end was covered with clear plastic cups filled with juice. "Strawberry or vanilla?" Mrs. Hughes held the ice cream scoop poised over the freezers.

"Vanilla, please." Kristin accepted the loaded bowl and licked the ice cream that was running over on one side.

"Let's go sit on the brick wall over there," her new friend suggested. "I'll trade a little strawberry for some of your vanilla before we start eating. Want to?"

Before Kristin could reply, something or someone crashed into her, knocking her feet right out from under her. The bowl of ice cream dumped down the front of her shirt. She jumped up sputtering. "What…who… YOU!" She spotted Jared standing there with a sheepish look on his face—and an empty plastic cup in his hand. "Why don't you watch where you're going!" Kristin tried to wipe the dripping mess off her shirt with the crumpled paper napkin she still clutched in one hand.

"I'm sorry," Jared said as he held out his napkin to Kristin. It wasn't in much better shape than her own. "I didn't see you there."

"You…you WHAT?" Kristin exploded. "Are you blind or something?"

"Here." The seventh-grade girl handed Kristin her clean napkin and bent to pick up the empty bowl and spoon. "Let's go ask Mrs. Hughes for a damp towel or something. Okay?"

Kristin nodded and turned toward the house. "What a jerk! He's such a complete idiot he can't put one foot in front of the other without causing a disaster! He's always been that way. Whenever there's a mess, you can be sure Jared caused it! Why, one time he…."

"Kristin, honey!" Mrs. Hughes handed the ice cream scoop to Carol when she spotted the soggy Kristin approaching. "Come on in the house and let's get you cleaned up." She ushered Kristin away while Kristin's new seventh-grade friend went to rejoin the party and eat her own melting ice cream.

"That's much better."

Story (continued)

Mrs. Hughes stood back and looked at the wet but clean front of Kristin's shirt.

"Thanks, Mrs. Hughes." Kristin smiled at her mother's friend and started out of the kitchen to rejoin the party.

She stopped in her tracks when Mrs. Hughes said, "Kristin, honey, that looks like juice on the back of your jeans." Kristin craned her neck to check it out. Sure enough, Jared's plastic cup had been empty because all the juice had gotten dumped on the back of her legs!

"You'd better ask your mother to take care of that right away, honey. That's grape juice and it will stain." She glanced at the clock on the kitchen wall. "Your dad should be here soon to pick you up. Otherwise I'd have you go ahead and change into something of Jared's so I could get those stains treated."

"I'll take care of it right away," Kristin assured the worried Mrs. Hughes. "But I'll do it myself," she added in her own mind. "I don't want Mom to know that my new jeans got messed up at the party after all."

Later that evening Kristin attempted to get the stains out. Bar soap from the bathtub didn't work well. Kristin squirted some liquid soap from the dispenser by the kitchen sink onto one of the larger spots and scrubbed some more. That didn't make the spots disappear either.

"How are you supposed to get grape juice stains out, anyway?" Kristin sat on the edge of the tub and stared at the dark spots on the jeans in the sink. "That Jared Hughes! He's an absolute pain! I can't stand him! He ruins everything! Why'd he have to go and ruin these jeans!"

When Kristin returned to her room Cathy was already in bed. "The party sure was fun, wasn't it?" Cathy yawned and turned on her side to talk to her big sister.

"It was until Jared decided to ruin it," Kristin muttered.

"That's not fair, Kristin."

Cathy sat up in bed. "You know he didn't mean to run into you. It was an accident! And besides, Mrs. Hughes got all the ice cream off your shirt."

"Yeah, my shirt's fine." Kristin jerked the bedspread off her bed. "But my jeans aren't!"

"What are you talking about?" Cathy pulled her knees up and looped her arms around them. "I didn't see anything on your jeans."

"Of course not!" Kristin shook her head angrily. "I made sure no one saw the back of my jeans during the last of the party and all the way home! I didn't want Mom to know that they're ruined!" Kristin's voice rose. "I thought I could get out the grape juice that Jared dumped on me all by myself, but I can't! My jeans are RUINED and it's all Jared's fault! If he wasn't such a jerk it wouldn't have happened. Life would be a lot nicer if he just…didn't exist!"

Cathy stared quietly at her sister for so long that Kristin grew uncomfortable. Finally Cathy shook her head and laid back down. "Maybe Mom could get the grape juice out—or maybe your jeans are ruined, I don't know." She pulled her covers up. "But I think the stuff you're saying about Jared is worse than any old stain." Cathy turned over and closed her eyes.

"But…" Kristin began and then stopped. What could she say? Cathy was right. She sat on the side of her bed and stared at the back of her sister's head. She was still upset and mad, but perhaps, if she was really honest, she was mostly upset that her new jeans—the brand everyone was wearing now—were ruined. She was upset with herself for wearing her jeans when she probably shouldn't have. She was upset with herself for saying such mean things about Jared, too, especially to the seventh-grade girl she'd just met. After all, she'd known Jared all her life and they'd been good friends even though he was one grade behind her. Sure, he made her mad sometimes, but he really wasn't so bad. She really liked Jared.

She really liked those jeans, too—and now they were ruined. Kristin envisioned those ugly grape juice stains on the back of her jeans. Then she was struck with an even more sobering thought, "Am I stained like that inside?"

Kristin jumped up and got her jeans out of the bathroom where she'd hidden them. She'd see if Mom could do anything about those stains.

"I already know Someone who can take care of the stains inside me, and I'll ask Him to give me a new, clean heart right now," she whispered to herself. "That's even more important than spots on my jeans."

2 Discussion Time

Check understanding of the story and development of personal values.

- Why had Kristin begged her mother to get a certain brand of jeans even though they were expensive?
- Where were Kristin and her family going?
- Why did Kristin want to wear her new jeans?
- Why did Mrs. Wright suggest Kristin wear something else?
- What happened to Kristin's jeans?
- How did Kristin feel about Jared?
- Was it Jared's fault that the jeans were stained? Why or why not?
- How could Kristin get rid of the stains in her heart?
- Have you ever blamed someone for something that was really your fault?

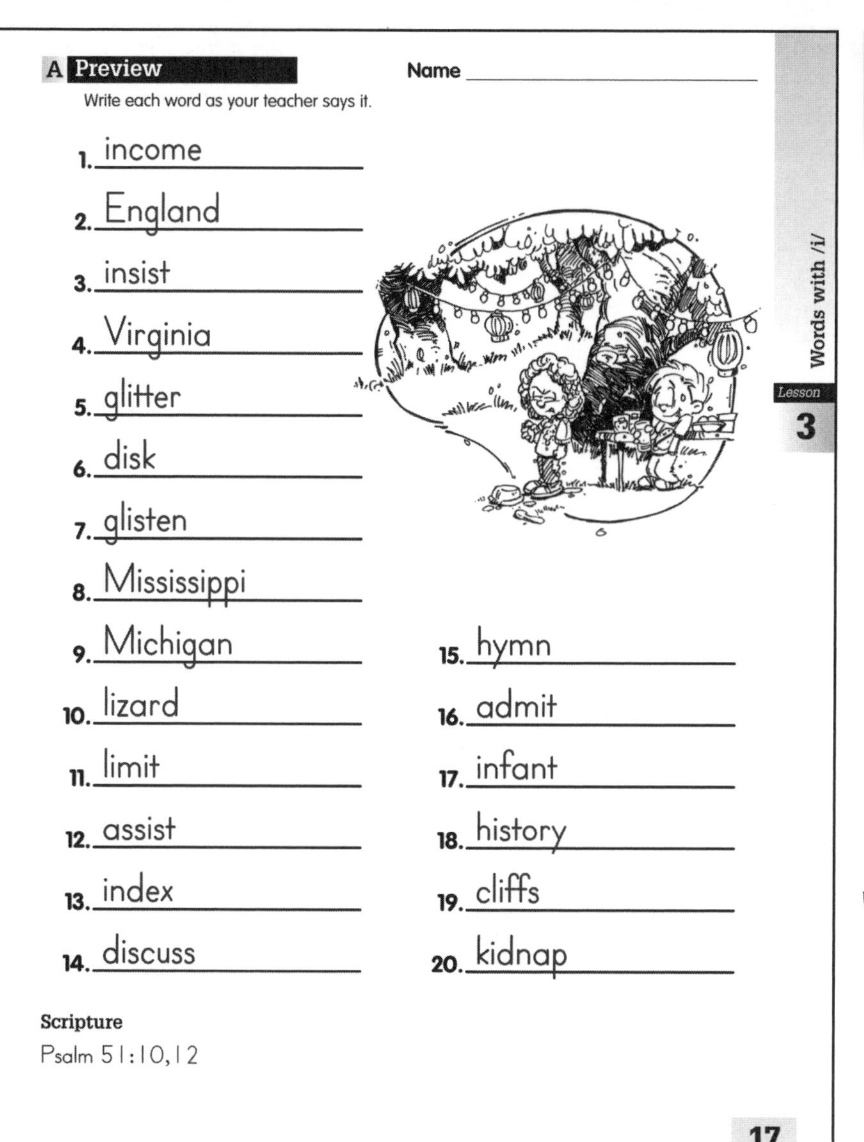

3 Preview

Test for knowledge of the correct spellings of these words.

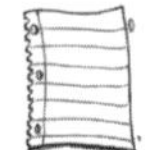

Customize Your List

On a separate sheet of paper, additional words of your choice may be tested.

I will say each word once, use the word in a sentence, then say the word again. Write the words on the lines in your Worktext.

Correct Immediately!

Let's correct our Preview. I will spell each word out loud. If you spelled a word incorrectly, rewrite it correctly.

Progress Chart

Students may record scores. (Reproducible master provided in Appendix B.)

1.	income	"I don't intend to spend all of our **income** on clothes," Mom said.
2.	England	The jeans were designed in **England.**
3.	insist	Kristin did **insist** on wearing them even after her mom said she shouldn't.
4.	Virginia	The Hughes family had moved from **Virginia** three years before.
5.	glitter	Their backyard seemed to **glitter** with color.
6.	disk	Mrs. Hughes had put a **disk** of circus music in the CD player.
7.	glisten	She saw the ice cubes **glisten** in the punch bowl.
8.	Mississippi	In the "Name That State" game Cathy said **Mississippi.**
9.	Michigan	Jared knew the answer to the next question was **Michigan.**
10.	lizard	A tiny **lizard** wriggled up the ivy near Kristin and her new friend.
11.	limit	There was almost no **limit** to the anger she felt towards Jared.
12.	assist	Mrs. Hughes tried to **assist** Kristin in getting the ice cream off her shirt.
13.	index	Kristin ran her **index** finger over the dark grape-juice stain.
14.	discuss	She did not want to **discuss** her stained jeans with her mom.
15.	hymn	The words of a **hymn** they had sung at church went through her mind.
16.	admit	Kristin had to **admit** that the way she had treated Jared was wrong.
17.	infant	She realized she'd behaved like an **infant.**
18.	history	She did not want to have a **history** of disobedience.
19.	cliffs	There are no **cliffs** in the Hugheses' backyard.
20.	kidnap	She had let Satan **kidnap,** or take control of, her thoughts and actions.

Day 1 | Lesson 3

4 Word Shapes

Help students form a correct image of whole words.

Say: Look at each word and think about its shape. Now, write the word in the correct word Shape Boxes. You may check off each word as you use it.

(Short vowels are usually found in syllables in which a vowel is immediately preceded and followed by a consonant, consonant cluster, or digraph.)

Say: In the word shape boxes, fill in the boxes containing the letter or letters that spell the sound of **/i/** in each word.

Take a minute to memorize...

Psalm 51:10,12

Lesson 3 — Words with /i/

B Word Shapes Name ______________

Using the word bank below, write each word in the correct word shape boxes. Next, in the word shape boxes, fill in the boxes containing the letter or letters that spell the sound of /i/ in each word.

1. assist
2. 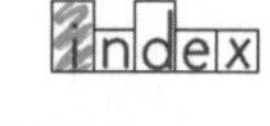 index
3. 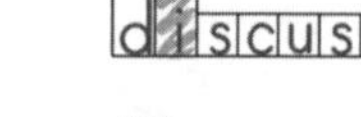 discuss
4. income
5. hymn
6.  limit
7.  insist
8. glisten
9.  Virginia
10.  Mississippi
11.  disk
12. kidnap
13. 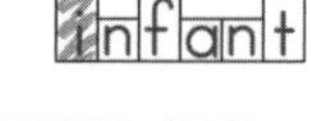 infant
14. Michigan
15. lizard
16.  cliffs
17. admit
18. 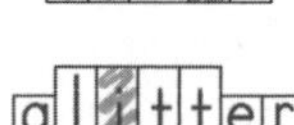 glitter
19.  England
20.  history

Word Bank

admit	disk	history	infant	lizard
assist	England	hymn	insist	Michigan
cliffs	glisten	income	kidnap	Mississippi
discuss	glitter	index	limit	Virginia

18

Answers may vary for duplicate word shapes.

Be Prepared For Fun

Check these supply lists for **Fun Ways to Spell** - presented **Day 2**.
Purchase and/or gather these items ahead of time!

General
- Pencil
- 3 X 5 Cards cut in half (20 per child)
- Spelling List

Auditory
- Spelling List

Visual
- Pencil
- Notebook Paper
- Spelling List

Tactile
- Blackboard and Chalk
  -OR-
- White Board and Marker
- Spelling List

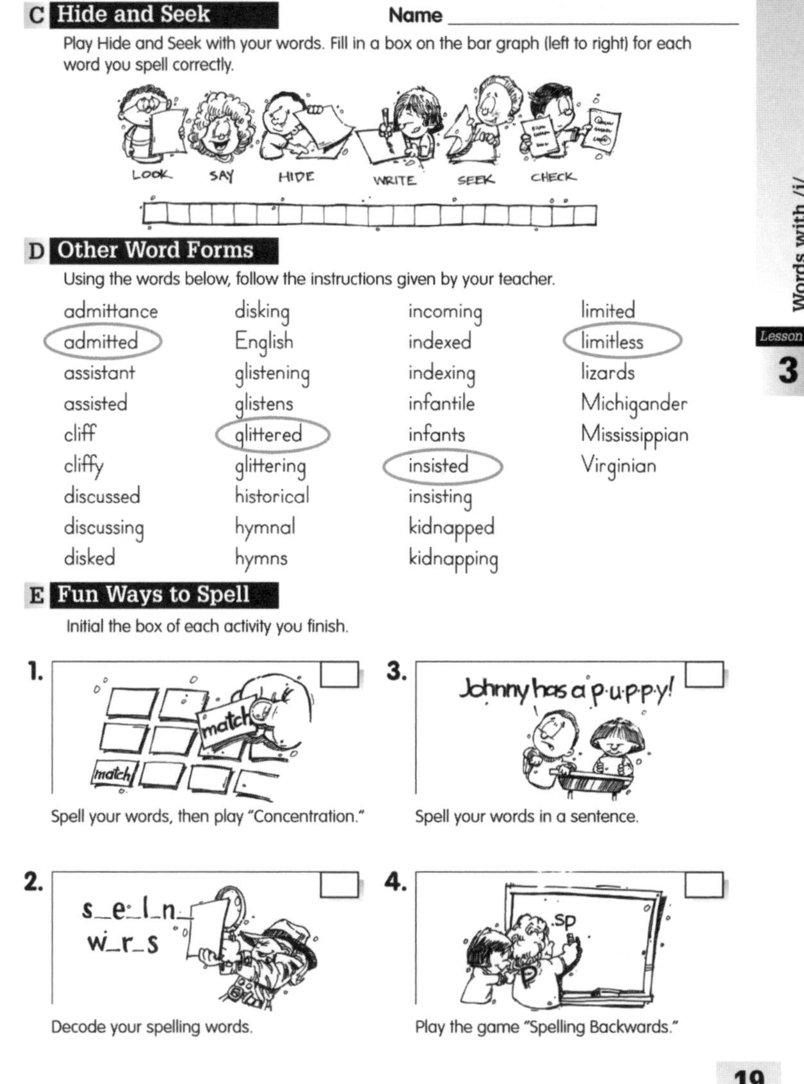

C Hide and Seek Name ______________________

Play Hide and Seek with your words. Fill in a box on the bar graph (left to right) for each word you spell correctly.

D Other Word Forms

Using the words below, follow the instructions given by your teacher.

admittance	disking	incoming	limited
admitted	English	indexed	limitless
assistant	glistening	indexing	lizards
assisted	glistens	infantile	Michigander
cliff	glittered	infants	Mississippian
cliffy	glittering	insisted	Virginian
discussed	historical	insisting	
discussing	hymnal	kidnapped	
disked	hymns	kidnapping	

E Fun Ways to Spell

Initial the box of each activity you finish.

1.
Spell your words, then play "Concentration."

2.
Decode your spelling words.

3.
Spell your words in a sentence.

4.
Play the game "Spelling Backwards."

Words with /i/ — Lesson 3

19

1 Hide and Seek

Reinforce spelling by using multiple styles of learning.

On a white board, Teacher writes each word — one at a time. **Have students:**

- **Look** at the word.
- **Say** the word out loud.
- **Spell** the word out loud.
- **Hide** (teacher erases word.)
- **Write** the word on paper.
- **Seek** (teacher rewrites word.)
- **Check** spelling. If incorrect, rewrite word correctly.

Day 2

Lesson 3

2 Other Word Forms

This activity is optional. Have students find and circle the Other Word Forms that are most nearly synonyms of the following:

granted access
sparkled
demanded
boundless

3 Fun Ways to Spell

Four activities are provided. Use one, two, three, or all of the activities. Have students initial the box for each activity they complete.

Options:

- assign activities to students according to their learning styles
- set up the activities in learning centers for the students to do throughout the day
- divide students into four groups and assign one activity per group
- do one activity per day

General

Spell your words; then play "Concentration"...
- Write each spelling word on a card. Mix your cards and a classmate's cards together. Arrange them face down in five rows of eight. Pick up two cards. If the cards match, play again. If the cards do not match, turn them back over. It is your classmate's turn. Continue taking turns until all the cards are matched. The player with the most cards wins!

Auditory

To spell your words in a sentence...
- Ask a classmate to read a spelling word to you from the list.
- Spell the word aloud and use it in a sentence.
- Ask your classmate to check your spelling.
- Each correctly spelled word that is used properly in a sentence counts as one point.
- Switch with a classmate and continue taking turns.

Visual

To decode your spelling words...
- Look at the first word on your list.
- Write every other letter of the word on your paper, putting a blank where each missing letter belongs.
- Trade papers with a classmate and fill in the missing letters.
- Check your spelling.

Tactile

To play the game "Spelling Backwards"...
- Ask a classmate to stand behind you and draw the letters to spell a word from your list on your back.
- Write the spelling word on the board as your classmate traces the letters on your back.
- Ask your classmate to check your spelling.
- Trade places and take turns until you have each spelled all the words.

Lesson 3 | Day 3

1 Working with Words

Familiarize students with word meaning and usage.

Clues

Write this incomplete sentence on the board:

To imagine events while you are asleep is to __________.

Guide the students in choosing the word **dream**.

Say: Read each sentence and choose a spelling word for each definition. You may use a dictionary to help you. Write the word in the blank.

Take a minute to memorize...

Psalm 51:10,12

Words with /i/ — Lesson 3

F Working with Words Name __________________

Clues

Write a spelling word for each clue.

1. Something that shines or sparkles is said to glisten or glitter.
2. To carry someone away against his will is to kidnap him.
3. The state that is abbreviated MI is Michigan.
4. Someone who is a baby is called an infant.
5. To glitter or glisten means to be sparkling, showy, or attractive.
6. To argue or consider carefully is to discuss.
7. A flat plate on which data for a computer is stored is a disk.
8. A hymn is a song of praise to God.
9. To take a resolute stand is to insist.
10. Virginia was one of the original thirteen colonies.
11. High steep faces of rock, earth, or ice are called cliffs.
12. History is a record of significant events of the past.
13. A gain in money from labor, business, or property is income
14. To help or aid people is to assist them.
15. England is a country in Europe.
16. An index is an alphabetical list with page numbers indicating where items can be found in a book.
17. To restrict in quantity or extent is to limit.
18. To allow someone to enter is to admit her.
19. Jackson is the capitol of Mississippi, a state of the Deep South.
20. A four-legged reptile with a long tapering tail is a lizard.

Word Bank

admit	disk	history	infant	lizard
assist	England	hymn	insist	Michigan
cliffs	glisten	income	kidnap	Mississippi
discuss	glitter	index	limit	Virginia

20

G Dictation

Name ______________________

Write each sentence as your teacher dictates. Use correct punctuation.

1. If you insist on wearing those pants, you will just have to limit the games you play.
2. Kristin knows she is wrong, but she does not like to admit it.
3. Mom knows a lady who can follow her family history back to a small county in England.

Words with /i/

Lesson 3

H Proofreading

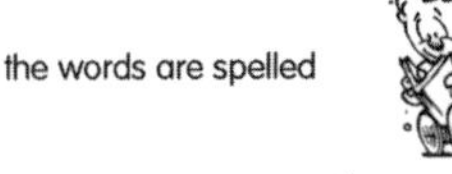

If a word is misspelled, fill in the oval by that word. If all the words are spelled correctly, fill in the oval by **no mistake**.

1. ○ kidnap ○ weapon ○ heifer ● no mistake
2. ○ cliffs ● hym ○ healthy ○ no mistake
3. ○ selfish ○ limit ● england ○ no mistake
4. ○ income ○ umbrella ○ index ● no mistake
5. ● infent ○ Virginia ○ tennis ○ no mistake
6. ○ assist ● disck ○ shelter ○ no mistake
7. ○ New Mexico ○ discuss ○ glisten ● no mistake
8. ● histry ○ Texas ○ insist ○ no mistake
9. ○ strength ● Missisippi ○ weather ○ no mistake
10. ○ glitter ● lizerd ○ Maryland ○ no mistake
11. ○ denim ○ tense ○ admit ● no mistake
12. ○ attend ○ method ● michigen ○ no mistake

21

1 Dictation

Reinforce correct spelling by using current and previous words in context.

Listen as I read each sentence and then write it in your Worktext. Remember to use correct capitalization and punctuation. (Slowly read each sentence twice. Sentences are found in the Student Worktext to the left.)

Day 4

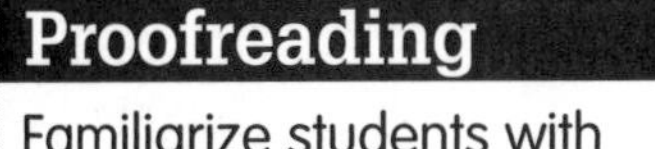

2 Proofreading

Familiarize students with standardized test format and reinforce recognition of misspelled words.

Lesson 3

Look at each set of words. If a word is misspelled, fill in the oval by that word. If all the words are spelled correctly, fill in the oval by **no mistake**.

Hide and Seek

Reinforce correct spelling of current spelling words. Repeat this activity from Day 2.

Vocabulary Extension

Have your students complete this activity to strengthen spelling ability and expand vocabulary. The reproducible master is provided in Appendix A as shown on the inset page to the right.

Posttest

Test mastery of the spelling words.

I will say the word once, use it in a sentence, then say it again. Write your words on a separate sheet of paper.

Progress Chart
Students may record scores. (Reproducible master in Appendix B.)

Personal Dictionary
Students may add any words they have misspelled to their personal dictionaries for reference when writing. (Cover in Appendix B.)

Hide and Seek

Play Hide and Seek with your words. Fill in a bar graph (left to right) for each word you spell correctly.

Vocabulary Extension

Multiple Choice

Fill in the oval by the word(s) with the same or nearly the same meaning as the word in bold type.

1. **consider**
   - ● ponder
   - ○ babble
   - ○ thoughtless
   - ○ balance
2. **Timothy**
   - ○ Old Testament book
   - ● companion of Paul
   - ○ first king of Israel
   - ○ town in western Judah
3. **convince**
   - ○ chosen one
   - ○ lenses for your eyes
   - ○ prisoner
   - ● persuade
4. **Corinthians**
   - ○ friends of Isaiah
   - ○ Old Testament book
   - ● people who lived in Corinth
   - ○ *Abraham's nephew*
5. **initials**
   - ● beginning letters of a name
   - ○ first book of the Bible
   - ○ important document
   - ○ good judgment
6. **political**
   - ○ ethical
   - ● governmental
   - ○ noticeable
   - ○ license
7. **friction**
   - ○ smoothness
   - ● disagreement
   - ○ roll carefully
   - ○ flattering
8. **grimace**
   - ● expression
   - ○ enemy
   - ○ lonely
   - ○ frightening
9. **minimum**
   - ○ receive
   - ○ administer
   - ● smallest
   - ○ record
10. **Kings**
    - ○ to take an oath
    - ○ to persuade
    - ○ prophet of Israel
    - ● Old Testament books

Vocabulary Extension — Lesson 3

327

1.	income	"Dad's **income** can't all be spent on clothes," said Mom.
2.	England	Kristin wanted a pair of the jeans designed in London, **England.**
3.	insist	Kristin did **insist** on going against her mom's wishes.
4.	Virginia	Three years earlier the Hughes had moved from **Virginia.**
5.	glitter	The colored lights strung around the yard seemed to **glitter.**
6.	disk	A **disk** of circus-style music played in the background.
7.	glisten	Kristin saw the flower-shaped ice cubes **glisten** in the punch bowl.
8.	Mississippi	Jared's answer in the "Name That State" game was **Mississippi.**
9.	Michigan	Cathy knew the answer to the third question was **Michigan.**
10.	lizard	Kristin did not want to touch the **lizard** on the ivy.
11.	limit	Kristin felt there was no **limit** to her anger toward Jared.
12.	assist	Mrs. Hughes was quick to **assist** Kristin in cleaning her shirt.
13.	index	Kristin rubbed soap into the stain with her **index** finger.
14.	discuss	Kristin knew it would be hard to **discuss** the accident with her mom.
15.	hymn	A verse from a **hymn** she had just learned ran through her head.
16.	admit	Kristin had to **admit** her attitude had been very bad.
17.	infant	She had behaved like an **infant** in front of all the guests.
18.	history	She did not want to have a **history** of saying mean things.
19.	cliffs	There aren't any **cliffs** in the Hugheses' backyard.
20.	kidnap	Kristin did not want to let Satan **kidnap** her thoughts.

Words with /i/

Lesson 3

I Game Name ______________________

Complete the secret phrase by spelling the words from this week's word list.

Remember: Ask God for a clean and willing heart.

J Journaling

In your journal, write what you think Kristin learned in this story. Tell why you think this is an important lesson for everyone to learn.

22

2 Game

Reinforce spelling skills and provide motivation and interest.

Materials

- game page (from student text)
- pencils (1 per child)
- game word list

Game Word List

Team A	Team B
1. **kidnap (R)**	1. **disk (R)**
2. **cliffs (E)**	2. **discuss (E)**
3. **hymn (A)**	3. **glisten (A)**
4. **limit (T)**	4. **history (T)**
5. **England (E)**	5. **insist (E)**
6. **income (I)**	6. **Mississippi (I)**
7. **index (N)**	7. **Michigan (N)**
8. **infant (M)**	8. **admit (M)**
9. **Virginia (E)**	9. **glitter (E)**
10. **assist (A)**	10. **lizard (A)**
11. **disk (C)**	11. **kidnap (C)**
12. **discuss (L)**	12. **cliffs (L)**
13. **glisten (E)**	13. **hymn (E)**
14. **history (A)**	14. **limit (A)**
15. **insist (N)**	15. **England (N)**
16. **Mississippi (H)**	16. **income (H)**
17. **Michigan (E)**	17. **index (E)**
18. **admit (A)**	18. **infant (A)**
19. **glitter (R)**	19. **Virginia (R)**
20. **lizard (T)**	20. **assist (T)**

How to Play:

- Divide the class into two teams, and decide which team will go first.
- Have a student from team A choose a number from 1 to 20.
- Say the word that matches that number from the team's word list.
- Have the student write the word on the board.
- If correct, have each member of team A write the given letter in the matching space on his/her game page.
- Alternate between teams A and B having the students choose a number of a blank space.
- The team to complete the secret phrase first is the winner.

3 Journaling

Provide a meaningful reason for correct spelling through personal writing.

Review the story using discussion leads provided on the following page. Encourage students to apply the Scriptural value in their journaling.

Journaling (continued)

- Is there something you've wanted just because everyone else seemed to be getting it, like Kristin's jeans?
- Where was the party the Wright family attended? (In the backyard of the Hugheses' home.)
- What was the party like? (Lots of activities for all age levels including water balloon toss, bobbing for apples, a dart throw and pie-eating. Colored lights were strung and there was home made ice cream and juice.)
- Do you think Kristin enjoyed the party? Why or why not?
- What happened to Kristin's jeans? (Jared bumped into her and spilled his grape juice on the back of her jeans.)
- What kinds of things might "stain" our hearts like the jeans were stained? (Unkind thoughts about others, lying, selfishness, etc.)
- Why didn't Kristin ask her mom to get the stains out right away? (She didn't want her mom to know that the jeans were stained.)
- How did Kristin try to get the stains out and did it work? (She tried bar soap and hand soap. It didn't work.)
- Can we get the stains out of our own hearts by ourselves? (No.)
- How can we get rid of them? (By asking God to give us new, clean hearts.)

There are only 12 letters in the Hawaiian alphabet.

Topic: Being pleasant in the morning
Theme Text: Psalm 92:2, 4

Don't Call Me in the Morning

Tommy is a real grouch in the mornings. Can anything help him change?

"Good morning, Tommy! Time to get up. Breakfast will be ready when you get downstairs." Tommy groaned and rolled over, burying his head in the covers when he heard his dad's familiar wake-up call.

"Tommy!" Dad's voice was now closer to the bed, "You've got to get up, young man! You'll be late for school if you don't get moving." Tommy grabbed for the covers when his dad started to tug them off him.

"'Kay." Tommy mumbled, "I'm up."

"Well, I wouldn't say you're really up yet," Dad chuckled, "but at least you seem to be alive. See you downstairs!" Mr. Rawson tickled Tommy's ribs, then left to call Lisa. He didn't notice the frown on his son's face.

When Tommy finally dragged himself out of his cozy bed and across the upstairs landing to the bathroom door, it was shut. Tommy banged on it.

"Just a minute!" Lisa, his older sister, called cheerfully. "I'll be out soon."

Tommy sagged against the wall for what he thought was a minute and then banged louder. "Hurry up, Lisa! Other people live in this house besides you!"

"It's all yours," Lisa said as she held the door open for him with a smile. "Hey, look at that sunshine!" She pointed at the light streaming through the bathroom window. "Isn't it great? The weather man said it was going to rain today, but it looks like he was wrong!"

Tommy grunted and shuffled into the bathroom. "LISA!" he bellowed. "You left your curling iron right next to the sink! I could've burned myself! And look at all this other junk you left out." He glowered at his sister when she came back to see what he was yelling about.

"Sorry, Tommy. I thought you wanted me to hurry after my shower, so I left this to put away later when you were through in the bathroom." Lisa picked up the offending curling iron and said lightly, "This wasn't even plugged in." She stuck it in her drawer and left.

"Yeah, yeah, yeah," Tommy muttered as he closed the door harder than he needed to.

He'd finished his shower and was back in his room searching for his shoes when his dad called again from downstairs. "Tommy! Time to eat!"

"I'm coming! I'm coming!" Tommy practically shouted. He frowned fiercely as he located a shoe and started to put it on only to discover a knot in the lace. He threw it across the room, and it thunked against the wall. He kicked the other shoe out of his way and went downstairs for breakfast in his socks, muttering all the way.

A few mornings later, the rest of the family was already gathered around the table when Tommy slid into the kitchen. "Good morning, Tommy." Mrs. Rawson smiled at her son as she poured orange juice for him. Tommy just grunted.

Dad's voice was stern when he said, "Tommy, you will treat my wife with the respect she deserves."

"Yes, sir." Tommy slipped into his chair. "I'm sorry, Mom. Good morning." Mom patted his shoulder when she placed the juice in front of him.

"What's the problem, Tommy?" Dad's voice was more relaxed. "Seems like you've had some rough mornings lately."

"He sure has!" Lisa agreed. "For the last couple of weeks he practically bites my head off whenever he sees me in the morning!"

"So what's going on?" Dad leaned back in his chair and waited for an answer.

"Well, I'm just so tired. It's hard to get up, and I feel angry when I wake up." Tommy picked up his napkin and tore off a little piece. "I just wish I could sleep as long as I wanted to and not have anybody telling me to get up and stuff!"

"Hmmm. I see." Dad changed the subject, "Lisa, will you ask the blessing on our food?"

"Dear God, thank You for the food we're about to eat. Help it make us strong to serve You today. And please help Tommy not to be so grumpy in the mornings. Amen."

Tommy frowned at Lisa, but she just grinned at him and took a sip of her orange juice.

"Mr. Canfield said that sometimes kids get really tired when they're growing fast," Tommy said, picking up his glass and taking a big swallow. "I'm growing a lot right now, don't you think?"

"Yes, that's pretty obvious from the clothes you keep outgrowing." Mom reached over to cut up Grandma's waffle.

"True." Dad dipped strawberries onto his waffle. "However, while I think that's something to be happy about, I don't think it's an acceptable excuse for bad behavior every morning."

Tommy dropped the conversation and turned his attention back to his own plate.

Several mornings later Tommy stirred and stretched in his bed. Something had awakened him. Blinking open blurry eyes, he looked around his room. Daylight, but Dad wasn't there calling him to get up for school or for breakfast or anything. Good. Tommy settled into a comfortable position and drifted back to sleep. When he woke up again, he looked

Story (continued)

around and figured it must be time to get up, but since no one had called him yet, he closed his eyes and dozed off again.

When Tommy finally decided to get up, he headed for the bathroom. The door was open and Lisa was nowhere to be seen. After a quick shower, Tommy was more alert. When he returned to his room he glanced at the clock. 10:30! That couldn't be right, could it? Tommy was frightened until he reminded himself it must be the weekend.

He bounced down the stairs and into an empty kitchen. "Mom!" Tommy called. "Mom, where are you?" No answer. Tommy checked the living room and Grandma's room. Nobody there. He checked the laundry room and the dining room. No one. He ran back upstairs to check the bedrooms. "MOM! DAD!"

Tommy started to panic as he dashed back down the stairs and repeated his search through each room. Where was everyone? Mom, Dad, Lisa—even Grandma—had all vanished without a trace. Tommy flung open the door to the garage. No one there. There was no one anywhere! "DAD!" Tommy's throat hurt from yelling so loudly.

Suddenly he felt someone shaking him. "Huh, what?" Tommy's eyes flew open. Slowly his own room came into focus. Dad stood by the side of the bed, gently shaking his shoulder.

"Come on, lazy bones, better get up or you're going to miss breakfast," Mr. Rawson called as he left the room. "I'll save you a few of Mom's blueberry pancakes if you hurry!"

Tommy looked at the clock, then rubbed his eyes and checked again, 6:30. He propped himself up on his elbows and looked around, trying to get his bearings. His racing heart began to beat more normally as he realized he could hear voices from downstairs. A dream! Tommy flopped back down on the bed in relief. It had all been an awful dream! He grinned at the sound of Lisa's voice warbling her favorite song in the bathroom.

"Hm." Tommy tucked both hands behind his head and stretched his long legs. "Never thought I'd be so glad to hear Lisa's screeching!" He sat up and reached for his Bible. "Think I'll read for a minute since she beat me to the bathroom as usual." He opened the Scriptures and flipped a few pages. "Let's see. This book is Psalms. Mr. Canfield said the Psalms were like songs." Tommy chose a chapter and began to read silently to himself. "Psalm 92:2. Every morning tell him, 'Thank you for your kindness,' and every evening rejoice in all his faithfulness...."

Tommy stopped reading and stared out the window while he thought about that Scripture. "I sure haven't been doing a very good job of thanking God for His kindness every morning lately. I've been grumping and growling at everyone like I have nothing at all to be thankful for!"

Yummy smells drifted up from the kitchen. Tommy sniffed appreciatively. "Mom's good food is one thing I should be thankful for instead of taking it for granted. Family is another." Tommy shivered. "Until my family all disappeared in my nightmare, I hadn't thought about how important our family is to me."

"Troublesome Tommy!" Lisa called as she passed his open bedroom door. "Bathroom's free now."

"Thanks, Lisa." Tommy grinned when he caught the look of astonishment on his older sister's face. "See you at breakfast!"

"Maybe I'm growing in more than one way!" he thought. "At least I hope I am."

2 Discussion Time

Check understanding of the story and development of personal values.

- How did Tommy react when Mr. Rawson woke him up in the morning?
- Why did Tommy yell at his sister Lisa?
- When his mom said "Good morning" and Tommy just grunted in reply, what did his dad say?
- Describe Tommy's dream.
- How did the dream change Tommy's feelings?
- What is it like around your house in the mornings?
- How could you make it better?

A Preview Name ____________________

Write each word as your teacher says it.

1. automatic
2. crawl
3. astronaut
4. launch
5. somersault
6. laundry
7. exhaust
8. audience
9. precaution
10. clause
11. Australia
12. coffee
13. strawberry
14. Vermont
15. awkward
16. automobile
17. on–line
18. lawyers
19. Washington
20. alcohol

Scripture
Psalm 92:2,4

Words with /ô/ or /o/ | Lesson 4

23

3 Preview

Test for knowledge of the correct spellings of these words.

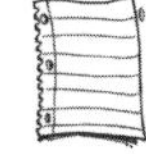

Customize Your List

On a separate sheet of paper, additional words of your choice may be tested.

I will say each word once, use the word in a sentence, then say the word again. Write the words on the lines in your Worktext.

Correct Immediately!

Let's correct our Preview. I will spell each word out loud. If you spelled a word incorrectly, rewrite it correctly.

Progress Chart

Students may record scores. (Reproducible master provided in Appendix B.)

Lesson 4 | Day 1

1.	automatic	It was almost **automatic** for Tommy to wake up grumpy.
2.	crawl	Tommy's dad heard him finally **crawl** out of bed.
3.	astronaut	Tommy had been dreaming that he was an **astronaut.**
4.	launch	His shuttle had just experienced a successful **launch.**
5.	somersault	He didn't exactly feel like doing a **somersault** now.
6.	laundry	He grumbled as he looked for his favorite socks in the **laundry.**
7.	exhaust	Tommy's foul moods were about to **exhaust** his family's patience.
8.	audience	They did not enjoy being the **audience** for his bad morning moods.
9.	precaution	Lisa took every **precaution** to stay out of Tommy's way.
10.	clause	"We need a 'no-grumpiness' **clause** added to our family constitution," she said.
11.	Australia	"Or we could just send him to **Australia** for a while," Lisa teased.
12.	coffee	"Here, will some black **coffee** help any?" she joked.
13.	strawberry	Tommy usually enjoys **strawberry** jam on his waffles.
14.	Vermont	Lisa loves the maple syrup they get from **Vermont.**
15.	awkward	Tommy felt **awkward** and embarrassed after being rude to his mom.
16.	automobile	The Rawson family **automobile** is a red sedan.
17.	on–line	Tommy enjoys getting **on–line** after he's done with his homework.
18.	lawyers	Mr. Canfield told the class about several presidents that started out as **lawyers.**
19.	Washington	Lincoln studied law, but **Washington** learned surveying skills.
20.	alcohol	No one in Tommy's family drinks **alcohol.**

4 Word Shapes

Help students form a correct image of whole words.

Say: Look at each word and think about its shape. Now, write the word in the correct word Shape Boxes. You may check off each word as you use it.

(In some words /ô/ is spelled with **a**, and it is often spelled this way when it is followed by **l** or **ll**. In other words /ô/ is spelled with **aw**, **o**, or **au**. The sound of /o/ can be spelled with **o**. Sometimes /o/ is spelled with **a**, especially when it follows **w**.)

Say: In the word shape boxes, fill in the boxes containing the letter or letters that spell the sound of /o/ or /ô/ in each word.

Take a minute to memorize...

Psalm 92:2,4

Words with /ô/ or /o/ — Lesson 4

B Word Shapes Name ______________

Using the word bank below, write each word in the correct word shape boxes. Next, in the word shape boxes, fill in the boxes containing the letter or letters that spell the sound of /ô/ or /o/ in each word.

1. astronaut
2. Vermont
3. lawyers
4. automobile
5. laundry
6. strawberry
7. on-line
8. clause
9. audience
10. launch
11. awkward
12. crawl
13. somersault
14. exhaust
15. precaution
16. coffee
17. automatic
18. alcohol
19. Australia
20. Washington

Word Bank

alcohol	automatic	coffee	laundry	somersault
astronaut	automobile	crawl	lawyers	strawberry
audience	awkward	exhaust	on-line	Vermont
Australia	clause	launch	precaution	Washington

24

Answers may vary for duplicate word shapes.

Be Prepared For Fun

Check these supply lists for **Fun Ways to Spell** - presented **Day 2**. Purchase and/or gather these items ahead of time!

General
- Pencil
- Notebook Paper
- Spelling List

Auditory
- Pencil
- 3 X 5 Cards Cut in half lengthwise (20 per child)
- Spelling List

Visual
- Colored Pencils
- Graph Paper (2 sheets per child)
- Spelling List

Tactile
- Clay
- Spelling List

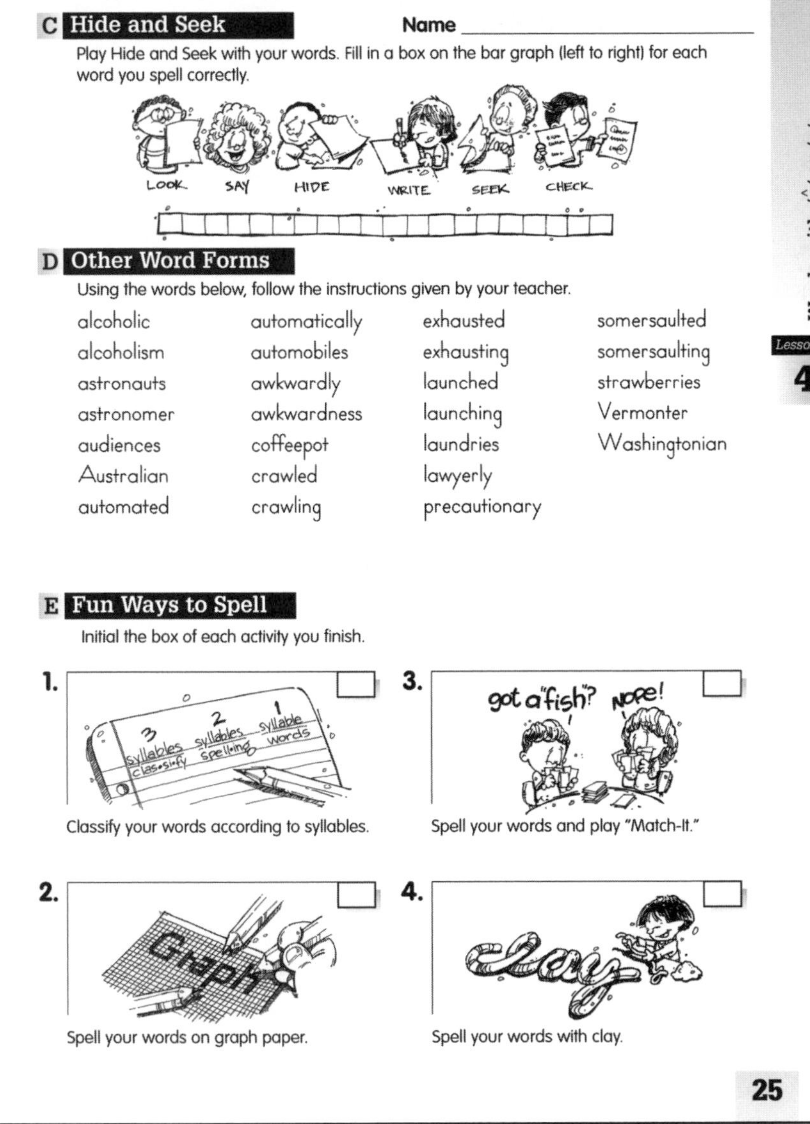

C Hide and Seek Name ____________________

Play Hide and Seek with your words. Fill in a box on the bar graph (left to right) for each word you spell correctly.

D Other Word Forms

Using the words below, follow the instructions given by your teacher.

alcoholic	automatically	exhausted	somersaulted
alcoholism	automobiles	exhausting	somersaulting
astronauts	awkwardly	launched	strawberries
astronomer	awkwardness	launching	Vermonter
audiences	coffeepot	laundries	Washingtonian
Australian	crawled	lawyerly	
automated	crawling	precautionary	

E Fun Ways to Spell

Initial the box of each activity you finish.

1. Classify your words according to syllables.

3. Spell your words and play "Match-It."

2. Spell your words on graph paper.

4. Spell your words with clay.

Words with /ô/ or /o/

Lesson 4

25

1 Hide and Seek

Reinforce spelling by using multiple styles of learning.

On a white board, Teacher writes each word — one at a time. **Have students:**

- **Look** at the word.
- **Say** the word out loud.
- **Spell** the word out loud.
- **Hide** (teacher erases word.)
- **Write** the word on paper.
- **Seek** (teacher rewrites word.)
- **Check** spelling. If incorrect, rewrite word correctly.

2 Other Word Forms

This activity is optional. Have students write original sentences using these Other Word Forms:

somersaulted
automated
precautionary
awkwardly

3 Fun Ways to Spell

Four activities are provided. Use one, two, three, or all of the activities. Have students initial the box for each activity they complete.

Options:

- assign activities to students according to their learning styles
- set up the activities in learning centers for the students to do throughout the day
- divide students into four groups and assign one activity per group
- do one activity per day

General

To classify your words according to syllables...
- Write three headings on your paper: One-syllable, Two-syllable, and Three-syllable.
- Write the first word on your list under the proper heading.
- Draw a line through the word to divide it into syllables.
- Do this with each word.

Auditory

To spell your words and play "Match-It"...
- Write each word on a card. Mix your word-cards and a classmate's together. Deal six cards to each player; the rest face down between you. Ask your classmate for a word-card. If the word-card matches, take it and play again. If not, draw from the stack, and it is your classmate's turn. Take turns until all cards are matched.

Visual

To spell your words on graph paper...
- Look at the first word on your list.
- Shade in squares to form the letters of each word.
- Check your spelling.
- Do this with each word.

Tactile

To spell your words with clay...
- Roll pieces of clay into ropes.
- Use the ropes to make the letters of each word.
- Put them in the right order to spell each word.
- Check your spelling.

Working with Words

Familiarize students with word meaning and usage.

Secret Words

The boxed letters in the acrostic are a phrase from the Scripture verse for this week.

Use the clues to write the words in the puzzle. You may use a dictionary to help you. Then write the boxed letters on the lines below to find the secret words from this week's Scripture.

Take a minute to memorize...

Psalm 92:2,4

Lesson 4 | Day 3

Words with /ô/ or /o/ — Lesson 4

F Working with Words Name ______________________

Secret Words

Use the clues to write the words in the puzzle. Then write the boxed letters on the lines below to find the secret words from this week's Scripture.

1. automatic
2. exhaust
3. crawl
4. astronaut
5. laundry
6. alcohol
7. launch
8. coffee
9. automobile
10. Vermont
11. lawyers
12. somersault
13. precaution
14. Australia
15. awkward
16. on-line
17. Washington
18. audience
19. strawberry
20. clause

1. instinctive
2. to fatigue or tire
3. creep about on all fours
4. space aviator
5. washing
6. colorless liquid used in making medicines and fuels
7. start
8. caffeine drink
9. car
10. New England state
11. attorneys
12. flip
13. forethought
14. smallest continent
15. clumsy
16. using the Internet
17. only state named for a president
18. congregation
19. small red fruit
20. part of a sentence

Write the secret phrase:

Thank you for your kindness.

Word Bank

alcohol	automatic	coffee	laundry	somersault
astronaut	automobile	crawl	lawyers	strawberry
audience	awkward	exhaust	on-line	Vermont
Australia	clause	launch	precaution	Washington

26

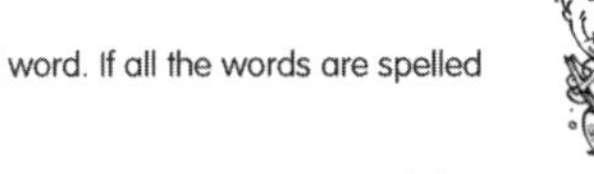

G **Dictation** Name ____________

Write each sentence as your teacher dictates. Use correct punctuation.

1. Tommy crawled out of bed exhausted and cross every day.
2. "My best pants are in the laundry, so I have to wear old ones," he growled.
3. Doing somersaults felt awkward, so he practiced a lot.

Words with /ô/ or /o/ — Lesson 4

H **Proofreading**

If a word is misspelled, fill in the oval by that word. If all the words are spelled correctly, fill in the oval by **no mistake**.

1. ● audiunce ○ cliffs ○ kidnap ○ no mistake
2. ○ hymn ○ launch ● summersalt ○ no mistake
3. ○ limit ○ laundry ○ Australia ● no mistake
4. ● clauze ○ exhaust ○ England ○ no mistake
5. ● astrunot ○ automobile ○ income ○ no mistake
6. ○ infant ● precaushun ○ index ○ no mistake
7. ○ awkward ○ crawl ○ Virginia ● no mistake
8. ○ lawyers ● strawberrie ○ assist ○ no mistake
9. ○ disk ○ history ● cofee ○ no mistake
10. ● alcohaul ○ on-line ○ Vermont ○ no mistake
11. ○ insist ○ Mississippi ● washington ○ no mistake
12. ○ automatic ○ discuss ○ glisten ● no mistake

27

1 Dictation

Reinforce correct spelling by using current and previous words in context.

Say: Listen as I read each sentence and then write it in your Worktext. Remember to use correct capitalization and punctuation. (Slowly read each sentence twice. Sentences are found in the Student Worktext to the left.)

2 Proofreading

Familiarize students with standardized test format and reinforce recognition of misspelled words.

Say: Look at each set of words. If a word is misspelled, fill in the oval by that word. If all the words are spelled correctly, fill in the oval by **no mistake**.

3 Hide and Seek

Reinforce correct spelling of current spelling words. Repeat this activity from Day 2.

4 Vocabulary Extension

Have your students complete this activity to strengthen spelling ability and expand vocabulary. The reproducible master is provided in Appendix A as shown on the inset page to the right.

1 Posttest

Test mastery of the spelling words.

I will say the word once, use it in a sentence, then say it again. Write your words on a separate sheet of paper.

Progress Chart

Students may record scores. (Reproducible master in Appendix B.)

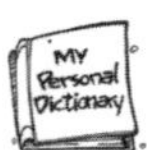

Personal Dictionary

Students may add any words they have misspelled to their personal dictionaries for reference when writing. (Cover in Appendix B.)

Vocabulary Extension — Lesson 4

Hide and Seek

Play Hide and Seek with your words. Fill in a bar graph (left to right) for each word you spell correctly.

Vocabulary Extension

Cause and Effect

Write a word from the word bank to complete each sentence.

1. If you are reading the fifth book of the Bible, you are reading Deuteronomy.
2. If a machine runs by mechanical or computerized means, it is an electronic device.
3. If you are reading a collection of sacred hymns from the Bible, you are reading the Psalms.
4. If someone brings something to completion, they were able to accomplish it.
5. If someone pretends to be very good but is not, he is guilty of hypocrisy.
6. If something is too small to see without using a special magnifying lens, it is microscopic.
7. If you are reading a poetical book of essays and practical statements, you are reading Proverbs.
8. If you live where there is government rule by the people, you live in a democracy.
9. If you want to learn about the reign of King David, you may read the books of Chronicles.
10. If you wanted to read about Jesus' cousin, you would read about John the Baptist.
11. If you wanted to read a letter written by Paul, you could read the book of Colossians.
12. If you wanted to learn more about the man who led the Israelites after Moses, you would learn about Joshua.

Word Bank

accomplish	democracy	hypocrisy	microscopic
Chronicles	Deuteronomy	John	Proverbs
Colossians	electronic	Joshua	Psalms

328

1.	automatic	It seemed **automatic** for Tommy to wake up grumpy.
2.	astronaut	He didn't want his dream of being an **astronaut** to end.
3.	launch	His dream began with a successful **launch.**
4.	somersault	Next he was doing a **somersault** in outer space.
5.	laundry	He complained as he looked through his clean, folded **laundry.**
6.	precaution	Lisa took an extra **precaution** to avoid Tommy in the bathroom.
7.	audience	Tommy's family did not enjoy being the **audience** for his morning moods.
8.	on-line	Mr. Wright may take away Tommy's **on-line** privileges.
9.	Australia	"Let's buy him a one-way ticket to **Australia,**" Lisa teased.
10.	coffee	"I'll get you some **coffee** if it'll help you get out of this mood," she offered.
11.	Vermont	Lisa smothered her waffle in butter and **Vermont** maple syrup.
12.	strawberry	Mom had put the **strawberry** jam on the table just for Tommy.
13.	awkward	Tommy felt **awkward** and ashamed under his dad's reproach.
14.	clause	"Let's add a 'no-grumpiness' **clause** to our family constitution," said Lisa.
15.	automobile	In Tommy's nightmare their **automobile** wasn't even in the garage.
16.	crawl	It was awful to **crawl** out of bed and find everyone gone!
17.	exhaust	"A nightmare can **exhaust** you and make you thankful!" Tommy said.
18.	alcohol	Tommy's family does not drink any kind of **alcohol.**
19.	Washington	Mr. Canfield told his class that **Washington** had been a surveyor.
20.	lawyers	He said some presidents were **lawyers** before they took office.

Lesson 4

I Game

Name ______________________

Record points for each word you or your team spells correctly. Earn bonus points for each row in which all four words are spelled correctly.

	1.	2	3	4	Row Totals
Row A					
Row B					
Row C					
Row D					
Row E					
				TOTAL	
				BONUS	
				GRAND	

Remember: God wants you to be thankful and cheerful...even in the morning!

J Journaling

In your journal, write about the morning routine at your house. Tell who wakes you up and when, what things you do to get ready for the day, and in what order you do them.

28

How to Play:

- Divide the class into two teams.
- Have a student from team A choose a square on the grid by indicating the row letter and number.
- Say the word that matches that row letter and number from the team's word list.
- Have the student write the word on the board.
- If correct, have each member of that team record the awarded points (in parentheses by the word) in the circle in that box. If the word is misspelled, have him/her put an **X** in that circle. That square may not be chosen again.
- Repeat this process with the second team.
- When all the words have been spelled by both teams, have each team tally its score. Award a bonus of 5 points for each row in which all four words were spelled correctly.
- Have the teams record their grand totals. The team with the highest score is the winner.

2 Game

Reinforce spelling skills and provide motivation and interest.

Materials

- game page (from student text)
- pencils (1 per child)
- game word list

Game Word List

Team A		Team B
E4	**audience (2)**	A1
E3	**somersault (3)**	A2
E2	**launch (1)**	A3
E1	**laundry (4)**	A4
D4	**Australia (1)**	B1
D3	**clause (3)**	B2
D2	**exhaust (4)**	B3
D1	**astronaut (2)**	B4
C4	**automobile (3)**	C1
C3	**automatic (4)**	C2
C2	**precaution (1)**	C3
C1	**awkward (2)**	C4
B4	**crawl (4)**	D1
B3	**lawyers (3)**	D2
B2	**strawberry (2)**	D3
B1	**Washington (1)**	D4
A4	**coffee (4)**	E1
A3	**alcohol (2)**	E2
A2	**on-line (1)**	E3
A1	**Vermont (3)**	E4

3 Journaling

Provide a meaningful reason for correct spelling through personal writing.

Review the story using discussion leads provided on the following page. Encourage students to apply the Scriptural value in their journaling.

Journaling (continued)

- What kinds of nicknames did Lisa use for her brother? (Troublesome Tommy, Terrible Tommy, Tommy the Terror, etc.)
- How did these names fit the way Tommy was acting in the mornings? (He was being a real grouch every morning to his whole family.)
- What did Tommy tell his family Mr. Canfield had said about being tired? (That kids who are growing fast sometimes get really tired.)
- Is it okay to be grumpy and grouchy if we're really tired? Why or why not? (No. Even when we feel bad we shouldn't be unkind to those around us—including our families.)
- How did Tommy's dream help him change? (When everyone disappeared in his dream he realized how important his family was to him and how badly he'd been treating them.)
- How do you feel and act when it's time to get up in the morning?
- Try thanking God for something the first thing each morning and let Him help you be joyful instead of grouchy.

Upper and lower case letters are named 'upper' and 'lower,' because in the time when all original print had to be set in individual letters, the 'upper case' letters were stored in the top or upper part of the case and the 'lower case' letters were stored in the bottom or lower part of the case.

Word Wow!

1 **Literature Connection**
Topic: Being content with how God made us
Theme Text: Psalm 16:8, 9

Casing the Jump

Tony learns about good friends, BMX racing, and being content with his height.

"Mama! Where's my helmet? Stephen and I want to ride bikes in Mr. Sample's empty lot." Tony stood in the doorway to the garage.

"On the shelf in your closet, Tony-O." Maria Vanetti continued to stir the gravy she was making for dinner. "Be back by 5:00. Your papa is coming at 6:00 to pick you up for the weekend—remember?"

"He'll be late," Tony said as he passed by the kitchen. He grabbed the stool out of the bathroom and carried it into his bedroom. He pushed his shoes aside so the legs would rest evenly on his closet floor. "I think I'll be short forever!" He stepped onto the stool and slid his blue helmet off the top shelf.

In the garage Tony jumped onto his blue six-speed mountain bike. He fastened the strap securely beneath his chin before peddling out to the sidewalk.

Stephen met him in front of his duplex. "What took you so long? I think Laney's coming too."

Tony squirmed. "Laney's always fun; but she's a girl and towers over me," he thought. "She never teases me about my size—or calls me Little Italy, Tiny Tony, or Cut Spaghetti Vanetti. Maybe that's why I like being around her. I wonder if I'll still be this short in eighth grade. Mama keeps saying I'll have a growth spurt. I hope it's soon." Tony quit thinking about Laney as he slammed on his brakes and skidded to keep from hitting Stephen's bike at the intersection.

"You trying to T-bone me, Tony? Save some tread for the trail."

"T-bone?" Tony wrinkled his forehead.

"Yeah, that's what Laney calls it when you slam into another biker from the side."

The three friends had a good time in the empty lot. They made some ramps for jumping and worked on the berm for one of the track's corners. Before they parted, they promised to meet the next Monday after school.

"I've got a surprise for you!" Mr. Vanetti headed around to the back of the LandCruiser. "Give me your bag."

Tony handed the green duffel bag to his papa and turned to wave to the slim woman standing on the front porch. "See you Sunday night, Mama!" He crawled up into the LandCruiser and buckled his seat belt. "Where were you, Papa? You were supposed to be here at 6:00."

"Merilee needed some help with the baby. Hey, take a look at this." Marcus Vanetti tossed an issue of Bicycles Today onto Tony's lap. "It's the latest issue of the NBL's newspaper. It's loaded with pictures, stories of big races, news from state and local tracks, and, of course, the standings of all NBL members. Whatdaya think?"

Tony squirmed and looked at the floor. "Are you talking about baseball?"

Papa grinned, "National Bicycle League, Tony-O. I've signed you up! Here's your membership card and NBL number." Mr. Vanetti reached behind his seat to retrieve the membership card and number for his son. "With this number, the NBL tabulates and posts the points you earn on ANY of their tracks. You can compete in local, state and national events and will be eligible for year-end awards."

"What are you talking about? There aren't any tracks around here, so how could I earn points?"

"We're going to your first BMX race this weekend! They've built a track near Fayetteville. You've been cruisin' around the neighborhood rompin' and stompin' with your buddies and racing on homemade tracks in the backyard long enough. That's how BMX racing got started, but now we've got a competitive track in Fayetteville. Whatdaya think?"

Tony arched his eyebrows, "I don't have a BMX bike."

"BMX isn't a kind of bike. It stands for bicycle motocross. It's the type of racing you and Stephen do on your bikes all the time. You're already a great BMXer. You do jumps, make dirt berms, and create tricks. That girl from New York rides with you guys, too, doesn't she? What's her name?" Mr. Vanetti pulled out on the highway leading to his home in Fayetteville.

"Laney Ausherman. We have a great time, but I don't have the right stuff for real racing. We just have fun with our mountain bikes from Wal-Mart®. Don't you have to have a special helmet and a bike that costs a lot of money? Laney said that bikes for real racing cost anywhere from $300 to $3000."

"Check out that box back there, Tony-O." Papa pointed over his shoulder to a large cardboard carton on the floor behind his seat.

Tony discovered a new helmet with mouth protection and a pair of gloves. "Thanks, Papa, but I didn't bring my bike. Even if I did it's not a bike for moto-whatever. I don't know much about them, but I know I don't want to race with mine. Everyone would laugh."

Papa just smiled. "I have something in the garage at home that might work for you. You'll have to make the final decision. No matter what you decide, Stephen and his dad are going to meet us at the new track tomorrow evening and you're going to see a real BMX race. It's sponsored by the NBL. Sound fun?"

Tony nodded and tried on his new gloves.

He couldn't believe his good fortune when he saw the new 20-inch Schwinn BMX

Story (continued)

bike in the garage. It was shiny black. There were no chain guard, reflectors, kickstand, or other gadgets. The crossbars and handle bars were padded, as well as the frame and gooseneck "Is this really mine?" was all he could say.

Tony was embarrassed when Papa had to adjust the seat as low as it would go. But he got over it after he hopped on and felt how easy it was to maneuver and ride. He pinched himself to make sure he wasn't dreaming.

The next evening Tony sat between Laney and Stephen to watch their first BMX race. Coach Larkin and Laney had come with Stephen and his dad. The three friends were really excited.

"Ewww! That guy did a face plant." Laney pointed to a kid who'd flipped over his handlebars and landed on his face. "Look at that ramp. I don't think I'm ready for that."

The group watched the bikers head for the starting gate below them.

"Oh! Did you see her case that jump? She flattened her rim. I hope she has a spare or she won't be racing today." Coach Larkin nodded toward a girl who was leaning back to check out her rear wheel.

Laney leaned over toward Tony. "Stephen said you might race in the open class today with the new bike your dad got you."

Tony shrugged, "We haven't had time to look at the whole track or practice, but it looks pretty easy."

"I dare you, Tony," Stephen grinned.

Tony looked over at Laney. "Maybe she'll be impressed if I do well in the race," he thought. "Maybe she'll forget that she towers over me. It really shouldn't be too hard on my new bike."

"Sure. Why not?" he said aloud.

Laney frowned. "I think you should practice, Tony. This track is harder than it looks. The ramps are high and there're some double jumps, too. The Skatepark in New York had some of this stuff. It's tricky."

Tony shrugged. "I think I can do it. There are no points in the open class, so it'll be good practice."

"It may not feel like good practice if you fall or someone T-bones you from the side," Laney warned.

Tony balanced his front wheel against the gate, which kept it from crossing the starting line. A gun went off, and the starting gate dropped. The race was on!

Tony shot out in front of the pack. "Go for it, Tony!" Coach Larkin yelled. "This is his first race—and he's in the lead!"

Tony rounded the curve and came up to the first set of doubles. It looked like two humps of dirt. From Tony's new perspective, the humps looked bigger than they had from the stands. As soon as he was airborne, he knew he was in trouble.

"That's a dead sailor," someone in the stands yelled.

Stephen turned to Laney, "What's a 'dead sailor?'"

"Tony," she said as she closed her eyes. "He's all stiff and out of control."

"The little kid out front is gonna case the jump!" a man shouted.

Laney heard a sickening thud and opened her eyes. "His bike's broken in now!"

"The rear wheel has a flat spot." Stephen grimaced, "I shouldn't have dared him. He's got this complex about being short. I knew if I dared him he'd do it."

Somehow Tony managed not to get smashed by the other racers. When they had all passed him, he wheeled his bike off the track and over to where Laney and Stephen were standing. Their fathers waited in the stands.

Stephen playfully punched his friend on the shoulder. "What happened, Tony? Were you thinking about Laney?"

Tony smiled sheepishly. "I was thinking about how I wanted to prove I could do this—but all I proved is how much more practice I need." Tony swept his hand in the direction of the spectators in the stands. "I should've concentrated on what I was doing, instead of who was watching."

"We like you, Tony. You don't have to prove anything to us." Laney bent down to look at the bent rim. "Maybe you should think of the Lord, like in the Scripture verse Mr. Canfield taught us. You fell because you were tense and nervous. Relax. Just be happy with who you are. You'll race better. You'll do everything better."

"Preach on!" Stephen teased.

Laney stood up and smiled, "I can't believe I said that."

"Neither can I." Tony grinned. "But you're okay. Thanks."

2 Discussion Time

Check understanding of the story and development of personal values.

- Raise your hand if you've ever watched a BMX race or have been to a track.
- What was it like?
- What did Tony's dad give him?
- How did Tony feel when his dad had to lower the seat all the way?
- Why did Tony decide to race with his new bike without practicing?
- What happened?
- How did Laney react when Tony cased the jump?

A Preview Name ____________

Write each word as your teacher says it.

1. minutes
2. construct
3. circuit
4. freedom
5. summary
6. shrug
7. District of Columbia
8. opossum
9. umpire
10. pulse
11. adult
12. numb
13. crumb
14. gruffly
15. museum
16. hungry
17. wisdom
18. album
19. tundra
20. suffix

Words with /u/, /e/, or /i/

Lesson 5

Scripture
Psalm 16:8,9

29

3 Preview

Test for knowledge of the correct spellings of these words.

Customize Your List

On a separate sheet of paper, additional words of your choice may be tested.

I will say each word once, use the word in a sentence, then say the word again. Write the words on the lines in your Worktext.

Correct Immediately!

Let's correct our Preview. I will spell each word out loud. If you spelled a word incorrectly, rewrite it correctly.

Progress Chart

Students may record scores. (Reproducible master provided in Appendix B.)

Lesson 5 | Day 1

1.	minutes	Laney arrived at the empty lot within **minutes** of Stephen and Tony.
2.	construct	They discussed how to **construct** a berm for one corner of the track.
3.	circuit	A diagram of an electric **circuit** ran across Tony's old blue helmet.
4.	freedom	Tony's papa has the financial **freedom** to buy very expensive gifts.
5.	summary	He gave Tony a **summary** of BMX racing.
6.	shrug	Tony gave a **shrug** when his dad asked him what the NBL was.
7.	District of Columbia	Do they print the BMX magazine in the **District of Columbia**?
8.	opossum	A **opossum** waddled across the road as they drove to the race.
9.	umpire	There is no **umpire** at a BMX race.
10.	pulse	Tony felt his **pulse** race as he put the front wheel of his bike in the gate.
11.	adult	Another **adult** shouted, "He's gonna case the jump!"
12.	numb	He felt **numb** for a few seconds after his crash on the track.
13.	crumb	He felt small and unimportant, like a **crumb** under the table.
14.	gruffly	Stephen and Laney did not speak **gruffly** to Tony.
15.	museum	"Hey, you should donate your bike to a BMX **museum**," Stephen teased.
16.	hungry	"Don't be so **hungry** to be different. Be happy with who you are."
17.	wisdom	There was a lot of **wisdom** in Laney's advice.
18.	album	He will put the picture his dad took in his photo **album** at home.
19.	tundra	Mr. Canfield defined and showed pictures of the **tundra**.
20.	suffix	Tony is getting better at spelling a word correctly when adding a **suffix**.

Lesson 5 | Day 1

4 Word Shapes

Help students form a correct image of whole words.

Look at each word and think about its shape. Now, write the word in the correct word Shape Boxes. You may check off each word as you use it.

(The sound of **/u/** or **/ə/** is often spelled with **a**, **o**, or **u**. The sound of **/i/** is usually spelled with **i**.)

In the word shape boxes, fill in the boxes containing the letter or letters that spell the sound of **/u/**, **/ə/**, or **/i/** in each word.

Take a minute to memorize...

Psalm 16:8,9

Words with /u/, /ə/, or /i/ — Lesson 5

B Word Shapes Name ____________

Using the word bank below, write each word in the correct word shape boxes. Next, in the word shape boxes, fill in the boxes containing the letter or letters that spell the sound of **/u/**, **/ə/**, or **/i/** in each word.

1. adult
2. minutes
3. suffix
4. shrug
5. crumb
6. album
7. circuit
8. construct
9. opossum
10. District of Columbia
11. museum
12. numb
13. umpire
14. wisdom
15. hungry
16. gruffly
17. pulse
18. freedom
19. summary
20. tundra

Word Bank

adult	crumb	hungry	opossum	summary
album	District of Columbia	minutes	pulse	tundra
circuit	freedom	museum	shrug	umpire
construct	gruffly	numb	suffix	wisdom

30

Answers may vary for duplicate word shapes.

Be Prepared For Fun

Check these supply lists for **Fun Ways to Spell** - presented **Day 2**. Purchase and/or gather these items ahead of time!

General
- Pencil
- Graph Paper (1 sheet per child)
- Spelling List

Auditory
- Pencil
- Notebook Paper
- Spelling List

Visual
- Colored Pencils
- Alphabet Stencils
- Paper

Tactile
- Uncooked Rice
- Art Paper (1 sheet per child)
- Glue
- Spelling List

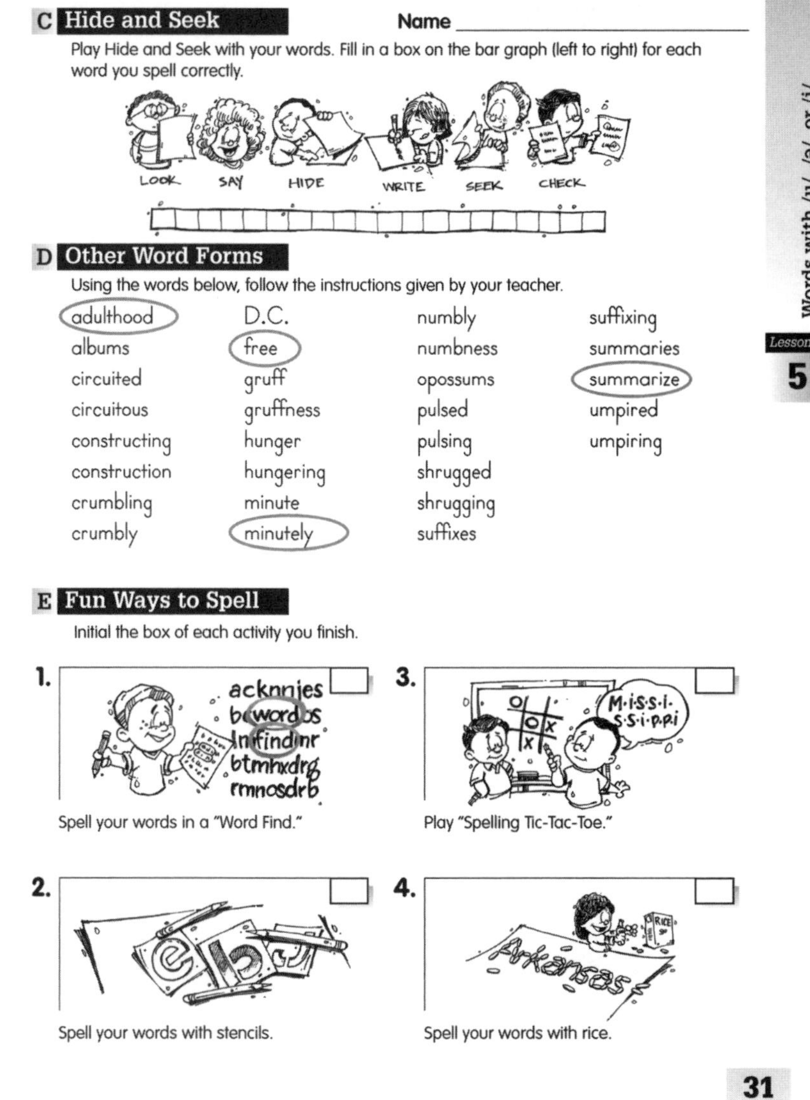

C Hide and Seek Name ____________________

Play Hide and Seek with your words. Fill in a box on the bar graph (left to right) for each word you spell correctly.

D Other Word Forms

Using the words below, follow the instructions given by your teacher.

adulthood	D.C.	numbly	suffixing
albums	free	numbness	summaries
circuited	gruff	opossums	summarize
circuitous	gruffness	pulsed	umpired
constructing	hunger	pulsing	umpiring
construction	hungering	shrugged	
crumbling	minute	shrugging	
crumbly	minutely	suffixes	

E Fun Ways to Spell

Initial the box of each activity you finish.

1. Spell your words in a "Word Find."

3. Play "Spelling Tic-Tac-Toe."

2. Spell your words with stencils.

4. Spell your words with rice.

Words with /u/, /ə/, or /i/

Lesson 5

31

Day 2 | Lesson 5

1 Hide and Seek

Reinforce spelling by using multiple styles of learning.

On a white board, Teacher writes each word — one at a time. **Have students:**

- **Look** at the word.
- **Say** the word out loud.
- **Spell** the word out loud.
- **Hide** (teacher erases word.)
- **Write** the word on paper.
- **Seek** (teacher rewrites word.)
- **Check** spelling. If incorrect, rewrite word correctly.

2 Other Word Forms

This activity is optional. Have students find and circle the Other Word Forms that are most nearly antonyms of the following:

elongate
enormously
restrained
childhood

3 Fun Ways to Spell

Four activities are provided. Use one, two, three, or all of the activities. Have students initial the box for each activity they complete.

Options:

- assign activities to students according to their learning styles
- set up the activities in learning centers for the students to do throughout the day
- divide students into four groups and assign one activity per group
- do one activity per day

General

To spell your words in a "Word Find"...
- Arrange your words on a piece of graph paper.
- Put one letter of each word in a square.
- Words may be written backwards, forwards, or diagonally.
- Outline your puzzle.
- Hide your words by filling in all the spaces inside the puzzle with random letters.
- Trade grids with a classmate and find the hidden words.

Auditory

To play "Spelling Tic-Tac-Toe"...
- Draw a Tic-Tac-Toe grid.
- Ask a classmate to read a spelling word.
- Spell the word aloud.
- If the word is spelled correctly, place your mark on the grid.
- Take turns with your classmate.

Visual

To spell your words with stencils...
- Look at the first letter of a word on your list.
- Place the stencil for the proper letter over your paper.
- Shade inside the stencil.
- Choose the proper stencil for the next letter of the word and shade it in next to the first letter.
- Finish the word in this way.
- Do this with each word.

Tactile

To spell your words with rice...
- Choose a word from your spelling list.
- Shape the letters of your word with rice.
- Glue the rice to art paper.
- Do this for each word on your list.

Working with Words

Familiarize students with word meaning and usage.

Drawing Conclusions

Explain that to figure something out using logic is to draw a conclusion. On the board write:

This area is hot, dry, and barren. It is a ____________ region.

Have a volunteer supply the word **desert**.

Complete each conclusion by writing a word from the word bank. You may use a dictionary to help you.

Take a minute to memorize...

Psalm 16:8,9

F Working with Words — Name ____________

Drawing Conclusions

Complete each conclusion by writing a word from the word bank.

1. My raccoon doesn't like its cage. Most likely it wants its freedom.
2. I feel a rhythmical beat in my wrist. This is my pulse.
3. We are going to see some paintings. We will go to a museum.
4. I dropped the plate of cookies. I had to clean up every crumb.
5. My stomach is rumbling. I am probably hungry.
6. We have a book of pictures. It is a photo album.
7. He is 24 years old. He is considered an adult.
8. He will come soon. It will only be a few minutes.
9. Washington, D.C. is the United States capitol. D.C. stands for District of Columbia.
10. This short statement gives the main ideas. It is a summary of the story.
11. He found a gray, furry marsupial that was playing dead. It is probably an opossum.
12. He felt grouchy. He probably answered her gruffly.
13. If you have knowledge, experience, and good judgment you have wisdom.
14. He is ruling on the plays in the ball game. He is the umpire.
15. He is building a house. He will construct it.
16. She doesn't seem to care. She shows this with a shrug.
17. The soil under the surface is permanently frozen. This area is a tundra.
18. We can add ing to some words. We can add a suffix.
19. You can't turn on the light. There may be a break in the circuit.
20. My toes are so cold I can't move them. They are numb.

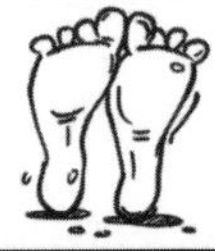

Word Bank

adult	crumb	hungry	opossum	summary
album	District of Columbia	minutes	pulse	tundra
circuit	freedom	museum	shrug	umpire
construct	gruffly	numb	suffix	wisdom

G Dictation

Name ____________________

Write each sentence as your teacher dictates. Use correct punctuation.

1. Tony's pulse raced as he headed for the first jump in the track.
2. The three kids worked hard to construct a track on which to ride their bicycles.
3. Laney had an album of pictures showing a museum she had visited in the District of Columbia.

Words with /u/, /ə/, or /i/ Lesson 5

H Proofreading

If a word is misspelled, fill in the oval by that word. If all the words are spelled correctly, fill in the oval by **no mistake**.

1.	○ gruffly	**5.**	● crum	**9.**	○ audience		
	● sufix		○ precaution		○ launch		
	○ strawberry		○ awkward		● sumary		
	○ no mistake		○ no mistake		○ no mistake		
2.	○ shrug	**6.**	● freedum	**10.**	○ laundry		
	○ lawyers		○ coffee		○ wisdom		
	○ Washington		○ numb		○ hungry		
	● no mistake		○ no mistake		● no mistake		
3.	○ adult	**7.**	○ crawl	**11.**	○ Australia		
	○ alcohol		● muzeum		● circut		
	○ pulse		○ construct		○ tundra		
	● no mistake		○ no mistake		○ no mistake		
4.	○ album	**8.**	○ umpire	**12.**	○ clause		
	○ Vermont		○ somersault		○ exhaust		
	● district of Columbia		● opposum		● minites		
	○ no mistake		○ no mistake		○ no mistake		

33

1 Dictation

Reinforce correct spelling by using current and previous words in context.

Listen as I read each sentence and then write it in your Worktext. Remember to use correct capitalization and punctuation. (Slowly read each sentence twice. Sentences are found in the Student Worktext to the left.)

Day 4

2 Proofreading

Familiarize students with standardized test format and reinforce recognition of misspelled words.

Lesson 5

Look at each set of words. If a word is misspelled, fill in the oval by that word. If all the words are spelled correctly, fill in the oval by **no mistake**.

3 Hide and Seek

Reinforce correct spelling of current spelling words. Repeat this activity from Day 2.

4 Vocabulary Extension

Have your students complete this activity to strengthen spelling ability and expand vocabulary. The reproducible master is provided in Appendix A as shown on the inset page to the right.

Hide and Seek

Play Hide and Seek with your words. Fill in a bar graph (left to right) for each word you spell correctly.

Vocabulary Extension

Fill in the Blanks

Choose a word from the word bank that best fits each sentence clue.

1. If you want the cookies to turn out well, you must follow the instructions.
2. The seventh book of the Bible, Judges, is named for the way Israel was ruled during this time.
3. I had to struggle to get the saddle on the huge horse, but I finally was successful.
4. Numbers, the fourth book of the Bible, begins with a census taken at Sinai.
5. The art class I want to sign up for allows a maximum of twenty students.
6. When our sink developed a leak underneath, we called a plumber.
7. It felt absolutely wonderful to go swimming in the middle of the hot day.
8. Someday she would like to travel to several other countries for a visit.
9. The stray cat soon became a regular visitor to our dog's bowl on the back porch.
10. The motel where we stayed provided shuttle service to the nearby shopping malls.
11. Several companies sent me their catalogs of outdoor gear when I subscribed to a ski magazine.
12. Mom is looking forward to the luxury of a long soak in the whirlpool.

Word Bank

companies	Judges	Numbers	shuttle
countries	luxury	plumber	struggle
instructions	maximum	regular	wonderful

Lesson 5 — Vocabulary Extension — 329

1 Posttest

Test mastery of the spelling words.

I will say the word once, use it in a sentence, then say it again. Write your words on a separate sheet of paper.

Progress Chart

Students may record scores. (Reproducible master in Appendix B.)

Personal Dictionary

Students may add any words they have misspelled to their personal dictionaries for reference when writing. (Cover in Appendix B.)

1. minutes	Only a few **minutes** passed before Laney met the boys at the lot.
2. construct	The three friends helped each other **construct** a berm for the track.
3. circuit	A bright electrical **circuit** decorated Tony's blue helmet.
4. freedom	Tony's mom doesn't have the **freedom** to buy expensive gifts like his dad.
5. summary	Tony's papa gave him a brief but exciting **summary** of BMX racing.
6. shrug	By Tony's **shrug**, his dad knew he needed to explain more about BMX racing.
7. District of Columbia	Was the BMX periodical printed in the **District of Columbia**?
8. opossum	Tony saw a **opossum** as they drove to the race.
9. umpire	There is no **umpire** to make calls during a BMX race.
10. pulse	Tony's **pulse** began to race as he neared the starting gate.
11. adult	An **adult** high in the stands shouted, "That's a dead sailor!"
12. numb	Tony's mind went **numb** as he realized he was going to crash.
13. crumb	He wanted to crawl under a table like a **crumb**.
14. gruffly	None of his friends or their parents spoke **gruffly** to Tony.
15. museum	"Wanna donate your bike to the BMX **museum**?" teased Stephen.
16. album	Tony will put the picture of him before the race in his **album** at home.
17. hungry	"Don't be too **hungry** to be different than you are," encouraged Laney.
18. wisdom	"You've got a lot of **wisdom** for a girl," joked Tony with a grin.
19. suffix	Tony is learning how a **suffix** can change the meaning of a word.
20. tundra	Mr. Canfield showed slides of plant life that thrives in the **tundra**.

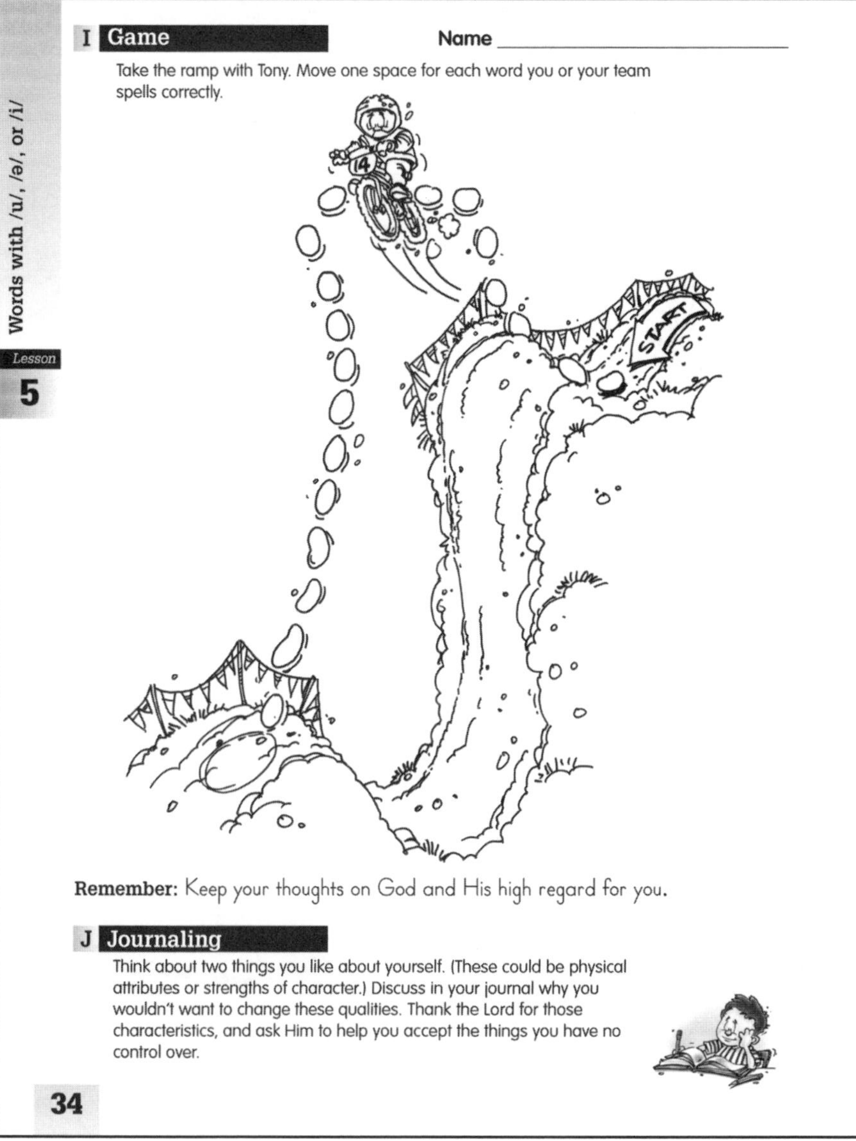

Words with /u/, /e/, or /i/

Lesson 5

I Game Name ______________________

Take the ramp with Tony. Move one space for each word you or your team spells correctly.

Remember: Keep your thoughts on God and His high regard for you.

J Journaling

Think about two things you like about yourself. (These could be physical attributes or strengths of character.) Discuss in your journal why you wouldn't want to change these qualities. Thank the Lord for those characteristics, and ask Him to help you accept the things you have no control over.

34

How to Play:

- Divide the class into two teams.
- Have each student place his/her game piece on Start.
- Have a student from team A go to the board.
- Say the spelling word.
- Have the student write the word on the board.
- If correct, instruct each member of team A to move his/her game piece forward one space.
- Alternate between teams A and B.
- The team to complete the jump first is the winner.
- **Small Group Option**: Students may play this game without teacher direction in small groups of two or more.

2 Game

Reinforce spelling skills and provide motivation and interest.

Materials

- game page (from student text)
- game pieces (1 per child)
- game word list

Game Word List

1. **construct**
2. **gruffly**
3. **suffix**
4. **shrug**
5. **adult**
6. **pulse**
7. **album**
8. **District of Columbia**
9. **crumb**
10. **freedom**
11. **museum**
12. **numb**
13. **opossum**
14. **summary**
15. **umpire**
16. **wisdom**
17. **hungry**
18. **tundra**
19. **circuit**
20. **minutes**

3 Journaling

Provide a meaningful reason for correct spelling through personal writing.

Review the story using discussion leads provided on the following page. Encourage students to apply the Scriptural value in their journaling.

Lesson 5 | Day 5

Journaling (continued)

- How did Tony reach the helmet high on his closet shelf? (A stool)
- What names did Tony's classmates sometimes call him? (Little Italy, Tiny Tony, Cut Spaghetti Vanetti)
- How did Tony feel about Laney towering over him? (He didn't like it.)
- Was Tony's dad on time to pick him up? (No.)
- What did Tony's dad get for him? (A helmet, gloves, and racing bike)
- What did Stephen do to get Tony to race? (Dared him to.)
- How did Laney feel about Tony racing without practicing? (She didn't think it was a good idea.)
- What happened to Tony on the first jump of the race? (He cased the jump.)
- What did Laney say to Tony after he crashed on the jump? ("Maybe you should think of the Lord. You fell because you were tense and nervous. Relax. Just be happy with who you are. You'll race better. You'll do everything better.")

In English, "four" is the only digit that has the same number of letters as its value.

Word Wow!

Topic: God's guidance
Theme Text: Psalm 119:33, 34

Invisible Instructor

When Christopher gets an opportunuty to fly in a small plane, he learns what it means to depend on God's guidance.

Christopher was so excited he was speechless—for a change. Dad pulled the green station wagon into a parking spot and opened his door. "You coming, Son?"

Christopher nodded and jumped out of the car as if it were on fire. He soaked in the smells and sounds around him as he walked beside his dad across the tarmac and into an air-conditioned terminal. His eyes darted this way and that way, trying to see as much as he could. With each step he lagged a little further behind his dad as he tried to take everything in.

Halfway down the corridor he cannoned into his father, who'd suddenly stopped. "Good afternoon, Mr. Wright." Christopher stuck his head around his dad to see who was talking. "And you must be Christopher!" The man was tall and lean. His blond hair and mustache were neatly trimmed. He shook Mr. Wright's hand and then stuck out his hand to Christopher. "Glad you could join us today."

"Christopher, this is Paul McInley." Dad nudged Christopher forward to shake the man's hand.

"H-hello, sir." Christopher managed to greet the man in uniform.

"It sure was kind of you to let my son come along, Paul." Mr. Wright rested a hand on Christopher's shoulder as the three of them walked toward a glass door. "But I should probably warn you that once he gets started he's likely to talk your ear off asking questions. Airplanes are his favorite subject—and this is his first flight in a small plane."

"Nothing I like to talk about more!" Mr. McInley laughed and held open the door for Christopher and his dad before leading the way across the tarmac to a blue and white airplane. A beautiful blue and white airplane. Christopher could hardly believe his good fortune. Dad had to make a brief business trip. It was a great opportunity for Christopher to tag along since it would be only a two-hour flight each way, with a short stop for business.

"You sit up here by me," Mr. McInley motioned Christopher into the seat across from his right, in front of the instruments. "After I get the preflight inspection complete and get this thing in the air, you just ask any questions you like. I'm always happy to meet someone who loves airplanes as much as I do."

Christopher absorbed details about the instrument panel while the pilot went through the preflight checklist. After the thrill of takeoff, Christopher began firing questions. "What's that thing for? Why did you do that? What do these gauges tell you? How do you control the altitude?"

Paul McInley patiently answered each question. He explained that they were flying a Cessna Skylane 182R RG that was built in 1987. He told Christopher that the RG stands for retractable gear, which means that the wheels fold up when the airplane is in flight. He explained that the Skylane is one of the most widely produced airplanes in history—more than 2,000 of them rolled out of the Cessna plant. Christopher learned that the Skylane featured a constant speed propeller and had a wingspan of 36 feet.

"How high can we go?" Christopher peered out at the patchwork earth far below.

"From sea level this baby can climb to 14,300 feet. Normal cruising altitude is about half that, though." Mr. McInley tapped a gauge on the instrument panel. "This is the altimeter. It indicates our altitude, or height."

Christopher pointed at a gauge in the middle, "What's that instrument for—that one that looks like a plane sitting on a runway?"

"It's called an attitude indicator. Watch this." Mr. McInley moved a control and suddenly the tiny plane on the attitude indicator flipped sideways at the same time that Christopher felt the plane tip to the right. One instant there was clear blue sky out Christopher's window; the next instant his window was pointed at the ground and he was gazing in fascination at the tiny hills far below. Just as quickly, Mr. McInley righted the plane again and the tiny plane on the attitude indicator faithfully reflected the change—its wings leveling out even with the horizontal lines across it once again.

"ALL RIGHT!" Christopher grinned across at the pilot. "Do some more stuff like that, please?"

Mr. McInley chuckled. "How about a quick course in landing this beauty instead? We're approaching the airport in a couple of minutes."

"Already?" Christopher peered out his window in dismay. Sure enough, way down there more roads converged and a bunch of tiny buildings appeared. Christopher listened intently as Mr. McInley spoke over the radio and prepared to land. He consoled himself with the thought that they still got to fly back home that night.

By the time Mr. Wright finished his business and he and Christopher arrived back at the airport, it was getting dark and cloudy. "We may be in for a bit of a rough ride on the return trip," Mr. McInley commented as they climbed in the Cessna. "That storm they've predicted for tomorrow morning is blowing in sooner than expected. Shouldn't cause a real problem—just be a little bumpy."

Christopher sat quietly in his seat as the pilot put

Story Continued

the small plane into motion. As they taxied down the runway gaining speed, the aircraft worked extra hard dragging itself up into the wind. The lights on the ground winked and then disappeared as the Cessna rose into the gathering darkness of the clouds. The three of them in the small airplane seemed to be the only things that existed anymore. By the light from the instrument panel, Christopher watched Paul McInley maneuver the plane.

"Mr. McInley, how do you know where you're going?" Christopher waved a hand at the blackness surrounding all the windows. "How do you find the airport?"

"The instruments, Christopher." Mr. McInley smiled and explained, "I don't have to be able to see where I'm going, because these instruments tell me."

"Do they tell you where other airplanes are?" Christopher stared out his window toward the light on the wing tip. Wisps of cloud often obscured its blinking glow. "There were a whole bunch of planes landing and taking off back at the airport. How do you keep from crashing into each other in the air when you can't see anything?"

"That's why I talk to the guy in the tower, the one who knows where everyone's headed." The pilot checked his airspeed and altitude. "That person is called an air traffic controller. At larger airports, like the one we just left, air traffic controllers keep track of every airplane in the area. If I follow the directions they give me, I'll stay out of trouble by keeping clear of the flight path of other…"

His voice trailed off as the plane lurched wildly. The turbulence required all of Mr. McInley's attention and skill. Christopher was happy to be quiet and let the pilot concentrate on flying the plane—especially when it continued to buck and drop in the currents of air.

Christopher assured himself that he wasn't really scared. After all, anyone would feel a little strange when their airplane was acting more like a roller-coaster!

Christopher was glad he was wearing a seat belt and he was glad Mr. McInley knew what he was doing. The thin aluminum walls shuddered and seemed pretty fragile when the wind buffeted the Skylane around. Well, maybe he was scared. Just a little bit.

"So, here's my aspiring young pilot!" Mom met Christopher and his dad at the door later that night. "Was it fun? Did you learn a lot?"

"Sure did!" Christopher grinned. "Especially how important it is to pay attention to your instruments and to obey the…the…, you know, that person who knows what's best for everyone."

"You're talking about air traffic controllers, aren't you?" Mom ruffled Christopher's hair like she used to when he was little and laughed at the look on his face. "Since the air traffic controllers know what all the planes around an airport are doing, pilots who obey their instructions stay on the right course."

"That's it! Air traffic controllers," Christopher repeated. He ran a hand through his wavy brown hair to smooth it back down.

"Well, I was sure glad to know someone out there could tell Mr. McInley where to go tonight." Mr. Wright laid his briefcase on the table and stretched. He thought aloud for a moment, "Someone who can keep us safely on the right course even when we're not flying…Hmmm. You know, that's a lot like life."

He grinned at his wife and son and finished his thought. "We obey God because He knows everything about us—even where we're headed. Obeying His instructions keeps us on the right track. See what I mean?"

His son returned the grin. "Gonna keep us flyin' straight, Dad."

2 Discussion Time

Check understanding of the story and development of personal values.

- Where did Christopher go with his dad?
- Why was he so excited about it?
- In what kind of plane were they flying?
- Did the pilot mind having Christopher come along?
- What happened on the flight back home?
- How did Christopher feel when the storm made the flight rough?
- How did Mr. McInley know how to fly the plane when he couldn't see anything?
- How can you keep on the right track when life is rough?

A Test-Words Name ____________

Write each spelling word on the line as your teacher says it.

1. lizard
2. glitter
3. income
4. index
5. discuss
6. assist
7. history
8. camera
9. album
10. limit
11. England
12. cliffs
13. Mississippi
14. infant
15. glisten
16. on-line

Review Lesson 6

B Test-Sentences

Write the sentences on the lines below, correcting each misspelled word, as well as all capitalization and punctuation errors. Two words are misspelled in each sentence.

with great skill the astronot began the lawnch

1. With great skill, the **astronaut** began the **launch.**

the dentist grufly told the boy that he had a cavitie?

2. The dentist **gruffly** told the boy that he had a **cavity.**

do you have friends in virginya and michigin.

3. Do you have friends in **Virginia** and **Michigan?**

Our teacher gave us freadum at the muzeam

4. Our teacher gave us **freedom** at the **museum.**

35

4 Test-Sentences

Reinforce recognizing misspelled words.

Read each sentence carefully. Write the sentences on the lines in your Worktext. There are two misspelled words in each sentence. Correct each misspelled word, as well as all capitalization and punctuation errors.

Take a minute to memorize...

Psalm 119:33,34

Day 1 | Review 6

3 Test-Words

Test for knowledge of the correct spellings of these words.

I will say each word once, use the word in a sentence, then say the word again. Write the words on the lines in your Worktext.

1.	lizard	Christopher saw a **lizard** sunning himself on the tarmac.
2.	glitter	The **glitter** in the stripes on the plane made it sparkle in the sun.
3.	income	Mr. McInley earns an **income** flying people in his plane.
4.	index	Christopher ran his **index** finger along the instrument panel.
5.	discuss	Mr. McInley was very eager to **discuss** airplanes and flying.
6.	assist	"These instruments **assist** me in knowing my altitude or height."
7.	history	He explained the **history** of the Cessna Skylanes.
8.	camera	Christopher pulled his **camera** out of his backpack.
9.	album	He had his dad take a picture of himself and the pilot for his **album.**
10.	limit	There was no **limit** to the questions Christopher wanted to ask.
11.	England	"Have you ever flown to **England**?" he asked Mr. McInley.
12.	cliffs	"Yes, I flew over some gorgeous **cliffs** over there!" he exclaimed.
13.	Mississippi	"I've flown across the **Mississippi** River too many times to count."
14.	infant	It seemed that Christopher had loved planes since he was an **infant.**
15.	glisten	He loved to see a plane **glisten** in the sunlight as it landed.
16.	on-line	He could hardly wait to get **on-line** and learn more about the Cessna Skylane.

1 Test-Dictation

Reinforce correct spelling by using current and previous words in context.

Say: Listen as I read each sentence, then write it in your worktext. Remember to use correct capitalization and punctuation. (Slowly read each sentence twice. Sentences are found in the student text to the right. The words **banana**, **lawyers**, **construct**, and **Washington** are found in this unit.)

2 Test-Proofreading

Familiarize students with standardized test format and reinforce recognizing misspelled words.

Say: Look at each set of words. If a word is misspelled, fill in the oval by that word. If all the words are spelled correctly, fill in the oval by **no mistake**.

C Test-Dictation

Name ______________________

Write each sentence as your teacher dictates. Use correct punctuation.

1. There is a yellow banana on the sidewalk.
2. Both of those lawyers are in my employ.
3. They plan to construct a wide gate here.
4. When in Washington, I saw my grandmother.

D Test-Proofreading

If a word is misspelled, fill in the oval by that word. If all the words are spelled correctly, fill in the oval by **no mistake**.

1. ● sufix ○ lizard ○ glitter ○ no mistake
2. ○ income ○ automobile ○ index ● no mistake
3. ○ discuss ○ assist ● austraila ○ no mistake
4. ○ history ● opposum ○ limit ○ no mistake
5. ● wepon ○ album ○ England ○ no mistake
6. ○ cliffs ○ Mississippi ● minites ○ no mistake
7. ● strawberrie ○ infant ○ glisten ○ no mistake
8. ○ on–line ○ disk ● hymm ○ no mistake
9. ○ somersault ● acsent ○ pulse ○ no mistake
10. ○ exhaust ○ camera ○ weather ● no mistake
11. ○ automatic ○ insist ○ strength ● no mistake
12. ○ admit ● circut ○ adapt ○ no mistake

E Test-Table

Name ______________________________

If a word is misspelled, fill in the space on the grid.

Montanna	assid	lacth	alcohaul
crumb	method	aspekt	vermont
denim	kiddnap	credit	tundra
planit	clause	selfish	cavern

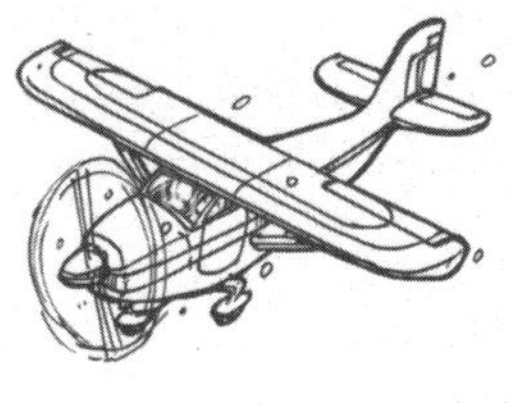

Review

Lesson 6

F Writing Assessment

Write about a flight you have taken. Tell all about the experience including when you flew, where you were going, and what the plane was like. If you haven't flown, write about how you would feel if you were in the plane with Christopher when the airplane felt more like a roller coaster than a plane.

Scripture

Psalm 119:33,34

37

A rubric for scoring is provided in Appendix B.

"I am."
is the shortest sentence
in the English language.

Test-Table

Test mastery of words in this unit.

If a word is misspelled, fill in the space on the grid.

Writing Assessment

Assess student's spelling, grammar, and composition skills through personal writing.

- Have you ever flown in an airplane? (Allow time to share experiences.)
- Why did Christopher get to go on the trip with his dad? (It was a two hour flight each way with a short stop for business at the other end and there was room in the plane.)
- What kinds of questions did Christopher have for Mr. McInley, the pilot? (What's that? What do these gauges tell you? How do you control the altitude? How high can we go? etc.)
- How did Mr. McInley show Christopher what the attitude indicator was for? (He tipped the plane on it's side so Christopher's window was facing the ground.)
- Why was the flight rough on the way back? (A storm had moved into the area.)
- How was Mr. McInley able to keep the plane on the right track even in the thick clouds? (By using his instruments and paying attention to and doing what the air traffic controller said to do.)
- How can you keep on the right track? (By paying attention to and doing what God says to do.)

Test-Sentences

Reinforce recognizing misspelled words.

Read each sentence carefully. Write the sentences on the lines in your Worktext, correcting each misspelled word, as well as all capitalization and punctuation errors.

G Test-Sentences Name ______________________

Write the sentences on the lines below. Correct each misspelled word, as well as all capitalization and punctuation errors. Two words are misspelled in each sentence.

the audiunse can often read a sumery of the play!

1. The audience can often read a summary of the play.

feeling awkwerd she swung at the tinnis ball,

2. Feeling awkward, she swung at the tennis ball.

they hung a baner to welcome the athleat

3. They hung a banner to welcome the athlete.

is the heffer helthy enough to show at the state fair.

4. Is the heifer healthy enough to show at the state fair?

H Test-Words

Write each spelling word on the line as your teacher says it.

1. disk
2. somersault
3. pulse
4. weather
5. insist
6. admit
7. strength
8. adapt
9. precaution
10. panic
11. lever
12. wisdom
13. respect
14. batch
15. hungry
16. coffee

38

2 Test-Words

Test for knowledge of the correct spellings of these words.

I will say the word once, use the word in a sentence, then say the word again. Write the word on the lines in your Worktext.

1.	disk	Christopher planned to save all he'd learned on a compact **disk.**
2.	somersault	During the storm, he felt like the plane might do a **somersault.**
3.	pulse	He could feel his **pulse** pounding in his temples.
4.	weather	It was a relief to everyone to be out of the rough **weather.**
5.	insist	I **insist** you let us buy you some dinner," said Mr. Wright to Paul.
6.	admit	Christopher had to **admit** he was a little scared during the storm.
7.	strength	His legs were shaking so he wasn't sure he had the **strength** to stand.
8.	adapt	Mr. McInley will **adapt** his course if instructed to do so.
9.	precaution	"The tower informs me of each **precaution** I need to take to land safely."
10.	panic	Storm clouds and dense fog can cause pilots to **panic.**
11.	lever	"He always knew just which **lever** to move," said Christopher in awe.
12.	wisdom	"I saw the **wisdom** in listening to the tower," he told his mom.
13.	respect	It is clear to see that Christopher has great **respect** for the pilot.
14.	batch	Mom had a **batch** of oatmeal cookies hot out of the oven.
15.	hungry	"Hope you're **hungry** for some cookies and milk," she said.
16.	coffee	"I'd love a cup of **coffee** myself," said Mr. Wright.

I Test-Editing		Name	

If a word is spelled correctly, fill in the oval under **Correct**. If the word is misspelled, fill in the oval under **Incorrect**, and spell the word correctly on the blank.

	Correct	Incorrect	
1. gram	●	○	
2. cannada	○	●	Canada
3. mass	●	○	
4. California	●	○	
5. atlus	○	●	atlas
6. delta	●	○	
7. shellter	○	●	shelter
8. attend	●	○	
9. tinse	○	●	tense
10. Marylund	○	●	Maryland
11. New Mexico	●	○	
12. laundry	●	○	
13. umbrela	○	●	umbrella
14. crawl	●	○	
15. texas	○	●	Texas
16. shrugg	○	●	shrug
17. adult	●	○	
18. District of Columbia	●	○	
19. numm	○	●	numb
20. umpire	●	○	

Review Lesson 6

39

3 Test-Editing

Reinforce recognizing and correcting misspelled words.

4 Action Game

Reinforce spelling skills and provide motivation and interest.

Materials

- masking tape
- four square ball
- word list on certificate at end of unit

BOUNCE BACK

Use tape to mark a two-square game grid on the classroom floor. Divide the class into two teams. Line up the two teams on opposite sides of the two-square court. The first player from each team steps into the court, one player holding a ball. Call out the first spelling word to be reviewed. The player with the ball says the first letter of the word as he or she hits the ball into the opposite square. The player in that square says the second letter of the word as he or she hits the ball back. This continues until the word has been spelled. If a player misspells a word by saying an incorrect letter, play stops and the other team gets a point. If the word is spelled correctly, both teams get a point. Give a new word to the next two players and continue in this pattern. The team with the most points wins!

1 Game

Reinforce spelling skills and provide motivation and interest.

Materials

- game page (from student text)
- colored pencils (1 per child)
- game word list

Game Word List

Check off each word lightly in pencil as it is used.

The Pipers

1. automobile
2. Australia
3. opossum
4. weapon
5. minutes
6. strawberry
7. hymn
8. denim
9. planet

The Bonanzans

1. acid
2. method
3. kidnap
4. clause
5. latch
6. aspect
7. credit
8. selfish
9. alcohol

The Cessnas

1. Vermont
2. tundra
3. cavern
4. accent
5. exhaust
6. automatic
7. circuit
8. Montana
9. crumb

How to Play:

- Divide the class into three teams. Name one team **The Pipers**, one **The Cessnas**, and one **The Bonanzas**. (Option: You may wish to seat students in groups of three, each student from a different team. They should share one game page.)
- Have a student from the first team go to the board.
- Say the spelling word.
- Have the student write the word on the board.
- If the word is spelled correctly, have each team member color a point symbol by his/her team name. If the word is misspelled, have him/her put an **X** through one point symbol. That word may not be given again.
- Repeat this process with the second team and then the third.
- When the words from all three lists have been used, the team with the most points is the winner.
- Play another round using Other Word Forms.

Date ____________________

This certificate is awarded to

____

for completing fun activities using the following spelling words!

accent	attend	admit	alcohol	adult
acid	credit	assist	astronaut	album
adapt	delta	cliffs	audience	circuit
aspect	denim	discuss	Australia	construct
athlete	healthy	disk	automatic	crumb
atlas	heifer	England	automobile	District of Columbia
banana	lever	glisten	awkward	freedom
banner	Maryland	glitter	clause	gruffly
batch	method	history	coffee	hungry
California	New Mexico	hymn	crawl	minutes
camera	respect	income	exhaust	museum
Canada	selfish	index	launch	numb
cavern	shelter	infant	laundry	opossum
cavity	strength	insist	lawyers	pulse
gram	tennis	kidnap	on-line	shrug
latch	tense	limit	precaution	suffix
mass	Texas	lizard	somersault	summary
Montana	umbrella	Michigan	strawberry	tundra
panic	weapon	Mississippi	Vermont	umpire
planet	weather	Virginia	Washington	wisdom

2 Certificate

Provide an opportunity for parents or guardians to encourage and assess their child's progress.

Fill in today's date and your name on your certificate.

Take a minute to memorize...

Psalm 119:33,34

3 Letter

Provide the parent or guardian with the spelling word lists for the next unit.

Give your parents or guardian this letter that lists your spelling words for the next unit. Put it where you will remember to practice the words together.

Dear Parent,

We are about to begin a new spelling unit containing five weekly lessons. A set of twenty words will be studied each week. All the words will be reviewed in the sixth week. Values based on the Scriptures listed below will be taught in each lesson.

Lesson 7	Lesson 8	Lesson 9	Lesson 10	Lesson 11
Asia	appeal	admire	banjo	accuse
chase	brief	alibi	boldly	canoe
contain	creep	arrive	buffalo	confuse
crater	deceit	byte	cargo	crew
debate	eager	diary	control	cue
decade	Hawaii	diet	dome	dune
decay	idea	geyser	donate	flu
detail	liter	guide	enroll	foolish
escape	Louisiana	guys	flamingo	funeral
estate	meter	height	macro	future
flavor	piece	Idaho	Minnesota	igloo
labor	Puerto Rico	Iowa	Oklahoma	include
Maine	relief	isle	patrol	Massachusetts
mesa	reveal	liar	portfolio	raccoon
Pennsylvania	shield	minor	soldier	tomb
prey	shriek	Ohio	sole	truly
ratio	skiing	recital	stereo	tulip
stray	Tennessee	riot	studio	useless
veil	vetoes	silence	voltage	Utah
vein	wield	wife	Wyoming	view
Psalm 37:4,5	Psalm 62:8	Psalm 89:14	Psalm 62:7	Psalm 119:96-98

1 Literature Connection

Topic: Fear of public speaking
Theme Text: Psalm 37: 4, 5

Funny Money

Matthew's little sister reminds him to trust the Lord, who is able to give him his heart's desire.

(Note: Your class might enjoy looking at a real $100 bill. Lower denominations have also been redesigned. It might be fun for them to find all the things found in this story that make counterfeiting more difficult.)

"Believe me, I'd rather play Monopoly than practice this report." Matthew spread the World magazine open on the floor in front of him. "I'd rather do 'most anything," he mumbled under his breath.

"Can't you just play with us for a little while? We don't have to finish the game." Alex took the game board out of the box and put it on the table.

Matthew tried to hide his discomfort. "Did you know…" His voice cracked. He paused to lick his lips. His tongue felt thick and dry. "…U.S. currency is used more than any other kind of money in the world?"

"No," nine-year-old Alex answered. "I thought our money was only good here. Don't all countries make their own?"

Matthew rubbed his clammy hands across the carpet. "Yeah, but I guess our money is safer because its value doesn't make extreme changes all the time. It says here Russians use it for their savings and Africans use it in business transactions." He hesitated again to wipe the beads of perspiration off his upper lip. "Here's another trivia question for you two." He took a deep breath and let it out slowly—trying to control his rising anxiety. "What bill is used the most?"

"The one dollar bill," Alex guessed, tucking his allotment of Monopoly money under the edge of the game board.

Matthew shook his head. "Nope, try again."

Alex looked down at Matthew. "Are you okay?"

Matthew ignored the question and wrote something down on a piece of notebook paper.

"Hundreds," his first-grade sister guessed.

Matthew's eyebrows shot up. "How did you know that, Em?"

Emily shrugged. "I doe know—just do… maybe the Money Town game on the computah."

Matthew smiled at his little sister. "You're right."

"Are you sick? I thought you couldn't play Monopoly because you had homework." Alex put three game pieces on "Go."

"I do. I need to practice this report. I have to read it in front the class." Matthew felt a lump in his throat, and his stomach felt funny too. "The best ones have to do theirs again for the whole school."

"I can't even imagine doing that," Matthew thought. "My hands shake so much I can't read my paper in front of my own class. My tongue gets thick and dry and I stumble over the words. I feel so stupid. I wish Mrs. Burton was still our teacher. She never made us do stuff like this." Matthew's heart started to pound just thinking about the coming ordeal.

"Is youah wepoaht about money?" Emily rolled the dice and moved the silver dog to Baltic.

Matthew didn't even notice how his sister still mispronounced her r's. He focused on what she said and tried not to think about giving the report. He knew his fear was unreasonable, but he couldn't stop it. Getting up in front of the whole class just terrified him. Finally he answered, "Yeah, my report's about money."

"Well, wead it to us. I like money." Emily got up from the table and came over to sit beside her brother. She picked up the magazine and examined the picture on the cover. It was of a girl peeking around the edge of a huge sheet of $100 bills hot off the press. Then she looked up at Matthew's face. "What's the mattah, Matt?"

Matthew ignored her question and started to read from his notebook. "Benjamin Franklin looks better than ever! The Treasury decided to make new currency because of 'funny money'—those fake bills counterfeiters try to pass off as real. A counterfeiter once needed special engraving skills—now all he needs is a good color copier."

Emily moved closer to Matthew and put her hand on his back.

Matthew stopped reading and looked up at her before he continued. "The new $100 bill has two pictures of Ben Franklin. One shows up only when the bill is held up to a light. It's called a watermark and a copy machine can't see it. Details in the new bigger picture of Ben make the face easier to recognize and the bill harder to copy. Tiny letters spelling 'United States of America' are hidden in Franklin's coat collar." Matthew stopped reading and pointed to a picture of the magnified words in the magazine.

Alex got up from the table and came over to look at the pictures too.

Matthew continued, "To the left of Ben's face there is a security thread that touches the last zeros of the hundreds at the top and bottom of the bill. It is a fine band with tiny letters and 100s printed on it. The band runs through the paper. You can only see it when you hold the money up to light. It can't be photocopied, either. There are some special things about the 100s printed on the two lower corners below Ben Franklin's

Story (continued)

picture. You'll need a magnifying glass to see one of them. All U.S. money is printed on special paper made from a secret formula."

"This is cool." Alex bent down to take a look at the 100 printed in the lower-left corner of the bill in the magazine. "What's different about this hundred?"

Matthew could feel the tension leaving his body. His brother and sister liked his report—even more than playing Monopoly. He smiled. "I'm not going to tell. You have to figure it out. You want to hear the rest of this?"

Both kids nodded, so Matthew read the last paragraph. "Don't get any ideas about copying your own money. The Secret Service was formed in 1865 to fight counterfeiting. (It has other jobs too.) It investigates every counterfeit case immediately and 99.1 percent of the bad guys are caught. Unless your copy of paper money is one-sided and less than three-fourths the bill's actual size, or greater than one and one-half times the bill's actual size, you're counterfeiting—and counterfeiting is against the law. When in doubt stick with Monopoly money!"

Emily clapped her hands. "That's good, Matthew. I want to look at a weal $100 bill now." She bent down and looked at Matthew's face. "You feeling bettah?"

Matthew nodded.

"Aah you scaaahed? You don't want to say youah wepoaht to youah class?"

Alex returned to the game table. "That's a good report. Yours will be one of the best. I think you should play Monopoly with us now and quit worrying."

Matthew's eyes got big.

Emily patted his hand. "Pway, Matt. Twust Jesus to help you do it. He will." A smile spread across the little girl's face.

The words blurred on the report in his hand. "I sure need your help, God. But it's okay if You help me just enough to do it in front of my own class," he prayed silently.

Matthew closed his notebook. "Thanks for listening to my report, guys. I think I can play Monopoly now. Pass me some of that real 'funny money!'"

2 Discussion Time

Check understanding of the story and development of personal values.

- How many of you have ever saved one hundred dollars?
- Raise your hand if you've held a one hundred dollar bill recently?
- What are some of the things Matthew talked about that make the one hundred dollar bill harder to counterfeit?
- Why do you think Matthew was afraid to give his report in front of the class?
- What did Emily do to encourage her older brother?
- Tell about a time you learned something or were reminded of it by someone younger.

A Preview Name ______________________

Write each word as your teacher says it.

1. labor
2. detail
3. estate
4. Pennsylvania
5. Asia
6. Maine
7. decay
8. escape
9. crater
10. stray
11. decade
12. mesa
13. prey
14. ratio
15. flavor
16. vein
17. contain
18. debate
19. chase
20. veil

Scripture
Psalm 37:4,5

Words with /ā/

Lesson 7

3 Preview

Test for knowledge of the correct spellings of these words.

Customize Your List

On a separate sheet of paper, additional words of your choice may be tested.

I will say each word once, use the word in a sentence, then say the word again. Write the words on the lines in your Worktext.

Correct Immediately!

Let's correct our Preview. I will spell each word out loud. If you spelled a word incorrectly, rewrite it correctly.

Progress Chart

Students may record scores. (Reproducible master provided in Appendix B.)

Lesson 7 | Day 1

1.	labor	It was a great **labor** for Matthew to prepare to speak publicly.
2.	detail	He carefully researched every **detail** of how money is printed.
3.	estate	Ben Franklin, pictured on the hundred dollar bill, did not live on an **estate.**
4.	Pennsylvania	There is a mint in Philadelphia, **Pennsylvania.**
5.	Asia	Our money is not printed on the continent of **Asia**, but in North America.
6.	Maine	There are no mints in **Maine.**
7.	decay	Matthew's enthusiasm about his report began to **decay** as fear overcame him.
8.	escape	He wished there was a way to **escape** this assignment.
9.	crater	Matthew thought a **crater** on the moon would be a good place to hide!
10.	stray	He tried not to allow his thoughts to **stray.**
11.	decade	To Matthew, every minute in front of the class felt like a **decade.**
12.	mesa	The platform at the front of the room felt like a huge **mesa.**
13.	prey	Matthew's nerves fell **prey** to his fears.
14.	ratio	His **ratio** of confidence to fear was very low.
15.	flavor	Em's favorite **flavor** of ice cream is mint chocolate chip.
16.	vein	"Why is the **vein** on your forehead popping out?" asked Alex.
17.	contain	"Your report sure does **contain** some great stuff!" he encouraged.
18.	debate	Em said there was no **debate;** he just needed to trust God to help him.
19.	chase	God can **chase** away our fears and replace them with strength and peace.
20.	veil	He lifted the **veil** of fear in front of Matthew's eyes.

Day 1

Lesson 7

Word Shapes

Help students form a correct image of whole words.

Look at each word and think about its shape. Now, write the word in the correct word Shape Boxes. You may check off each word as you use it.

(In many words, the sound of **/ā/** is spelled with **a** at the end of a syllable, or with **a-consonant-e**, **ai**, **ay**, **ey**, and occasionally **ei**.)

In the word shape boxes, fill in the boxes containing the letter or letters that spell the sound of **/ā/** in each word.

Take a minute to memorize...
Psalm 37:4,5

Lesson 7 — Words with /ā/

B Word Shapes Name ______________________

Using the word bank below, write each word in the correct word shape boxes. Next, in the word shape boxes, fill in the boxes containing the letter or letters that spell the sound of **/ā/** in each word.

1.	ratio	11.	crater
2.	Maine	12.	veil
3.	escape	13.	debate
4.	prey	14.	Pennsylvania
5.	stray	15.	estate
6.	labor	16.	vein
7.	decade	17.	chase
8.	detail	18.	flavor
9.	decay	19.	mesa
10.	Asia	20.	contain

Word Bank

Asia	debate	escape	Maine	ratio
chase	decade	estate	mesa	stray
contain	decay	flavor	Pennsylvania	veil
crater	detail	labor	prey	vein

44

Answers may vary for duplicate word shapes.

Be Prepared For Fun

Check these supply lists for **Fun Ways to Spell** - presented **Day 2**. Purchase and/or gather these items ahead of time!

General
- Pencil
- Graph Paper (1 sheet per child)
- Spelling List

Auditory
- Voice Recorder
- Spelling List

Visual
- American Sign Language reproducible master (provided in Appendix B)
- Spelling List

Tactile
- Soccer Ball, Basketball, Tennis Ball, or 4-Square Ball
- Spelling List

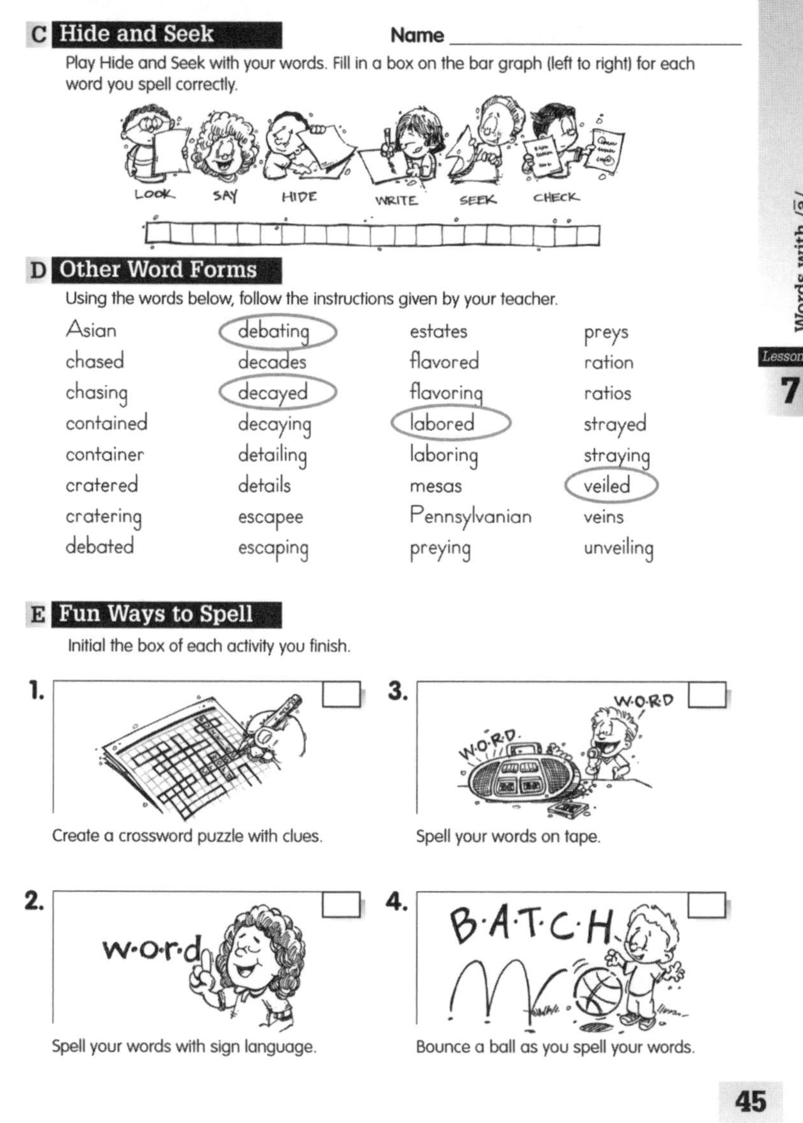

C Hide and Seek Name ____________________

Play Hide and Seek with your words. Fill in a box on the bar graph (left to right) for each word you spell correctly.

D Other Word Forms

Using the words below, follow the instructions given by your teacher.

Asian	debating	estates	preys
chased	decades	flavored	ration
chasing	decayed	flavoring	ratios
contained	decaying	labored	strayed
container	detailing	laboring	straying
cratered	details	mesas	veiled
cratering	escapee	Pennsylvanian	veins
debated	escaping	preying	unveiling

E Fun Ways to Spell

Initial the box of each activity you finish.

1. Create a crossword puzzle with clues.

3. Spell your words on tape.

2. Spell your words with sign language.

4. Bounce a ball as you spell your words.

45

Words with /ā/

Lesson 7

Day 2 · Lesson 7

1 Hide and Seek

Reinforce spelling by using multiple styles of learning.

On a white board, Teacher writes each word — one at a time. **Have students:**

- **Look** at the word.
- **Say** the word out loud.
- **Spell** the word out loud.
- **Hide** (teacher erases word.)
- **Write** the word on paper.
- **Seek** (teacher rewrites word.)
- **Check** spelling. If incorrect, rewrite word correctly.

2 Other Word Forms

This activity is optional. Have students find and circle the Other Word Forms that are most nearly synonyms of the following:

arguing
toiled
rotten
covered

3 Fun Ways to Spell

Four activities are provided. Use one, two, three, or all of the activities. Have students initial the box for each activity they complete.

Options:

- assign activities to students according to their learning styles
- set up the activities in learning centers for the students to do throughout the day
- divide students into four groups and assign one activity per group
- do one activity per day

General

To create a crossword puzzle...
- Use a pencil to arrange your words on graph paper.
- Overlap words where letters are shared.
- Don't create any new words.
- Outline each word with a marker and number it.
- Write a clue for each word.
- Erase your words.
- Trade with a classmate and work each other's puzzles.

Auditory

To spell your words using a voice recorder...
- Record yourself as you say and spell each word on your spelling list.
- Listen to your recording and check your spelling.

Visual

To spell your words with sign language...
- Have a classmate read a spelling word to you from the list.
- Spell the word using the American Sign Language alphabet.
- Do this with each word on your list.

Tactile

To bounce a ball as you spell your words...
- Look at the first word on your list.
- Bounce the ball as you say each letter of the word aloud.
- Do this with each word on your list.

1 Working with Words

Familiarize students with word meaning and usage.

Word Building

Write the endings **s**, **ed**, and **ing**, and the word **glisten** on the board. Have a volunteer add each suffix to the word until you have **glistens**, **glistened**, and **glistening**.

You will be adding each suffix to these spelling words to make other word forms.

The A's Have It

Answer each question with an **/ā/** word from the word bank. You may use a dictionary to help you. Write the word in the blank.

Take a minute to memorize...

Psalm 37:4,5

Words with /ā/ — Lesson 7

F Working with Words Name ____________

Word Building

Add each suffix to the word in each row to make a new word. Remember, when words have the consonant-vowel-consonant-**e** pattern, drop the **e** when adding an ending that begins with a vowel.

	+s or es	+d or ed	+ing
1. debate	debates	debated	debating
2. stray	strays	strayed	straying
3. labor	labors	labored	laboring
4. detail	details	detailed	detailing
5. veil	veils	veiled	veiling
6. prey	preys	preyed	preying
7. chase	chases	chased	chasing
8. flavor	flavors	flavored	flavoring
9. vein	veins	veined	veining
10. decay	decays	decayed	decaying
11. contain	contains	contained	containing
12. escape	escapes	escaped	escaping

The A's Have It

Answer each question with an **/ā/** word from the word bank. Write the word in the blank.

1. What /ā/ word means flat-topped hill with steep sides? mesa
2. What /ā/ word is the name of the world's largest continent? Asia
3. What /ā/ word means a number relationship between two things? ratio
4. What /ā/ word is a state whose capitol is Augusta? Maine
5. What /ā/ word means a period of ten years? decade
6. What /ā/ word is a state whose southern boundary is part of the Mason-Dixon line? Pennsylvania
7. What /ā/ word means a depression formed by an explosion? crater
8. What /ā/ word means a person's land and property? estate

Word Bank

Asia	debate	escape	Maine	ratio
chase	decade	estate	mesa	stray
contain	decay	flavor	Pennsylvania	veil
crater	detail	labor	prey	vein

46

G Dictation

Name ______________________

Write each sentence as your teacher dictates. Use correct punctuation.

1. "The money has many details so people can not copy it," he said.
2. He wanted to escape and not have to speak in front of his class.
3. We read about some children in Asia who had to work in a labor camp all day.

Words with /ā/

Lesson 7

H Proofreading

If a word is misspelled, fill in the oval by that word. If all the words are spelled correctly, fill in the oval by **no mistake**.

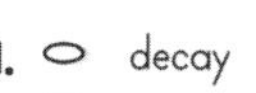
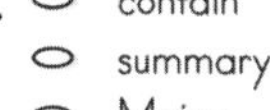

1. ○ decay ○ prey ○ wisdom ● no mistake	**5.** ○ contain ○ summary ○ Maine ● no mistake	**9.** ● rashio ○ crater ○ construct ○ no mistake	
2. ○ stray ● laber ○ minutes ○ no mistake	**6.** ● Pensylvania ○ opossum ○ tundra ○ no mistake	**10.** ○ gruffly ○ suffix ● debait ○ no mistake	
3. ○ umpire ○ circuit ● dekade ○ no mistake	**7.** ○ vein ○ escape ○ crumb ● no mistake	**11.** ○ pulse ○ estate ● flaver ○ no mistake	
4. ○ hungry ● detale ○ veil ○ no mistake	**8.** ○ chase ● messa ○ numb ○ no mistake	**12.** ○ shrug ○ adult ● asia ○ no mistake	

1 Dictation

Reinforce correct spelling by using current and previous words in context.

Say: Listen as I read each sentence and then write it in your Worktext. Remember to use correct capitalization and punctuation. (Slowly read each sentence twice. Sentences are found in the Student Worktext to the left.)

Day 4

2 Proofreading

Familiarize students with standardized test format and reinforce recognition of misspelled words.

Say: Look at each set of words. If a word is misspelled, fill in the oval by that word. If all the words are spelled correctly, fill in the oval by **no mistake**.

Lesson 7

3 Hide and Seek

Reinforce correct spelling of current spelling words. Repeat this activity from Day 2.

4 Vocabulary Extension

Have your students complete this activity to strengthen spelling ability and expand vocabulary. The reproducible master is provided in Appendix A as shown on the inset page to the right.

1 Posttest

Test mastery of the spelling words.

I will say the word once, use it in a sentence, then say it again. Write your words on a separate sheet of paper.

Progress Chart
Students may record scores. (Reproducible master in Appendix B.)

Personal Dictionary
Students may add any words they have misspelled to their personal dictionaries for reference when writing. (Cover in Appendix B.)

Vocabulary Extension — Lesson 7

Hide and Seek

Play Hide and Seek with your words. Fill in a bar graph (left to right) for each word you spell correctly.

Vocabulary Extension

Crossword Puzzle

Use the clues below to complete the puzzle.

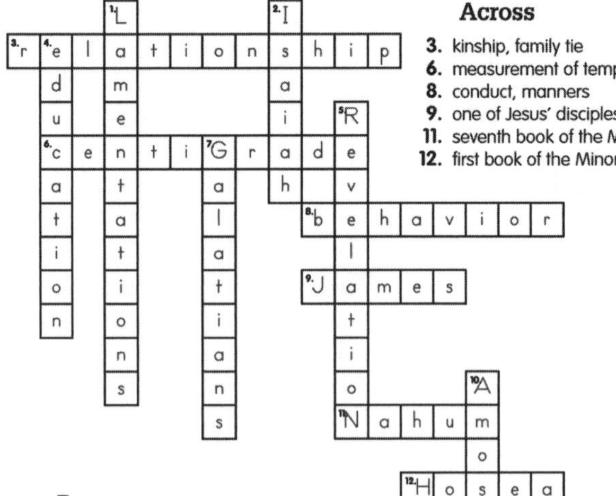

Across

3. kinship, family tie
6. measurement of temperature
8. conduct, manners
9. one of Jesus' disciples
11. seventh book of the Minor Prophets
12. first book of the Minor Prophets

Down

1. Old Testament book following Jeremiah
2. Old Testament book before Jeremiah
4. instruction, schooling
5. last book of the Bible
7. letter written by Paul
10. third book of the Minor Prophets

Word Bank

Amos	education	Isaiah	Nahum
behavior	Galatians	James	relationship
centigrade	Hosea	Lamentations	Revelation

330

1.	labor	Matthew did not mind the **labor** of preparing the written report.
2.	detail	He went over his report in **detail**, checking spelling and grammar.
3.	estate	Ben Franklin, the man on the hundred dollar bill, did not own a large **estate.**
4.	Pennsylvania	One of our nation's mints is in Philadelphia, **Pennsylvania.**
5.	Asia	We do not have our money printed in **Asia.**
6.	Maine	There is not a mint in **Maine,** but there is one in Colorado.
7.	decay	Matthew felt his excitement over his report **decay.**
8.	prey	His mind fell **prey** to the fear of public speaking.
9.	decade	When he spoke in front of his class, a minute felt like a **decade** to him.
10.	mesa	The platform seemed like an enormous **mesa**!
11.	stray	Matthew allowed his thoughts to **stray** from reality for a moment.
12.	escape	He thought of wild ways to **escape** his oral report.
13.	crater	"I could fly to the moon and hide in a **crater**!" he said.
14.	ratio	His **ratio** of fear to confidence was not good.
15.	flavor	The **flavor** of ice cream Em served to the boys was chocolate chip.
16.	vein	"Relax so that **vein** in your neck doesn't bulge," said Alex.
17.	contain	"Your report sure does **contain** interesting facts!" he continued.
18.	debate	Em knew there was no **debate;** Matthew needed to trust God for His help.
19.	chase	God can and will **chase** away your fears.
20.	veil	He removed the **veil** of fear from Matthew's eyes and gave him strength.

I Game Name ______________________

Support Matthew as he gives his oral report to the class. Move one space for each word you or your team spells correctly.

Remember: Trust God to help you do the things you must.

J Journaling

Write in your journal about something you are afraid to do. How do you feel? Is it all "in your head" or do you have other symptoms like clammy hands or a pounding heart?

48

2 Game

Reinforce spelling skills and provide motivation and interest.

Materials

- game page (from student text)
- game pieces (1 per child)
- game word list

Game Word List

1. **decay**
2. **prey**
3. **stray**
4. **labor**
5. **decade**
6. **detail**
7. **veil**
8. **contain**
9. **Maine**
10. **Pennsylvania**
11. **vein**
12. **escape**
13. **chase**
14. **mesa**
15. **ratio**
16. **crater**
17. **debate**
18. **estate**
19. **flavor**
20. **Asia**

How to Play:

- Divide the class into two teams.
- Have each student place his/her game piece on Start.
- Have a student from team A go to the board.
- Say the spelling word.
- Have the student write the word on the board.
- If correct, instruct each member of team A to move his/her game piece forward one space.
- Alternate between teams A and B.
- The team to reach the platform first is the winner.
- **Small Group Option**: Students may play this game without teacher direction in small groups of two or more.

3 Journaling

Provide a meaningful reason for correct spelling through personal writing.

Review the story using discussion leads provided on the following page. Encourage students to apply the Scriptural value in their journaling.

Journaling (continued)

- What game did Alex and Emily want Matthew to play? (Monopoly)
- Why couldn't Matthew play with his brother and sister? (He was practicing a report he had to present.)
- Why did Matthew's voice crack, his lips and tongue feel dry, his stomach feel queasy, and his palms feel clammy? (He was very anxious even thinking about reading the report in front of his class.)
- Why was Matthew afraid to give such an interesting report? (It was an unreasonable fear. He just didn't want to do it.)
- What did Emily suggest he do? ("Pway, Matt. Twust Jesus to help you do it. He will.")
- What are some things you are afraid to do?

Have you ever wondered. . .

Why do we park on driveways and drive on parkways?

Why is "abbreviation" such a long word?

What's another word for Thesaurus?

1 Literature Connection

Topic: Trusting God
Theme Text: Psalm 62:8

Under the Influence

While her mother's drinking problem causes more and more difficulties, Sarah chooses to keep trusting God.

"Now, don't forget to give these notes to your parents!" Mr. Canfield picked up a sheat of papers and began passing them out. "Over the next few weeks we want as many parents as possible to come tell us about their jobs. I'll be getting in touch with each of them later by phone or in person, but I want to give them some time to think about this project." He reached over Tony's head to hand a note to Stephen. "And don't forget your science assignment!"

"Mr. Canfield!" Katelynn caught the teacher's attention as he handed out the last few notes. "Both of my parents work. Are they both supposed to come?"

"Sure, if it's possible," Mr. Canfield replied as he handed the last note to Sarah and the kids began to stream toward the door. "The more the merrier!"

Setsuko rested her denim backpack on the corner of Sarah's desk. "Maybe my father can bring some X rays to show everyone. He could even bring a view box so everyone could see real well. You ready?"

"Just a second." Sarah reached for her library book and stuffed it into her tattered book bag along with her science book. "Are you done with your science assignment?"

"No, but I think I can finish it tonight." Setsuko swung her backpack over one shoulder and fell into step with Sarah as the girls left the classroom. "I wonder if there's anything my mother could bring to show. Probably not, but she sure could tell some stories."

Setsuko held the glass door open for Sarah and then followed her out. "There was a lady that tried on everything in her size in the whole store. She was there for hours and after all that she left without buying a single thing! Then there's the lady who…" Her voice trailed off when she noticed her friend's face. "What's wrong, Sarah?"

"Nothing, really." Sarah shrugged. "It's just that your dad's an X-ray technician and your mom's in charge of the women's department at a big store. Those are interesting, important jobs all the kids will like hearing about." She kicked at a small pebble on the sidewalk and mumbled, "My momma cleans bathrooms."

"Well, that's important, too." Setsuko shifted her backpack. "But I see what you mean. It's probably not the most interesting of jobs. There's my mother. See you tomorrow!"

Sarah waved and dropped to the curb in her usual spot. A steady stream of cars came and went. Not all were new, but most were shiny and well kept. Those people were probably secretaries and doctors and lawyers and clerks and interesting things like that. She held Mr. Canfield's note between two fingers and let it flap in the light wind.

"Oh, no!" Her sister Nellie's exclamation jerked Sarah's attention from the note in her hand. "Just look!" Nellie pointed toward a car turning into the school drive. "Momma's wrecked the car!"

The battered old car had once been red. Long ago it had lost its shine and shape, but today it looked much worse for the wear. Both passenger-side doors were smashed in and the glass was broken out. The right front wheel was turned a bit outwards so that it looked like the car was trying to go two ways at once. A headlight was missing and the fender was crumpled. The girls rushed over when the car shuddered to a stop.

"What happened?" Nellie demanded as she opened the back door on the driver's side and slid across the back seat. Sarah followed and pulled the door closed.

Mrs. Johansen's voice was strained. "Watch out for glass. I think it's all cleaned up, but be careful anyway." Sarah caught a glimpse of her mother's eyes in the mirror. They were puffy and red as if she'd been crying. Mrs. Johansen finally spoke. "There was an accident. A car hit me from the left side and knocked my car into a telephone pole. No one was injured."

Nobody spoke as the car rattled down the street. Mrs. Johansen didn't add any details, and Nellie and Sarah didn't ask any questions. Sarah was sure Nellie was thinking pretty much the same thoughts that were spinning through her own head. "Momma's probably been drinking." A number of the sedan's bumps and scrapes were a result of their mother's drinking habit, but this time the damage was severe.

Later that evening, Sarah yawned and closed her library book. When she replaced it in her backpack, the note from Mr. Canfield caught her attention. "Back to reality, Sarah Johansen," she whispered to herself. "From the wonderful adventures of the Barton twins in my library book to real-life problems."

Sarah flopped on her bed. "I really, really, really don't want Momma to come talk to my class about cleaning bathrooms. How embarrassing! But Mr. Canfield's going to talk to her about it so I've got to give the note to her." Sarah dragged herself off the bed and toward the kitchen. "Maybe she'll get drunk and forget to show up at the right time." That thought was comforting for a second until she realized her mother might get drunk and show up at the right time! "Talk about embarrassing!"

"Momma, Mr. Canfield said to give you this note." Mrs. Johansen leaned against the kitchen counter and read it. When she was

Story (continued)

finished, she folded it carefully in half and laid it on the table where Nellie was working on her homework.

"Nellie. Sarah." Mrs. Johansen cleared her throat. "There's something you should know. I won't be coming to your classroom for this, Sarah, because I don't have a job anymore. I lost my job today." She sank into a chair. "A few days ago my boss told me if I was late again he'd fire me. Because of the accident this morning, I was late to work."

Sarah's ears were buzzing. She felt like screaming. From what seemed like far away she heard Nellie ask, "Was the accident your fault, Momma? Had you been drinking?" She didn't really need to see her mother nod her head to know the truth. Of course her mother was drunk again. And now instead of an embarrassing, low-paying job she had no job at all!

Sarah rushed away as Nellie asked something else. She locked herself in the bathroom. Her hand shook a little when she squirted toothpaste on her toothbrush. "Better not use very much toothpaste. It was bad enough before, when Momma spent so much of her pay on liquor. Now we won't have any money at all." She brushed her teeth with jerky strokes. "I've prayed and prayed and asked God for help. I'm so tired of Momma's drinking! When she's drunk she's not like my mom at all. I miss the mom I used to have. I'm tired of keeping her drinking a secret. I'm tired of never having nice clothes and food and all the stuff most kids have."

A single tear trickled down Sarah's cheek, quickly followed by a torrent. "I'm so tired of it all! God, why aren't you helping? We need help so bad. Please, please help us." Sarah rinsed her mouth and then stared into the small mirror above the sink. "I know you don't promise to take away all the bad things in this world like alcohol. And I know you don't force people to do right, but I wish you would do something to make Momma want to quit drinking!" Sarah leaned over the sink and splashed cold water on her face. "You do promise to be with me always and help me through whatever happens. So, even though things are getting worse and worse, I'll keep trusting you. But, God, I'd really, really, really, really appreciate it if you would help Momma quit drinking."

Sarah dried her face and unlocked the bathroom door. Squaring her shoulders, she walked back into the kitchen. Nellie sat alone at the kitchen table. "Where's Momma?" Sarah reached into the cupboard for a glass.

Nellie laid down her pencil and grinned. "You'll never guess!"

Sarah set the glass down on the counter, forgetting all about getting a drink of water. She stared at her obviously elated sister. "I don't have a clue, so just tell me!"

"Okay. Listen to this!" Nellie leaned forward. "Our mother, Mrs. Johansen,
is... at..." Nellie drew out the suspense, "... an Alcoholics Anonymous meeting for people who want to quit drinking!"

Sarah's mouth dropped open. "Told you you'd never guess!" Nellie bounced around the small kitchen in excitement. "After you left, she told me she knew we were upset about her drinking and that we were praying for her, but she'd always thought it wasn't really such a big deal. She thought she kinda deserved to drink since our father left when we were so little and all."

Nellie picked up Sarah's abandoned glass and filled it with water. "Anyway, she said when she met Setsuko's mom she started realizing how her drinking was ruining our lives, how really bad it was for us." Nellie handed the glass of water to her sister. "She wanted to be more like Mrs. Noma, but she couldn't seem to make a change—till today when she lost her job, smashed the car, and was arrested for driving under the influence of alcohol!"

A few weeks later Sarah sat with her class and listened to her mother tell about her new job in the hospital kitchen. The kids were interested and asked a lot of questions. Sarah wasn't embarrassed at all—in fact she could hardly quit smiling.

She found herself smiling again when it was time for handwriting. The Scripture for the week was "Oh my people, trust him all the time. Pour out your longings before him, for he can help!" Psalm 62:8.

Sarah thoroughly enjoyed writing that verse because she knew from experience that He can and does help those who trust Him.

2 Discussion Time

Check understanding of the story and development of personal values.

- Why was Mr. Canfield inviting all the parents to come to the classroom?
- How did Sarah feel about having her mother come talk to the class? Why?
- What happened to Mrs. Johansen's car?
- Why did Mrs. Johansen lose her job?
- How did Sarah feel about her mother's drinking problem?
- Where did Mrs. Johansen go to get help to stop drinking?
- What new job did Mrs. Johansen get?

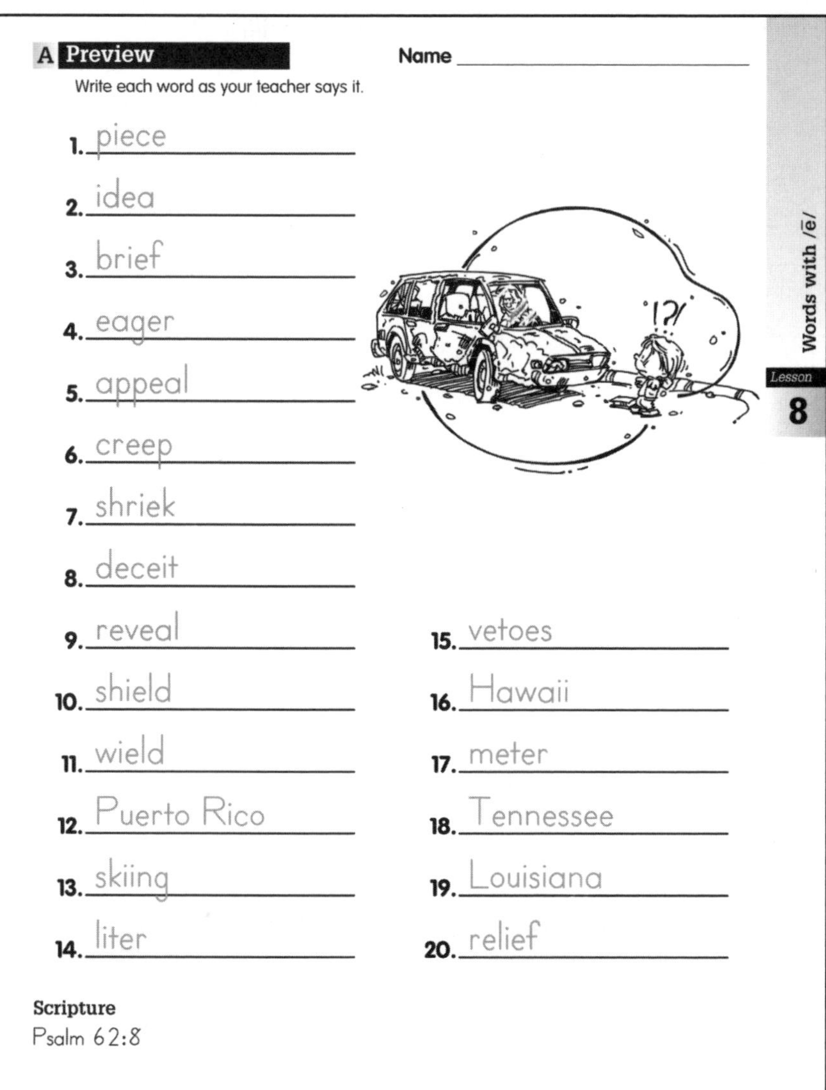

A Preview Name ____________

Write each word as your teacher says it.

1. piece
2. idea
3. brief
4. eager
5. appeal
6. creep
7. shriek
8. deceit
9. reveal
10. shield
11. wield
12. Puerto Rico
13. skiing
14. liter
15. vetoes
16. Hawaii
17. meter
18. Tennessee
19. Louisiana
20. relief

Scripture
Psalm 62:8

Words with /ē/ Lesson 8

49

3 Preview

Test for knowledge of the correct spellings of these words.

Customize Your List

On a separate sheet of paper, additional words of your choice may be tested.

I will say each word once, use the word in a sentence, then say the word again. Write the words on the lines in your Worktext.

Day 1

Correct Immediately!

Let's correct our Preview. I will spell each word out loud. If you spelled a word incorrectly, rewrite it correctly.

Lesson 8

Progress Chart

Students may record scores. (Reproducible master provided in Appendix B.)

1. **piece** Mr. Canfield gave a **piece** of paper to each student.
2. **idea** He had a great **idea** to inform the class of a variety of jobs.
3. **brief** His note to the parents was a **brief** description of his plan.
4. **eager** He was **eager** to have parents tell the class about their jobs.
5. **appeal** The idea of having her mom come to her class did not **appeal** to Sarah.
6. **creep** She wanted to **creep** out of the classroom without taking a note.
7. **shriek** She felt like letting out a **shriek** and a groan when she saw the battered car.
8. **deceit** Sarah knew the **deceit** her mom often practiced to get and keep a job.
9. **reveal** Slowly Mrs. Johansen began to **reveal** the story of her wreck.
10. **shield** Their mother did not try to **shield** the girls from the effects of her drinking.
11. **wield** "What does **wield** mean?" asked Sarah.
12. **Puerto Rico** Sarah enjoyed reading about the Barton twins' trip to **Puerto Rico.**
13. **skiing** Sarah and Nellie have never been **skiing** in the mountains.
14. **liter** They think just buying a **liter** of pop and some ice cream would be fun!
15. **vetoes** Lack of money often **vetoes** their plans.
16. **Hawaii** Sarah didn't even allow herself to dream of vacationing in **Hawaii.**
17. **meter** Mr. Canfield defined the measurement called a **meter.**
18. **Tennessee** He also read the first chapter in a book by a man from **Tennessee.**
19. **Louisiana** The man journaled his travels through Mississippi and **Louisiana.**
20. **relief** Sarah and Nellie felt a great **relief** at the good news about their mom.

Word Shapes

Help students form a correct image of whole words.

Look at each word and think about its shape. Now, write the word in the correct word Shape Boxes. You may check off each word as you use it.

(In many words, the sound of **/ē/** is spelled with **e** at the end of a syllable, or with **ea**, **ee**, **ei**, **ie**, and occasionally **i**. The spelling **y** can be used at the end of a word.)

Lesson 8 Day 1

In the word shape boxes, fill in the boxes containing the letter or letters that spell the sound of **/ē/** in each word.

Take a minute to memorize...

Psalm 62:8

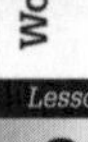

Words with /ē/ Lesson 8

B Word Shapes Name ____________________

Using the word bank below, write each word in the correct word shape boxes. Next, in the word shape boxes, fill in the boxes containing the letter or letters that spell the sound of **/ē/** in each word.

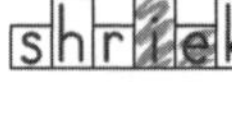
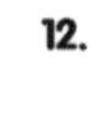
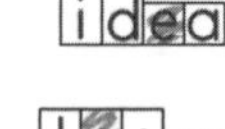

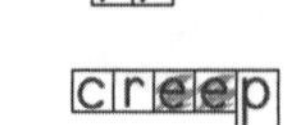

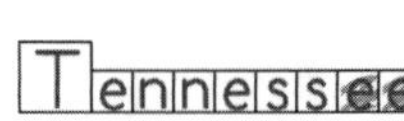

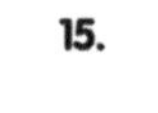
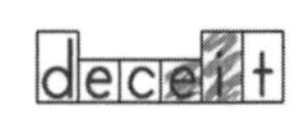

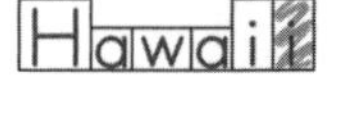

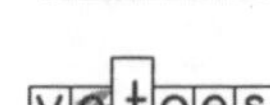

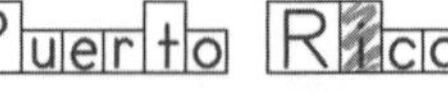

1. reveal
2. skiing
3. appeal
4. creep
5. eager
6. Louisiana
7. shield
8. wield
9. relief
10. brief
11. shriek
12. idea
13. liter
14. Tennessee
15. deceit
16. Hawaii
17. meter
18. vetoes
19. Puerto Rico
20. piece

Word Bank

appeal	eager	Louisiana	relief	skiing
brief	Hawaii	meter	reveal	Tennessee
creep	idea	piece	shield	vetoes
deceit	liter	Puerto Rico	shriek	wield

50

Answers may vary for duplicate word shapes.

Be Prepared For Fun

Check these supply lists for **Fun Ways to Spell** - presented **Day 2**.
Purchase and/or gather these items ahead of time!

General
- Pencil
- Notebook Paper
- Spelling List

Auditory
- Pencil
- Notebook Paper
- Dictionary
- Spelling List

Visual
- Pencil
- Notebook Paper
- Spelling List

Tactile
- Computer Keyboard
- Spelling List

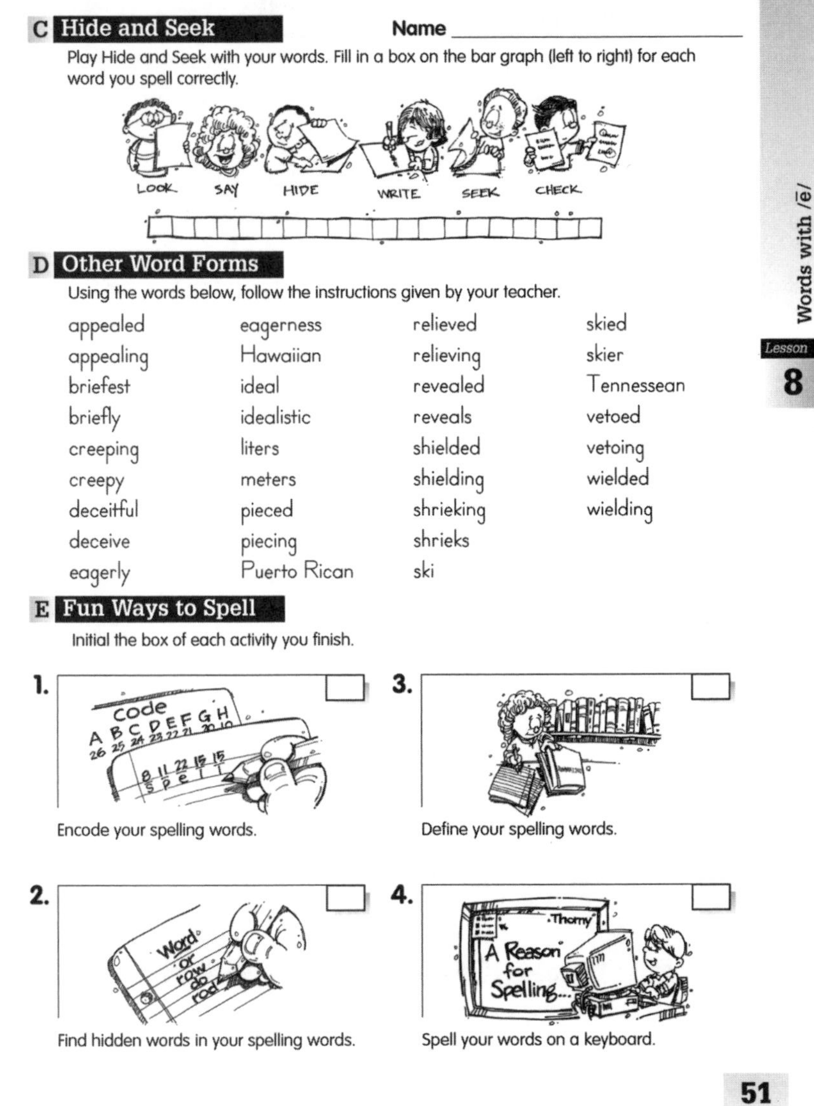

C Hide and Seek Name ____________________

Play Hide and Seek with your words. Fill in a box on the bar graph (left to right) for each word you spell correctly.

D Other Word Forms

Using the words below, follow the instructions given by your teacher.

appealed	eagerness	relieved	skied
appealing	Hawaiian	relieving	skier
briefest	ideal	revealed	Tennessean
briefly	idealistic	reveals	vetoed
creeping	liters	shielded	vetoing
creepy	meters	shielding	wielded
deceitful	pieced	shrieking	wielding
deceive	piecing	shrieks	
eagerly	Puerto Rican	ski	

E Fun Ways to Spell

Initial the box of each activity you finish.

1.
Encode your spelling words.

2.
Find hidden words in your spelling words.

3. Define your spelling words.

4.
Spell your words on a keyboard.

Words with /ē/

Lesson 8

51

1 Hide and Seek

Reinforce spelling by using multiple styles of learning.

On a white board, Teacher writes each word — one at a time. **Have students:**

- **Look** at the word.
- **Say** the word out loud.
- **Spell** the word out loud.
- **Hide** (teacher erases word.)
- **Write** the word on paper.
- **Seek** (teacher rewrites word.)
- **Check** spelling. If incorrect, rewrite word correctly.

Day 2

Lesson 8

2 Other Word Forms

This activity is optional. Have students write original sentences using these Other Word Forms:

eagerness
appealed
wielded
liters

3 Fun Ways to Spell

Four activities are provided. Use one, two, three, or all of the activities. Have students initial the box for each activity they complete.

Options:

- assign activities to students according to their learning styles
- set up the activities in learning centers for the students to do throughout the day
- divide students into four groups and assign one activity per group
- do one activity per day

General

To encode your spelling words...
- Write the alphabet on your paper.
- Write your own code for each letter underneath it.
- Write your spelling words in your code.
- Trade papers with a classmate and decode the words.
- Check to make sure your classmate spelled the words correctly.

Auditory

To define your spelling words...
- Ask a classmate to look up a word from the spelling list in the dictionary and read the definition to you, but not the spelling word.
- Decide which word on your list matches this definition and write the word.
- Ask your classmate to check your spelling.
- Switch and continue taking turns.

Visual

To find hidden words in your spelling words...
- Choose a word from your spelling list.
- Write it on your paper.
- Find and write as many smaller words as you can that are contained within your spelling word.
- Do this with each word.

Tactile

To spell your words on a keyboard...
- Type your spelling words on a keyboard.
- Check your spelling.

Day 3 | Lesson 8

1 Working with Words

Familiarize students with word meaning and usage.

Scrambled Words

Write the letters **acehs** on the board. Have a student unscramble the letters to make the word **chase**.

Unscramble each spelling word. Write the word correctly on the line. Remember to use capital letters where they are needed.

Word Clues

Use your word bank to help you match the spelling words to the clues. Some of the clues are synonyms, words that have the same meaning as the spelling word. You may use a dictionary or thesaurus to help you.

Take a minute to memorize...

Psalm 62:8

Words with /ē/ — Lesson 8

F Working with Words Name ______________

Scrambled Words

Unscramble each word. Write the unscrambled word on the line. Use capital letters and a space where they are needed.

1. aeegr — eager
2. aahiiw — Hawaii
3. aaiilnosu — Louisiana
4. cdeeit — deceit
5. adei — idea
6. befir — brief
7. eemrt — meter
8. deilw — wield
9. ceepr — creep
10. eeostv — vetoes
11. ceeip — piece
12. aaelpp — appeal
13. eeeennsst — Tennessee
14. eilrt — liter
15. eefilr — relief
16. giikns — skiing
17. eoprtu cior — Puerto Rico
18. dehils — shield
19. aeelrv — reveal
20. ehikrs — shriek

Word Clues

Match the spelling words to the clues. You may use a dictionary or thesaurus to help you.

1. sneak, prowl — creep
2. cheating, trickery — deceit
3. disclose, make known — reveal
4. the island state — Hawaii
5. liquid measure — liter
6. southeastern state — Tennessee
7. enthusiastic, zealous — eager
8. rhythm, measure — meter
9. fragment, part — piece
10. Caribbean island — Puerto Rico
11. request, plead — appeal
12. assistance, comfort — relief
13. protect, conceal — shield
14. scream, yell — shriek
15. momentary, fleeting — brief
16. sliding, gliding — skiing
17. belief, thought — idea
18. southern state — Louisiana
19. prohibits, denies — vetoes
20. raise, brandish — wield

Word Bank

appeal	eager	Louisiana	relief	skiing
brief	Hawaii	meter	reveal	Tennessee
creep	idea	piece	shield	vetoes
deceit	liter	Puerto Rico	shriek	wield

52

G Dictation

Name ____________________

Write each sentence as your teacher dictates. Use correct punctuation.

1. Setsuko is eager for her dad to visit her classroom to tell about the work he does.
2. Sarah had no idea why her sister would look so happy, or where Mom could be.
3. What a relief it was to the girls when Mom was able to get some help and find work.

Words with /ē/

Lesson 8

H Proofreading

If a word is misspelled, fill in the oval by that word. If all the words are spelled correctly, fill in the oval by **no mistake**.

1.	○ idea ○ crater ● peice ○ no mistake	**5.**	○ chase ● appiel ○ reveal ○ no mistake	**9.**	○ deceit ○ contain ● lieter ○ no mistake
2.	○ debate ○ estate ● sking ○ no mistake	**6.**	● weild ○ shield ○ flavor ○ no mistake	**10.**	○ meter ○ labor ○ veil ● no mistake
3.	● breef ○ relief ○ Asia ○ no mistake	**7.**	○ Puerto Rico ● kreep ○ decay ○ no mistake	**11.**	○ Maine ○ stray ○ vetoes ● no mistake
4.	○ ratio ● eeger ○ shriek ○ no mistake	**8.**	● Hawai ○ Tennessee ○ prey ○ no mistake	**12.**	● Louiziana ○ decade ○ detail ○ no mistake

53

1 Dictation

Reinforce correct spelling by using current and previous words in context.

Listen as I read each sentence and then write it in your Worktext. Remember to use correct capitalization and punctuation. (Slowly read each sentence twice. Sentences are found in the Student Worktext to the left.)

Day 4

2 Proofreading

Familiarize students with standardized test format and reinforce recognition of misspelled words.

Look at each set of words. If a word is misspelled, fill in the oval by that word. If all the words are spelled correctly, fill in the oval by **no mistake**.

Lesson 8

3 Hide and Seek

Reinforce correct spelling of current spelling words. Repeat this activity from Day 2.

4 Vocabulary Extension

Have your students complete this activity to strengthen spelling ability and expand vocabulary. The reproducible master is provided in Appendix A as shown on the inset page to the right.

1 Posttest

Test mastery of the spelling words.

I will say the word once, use it in a sentence, then say it again. Write your words on a separate sheet of paper.

Progress Chart

Students may record scores. (Reproducible master in Appendix B.)

Personal Dictionary

Students may add any words they have misspelled to their personal dictionaries for reference when writing. (Cover in Appendix B.)

Vocabulary Extension — Lesson 8

Hide and Seek

Play Hide and Seek with your words. Fill in a bar graph (left to right) for each word you spell correctly.

Vocabulary Extension

Trade-off

Choose a word from the word bank to replace the word(s) in parentheses. Write the word in the blank.

1. Descendants of Jacob became known as Hebrews (Israelites).
2. Levers, screws, pulleys, and gears are all simple machines (devices).
3. Anne has always done very well. She will succeed (triumph) now.
4. Dad yielded (surrendered) to the other car so we would not have an accident.
5. When we go out in the extreme (excessive) cold, we dress in many layers of clothes.
6. Paul wrote a letter to Philemon (Onesimus' master) asking him to treat the slave as a brother in Christ.
7. Brushing your teeth after every meal is an example of good hygiene (health habits).
8. Peter (Simon) was an eager, earnest, and courageous disciple of Jesus Christ.
9. We quickly called the police and hoped they would catch the thieves (burglars) who had robbed us.
10. I am teaching my dog how to retrieve (fetch) a stick when I throw it for him.
11. Ecclesiastes (Old Testament book) was written by King Solomon and tells his view of life.
12. She has the gift of leadership (administration), so she is the yearbook editor.

Word Bank

Ecclesiastes	hygiene	Peter	succeed
extreme	leadership	Philemon	thieves
Hebrews	machines	retrieve	yielded

331

---

1. piece — The **piece** of paper Mr. Canfield handed out was a note to the parents.
2. idea — Most of the students were excited about their teacher's **idea.**
3. eager — Setsuko was **eager** for her dad to show the class his X-ray machine.
4. brief — The **brief** note told the parents to expect a phone call from Mr. Canfield.
5. relief — Sarah let out a sigh of **relief** when she remembered they did not have a phone.
6. appeal — "I'll make my **appeal** to your mom after school one day," smiled her teacher.
7. Puerto Rico — Sarah wished she could move to **Puerto Rico** that very moment.
8. creep — She wanted to **creep** out of the room without taking a note from Mr. Canfield.
9. shriek — A **shriek** slipped out of her mouth when she saw the battered car.
10. reveal — As she drove, Mrs. Johansen began to **reveal** the details of her accident.
11. shield — She could not **shield** her daughters form the ill effects of her drinking.
12. deceit — Mrs. Johansen often practiced **deceit** to get a new job.
13. skiing — The girls have a picture of their mom snow **skiing** when she was young.
14. vetoes — Lack of money always **vetoes** their plans to learn to ski.
15. liter — There was not even a **liter** of cheap soda in the refrigerator.
16. wield — Sarah did not know what **wield** meant.
17. Hawaii — Nellie and Sarah didn't even daydream about traveling to **Hawaii.**
18. Tennessee — Mr. Canfield read the first chapter in a book by a man from **Tennessee.**
19. Louisiana — The book chronicled his explorations through the state of **Louisiana.**
20. meter — During math, Mr. Canfield defined the measurement called a **meter.**

Words with /ē/

Lesson 8

I Game Name ______________________

Complete the secret phrase by spelling the words from this week's word list.

TRUST
HIM ALL
THE TIME
HE CAN
HELP!

Remember: Pour out your heart to God; He can do great things!

J Journaling

In your journal, write about what kind of work you would like to do when you become an adult and why the job interests you.

54

How to Play:

- Divide the class into two teams, and decide which team will go first.
- Have a student from team A choose a number from 1 to 20.
- Say the word that matches that number from the team's word list.
- Have the student write the word on the board.
- If correct, have each member of team A write the given letter in the matching space on his/her game page.
- Alternate between teams A and B having the students choose a number of a blank space.
- The team to complete the secret phrase first is the winner.

2 Game

Reinforce spelling skills and provide motivation and interest.

Materials

- game page (from student text)
- pencils (1 per child)
- game word list

Game Word List

Team A	Team B
1. **idea (R)**	1. **wield (R)**
2. **piece (U)**	2. **Puerto Rico (U)**
3. **skiing (S)**	3. **creep (S)**
4. **brief (T)**	4. **Hawaii (T)**
5. **relief (I)**	5. **Tennessee (I)**
6. **eager (M)**	6. **deceit (M)**
7. **shriek (A)**	7. **liter (A)**
8. **appeal (L)**	8. **meter (L)**
9. **reveal (L)**	9. **vetoes (L)**
10. **shield (T)**	10. **Louisiana (T)**
11. **wield (H)**	11. **idea (H)**
12. **Puerto Rico (E)**	12. **piece (E)**
13. **creep (T)**	13. **skiing (T)**
14. **Hawaii (I)**	14. **brief (I)**
15. **Tennessee (M)**	15. **relief (M)**
16. **deceit (E)**	16. **eager (E)**
17. **liter (E)**	17. **shriek (E)**
18. **meter (E)**	18. **appeal (E)**
19. **vetoes (L)**	19. **reveal (L)**
20. **Louisiana (P)**	20. **shield (P)**

3 Journaling

Provide a meaningful reason for correct spelling through personal writing.

Review the story using discussion leads provided on the following page. Encourage students to apply the Scriptural value in their journaling.

Journaling (continued)

- What kind of work do your parents do? (Allow time to share information.)
- Why was Sarah embarrassed to have her mother come tell the class about her job? (Her mother cleaned bathrooms. Sarah felt that it wasn't an interesting or important job and she was afraid her mother would be drunk when she came to the school.)
- Is cleaning bathrooms a less important job than others? Explain. (No. Any job is important and should be done to the best of our abilities.)
- What caused Mrs. Johansen to have a wreck? (She had been drinking.)
- What other bad things happened because of her drinking? (She lost her job and had to go to court for driving under the influence of alcohol. She didn't act the same towards her children and didn't provide them with enough food or clothes.)
- Could God make Mrs. Johansen quit drinking? (He could but He doesn't make anyone do right.)
- Why did Sarah decide to keep trusting God even though things just kept getting worse? (She knew that when we tell God about our troubles He promises to help us through them.)

Beijing has three dotted letters in a row (in lower case), as do Fiji, and hijinks. Four dotted letters in a row occur in Ujiji where Stanley found Livingstone in 1871.

Topic: Shoplifting
Theme Text: Psalm 89:14

A High Price to Pay

Katelynn discovers some unwanted justice that comes with God's unconditional forgiveness.

"Katelynn, you wore that shirt yesterday!" Jennifer ran a brush through her long hair. "Why are you wearing it again?"

"I like it—everybody does."

"That's disgusting! It can't be clean after you wore it all day long. Mom just did the laundry, so wear something else—everything's clean."

"Including this," Katelynn muttered, looking down at her favorite shirt. "Remember we have chapel this morning, and I want to look good." Katelynn examined her reflection in the bathroom mirror.

"Your hair is really getting long. I like it." Katelynn's older sister reached in front of her to get the toothpaste. "I like your shirt too—just not every day. I hope Grandma sends me one for my birthday."

"So you don't think I should wear it today?" Katelynn sought the reflection of her sister's dark eyes in the mirror.

"I guess if it's clean...." Jennifer sighed.

"Let's go, girls or you'll be late for school." Mr. Hatasaki called from the living room.

"Coming," the girls chorused.

Later that afternoon Mrs. Hatasaki trudged up the apartment stairs. She stopped in front of the red door marked 308-B and unlocked it. The big gold chain kept her from completely opening the door. "Katie, I'm home."

Katelynn ran to let her mother in.

Mrs. Hatasaki gave her daughter a hug. "Let's hurry and get supper ready so we can eat as soon as your dad and Jennifer get home. I need to go to the mall and look for some new shoes. These black ones are really worn, and there are some good sales at several of the department stores this week. You want to come?"

Katelynn nodded.

On their way through the mall, Jennifer saw a classmate from school trying on jackets in one of the more exclusive stores.

"Hi, Jen!" Sandra SaintClair gushed, "Look at these jackets. They're just what I've been looking for. Everyone has them. Which do you like better?" The girl held up two she liked.

Jennifer shrugged. "I don't know—they're both nice." She picked up the nearest jacket and gasped when she saw the price. Their family never spent that much money on clothes—ever!

"You don't like them?"

"Sure. I just think...."

"I can't make up my mind," Sandra interrupted as she turned back and forth in front of the three-way mirror.

Mrs. Hatasaki and Sandra's mother were soon engaged in a serious discussion about the pros and cons of the new school dress code.

Katelynn and Jennifer watched silently as Sandra admired her reflection. After a while, they tired of waiting for her to try on all the different styles and colors. They began to examine the other beautifully displayed clothes. "Here's a shirt just like Grandma got you." Jennifer held it up for her sister to see.

"Did you girls find something?" Mom and Mrs. SaintClair walked up behind the girls.

"Sandra can't decide what jacket she likes, but we like these shirts. They're like the one Grandma sent Katelynn. Look! They're on sale." Jennifer held up the shirt.

Mom raised her eyebrows when she checked the price tag. Mrs. SaintClair excused herself and went over to look at jackets with Sandra.

"Do you girls have enough money for these? They are quite pricey even when they're on sale," Mrs. Hatasaki whispered. "We'll go to the outlet mall later this week."

"I have baby-sitting money." Jennifer picked a shirt to try on and headed to the dressing room. Mrs. SaintClair chose some more clothes for Sandra to try and followed Jennifer.

Sandra paused and looked over the pile of clothes in her arms. "Wait just a minute. I want you to tell me which one of these looks best with my blond hair."

Katelynn glanced up at her mom, who nodded and smiled. Sandra and Jennifer finally came out. "That's my favorite." Katelynn smiled and looked at Jennifer. "I think you should definitely get that one."

"Why don't you get one?" Sandra pulled a shirt off the rack for Katelynn to try on.

"Oh. I like this one," Katelynn said as she held up a different color.

"Try it on, Katelynn," Mrs. SaintClair suggested as she walked up beside the trio with more clothes on her arm. "It's the perfect color for your dark hair and eyes."

Katelynn shook her head. "I don't think so."

Sandra eventually chose a jacket, as well as several other new outfits. Katelynn leaned against the counter, waiting for Jennifer to pay for her shirt. Sandra stood beside her—arms loaded with clothes "Aren't you going to get that shirt you tried on? It looks so great on you."

"I didn't try it on—and no." Katelynn stood on the side of her feet. "I don't have enough money."

"There are other ways to get what you want," whispered Sandra. "My friend Elizabeth and I do this all the time. Watch."

Katelynn wrinkled her forehead.

Story (continued)

Sandra glanced at the clerk, who was now busy ringing up all the SaintClairs' purchases. The blond girl casually took the shirt Katelynn liked off the rack and walked back into the dressing room. She returned minutes later—patting a bag from J C Penney®.

As the three girls walked down the mall behind their mothers (who were still discussing Knowlton Elementary), Sandra pulled out "Katelynn's" shirt from the Penney's bag. When Jennifer stopped to examine some purses, Sandra quietly stuffed it into one of Katelynn's bags.

"Consider it a gift," Sandra said, smiling sweetly.

Katelynn jumped when Jennifer turned around to show her a purse. Her stomach didn't feel so good.

Mom was already at work the next morning when Katelynn cut the tags off the stolen shirt. When she put it on and looked in the mirror, there was an unexpected pit in the bottom of her stomach. "Jennifer will know it's the shirt from the mall and Mom will wonder where it came from when she sees it in the wash. What am I going to do? If I take it back Sandra will get in trouble. If I don't tell on Sandra, how will I explain to the store why I didn't steal it but want to bring it back?" Katelynn slowly took off the shirt and tucked the tags in her notebook.

When Dad dropped the girls off in front of Knowlton Elementary, Katelynn lingered in the car until Jennifer was out of earshot. Big tears slipped down her cheeks. "My stomach really hurts. I have to tell you something really bad. Will you help me make it right?"

After school Katelynn and her dad returned to the mall for a much-less-fun excursion than the one the previous evening. An hour later they left the mall security office—minus one shirt. Katelynn took a deep breath of the fresh fall air. She slowly exhaled as she leaned up against a big cement pillar at the arched entrance to the mall. She fumbled with the zipper of her jacket. Dad looked solemn. Neither spoke for a while.

Katelynn finally broke the silence. "I can't believe they put my name in their computer when I brought the shirt back. I didn't steal it."

Mr. Hatasaki wiped his hand across his upper lip. "You carried it out of the mall without paying for it, Katie. God's government has two important principles that hold it up—kind of like the pillar you're leaning against helps hold up this archway." Dad patted the huge cement column. "One of God's principles is righteousness, and the other is justice."

When Katelynn look puzzled, her father explained, "God's righteousness will cover your sins—He forgives you no matter what. But don't forget that the other pillar is justice. He will forgive you, but He doesn't erase the pain your mistakes cause. If mall security ever catches you shoplifting, you'll be in serious trouble because your name is already in the computer system."

Katelynn smiled weakly. "I think I like the righteousness part of God's government better than the justice. And I wouldn't even dream of shoplifting. This experience was bad enough," she shuddered.

Her dad agreed. "I'm sorry they entered your name into their database today, but I can see why they want it. Stores lose millions of dollars a year from shoplifting. It's honest people who pay for the stolen items, because the stores raise their prices to cover their losses and insure a profit. Every time a shoplifter is caught, it helps keep prices down."

Dad squeezed Katelynn's shoulder as they headed toward the parking lot. "Just remember, 'Character is made by what you stand for; reputation, by what you fall for.' I'm proud of the stand you took today."

"Thanks," Katelynn said as she climbed into the car.

2 Discussion Time

Check understanding of the story and development of personal values.

- Who is the nicest person you know in school?
- What made you think of that person?
- Who is someone you know that always dresses well?
- Why did you choose that particular person?
- Which is more important—character or appearance?
- How did Katelynn get her priorities out of balance?
- Who can help you keep things in the proper perspective?

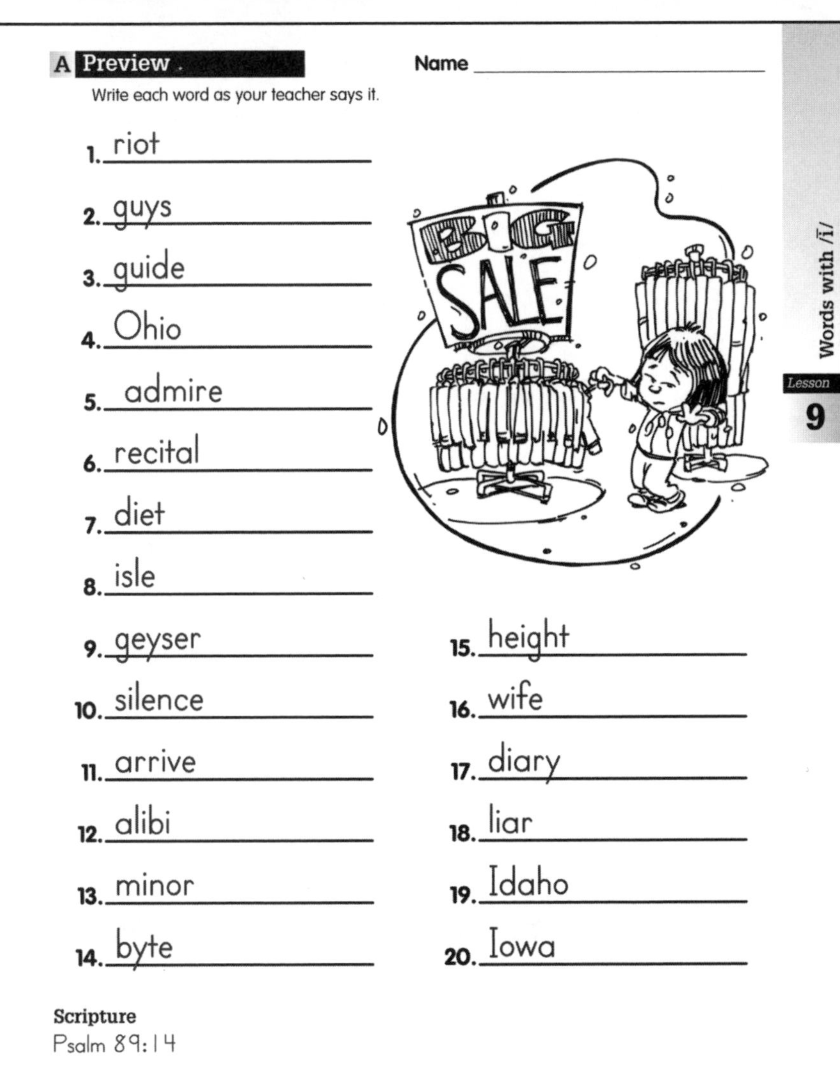

A Preview

Name ______________________

Write each word as your teacher says it.

1. riot
2. guys
3. guide
4. Ohio
5. admire
6. recital
7. diet
8. isle
9. geyser
10. silence
11. arrive
12. alibi
13. minor
14. byte
15. height
16. wife
17. diary
18. liar
19. Idaho
20. Iowa

Words with /ī/

Lesson 9

Scripture
Psalm 89:14

55

3 Preview

Test for knowledge of the correct spellings of these words.

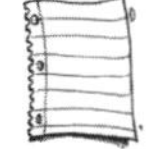

Customize Your List

On a separate sheet of paper, additional words of your choice may be tested.

I will say each word once, use the word in a sentence, then say the word again. Write the words on the lines in your Worktext.

Correct Immediately!

Let's correct our Preview. I will spell each word out loud. If you spelled a word incorrectly, rewrite it correctly.

Progress Chart

Students may record scores. (Reproducible master provided in Appendix B.)

1. riot	There was a small **riot** outside in the mall parking lot.
2. guys	Several **guys** were protesting the sale of certain products in the mall.
3. guide	"I can be your personal fashion **guide**," Sandra teased Katelynn.
4. Ohio	"Our mall in **Ohio** was three times the size of this one," she bragged.
5. admire	Katelynn watched Sandra **admire** herself in the dressing-room mirror.
6. recital	"I think I'll wear this at my piano **recital**," she told Katelynn.
7. diet	Sarah already talks about going on a **diet** to stay thin.
8. isle	The Saint Clairs spent the summer vacationing on an **isle** in the Mediterranean.
9. geyser	Sandra hoped to see a huge **geyser** on the island.
10. silence	There was a long **silence** after Katelynn confessed to her dad.
11. arrive	She was dreading the moment they would **arrive** at the mall office.
12. alibi	Katelynn did not have an **alibi**.
13. minor	Since Katelynn is a **minor** and returned the shirt, the mall did not press charges.
14. byte	She felt like every **byte** of memory in the mall computer had stored her name!
15. height	She was sure that this was the **height** of embarrassment and shame!
16. wife	Mr. Hatasaki called his **wife** at work to tell her about Katelynn.
17. diary	Katelynn recorded the awful event in her **diary**.
18. liar	She realized that she did not want to be a thief and a **liar**.
19. Idaho	The state of **Idaho** is famous for its hardy crops of delicious potatoes.
20. Iowa	Many of us associate the growing of corn with the state of **Iowa**.

Lesson 9 | Day 1

4 Word Shapes

Help students form a correct image of whole words.

Look at each word and think about its shape. Now, write the word in the correct word Shape Boxes. You may check off each word as you use it.

(In many words, the sound of /ī/ is spelled with **i** at the end of a syllable, or with **ie**, or **i-consonant-e**. It is sometimes spelled with **y**.)

In the word shape boxes, fill in the boxes containing the letter or letters that spell the sound of /ī/ in each word.

Take a minute to memorize...

Psalm 89:14

Words with /ī/ — Lesson 9

B Word Shapes Name ____________________

Using the word bank below, write each word in the correct word shape boxes. Next, in the word shape boxes, fill in the boxes containing the letter or letters that spell the sound of /ī/ in each word.

1.	recital	11.	Iowa
2.	diet	12.	silence
3.	geyser	13.	minor
4.	alibi	14.	isle
5.	diary	15.	admire
6.	guys	16.	byte
7.	wife	17.	riot
8.	guide	18.	Ohio
9.	arrive	19.	Idaho
10.	height	20.	liar

Word Bank

admire	diary	guys	isle	recital
alibi	diet	height	liar	riot
arrive	geyser	Idaho	minor	silence
byte	guide	Iowa	Ohio	wife

56

Answers may vary for duplicate word shapes.

Be Prepared For Fun

Check these supply lists for **Fun Ways to Spell** - presented **Day 2**.
Purchase and/or gather these items ahead of time!

General
- Pencil
- 3 X 5 Cards cut in half (20 per child)
- Spelling List

Auditory
- Spelling List

Visual
- Pencil
- Notebook Paper
- Spelling List

Tactile
- Blackboard and Chalk
  -OR-
- White Board and Marker
- Spelling List

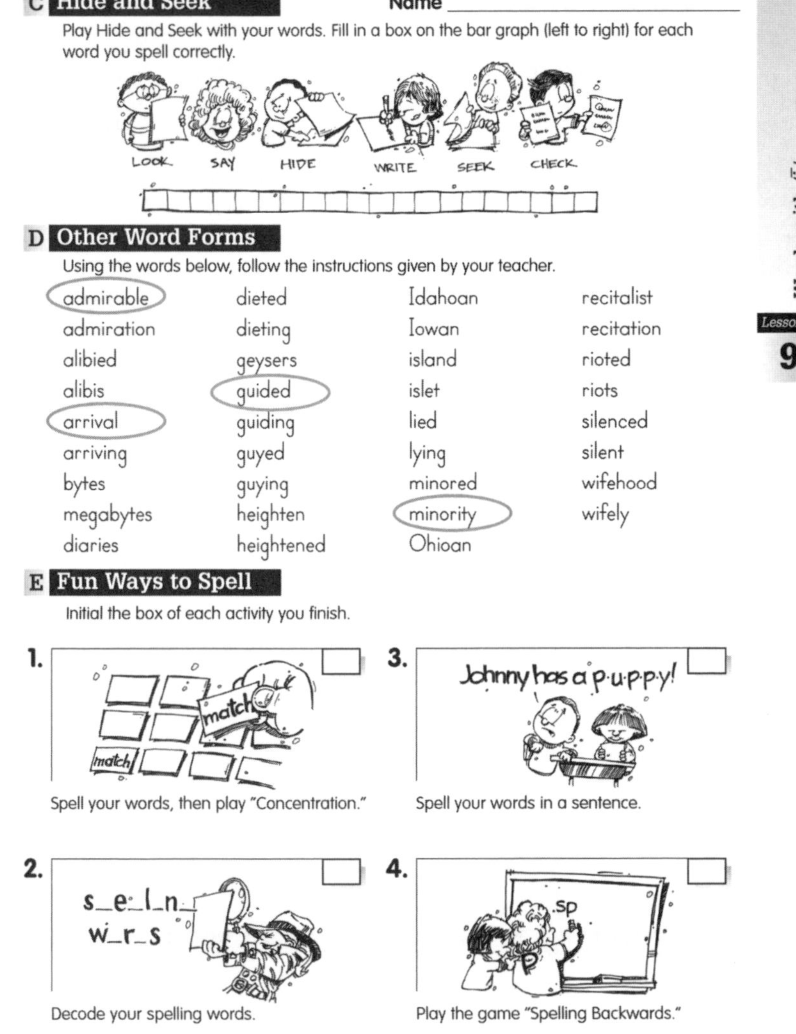

C Hide and Seek Name ______________________

Play Hide and Seek with your words. Fill in a box on the bar graph (left to right) for each word you spell correctly.

D Other Word Forms

Using the words below, follow the instructions given by your teacher.

admirable, admiration, alibied, alibis, arrival, arriving, bytes, megabytes, diaries, dieted, dieting, geysers, guided, guiding, guyed, guying, heighten, heightened, Idahoan, Iowan, island, islet, lied, lying, minored, minority, Ohioan, recitalist, recitation, rioted, riots, silenced, silent, wifehood, wifely

E Fun Ways to Spell

Initial the box of each activity you finish.

1. Spell your words, then play "Concentration."
2. Decode your spelling words.
3. Spell your words in a sentence.
4. Play the game "Spelling Backwards."

Words with /ī/

Lesson 9

57

1 Hide and Seek

Reinforce spelling by using multiple styles of learning.

On a white board, Teacher writes each word — one at a time. **Have students:**

- **Look** at the word.
- **Say** the word out loud.
- **Spell** the word out loud.
- **Hide** (teacher erases word.)
- **Write** the word on paper.
- **Seek** (teacher rewrites word.)
- **Check** spelling. If incorrect, rewrite word correctly.

Day 2

Lesson 9

2 Other Word Forms

This activity is optional. Have students find and circle the Other Word Forms that are most nearly antonyms of the following:

despicable
unassisted
departure
bulk

3 Fun Ways to Spell

Four activities are provided. Use one, two, three, or all of the activities. Have students initial the box for each activity they complete.

Options:

- assign activities to students according to their learning styles
- set up the activities in learning centers for the students to do throughout the day
- divide students into four groups and assign one activity per group
- do one activity per day

General

Spell your words; then play "Concentration"...
- Write each spelling word on a card. Mix your cards and a classmate's cards together. Arrange them face down in five rows of eight. Pick up two cards. If the cards match, play again. If the cards do not match, turn them back over. It is your classmate's turn. Continue taking turns until all the cards are matched. The player with the most cards wins!

Auditory

To spell your words in a sentence...
- Ask a classmate read a spelling word to you from the list.
- Spell the word aloud and use it in a sentence.
- Ask your classmate to check your spelling.
- Each correctly spelled word that is used properly in a sentence counts as one point.
- Switch and continue taking turns.

Visual

To decode your spelling words...
- Look at the first word on your list.
- Write every other letter of the word on your paper, putting a blank where each missing letter belongs.
- Trade papers with a classmate and fill in the missing letters.
- Check your spelling.

Tactile

To play the game "Spelling Backwards"...
- Ask a classmate to stand behind you and draw the letters to spell a word from the list on your back.
- Write the spelling word on the board as your classmate traces the letters on your back.
- Ask your classmate to check your spelling.
- Trade places and take turns until you have each spelled all the words.

Working with Words

Familiarize students with word meaning and usage.

Hidden Words

Explain that the spelling words for this week are hidden in the puzzle. After finding each word, the student should write the word under the correct heading.

Use the word bank to help you find each of the words in the puzzle. Words may go across, down, or diagonally. Circle, then write the words.

Take a minute to memorize...

Psalm 89:14

Lesson 9 | Day 3

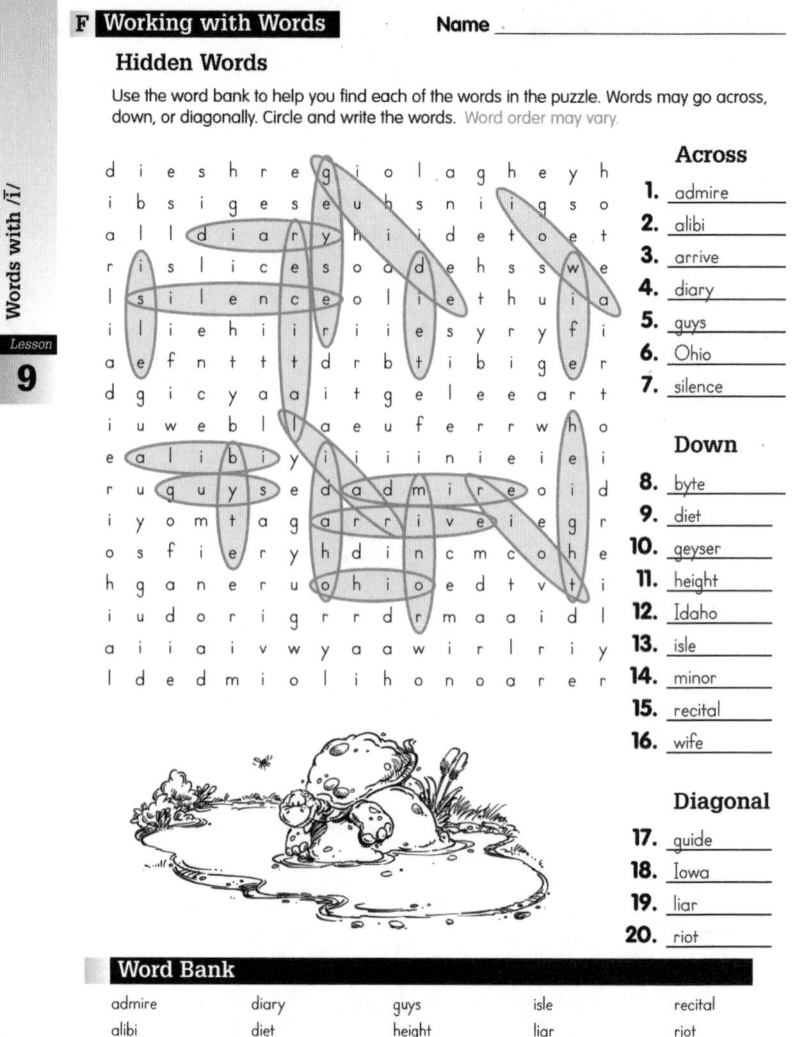

F **Working with Words** Name ____________

Words with /ī/ — Lesson 9

Hidden Words

Use the word bank to help you find each of the words in the puzzle. Words may go across, down, or diagonally. Circle and write the words. Word order may vary.

```
d i e s h r e g i o l a g h e y h
i b s i g e s e u h s n i i g s o
a l l d i a r y h i i d e t o e t
r i s l i c e s o a d e h s s w e
l s i l e n c e o l i e t h u i a
i l i e h i i r i i e s y r y f i
a e f n t t t d r b t i b i g e r
d g i c y a a i t g e l e e a r t
i u w e b l l a e u f e r r w h o
e a l i b i y i i i i n i e i e i
r u g u y s e d a d m i r e o i d
i y o m t a g a r r i v e i e g r
o s f i e r y h d i n c m c o h e
h g a n e r u o h i o e d t v t i
i u d o r i g r r d r m a a i d l
a i i a i v w y a a w i r l r i y
l d e d m i o l i h o n o a r e r
```

Across

1. admire
2. alibi
3. arrive
4. diary
5. guys
6. Ohio
7. silence

Down

8. byte
9. diet
10. geyser
11. height
12. Idaho
13. isle
14. minor
15. recital
16. wife

Diagonal

17. guide
18. Iowa
19. liar
20. riot

Word Bank

admire	diary	guys	isle	recital
alibi	diet	height	liar	riot
arrive	geyser	Idaho	minor	silence
byte	guide	Iowa	Ohio	wife

58

G Dictation

Name ______________________

Write each sentence as your teacher dictates. Use correct punctuation.

1. Sandra looked in the mirror to admire the clothes.
2. Katelynn did not want to take clothes from the shop, but she looked on in silence.
3. Dad guided her back to the car, and they soon arrived at school.

Words with /ī/ Lesson 9

H Proofreading

If a word is misspelled, fill in the oval by that word. If all the words are spelled correctly, fill in the oval by **no mistake**.

1. ○ diary ○ Tennessee ○ deceit ● no mistake
2. ○ liar ○ diet ○ Louisiana ● no mistake
3. ○ creep ○ Hawaii ● riut ○ no mistake
4. ● ohio ○ alibi ○ shield ○ no mistake
5. ○ guide ● Idahoe ○ vetoes ○ no mistake
6. ○ wife ○ isle ○ liter ● no mistake
7. ● silense ○ Puerto Rico ○ eager ○ no mistake
8. ○ admire ○ idea ● minnor ○ no mistake
9. ○ byte ● heit ○ piece ○ no mistake
10. ○ recital ● arive ○ skiing ○ no mistake
11. ● iowa ○ guys ○ reveal ○ no mistake
12. ○ brief ○ relief ● gyser ○ no mistake

59

1 Dictation

Reinforce correct spelling by using current and previous words in context.

Listen as I read each sentence and then write it in your Worktext. Remember to use correct capitalization and punctuation. (Slowly read each sentence twice. Sentences are found in the Student Worktext to the left.)

2 Proofreading

Familiarize students with standardized test format and reinforce recognition of misspelled words.

Look at each set of words. If a word is misspelled, fill in the oval by that word. If all the words are spelled correctly, fill in the oval by **no mistake**.

3 Hide and Seek

Reinforce correct spelling of current spelling words. Repeat this activity from Day 2.

4 Vocabulary Extension

Have your students complete this activity to strengthen spelling ability and expand vocabulary. The reproducible master is provided in Appendix A as shown on the inset page to the right.

Hide and Seek

Play Hide and Seek with your words. Fill in a bar graph (left to right) for each word you spell correctly.

Vocabulary Extension

Multiple Choice

Fill in the oval by the word(s) with the same or nearly the same meaning as the word in bold type.

1. Obadiah
- ○ New Testament prophet
- ○ son of Ruth and Boaz
- ● the shortest book in the Old Testament
- ○ the longest book in the Old Testament

2. sacrifice
- ○ to commandeer an airplane
- ● an offering
- ○ to communicate
- ○ resemblance

3. satellite
- ○ to soak thoroughly
- ○ uncivilized
- ● an object that orbits a heavenly body
- ○ sixth planet from the sun

4. Nehemiah
- ● Old Testament book before Esther
- ○ Old Testament book after Esther
- ○ New Testament book after Ezra
- ○ follower of Jesus who called Peter

5. Jeremiah
- ○ important city in the Jordan Valley
- ○ city where the temple stood
- ○ first king of Israel
- ● the "weeping prophet"

6. Micah
- ○ an archangel
- ○ a town near Bethel
- ● book of the minor prophets
- ○ last Old Testament book

7. Zephaniah
- ○ prophet in the days of King Josiah
- ○ ninth book of the Bible
- ○ last book of the Old Testament
- ● son of Zilpah

8. Zechariah
- ○ next to the last book of the Bible
- ● Old Testament book following Haggai
- ○ a man who climbed a tree to see Jesus
- ○ a town in Shephelah in Judah

9. variety
- ○ undue pride in oneself
- ○ an animal considered a pest
- ● assortment of different things
- ○ fine particles floating in the air

10. Titus
- ○ the 10th part of one's increase
- ○ letter written by Peter
- ○ a covenant
- ● New Testament book before Philemon

1 Posttest

Test mastery of the spelling words.

I will say the word once, use it in a sentence, then say it again. Write your words on a separate sheet of paper.

Progress Chart

Students may record scores. (Reproducible master in Appendix B.)

Personal Dictionary

Students may add any words they have misspelled to their personal dictionaries for reference when writing. (Cover in Appendix B.)

1. guys — Some rough-looking **guys** were hanging around the mall entrance.
2. diet — Even though Sandra does not need to **diet**, she talks about it a lot.
3. riot — Katelynn hoped they would not start a **riot**.
4. Ohio — "This mall is tiny compared to the one we shopped at in **Ohio**," Sandra said.
5. guide — "I read the fashion **guide** in each of the magazines my mom gets."
6. admire — Sandra likes people to **admire** her hair and clothes.
7. recital — "This would look terrific for my piano **recital**," Sandra bragged.
8. isle — "We spent the summer on an **isle** in the Mediterranean," said Sandra's mom.
9. geyser — "We all hoped to see a **geyser**," said Mrs. Saint Clair.
10. silence — There was a long, awkward **silence** after she told her dad what she had done.
11. alibi — She had no **alibi**.
12. minor — Katelynn is a **minor** and, so, was not charged with shoplifting.
13. byte — "My name is in every **byte** of their computer's memory," groaned Katelynn.
14. height — "This has to be the **height** of embarrassment," she told her dad.
15. arrive — She dreaded the moment they would **arrive** at the mall office.
16. wife — Mr. Hatasaki sadly told his **wife** about Katelynn's bad choice.
17. diary — Katelynn cried as she recorded the terrible events of the day in her **diary**.
18. liar — She had no desire to be a thief or a **liar**.
19. Idaho — Katelynn loves baked **Idaho** potatoes with butter and sour cream.
20. Iowa — Some of the corn grown in **Iowa** is used for animal feed.

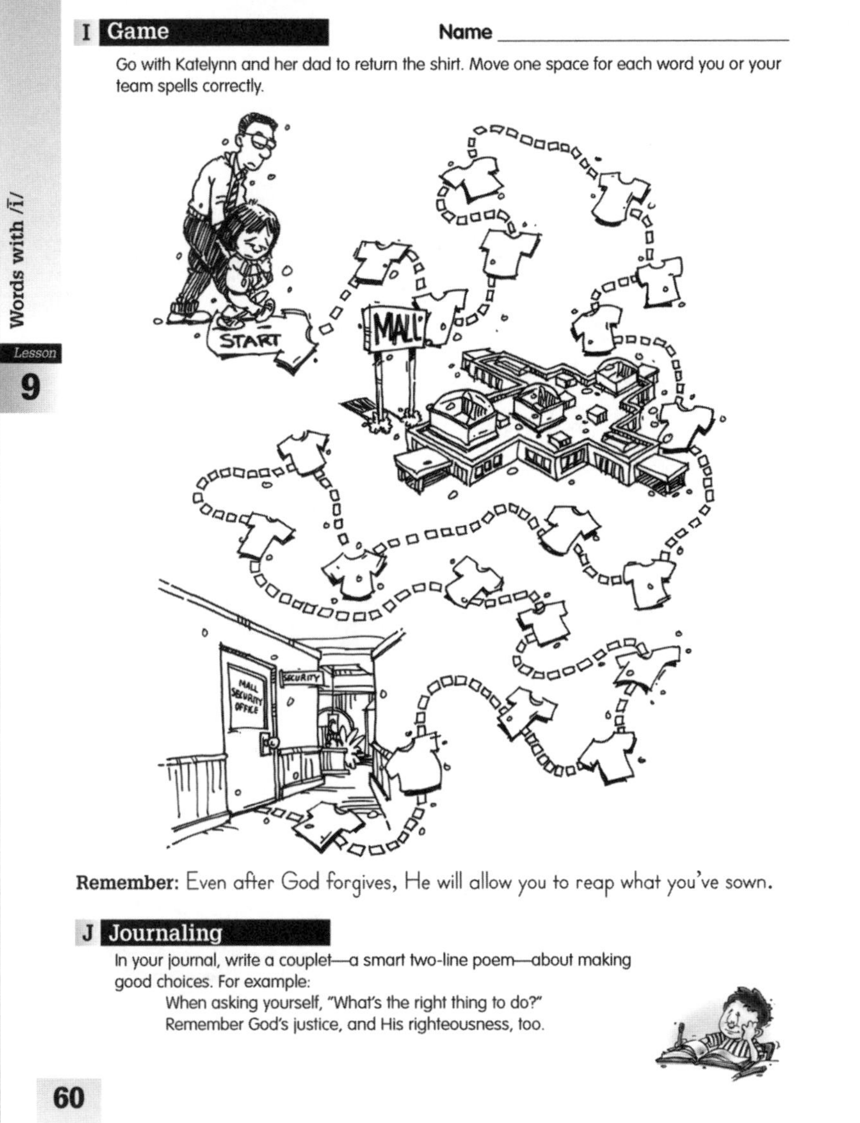

I Game Name ______________________

Go with Katelynn and her dad to return the shirt. Move one space for each word you or your team spells correctly.

Remember: Even after God forgives, He will allow you to reap what you've sown.

J Journaling

In your journal, write a couplet—a smart two-line poem—about making good choices. For example:

When asking yourself, "What's the right thing to do?"
Remember God's justice, and His righteousness, too.

Words with /ī/ Lesson 9

60

2 Game

Reinforce spelling skills and provide motivation and interest.

Materials

- game page (from student text)
- game pieces (1 per child)
- game word list

Game Word List

1. **diary**
2. **liar**
3. **diet**
4. **riot**
5. **Ohio**
6. **alibi**
7. **guide**
8. **Idaho**
9. **wife**
10. **isle**
11. **silence**
12. **minor**
13. **admire**
14. **byte**
15. **height**
16. **recital**
17. **arrive**
18. **Iowa**
19. **guys**
20. **geyser**

How to Play:

- Divide the class into two teams.
- Have each student place his/her game piece on Start.
- Have a student from team A go to the board.
- Say the spelling word.
- Have the student write the word on the board.
- If correct, instruct each member of team A to move his/her game piece forward one space.
- Alternate between teams A and B.
- The team to reach the mall security office first is the winner.
- **Small Group Option**: Students may play this game without teacher direction in small groups of two or more.

3 Journaling

Provide a meaningful reason for correct spelling through personal writing.

Review the story using discussion leads provided on the following page. Encourage students to apply the Scriptural value in their journaling.

Journaling (continued)

- What do you think Mr. Hatasaki meant when he said, "Character is made by what you stand for; reputation, by what you fall for?" (When you make wise choices you are strengthening a good character. When you make a mistake people often hear about it and your reputation can be damaged.)
- How did Katelynn damage her reputation? (She took the shirt Sandra handed her even though she knew it hadn't been paid for.)
- What did Katelynn do that showed her strength of character? (She went to the mall and returned the shirt.)
- Why was Katelynn's dad proud of her? (Katelynn had recognized her mistake, asked forgiveness, and made it right.)
- In poetry a couplet is a two-line verse. Usually the last words of each line rhyme. Couplets can be sophisticated, simple, silly, or fun. Some examples are:

  There are times when two together,
  Add up to one—one thing that's better!
  —Leah Knowlton

  But if the while I think on thee, dear friend,
  All losses are restored and sorrows end.
  —Shakespeare

- Write the first line of a possible couplet on the board: **When asking yourself, "What's the right thing to do?"** Help students think of words that rhyme with do. Together, compile a list of possible rhyming words.

CATERCORNER has eight spellings in the third edition of Websters Dictionary: catercorner, cater-cornered, cata-corner, cata-cornered, catty-corner, catty-cornered, kitty-corner, and kitty-cornered.

1 **Literature Connection**
Topic: Saying no to drug abuse
Theme Text: Psalm 62:7

The Suspect

Stephen learns about drug abuse and whom he can always depend on for help.

"Beth!" Tony skidded to a stop beside his friend. "Have you noticed all the awesome clothes Brutus has been wearing?"

Beth looked across the playground at the big eighth grader talking to a younger child. "Yeah. He's changed since he flunked eighth grade last year."

"Who're you talkin' about? Rudest Brutus?" Stephen said as he joined his friends.

Beth nodded. "Who else?"

"I'm just thankful he's been leaving us alone; and I, for one, am going to keep out of his way," Stephen said.

"I still wonder where he gets such expensive clothes. He used to wear old hand-me-downs." Tony took the comb out of his back pocket and ran it through his hair.

"No one's big enough to give him hand-me-downs anymore," Beth observed.

"No, that's just it. The clothes he wore last year didn't look like kid-clothes. They looked like stuff even grown-ups didn't want to wear any more. And I'd wear what he has on today—if it were a little smaller," Tony grinned. "It just doesn't make sense."

"Maybe his dad got a new job or something?" Beth suggested.

"No," Tony bent down to tie his shoe. "He lives with his mom. I think his dad's in jail or something."

"I'm not getting close enough to ask him." Stephen watched the big boy as he put his hand on the shoulder of a seventh-grade girl and bent over to say something into her ear.

"We could be detectives!" suggested Beth.

"Later!" Tony said. "Looks like Mr. Canfield is ready to play soccer. Race you to the goal!"

After recess Mr. Canfield walked to the front of the class and waited for them to settle down before he spoke. "We're going to have a guest every Monday afternoon for a while. He'll be here for about an hour. His name is Officer Klein and he's going to dare you to do something."

A brisk knock sounded at the door, and Mr. Canfield went to answer it. A blue-clad police officer entered, followed by a very big German shepherd. "Kelly, sit," the officer commanded. The dog obeyed instantly. "Kelly, stay," Officer Klein made eye contact with his dog, then turned his attention to the class.

"How many of you have ever been told no?" Every hand in the class shot up in the air. "Is it hard for you to tell a friend no?" Heads nodded around the room. "Your school has invited me to come to your classroom to teach you how to say no! Raise your hand if you believe me." Everyone looked around to see how everyone else was voting. Thorny raised his hand first. Matthew followed. Everyone else wasn't sure. The officer continued. "I want to teach you about a program called D.A.R.E. D.A.R.E. is an acronym. Does anyone know what an acronym is?" Thorny and Matthew raised their hands. Mr. Klein pointed to Thorny.

"An acronym is a word formed from the initial letter or letters of a series of words."

"I think what Thorny's trying to say is an acronym comes from the beginning letters of words to make a new word. You know, like SWAK for Sealed With A Kiss," Matthew interpreted. The class burst out laughing. Matthew's face turned red. "That's what my grandma always writes on the back of the envelope when she sends me a letter," he explained.

"Good job, boys! Have any of you heard of the acronym D.A.R.E.?" Officer Klein reached down and patted his dog on the head.

No one raised a hand.

He wrote on the board while he spoke, "D.A.R.E. stands for Drug Abuse Resistance Education." When he was finished he underlined the first letter of each word he had written. "So what's the acronym for drug abuse resistance education?"

"D.A.R.E.!" Kristin blurted.

"Great," Officer Klein nodded. "I'm here today because I don't want drugs to be the *last* thing you do! I dare you to say no to drug abuse!"

"My dog Kelly is trained to smell illegal drugs. If I were to give her the command, she would use her sensitive nose to detect if there were any drugs in a car, a locker, or even on a person. She's rarely wrong!" The big dog wopped her tail on the carpet as if she understood what her master was saying about her.

"Over the next few weeks we're going to be role-playing eight different ways to say no to drugs. I would hate for Kelly to find drugs on you—ever!"

"I need a volunteer." Laney waved her hand in the air and Officer Klein motioned her to the front of the room. "What would you say if one of your friends came up to you and said, 'Wanna try some marijuana? It isn't as strong as it used to be. It stays in your body less than 24 hours. Come on—it's harmless. It's not addictive and everyone's doing it!'"

Laney looked over at the dog. "No?"

"Great job," Officer Klein shook Laney's hand. "Next time try to say it more forcefully—like you really mean it."

The class continued to role-play different situations. They divided into small groups and did some cooperative learning activities before Officer Klein and Kelly went on to the eighth-grade classroom.

Later that evening Tony and Stephen collapsed on the ground after their fifth run through a soccer drill they'd set up in Mason Springs Park. "I wonder if Kelly could smell drugs in someone's desk or locker after they took them out," Tony said thoughtfully.

"Worried?" Stephen teased.

"No. I was thinking about Brutus. On the way home from school today I saw him talking to some guys from the high school—older, like maybe juniors or seniors. They were in a new Corvette. It kinda looked like they handed him something. Maybe he's into drugs. That would explain all his new clothes."

"Just because we don't like Brutus doesn't mean he deals drugs," Stephen reasoned. "I know he's mean and everything, but I don't think he's dumb enough to do drugs."

"Maybe he just sells them—to get what he wants, ya know."

"We could watch him like Beth said today. If we don't catch him, I'm sure Kelly could." The two boys stood up.

During lunch break the next day, Beth, Tony, and Stephen halfheartedly kicked the soccer ball back and forth. They kept watching for the suspect, Brutus. "I think we should talk to that seventh-grade girl we saw him with yesterday. What's her name? Sandra?" Beth picked up the soccer ball.

"Well, that would be a start," Tony agreed. "He probably doesn't bring the drugs to school, especially now that Officer Klein and Kelly are here every day."

"Sandra's right over there. Maybe she'll know something about the suspect's new clothes." Beth headed off across the playground.

Tony and Stephen followed at a distance. Brutus almost ran them down as he rushed around the corner of the school. "Get out of my way, you little rug rats. Who gave you permission to live? I want you and your little friends to stay away from my girl—or I'll bounce you across that cement over there like I did your little cars last year! Any questions?" Both boys shook their heads and looked down submissively at the toes of Brutus' new shoes. "Here let me give you a sample of what I mean." Brutus grabbed each boy by the coat and lifted them a foot off the ground.

Stephen knew his head was going to be smashed against the brick wall beside them, and he shut his eyes. "Save us, God" he breathed.

"What'd you say?" Brutus glared at Stephen as he lifted the boys higher.

A booming voice answered, "I said put them down and come with me, Brutus!"

Brutus let go of their coats, and Stephen opened his eyes a crack as he crumpled to the ground.

He watched Mr. Canfield sling his big arm over Brutus' shoulder.

"'Your protection and success come from God alone. He is your refuge, a Rock where no enemy can reach you,'" the big black man recited a Scripture verse as he guided the eighth grader toward the front of the building.

"Was he talking to us or Brutus?" Tony asked.

"I don't know. I prayed for protection. I think Brutus may need it now though. He even looks small compared to Mr. Canfield." Stephen laughed. "And Mr. Canfield doesn't look too happy."

"Do you think he believes in God?" Tony dusted off his clothes and took the comb out of his pocket.

"Who—Brutus?" Stephen stood up slowly.

Tony nodded.

"He sure doesn't act like it." Stephen frowned. "And Mr. Canfield can't be everywhere...."

"But God can." Tony remembered what his Grandma had told him. "All we have to do is ask."

(To be continued...)

2 Discussion Time

Check understanding of the story and development of personal values.

- Tell about a time God protected you.
- How did you feel as you asked God for help?
- What is a refuge?
- Why do you think David compared God to a rock in Psalm 62:7?
- How did God answer Stephen's prayer for protection?
- Do you think Mr. Canfield can always successfully protect Stephen and Tony?
- How do you think God might continue to protect them?

A Preview

Name ______________________

Write each word as your teacher says it.

1. banjo
2. Wyoming
3. buffalo
4. soldier
5. cargo
6. stereo
7. boldly
8. studio
9. flamingo
10. enroll
11. patrol
12. sole
13. macro
14. control
15. portfolio
16. voltage
17. dome
18. Oklahoma
19. Minnesota
20. donate

Scripture
Psalm 62:7

Words with /ō/

Lesson 10

61

3 Preview

Test for knowledge of the correct spellings of these words.

Customize Your List

On a separate sheet of paper, additional words of your choice may be tested.

I will say each word once, use the word in a sentence, then say the word again. Write the words on the lines in your Worktext.

Correct Immediately!

Let's correct our Preview. I will spell each word out loud. If you spelled a word incorrectly, rewrite it correctly.

Progress Chart

Students may record scores. (Reproducible master provided in Appendix B.)

Day 1 | Lesson 10

1.	banjo	None of the students in Mr. Canfield's class plays the **banjo.**
2.	Wyoming	Mr. Canfield read a terrific story set in **Wyoming** in the early 1800's.
3.	buffalo	It described the huge herds of mighty **buffalo** that roamed the land.
4.	soldier	The story told about a **soldier** that settled his family there.
5.	cargo	Mr. Canfield read about enormous steam engines that hauled **cargo** to the west.
6.	stereo	After the story, he played music by a famous composer on the **stereo.**
7.	boldly	The music of the tuba **boldly** represented trains in the first piece.
8.	studio	Mr. Canfield has one corner of the room set up like an art **studio.**
9.	flamingo	Sarah's painting of a **flamingo** is hanging on the wall.
10.	enroll	Knowlton Elementary was eager to **enroll** its classes in Officer Klein's program.
11.	patrol	Officer Klein takes his dog Kelly on **patrol** with him every day.
12.	sole	He can tap a signal to Kelly with the **sole** of his shoe.
13.	macro	When Stephen said Kelly was a **macro** dog, Officer Klein laughed.
14.	control	His work is invaluable to the **control** of illegal drug distribution.
15.	portfolio	At his office he keeps a file or **portfolio** of cases he has solved.
16.	voltage	He carries a stun gun that shocks a fleeing criminal with low **voltage.**
17.	dome	The lights on top of a squad car are no longer **dome** shaped, but rectangular.
18.	Oklahoma	Officer Klein said he grew up in the state of **Oklahoma.**
19.	Minnesota	He has a good friend on the police force in **Minnesota.**
20.	donate	Some parents **donate** their time and money to promote the D.A.R.E. program.

Lesson 10 | Day 1

4 Word Shapes

Help students form a correct image of whole words.

Look at each word and think about its shape. Now, write the word in the correct word Shape Boxes. You may check off each word as you use it.

(In many words, the sound of **/ō/** is spelled with **o** or **o-consonant-e**.)

In the word shape boxes, fill in the boxes containing the letter or letters that spell the sound of **/ō/** in each word.

Take a minute to memorize...

Psalm 62:7

Lesson 10 — Words with /ō/

B Word Shapes Name ______________________

Using the word bank below, write each word in the correct word shape boxes. Next, in the word shape boxes, fill in the boxes containing the letter or letters that spell the sound of **/ō/** in each word.

1. patrol
2. studio
3. cargo
4. portfolio
5. boldly
6. dome
7. stereo
8. banjo
9. flamingo
10. control
11. soldier
12. enroll
13. Oklahoma
14. voltage
15. Wyoming
16. donate
17. sole
18. Minnesota
19. buffalo
20. macro

Word Bank

banjo	control	flamingo	patrol	stereo
boldly	dome	macro	portfolio	studio
buffalo	donate	Minnesota	soldier	voltage
cargo	enroll	Oklahoma	sole	Wyoming

62

Answers may vary for duplicate word shapes.

Be Prepared For Fun

Check these supply lists for **Fun Ways to Spell** - presented **Day 2**.
Purchase and/or gather these items ahead of time!

General
- Pencil
- Notebook Paper
- Spelling List

Auditory
- Pencil
- 3 X 5 Cards Cut in half lengthwise (20 per child)
- Spelling List

Visual
- Colored Pencils
- Graph Paper (2 sheets per child)
- Spelling List

Tactile
- Clay
- Spelling List

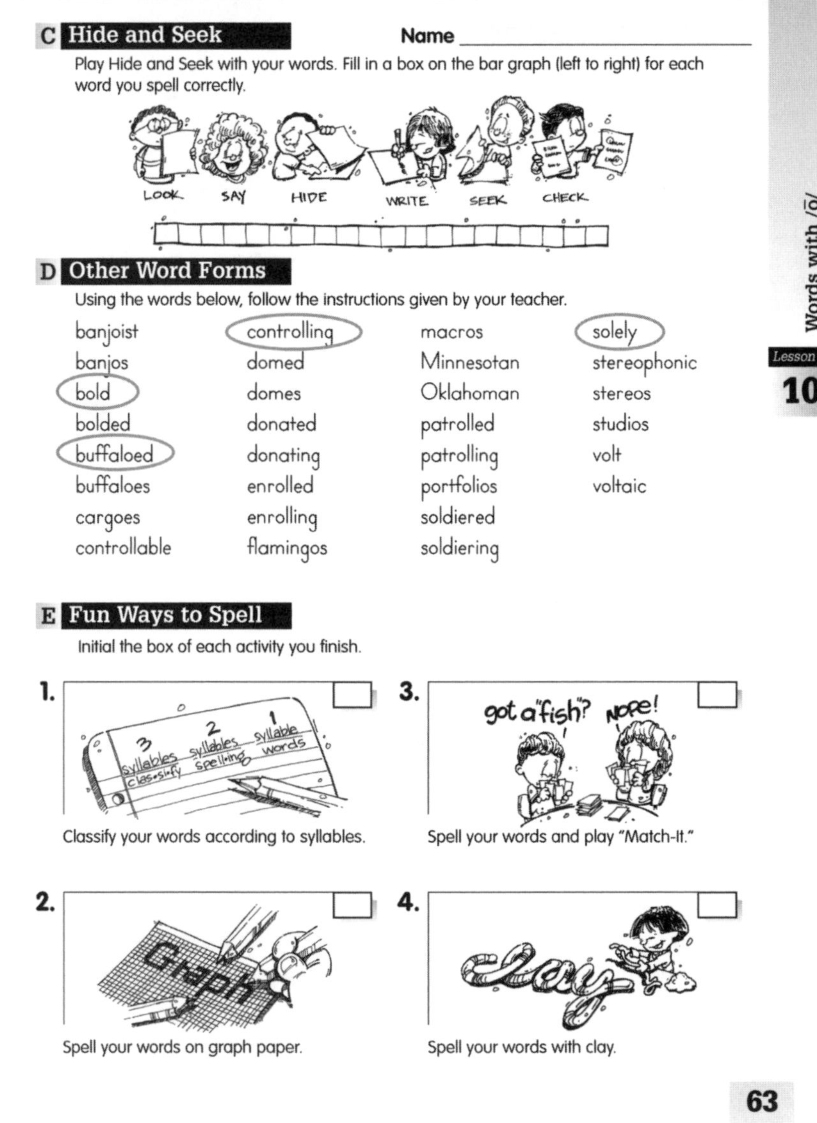

C Hide and Seek Name ______________________

Play Hide and Seek with your words. Fill in a box on the bar graph (left to right) for each word you spell correctly.

D Other Word Forms

Using the words below, follow the instructions given by your teacher.

banjoist	controlling	macros	solely
banjos	domed	Minnesotan	stereophonic
bold	domes	Oklahoman	stereos
bolded	donated	patrolled	studios
buffaloed	donating	patrolling	volt
buffaloes	enrolled	portfolios	voltaic
cargoes	enrolling	soldiered	
controllable	flamingos	soldiering	

E Fun Ways to Spell

Initial the box of each activity you finish.

1\.

Classify your words according to syllables.

2\.

Spell your words on graph paper.

3\.

Spell your words and play "Match-It."

4\.

Spell your words with clay.

Words with /ō/

Lesson 10

63

1 Hide and Seek

Reinforce spelling by using multiple styles of learning.

On a white board, Teacher writes each word — one at a time. **Have students:**

- **Look** at the word.
- **Say** the word out loud.
- **Spell** the word out loud.
- **Hide** (teacher erases word.)
- **Write** the word on paper.
- **Seek** (teacher rewrites word.)
- **Check** spelling. If incorrect, rewrite word correctly.

2 Other Word Forms

This activity is optional. Have students find and circle the Other Word Forms that are synonyms of the following:

brazen
bamboozled
singularly
manipulating

3 Fun Ways to Spell

Four activities are provided. Use one, two, three, or all of the activities. Have students initial the box for each activity they complete.

Day 2

Lesson 10

Options:

- assign activities to students according to their learning styles
- set up the activities in learning centers for the students to do throughout the day
- divide students into four groups and assign one activity per group
- do one activity per day

General

To classify your words according to syllables...
- Write three headings on your paper: One-syllable, Two-syllable, and Three-syllable.
- Write the first word on your list under the proper heading.
- Draw a line through the word to divide it into syllables.
- Do this with each word.

Auditory

To spell your words and play "Match-It"...
- Write each word on a card. Mix your word-cards and a classmate's together. Deal six cards to each player; the rest face down between you. Ask your classmate for a word-card. If the word-card matches, take it and play again. If not, draw from the stack, and it is your classmate's turn. Take turns until all cards are matched.

Visual

To spell your words on graph paper...
- Look at the first word on your list.
- Shade in squares to form the letters of each word.
- Check your spelling.
- Do this with each word.

Tactile

To spell your words with clay...
- Roll pieces of clay into ropes.
- Use the ropes to make the letters of each word.
- Put them in the right order to spell each word.
- Check your spelling.

Lesson 10 | Day 3

Working with Words

Familiarize students with word meaning and usage.

Clues

Write this incomplete sentence on the board:

An underground prison is called a ____________.

Guide the students in choosing the word **dungeon**.

Read each sentence and choose a spelling word for each definition. You may use a dictionary to help you. Write the word in the blank.

Take a minute to memorize...

Psalm 62:7

Lesson 10 | Words with /ō/

F Working with Words Name ____________________

Clues

Write a spelling word for each clue.

1. The force of electrical current is called voltage.
2. A large shaggy-maned mammal with a big muscular hump is a buffalo.
3. The bottom of your foot is called the sole.
4. A banjo is a musical instrument with a long neck and usually five strings.
5. A person who is in the army is called a soldier.
6. To donate is to make a contribution or gift.
7. Macro relates to something with very large quantities.
8. To have direct influence over something is to control it.
9. A patrol checks an area for maintenance or security.
10. The freight carried in a ship, airplane, or vehicle is called cargo.
11. A studio is the place where an artist works.
12. Saint Paul is the capitol of Minnesota.
13. A flamingo is a long-legged long-necked tropical water bird with scarlet wings.
14. A sports building with a roof is known as a dome.
15. One of the mountain states of the United States is Wyoming.
16. A portable case for papers and drawings is called a portfolio.
17. The state bordered by Colorado, Kansas, Missouri, and Arkansas is Oklahoma.
18. To do something courageously and valiantly is to do it boldly.
19. To put your name on a list to join a club or class is to enroll.
20. A stereo is a sound system that uses two or more channels of sound.

Word Bank

banjo	control	flamingo	patrol	stereo
boldly	dome	macro	portfolio	studio
buffalo	donate	Minnesota	soldier	voltage
cargo	enroll	Oklahoma	sole	Wyoming

64

G Dictation

Name ______________________

Write each sentence as your teacher dictates. Use correct punctuation.

1. Kelly, the patrol dog, was the picture of control since she had been well trained.
2. Stephen looked in his portfolio to find his report on buffalo.
3. People used to donate clothes to the older boy, but now he dressed in style.

Words with /ō/

Lesson 10

H Proofreading

If a word is misspelled, fill in the oval by that word. If all the words are spelled correctly, fill in the oval by **no mistake**.

1. ● banjoe ○ arrive ○ Iowa ○ no mistake
2. ○ guys ○ flamingo ● cargoe ○ no mistake
3. ○ admire ● buffaloe ○ byte ○ no mistake
4. ○ geyser ○ macro ○ stereo ● no mistake
5. ○ boldly ● enrole ○ recital ○ no mistake
6. ○ control ○ alibi ● patroll ○ no mistake
7. ○ donate ○ Minnesota ○ diary ● no mistake
8. ○ portfolio ● soldyer ○ guide ○ no mistake
9. ○ sole ● voltige ○ height ○ no mistake
10. ● doam ○ studio ○ liar ○ no mistake
11. ○ Oklahoma ○ Ohio ○ diet ● no mistake
12. ● Wyomng ○ riot ○ Idaho ○ no mistake

65

1 Dictation

Reinforce correct spelling by using current and previous words in context.

Listen as I read each sentence and then write it in your Worktext. Remember to use correct capitalization and punctuation. (Slowly read each sentence twice. Sentences are found in the Student Worktext to the left.)

2 Proofreading

Familiarize students with standardized test format and reinforce recognition of misspelled words.

Look at each set of words. If a word is misspelled, fill in the oval by that word. If all the words are spelled correctly, fill in the oval by **no mistake**.

Day 4 / Day 5

Lesson 10

Hide and Seek

Reinforce correct spelling of current spelling words. Repeat this activity from Day 2.

Vocabulary Extension

Have your students complete this activity to strengthen spelling ability and expand vocabulary. The reproducible master is provided in Appendix A as shown on the inset page to the right.

Posttest

Test mastery of the spelling words.

I will say the word once, use it in a sentence, then say it again. Write your words on a separate sheet of paper.

Progress Chart

Students may record scores. (Reproducible master in Appendix B.)

Personal Dictionary

Students may add any words they have misspelled to their personal dictionaries for reference when writing. (Cover in Appendix B.)

Hide and Seek

Play Hide and Seek with your words. Fill in a bar graph (left to right) for each word you spell correctly.

Vocabulary Extension

Cause and Effect

Write a word from the word bank to complete each sentence.

1. If you wanted to approach someone, you would go up and talk to them.
2. If a family had lived in the city of Thessalonica, they would be known as Thessalonians.
3. If you want to look at something that is very small, you would use a microscope.
4. If you want to read the book of the Bible between Hosea and Amos, you would read the book of Joel.
5. If you wanted to describe the brilliance that radiates from a heavenly angel, you might use the word glory.
6. If a carpenter wanted to hold up the roof of a porch, he might use pillars to support it.
7. If you wanted to describe someone who had suffered a lot, you might compare them to a man in the Bible named Job.
8. If you want to go into a cave to discover what it is like, you will explore it.
9. If you were telling a story about a man who had been swallowed by a large fish, you would be telling the story of Jonah.
10. If you had written a letter to a friend and needed to mail it, you would write the address on an envelope.
11. If you challenged a friend to a game of tennis, you would play at a tennis court.
12. If your family were citizens of Rome, they would be known as Romans.

Word Bank

approach	explore	Joel	Romans
court	glory	Jonah	support
envelope	Job	microscope	Thessalonians

Vocabulary Extension — Lesson 10 — 333

1.	banjo	Mr. Canfield brought a **banjo**, guitar, and violin for the class to see.
2.	stereo	He also set up a **stereo** in the classroom to encourage music appreciation.
3.	donate	Many parents were willing to **donate** CD's of music by famous composers.
4.	Wyoming	One composer wrote a piece to describe the beauty he saw in **Wyoming.**
5.	studio	The kind officer admired the students' paintings in the **studio** area.
6.	buffalo	Using a charcoal pencil, Thorny sketched a very realistic **buffalo.**
7.	flamingo	He complimented Sarah on her beautiful **flamingo.**
8.	Oklahoma	He told the class that he moved from **Oklahoma** when he was twenty-one.
9.	soldier	He had thought about being a **soldier** in the armed forces.
10.	enroll	He said that God wanted him to **enroll** in the police academy instead.
11.	boldly	In his training, he had to learn to **boldly** face danger.
12.	control	His teachers also trained him to exercise self-**control.**
13.	voltage	He has a stun gun that can shock a fleeing criminal with low **voltage.**
14.	patrol	Officer Klein is glad to have Kelly as his partner on **patrol.**
15.	sole	He tapped the floor twice with the **sole** of his shoe and Kelly sat down.
16.	macro	"You'd probably laugh again if I said the dog has **macro** teeth."
17.	cargo	He and Kelly often check the **cargo** of boats for illegal drugs.
18.	portfolio	Officer Klein showed the class his **portfolio** of newspaper clippings.
19.	dome	Newer patrol cars do not have **dome** lights; they are rectangular instead.
20.	Minnesota	His best friend from school is an officer in **Minnesota.**

Lesson 10 — Words with /ō/

I Game Name ____________

Record points for each word you or your team spells correctly. Earn bonus points for each row in which all four words are spelled correctly.

	1	2	3	4	Row Totals
Row A	○	○	○	○	⬭
Row B	○	○	○	○	⬭
Row C	○	○	○	○	⬭
Row D	○	○	○	○	⬭
Row E	○	○	○	○	⬭
				TOTAL	⬭
				BONUS	⬭
				GRAND	⬭

Remember: Hide behind the Rock; you're safe there!

J Journaling

In your journal, write another chapter to the story. How do you think God might continue to protect Beth, Tony, and Stephen from Brutus?

66

How to Play:

- Divide the class into two teams.
- Have a student from team A choose a square on the grid by indicating the row letter and number.
- Say the word that matches that row letter and number from the team's word list.
- Have the student write the word on the board.
- If correct, have each member of that team record the awarded points (in parentheses by the word) in the circle in that box. If the word is misspelled, have him/her put an **X** in that circle. That square may not be chosen again.
- Repeat this process with the second team.
- When all the words have been spelled by both teams, have each team tally its score. Award a bonus of 5 points for each row in which all four words were spelled correctly.
- Have the teams record their grand totals. The team with the highest score is the winner.

2 Game

Reinforce spelling skills and provide motivation and interest.

Materials

- game page (from student text)
- pencils (1 per child)
- game word list

Game Word List

Team A		Team B
E4	**banjo (4)**	A1
E3	**buffalo (3)**	A2
E2	**cargo (2)**	A3
E1	**flamingo (1)**	A4
D4	**macro (2)**	B1
D3	**stereo (4)**	B2
D2	**studio (1)**	B3
D1	**boldly (3)**	B4
C4	**control (2)**	C1
C3	**enroll (1)**	C2
C2	**patrol (3)**	C3
C1	**portfolio (4)**	C4
B4	**soldier (1)**	D1
B3	**sole (4)**	D2
B2	**voltage (3)**	D3
B1	**dome (2)**	D4
A4	**Oklahoma (4)**	E1
A3	**Wyoming (3)**	E2
A2	**donate (1)**	E3
A1	**Minnesota (2)**	E4

3 Journaling

Provide a meaningful reason for correct spelling through personal writing.

Review the story using discussion leads provided on the following page. Encourage students to apply the Scriptural value in their journaling.

Journaling (continued)

- Whom is Brutus still being mean to? (Stephen and Tony)
- Why does Beth suggest they should be detectives? (Brutus is wearing nice clothes this year and they can't figure out how he affords them.)
- Whom did Tony see Brutus talking to on the way home from school? (Some high school boys in a Corvette.)
- What do Stephen, Beth, and Tony suspect Brutus is doing? (Making money from illegal drugs.)
- Do you think Brutus is selling drugs?
- Do you think Tony and Stephen will need protection again?

The words erroneousnesses and verrucosenesses are the longest ones consisting of only short letters.

1 Literature Connection

Topic: Focusing on God's perfect words
Theme Text: Psalm 119:96-98

Smart Mouths

When they have a substitute teacher, Rosa and her classmates learn to be careful what they say about people.

Carlos walked into the kitchen, head down, pawing through his backpack. "Have you guys seen my history paper? I finished it last night. It's gotta be here somewhere!" He pulled his history book out and frantically flipped through it.

"Well, don't panic." Maria glanced up from her place at the breakfast table. "Where'd you leave it, anyway?"

"Right here on the table where I was working!" 16-year-old Carlos stuffed the book back in his pack before dropping the whole thing on the floor and slumping into his seat at the table.

"That's strange," said their father, turning from the refrigerator with a jar of jam. "Did you see anything when you set the table for breakfast, Rosa?"

"Jisss bum unch fapers." Rosa answered around a mouthful of Yummy O's.

Mr. Vasquez frowned across the table at her. "Try that again, please, without the food in your mouth."

Rosa nodded and swallowed rapidly. "I said, just a bunch of papers." She spooned another bite of cereal into her mouth.

"Rosa, would you quit stuffing yourself for just a minute?" Carlos demanded. "Where's my history paper!?"

Rosa washed down the cereal with orange juice. She shrugged. "I don't know if it was your history paper, Carlos. There was a stack of papers on the table when I was supposed to set it for breakfast, so I moved them." Rosa took another bite of Yummy O's.

"Moved them where?" Carlos clunked his spoon down on the table and glared at his little sister. When she pointed to her full mouth instead of answering immediately, Carlos exploded. "Are you deaf and dumb—or just dumb?!"

Mr. Vasquez spoke sternly, "Carlos, you may leave the table or make a sincere apology to your sister. You will not use words that belittle others."

For a moment it was so quiet that Rosa's chewing sounded loud. Then Carlos sighed. "I'm sorry, Rosa. That report's real important and it's due today."

Rosa fumed as she picked up her glass of orange juice. "I put the papers on the coffee table in the living room, but I'm so dumb I didn't look to see if your history report was with them." She glared across the table at her older brother.

"Why don't you go check right now, Carlos?" Mr. Vasquez shook his head at Rosa. "I'm sure we'll all enjoy our breakfast more once that report is found."

Later that morning Carlos slowed the blue Jeep to a stop in front of Knowlton Elementary School. "I'll pick you up here right after school," he said as his sisters got out.

"Okay!" Rosa scrambled out after Maria. "Do you still have your history paper, Carlos? I really don't think someone who can't keep track of their work should be driving! See you!" She grinned impishly and slammed the door, drowning out Carlos' reply.

"Hey, Rosa, hurry up!" Rosa's friend, Kristin, motioned from halfway up the sidewalk. When Rosa caught up with her, Kristin wiped the back of her hand across her forehead. "Whew! I'm sure glad you got here safely. It takes years off my life just thinking about Carlos driving a car!"

"I just close my eyes and hold on!" Rosa laughed as the girls walked into the building. "Hey, you think Mr. Canfield will let us sit together for art today like he did last week?"

"Probably. Let's ask.... Who's that?" Kristin stopped just inside the classroom door and pointed at someone writing on the board.

"That is our substitute teacher," Beth whispered as she walked by. "Can you believe that hair?"

Kristin whispered back, "It, um, it's certainly a long, straight ponytail. And thick. Like a horse's tail!"

"Just wait till she turns around!" Beth moved on to her desk.

Kristin snickered when the substitute teacher turned around. Her face was long and thin with large brown eyes—just like a horse's face. Kristin cleared her throat to keep from laughing when she read the name written on the board: Miss Horace.

"Good morning, children. I'm Miss Horace, your teacher for today. Now, please stand and repeat the pledge of allegiance."

Rosa stood with her class and faced the flag, but she rolled her eyes to study the substitute teacher. Miss Horace didn't appear to be very old, although her mane of hair was streaked with gray. Her face was smooth and unlined, not a smile, wrinkle or a laugh line to be found. "...with liberty and justice for all." Rosa finished the pledge with her classmates and started to sit back down.

"Young man!" The substitute teacher's voice snapped across the room. "Yes, you in the black shirt." Everyone turned to see who she was talking to. Christopher Wright, Kristin's twin brother, stood in the aisle clutching his pencil with the jet eraser on the end. "Sit down."

"I was just going to sharpen my pencil, Miss Horace." Christopher held up the red pencil so the teacher could see its dull point.

Miss Horace frowned

Story (continued)

and barked, "I said, sit down."

"Um, Miss Horace?" Christopher tried once more to explain. "I need my pencil for this first class and Mr. Canfield lets us sharpen our pencils whenever we need to."

Miss Horace stared at Christopher without saying a word before walking across the room to stand directly in front of him. "I said, SIT DOWN." Christopher turned quickly and bolted to his desk.

Miss Horace returned to the front of the room. "I am your teacher today and I am not Mr. Canfield. Now get out your books and turn to page 79."

"She can sure say that again!" Tommy whispered to a red-faced Christopher as he handed a sharp pencil across the aisle to him.

"Yep, this day is gonna be as much fun as a paper cut!" Daniel whispered from the back row.

The day dragged on minute by minute. By art time, Rosa knew better than to ask Miss Horace if she could sit with Kristin. Usually art class was noisy and fun. Mr. Canfield encouraged them to talk about ideas and to try new things. Today the room was much quieter. Miss Horace was busy at the front of the room writing on the board.

"Psst, Katelynn." Rosa nudged the girl in front of her. "Look at my sculpture."

Katelynn studied the lump of clay balanced on four wobbly clay legs. "What is it?"

Rosa leaned forward and whispered, "I call it Miss Horse." Katelynn slapped her hand over her mouth to hold her giggles in. Nearby, Beth choked on her laughter and went into a fit of coughing.

Beth poked Stephen and pointed at Rosa's sculpture. "That's Miss Horse." She tossed her own short ponytail and raised her eyebrows at the substitute teacher's long one.

Stephen grinned and caught Tommy's attention. "Miss Horse," he mouthed and nodded at Rosa's lopsided clay horse.

"Miss Horse looks like what my grandma used to call 'one brick short of a load.'" Tommy whispered back.

Christopher jabbed at his own lump of clay and muttered, "I'd say more like two or three bricks short."

Rosa wiggled her eyebrows. "Maybe she's a donut short of a dozen."

"I believe the expression 'a bubble off plumb' is used by those in the building profession to represent the same idea you are suggesting." Thorny divided his clay precisely into equal parts.

Stephen rolled his eyes. "You mean, like, she's a throwback from the gene pool?"

Daniel held up his hand to get the attention of everyone around him. He motioned toward the woman writing on the board at the front of the room, her long ponytail swishing back and forth down her back. "I can't figure out if Miss Horse is deaf and dumb—or just dumb."

At that exact moment, Miss Horace turned around. "Daniel, did you have a question?"

"Nay." Daniel grinned as his classmates almost burst trying to hold in their laughter. "I mean, no, Miss Horace."

Miss Horace frowned around the room and turned back to finish what she was writing.

Tommy read the words the substitute teacher had written. "Oops," he whispered. "Check that out, guys." He pointed his pencil at the board.

"At your service, sir!" Daniel leaned over in his seat and bowed to Tommy. "'Nothing is perfect except your words. Oh, how I love them. I think about them all day long.'" Daniel's whisper lost it's cocky tone as he read, "'They make me wiser than my enemies, because….'" His voice trailed off. Then he turned to his classmates and added, "'Oops' is right."

At last Thorny broke the silence in the classroom. He chose his words even more carefully than usual. "Our words have been anything but perfect," Thorny said, frowning at the neat clay birdhouse on his desk. "We appear to have given little thought to what is right and thus have made a significant error."

"Thorny, what are you talking about?" Christopher rubbed his face and left a streak of clay.

Stephen's eyes rolled again. "He means we blew it."

Rosa nodded, "Blew it big time."

"I knew how bad it felt when Carlos said mean things to me this morning. But I did the same thing to somebody else. I think I need a fresh start—in more ways than one." Rosa smiled, then wadded the clay horse into a ball and started her art project over again.

2 Discussion Time

Check understanding of the story and development of personal values.

- What was Carlos looking for at breakfast time?
- Why was he upset with Rosa?
- When Carlos called Rosa "dumb," how did Mr. Vasquez respond?
- Describe the substitute teacher Rosa's class had that day.
- What did Miss Horace do when Christopher got up to sharpen his pencil?
- What did Rosa make during art time?
- What made Rosa and her classmates realize that they were doing wrong?

A Preview Name ______________

Write each word as your teacher says it.

1. flu
2. useless
3. foolish
4. view
5. cue
6. include
7. funeral
8. confuse
9. canoe
10. dune
11. tulip
12. tomb
13. raccoon
14. crew
15. accuse
16. igloo
17. truly
18. future
19. Utah
20. Massachusetts

Words with /ü/ or /ū/

Lesson 11

Scripture

Psalm 119:96-98

67

3 Preview

Test for knowledge of the correct spellings of these words.

Customize Your List

On a separate sheet of paper, additional words of your choice may be tested.

I will say each word once, use the word in a sentence, then say the word again. Write the words on the lines in your Worktext.

Correct Immediately!

Let's correct our Preview. I will spell each word out loud. If you spelled a word incorrectly, rewrite it correctly.

Progress Chart

Students may record scores. (Reproducible master provided in Appendix B.)

Day 1

Lesson 11

1. flu — The whole class thought having Miss Horace for a teacher was as bad as having the **flu.**
2. useless — They felt like trying to please Miss Horace was **useless.**
3. foolish — Christopher felt **foolish** when she would not let him sharpen his pencil.
4. view — Rosa got Katelynn's attention so she could **view** her sculpture.
5. cue — Her classmate began to snicker right on **cue.**
6. include — Mr. Canfield always tried to **include** everyone in interesting discussions.
7. funeral — Miss Horace looked like she had just come from a **funeral.**
8. confuse — It was impossible to **confuse** the two teachers' methods as they are opposite.
9. canoe — Talking to her was like paddling a **canoe** upstream.
10. dune — Daniel compared being in her class to climbing a **dune** without any water!
11. tulip — Setsuko carefully shaped a small piece of clay into a **tulip.**
12. tomb — Thorny made a realistic Egyptian **tomb** out of his lump of clay.
13. raccoon — Beth made an adorable **raccoon** family sitting on a log.
14. crew — A road **crew** was repairing a portion of the school parking lot.
15. accuse — "Did she **accuse** you of talking during the test?" Daniel asked Tommy.
16. igloo — Sarah made a miniature **igloo** out of clay.
17. truly — They were **truly** sorry they had made fun of Miss Horace.
18. future — "In the **future,** we need to let God's words be in our mouths," said Tommy.
19. Utah — Miss Horace's parents live in **Utah** where she used to teach.
20. Massachusetts — She is hoping to get a job in **Massachusetts.**

Day 1

Lesson 11

4 Word Shapes

Help students form a correct image of whole words.

Look at each word and think about its shape. Now, write the word in the correct word Shape Boxes. You may check off each word as you use it.

(In most words, the sound of **/ü/** is spelled with **oo**, or **u**. However, the sound of **/ü/** can also be spelled with **o**, **oe**, **ew**, or **u-consonant-e**.) The sound of **/ū/** can be spelled with **ue**, **ew**, **eu**, or **ie**.

In the word shape boxes, fill in the boxes containing the letter or letters that spell the sound of **/ū/** or **/ü/** in each word.

Take a minute to memorize...

Psalm 119:96-98

Words with /ü/ or /ū/ — Lesson 11

B Word Shapes Name ____________

Using the word bank below, write each word in the correct word shape boxes. Next, in the word shape boxes, fill in the boxes containing the letter or letters that spell the sound of **/ü/** or **/ū/** in each word.

1. foolish
2. igloo
3. dune
4. cue
5. truly
6. tulip
7. canoe
8. view
9. Massachusetts
10. confuse
11. include
12. crew
13. funeral
14. Utah
15. future
16. flu
17. useless
18. tomb
19. accuse
20. raccoon

Word Bank

accuse	cue	funeral	Massachusetts	tulip
canoe	dune	future	raccoon	useless
confuse	flu	igloo	tomb	Utah
crew	foolish	include	truly	view

68

Answers may vary for duplicate word shapes.

Be Prepared For Fun

Check these supply lists for **Fun Ways to Spell** - presented **Day 2**. Purchase and/or gather these items ahead of time!

General
- Pencil
- Graph Paper (1 sheet per child)
- Spelling List

Auditory
- Pencil
- Notebook Paper
- Spelling List

Visual
- Colored Pencils
- Alphabet Stencils
- Paper

Tactile
- Uncooked Rice
- Art Paper (1 sheet per child)
- Glue
- Spelling List

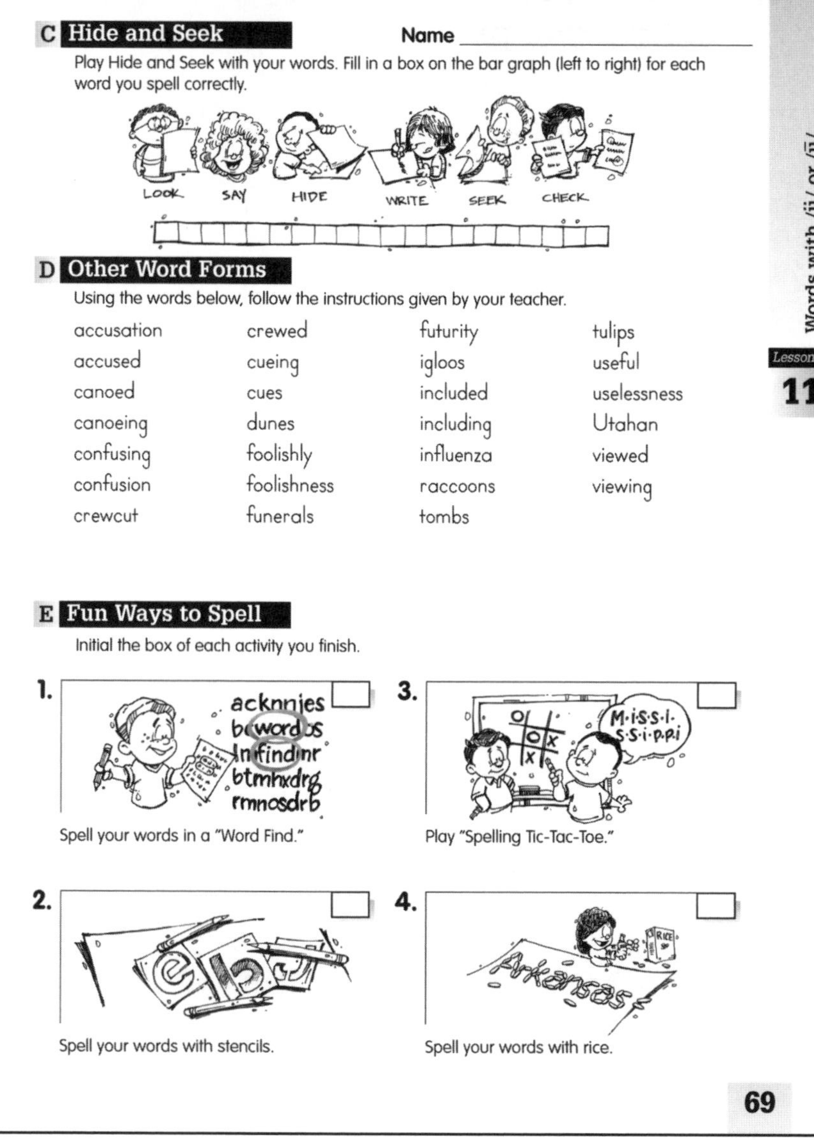

C Hide and Seek Name ____________

Play Hide and Seek with your words. Fill in a box on the bar graph (left to right) for each word you spell correctly.

D Other Word Forms

Using the words below, follow the instructions given by your teacher.

accusation	crewed	futurity	tulips
accused	cueing	igloos	useful
canoed	cues	included	uselessness
canoeing	dunes	including	Utahan
confusing	foolishly	influenza	viewed
confusion	foolishness	raccoons	viewing
crewcut	funerals	tombs	

E Fun Ways to Spell

Initial the box of each activity you finish.

1.

Spell your words in a "Word Find."

3.

Play "Spelling Tic-Tac-Toe."

2. Spell your words with stencils.

4.

Spell your words with rice.

Words with /ü/ or /ū/

Lesson 11

69

1 Hide and Seek

Reinforce spelling by using multiple styles of learning.

On a white board, Teacher writes each word — one at a time. **Have students:**

- **Look** at the word.
- **Say** the word out loud.
- **Spell** the word out loud.
- **Hide** (teacher erases word.)
- **Write** the word on paper.
- **Seek** (teacher rewrites word.)
- **Check** spelling. If incorrect, rewrite word correctly.

Day 2 | Lesson 11

2 Other Word Forms

This activity is optional. Have students write original sentences using these Other Word Forms:

viewed
dunes
uselessness
confusion

3 Fun Ways to Spell

Four activities are provided. Use one, two, three, or all of the activities. Have students initial the box for each activity they complete.

Options:

- assign activities to students according to their learning styles
- set up the activities in learning centers for the students to do throughout the day
- divide students into four groups and assign one activity per group
- do one activity per day

General

To spell your words in a "Word Find"...
- Arrange your words on a piece of graph paper.
- Put one letter of each word in a square.
- Words may be written backwards, forwards, or diagonally.
- Outline your puzzle.
- Hide your words by filling in all the spaces inside the puzzle with random letters.
- Trade grids with a classmate and find the hidden words.

Auditory

To play "Spelling Tic-Tac-Toe"...
- Draw a Tic-Tac-Toe grid.
- Ask a classmate to read a word from the list.
- Spell the word aloud.
- If the word is spelled correctly, place your mark on the grid.
- Take turns with your classmate.

Visual

To spell your words with stencils...
- Look at the first letter of a word on your list.
- Place the stencil for the proper letter over your paper.
- Shade inside the stencil.
- Choose the proper stencil for the next letter of the word and shade it in next to the first letter.
- Finish the word in this way.
- Do this with each word.

Tactile

To spell your words with rice...
- Choose a word from your spelling list.
- Shape the letters of your word with rice.
- Glue the rice to art paper.
- Do this for each word on your list.

Working with Words

Familiarize students with word meaning and usage.

Secret Words

The boxed letters in the acrostic are a phrase from the Scripture verse for this week.

Use the clues to write the words in the puzzle. You may use a dictionary to help you. Then write the boxed letters on the lines below to find the secret words from this week's Scripture.

Take a minute to memorize...

Psalm 119:96-98

F Working with Words Name ____________________

Secret Words

Use the clues to write the words in the puzzle. Then write the boxed letters on the lines below to find the secret words from this week's Scripture.

1. t r u l y
2. c o n f u s e
3. c u e
4. f u t u r e
5. c r e w
6. c a n o e
7. r a c c o o n
8. i n c l u d e
9. M a s s a c h u s e t t s
10. U t a h
11. f u n e r a l
12. v i e w
13. t o m b
14. y
15. i g l o o
16. a c c u s e
17. t u l i p
18. d u n e
19. u s e l e s s

1. absolutely, really
2. bewilder, baffle
3. suggestion, hint
4. afterward, by-and-by
5. group, gang
6. dugout, kayak
7. masked animal
8. involve, comprise
9. New England state
10. mountain state north of Arizona
11. burial ceremony
12. scene, vista
13. grave, memorial
14. 25th letter of the alphabet
15. ice house
16. blame, reproach
17. spring flower
18. small round hill
19. futile, hopeless

Write the secret phrase:

Y o u r w o r d s a r e m y g u i d e.

Word Bank

accuse	cue	funeral	Massachusetts	tulip
canoe	dune	future	raccoon	useless
confuse	flu	igloo	tomb	Utah
crew	foolish	include	truly	view

G Dictation

Name ______________________

Write each sentence as your teacher dictates. Use correct punctuation.

1. Carlos read his paper about how Indians built canoes and igloos.
2. Christopher found that it was useless to argue with the teacher.
3. Once the children read the words, they quit saying foolish and unkind things.

Words with /ü/ or /ū/

Lesson 11

H Proofreading

If a word is misspelled, fill in the oval by that word. If all the words are spelled correctly, fill in the oval by **no mistake**.

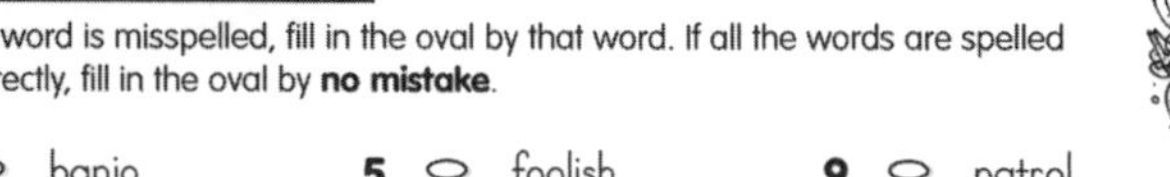

1.	○ banjo ○ crew ● canoo ○ no mistake	**5.**	○ foolish ○ truly ○ flamingo ● no mistake	**9.**	○ patrol ○ raccoon ○ useless ● no mistake
2.	● confuze ○ studio ○ boldly ○ no mistake	**6.**	○ tomb ● tullip ○ dome ○ no mistake	**10.**	○ portfolio ○ future ● Utaw ○ no mistake
3.	○ igloo ○ voltage ○ stereo ● no mistake	**7.**	○ dune ● funneral ○ macro ○ no mistake	**11.**	○ cue ○ flu ○ buffalo ● no mistake
4.	● veiw ○ include ○ cargo ○ no mistake	**8.**	○ control ○ enroll ● Massachusitts ○ no mistake	**12.**	● accuze ○ soldier ○ sole ○ no mistake

71

1 Dictation

Reinforce correct spelling by using current and previous words in context.

Listen as I read each sentence and then write it in your Worktext. Remember to use correct capitalization and punctuation. (Slowly read each sentence twice. Sentences are found in the Student Worktext to the left.)

Day 4

2 Proofreading

Familiarize students with standardized test format and reinforce recognition of misspelled words.

Look at each set of words. If a word is misspelled, fill in the oval by that word. If all the words are spelled correctly, fill in the oval by **no mistake**.

Lesson 11

3 Hide and Seek

Reinforce correct spelling of current spelling words.
Repeat this activity from Day 2.

4 Vocabulary Extension

Have your students complete this activity to strengthen spelling ability and expand vocabulary. The reproducible master is provided in Appendix A as shown on the inset page to the right.

1 Posttest

Test mastery of the spelling words.

I will say the word once, use it in a sentence, then say it again. Write your words on a separate sheet of paper.

Progress Chart
Students may record scores. (Reproducible master in Appendix B.)

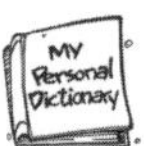

Personal Dictionary
Students may add any words they have misspelled to their personal dictionaries for reference when writing. (Cover in Appendix B.)

Vocabulary Extension | Lesson 11

Hide and Seek

Play Hide and Seek with your words. Fill in a bar graph (left to right) for each word you spell correctly.

Vocabulary Extension

Fill in the Blanks

Choose a word from the word bank that best fits each sentence clue.

1. When I saw my brother playing with my yo-yo, I had to conclude that he had taken it.
2. We did not mean to exclude you; we accidentally left you out of the game.
3. Grandma always smells like a rose garden. I like the perfume she wears.
4. When my sister broke her leg, lots of people sent flowers to her. Their kindness was abundant and profuse.
5. I am memorizing a verse in the 26th book of the New Testament. I am learning a verse in the book of Jude.
6. My grandfather thinks I look very young. He comments on how youthful I seem.
7. I have good opinions and feelings about school. I have a positive attitude.
8. My mother-in-law's name was Naomi. I was kind to her. I later married Boaz. My name was Ruth.
9. The round black part of your eye that lets light travel through it is called the pupil.
10. I was a doctor and wrote the third gospel. I also traveled with Paul. My name was Luke.
11. The earth, the planets, the stars and everything in space make up the universe.
12. My brother likes to make funny little drawings. He likes to draw cartoons.

Word Bank

attitude	exclude	perfume	Ruth
cartoon	Jude	profuse	universe
conclude	Luke	pupil	youthful

334

---

1. **crew** The class saw the road **crew** working to repair the school parking lot.
2. **funeral** Miss Horace looked as cheerful as if she'd just come from a **funeral.**
3. **canoe** "Talking to her is like paddling your **canoe** upstream," exclaimed Beth.
4. **useless** "Pleasing her is **useless,** I'd say" replied Rosa.
5. **view** Daniel thought he was out of her **view** as he made his silly faces.
6. **flu** "I'd rather have the **flu** than have her for a teacher," he said with a groan.
7. **cue** As if on **cue,** Miss Horace turned around to see what Daniel was doing.
8. **include** She did not make an attempt to **include** the class in any exciting discussions.
9. **foolish** Her harshness made Christopher feel **foolish.**
10. **accuse** "I don't want her to **accuse** me of anything," worried Tony.
11. **confuse** On the quiz, Matthew found it easy to **confuse** adjectives and adverbs.
12. **tulip** Setsuko made more than one **tulip** and arranged them in a clay vase.
13. **tomb** Thorny scored the sides of his Egyptian **tomb** to look like stone.
14. **raccoon** "Do you like my **raccoon,** Laney?" Beth asked.
15. **igloo** Sarah shaped several little Eskimos to stand outside her **igloo.**
16. **dune** At lunch, Thorny said Miss Horace's teaching delivery was as dry as a desert **dune.**
17. **truly** When the class saw the verse on the board they were **truly** sorry.
18. **future** "Our words should be more carefully chosen in the **future,**" commented Thorny.
19. **Massachusetts** Miss Horace is looking for a teaching position in **Massachusetts.**
20. **Utah** She recently visited her parents in **Utah.**

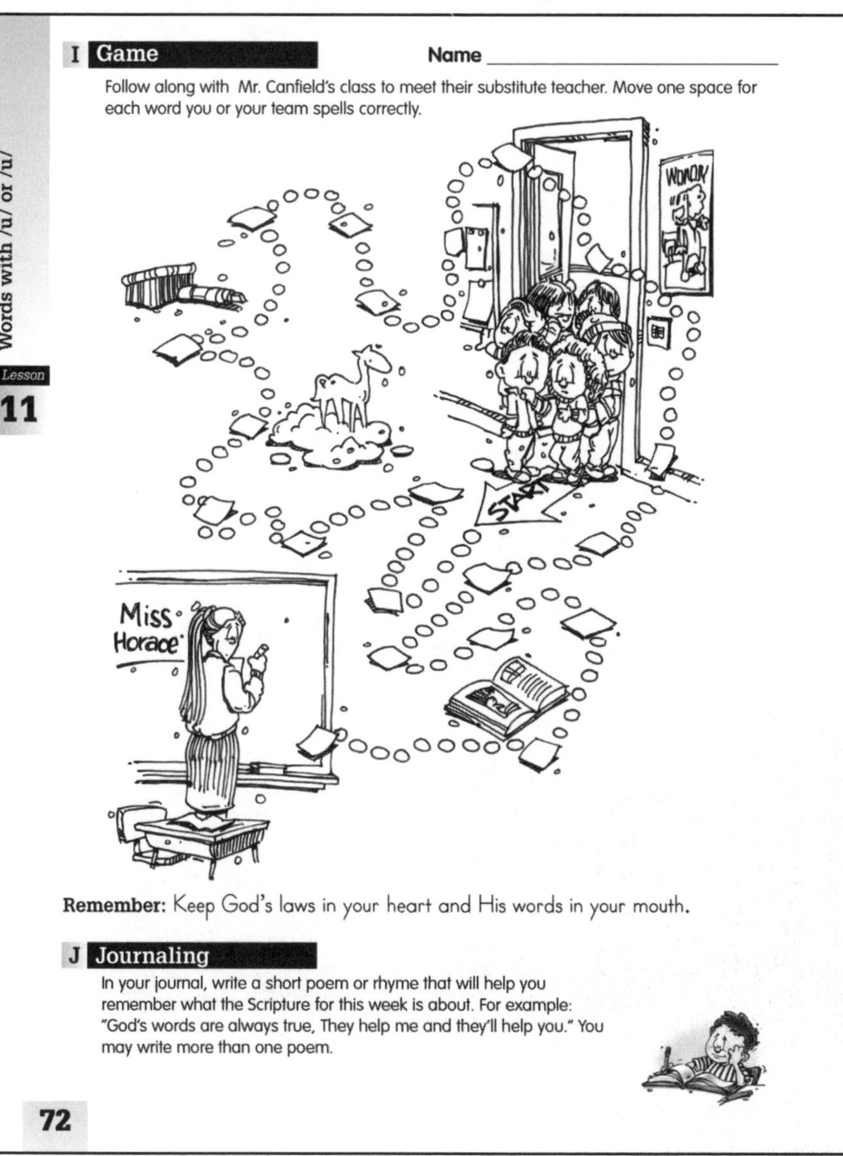

Words with /ü/ or /ū/

Lesson 11

I Game Name ______________________

Follow along with Mr. Canfield's class to meet their substitute teacher. Move one space for each word you or your team spells correctly.

Remember: Keep God's laws in your heart and His words in your mouth.

J Journaling

In your journal, write a short poem or rhyme that will help you remember what the Scripture for this week is about. For example: "God's words are always true, They help me and they'll help you." You may write more than one poem.

72

How to Play:

- Divide the class into two teams.
- Have each student place his/her game piece on Start.
- Have a student from team A go to the board.
- Say the spelling word.
- Have the student write the word on the board.
- If correct, instruct each member of team A to move his/her game piece forward one space.
- Alternate between teams A and B.
- The team to reach Miss Horace first is the winner.
- **Small Group Option**: Students may play this game without teacher direction in small groups of two or more.

2 Game

Reinforce spelling skills and provide motivation and interest.

Materials

- game page (from student text)
- game pieces (1 per child)
- game word list

Game Word List

1. **canoe**
2. **crew**
3. **cue**
4. **flu**
5. **igloo**
6. **view**
7. **include**
8. **foolish**
9. **truly**
10. **tulip**
11. **tomb**
12. **dune**
13. **funeral**
14. **raccoon**
15. **Massachusetts**
16. **useless**
17. **accuse**
18. **confuse**
19. **future**
20. **Utah**

3 Journaling

Provide a meaningful reason for correct spelling through personal writing.

Review the story using discussion leads provided on the following page. Encourage students to apply the Scriptural value in their journaling.

Journaling (continued)

- Do you sometimes have disagreements with your brother or sister like Rosa and Carlos did? (Allow time to share experiences.)
- What things gave Rosa the idea of calling her substitute "Miss Horse?" (The teacher had a long straight brown pony tail, a long thin face, and her name was Miss Horace.)
- Why do you think the class made fun of Miss Horace? (They didn't like her because she was different from Mr. Canfield. She was strict and she didn't smile much.)
- Is it okay to make fun of people that aren't nice? Why or why not? (No. It is never okay to say things that belittle others whether they are nice or not.)
- How do you feel when people make fun of you or say unkind things about you?
- How can we be sure we never belittle others? (By making God's words our constant guide.)

A GOOGOL is the figure 1 followed by 100 zeros. Mathematician Edward Kasner supposedly asked his nephew Milton Sirotta to suggest a name for the number, and he came up with this word, which is now found in many dictionaries. The million, billion, trillion, quadrillion system skips over this number.

Word Wow!

1 Literature Connection
Topic: Dealing with a bully
Theme Text: Psalm 63:3-5

A Satisfying Solution

Stephen learns to be satisfied with God's answers to his prayer in God's time.

"Hey, Wimp!"

Stephen quickened his pace at the sound of the voice behind him. His hands shook as he grabbed the handle on the glass door.

A big hand reached out and seized his arm; a gruff voice snarled in his ear, "Watch yourself! Mr. Canfield can't be everywhere!" The big eighth grader glared down at Stephen before the younger boy darted into the gym behind his classmates.

"I want you to line up behind the free-throw line," Mr. Canfield was saying as Stephen joined his classmates. The big teacher spun the basketball in his hand, dribbled it under his right leg, then arched it effortlessly toward the basket. The ball swished through the net before it bounced toward the group of kids lining up.

Tony darted out of line, grabbed the orange ball, and passed it back to his teacher. Mr. Canfield dribbled the ball all around himself as he walked to the head of the line. He easily made 10 shots in a row before one bounced off the rim without swishing through the net. "Everyone gets 10 free-throws today," he said. "After the tenth, try a layup, then go to the end of the line."

Mr. Canfield grinned and threw the ball to Beth before he took another one out of the equipment bag and positioned himself underneath the backboard. When Beth's ball arched through the air toward the basket, Mr. Canfield threw her the next one.

"He's amazing!" Tony looked at his teacher in awe. "If he can't help us improve our game, nobody can. Laney says they pay him to ref at Mason Springs Park, so we can't complain about him not knowing the rules." Tony watched Beth continue to shoot.

Stephen ignored his friend's comments and absently rubbed his arm where Brutus had grabbed him. He shook his head as if to rid his brain of the bully's warning.

After her layup, Beth joined her friends at the end of the line. "I got four. Do you think you can beat that?"

"No one can beat Mr. Canfield!" Tony declared. "Even Brutus!"

Tony noticed Stephen wasn't joining in the conversation. "What's wrong with you, Stephen? You in trouble?"

"Brutus," Stephen whispered. "He caught me in the hall as I was coming in here. No one else was around. I don't know how he does that."

"Wha'd he say?" Beth asked.

"He said, 'Watch yourself! Mr. Canfield can't be everywhere!'"

"I think we should tell Mr. Canfield," declared Beth.

"I think if Brutus finds out we told, we'll be dead meat." Stephen rubbed his arm again. "He's right, you know—Mr. Canfield can't be everywhere."

After school that afternoon Stephen didn't linger in the hall. He rushed to the curb when he saw the family car pull up.

"Surprise!" Mom said as he slipped in the back seat and slammed the door. "Look who's here!" Tony peered around the headrest and grinned when he saw his grandma.

"When did you get here? How long can you stay? Did you drive? Is Grandpa here too? Why didn't you tell me you were coming? Can you come to my basketball game?"

"Just a minute, Stephen, my boy. One question at a time. We got here about noon. We drove…." The three chatted happily all the way home. Stephen almost forgot about his trouble with Brutus.

After supper Mom and Dad were in deep discussion with Grandpa about a church issue. They'd gone into the living room to look something up in the Scriptures.

Grandma joined Stephen at the sink. "How 'bout I wash and you dry, my boy?" The older woman smiled down at her grandson. "How's your problem with Brutus goin'? You haven't mentioned him lately." Grandma filled the sink with hot water. Stephen didn't answer immediately.

"I guess he graduated since he was in eighth grade last year," Grandma continued. "Praise the Lord! He never gives us more than we can bear. Did you ever tell your teacher about what he did last year?" The gray-haired woman squirted soap into the steamy water.

"Nope," Stephen finally answered. "We just tried to keep out of his way. I don't know what Mrs. Burton could have done anyway. Brutus is a lot bigger than she is."

"The Lord answers prayer, Stephen. In His own time." Grandma plunged her hands into the soapy dishwater and tackled the dinner plates. "When I look back, I'm always satisfied."

"You sound like the Scripture we're learning in school this week, Grandma." Stephen picked up a plate from the dish rack. "It goes something like this, 'I will bless you as long as I live, lifting up my hands to you in prayer. At last I shall be fully satisfied.'"

After a short pause Stephen said thoughtfully, "I'm glad He answers your prayers, but he doesn't seem to do that for me. Brutus flunked last year! He's back and he's worse than ever. I think he might be dealing drugs, but we can't prove it. A few weeks ago he grabbed me and Tony, and was about to slam us into the wall when our teacher caught him. He got in trouble, and now he's really out

Story Continued

to get me. For some reason he always picks on me. Today he grabbed my arm and said, 'Watch yourself! Mr. Canfield can't be everywhere.'" Stephen lifted his shirtsleeve to reveal the black-and-blue handprint, "Look what he did to my arm, Grandma."

Grandma sucked in her breath and carefully controlled her facial features. "My boy, this is soundin' serious. I think it's 'bout time you should be tellin' someone, like your teacher. You want me to go with you?"

"No, Grandma." Stephen put the clean plate in the cupboard. "I can tell Mr. Canfield. He's bigger than Brutus. You should see him play basketball! But if Brutus ever found out I told on him, I'd be dead meat. And he always seems to find me."

"Maybe you could telephone your teacher. Brutus can't see you do that. You should always stick with a friend, too. Never go anywhere at school alone. That way if Brutus ever did anything to you, it wouldn't just be your word against his. If Mr. Canfield understands what's happenin'—I'm sure he'll help you."

Stephen nodded thoughtfully and picked up another plate to dry.

"I'll be prayin' for you, Stephen. I'll ask the good Lord to surround you with angels that excel in strength. I'll be prayin' that you'll be fully satisfied when this is over. I'll finish the dishes here. You better be makin' that phone call."

At lunch recess the next day no one paid much attention when a police car parked in front of Knowlton Elementary. Everyone was used to seeing Officer Klein and Kelly coming to the school every afternoon for D.A.R.E. classes. They were surprised, though, when he came out a few minutes later, followed by Brutus and an officer they didn't recognize. Brutus tried to jerk away from the officer, and kicked at his shins. The officers put Brutus into the back seat of the police car, and drove away.

All kinds of rumors flew around the school. Some eighth graders said Brutus had been caught selling drugs. Sandra was telling everyone he'd been framed by older high school guys who drove a Corvette. Some younger kids thought he'd smoked marijuana and flunked a drug test. One kid thought Officer Klein's dog had found drugs in his desk. None of the teachers at Knowlton Elementary would say why Brutus was taken away by the police.

The next day it was spread across the front page of the local newspaper for everyone to see. "Local Youth Arrested on Drug Charges," screamed the bold, black headline.

"It doesn't look like Brutus will be back to school," Grandma said as she showed Stephen the newspaper that evening. "I think we can praise the Lord with great joy for solving your problem."

"I know, but I'm kinda in the habit of praying for him now, Grandma."

"I don't think you have to stop just because you're satisfied he won't be botherin' you any more. I'm sure he needs your prayers more than ever now. Poor boy, it says here his mama works in a bar and his daddy is already servin' time for armed robbery up north somewhere. Why don't you come in here to my room and we'll praise the Lord for solving your problem—and ask Him to keep workin' on Brutus' problem?" The older woman put her arm around Stephen's broadening shoulders and gave her grandson a tight squeeze. "There is tremendous power in prayer, my boy—tremendous power."

2 Discussion Time

Check understanding of the story and development of personal values.

- How did Stephen feel when he saw his grandma in the car?
- What did Grandma ask him about when they were finally alone?
- What are some things you might pray about over an extended period of time?
- Talk about how long it has taken God to answer some of your prayers.
- How does Stephen feel now that he doesn't have to worry anymore about Brutus?
- What are some ways you can praise God.

A Test-Words

Name ______________________

Write each spelling word on the line as your teacher says it.

1.	escape	9.	accuse
2.	chase	10.	height
3.	prey	11.	admire
4.	arrive	12.	include
5.	shriek	13.	guys
6.	brief	14.	sole
7.	silence	15.	useless
8.	foolish	16.	soldier

Review

Lesson 12

B Test-Sentences

Write the sentences on the lines below, correcting each misspelled word, as well as all capitalization and punctuation errors. Two words are misspelled in each sentence.

it has been a deckade since we have been to maine?

1. It has been a decade since we have been to Maine.

everyone is eeger to leave on the skying trip:

2. Everyone is eager to leave on the skiing trip.

he painted the bufaloe on the plains of whyoming

3. He painted the buffalo on the plains of Wyoming.

the racoon jumped into the canoo

4. The raccoon jumped into the canoe.

73

4 Test-Sentences

Reinforce recognizing misspelled words.

Read each sentence carefully. Write the sentences on the lines in your Worktext. There are two misspelled words in each sentence. Correct each misspelled word, as well as all capitalization and punctuation errors.

Take a minute to memorize...

Psalm 63:3-5

Day 1

Review 12

3 Test-Words

Test for knowledge of the correct spellings of these words.

I will say each word once, use the word in a sentence, then say the word again. Write the words on the lines in your Worktext.

1. escape — Stephen thought there might be no **escape** from Brutus.
2. chase — He knew Brutus could **chase** him down easily.
3. prey — Stephen felt like Brutus was a lion and he was his **prey**!
4. arrive — Stephen was afraid and eager to **arrive** safely in the gym.
5. shriek — He stifled a **shriek** when Brutus grabbed him by the arm.
6. brief — For one **brief** moment, Stephen thought Brutus might hit him.
7. silence — There was an awkward **silence** after Brutus made his threat.
8. foolish — Stephen felt **foolish** and shaken after his meeting with the bully.
9. accuse — Stephen knew that Brutus would **accuse** him of telling.
10. height — Mr. Canfield suggested that Matthew put some **height** on the ball.
11. admire — The class does greatly **admire** Mr. Canfield.
12. include — Mr. Canfield is always eager to **include** all his students.
13. guys — All the **guys** would like to be tall and athletic like their teacher.
14. sole — Sometimes he is the **sole** referee at the games in the park.
15. useless — "Are my prayers **useless**?" he asked himself.
16. soldier — Stephen's grandmother is a faithful **soldier** in the Lord's army.

Review 12 Day 2

Test-Dictation

Reinforce correct spelling by using current and previous words in context.

Listen as I read each sentence, then write it in your worktext. Remember to use correct capitalization and punctuation. (Slowly read each sentence twice. Sentences are found in the student text to the right. The words **diary**, **idea**, **vein**, and **Pennsylvania** are found in this unit.)

2 Test-Proofreading

Familiarize students with standardized test format and reinforce recognizing misspelled words.

Look at each set of words. If a word is misspelled, fill in the oval by that word. If all the words are spelled correctly, fill in the oval by **no mistake**.

Review Lesson 12

C Test-Dictation

Name ____________________

Write each sentence as your teacher dictates. Use correct punctuation.

1. She will write everything in her diary.
2. It was a good idea to have our neighbor over.
3. Can you see the vein carrying the blood?
4. Take your camera to beautiful Pennsylvania.

D Test-Proofreading

If a word is misspelled, fill in the oval by that word. If all the words are spelled correctly, fill in the oval by **no mistake**.

1. ○ escape ● meater ○ chase ○ no mistake
2. ● Huwaii ○ prey ○ arrive ○ no mistake
3. ○ shriek ○ brief ● viel ○ no mistake
4. ○ silence ● aliby ○ foolish ○ no mistake
5. ○ accuse ○ height ● beyte ○ no mistake
6. ○ flamingo ○ admire ○ include ● no mistake
7. ○ guys ● doughnate ○ sole ○ no mistake
8. ● leeter ○ useless ○ soldier ○ no mistake
9. ● appeel ○ boldly ○ patrol ○ no mistake
10. ○ crater ○ view ○ relief ● no mistake
11. ○ detail ● rashio ○ contain ○ no mistake
12. ○ stereo ○ decay ● maysa ○ no mistake

74

E **Test-Table** Name ____________

If a word is misspelled, fill in the space on the grid.

voltige	iglue	iowa	strae
Asia	debate	creep	Ohio
louiziana	istate	recitle	truely
tomb	tullip	studio	crew

Stephen Prayer Journal

Review

Lesson 12

F **Writing Assessment**

Write what you think Stephen might have written in his prayer journal when he returned to his room after drying the dishes with his grandma.

Scripture

Psalm 63:3-5

75

A rubric for scoring is provided in Appendix B.

I is the most commonly spoken word in English, followed by YOU, THE, and A.

Word Wow!

1 Test-Table

Test mastery of words in this unit.

If a word is misspelled, fill in the space on the grid.

2 Writing Assessment

Assess student's spelling, grammar, and composition skills through personal writing.

- What do you think would cause someone to be a bully? (Students may suggest: home environment, lack of good role models, dissatisfaction with size, low self-esteem, desire to dominate, wish to have own way, or perception of unfairness)
- What did Grandma think Stephen should do about Brutus? (Call and tell Mr. Canfield what was happening.)
- When Grandma told Stephen why Brutus had been arrested, how did Stephen feel? (He was relieved but also thought he'd keep praying for him.)

1 Test-Sentences

Reinforce recognizing misspelled words.

Read each sentence carefully. Write the sentences on the lines in your Worktext, correcting each misspelled word, as well as all capitalization and punctuation errors.

Review Lesson 12

G Test-Sentences Name ________________

Write the sentences on the lines below. Correct each misspelled word, as well as all capitalization and punctuation errors. Two words are misspelled in each sentence.

we plan to visit a mackro gyser in this state park?

1. We plan to visit a macro geyser in this state park.

he held up his sheald and began to weild his sword

2. He held up his shield and began to wield his sword.

the peice of cake was moist and had great flaver

3. The piece of cake was moist and had great flavor!

the ship took the cargoe to a small ile nearby

4. The ship took the cargo to a small isle nearby.

H Test-Words

Write each spelling word on the line as your teacher says it.

1. boldly	9. deceit
2. patrol	10. minor
3. view	11. liar
4. relief	12. wife
5. detail	13. guide
6. contain	14. control
7. stereo	15. confuse
8. decay	16. future

76

2 Test-Words

Test for knowledge of the correct spellings of these words.

I will say the word once, use the word in a sentence, then say the word again. Write the word on the lines in your Worktext.

1.	boldly	"You've got to keep comin' **boldly** before the Lord," said Grandma.
2.	patrol	No one was surprised to see the **patrol** car parked in front of the school.
3.	view	The kids crowded around the window to get a **view** of Brutus.
4.	relief	Stephen felt a great **relief** when the officer took Brutus away.
5.	detail	The next morning's newspaper told every **detail** of Brutus' arrest.
6.	contain	The story did **contain** a lot of details Stephen didn't know.
7.	stereo	The police found a **stereo** and other expensive things in Brutus' house.
8.	decay	Brutus' teacher had noticed an even greater **decay** in his attitude.
9.	deceit	He regularly practiced **deceit** with his mom and his teachers.
10.	minor	Since Brutus is a **minor**, it was not clear what charges would be pressed.
11.	liar	The newspaper described his dad as a **liar** and a thief.
12.	wife	It said his **wife**, Brutus' mother, worked in a bar.
13.	guide	Neither his dad nor his mom has been a good **guide** for him.
14.	control	Brutus has never given God **control** of his life.
15.	confuse	It was easy for Brutus to **confuse** having things with having security.
16.	future	"We need to be prayin' for Brutus and his **future**," encouraged Grandma.

I **Test-Editing** Name ____________

If a word is spelled correctly, fill in the oval under **Correct**. If the word is misspelled, fill in the oval under **Incorrect**, and spell the word correctly on the blank.

	Correct	Incorrect	
1. labor	●	○	
2. reveel	○	●	reveal
3. porto reeco	○	●	Puerto Rico
4. Tennessee	●	○	
5. vetoes	●	○	
6. diet	●	○	
7. reiut	○	●	riot
8. idahoe	○	●	Idaho
9. banjo	●	○	
10. inrole	○	●	enroll
11. portfolio	●	○	
12. cue	●	○	
13. flu	●	○	
14. doone	○	●	dune
15. funral	○	●	funeral
16. massechusettes	○	●	Massachusetts
17. Utah	●	○	
18. dome	●	○	
19. Oklahoma	●	○	
20. Minnisoda	○	●	Minnesota

Review Lesson 12

77

3 Test-Editing

Reinforce recognizing and correcting misspelled words.

4 Action Game

Reinforce spelling skills and provide motivation and interest.

Day 4

Review 12

Materials

- masking tape
- two 9 x 13 inch pans of damp sand
- word list on certificate at end of unit

SAND RELAY

Divide the class into two teams. Mark a line on the floor and line each team up behind that line. Place two containers of sand a few yards on the other side of the line. Choose a team leader for each team. Each team leader holds a list of spelling words to be reviewed and stands by his or her team's sand. When you give the signal to begin, the first player from each team runs to the sand where his or her team leader will say a spelling word. The player will write the word in the sand while the team leader checks the spelling. If the word is misspelled the player is given a different word to spell. If the word is spelled correctly, the player runs back to the line. When the player crosses the line, the next player runs to the sand to spell a word. The first team to finish wins!

Game

Reinforce spelling skills and provide motivation and interest.

Materials

- game page (from student text)
- colored pencils (1 per child)
- game word list

Game Word List

Check off each word lightly in pencil as it is used.

Stephen's Team

1. **meter**
2. **Hawaii**
3. **veil**
4. **alibi**
5. **byte**
6. **flamingo**
7. **donate**
8. **liter**
9. **appeal**

Officer Klein's Team

1. **crater**
2. **ratio**
3. **mesa**
4. **voltage**
5. **Asia**
6. **Louisiana**
7. **tomb**
8. **igloo**
9. **debate**

Mr. Canfield's Team

1. **estate**
2. **tulip**
3. **Iowa**
4. **creep**
5. **recital**
6. **studio**
7. **stray**
8. **Ohio**
9. **truly**

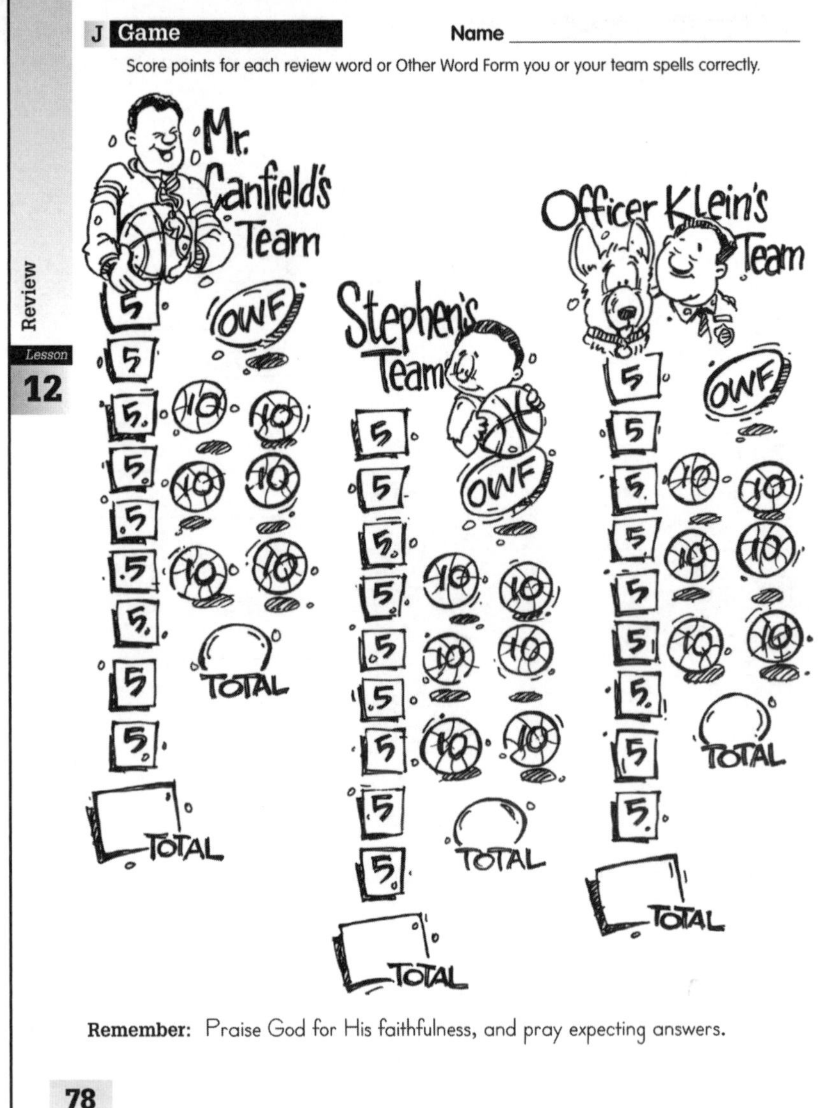

How to Play:

- Divide the class into three teams. Name one team **Stephen's Team**, one **Officer Klein's Team**, and one **Mr. Canfield's Team**. (Option: You may wish to seat students in groups of three, each student from a different team. They should share one game page.)
- Have a student from the first team go to the board.
- Say the spelling word.
- Have the student write the word on the board.
- If the word is spelled correctly, have each team member color a point symbol by his/her team name. If the word is misspelled, have him/her put an **X** through one point symbol. That word may not be given again.
- Repeat this process with the second team and then the third.
- When the words from all three lists have been used, the team with the most points is the winner.
- Play another round using Other Word Forms.

Date ______________________

This certificate is awarded to

____

for completing fun activities using the following spelling words!

Asia	appeal	admire	banjo	accuse
chase	brief	alibi	boldly	canoe
contain	creep	arrive	buffalo	confuse
crater	deceit	byte	cargo	crew
debate	eager	diary	control	cue
decade	Hawaii	diet	dome	dune
decay	idea	geyser	donate	flu
detail	liter	guide	enroll	foolish
escape	Louisiana	guys	flamingo	funeral
estate	meter	height	macro	future
flavor	piece	Idaho	Minnesota	igloo
labor	Puerto Rico	Iowa	Oklahoma	include
Maine	relief	isle	patrol	Massachusetts
mesa	reveal	liar	portfolio	raccoon
Pennsylvania	shield	minor	soldier	tomb
prey	shriek	Ohio	sole	truly
ratio	skiing	recital	stereo	tulip
stray	Tennessee	riot	studio	useless
veil	vetoes	silence	voltage	Utah
vein	wield	wife	Wyoming	view

Certificate

Provide an opportunity for parents or guardians to encourage and assess their child's progress.

Fill in today's date and your name on your certificate.

Take a minute to memorize...

Psalm 63:3-5

3 Letter

Provide the parent or guardian with the spelling word lists for the next unit.

Give your parents or guardian this letter that lists your spelling words for the next unit. Put it where you will remember to practice the words together.

Dear Parent,

We are about to begin a new spelling unit containing five weekly lessons. A set of twenty words will be studied each week. All the words will be reviewed in the sixth week. Values based on the Scriptures listed below will be taught in each lesson.

Lesson 13	Lesson 14	Lesson 15	Lesson 16	Lesson 17
Alabama	adopt	Antarctica	aerobics	aisle
Colorado	atomic	argument	area	aspire
combat	borrow	Arkansas	Arizona	biceps
gallon	bottom	artery	aware	climate
gallop	college	artichoke	barracks	combine
gather	colonies	bargain	barren	compile
Indiana	comment	cardiac	barrier	coyote
inhabit	commerce	cartilage	caramel	crime
mammal	compost	carton	compare	crisis
Nevada	concentrate	chart	Delaware	decline
New Hampshire	contact	compartment	embarrassed	device
perhaps	continent	dart	librarian	dining
random	conversation	department	marriage	entice
rascal	crocodile	harbor	narrate	eyeing
savanna	demolish	hardship	narrow	fiery
scallop	deposit	harmony	Ontario	haiku
soprano	doctor	hearty	parakeet	iceberg
static	geometry	partner	parallel	imply
valley	glossary	radar	prepare	migrant
valve	Wisconsin	snarl	software	pride
Psalm 119:29,30	Psalm 127:1	Psalm 98:7	Psalm 57:10	Psalm 18:30

1 **Literature Connection**

Topic: Doing the right thing

Theme Text: Psalm 119:29, 30

Lost in Space

Christopher gets a new computer program and finds out that doing right may not mean just avoiding wrong.

Mr. Wright caught the sales clerk's attention. "Excuse me, sir. Do you carry the latest version of Tax Manager?"

"I believe that's in. Just a moment, please, and I'll check."

Christopher wandered over to a display of game software while his dad rested an elbow on the checkout counter to wait for the clerk. Some of the learning games looked familiar, such as *Somewhere in Time* and *Reading Roundup*. Some of the other games looked kind of creepy, such as *Absolute Annihilation*. Why would anyone want to destroy the world, anyway—even a virtual world?

Then he spotted it. *Masteroid!* Christopher grabbed the shiny black box with the gleaming, streamlined space vehicle in 3-D on the front. "Dad, the Hugheses have got this program. It's fantastic! Jared and I played when we were over at their house last week. May I buy it?"

"Let's see that." Mr. Wright turned the box over and read the description of the game. "Hmmm. Choose from six spaceships or design your own…32 missions…Unexpected challenges….

"I apologize for the wait, sir." The sales clerk rushed back over. "Would you prefer the CD-ROM or disk version of Tax Manager 4.0?" He placed two cartons on the counter in front of Mr. Wright.

"CD-ROM." Mr. Wright tapped one of the boxes.

"Will that be all, sir?" The clerk began ringing up the sale.

"No, we'll take this as well." Dad handed the Masteroid box to the clerk and turned to his son, "You'll have to teach me how to play it sometime."

"All right!" Christopher raised a hand and gave his dad a high five. "It's a really great game! You'll see."

"Christopher, come play with me." Six-year-old Cory leaned on the back of Christopher's computer chair.

Christopher's eyes never left the screen in front of him. "Not now, Cory." He shrugged his little brother's hands off his shoulders.

"But I haven't had anyone to play with all day while you guys were at school." Cory leaned over the chair to look up into his big brother's face.

"Cory! Get out of the way! I'm right in the middle of this *Stars End* mission!" Christopher's fingers worked the controls rapidly. He didn't notice when Cory finally gave up and left the room.

One afternoon later that week, Mrs. Wright called to her son, "Christopher, we're going for a walk since it's such nice weather. Want to go with us?"

"Not right now, Mom." Christopher took evasive action to avoid having his Starship pulled into a gravitational field. "I'm busy!"

A few days later, Cathy, Christopher's nine-year-old sister, popped her head around the door. "Christopher, come play *Sorry!*®, with us."

Christopher just shook his head while he checked the fuel levels of his Space Ranger and judged the distance to the next planetary settlement.

"Christopher, come on!" Cathy persisted, "Cory and Kristin and I all want to play *Sorry!*®, and it's a lot more fun with four people. Pleeeeeze?"

"Sorry, but I said no!" Christopher changed his speed and watched carefully for enemy craft in this sector. "Can't you see I'm already playing a game?"

"Of course!" Cathy tossed her head. "That's hard to miss. You've been playing that silly computer game constantly for two weeks!"

"Christopher, it's for you!" Mrs. Wright handed the cordless phone to her son where he sat at the computer and went on toward the laundry room with her load of wash.

"Hello?" Christopher hit F2 to pause the *Masteroid* game. "Hey, Jared!" He greeted his friend with enthusiasm. "Guess what? I'm already on level 12!… Yeah, the special effects are great!… Really?… Awesome!… Just a minute, let me ask my mom." Christopher hopped up to find his mother, taking the phone with him. "Yeah, that one almost caught me off guard on level 5…Did you manage to make it through sector seven-zero?… Oh, just a sec!"

Christopher dropped the phone from his ear when he arrived in the laundry room. "Mom, can I go to the mall with the Hughes family this afternoon?"

Mrs. Wright scooped the last few fresh-smelling items out of the dryer and stood up. "Probably. Let me talk to Jared's mom for a minute and we'll see."

"Hey, Jared!" Christopher spoke into the phone. "Did you hear that?… Yeah, she wants to talk to your mom first, but I can probably go…Okay! See you soon." Christopher handed the phone over to his mom and rushed back to finish his *Masteroid* game before the Hugheses came to pick him up.

"Check this out, Chris." Jared and Christopher stopped in front of an eye-catching display in the software store. "*Masteroid II: The Next Generation* is out!"

"Amazing! Look at this," Christopher pointed to the list of capabilities and new

Story (continued)

challenges the next version of the game provided. "Awesome! I'm gonna get this."

"Dad said he'd take us to the arcade as soon as he was done looking here. Why don't you wait till afterwards to get it?" Jared suggested. "That way you won't have to worry about hanging on to a package while you're playing. Remember that *Space Chasers* game I told you about? They have it at this arcade. It is INCREDIBLE!"

Christopher was ready. "Let's go!"

"Let's see if Dad's done!"

The next evening, Kristin frowned at the wrong answer she'd just written in her spelling book. "Christopher, let me use your eraser."

"Use your own." Christopher propped his elbow on the kitchen table and rested his chin in his hand.

"The eraser is worn off this pencil." Kristin held it up for her twin to see.

"Well, go get another one." Christopher waved his sister away with one hand. "I'm busy and I shouldn't have to do everything for you."

"That's it!" Kristin slapped the pencil down on the table. "You're always busy and you never do anything for anyone anymore!"

Christopher frowned. "What're you talking about?"

"This!" Kristin thumped the spelling book in front of her. "Remember this Scripture?"

"Yeah," Christopher shrugged. "So?"

"Then you know it says you should obey and not do anything wrong. Don't you think spending your life playing *Masteroid* is wrong?" Kristin demanded.

"Of course not!" Christopher shook his head and rolled his eyes. "It's not all bloody and gross or satanic or anything! It's just a really great game!"

"Well, this Scripture says to 'keep me far from every wrong' not just 'keep me from doing wrong.'" Kristin stood up and brushed her hair back behind her ear. "It seems to me you're not far from being addicted to that kind of game. You've spent every spare minute for the last two weeks playing it. You spent all your money playing some space game in the arcade. That was what—$30? On one afternoon at the arcade?"

Kristin shook her head, still fuming at her twin. "You don't play with Cory, or Cathy, or me. You rush through your homework and chores. You barely answer when someone talks to you." Kristin ticked each item off on her fingers. "You didn't even want to take time to talk to Dad on the phone when he called from LA! Seems to me that computer game is all you care about. Maybe it's not violent or evil, but it's sure taken over your whole life."

Kristin walked a few steps toward the door, then turned back. "It may not be wrong—but it can't be far from it."

"Sisters!" Christopher muttered as she disappeared down the hall. "Now, where was I?" He ran his finger down the page of his book till he found where he'd been. "The desert was so still," Christopher read aloud. "Silence. Silence all around. Johnny could hear himself breathing. But what was that? A soft hiss…."

Christopher lapsed into silent reading when Kristin came back with an eraser. When he finished the story, Christopher picked up his pencil to write the report Mr. Canfield had assigned, but he couldn't remember what the story was about! Instead of the desert adventure he'd been reading about, his head was filled with scenes from *Masteroid*!

Christopher shook his head, trying to clear it of space vehicles. "Uh, Kristin?" He grinned sheepishly when his twin looked up. "Maybe you had a good point. When this homework's done, you want to go shoot some baskets or something before dark?"

2 Discussion Time

Check understanding of the story and development of personal values.

- What was Christopher's dad looking for at the software store?
- What game did he get for Christopher?
- What did Christopher do when Cory wanted to play with him?
- What did Christopher do when the family went for a walk?
- What did Christopher do when Cathy, Kristin, and Cory wanted him to play Sorry!®?
- How much money did Christopher spend playing video games at the arcade in the mall?
- Is it wrong to spend all your time doing one thing, even if that thing isn't a bad thing?

A Preview

Name ______________

Write each word as your teacher says it.

1. soprano
2. Nevada
3. scallop
4. Alabama
5. gather
6. Colorado
7. random
8. valve
9. inhabit
10. gallon
11. combat
12. Indiana
13. valley
14. mammal
15. New Hampshire
16. savanna
17. static
18. perhaps
19. rascal
20. gallop

SIGH!

Words with /a/

Lesson 13

Scripture

Psalm 119: 29,30

81

3 Preview

Test for knowledge of the correct spellings of these words.

Customize Your List

On a separate sheet of paper, additional words of your choice may be tested.

I will say each word once, use the word in a sentence, then say the word again. Write the words on the lines in your Worktext.

Correct Immediately!

Let's correct our Preview. I will spell each word out loud. If you spelled a word incorrectly, rewrite it correctly.

Progress Chart

Students may record scores. (Reproducible master provided in Appendix B.)

Day 1

Lesson 13

1. **soprano** — Kristin practices the **soprano** part of the choral arrangement.
2. **Nevada** — The new choir director from **Nevada** thinks Kristin has a real talent.
3. **scallop** — She plans to take a **scallop** shell to school when they discuss marine life.
4. **Alabama** — She found it on a beach in **Alabama** while they were on vacation last summer.
5. **gather** — Kristin was able to **gather** many beautiful shells that day.
6. **Colorado** — Christopher's cousin in **Colorado** e-mailed him about the new computer game.
7. **random** — Selecting Masteroid was not a **random** choice.
8. **valve** — "I need to go by the auto supply store for a new **valve**," said his dad.
9. **inhabit** — "Earn 1000 points if you **inhabit** Mars within 48 hours," Christopher read.
10. **gallon** — He received points for each **gallon** of fuel he conserved on a mission.
11. **combat** — The **combat** mode of the game was really exciting!
12. **Indiana** — "I'd love to go to **Indiana** to meet the team that wrote this game," he exclaimed.
13. **valley** — The goal of the next mission was to attack a station in a **valley** on Venus.
14. **mammal** — "Which **mammal** did you decide to research for your paper?" she asked.
15. **New Hampshire** — "Something that lives in **New Hampshire**," was his rude remark.
16. **savanna** — "Or maybe something that lives on a **savanna** on Pluto," he snickered.
17. **static** — "Do you have a channel I can talk to you on that's not all **static**?" asked Kristin.
18. **perhaps** — "**Perhaps** you shouldn't spend all your spare time in front of the computer!"
19. **rascal** — Christopher knew he was being a **rascal** and ignoring his family.
20. **gallop** — Kristin laughed when Christopher began to **gallop** around the driveway.

4 Word Shapes

Help students form a correct image of whole words.

Look at each word and think about its shape. Now, write the word in the correct word Shape Boxes. You may check off each word as you use it.

(Short vowels are usually found in syllables in which a vowel is immediately preceded and followed by a consonant, consonant cluster, or digraph.)

In the word shape boxes, fill in the boxes containing the letter or letters that spell the sound of **/a/** in each word.

Take a minute to memorize...

Psalm 119: 29,30

Lesson **13** | Day 1

Words with /a/ — Lesson 13

B Word Shapes Name ______________________

Using the word bank below, write each word in the correct word shape boxes. Next, in the word shape boxes, fill in the boxes containing the letter or letters that spell the sound of **/a/** in each word.

1. New Hampshire
2. Colorado
3. Nevada
4. mammal
5. savanna
6. static
7. Indiana
8. scallop
9. Alabama
10. gallon
11. gallop
12. valley
13. valve
14. soprano
15. combat
16. rascal
17. gather
18. inhabit
19. random
20. perhaps

Word Bank

Alabama	gallop	mammal	random	soprano
Colorado	gather	Nevada	rascal	static
combat	Indiana	New Hampshire	savanna	valley
gallon	inhabit	perhaps	scallop	valve

82

Answers may vary for duplicate word shapes.

Be Prepared For Fun

Check these supply lists for **Fun Ways to Spell** - presented **Day 2**.
Purchase and/or gather these items ahead of time!

General
- Pencil
- Graph Paper (1 sheet per child)
- Spelling List

Auditory
- Voice Recorder
- Spelling List

Visual
- American Sign Language reproducible master (provided in Appendix B)
- Spelling List

Tactile
- Soccer Ball, Basketball, Tennis Ball, or 4-Square Ball
- Spelling List

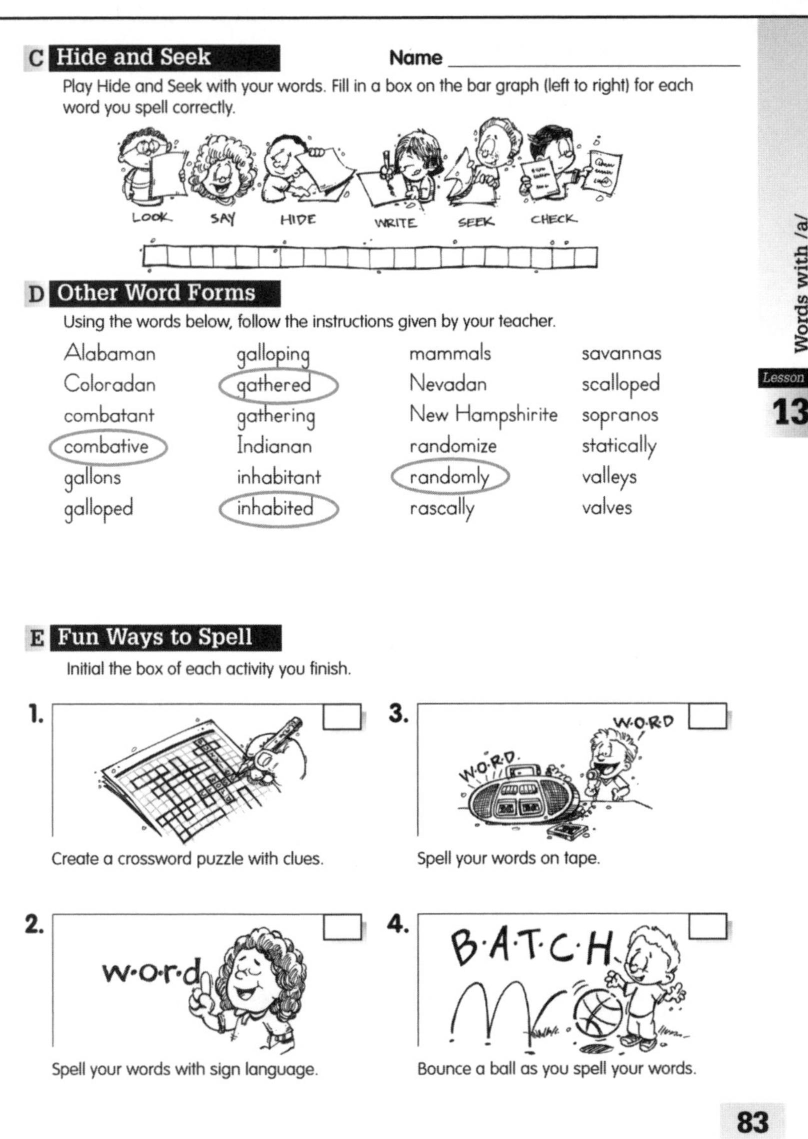

C Hide and Seek Name ____________________

Play Hide and Seek with your words. Fill in a box on the bar graph (left to right) for each word you spell correctly.

D Other Word Forms

Using the words below, follow the instructions given by your teacher.

Alabaman	galloping	mammals	savannas
Coloradan	(gathered)	Nevadan	scalloped
combatant	gathering	New Hampshirite	sopranos
(combative)	Indianan	randomize	statically
gallons	inhabitant	(randomly)	valleys
galloped	(inhabited)	rascally	valves

E Fun Ways to Spell

Initial the box of each activity you finish.

1. Create a crossword puzzle with clues.

2. Spell your words with sign language.

3. Spell your words on tape.

4. Bounce a ball as you spell your words.

Words with /a/

Lesson 13

83

1 Hide and Seek

Reinforce spelling by using multiple styles of learning.

On a white board, Teacher writes each word — one at a time. **Have students:**

- **Look** at the word.
- **Say** the word out loud.
- **Spell** the word out loud.
- **Hide** (teacher erases word.)
- **Write** the word on paper.
- **Seek** (teacher rewrites word.)
- **Check** spelling. If incorrect, rewrite word correctly.

2 Other Word Forms

This activity is optional. Have students find and circle the Other Word Forms that are antonyms of the following:

peaceful
dispersed
intentionally
deserted

3 Fun Ways to Spell

Four activities are provided. Use one, two, three, or all of the activities. Have students initial the box for each activity they complete.

Options:

- assign activities to students according to their learning styles
- set up the activities in learning centers for the students to do throughout the day
- divide students into four groups and assign one activity per group
- do one activity per day

General

To create a crossword puzzle...
- Use a pencil to arrange your words on graph paper.
- Overlap words where letters are shared.
- Don't create any new words.
- Outline each word with a marker and number it.
- Write a clue for each word.
- Erase your words.
- Trade with a classmate and work each other's puzzles.

Auditory

To spell your words using a voice recorder...
- Record yourself as you say and spell each word on your spelling list.
- Listen to your recording and check your spelling.

Visual

To spell your words with sign language...
- Have a classmate read a spelling word to you from the list.
- Spell the word using the American Sign Language alphabet.
- Do this with each word on your list.

Tactile

To bounce a ball as you spell your words...
- Look at the first word on your list.
- Bounce the ball as you say each letter of the word aloud.
- Do this with each word on your list.

1 Working with Words

Familiarize students with word meaning and usage.

Drawing Conclusions

Explain that to figure something out using logic is to draw a conclusion. On the board write:

You are using a tool to make holes in wood. You are probably using a ____________.

Have a volunteer supply the word **drill**.

Complete each conclusion by writing a word from the word bank. You may use a dictionary to help you.

Take a minute to memorize...

Psalm 119: 29,30

F Working with Words Name ____________________

Drawing Conclusions

Complete each conclusion by writing a word from the word bank.

1. You choose by saying "Eeny, Meeny, Miny, Moe." You choose at random.
2. You hear noise on your cell phone. You may have static.
3. A singer has a high voice. She probably sings soprano.
4. You are moving to Concord. You may be going to New Hampshire.
5. You live in a house. This means you inhabit it.
6. You are in a state whose name means "reddish-colored." You are in Colorado.
7. A farm girl has gone out to collect eggs. She will gather them.
8. That baby animal is drinking milk from its mother. It is a mammal.
9. Your dad brought home a jug of milk. He probably bought a gallon.
10. A gazelle is grazing on grass. It is probably on the savanna.
11. The soldiers are digging trenches. They are about to enter combat.
12. One student is very mischievous. He could be considered a rascal.
13. We camped in a low place between two mountains. We were in a valley.
14. One state is called "The Heart of Dixie." It is the state of Alabama.
15. You think you possibly might do something. You think perhaps you might.
16. Your horse is running fast. He is probably going at a gallop.
17. You may want to visit the midwest state nicknamed "The Hoosier State." You may want to visit Indiana.
18. He closed something to keep the liquid flowing in the right direction. He closed a valve.
19. You will be driving through Las Vegas to get to Hoover Dam. You will be in the state of Nevada.
20. You cut a fancy rounded edge on your Valentine. You may have cut a scallop.

Word Bank

Alabama	gallop	mammal	random	soprano
Colorado	gather	Nevada	rascal	static
combat	Indiana	New Hampshire	savanna	valley
gallon	inhabit	perhaps	scallop	valve

84

G Dictation Name ______________

Write each sentence as your teacher dictates. Use correct punctuation.

1. Christopher set the controls as his astronaut flew over the combat field.
2. Christopher read about several kinds of mammals that inhabit Colorado.
3. Perhaps Dad will take us to the store to get that game.

Words with /a/

Lesson 13

H Proofreading

If a word is misspelled, fill in the oval by that word. If all the words are spelled correctly, fill in the oval by **no mistake**.

1.	○ inhabit	● Colorado	○ igloo	○ no mistake
2.	● nevada	○ include	○ foolish	○ no mistake
3.	● gallun	○ gallop	○ tulip	○ no mistake
4.	○ valley	○ valve	○ raccoon	● no mistake
5.	○ Alabama	○ useless	● scallup	○ no mistake
6.	● mammel	○ New Hampshire	○ accuse	○ no mistake
7.	○ Indiana	● randum	○ Utah	○ no mistake
8.	● sevanna	○ gather	○ crew	○ no mistake
9.	○ perhaps	○ cue	● sopranoe	○ no mistake
10.	● rasckal	○ flu	○ view	○ no mistake
11.	● combatt	○ truly	○ tomb	○ no mistake
12.	○ future	● statick	○ confuse	○ no mistake

85

1 Dictation

Reinforce correct spelling by using current and previous words in context.

Listen as I read each sentence and then write it in your Worktext. Remember to use correct capitalization and punctuation. (Slowly read each sentence twice. Sentences are found in the Student Worktext to the left.)

2 Proofreading

Familiarize students with standardized test format and reinforce recognition of misspelled words.

Look at each set of words. If a word is misspelled, fill in the oval by that word. If all the words are spelled correctly, fill in the oval by **no mistake**.

3 Hide and Seek

Reinforce correct spelling of current spelling words. Repeat this activity from Day 2.

4 Vocabulary Extension

Have your students complete this activity to strengthen spelling ability and expand vocabulary. The reproducible master is provided in Appendix A as shown on the inset page to the right.

1 Posttest

Test mastery of the spelling words.

I will say the word once, use it in a sentence, then say it again. Write your words on a separate sheet of paper.

Progress Chart

Students may record scores. (Reproducible master in Appendix B.)

Personal Dictionary

Students may add any words they have misspelled to their personal dictionaries for reference when writing. (Cover in Appendix B.)

Vocabulary Extension | Lesson 13

Hide and Seek

Play Hide and Seek with your words. Fill in a bar graph (left to right) for each word you spell correctly.

Vocabulary Extension

Crossword Puzzle

Use the clues below to complete the puzzle.

Down

1. questionnaire, test
3. pass blood into a vein of someone
4. done with extraordinary skill
5. catastrophe, misfortune
6. tenderness, mercy
7. six-pointed star
9. insufficient, imperfect

Across

2. writing or printing in uppercase letters
5. immature, juvenile
8. contentment, happiness
10. display, show
11. scarf, tissue

Word Bank

accident	capitalization	handkerchief	pageant
adolescent	compassion	inadequate	satisfaction
asterisk	examination	masterpiece	transfusion

335

1.	soprano	Kristin is learning to sing **soprano** in the school choir.
2.	Nevada	The new music director is from **Nevada.**
3.	New Hampshire	The choir may compete in a choral competition in **New Hampshire.**
4.	mammal	Kristin and Christopher each have a report to prepare about a **mammal.**
5.	gather	"Did you **gather** any of the information you need for your paper?" she asked.
6.	random	Christopher did not choose Masteriod at **random.**
7.	combat	He had heard the **combat** mode was awesome.
8.	Colorado	Even Christopher's cousin in **Colorado** said the game was terrific.
9.	Alabama	The sales clerk had worked at a computer store in **Alabama.**
10.	inhabit	The instructions on the screen read, "Conquer and **inhabit** Mars."
11.	valley	He felt as if he were really guiding his spaceship through a **valley** on Venus.
12.	savanna	Finding the hidden base in a **savanna** on Saturn was the next mission.
13.	Indiana	The team that wrote the computer game is located in **Indiana.**
14.	scallop	Kristin has a **scallop** shell she found on the beach during vacation.
15.	valve	This marine mollusk has not one **valve,** but two.
16.	static	"Talking to you is like being on a cell phone with a lot of **static,**" Kristin frowned.
17.	rascal	After Kristin's reprimand, Christopher realized he had been a **rascal.**
18.	perhaps	"I have, **perhaps,** been a little consumed with the computer game," he said.
19.	gallop	He liked to **gallop** around the driveway to make his sister laugh.
20.	gallon	After a game of one on one, he felt like he could drink a **gallon** of water.

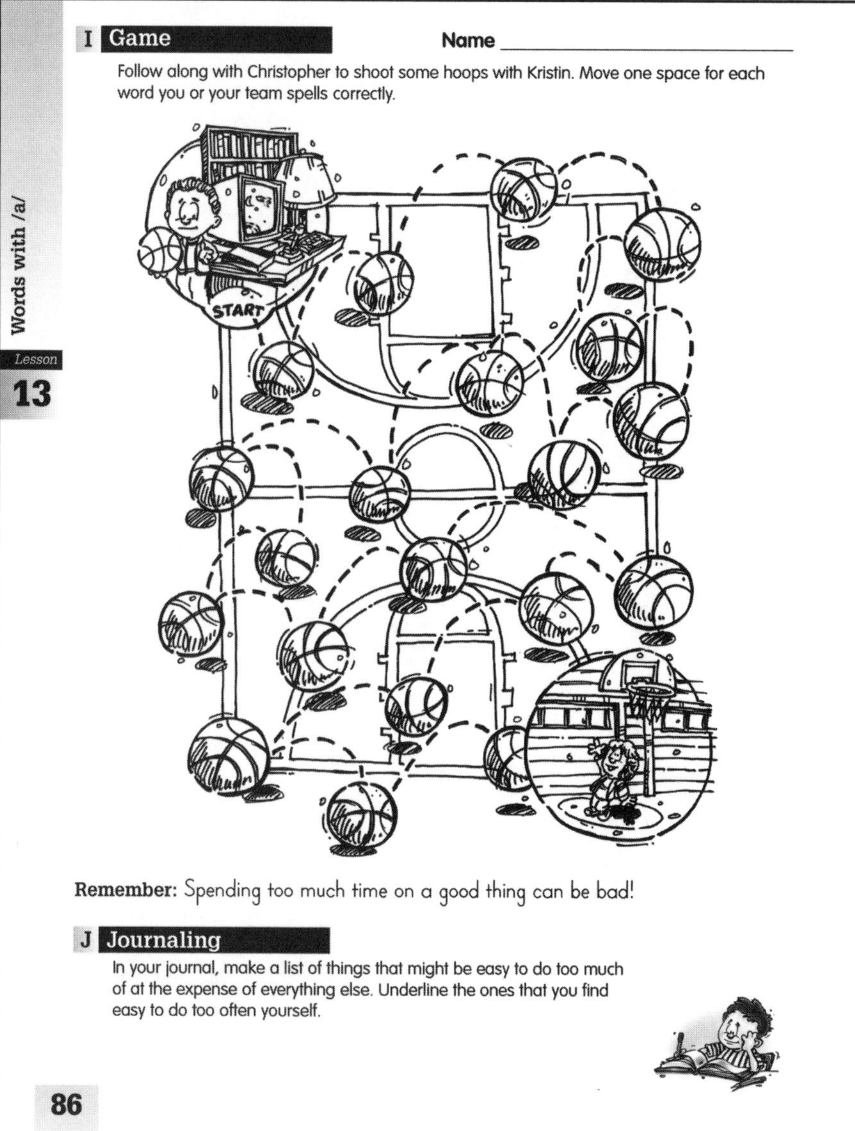

2 Game

Reinforce spelling skills and provide motivation and interest.

Materials

- game page (from student text)
- game pieces (1 per child)
- game word list

Game Word List

1. **inhabit**
2. **Colorado**
3. **Nevada**
4. **gallon**
5. **gallop**
6. **valley**
7. **valve**
8. **scallop**
9. **Alabama**
10. **mammal**
11. **New Hampshire**
12. **Indiana**
13. **random**
14. **savanna**
15. **soprano**
16. **perhaps**
17. **rascal**
18. **gather**
19. **combat**
20. **static**

How to Play:

- Divide the class into two teams.
- Have each student place his/her game piece on Start.
- Have a student from team A go to the board.
- Say the spelling word.
- Have the student write the word on the board.
- If correct, instruct each member of team A to move his/her game piece forward one space.
- Alternate between teams A and B.
- The team to reach Kristin at the basketball goal first is the winner.
- **Small Group Option**: Students may play this game without teacher direction in small groups of two or more.

3 Journaling

Provide a meaningful reason for correct spelling through personal writing.

Review the story using discussion leads provided on the following page. Encourage students to apply the Scriptural value in their journaling.

Journaling (continued)

- Have you ever played Nintendo®, or some other computer game? (Allow time to share experiences.)
- What kind of things did Christopher's Masteroid game include? (Choosing or designing space ships and flying them through challenging missions.)
- Was it a bad game, violent or satanic? (No.)
- What was the problem with Christopher playing it, then? (He played it all the time and didn't do anything else.)
- Can you think of some other things that might be easy to do too much? (Sports, TV, reading, etc.—even talking on the phone!)

The most commonly used words in written English, according to the 1971 American Heritage Word Frequency Book are: the, of, and, a, to, in, is, you, that, it, he, for, was, on, are, as, with, his, they, at, be, this, from, I, have, or, by, one, had, not, but, what, all, were, when, we, there, can, an, your, which, their, said, if, do.

Word Wow!

Tony in Training

Tony painfully determines to learn more about the limitations of the mentally challenged and resolves to work on his predjudice.

"Mr. Canfield is unbelievable! Is there any sport he isn't good at?" Tony watched his teacher sprint down the track. "He's fast! So far this year, he's been good at everything. Do you think he plays baseball too?"

"Probably," Stephen smiled. "He's awesome."

"Let's stretch before you do any running," Mr. Canfield said as he stood in front of the class and jogged in place. "Toe touches! Everybody reach for your right toe. No bouncing. Hold it right there. One, two, three, four, five, six, seven, eight, nine and ten. Now reach for your left toe. Hold it! One, two....

"Are you going to run in the Turkey Trot to help raise money for the mentally-messed-up-mongoloids?" Stephen looked through his legs at Tony.

"You mean the retards at the Cole County Sunshine School?" Tony laughed.

"Yeah!" Stephen smirked.

Tony touched the top of his running shoes with the palms of his hands. "I've been practicing. Five miles is long way to run for retards, but Grandma wants me to enter. She's already paid the registration fee."

"I bet Mr. Canfield wins!" Stephen stretched toward the ground between his toes.

"Is he entering?"

"That's what I heard him telling Mrs. Bently in the office this morning."

"No wonder he's been running every night at Mason Springs Park! He must be getting ready for the Turkey Trot." Tony straightened his back and reached for the sky. "Maybe he'd give me some training tips."

Tony fell in step beside Mr. Canfield as they returned to the classroom after PE. "What are you doing to get ready for the Turkey Trot, Mr. Canfield?"

The teacher looked down and smiled at Tony's eagerness. "Well I'm drinking lots of water, getting plenty of sleep, and eating a balanced diet. I've been running a couple miles every night, too." He playfully punched Tony's shoulder. "You gonna run?"

"Aren't the kids at the Sunshine School like—one brick short of a load?" Tommy interrupted.

"Thorny says they're a bubble off plumb," Daniel laughed.

Tony nodded. "I don't know if I can run the whole five miles. My grandma thinks it's a good idea to help the retar... um...mentally challenged. She's been helping me line up sponsors."

"Why? You mentally challenged?" Stephen joked.

"No! She says serving others is the only way to happiness."

Mr. Canfield smiled, "Smart lady."

"Winning would make me happy," Tony declared.

Tommy laughed and gave the smaller boy a playful shove.

After supper that evening Tony put on his jacket. "I'm going to wait for Mr. Canfield on the front steps, Grandma." He whispered to himself, "I hope he runs tonight."

"Don't you want some ice cream, Tony?" Grandma asked.

"No, 'cause I'm in training for the Turkey Trot. Ice cream will clog my system," Tony said as he ran out the door. He sat down on the grass in the front yard to do warm-up stretches while he watched for Mr. Canfield. He'd just about given up when he saw his teacher's black compact car round the corner. He sprinted across the street and skidded to a stop as the car pulled to the curb.

Mr. Canfield kissed his wife, then hopped out of the car. He stuck his head back inside, "Get me in half an hour, Hon? I'll meet you here." He slammed the car door and waved to the two kids in the back seat as his wife pulled away from the curb. "I love you," he mouthed.

"Well, hi, Tony." The big man looked down at his student and slung an arm across his shoulders. "Are you here to train with me?"

Tony looked over his shoulder at the little car. "I didn't know you had two kids."

"Yup! J.J. will be seven this year and Jessica is five. You ready?"

"I've seen Jessica at school, but J.J. doesn't go to Knowlton Elementary does he?"

"Nope." Jason Canfield sprinted down the trail.

Tony ran to catch up. All his energy focused on matching his teacher's pace, and soon he was breathing too hard to ask any of the questions popping into his head.

After the first mile Tony was dragging. "I gotta quit. You're fast," he panted.

"Why don't you walk a lap and then see how you feel? If you're up to it, jog the third mile at your own pace. Then walk until you cool down. Jogging up a hill would help build your leg muscles and increase your endurance, too. Relax, do your best, and leave it with the Lord!" Mr. Canfield waved as he took off on his second lap around the park.

After finishing the third mile, Tony trudged up the steps of the duplex and gulped down three tall glasses of water. "Grandma, does Mama still have some of those high-protein drinks?"

"I don't think so, unless they're in the pantry. I'll check."

"Grandma, where are those ankle weights Mama used in her aerobics class?"

Story (continued)

"Probably out in the garage somewhere, Tony-O." Grandma wiped her hands on her apron and closed the pantry door. "No drinks. I'll get some when I go grocery shopping."

Tony rummaged around in the garage without success. "I can't find them. Maybe Mama knows where they are. I think I'll run up to Stephen's. They have some of those little dumbbells you hold in your hands when you exercise. Maybe I can borrow them."

Grandma Miller smiled and shook her head as she watched Tony run out the door. "I'm glad he's interested in bodybuilding and training, but I hope it's for the right reasons." She began a silent prayer. "Lord, help my grandson. He's short and wants so badly to prove himself to his peers. Help him realize the builder's work is useless without You, Lord." The gray-haired woman wiped the corner of her eye with a wrinkled hand and sat down on the couch.

Tony trained faithfully every day after school—with or without Mr. Canfield. Friday afternoon he strapped on his ankle weights and took the blue plastic dumbbells he'd borrowed from Stephen and headed out the door. "I'm going to run up to Stephen's, Grandma," he yelled.

The run to Stephen's was getting easier, but his friend wasn't home. Tony jogged up and down the hill until his legs ached. He finally collapsed on his front lawn. He absently watched a woman and two children coming toward him across Mason Springs Park. The little girl's hair was braided in tiny braids that swung around her face as she danced around a bigger boy. The boy's head was tilted at an odd angle and he was walking with a peculiar gait.

Tony kept watching. He jumped up and waved wildly when he saw Mr. Canfield zip around the corner and park his black car at the curb.

Tony recognized the woman first. It was Mrs. Canfield! And the little girl was Jessica. She ran to meet her daddy and jumped up into his arms. Tony could hear her laughing. He still didn't recognize the boy and was surprised when he walked around the car and fumbled with the door handle. Mr. Canfield came over and watched him slowly get into the car, then buckled the boy's seat belt and kissed him on the forehead.

Suddenly Tony knew! "That's J.J.! He doesn't go to Knowlton Elementary becau….Mr. Canfield's son is mentally challenged. And we called those kids with Down's syndrome and stuff mongoloids and retards! We all joked about it in front of him!" Tony was mortified.

"I'm running in the Turkey Trot because I want to win and look good. Mr. Canfield is running because he wants to help his own kid and others like him." Tony didn't feel like talking to his teacher anymore. He turned and rushed into the house. He wanted to hide.

He sat on the edge of his bed in the darkening room. "I'm so sorry, Lord," he prayed. "I've been a fool."

Grandma Miller came in quietly and sat down beside him. After looking at his face she said, "I see you found out."

Tony nodded. "I sure made a fool out of myself, Grandma. Mr. Canfield probably thinks I'm the retard—but he's been nice. He's helping me train for the race even after he heard us joke about the Sunshine School kids."

"Body building and winning are useless without the Lord, Tony-O." Grandma put her arm around her dejected grandson and squeezed. "Ask Him to be with you and do your best."

"But Grandma, how do the Canfields stand it? I mean, it's so awful to watch J.J.," Tony whispered.

"The Canfields have been dealing with the limitations of Down's syndrome for seven years now. The Lord has helped them accept their son's handicap, and they're handling people's ignorance and prejudice. I'm sure your teacher is proud of you for training hard and participating in a fund-raising project to help the mentally challenged."

Tony looked at his Grandma out of the corner of his eye. "I'm so embarrassed!"

"You should be!" The older woman got up slowly from the bed. "The Lord loves building projects, Tony-O, but I think you might want to let Him work on tearing down that prejudice you have."

"I see that now. Hey, Grandma, would you make me a T-shirt that says, 'Proudly Running for the Mentally Challenged?' I'd like to wear a special shirt when I run in the Turkey Trot!"

2 Discussion Time

Check understanding of the story and development of personal values.

- Have you ever participated in a race to raise money for a good cause?
- When and what for?
- Why was Tony participating in the Turkey Trot?
- Why was he training so hard?
- Was that a good reason to train so diligently?
- What does it mean when someone says you just put your foot in your mouth?
- How did Tony put his foot in his mouth?
- How did he feel when he realized Mr. Canfield's son was mentally challenged?
- How did Tony's reason for running change?

A Preview Name ______________________

Write each word as your teacher says it.

1. glossary
2. colonies
3. college
4. geometry
5. contact
6. doctor
7. conversation
8. continent
9. borrow
10. crocodile
11. Wisconsin
12. commerce
13. concentrate
14. atomic
15. deposit
16. adopt
17. comment
18. compost
19. bottom
20. demolish

Words with /o/

Lesson 14

Scripture

Psalm 127:1

87

3 Preview

Test for knowledge of the correct spellings of these words.

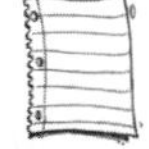

Customize Your List

On a separate sheet of paper, additional words of your choice may be tested.

I will say each word once, use the word in a sentence, then say the word again. Write the words on the lines in your Worktext.

Correct Immediately!

Let's correct our Preview. I will spell each word out loud. If you spelled a word incorrectly, rewrite it correctly.

Progress Chart

Students may record scores. (Reproducible master provided in Appendix B.)

1.	**glossary**	"Use the **glossary** to complete the assignment," instructed Mr. Canfield.
2.	**colonies**	"They may have had Turkey Trots in the **colonies**," he teased.
3.	**college**	"Did you run track in **college**, Mr. Canfield?" Tony asked.
4.	**geometry**	"Yes, and in high school I ran laps while I memorized **geometry** theorems."
5.	**contact**	"I never played a **contact** sport like football, though."
6.	**doctor**	"I was afraid I'd spend more time going to the **doctor** than playing the game."
7.	**conversation**	The boys really enjoyed having a **conversation** with their teacher.
8.	**continent**	"I think you could win a race on any **continent**!" exclaimed Stephen!
9.	**borrow**	"Can I **borrow** some of your energy?" Tony asked with admiration.
10.	**crocodile**	He sprawled out on the grass like a lazy **crocodile.**
11.	**Wisconsin**	"My brother recently won a 3-mile run in **Wisconsin**," he told the boys.
12.	**commerce**	During history, Mr. Canfield discussed international **commerce.**
13.	**concentrate**	"Some countries wanted to **concentrate** their energy on gaining power."
14.	**atomic**	"The power of an **atomic** weapon is potentially devastating," he explained
15.	**deposit**	"America had no plans to allow Russia to **deposit** a nuclear weapon here!"
16.	**adopt**	Senators urged congress to **adopt** new policies and increase the defense budget.
17.	**comment**	Tony regretted his mean **comment** about mentally handicapped kids.
18.	**compost**	"I'm so embarrassed I could hide in the **compost** pile," Tony told Gram.
19.	**bottom**	"From the **bottom** of my heart, I apologize for the things I said," Tony explained.
20.	**demolish**	"God, please **demolish** the prejudice in my heart," Tony prayed.

Lesson 14 | Day 1

Word Shapes

Help students form a correct image of whole words.

Look at each word and think about its shape. Now, write the word in the correct word Shape Boxes. You may check off each word as you use it.

(Short vowels are usually found in syllables in which a vowel is immediately preceded and followed by a consonant, consonant cluster, or digraph. The sound of **/o/** is usually spelled with **o** or **a**.)

In the word shape boxes, fill in the boxes containing the letter or letters that spell the sound of **/o/** in each word.

Words with /o/ — Lesson 14

B Word Shapes Name ____________

Using the word bank below, write each word in the correct word shape boxes. Next, in the word shape boxes, fill in the boxes containing the letter or letters that spell the sound of **/o/** in each word.

1.	college	11.	demolish
2.	comment	12.	contact
3.	geometry	13.	continent
4.	atomic	14.	glossary
5.	crocodile	15.	commerce
6.	doctor	16.	deposit
7.	adopt	17.	compost
8.	conversation	18.	Wisconsin
9.	borrow	19.	colonies
10.	concentrate	20.	bottom

Word Bank

adopt	college	compost	conversation	doctor
atomic	colonies	concentrate	crocodile	geometry
borrow	comment	contact	demolish	glossary
bottom	commerce	continent	deposit	Wisconsin

88

Answers may vary for duplicate word shapes.

Take a minute to memorize...

Psalm 127:1

Be Prepared For Fun

Check these supply lists for **Fun Ways to Spell** - presented **Day 2**. Purchase and/or gather these items ahead of time!

General
- Pencil
- Notebook Paper
- Spelling List

Auditory
- Pencil
- Notebook Paper
- Dictionary
- Spelling List

Visual
- Pencil
- Notebook Paper
- Spelling List

Tactile
- Computer Keyboard
- Spelling List

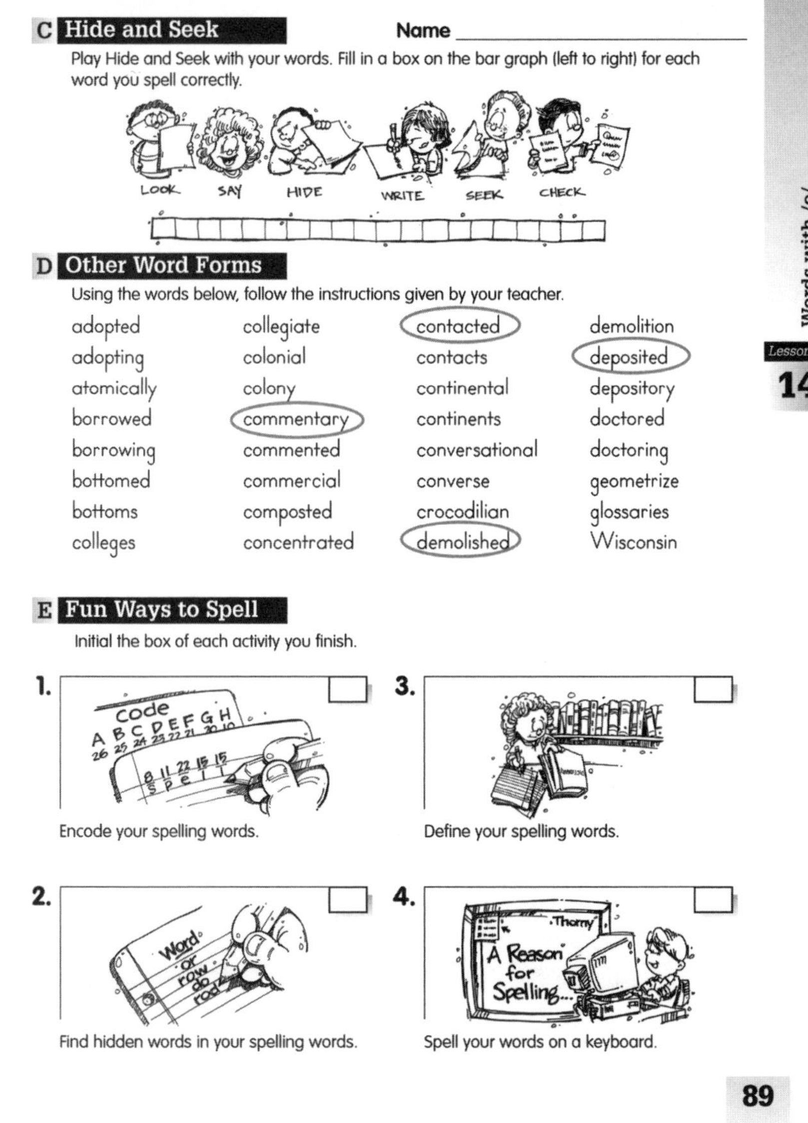

C Hide and Seek Name ______________________

Play Hide and Seek with your words. Fill in a box on the bar graph (left to right) for each word you spell correctly.

D Other Word Forms

Using the words below, follow the instructions given by your teacher.

adopted	collegiate	contacted	demolition
adopting	colonial	contacts	deposited
atomically	colony	continental	depository
borrowed	commentary	continents	doctored
borrowing	commented	conversational	doctoring
bottomed	commercial	converse	geometrize
bottoms	composted	crocodilian	glossaries
colleges	concentrated	demolished	Wisconsin

E Fun Ways to Spell

Initial the box of each activity you finish.

1. Encode your spelling words.

2. Find hidden words in your spelling words.

3. Define your spelling words.

4. Spell your words on a keyboard.

Words with /o/

Lesson 14

89

1 Hide and Seek

Reinforce spelling by using multiple styles of learning.

On a white board, Teacher writes each word — one at a time. **Have students:**

- **Look** at the word.
- **Say** the word out loud.
- **Spell** the word out loud.
- **Hide** (teacher erases word.)
- **Write** the word on paper.
- **Seek** (teacher rewrites word.)
- **Check** spelling. If incorrect, rewrite word correctly.

2 Other Word Forms

This activity is optional. Have students find and circle the Other Word Forms that are synonyms of the following:

laid waste
reached
dropped
critique

3 Fun Ways to Spell

Four activities are provided. Use one, two, three, or all of the activities. Have students initial the box for each activity they complete.

Options:

- assign activities to students according to their learning styles
- set up the activities in learning centers for the students to do throughout the day
- divide students into four groups and assign one activity per group
- do one activity per day

General

To encode your spelling words...
- Write the alphabet on your paper.
- Write your own code for each letter underneath it.
- Write your spelling words in your code.
- Trade papers with a classmate and decode the words.
- Check to make sure your classmate spelled the words correctly.

Auditory

To define your spelling words...
- Ask a classmate to look up a word from your spelling list in the dictionary and read the definition to you, but not the spelling word.
- Decide which word on your list matches this definition and write the word.
- Ask your classmate to check your spelling.
- Switch and continue taking turns.

Visual

To find hidden words in your spelling words...
- Choose a word from your spelling list.
- Write it on your paper.
- Find and write as many smaller words as you can that are contained within your spelling word.
- Do this with each word.

Tactile

To spell your words on a keyboard...
- Type your spelling words on a keyboard.
- Check your spelling.

Working with Words

Familiarize students with word meaning and usage.

Scrambled Words

Write the letters **aeghrt** on the board. Have a student unscramble the letters to make the word **gather**.

Unscramble each spelling word. Write the word correctly on the line. Remember to use capital letters where they are needed.

Word Clues

Use your word bank to help you match the spelling words to the clues. Some of the clues are synonyms, words that have the same meaning as the spelling word. You may use a dictionary or thesaurus to help you.

Take a minute to memorize...

Psalm 127:1

Words with /o/ — Lesson 14

F Working with Words Name ______________

Scrambled Words

Unscramble each word. Write the unscrambled word on the line. Use capital letters where they are needed.

1. cdoort	doctor	11. ceegllo	college
2. aceinnoorstv	conversation	12. eegmorty	geometry
3. ccdeiloor	crocodile	13. ceinnnott	continent
4. acimot	atomic	14. aglorssy	glossary
5. deiopst	deposit	15. bmoott	bottom
6. accnott	contact	16. podat	adopt
7. ciinnossw	Wisconsin	17. acceennortt	concentrate
8. wororb	borrow	18. cmoopst	compost
9. ceilnoos	colonies	19. cceemmor	commerce
10. cemmnot	comment	20. dehilmos	demolish

Word Clues

Match the spelling words to the clues. You may use a dictionary or thesaurus to help you.

1. microscopic, smallest	atomic	11. reptilian, alligator	crocodile
2. observation, remark	comment	12. destroy, wreck	demolish
3. get temporary use of	borrow	13. sediment, silt	deposit
4. lowest part, base	bottom	14. physician, M. D.	doctor
5. communities, settlements	colonies	15. take into one's family	adopt
6. business, trading	commerce	16. math about angles	geometry
7. decayed organic matter	compost	17. educational institution	college
8. pay attention, focus	concentrate	18. list of terms, dictionary	glossary
9. connection, touch	contact	19. talking together	conversation
10. land mass	continent	20. north-central state	Wisconsin

Word Bank

adopt	college	compost	conversation	doctor
atomic	colonies	concentrate	crocodile	geometry
borrow	comment	contact	demolish	glossary
bottom	commerce	continent	deposit	Wisconsin

90

G Dictation

Name ______________________

Write each sentence as your teacher dictates. Use correct punctuation.

1. Mr. Canfield did not say much as the boys laughed and made unkind comments.
2. Tony concentrated on eating healthy foods as he built his strength.
3. He looked in the glossary to find more about the commerce of the early colonies.

Words with /o/

Lesson 14

H Proofreading

If a word is misspelled, fill in the oval by that word. If all the words are spelled correctly, fill in the oval by **no mistake**.

1. ● convirsation ○ inhabit ○ Colorado ○ no mistake
2. ○ gallop ○ gallon ● crocadial ○ no mistake
3. ● docter ○ Nevada ○ valley ○ no mistake
4. ○ valve ● collige ○ scallop ○ no mistake
5. ● colonys ○ demolish ○ Alabama ○ no mistake
6. ○ mammal ○ New Hampshire ● attomic ○ no mistake
7. ● coment ○ Indiana ○ random ○ no mistake
8. ○ compost ● comerce ○ savanna ○ no mistake
9. ○ concentrate ● geometrey ○ perhaps ○ no mistake
10. ○ contact ○ Wisconsin ● continint ○ no mistake
11. ● addopt ○ bottom ○ borrow ○ no mistake
12. ○ soprano ○ deposit ● glossry ○ no mistake

91

1 Dictation

Reinforce correct spelling by using current and previous words in context.

Listen as I read each sentence and then write it in your Worktext. Remember to use correct capitalization and punctuation. (Slowly read each sentence twice. Sentences are found in the Student Worktext to the left.)

2 Proofreading

Familiarize students with standardized test format and reinforce recognition of misspelled words.

Look at each set of words. If a word is misspelled, fill in the oval by that word. If all the words are spelled correctly, fill in the oval by **no mistake**.

3 Hide and Seek

Reinforce correct spelling of current spelling words. Repeat this activity from Day 2.

4 Vocabulary Extension

Have your students complete this activity to strengthen spelling ability and expand vocabulary. The reproducible master is provided in Appendix A as shown on the inset page to the right.

1 Posttest

Test mastery of the spelling words.

I will say the word once, use it in a sentence, then say it again. Write your words on a separate sheet of paper.

Progress Chart

Students may record scores. (Reproducible master in Appendix B.)

Personal Dictionary

Students may add any words they have misspelled to their personal dictionaries for reference when writing. (Cover in Appendix B.)

Vocabulary Extension — Lesson 14

Hide and Seek

Play Hide and Seek with your words. Fill in a bar graph (left to right) for each word you spell correctly.

Vocabulary Extension

Trade-off

Choose a word from the word bank to replace the word(s) in parentheses. Write the word in the blank.

1. My teacher said that the composition (essay) I wrote was really good.
2. There was a lot of opposition (conflict) to the plans for the new gymnasium.
3. The lawyer for the prosecution (accuser) had plenty of evidence to convict the thief.
4. She was so upset that her arguments became very illogical (unreasonable).
5. The boys finally gave up on the go-cart they were trying to build. They decided it was impossible (hopeless).
6. The laws in our country that state the rights of the people and the powers of the government are known as the constitution (written laws).
7. The fraction 1 3/7 is an improper (incorrect) fraction because the numerator is greater than its denominator.
8. I love to look at the constellation (pattern of stars) Orion in the sky on a dark night.
9. Jeans are the most dominant (most common) kind of clothes in my closet.
10. We need to be tolerant (accepting) of others by showing respect for their customs, beliefs, or opinions.
11. I want to protect valuable things such as forests, wildlife, and natural resources. I believe in conservation (preservation).
12. If you have a conversation (discourse) with someone, you talk to them for a while.

Word Bank

composition	constitution	illogical	opposition
conservation	conversation	impossible	prosecution
constellation	dominant	improper	tolerant

336

1.	glossary	"Use the **glossary** at the back of your book," instructed Mr. Canfield.
2.	concentrate	"Please, **concentrate** on completing the first two pages," he continued.
3.	geometry	Mr. Canfield introduced his class to several principles of **geometry**.
4.	crocodile	Tony dropped to the grass, his mouth open like a giant **crocodile**.
5.	borrow	"I'd like to **borrow** some of his talent and ability!" exclaimed Tony.
6.	conversation	The boys thought it was neat to share **conversation** with their teacher.
7.	contact	"Did you play any **contact** sports?" inquired Stephen.
8.	doctor	"No, I thought I'd have to see the **doctor** too often," he laughed.
9.	college	"I ran track in high school and in **college**," said Mr. Canfield.
10.	colonies	"Think they used to have a Turkey Trot in the **colonies** way back when?"
11.	Wisconsin	"My brother who lives in **Wisconsin** recently won a race," he told the boys.
12.	bottom	J.J. did not stand evenly on the **bottom** of his right foot.
13.	atomic	"How did the knowledge of **atomic** power change the world?" he asked the students.
14.	commerce	"Tony, what effect did that have on international **commerce**?"
15.	compost	Tony felt low enough to crawl in the **compost** pile!
16.	continent	"What changes affected our **continent** specifically, Kristin?"
17.	deposit	He saw Mr. Canfield scoop up his son and **deposit** him safely in the car.
18.	adopt	"Did he **adopt** J.J.?" asked Tony.
19.	comment	Tony was so sorry for his unkind **comment** in front of his teacher.
20.	demolish	Tony wanted God to **demolish** any prejudice in his heart against the mentally handicapped.

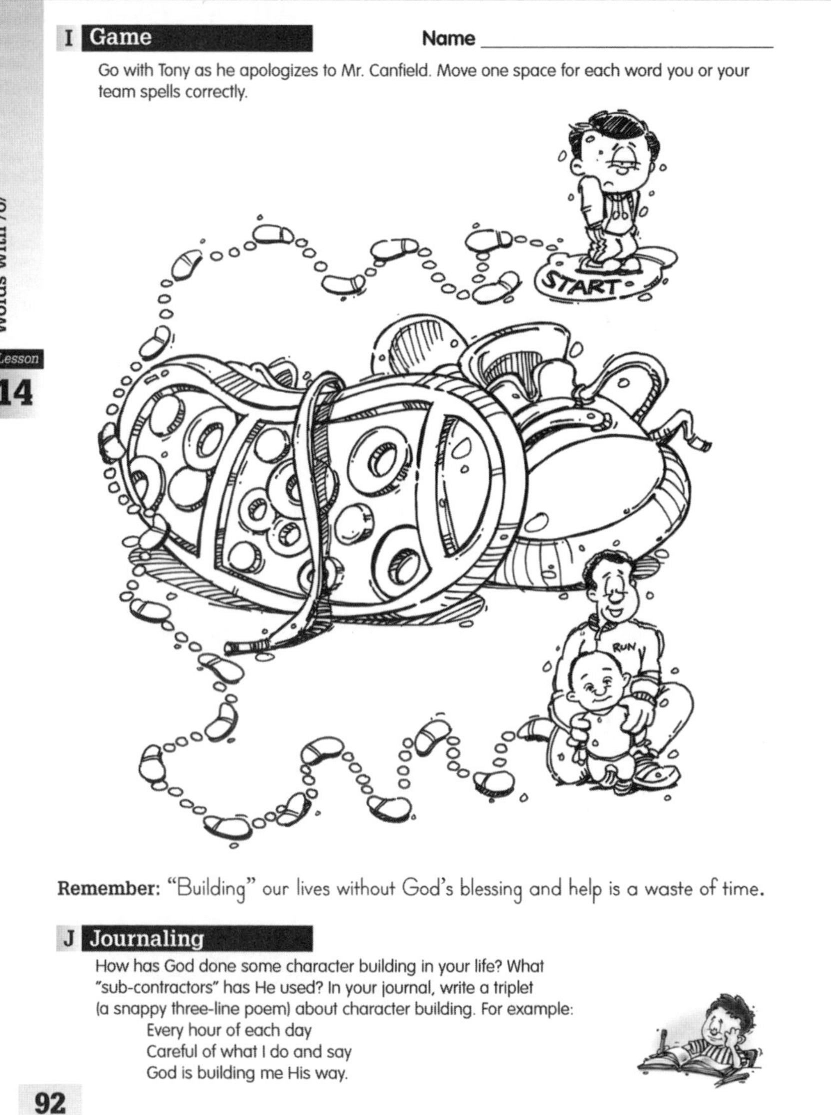

Words with /o/

Lesson 14

I Game Name ____________

Go with Tony as he apologizes to Mr. Canfield. Move one space for each word you or your team spells correctly.

Remember: "Building" our lives without God's blessing and help is a waste of time.

J Journaling

How has God done some character building in your life? What "sub-contractors" has He used? In your journal, write a triplet (a snappy three-line poem) about character building. For example:

Every hour of each day
Careful of what I do and say
God is building me His way.

92

Game

Reinforce spelling skills and provide motivation and interest.

Materials

- game page (from student text)
- game pieces (1 per child)
- game word list

Game Word List

1. **conversation**
2. **crocodile**
3. **doctor**
4. **college**
5. **colonies**
6. **demolish**
7. **atomic**
8. **comment**
9. **commerce**
10. **compost**
11. **geometry**
12. **concentrate**
13. **contact**
14. **continent**
15. **Wisconsin**
16. **adopt**
17. **borrow**
18. **bottom**
19. **deposit**
20. **glossary**

How to Play:

- Divide the class into two teams.
- Have each student place his/her game piece on Start.
- Have a student from team A go to the board.
- Say the spelling word.
- Have the student write the word on the board.
- If correct, instruct each member of team A to move his/her game piece forward one space.
- Alternate between teams A and B.
- The team to reach Mr. Canfield first is the winner.
- **Small Group Option**: Students may play this game without teacher direction in small groups of two or more.

3 Journaling

Provide a meaningful reason for correct spelling through personal writing.

Review the story using discussion leads provided on the following page. Encourage students to apply the Scriptural value in their journaling.

Journaling (continued)

- Why did Tony want to win the Turkey Trot? (To look good.)
- Why do you think Grandma Miller told Tony that body building and winning were useless without the Lord? (She knew serving others is the only way to happiness.)
- What does it mean when someone says you just put your foot in your mouth? (You've said something to embarrass yourself.)
- How did Tony put his foot in his mouth? (While Mr. Canfield was listening he started to call the mentally challenged "retards" and said winning was what would make him happy.)
- What character traits do you think the Lord helped Tony build? (Compassion, empathy, humility)
- Triplets are three-line poems. They're not as common as couplets (two-line poems) and quatrains (four-line poems). Sometimes triplets rhyme—sometimes they don't. When a triplet rhymes, all three lines may rhyme (aaa), the first and last lines may rhyme (aba), the first two lines can rhyme (aab), or just the last two may rhyme (abb).
- Write these incomplete triplets on the board. Ask students to complete them. Share results.
- **aaa** pattern (all three lines rhyme)

  Running is a lot of fun

  ____

  But is feels great when I am done
- **abb** pattern (the last two lines rhyme)

  Tony always combs his hair!

  He thinks it's out of place

  ____

ICEBOX is a word with horizontal symmetry when written in capital letters (it reflects itself across a horizontal line); some others are DECIDED, EXCEEDED, CHECK-BOOK, OKEECHOBEE, HIDE, CHOICE, DIOXIDE, CEBID (a type of monkey), and OBOE.

1 **Literature Connection**
Topic: Blended family relationships
Theme Text: Psalm 98:7

Protection in Paradise

Lany spends Christmas vacation in the Bahamas with her dad, his new wife, and daughter.

Dear Megan,

I have so much to tell you, but it's hard to get it out of my fingers and into the computer. Guess what? Three exciting things! First, Mom got a program to help me type faster. It's called Typing Tutor. I'll let you know if it works. Second, my dad is taking me to the Bahamas for Christmas vacation! I'll get out of this place for a while! He's already sent my tickets, so I know he won't forget our plans this time. I've been reading about the Bahamas on the Internet. Did you know there are 700 islands in the Bahamas? (I didn't either until yesterday.) The closest islands are only 50 miles off the Florida coast. I get to spend a day in New York on the way back. So the third exciting thing is—I'll get to see you!! ☺ Are you going to be home December 30?

Love,
Laney

Dear Laney,

I'll be here! I can hardly wait till you are! It seems like forever since you lived here and we went to school together. Your dad must be trying to make up for forgetting about your plans with him last spring. Glad you have your tickets! Lucky bird (as our friend Brittany would say)! I've always wanted to go snorkeling and sailing in the Bahamas. All that warm, blue water, those coral reefs, and crashing waves! Which of the 700 islands are you going to see? I've been learning to type in the computer lab at school. I'm getting better, but I'm not very fast either.
See ya!

Megan

Dear Megan,

I'm going to Paradise Island! We're flying into Nassau, the capital city of the Bahamas. The Internet said it was founded in 1670. Over half the people in the Bahamas live there. I don't know where we're going after that. The only reason I know we're going to Nassau is because of my ticket. You know how busy Dad always is. He probably won't tell me until we're in the air exactly what we're going to do. Maybe we'll stay in Paradise the whole time. Who knows? (Hopefully Dad.)

Love,
Laney

Dear Laney,

Brittany wants to know if she can come with you. You know how she loves birds. She said 60,000 West Indian flamingos live in the Bahamas. Flamingos are the national bird. Her brother said the exotic Abaco parrots live in one of the national parks. Do you get to sail and learn to scuba dive?

Megan

Dear Megan,

Tell Brittany I'd love for her to come. Which island do the flamingos live on? My stepdad gave me a whole list of things to take with me today! He says I need to wear lots of sunscreen. I told him Dad and Suzanne would bring stuff like that. He said nothing could ruin a trip to the beach more than a sunburn. He wants me to take some aloe vera and a hat. He says I need a jacket, too. I don't think I'll miss his hovering over me all the time trying to protect me. It gets kind of irritating. I'll be with my own dad. Mom says we get to go shopping tomorrow. I don't think it will do much good. Where will I get summer clothes in December?

Love,
Laney

Dear Laney,

Just tell Coach Larkin your real dad can take care of you in Paradise. Brittany said the flamingos are on the island that is farthest away—Iguana, I think she said. When do you leave? Can you e-mail on your trip?

Megan

Dear Megan,

I'm sure Dad will bring his laptop computer, beeper, and cell phone. He couldn't stand to stay away from his law practice for more than a day. Maybe he'll let me e-mail. Tell Brittany the island with the Flamingos is Great Inagua—I looked it up. Same letters as Iguana, just a different order.

Love,
Laney

Dear Laney

My Mom saw your dad's wife today in town. She said you were going on a cruise. You lucky duck! Are you sure you have an airline ticket?

Megan

Dear Megan,

You're right. I am going on a cruise! We'll leave from New York and sail all the way! Then we island hop. My stepdad says I need more than one swimming suit, and I should take some books to read on rainy days. He told me they drive on the wrong side of the road down there too. (He wants me to wear my seat belt because tourists aren't used to driving on the left side of the road.) Can you believe him? Gotta go.

Laney

Dear Megan,

I leave tomorrow. I'll miss Wicker. I really love that dog. Mom even lets him sleep on a big pillow bed in my room now—if I brush him before I let him in. He'll howl if they make him sleep out in his kennel again. Poor boy. It'll seem funny to

Story (continued)

have a warm Christmas. I'm used to snow. Mom and my stepdad gave me a Christmas present today. It's two swimming suits, a mask, and snorkel. (Mom found the swimming suits in a catalog.) They said 5 percent of the world's coral reefs are in Bermuda and they want me to get a good look at them. Is this for real? Matthew gave me money to buy him some stamps. (He collects them.) Heather wants me to send her some postcards. (She collects those.) Everyone in my class wants shells from the endless sandy beaches. I can hardly wait.

Love,
Laney

P.S. My friend Rachel said she would come over and play catch with Wicker every day so the poor dog won't get so lonely.

Dear Laney,

Have fun. I'm looking forward to seeing you.

Megan

Dear Megan,

I got here late last night. I don't know why I'm e-mailing. I can call you on the phone!

Love,
Laney

Dear Laney,

Good to hear your voice three days ago. Where are you? E-mail me.

Megan

Dear Megan,

We're here—on Paradise Island! We came into port last night. I couldn't e-mail you on the ship. Dad said it would be too expensive. It was good to actually talk to you last week. I'm looking forward to seeing you when we get back. Suzanne and Dad were seasick all the way here, but I wasn't, so I got to baby-sit Suzette. Too exciting. I think we go to the beach tomorrow. I'm not sure yet. Dad still doesn't feel well.

Laney

Dear Megan,

You won't believe this. I'm the only one in this family that's not sunburned. Dad Larkin was right. (I hate to put that in writing.) I'm glad he sent me my own sunscreen. It was waterproof. The stuff Suzanne brought wasn't. My dad was pretty mad at her. I let them use some of my aloe vera stuff. It helped. I didn't tell them Dad Larkin made me bring it.

Laney

Dear Megan,

I never thought I'd say this but I miss home—my new home. I miss Mom. I miss Wicker and I hate to admit it, but I even miss my stepdad. We've started having family worship every night—Dad Larkin, Mom, and me. Rachel's family does that. I told Mom I thought we should start. She told Dad, and now we do it. Sometimes it isn't very interesting or comes at a bad time, but usually I like it because we do it together. Nobody here gets into having family anything. We're so busy on this cruise we don't see each other some days. Dad goes off deep-sea fishing or scuba diving with Suzanne. I take Suzette and we go on some kids' trip with a tour guide. It's fun, but I wish Dad and Suzanne would do things with us. When Dad and Suzanne get back, Dad works or falls asleep because he's so tired.

The warm ocean is endless. I praise God for it—but I'll be glad to be home. I guess I'm learning that home is where your family is, and my real family now is Mom, Dad Larkin, and Wicker.

Love,
Laney

2 Discussion Time

Check understanding of the story and development of personal values.

- What three things was Laney so excited about?
- Raise your hand if you've ever been on a tropical island vacation.
- What are some things you like most about the ocean?
- What do you think this Scripture verse means? "Let the sea in all its vastness roar with praise! Let the earth and all those living on it shout, 'Glory to the Lord.'"
- What did Laney miss about being away from home?

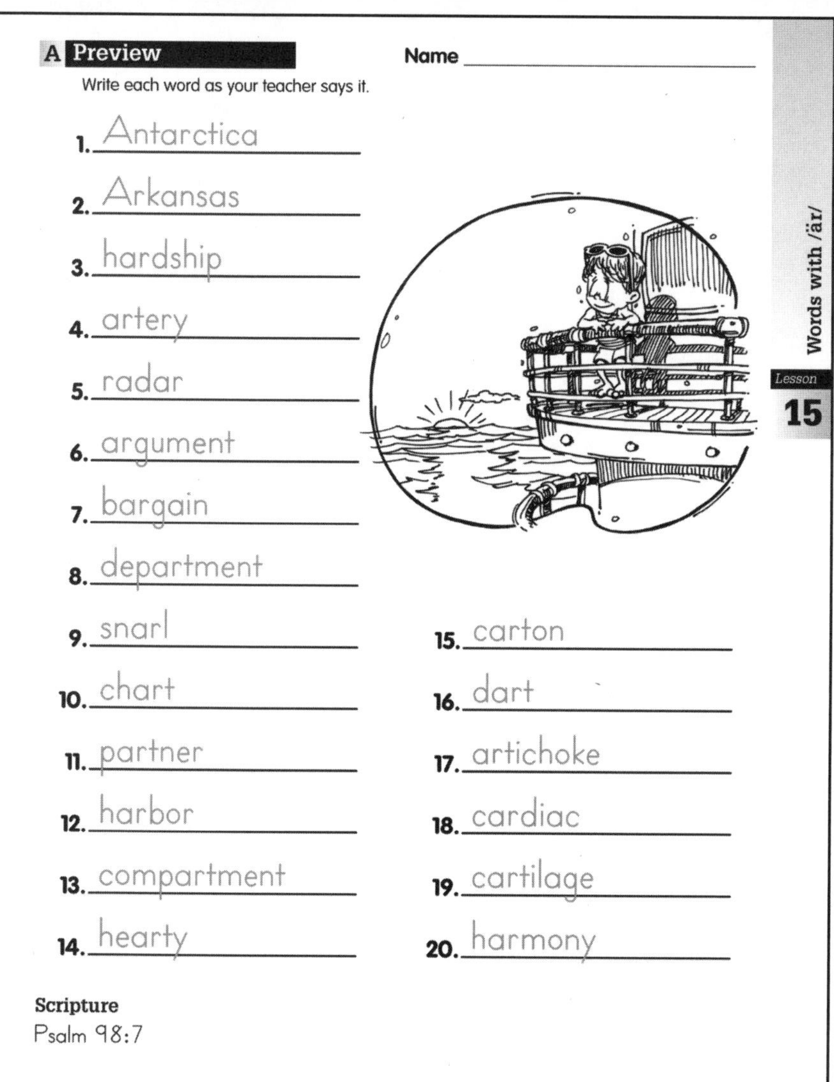

3 Preview

Test for knowledge of the correct spellings of these words.

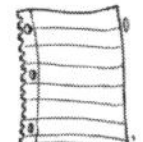

Customize Your List

On a separate sheet of paper, additional words of your choice may be tested.

I will say each word once, use the word in a sentence, then say the word again. Write the words on the lines in your Worktext.

Correct Immediately!

Let's correct our Preview. I will spell each word out loud. If you spelled a word incorrectly, rewrite it correctly.

Progress Chart

Students may record scores. (Reproducible master provided in Appendix B.)

1.	Antarctica	Laney is going to the Bahamas, not the **Antarctica.**
2.	Arkansas	Her dad lives in New York but grew up in **Arkansas.**
3.	hardship	"It will be such a **hardship** to spend a week in the Bahamas," her mom teased.
4.	artery	"Dad's going to clog an **artery** worrying about what I pack," she said disrespectfully.
5.	radar	"He has a built-in safety **radar,**" said Laney with a groan.
6.	argument	Laney knew she should not get into an **argument** with Dad Larkin.
7.	bargain	Her mom found a **bargain** or two in a mail-order catalog.
8.	department	They also went to a **department** store to shop for the trip.
9.	snarl	Laney heard Wicker **snarl** at a squirrel that stole a piece of his dog food.
10.	chart	The captain and his crew carefully **chart** the course for their voyage.
11.	partner	Laney's real dad has a **partner** that will see to business while he is away.
12.	harbor	The captain gave the orders to take the cruise ship slowly out of **harbor.**
13.	compartment	Laney liked her little sleeping **compartment.**
14.	hearty	They served a **hearty** breakfast each morning of the cruise.
15.	carton	She chose a small **carton** of milk to share with Suzette.
16.	dart	Laney threw a **dart** at the board on the upper deck.
17.	artichoke	At dinner, she took a bite of steamed **artichoke** and really liked it.
18.	cardiac	Laney's dad has had some **cardiac** trouble due to stress.
19.	cartilage	Even the **cartilage** in her dad's and Suzanne's ears felt sunburned!
20.	harmony	After the trip, Laney appreciated the **harmony** in her home.

Lesson 15 | Day 1

4 Word Shapes

Help students form a correct image of whole words.

Look at each word and think about its shape. Now, write the word in the correct word Shape Boxes. You may check off each word as you use it.

(In most words, the letters **ar** spell the sound of **/är/**, whether it is at the beginning, middle, or end of a word. There are a few exceptions.)

Say

In the word shape boxes, fill in the boxes containing the letters that spell the sound of **/är/** in each word.

Take a minute to memorize...

Psalm 98:7

Words with /är/ — Lesson 15

B Word Shapes Name ______________________

Using the word bank below, write each word in the correct word shape boxes. Next, in the word shape boxes, fill in the boxes containing the letter or letters that spell the sound of **/är/** in each word.

1.	artichoke	11.	harmony
2.	compartment	12.	chart
3.	snarl	13.	hearty
4.	partner	14.	dart
5.	Antarctica	15.	Arkansas
6.	harbor	16.	carton
7.	hardship	17.	bargain
8.	radar	18.	artery
9.	argument	19.	department
10.	cardiac	20.	cartilage

Word Bank

Antarctica	artichoke	carton	department	hearty
argument	bargain	chart	harbor	partner
Arkansas	cardiac	compartment	hardship	radar
artery	cartilage	dart	harmony	snarl

94

Answers may vary for duplicate word shapes.

Be Prepared For Fun

Check these supply lists for **Fun Ways to Spell** - presented **Day 2**. Purchase and/or gather these items ahead of time!

General
- Pencil
- 3 X 5 Cards cut in half (20 per child)
- Spelling List

Auditory
- Spelling List

Visual
- Pencil
- Notebook Paper
- Spelling List

Tactile
- Blackboard and Chalk
  -OR-
- White Board and Marker
- Spelling List

C Hide and Seek

Name ______________________

Play Hide and Seek with your words. Fill in a box on the bar graph (left to right) for each word you spell correctly.

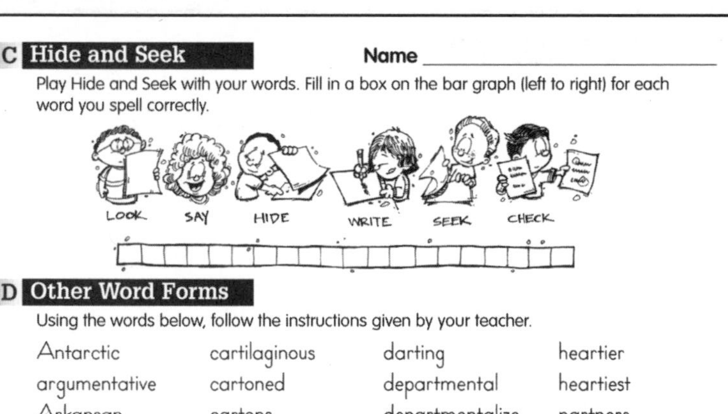

D Other Word Forms

Using the words below, follow the instructions given by your teacher.

Antarctic	cartilaginous	darting	heartier
argumentative	cartoned	departmental	heartiest
Arkansan	cartons	departmentalize	partners
arteries	charted	harbored	partnership
artichokes	charts	harboring	snarled
bargained	compartmentalize	hardships	snarling
bargaining	compartmented	harmonies	
cardiology	darted	harmonize	

E Fun Ways to Spell

Initial the box of each activity you finish.

1. 

Spell your words, then play "Concentration."

3. 

Spell your words in a sentence.

2. 

Decode your spelling words.

4. 

Play the game "Spelling Backwards."

Words with /är/

Lesson 15

95

1 Hide and Seek

Reinforce spelling by using multiple styles of learning.

On a white board, Teacher writes each word — one at a time. **Have students:**

- **Look** at the word.
- **Say** the word out loud.
- **Spell** the word out loud.
- **Hide** (teacher erases word.)
- **Write** the word on paper.
- **Seek** (teacher rewrites word.)
- **Check** spelling. If incorrect, rewrite word correctly.

2 Other Word Forms

This activity is optional. Have students write original sentences using these Other Word Forms:

snarled
cartoned
departmental
partnership

3 Fun Ways to Spell

Four activities are provided. Use one, two, three, or all of the activities. Have students initial the box for each activity they complete.

Options:

- assign activities to students according to their learning styles
- set up the activities in learning centers for the students to do throughout the day
- divide students into four groups and assign one activity per group
- do one activity per day

General

Spell your words; then play "Concentration"...
- Write each spelling word on a card. Mix your cards and a classmate's cards together. Arrange them face down in five rows of eight. Pick up two cards. If the cards match, play again. If the cards do not match, turn them back over. It is your classmate's turn. Continue taking turns until all the cards are matched. The player with the most cards wins!

Auditory

To spell your words in a sentence...
- Ask a classmate to read a spelling word to you from the list.
- Spell the word aloud and use it in a sentence.
- Ask your classmate to check your spelling.
- Each correctly spelled word that is used properly in a sentence counts as one point.
- Switch and continue taking turns.

Visual

To decode your spelling words...
- Look at the first word on your list.
- Write every other letter of the word on your paper, putting a blank where each missing letter belongs.
- Trade papers with a classmate and fill in the missing letters.
- Check your spelling.

Tactile

To play the game "Spelling Backwards"...
- Ask a classmate to stand behind you and draw the letters to spell a word from your list on your back.
- Write the spelling word on the board as your classmate traces the letters on your back.
- Ask your classmate to check your spelling.
- Trade places and take turns until you have each spelled all the words.

1 Working with Words

Familiarize students with word meaning and usage.

Rhyming Clues

Write the words **farmstead**, **freewheeler**, **forehead**, and **cartwheel** on the board. Have a volunteer underline the two words that rhyme (**farmstead**, **forehead**). Tell students that, for this exercise, words need to rhyme on at least the last syllable to be considered rhyming words. Explain that students will be matching some of their spelling words to a rhyming word.

Write the spelling word that rhymes with each word below.

The AR's Have It

Each spelling word in this lesson has the **/är/** sound. Answer each question with a word from the word bank. You may use a dictionary to help you. Write the word in the blank.

Take a minute to memorize...

Psalm 98:7

Words with /är/ — Lesson 15

F Working with Words Name ____________________

Similiar Sounds

Write the spelling word that rhymes with the last syllable of each word below.

1. message cartilage
2. kindergartner partner
3. battery artery
4. horsewhip hardship
5. tailspin bargain
6. start dart or chart
7. tartan carton
8. replica Antarctica
9. smart chart or dart
10. maniac cardiac
11. barber harbor
12. womenfolk artichoke
13. symphony harmony
14. party hearty
15. overdraw Arkansas
16. bizarre radar
17. gnarl snarl
18. confident argument, compartment, or department

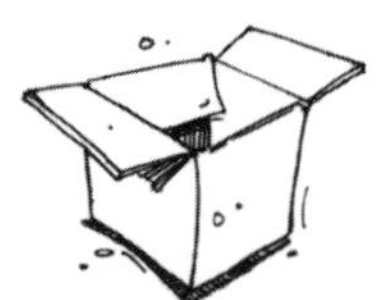

The AR's Have It

Answer each question with an **/är/** word from the word bank. Write the word in the blank.

1. What /är/ word means a pleasing blend of sounds? harmony
2. What /är/ word means to strike an agreement? bargain
3. What /är/ word means vigorously healthy? hearty
4. What /är/ word means a quarrel or disagreement? argument
5. What /är/ word is a continent centered on the South Pole? Antarctica
6. What /är/ word means relating to the heart? cardiac
7. What /är/ word means a place to safely anchor boats? harbor
8. What /är/ word is what your outer ear is made of? cartilage
9. What /är/ word means a tube that carries blood from the heart? artery
10. What /är/ word means a section of enclosed space? compartment
11. What /är/ word is a state whose eastern border is the Mississippi River? Arkansas

Word Bank

Antarctica	artichoke	carton	department	hearty
argument	bargain	chart	harbor	partner
Arkansas	cardiac	compartment	hardship	radar
artery	cartilage	dart	harmony	snarl

96

G Dictation Name ______________________

Write each sentence as your teacher dictates. Use correct punctuation.

1. Mom and I went to a big department store to shop for clothes to take with me.
2. Suzanne and Dad had an argument over the sunscreen she had brought.
3. As the huge ship sailed into the harbor, we saw people selling many things.

Words with /är/

Lesson 15

H Proofreading

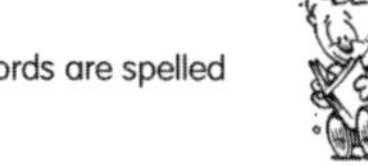

If a word is misspelled, fill in the oval by that word. If all the words are spelled correctly, fill in the oval by **no mistake**.

1. ○ crocodile ○ doctor ● harber ○ no mistake
2. ● cardiack ○ hardship ○ comment ○ no mistake
3. ● antarctica ○ compost ○ contact ○ no mistake
4. ○ Hawaii ● Arkansaw ○ college ○ no mistake
5. ○ deposit ○ glossary ● argumint ○ no mistake
6. ● bargin ○ snarl ○ bottom ○ no mistake
7. ○ radar ○ colonies ● harmonie ○ no mistake
8. ● arttery ○ artichoke ○ demolish ○ no mistake
9. ○ atomic ○ commerce ● cartillage ○ no mistake
10. ● cartin ○ geometry ○ chart ○ no mistake
11. ○ dart ● compartmint ○ partner ○ no mistake
12. ● departmint ○ hearty ○ concentrate ○ no mistake

97

1 Dictation

Reinforce correct spelling by using current and previous words in context.

Listen as I read each sentence and then write it in your Worktext. Remember to use correct capitalization and punctuation. (Slowly read each sentence twice. Sentences are found in the Student Worktext to the left.)

2 Proofreading

Familiarize students with standardized test format and reinforce recognition of misspelled words.

Look at each set of words. If a word is misspelled, fill in the oval by that word. If all the words are spelled correctly, fill in the oval by **no mistake**.

3 Hide and Seek

Reinforce correct spelling of current spelling words. Repeat this activity from Day 2.

4 Vocabulary Extension

Have your students complete this activity to strengthen spelling ability and expand vocabulary. The reproducible master is provided in Appendix A as shown on the inset page to the right.

1 Posttest

Test mastery of the spelling words.

I will say the word once, use it in a sentence, then say it again. Write your words on a separate sheet of paper.

Progress Chart
Students may record scores. (Reproducible master in Appendix B.)

Personal Dictionary
Students may add any words they have misspelled to their personal dictionaries for reference when writing. (Cover in Appendix B.)

Hide and Seek

Play Hide and Seek with your words. Fill in a bar graph (left to right) for each word you spell correctly.

Vocabulary Extension

Multiple Choice

Fill in the oval by the word(s) with the same or nearly the same meaning as the word in bold type.

1. **pharmacist**
   - ○ large, brightly colored bird
   - ● person who prepares and sells medicines
   - ○ one who grows crops
   - ○ machine that reproduces sounds
2. **carpenter**
   - ○ thick floor covering made of fabric
   - ○ vehicle pulled by horses
   - ○ part of the engine in a car
   - ● someone who works with wood
3. **bargain**
   - ● discuss the price of something
   - ○ to trade food for other goods
   - ○ land where crops will not grow
   - ○ common cereal plant
4. **margin**
   - ○ something made of stone or cement
   - ○ dark reddish brown color
   - ○ place where people buy and sell food
   - ● blank space down the edge of a page
5. **article**
   - ○ disease the makes people's joints swell
   - ○ false, not real or natural
   - ● piece of writing published in a newspaper
   - ○ conceited and proud
6. **charming**
   - ● enchanting and appealing
   - ○ document that states the rights of people
   - ○ raising money to help people in need
   - ○ deep crack in the surface of the earth
7. **regard**
   - ○ in spite of everything
   - ● opinion; esteem
   - ○ to give money back to someone
   - ○ person who is forced to leave their home
8. **darkened**
   - ○ room with photography equipment
   - ○ someone who is dearly loved
   - ○ unpleasantly wet and damp
   - ● caused something to be without light
9. **enlarged**
   - ● made bigger or increased
   - ○ gave something all your attention
   - ○ mystery or puzzle
   - ○ made something better or greater
10. **guardian**
    - ○ person who is dirty or sloppy
    - ○ musical instrument with strings
    - ● person legally responsible for a child
    - ○ direction or supervision

Vocabulary Extension Lesson 15

337

1.	argument	Laney did not want to get into an **argument** with Dad Larkin.
2.	department	There weren't any swimsuits for sale in the **department** stores.
3.	bargain	The mail-order catalog had a **bargain** or two on summer clothing.
4.	snarl	Wicker began to **snarl** when the squirrel got too close to his dog food.
5.	cardiac	Laney hoped her dad's **cardiac** trouble would not flare up.
6.	hardship	The stress of his job is a real **hardship** on his heart.
7.	artery	He had a clogged **artery** and high blood pressure.
8.	partner	His law-firm **partner** will be in charge while Laney's dad is gone on vacation.
9.	Arkansas	Her dad grew up in **Arkansas,** but has not been there in years.
10.	Antarctica	They will not pass close to **Antarctica** on their way to the Bahamas.
11.	artichoke	At dinner, the waiter brought a platter of steamed **artichoke.**
12.	hearty	She enjoyed the **hearty** breakfast they served each morning.
13.	harbor	The ship docked safely in the **harbor.**
14.	carton	Laney opened a small **carton** of milk for Suzette as they relaxed on the deck.
15.	radar	A ship uses sonar rather than **radar** to detect objects in its path.
16.	cartilage	Laney's dad said even the **cartilage** inside his nose felt sunburned.
17.	chart	The captain and his crew carefully **chart** their course before the voyage.
18.	compartment	Laney's sleeping **compartment** was small but very comfortable.
19.	dart	Laney expertly threw a **dart** at the bull's-eye on the board.
20.	harmony	Laney realized she should thank God for the **harmony** in her home.

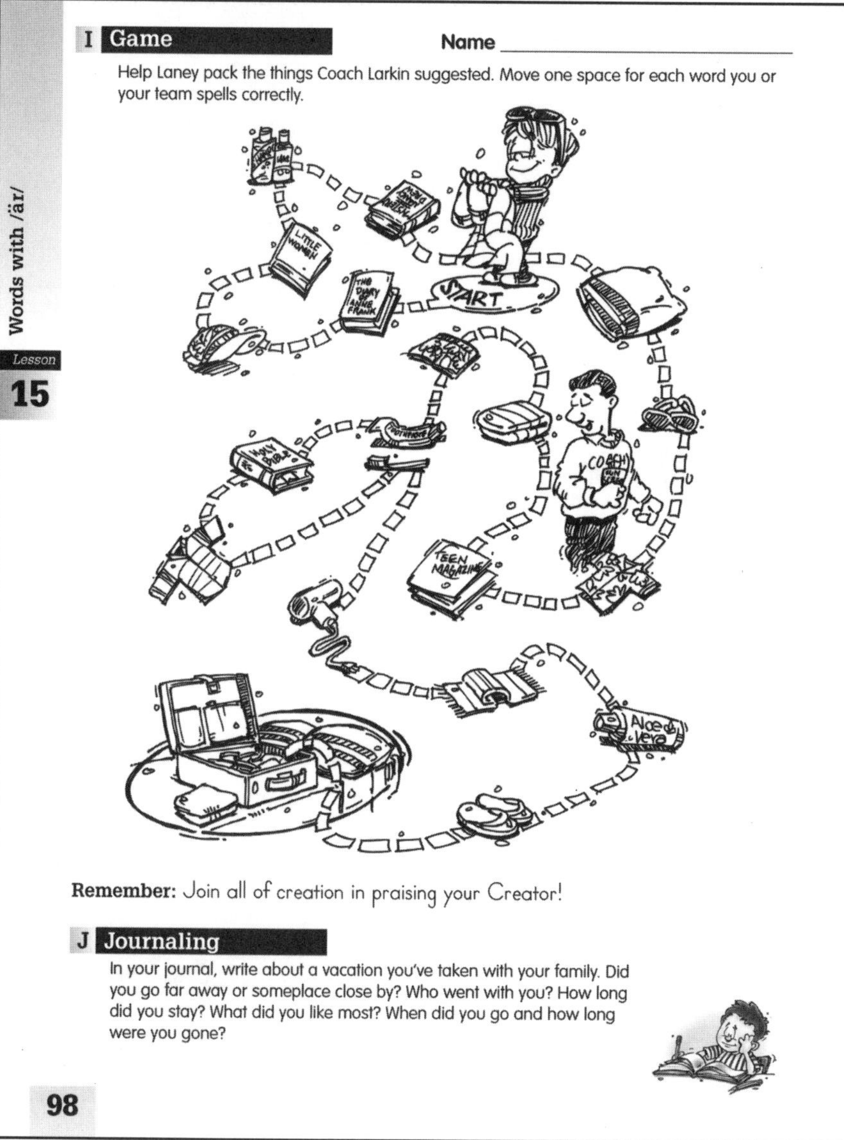

Words with /är/

Lesson 15

I Game Name ____________________

Help Laney pack the things Coach Larkin suggested. Move one space for each word you or your team spells correctly.

Remember: Join all of creation in praising your Creator!

J Journaling

In your journal, write about a vacation you've taken with your family. Did you go far away or someplace close by? Who went with you? How long did you stay? What did you like most? When did you go and how long were you gone?

98

2 Game

Reinforce spelling skills and provide motivation and interest.

Materials

- game page (from student text)
- game pieces (1 per child)
- game word list

Game Word List

1. **harbor**
2. **cardiac**
3. **hardship**
4. **Antarctica**
5. **Arkansas**
6. **argument**
7. **bargain**
8. **snarl**
9. **harmony**
10. **radar**
11. **artery**
12. **artichoke**
13. **cartilage**
14. **carton**
15. **chart**
16. **compartment**
17. **department**
18. **dart**
19. **hearty**
20. **partner**

How to Play:

- Divide the class into two teams.
- Have each student place his/her game piece on Start.
- Have a student from team A go to the board.
- Say the spelling word.
- Have the student write the word on the board.
- If correct, instruct each member of team A to move his/her game piece forward one space.
- Alternate between teams A and B.
- The team to reach Laney's suitcase first is the winner.
- **Small Group Option**: Students may play this game without teacher direction in small groups of two or more.

3 Journaling

Provide a meaningful reason for correct spelling through personal writing.

Review the story using discussion leads provided on the following page. Encourage students to apply the Scriptural value in their journaling.

Journaling (continued)

- Where did Laney go for Christmas vacation? (The Bahamas.)
- Where are some places you've been for Christmas vacation?
- How did Laney feel about leaving the small town where she lives with her mom and stepdad? (She was happy to get out of there for a while.)
- What were some of the things Laney was looking forward to seeing or doing in the Bahamas? (Coral reefs, sailing, snorkeling, clear blue water, crashing waves)
- Whom did Laney miss while she was gone? (Her mom, stepdad, and Wicker.)
- Why do you think she missed them so much?

IRAQ is one of the very few words ending in Q.

Word Wow!

1 Literature Connection
Topic: God's great love and faithfulness
Theme Text: Psalm 57:10

Fujiyama

When Setsuko and her parents climb Mount Fuji, she gets an idea of how truly incredible God is.

Setsuko checked the classroom clock. She had a few minutes free. Maybe she'd work on her spelling journal assignment. Pulling the worktext out of her desk, she flipped a few pages till she found the right spot. Silently she read the directions. "Read Psalm 57:10. Think about the words this Scripture uses to describe God's love. In your journal, write about something you think of when you read these descriptive words."

Setsuko turned the page and read the Scripture. "Vast as the heavens. Higher than the skies." She stared out the window as the words triggered a memory from last summer....

"Aren't we ready yet?" Setsuko tugged at her father's sleeve. "Look, those people are leaving."

Mr. Noma tucked a full water bottle in his small pack. "What's the hurry, Suzy-Q? You've been rushing from one thing to the next ever since we got to Japan. Afraid you'll miss something? You know, we'll be on Fujiyama (Mount Fuji) all night."

"I want to be sure we get to the top before the sun comes up." Setsuko stepped behind her father to get out of the way of a group of boisterous young men.

"Gomen kudasai (gō′ men kü dä′ sä i - excuse me)." Mrs. Noma worked her way through another group of climbers to reach her husband and daughter. "What a crowd!" She shook her head, "I think there are more climbers tonight than when we climbed Fuji-san before."

"Well, you know, Sweetheart, that was a long, long time ago," Mr. Noma teased. "Hey!" He barely caught the jacket she tossed at him. "When you and I climbed as teenagers, the weather was lousy. Since the climbing season only lasts from July 1 to August 31, whenever the weather's decent the mountain's crowded. And tonight it's almost perfect."

"So let's climb!" Setsuko urged.

"Put this on, Setsuko-chan." Mrs. Noma handed a jacket to her daughter. "Then we'll go." She glanced at her watch. "We'll have plenty of time to make it for the tradition of watching sunrise from the summit, especially since we're starting from the fifth station."

"How many stations are there?" Setsuko almost stepped on her father's heels as she eagerly followed him from the hut.

"Ten, dividing the climb into stages." Mr. Noma led his family onto the trail. "At each we can pay 200 yen and get another souvenir stamp burned into our climbing sticks."

"All right!" Setsuko admired the octagonal walking stick in her hand. "Do all the stamps look like this one?" She ran her hand over the rectangles filled with Japanese characters.

"No, they're all different." Mrs. Noma stopped and flicked her flashlight off for an instant to look into the sky. "Isn't the moon beautiful now that we're away from the lights of the hut?"

"Yeah." Setsuko glanced up. "But we could see it even better if some people weren't carrying those paper lanterns. Why do they do that, Otosan (ō tō sän - father)?"

"Pilgrimage." Mr. Noma moved at a steady pace, following the stream of people in front of him. "Climbing Mount Fuji began as a religious practice, and some people in Japan still consider the mountain to be sacred. See those climbers in grass sandals?"

Setsuko kicked a rock with the toe of her sturdy hiking boot. "I bet they're going to have really sore feet by the time they get to the top!" She walked in silence for a few moments. "How far is it to the top?"

"Well, the volcano is 12,395 feet high, the highest peak in Japan, and the path switches back and forth as it goes up the side." Mr. Noma shifted the pack on his back. "We'll be covering a lot of ground in the next few hours."

"What do we do if we get to the top before the sun comes up?" Setsuko's eyes followed a short Japanese man with a red and white handkerchief tied around his head. He passed the Nomas and trotted on.

"We probably won't get there too early," Mother chuckled. "The path is almost level right here at station 5, but that won't last for long!"

The trail turned steeply up the mountain. Mr. Noma called over his shoulder, "Watch your step."

Soon Setsuko was struggling to get enough air. "Is it pff...pff like this pff... pff all the way?"

Mr. Noma paused by a tall wooden sign and waited for Setsuko to catch up. "Some parts of the path are dirt, some gravel, some cobblestone. It's not a technical climb, but it certainly is a grueling hike, and lots of people that start out don't make it to the top." He motioned to the sign. "Look at these rules."

Setsuko read the list aloud, "'Avoid climbing during bad weather. Take refuge at nearby huts when lightning, strong wind, or heavy rain occurs. Do not stray from the route. Do not run when descending. Beware of falling rocks. Do not climb when tired. Be careful and enjoy a safe climb.' But, Otosan, I'm already tired!" she wailed.

"Come on, Suzy-Q! Where's all that energy we've seen while you've been dragging your mother and me all over Tokyo?" Mr. Noma teased.

"Gone," Setsuko sighed as they rejoined the stream

of climbers. She concentrated on placing one foot in front of the other and was surprised when they reached the sixth station. Setsuko revived a bit when she ate some sembeh (sem be - rice crackers) and watched in fascination as the station stamp was burned onto her stick with a small branding iron heated in an open fire. Then, back to the climb.

"Okasan (ō kä sän - mother), my feet slide back a step for every two steps forward!" Setsuko complained.

"That's because this part of the trail is volcanic ash." Mrs. Noma swept the light from her flashlight along the trail. "We take a different trail down the mountain. It's almost entirely an ash slide. One step down and you can slide for yards! It makes a quick trip down that you'll be glad for then, but I'll admit this is hard stuff to climb." Setsuko's mother used both hands and feet to make it up a particularly steep place.

Suddenly a young woman almost bowled over some climbers as she raced down the trail. Setsuko slipped and sat down hard on the trail when the girl flew past the Noma family. The woman's laughter rang out as she ran swiftly down the ash slide. Setsuko stared in horror when the young woman's laughter turned to screams of terror. She was going too fast and she couldn't stop! In seconds she would go over the sheer drop along the edge of the trail.

In an instant, two men on the trail below launched themselves upwards and sideways toward her, knocking her off her feet. Everyone along that stretch of trail held their breath as the three climbers slid in a tangle of arms and legs toward the edge. Inches away from thin air, they halted.

Setsuko took the hand her father offered and pulled herself up. "I guess that's why the rule says 'Do not run when descending.'" She shook her head and started carefully climbing once more.

It didn't get easier. Just before the seventh station they scaled a rock face. It was kind of scary finding handholds and pulling yourself up the chains that had been firmly placed along the rock face, especially since the weather had changed and occasional drops of freezing rain pelted the climbers. The crowded station was warm and the fire wonderful.

"Otosan, are we even going to be able to see the sunrise at all in this weather?" Setsuko shrugged into a thick sweatshirt. "I thought it would stay nice like it was when we started."

"Fuji-san is tall enough to create its own weather, Suzy-Q." Mr. Noma sipped hot tea gratefully. "But it could be clear on top. Somewhere around station eight the mountain usually breaks through the clouds. Ready?"

"I'm tired and sleepy and cold." Setsuko rubbed her gritty eyes. "I don't think I can make it," she grumbled.

"Sure you can." Mrs. Noma gave her daughter a hug. "We'll just keep up a slow, steady pace and be there before you know it."

But when they reached station eight Setsuko was still ready to quit. Parts of the hut were occupied by hikers sleeping on tatami mats. Effects of high altitude, stiff winds, and the hard night climb tempted Setsuko to join them.

"This should revive you, Setsuko-chan." Father handed her a bowl of deliciously warm, fragrant so-soba (sō sō bä - noodle soup).

The soup helped. Setsuko even found the energy to write a short message on a couple of postcards and to drop them in the mailbox at station eight, Mount Fuji Post Office. Then it was back to putting one foot in front of the other, trying to ignore the cold and her tired muscles.

"Seven hours—not bad." Setsuko bumped into her father when he suddenly stopped. "Whoa, there! Don't you want to stay a minute or two after working so hard to get here?"

"Here?" Setsuko squeaked. "This is it?" She looked around in dismay. A shrine, several mountain huts and a crowd of weary hikers. True, the sign on the shrine said "SUMMIT," but could this really be it? It seemed anti-climactic—that is until a few minutes later when the sun began to rise!

Mrs. Noma slipped her arm around her weary daughter and whispered the well known verse as they watched the sunrise, "The heavens declare the glory of God."

"Everything in heaven and earth is Yours, oh Lord," Mr. Noma added quietly, wrapping his arms around mother and daughter. Setsuko leaned back against her father, tiredness forgotten. The light and color were breathtaking, the view awesome as the sun slipped slowly into the heavens.

A bell rang. Setsuko blinked and looked around. She was at school, and her free time was up. Oh, well, at least she knew what she would write about in her journal this week!

2 Discussion Time

Check understanding of the story and development of personal values.

- Of what did Psalm 57:10 remind Setsuko?
- What mountain did Setsuko and her parents climb last summer in Japan?
- Why do most people climb the mountain at night?
- Why were there so many people climbing the mountain that night?
- At which station did the Noma family start their climb?
- What happened to the woman that ran down the trail?
- What did Setsuko think when they reached the summit?
- How did her thoughts change when the sun began to rise?

A Preview Name ____________________

Write each word as your teacher says it.

1. Arizona
2. librarian
3. prepare
4. software
5. narrate
6. marriage
7. Ontario
8. narrow
9. area
10. aware
11. caramel
12. parakeet
13. barracks
14. embarrassed
15. barrier
16. aerobics
17. Delaware
18. barren
19. compare
20. parallel

Scripture
Psalm 57:10

Words with /ar/ or /âr/

Lesson 16

99

3 Preview

Test for knowledge of the correct spellings of these words.

Customize Your List

On a separate sheet of paper, additional words of your choice may be tested.

I will say each word once, use the word in a sentence, then say the word again. Write the words on the lines in your Worktext.

Correct Immediately!

Let's correct our Preview. I will spell each word out loud. If you spelled a word incorrectly, rewrite it correctly.

Progress Chart

Students may record scores. (Reproducible master provided in Appendix B.)

Lesson 16 | Day 1

1. Arizona — Mt. Fuji is not in **Arizona.**
2. librarian — Before the trip, the **librarian** helped Setsuko find information on travel in Japan.
3. prepare — She wanted to **prepare** for the trip in every way possible.
4. software — The Nomas purchased special **software** that helped them plan their trip.
5. narrate — Setsuko listened to her father **narrate** an ancient tale about Mt. Fuji.
6. marriage — This was the first time since their **marriage** that the Nomas had been to Japan.
7. Ontario — A scientist from **Ontario** was there to make the climb.
8. narrow — The trail quickly became **narrow** and steep.
9. area — There was more than one rest **area** along the trail.
10. aware — Setsuko wasn't **aware** the climb would be so exhausting.
11. caramel — She chewed a sticky **caramel** as she rested.
12. parakeet — One woman carried her caged **parakeet** on the climb.
13. barracks — There are **barracks** or bunk houses at the foot of Mt. Fuji.
14. embarrassed — The Japanese woman was **embarrassed** about her fall.
15. barrier — The two Japanese men made a **barrier** with their bodies.
16. aerobics — Setsuko felt sure she would not feel like doing **aerobics** after this climb.
17. Delaware — Their friends from **Delaware** had made the long trip with them.
18. barren — The summit seemed like a dismal, **barren** place till the sun rose.
19. compare — Setsuko thought no sight could **compare** with this.
20. parallel — "Nothing can **parallel** God's majesty," said Mr. Noma.

Lesson 16 | Day 1

4 Word Shapes

Help students form a correct image of whole words.

Look at each word and think about its shape. Now, write the word in the correct word Shape Boxes. You may check off each word as you use it.

(In many words, the sounds of **/ar/** and **/âr/** are spelled with **are** or **ar**. Because spellers cannot rely on a phonetic way of remembering the various spellings, this sound is often difficult.)

In the word shape boxes, fill in the boxes containing the letters that spell the sound of **/ar/** or **/âr/** in each word.

Take a minute to memorize...

Psalm 57:10

Words with /ar/ or /âr/ — Lesson 16

B Word Shapes **Name** ____________________

Using the word bank below, write each word in the correct word shape boxes. Next, in the word shape boxes, fill in the boxes containing the letter or letters that spell the sound of **/ar/** or **/âr/** in each word.

1. Delaware
2. barren
3. narrow
4. Arizona
5. librarian
6. compare
7. narrate
8. marriage
9. aerobics
10. barrier
11. barracks
12. aware
13. caramel
14. embarrassed
15. area
16. parakeet
17. software
18. parallel
19. prepare
20. Ontario

Word Bank

aerobics	barracks	compare	marriage	parakeet
area	barren	Delaware	narrate	parallel
Arizona	barrier	embarrassed	narrow	prepare
aware	caramel	librarian	Ontario	software

100

Answers may vary for duplicate word shapes.

Be Prepared For Fun

Check these supply lists for **Fun Ways to Spell** - presented **Day 2**. Purchase and/or gather these items ahead of time!

General
- Pencil
- Notebook Paper
- Spelling List

Auditory
- Pencil
- 3 X 5 Cards Cut in half lengthwise (20 per child)
- Spelling List

Visual
- Colored Pencils
- Graph Paper (2 sheets per child)
- Spelling List

Tactile
- Clay
- Spelling List

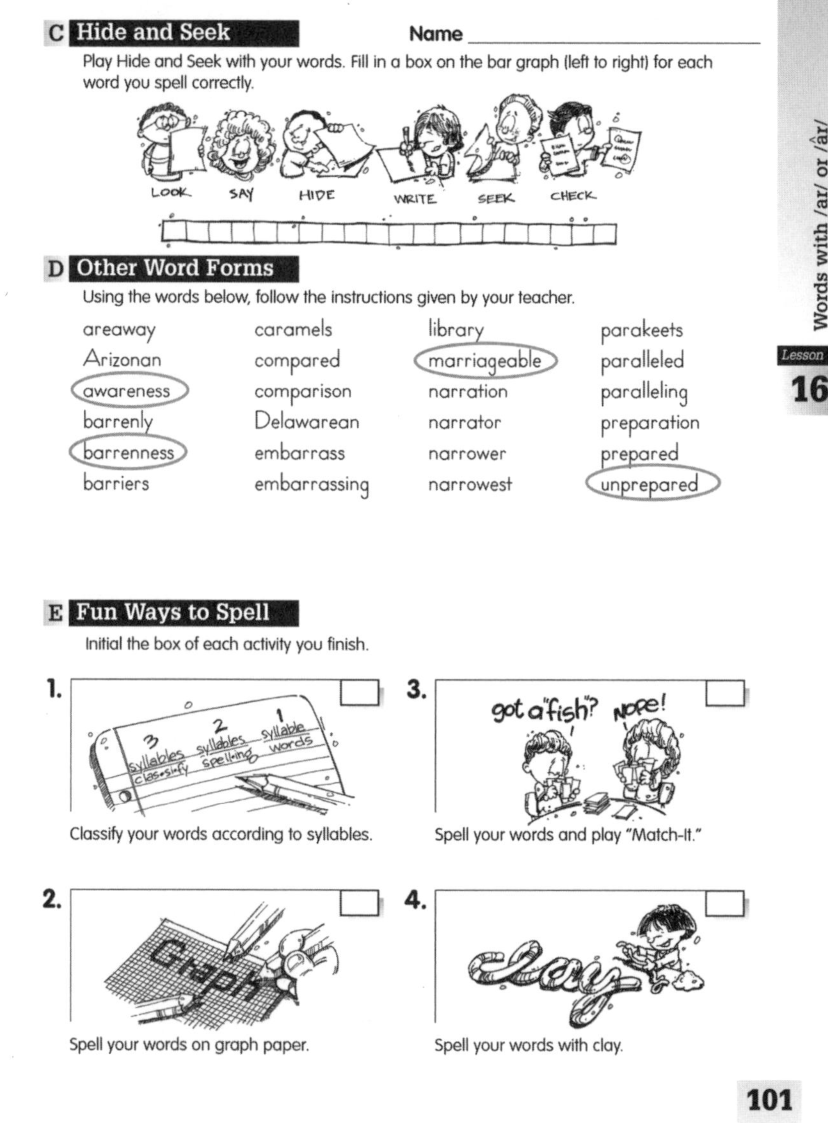

1 Hide and Seek

Reinforce spelling by using multiple styles of learning.

On a white board, Teacher writes each word — one at a time. **Have students:**

- **Look** at the word.
- **Say** the word out loud.
- **Spell** the word out loud.
- **Hide** (teacher erases word.)
- **Write** the word on paper.
- **Seek** (teacher rewrites word.)
- **Check** spelling. If incorrect, rewrite word correctly.

2 Other Word Forms

This activity is optional. Have students find and circle the Other Word Forms that are most nearly antonyms of the following:

ready
fruitfulness
ignorance
dissimilar

3 Fun Ways to Spell

Four activities are provided. Use one, two, three, or all of the activities. Have students initial the box for each activity they complete.

Options:

- assign activities to students according to their learning styles
- set up the activities in learning centers for the students to do throughout the day
- divide students into four groups and assign one activity per group
- do one activity per day

General

To classify your words according to syllables...
- Write three headings on your paper: One-syllable, Two-syllable, and Three-syllable.
- Write the first word on your list under the proper heading.
- Draw a line through the word to divide it into syllables.
- Do this with each word.

Auditory

To spell your words and play "Match-It"...
- Write each word on a card. Mix your word-cards and a classmate's together. Deal six cards to each player; the rest face down between you. Ask your classmate for a word-card. If the word-card matches, take it and play again. If not, draw from the stack, and it is your classmate's turn. Take turns until all cards are matched.

Visual

To spell your words on graph paper...
- Look at the first word on your list.
- Shade in squares to form the letters of each word.
- Check your spelling.
- Do this with each word.

Tactile

To spell your words with clay...
- Roll pieces of clay into ropes.
- Use the ropes to make the letters of each word.
- Put them in the right order to spell each word.
- Check your spelling.

Working with Words

Familiarize students with word meaning and usage.

Hidden Words

Explain that the spelling words for this week are hidden in the puzzle. After finding each word, the student should write the word under the correct heading.

Use the word bank to help you find each of the words in the puzzle. Words may go across, down, or diagonally. Circle, then write the words.

Take a minute to memorize...

Psalm 57:10

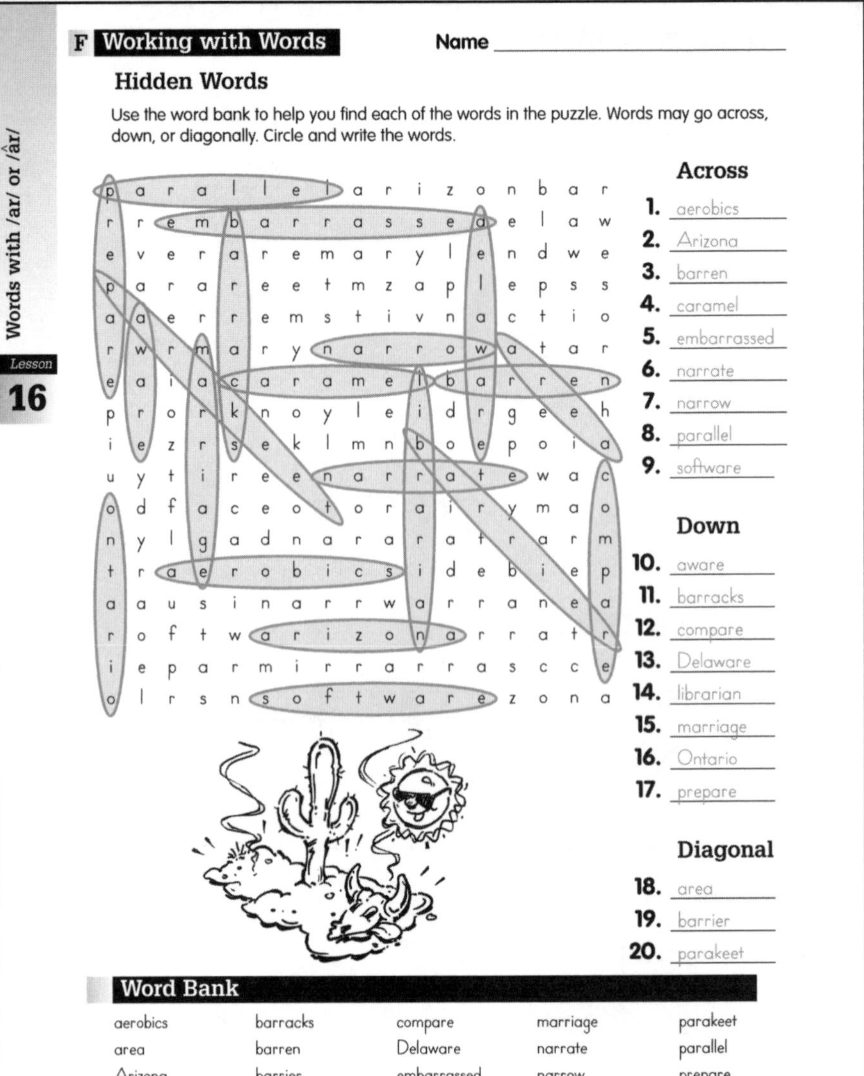

Words with /ar/ or /âr/ — Lesson 16

F Working with Words — Name ____________

Hidden Words

Use the word bank to help you find each of the words in the puzzle. Words may go across, down, or diagonally. Circle and write the words.

```
p a r a l l e l a r i z o n b a r
r r e m b a r r a s s e d e l a w
e v e r a r e m a r y l e n d w e
p a r a r e e t m z a p l e p s s
a a e r r e m s t i v n a c t i o
r w r m a r y n a r r o w a t a r
e a i a c a r a m e l b a r r e n
p r o r k n o y l e i d r g e e h
i e z r s e k l m n b o e p o i a
u y t i r e e n a r r a t e w a c
o d f a c e o t o r a i r y m a o
n y l g a d n a r a r a t r a r m
t r a e r o b i c s i d e b i e p
a a u s i n a r r w a r r a n e a
r o f t w a r i z o n a r r a t r
i e p a r m i r r a r r a s c c e
o l r s n s o f t w a r e z o n a
```

Across

1. aerobics
2. Arizona
3. barren
4. caramel
5. embarrassed
6. narrate
7. narrow
8. parallel
9. software

Down

10. aware
11. barracks
12. compare
13. Delaware
14. librarian
15. marriage
16. Ontario
17. prepare

Diagonal

18. area
19. barrier
20. parakeet

Word Bank

aerobics	barracks	compare	marriage	parakeet
area	barren	Delaware	narrate	parallel
Arizona	barrier	embarrassed	narrow	prepare
aware	caramel	librarian	Ontario	software

102

G Dictation Name ______________________

Write each sentence as your teacher dictates. Use correct punctuation.

1. Setsuko was so weary, she found it hard to climb up the narrow, slippery track.
2. Looking around the area, she became aware of the beautiful things God had made.
3. Setsuko asked the librarian to help her find books about famous places.

Words with /ar/ or /âr/

Lesson 16

H Proofreading

If a word is misspelled, fill in the oval by that word. If all the words are spelled correctly, fill in the oval by **no mistake**.

1. ○ area ● arizona ○ argument ○ no mistake	**5.** ○ bargain ● compair ○ Delaware ○ no mistake	**9.** ● airobics ○ narrate ○ narrow ○ no mistake	
2. ● awair ○ radar ○ snarl ○ no mistake	**6.** ● embarassed ○ hardship ○ Arkansas ○ no mistake	**10.** ○ Ontario ● parakeat ○ chart ○ no mistake	
3. ● baracks ○ barren ○ harmony ○ no mistake	**7.** ○ cartilage ○ department ● librarien ○ no mistake	**11.** ● parralel ○ carton ○ compartment ○ no mistake	
4. ○ caramel ○ artichoke ● barryer ○ no mistake	**8.** ○ cardiac ○ Antarctica ● marrige ○ no mistake	**12.** ○ prepare ● softwair ○ harbor ○ no mistake	

103

1 Dictation

Reinforce correct spelling by using current and previous words in context.

Listen as I read each sentence and then write it in your Worktext. Remember to use correct capitalization and punctuation. (Slowly read each sentence twice. Sentences are found in the Student Worktext to the left.)

2 Proofreading

Familiarize students with standardized test format and reinforce recognition of misspelled words.

Look at each set of words. If a word is misspelled, fill in the oval by that word. If all the words are spelled correctly, fill in the oval by **no mistake**.

Day 4 | Lesson 16

3 Hide and Seek

Reinforce correct spelling of current spelling words. Repeat this activity from Day 2.

4 Vocabulary Extension

Have your students complete this activity to strengthen spelling ability and expand vocabulary. The reproducible master is provided in Appendix A as shown on the inset page to the right.

1 Posttest

Test mastery of the spelling words.

I will say the word once, use it in a sentence, then say it again. Write your words on a separate sheet of paper.

Progress Chart
Students may record scores. (Reproducible master in Appendix B.)

Personal Dictionary
Students may add any words they have misspelled to their personal dictionaries for reference when writing. (Cover in Appendix B.)

Vocabulary Extension | Lesson 16

Hide and Seek

Play Hide and Seek with your words. Fill in a bar graph (left to right) for each word you spell correctly.

Vocabulary Extension

Cause and Effect

Write a word from the word bank to complete each sentence.

1. If you promise that something will work, you guarantee it.
2. If you study about the tubes that carry blood throughout your body, you are learning about arteries, veins, and capillaries.
3. If you want to write a letter to someone, you may write on some pretty stationery.
4. If you do not know what a word means, you can look it up in a dictionary.
5. If you are riding an exercise bike, it does not take you anywhere because it is stationary.
6. If you are sent to teach people about Jesus, you are being a missionary.
7. If you recite the details of something that has happened, you are being a narrator.
8. If you have a glass tank in which you keep fish, you have an aquarium.
9. If your mom says you must clean your room, it is necessary for you to do it.
10. If a country has a group of soldiers in the navy, air force, or army, they are known as a country's military.
11. If you are hired to handle records, mail, and routine work for another person, you are their secretary.
12. If you own a store that sells tools, bolts, nails, knobs, and other such things, you own a hardware store.

Word Bank

aquarium	guarantee	missionary	secretary
capillaries	hardware	narrator	stationary
dictionary	military	necessary	stationery

338

1. **librarian** — Setsuko asked the **librarian** for books about travel in Japan.
2. **prepare** — She and her family wanted to properly **prepare** for the trip.
3. **software** — There was a lot of **software** available for travel planning.
4. **marriage** — Since the beginning of their **marriage**, the Nomas had been planning a trip to Japan.
5. **Arizona** — Mt. Fuji is not in **Arizona**, but rather in Japan.
6. **narrow** — The path turned sharply and became **narrow** and steep.
7. **area** — Setsuko plopped down in the rest **area**, exhausted.
8. **caramel** — She pulled a **caramel** from her backpack and unwrapped it.
9. **aware** — She was not **aware** the climb would be so tiring.
10. **narrate** — While she rested, an elderly man began to **narrate** some of his childhood memories.
11. **parakeet** — One woman actually carried her **parakeet** in a cage as she climbed.
12. **barracks** — There were **barracks** at the foot of the mountain for spending the night.
13. **embarrassed** — The Japanese woman who fell was **embarrassed**, but very thankful.
14. **barrier** — She was very glad the two men formed a **barrier** to stop her fall.
15. **aerobics** — Setsuko knew she would not feel like attending **aerobics** after this climb.
16. **Delaware** — They met people from **Delaware** who had three young boys.
17. **Ontario** — The scientist from **Ontario** was a very strong climber.
18. **barren** — The summit looked **barren** and uninteresting at first.
19. **parallel** — Setsuko believed there was no **parallel** to the beauty before her.
20. **compare** — Nothing could **compare** with the majestic sunrise!

Words with /ar/ or /âr/

Lesson 16

I Game Name ____________________

Record points for each word you or your team spells correctly. Earn bonus points for each row in which all four words are spelled correctly.

	1	2	3	4	Row Totals
Row A	○	○	○	○	○
Row B	○	○	○	○	○
Row C	○	○	○	○	○
Row D	○	○	○	○	○
Row E	○	○	○	○	○
				TOTAL	○
				BONUS	○
				GRAND	○

Remember: God's love and faithfulness are even bigger than anything He created.

J Journaling

Read Psalm 57:10. Think about the words this Scripture uses to describe God's love. In your journal, write about something you think of when you read these descriptive words.

104

How to Play:

- Divide the class into two teams.
- Have a student from team A choose a square on the grid by indicating the row letter and number.
- Say the word that matches that row letter and number from the team's word list.
- Have the student write the word on the board.
- If correct, have each member of that team record the awarded points (in parentheses by the word) in the circle in that box. If the word is misspelled, have him/her put an **X** in that circle. That square may not be chosen again.
- Repeat this process with the second team.
- When all the words have been spelled by both teams, have each team tally its score. Award a bonus of 5 points for each row in which all four words were spelled correctly.
- Have the teams record their grand totals. The team with the highest score is the winner.

2 Game

Reinforce spelling skills and provide motivation and interest.

Materials

- game page (from student text)
- pencils (1 per child)
- game word list

Game Word List

Team A		Team B
E4	**aerobics (4)**	A1
E3	**area (2)**	A2
E2	**Arizona (3)**	A3
E1	**aware (1)**	A4
D4	**barracks (4)**	B1
D3	**barren (1)**	B2
D2	**barrier (3)**	B3
D1	**caramel (2)**	B4
C4	**compare (2)**	C1
C3	**Delaware (1)**	C2
C2	**embarrassed (3)**	C3
C1	**librarian (4)**	C4
B4	**marriage (3)**	D1
B3	**narrate (1)**	D2
B2	**narrow (4)**	D3
B1	**Ontario (2)**	D4
A4	**parakeet (1)**	E1
A3	**parallel (4)**	E2
A2	**prepare (2)**	E3
A1	**software (3)**	E4

3 Journaling

Provide a meaningful reason for correct spelling through personal writing.

Review the story using discussion leads provided on the following page. Encourage students to apply the Scriptural value in their journaling.

Day 5

Lesson 16

Journaling (continued)

- Have you ever climbed a mountain? (Allow time to share experiences.)
- Why is Mount Fuji special to the Japanese people? (It is the highest peak in Japan. Climbing the mountain began as a religious practice and many still consider the mountain to be sacred.)
- What were some of the rules for climbing Mount Fuji? (Avoid climbing during bad weather. Take refuge at nearby huts when lightning, strong wind, or heavy rain occurs. Do not stray from the route. Do not run when descending. Beware of falling rocks. Do not climb when tired. Be careful.)
- Why were so many people climbing that night? (The climbing season only lasts from July 1 to August 31, so many people climb whenever the weather is good during that time.)
- Why did Setsuko get so tired? (It got cold, they were climbing at a high altitude on steep trails, and they climbed all night.)
- What could you pay to have done to your walking stick at each station? (You could have a souvenir stamp from that station burned into the wooden walking stick.)
- What was different about Station 8? (There was a post office there on the mountain.)
- Do you think Setsuko was glad she made it to the top? Why or why not? (Yes. The view of the sunrise was awesome.)

OF is apparently the only word in which an F is pronounced like a V.

Word Wow!

The Promise of Peace

Setsuko learns that, although horrible things happen in this world, God always keeps his promises to be with us.

"Look, Okasan!" Setsuko pointed out the window of the train. "There's a river. I wonder if it's the Ota (ō tä) River. Aren't there six rivers here?"

"That's right." Mrs. Noma watched the changing scenes flash by. "Hiroshima means 'Wide Island' and its nickname is the 'City of Water' because it grew from five different villages that were settled on the river deltas. Now we usually remember it as the city destroyed by the first atomic bomb."

"Our stop is next—have you got everything together?" Mr. Noma asked Setsuko.

Setsuko grabbed her backpack, "Right here—camera, wallet, comb, extra film. Are we going to the museum first?"

"I think so." Father led the way toward the door. "Stick close, you two."

The triangular-shaped park was a peaceful island in the city between two rivers. Once an area filled with fashionable shops, it was demolished by the atomic bomb on August 6, 1945. Now there are flowers and more than 1,600 trees shading the various peace memorials in the area.

Walking into the park from the south, the Nomas passed a statue of a mother bending over to shield a small child she held in her arms, while reaching behind to protect her older child. Next, the massive Fountain of Peace sprayed constantly into the sky.

The Peace Memorial Hall was a long rectangular cement-and-glass building built on 10 cement columns. It was quiet inside the museum. Setsuko gazed in horrified fascination at the displays. She couldn't stop looking at the lunch boxes blackened by the blast, wristwatches stopped at the instant of the explosion, glass bottles melted together from the intense heat, and stone columns on which human shadows are permanently etched.

After a couple of hours it was nice to get out in the sun again, to hear birds singing and children laughing in the park. Setsuko pointed out an object at the end of a wide cement walkway. "What's that thing that looks kind of like the top part of a covered wagon?"

"A cenotaph. This booklet says that it's the shape of an ancient Japanese clay house and is there to keep the souls of those who died in the bombing out of the rain." Mr. Noma scanned the brochure while leading his family toward the strange monument.

Mrs. Noma read the inscription on the stone coffin under the arched shelter. "Let all the souls here rest in peace; For we shall not repeat the evil." She stepped back to let someone carrying flowers get close.

"Because of the bomb that was dropped here, almost 200 thousand people died," Mother told Setsuko quietly while they watched another person light incense. "A register of all their names is kept inside that stone coffin. Over the years the list has grown as people continue to die from illnesses caused by exposure to the radiation."

"Look at that building over there." Setsuko pointed at a ruined building that they could see by looking through the arch of the cenotaph. "Was that here when the atomic bomb hit?"

"Yes, it was." Mr. Noma explained while the three strolled around the large reflecting pool, "Nearly everything within a radius of two kilometers of ground zero was destroyed. After the blast only a few shells of reinforced concrete buildings were still standing. The one with the iron dome was the Hiroshima Prefecture Industrial Promotion Hall. Now it's called the A-Bomb Dome and is still standing as a sort of memorial."

They walked past the Fire of Peace at the far end of the pool and wandered through the rest of the park. Under a concrete arch a huge gong that could be struck for peace hung quietly.

A tall concrete monument by a covered rose garden caught Setsuko's attention. It was topped by a metal statue of a girl holding a giant origami crane. Inside the monument, shaped like an upside down cup with three large spaces cut out, hung thousands—maybe millions—of paper cranes.

Setsuko touched a bright red origami crane and asked her father, "What's this monument about?"

"Let's sit over there on that bench and I'll tell you about it," Mr. Noma suggested. "A two-year-old girl survived the bombing. At least she seemed to be okay until about 10 years later. In the fall of her twelfth year, Sadako Sasaki (sä dä kō sä sä ki) got leukemia, a kind of cancer, from the radiation of the A-bomb. She had one hope. She believed that if she could fold 1,000 paper cranes she'd be cured. She didn't live long enough. Her classmates were so sad and upset by her death they started a project which grew into a national one to build this monument, called the Children's Peace Monument. Now there are always new paper cranes symbolizing prayers for peace."

"That's so sad." Setsuko stared at the monument and thought of the girl, so close to her own age, who had fought so hard to live.

"Yes, it certainly is," Mrs. Noma agreed. "It's all so sad. When that atomic bomb exploded, people within a one-kilometer circle died. People as far away as three and one-half kilometers got terrible burns. Many suffer still from keloids or massive scars. In fact, your grandmother's

Story (continued)

cousins lived here then. Why don't you ask her to tell you about that when we get back to her house?"

The next day Setsuko sat on the tatami floor of her grandmother's small house in Yokohama and flipped through the postcards she'd purchased in Hiroshima. "Grandmother, look at this." She held up one of the cards for her grandmother to see. "Okasan told me about the girl who made origami cranes. Did you know her?"

Grandmother shook her head, "Iie (ē e - no)." She took the postcard and gazed at it for a long moment before handing it back. "So many people—so many dead and hurt."

"What was it like?" Setsuko placed the cards back in their folder. "Did you see it?"

Setsuko's grandmother shook her head again. "Futaba (fū tä bä, my itoko (i tō ko - cousin) told me how it was." Setsuko moved closer and listened intently. "The day before had been a holiday and she and her sister had gone swimming in the Kyobashigawa (kyō bä shē gä wä). They had had a wonderful time, but when she woke up on August 6 Futaba had a fever, so her mother kept her home from school. It was a beautiful, clear day. She watched her older sister go off to work at the factory."

Without pause, the small woman moved across the room to make ocha (Japanese tea), while continuing her story. Her hands moved through each task with the sure ease of much practice. "It was still early when Futaba stepped outside to get the newspaper out of the letter box for her mother. The sun was shining so brightly she almost didn't notice the plane flying very high, but its silver wings reflected the light and caught her attention. She thought she saw a parachute coming down from the plane, and then the whole sky flashed. She thought a fire had been set in her eyes—a purple-like spark a billion times stronger than anything she'd seen before. The explosion knocked her to the ground as buildings and their contents crashed all around.

"The beautiful day had vanished. It was like evening, and everything appeared vague and hazy. The house was gone—flattened—as were all the other houses in the area. Futaba managed to move some boards and other debris to help her mother out. When fires broke out soon after the explosion, the two of them struggled to a nearby river. They saw incredible suffering and devastation. Futaba now has keloid scars on her back and right arm from severe burns, but she and her mother survived. Many people did not. They never saw her father or sister again."

Grandmother handed a steaming cup of tea to her granddaughter. Setsuko sniffed the fragrant tea appreciatively, but looked up with a frown. "I don't see how God could let something so awful happen."

Grandmother took a sip of her own tea before replying. "It was awful, but many other awful, horrible things have happened—and will happen—in this world. We just have to remember that God has promised to help us through whatever happens to us, even the awful, horrible things. And you know, Setsuko-chan, that God always keeps his promises."

Setsuko carefully set down her teacup before giving her grandmother a tight hug. "I love you, Grandmother. I wish we could always be together."

The old woman smiled and held her granddaughter close. "Aishtimasu (ä ish ti mä sū - I love you)." She wiped away a tear. "This visit has been much too short, and you're growing so very fast. Soon you will be a young lady and I will be an even older one." She chuckled. "Already you are almost as tall as your grandmother." She stroked Setsuko's smooth black hair. "It is sad that we can't always be together, but remember the yakusoku (yä kü sō kü - promise)?" With one finger under Setsuko's chin, she tipped her granddaughter's face up towards her own.

"You mean that God will help us through whatever happens to us?"

"Hai, so desu yo! (hä ē sō de sū yō - yes!)" Grandmother reached for a piece of paper on the small table nearby and began to fold it expertly. "Do you trust God to keep that promise, Setsuko-chan?"

Setsuko nodded. She watched her grandmother's quick fingers shape the red paper. "Perhaps this will remind you that no matter how far apart we are, you are in my heart and that God is keeping His promises." Grandmother gave Setsuko a squeeze and handed her a tiny red origami crane.

2 Discussion Time

Check understanding of the story and development of personal values.

- On their trip to Japan, Setsuko and her parents visited a city that had been destroyed by an atomic bomb during World War II. What was its name?
- What things did Setsuko see in the Peace Memorial Hall museum?
- Why was one ruined building left standing at the park?
- Why did the little girl, Sadako Sasaki, try to make one thousand paper cranes?
- Who did Setsuko's grandmother know that had been in Hiroshima when the bomb fell?
- What did grandmother make and give to Setsuko?

A Preview Name ____________

Write each word as your teacher says it.

1. haiku
2. biceps
3. coyote
4. migrant
5. crisis
6. device
7. entice
8. iceberg
9. fiery
10. aisle
11. eyeing
12. compile
13. crime
14. climate
15. dining
16. combine
17. decline
18. pride
19. aspire
20. imply

Words with /ī/

Lesson 17

Scripture
Psalm 18:30

105

3 Preview

Test for knowledge of the correct spellings of these words.

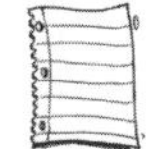

Customize Your List

On a separate sheet of paper, additional words of your choice may be tested.

I will say each word once, use the word in a sentence, then say the word again. Write the words on the lines in your Worktext.

Correct Immediately!

Let's correct our Preview. I will spell each word out loud. If you spelled a word incorrectly, rewrite it correctly.

Progress Chart

Students may record scores. (Reproducible master provided in Appendix B.)

Lesson 17 | Day 1

1. haiku	A **haiku** is a Japanese lyric poem that often points to something in nature.
2. biceps	The man who loaded their luggage on the train had large **biceps**.
3. coyote	There is not a single **coyote** in Japan.
4. migrant	Setsuko's father's father was a **migrant** worker when he first arrived in America.
5. crisis	The bombing of Hiroshima was no little **crisis** for the people of Japan.
6. device	There was no **device** on the ground that could save the Japanese people.
7. entice	The bombing did **entice** the people away from war and toward peace.
8. iceberg	The largest **iceberg** in the world could not have withstood the heat of the bomb.
9. fiery	There was more than one **fiery** explosion after the bomb fell.
10. aisle	In one memorial, there was an **aisle** running between two rows of flowers.
11. eyeing	Setsuko stood for a long while **eyeing** the monument filled with red paper cranes.
12. compile	Historians have tried to **compile** photos and documentation of the bombing.
13. crime	It is a **crime** to deface a war monument in Hiroshima.
14. climate	The **climate** in Hiroshima was favorable during their visit.
15. dining	After **dining** at an outdoor cafe, the Nomas continued their tour.
16. combine	The Japanese don't **combine** sugar and tea, but rather drink their tea plain.
17. decline	Setsuko did not **decline** the tea, but drank it gratefully.
18. pride	Setsuko felt a warm **pride** at her grandmother's ability to fold the paper.
19. aspire	She will **aspire** to learn origami as well as her grandmother has.
20. imply	Setsuko's grandmother did more than **imply** that God is faithful!

Lesson **17** | Day 1

4 Word Shapes

Help students form a correct image of whole words.

Look at each word and think about its shape. Now, write the word in the correct word Shape Boxes. You may check off each word as you use it.

(In many words, the sound of /ī/ is spelled with **i** at the end of a syllable, or with **ie**, or **i-consonant-e**. It is sometimes spelled with **y** at the end of a word.)

In the word shape boxes, fill in the boxes containing the letter or letters that spell the sound of /ī/ in each word.

Take a minute to memorize...

Psalm 18:30

Words with /ī/ — Lesson 17

B Word Shapes Name ____________

Using the word bank below, write each word in the correct word shape boxes. Next, in the word shape boxes, fill in the boxes containing the letter or letters that spell the sound of /ī/ in each word.

1. aisle
2. haiku
3. crisis
4. climate
5. aspire
6. dining
7. pride
8. fiery
9. decline
10. eyeing
11. combine
12. biceps
13. iceberg
14. compile
15. crime
16. device
17. migrant
18. coyote
19. imply
20. entice

Word Bank

aisle	combine	crisis	entice	iceberg
aspire	compile	decline	eyeing	imply
biceps	coyote	device	fiery	migrant
climate	crime	dining	haiku	pride

106

Answers may vary for duplicate word shapes.

Be Prepared For Fun

Check these supply lists for **Fun Ways to Spell** - presented **Day 2**.
Purchase and/or gather these items ahead of time!

General
- Pencil
- Graph Paper (1 sheet per child)
- Spelling List

Auditory
- Pencil
- Notebook Paper
- Spelling List

Visual
- Colored Pencils
- Alphabet Stencils
- Paper

Tactile
- Uncooked Rice
- Art Paper (1 sheet per child)
- Glue
- Spelling List

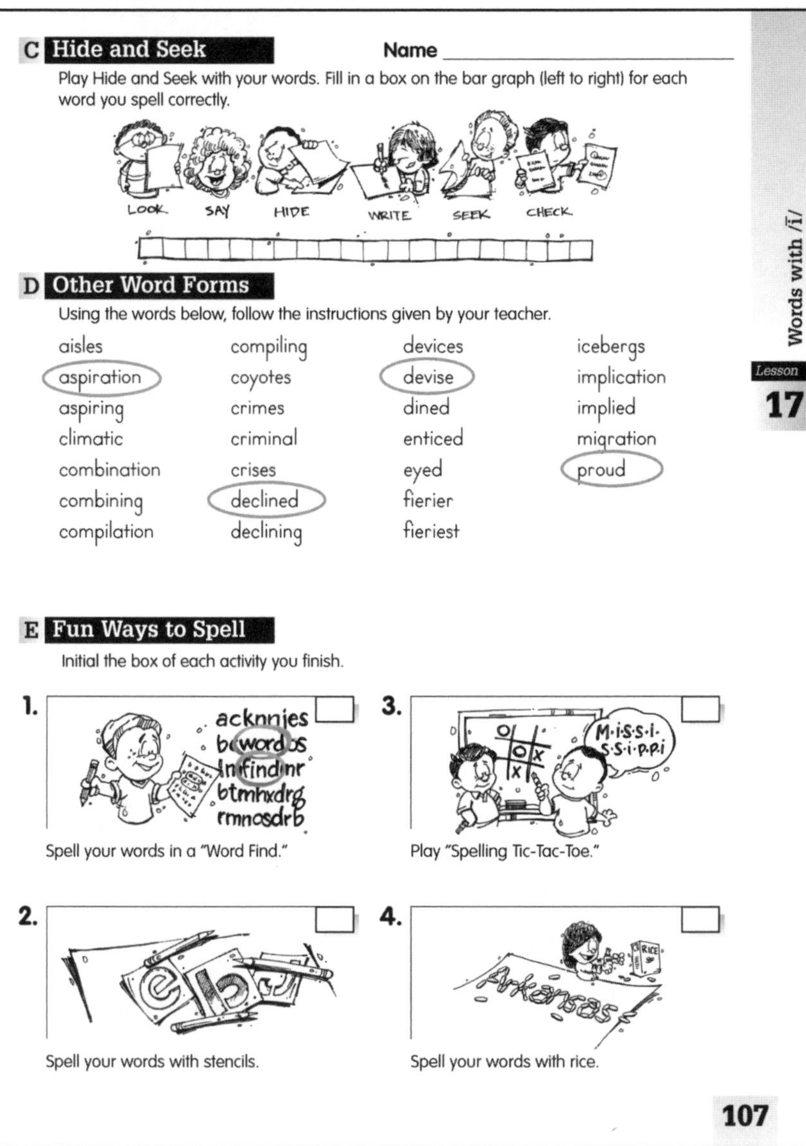

C Hide and Seek Name ______________

Play Hide and Seek with your words. Fill in a box on the bar graph (left to right) for each word you spell correctly.

D Other Word Forms

Using the words below, follow the instructions given by your teacher.

aisles	compiling	devices	icebergs
(aspiration)	coyotes	(devise)	implication
aspiring	crimes	dined	implied
climatic	criminal	enticed	migration
combination	crises	eyed	(proud)
combining	(declined)	fierier	
compilation	declining	fieriest	

E Fun Ways to Spell

Initial the box of each activity you finish.

1.
Spell your words in a "Word Find."

3.
Play "Spelling Tic-Tac-Toe."

2. Spell your words with stencils.

4.
Spell your words with rice.

Words with /ī/

Lesson 17

107

1 Hide and Seek

Reinforce spelling by using multiple styles of learning.

On a white board, Teacher writes each word — one at a time. **Have students:**

- **Look** at the word.
- **Say** the word out loud.
- **Spell** the word out loud.
- **Hide** (teacher erases word.)
- **Write** the word on paper.
- **Seek** (teacher rewrites word.)
- **Check** spelling. If incorrect, rewrite word correctly.

2 Other Word Forms

This activity is optional. Have students find and circle the Other Word Forms that are synonyms of the following:

ambition
contrive
haughty
rejected

3 Fun Ways to Spell

Four activities are provided. Use one, two, three, or all of the activities. Have students initial the box for each activity they complete.

Options:

- assign activities to students according to their learning styles
- set up the activities in learning centers for the students to do throughout the day
- divide students into four groups and assign one activity per group
- do one activity per day

General

To spell your words in a "Word Find"...
- Arrange your words on a piece of graph paper.
- Put one letter of each word in a square.
- Words may be written backwards, forwards, or diagonally.
- Outline your puzzle.
- Hide your words by filling in all the spaces inside the puzzle with random letters.
- Trade grids with a classmate and find the hidden words.

Auditory

To play "Spelling Tic-Tac-Toe"...
- Draw a Tic-Tac-Toe grid.
- Ask a classmate to read a word from the list.
- Spell the word aloud.
- If the word is spelled correctly, place your mark on the grid.
- Take turns with your classmate.

Visual

To spell your words with stencils...
- Look at the first letter of a word on your list.
- Place the stencil for the proper letter over your paper.
- Shade inside the stencil.
- Choose the proper stencil for the next letter of the word and shade it in next to the first letter.
- Finish the word in this way.
- Do this with each word.

Tactile

To spell your words with rice...
- Choose a word from your spelling list.
- Shape the letters of your word with rice.
- Glue the rice to art paper.
- Do this for each word on your list.

Lesson **17** | Day 3

1 Working with Words

Familiarize students with word meaning and usage.

Clues

Write this incomplete sentence on the board:

A larva that changes into a butterfly or moth is a __________.

Guide the students in choosing the word **caterpillar**.

Read each sentence and choose a spelling word for each definition. You may use a dictionary to help you. Write the word in the blank.

Take a minute to memorize...

Psalm 18:30

Lesson 17 — Words with /ī/

F Working with Words — Name ________________

Clues

Write a spelling word for each clue.

1. A <u>coyote</u> is a North American mammal related to a wolf.
2. A person who moves around doing seasonal work is a <u>migrant</u>.
3. To express indirectly, or hint at, is to <u>imply</u>.
4. An unrhymed Japanese poem of three lines is called <u>haiku</u>.
5. <u>Dining</u> means to be eating a meal.
6. The muscles in the front of the upper arm are called <u>biceps</u>.
7. Something that is burning or blazing is <u>fiery</u>.
8. To allure or tempt someone is to <u>entice</u> them.
9. To <u>aspire</u> is to try to attain or accomplish a certain goal.
10. Elation over an act or possession is called <u>pride</u>.
11. A <u>crisis</u> is a decisive or critical moment.
12. A piece of equipment for a special purpose is a <u>device</u>.
13. <u>Combine</u> means to put some things together to become one.
14. To collect and edit writings to make a book is to <u>compile</u>.
15. The <u>climate</u> is the average weather condition of a place.
16. To be looking at something or watching it is to be <u>eyeing</u> it.
17. A large floating mass of ice broken from a glacier is an <u>iceberg</u>.
18. A <u>crime</u> is a serious offense against the public law.
19. <u>Decline</u> is a gradual sinking and wasting away.
20. A passage between sections of seats is an <u>aisle</u>.

Word Bank

aisle	combine	crisis	entice	iceberg
aspire	compile	decline	eyeing	imply
biceps	coyote	device	fiery	migrant
climate	crime	dining	haiku	pride

108

G Dictation Name ____________________

Write each sentence as your teacher dictates. Use correct punctuation.

1. Setsuko listened as Grandmother told of the fiery atomic crisis.
2. Setsuko walked down the aisle of the museum, eyeing things without comment.
3. She began to compile a book of haiku to remind her of her homeland.

Words with /ī/

Lesson 17

H Proofreading

If a word is misspelled, fill in the oval by that word. If all the words are spelled correctly, fill in the oval by **no mistake**.

1. ○ imply ● biseps ○ area ○ no mistake
2. ○ crisis ○ device ○ Arizona ● no mistake
3. ● entise ○ parakeet ○ parallel ○ no mistake
4. ● iceburg ○ pride ○ software ○ no mistake
5. ○ migrant ● hiku ○ prepare ○ no mistake
6. ○ aisle ○ compile ○ crime ● no mistake
7. ● climit ○ combine ○ dining ○ no mistake
8. ○ narrow ○ Ontario ● dekline ○ no mistake
9. ● firey ○ aware ○ barracks ○ no mistake
10. ○ barrier ● cyote ○ barren ○ no mistake
11. ○ caramel ● aspier ○ compare ○ no mistake
12. ○ eyeing ○ embarrassed ○ librarian ● no mistake

109

Dictation

Reinforce correct spelling by using current and previous words in context.

Listen as I read each sentence and then write it in your Worktext. Remember to use correct capitalization and punctuation. (Slowly read each sentence twice. Sentences are found in the Student Worktext to the left.)

Day 4

2

Proofreading

Familiarize students with standardized test format and reinforce recognition of misspelled words.

Look at each set of words. If a word is misspelled, fill in the oval by that word. If all the words are spelled correctly, fill in the oval by **no mistake**.

Lesson 17

3 Hide and Seek

Reinforce correct spelling of current spelling words. Repeat this activity from Day 2.

4 Vocabulary Extension

Have your students complete this activity to strengthen spelling ability and expand vocabulary. The reproducible master is provided in Appendix A as shown on the inset page to the right.

1 Posttest

Test mastery of the spelling words.

I will say the word once, use it in a sentence, then say it again. Write your words on a separate sheet of paper.

Progress Chart

Students may record scores. (Reproducible master in Appendix B.)

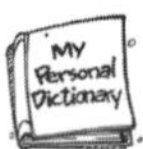

Personal Dictionary

Students may add any words they have misspelled to their personal dictionaries for reference when writing. (Cover in Appendix B.)

Vocabulary Extension | Lesson 17

Hide and Seek

Play Hide and Seek with your words. Fill in a bar graph (left to right) for each word you spell correctly.

Vocabulary Extension

Fill in the Blanks

Choose a word from the word bank that best fits each sentence clue.

1. I spoke to my mom in a rude manner. I'm afraid I was being impolite.
2. I have learned to ride my mountain bike well. I am a good bicyclist.
3. My dad had to get new glasses that have two sections in the lenses. He can see up close and far away with his new bifocals.
4. We had to change the plans for our tree house; however, we only needed to modify them a little.
5. We visited a refinery, a factory where raw materials are purified and made into finished products.
6. Your body needs foods that give you energy. Eat plenty of carbohydrates, such as bread, pasta, and potatoes.
7. We needed lightweight foods to take on our backpack trip, so Mom helped us dehydrate some in the food dryer.
8. Uncle Paul sure can eat a lot. He has a huge appetite because he works so hard.
9. My nephews play in the community orchestra. They are both good violinists.
10. I like to study about nature and the physical world. I really enjoy scientific experiments.
11. Some drivers travel too fast. This is a violation of the speed limit laws.
12. We watched a play in which the story was told through gestures, body movements, and facial expressions instead of words. It was called a pantomime.

Word Bank

appetite	carbohydrates	modify	scientific
bicyclist	dehydrate	pantomime	violation
bifocals	impolite	refinery	violinist

339

---

1. **biceps** — The man on the train used his strong **biceps** to lift the heavy luggage.
2. **crisis** — God is able to help us through any **crisis**, large or small.
3. **device** — There was a special **device** used to detonate the atomic bomb.
4. **fiery** — Many people in Hiroshima saw a **fiery** purple explosion in the sky.
5. **entice** — It seemed that nothing could **entice** the Japanese to peace.
6. **iceberg** — No **iceberg** of any size could withstand the heat of that blast.
7. **dining** — The Nomas knew they would be **dining** with Grandmother later that day.
8. **eyeing** — "I know it is hard to understand," Grandmother said, **eyeing** Setsuko's face.
9. **pride** — "We must never have the **pride** that says we know more than God," she said.
10. **imply** — The Bible does not **imply**, but states boldly, that God keeps his promises.
11. **compile** — Setsuko has tried to **compile**, or collect, many family stories.
12. **migrant** — She knew that her dad's father was a **migrant** worker his first years in America.
13. **aisle** — Setsuko quietly walked down the **aisle** of the huge peace memorial.
14. **crime** — It is a serious **crime** to deface any peace memorial in Hiroshima.
15. **climate** — The **climate** in Japan is much like that of the continental United States.
16. **combine** — She plans to **combine** information she reads with stories from her relatives.
17. **decline** — Setsuko would never **decline** her grandmother's offer to tell her a story.
18. **aspire** — Setsuko will **aspire** to be like her godly grandmother in many ways.
19. **haiku** — A **haiku** is a short 17–syllable Japanese poem.
20. **coyote** — There is not even one **coyote** in Japan.

Words with /ī/

Lesson 17

I Game Name ____________________

Complete the secret phrase by spelling the words from this week's word list.

Remember: God's ways are perfect and His promises true.

J Journaling

Setsuko's grandmother helped her remember to trust God's promises. In your journal, write about something one of your grandparents has done for you.

110

How to Play:

- Divide the class into two teams, and decide which team will go first.
- Have a student from team A choose a number from 1 to 20.
- Say the word that matches that number from the team's word list.
- Have the student write the word on the board.
- If correct, have each member of team A write the given letter in the matching space on his/her game page.
- Alternate between teams A and B having the students choose a number of a blank space.
- The team to complete the secret phrase first is the winner.

2 Game

Reinforce spelling skills and provide motivation and interest.

Materials

- game page (from student text)
- pencils (1 per child)
- game word list

Game Word List

	Team A		Team B
1.	**imply (O)**	1.	**compile (O)**
2.	**biceps (D)**	2.	**crime (D)**
3.	**crisis (L)**	3.	**climate (L)**
4.	**device (W)**	4.	**combine (W)**
5.	**entice (A)**	5.	**dining (A)**
6.	**iceberg (Y)**	6.	**decline (Y)**
7.	**pride (S)**	7.	**fiery (S)**
8.	**migrant (E)**	8.	**aspire (E)**
9.	**haiku (E)**	9.	**eyeing (E)**
10.	**aisle (P)**	10.	**coyote (P)**
11.	**compile (S)**	11.	**imply (S)**
12.	**crime (I)**	12.	**biceps (I)**
13.	**climate (S)**	13.	**crisis (S)**
14.	**combine (R)**	14.	**device (R)**
15.	**dining (O)**	15.	**entice (O)**
16.	**decline (M)**	16.	**iceberg (M)**
17.	**fiery (I)**	17.	**pride (I)**
18.	**aspire (S)**	18.	**migrant (S)**
19.	**eyeing (E)**	19.	**haiku (E)**
20.	**coyote (S)**	20.	**aisle (S)**

3 Journaling

Provide a meaningful reason for correct spelling through personal writing.

Review the story using discussion leads provided on the following page. Encourage students to apply the Scriptural value in their journaling.

Journaling (continued)

- Hiroshima means "Wide Island." How did it get its name? (Because the city grew from five different villages that were settled on six river deltas.)
- What was inside the cenotaph? (The names of the one hundred and ninety thousand people who died because of the atomic bomb.)
- Who makes the origami cranes that hang from the Children's Peace Monument? (School children all across Japan still make the cranes symbolizing prayers for peace.)
- What happened to grandmother's cousin, Futaba, when the bomb fell? (She was home from school because she had a fever. She was outside and saw the plane very high in the sky and then a purple light. She was badly burned, but managed to get her mother out of the rubble that used to be their house. Futaba survived, but never saw her father or sister again.)
- Why do such horrible, awful things happen in this world? (Because God doesn't force people to be good.)
- Why did grandmother make and give Setsuko the tiny origami crane? (To remind Setsuko that her grandmother loves her, that God loves her and has promised to be with her through whatever happens, and that God always keeps his promises.)

PIKES PEAK is spelled without an apostrophe by law. The Colorado legislature established the correct spelling in 1978. There are other cases in which spelling was established by law. The voters of Mullens, West Virginia, voted to retain the spelling, rather than switch to "Mullins," which is how the person for whom the town is named spelled his name. According to Willis Johnson, the Louisiana legislature enacted a law specifying that "crawfish" should not be spelled with a "y".

1 **Literature Connection**
Topic: Utilizing talents
Theme Text: Psalm 43:4

Federation of Praise

Heather looks at participating in the Piano Federation Competition.

"Jennifer is playing superbly," Beth whispered.

Heather nodded, absently adjusted her headband, and smoothed her skirt as she watched Jennifer Hatasaki's fingers fly up and down the keyboard.

Beth held up four fingers. "This judge should give her another superior plus."

"Her fourth?" Heather arched her eyebrows.

Beth nodded.

"You and Tony did well this morning. I liked your duet," Heather said softly. The music from the baby grand piano floated around her as her thoughts drifted back to the beginning of the school year when she and Beth had first talked about the Piano Federation.

"Aren't you done eating yet?" Beth squeezed the Velcro strips of her lunch bag together as she stood in front of Heather's desk.

"Mmmmm." Heather held up one finger while she chewed a mouthful of Fritos.

Beth waited impatiently for Heather to swallow. "Did Miss Paula talk to you about the Piano Federation?"

Heather nodded.

"Well, what are you going to play?" Beth arched her ball of trash into the wastebasket. "Your cousin Tony and I are going to do the duets together. Miss Paula is helping me pick the two solos to memorize. I'm entering in the "easy three" category. Mom said I could get a new dress, and Dad said he'd get our piano tuned. So are you going to tell me what you're playing—or keep chewing all afternoon?"

Heather held up her finger again and slowly wiped her mouth with her napkin before she answered, "Miss Paula wants me to enter, but this is the first year I've taken lessons."

"You play better than anyone else in our class," Beth encouraged. "I thought you'd taken lessons for years."

"I play by ear. Reading music and playing it the way it's written is new for me. And in front of a judge!" Heather laughed, "I'd probably forget what I memorized and start making it up as I went along. The judges would love that!" She looked down at her bag of chips and then put another handful into her mouth.

"Does Miss Paula want you to enter the medium or difficult category?"

"Mmmmm." Heather pointed to her mouth again.

"Well, I think you should enter." Beth walked toward the door. "You'd earn one of those gold certificates for sure."

Heather watched Beth put her lunch sack away and get a basketball. "I don't know how I'd practice," the redhead thought to herself. "We don't have a full keyboard. It works for lessons, but its too small to play a duet on. How would I learn my part? I don't have anything to wear either. Last year's winter church dress is too small and my school clothes aren't nice enough!"

She avoided Beth the rest of the day. She didn't really feel like telling her all the reasons she couldn't perform for the Piano Federation judges. She couldn't tell her mom she needed a new dress. Even if she found a way to practice a duet with someone, her parents were already stretching the family budget to pay the school bill at Knowlton Elementary—and now piano lessons. Heather tried to put the Piano Federation out of her mind, but it kept sneaking back in.

That afternoon Grandma Miller drove Heather and her brother, Collin, home after school. "The Jensen children are still asleep," the older woman explained, "so your mom called and asked me to bring you home today."

"Do you know the spelling Scripture?" Tony twisted around in the front seat to look at Heather.

Heather arched her eyebrows and recited, "'There I will go to the altar of God my exceeding joy, and praise him with my harp. Oh God— my God!'"

"Yeah, I guess you do. So who are you playing your duets with?" Tony asked.

"I'm not sure I'm going to do Federation." Heather looked out the car window.

"I'm playing with Beth. We both started lessons in first grade and are still at about the same level. Miss Paula will have the music ready at my lesson tomorrow. Papa promised to be there to hear me. I'm getting some new shoes and a tie with musical notes all over it. I saw it in the mall. Mama said she'd get it for me. What are you going to wear?"

The car stopped and Heather jumped out without answering Tony's questions.

The Stark children thanked Grandma Miller before they hurried up the sidewalk. Heather turned and waved to Tony and Grandma before she quietly opened the front door. She didn't want to wake up the children her mom baby-sat. Collin went on into the kitchen to talk to their mother about an upcoming field trip.

Heather unlocked her bedroom door and plopped down on the bed. The postcards Laney had mailed her from the Bahamas were sitting on the little table beside her. Heather picked them up and thumbed through the colorful pictures. There were pictures of flamingos, a beautiful parrot, white sandy beaches, a coral reef, shells, lots of blue water, and sailboats. Laney must have liked sailing. There was a

Story Continued

picture of the cruise ship she had sailed on from New York and then some of smaller sailboats. One card said, "Ships are safe in port, but that's not why they were built." Heather flopped back on her bed and studied the ceiling. "I guess it's safer not to play at the Piano Federation, but I don't see how I could do it even if I wanted to," she said out loud.

Two days later Grandma Miller took Heather home again. Collin had gone over to a friend's and Tony was at basketball practice, so the two were alone in the car. Grandma pulled the car to the curb in front of the Starks' small house. "Heather, why aren't you going to enter the Piano Federation competition?"

"Well, I've never played for judges. They're going to grade us on how accurately we play, smoothness, rhythm, and how it sounds. I'm not sure I'm ready for that."

"What does Miss Paula say?" The older woman prodded gently.

"She wants me to enter the difficult category."

"Then you should! God has blessed you with remarkable musical ability. You shouldn't keep it hidden. That's not why God gave you the talent. Your gift will never fully mature to bless others if you don't use it."

Heather thought about the postcard beside her bed. "'Ships are safe in port, but that's not why they were built.'"

"I never thought of Piano Federation as being a way to praise God," she said aloud.

"What was that Scripture verse you recited for Tony the other day?"

"'There I will go to the altar of God my exceeding joy, and praise him with my harp. Oh God—my God!'"

"That's the one. A harp has a lot in common with the piano," Grandma Miller pointed out.

"I never thought of that, either," Heather admitted.

The two were quiet for a while, Heather with her own thoughts, Grandma Miller praying to her God. Finally Heather broke the silence. "But I don't have a piano to practice the duets on."

"You can use mine."

"Well, that takes care of two problems." Heather looked at the floorboard of the car.

"What else?" the perceptive woman asked.

"I don't have a dress to wear. Miss Paula said we were supposed to wear church clothes. By Federation time it will be the middle of winter. I don't have a winter church dress, and I can't ask Mom to get me one."

"I see," Grandma said. "How about letting me worry about the dress, and you concentrate on practicing the pieces Miss Paula helps you pick out?"

A smile crept across Heather's face. "This is amazing!"

The noise of the applauding audience brought Heather back to reality. She watched Jennifer curtsy and exit the stage. Her hands felt damp, and her heart was beating loudly. She looked at the folded program in her hand. Maria was next. Then it would be her turn at the keyboard.

Grandma Miller came up behind her and touched her gently on the shoulder. "You'll do fine, Heather," the older woman encouraged. A warm smile crinkled her leathery face. "You look lovely, and I've heard you sail effortlessly through this hymn many times."

"Sail!" Heather thought of the words on the postcard Laney had sent. "'Ships are safe in port, but that's not why they were built.'" Grandma Miller squeezed her shoulders, "Go out there and praise God with your music!"

Heather rubbed the blue velvet of her new skirt between her fingers. "Thanks, Grandma Miller, thanks for everything. I hope I sail through again!"

2 Discussion Time

Check understanding of the story and development of personal values.

- What are the reasons Heather doesn't think she will play at the Piano Federation?
- Why does Beth think Heather should play?
- What did Tony ask that tells us he thought she was playing for the Federation?
- Who helps Heather decide to perform for the Piano Federation?
- What did Grandma Miller tell Heather about using her talent of musical ability?
- How did Grandma Miller help Heather be able to play for the Piano Federation?
- What talent has God given you to praise Him with?

A Test-Words Name ____________

Write each spelling word on the line as your teacher says it.

1. college
2. carton
3. caramel
4. combine
5. New Hampshire
6. random
7. librarian
8. barrier
9. parallel
10. crime
11. crisis
12. compartment
13. eyeing
14. aspire
15. pride
16. soprano

Review Lesson 18

B Test-Sentences

Write the sentences on the lines below, correcting each misspelled word, as well as all capitalization and punctuation errors. Two words are misspelled in each sentence.

in what climit does the artichoak plant grow.

1. In what climate does the artichoke plant grow?

the soldier heard the cyotee outside the bearicks

2. The soldier heard the coyote outside the barracks.

a crockidile will usually inhabitt the swamps

3. A crocodile will usually inhabit the swamps.

the ship will dock at a harber on Delewear's coast.

4. The ship will dock at a harbor on Delaware's coast.

111

4 Test-Sentences

Reinforce recognizing misspelled words.

Read each sentence carefully. Write the sentences on the lines in your Worktext. There are two misspelled words in each sentence. Correct each misspelled word, as well as all capitalization and punctuation errors.

Take a minute to memorize...

Psalm 43:4

3 Test-Words

Test for knowledge of the correct spellings of these words.

Say: I will say each word once, use the word in a sentence, then say the word again. Write the words on the lines in your Worktext.

1. college — "You're good enough to study music in **college**," complimented Beth.
2. carton — She drank the last bit of milk from the small **carton**.
3. caramel — Heather pulled a **caramel** candy out of her lunch bag.
4. combine — Beth and Tony will **combine** their talents in a piano duet.
5. New Hampshire — Miss Paula, their piano teacher, is originally from **New Hampshire**.
6. random — She does not choose the competition pieces at **random**.
7. librarian — Heather thanked the **librarian** for finding the book on famous musicians.
8. barrier — Heather's concerns were a **barrier** to her wanting to perform.
9. parallel — She was not sure her talents could **parallel** that of the other contestants.
10. crime — "It's not a **crime** not to play at Piano Federation, is it?" she asked.
11. crisis — Just getting a new dress for the competition seemed a **crisis**.
12. compartment — Grandma Miller put a box of tissues in the glove **compartment**.
13. eyeing — She was **eyeing** Heather in the mirror when she did not answer Tony.
14. aspire — When she practices, Heather does **aspire** to do her very best.
15. pride — It is good to take **pride** in your work and do it well.
16. soprano — Heather's mom has a lovely **soprano** singing voice.

Review 18 | Day 2

1 Test-Dictation

Reinforce correct spelling by using current and previous words in context.

Listen as I read each sentence, then write it in your worktext. Remember to use correct capitalization and punctuation. (Slowly read each sentence twice. Sentences are found in the student text to the right. The words **adopt**, **parakeet**, **Ontario**, and **snarl** are found in this unit.)

2 Test-Proofreading

Familiarize students with standardized test format and reinforce recognizing misspelled words.

Look at each set of words. If a word is misspelled, fill in the oval by that word. If all the words are spelled correctly, fill in the oval by **no mistake**.

Review Lesson 18

C Test-Dictation Name ______

Write each sentence as your teacher dictates. Use correct punctuation.

1. Do they plan to adopt a baby?
2. The big, green parakeet was very near our table.
3. My cousin lives in Ontario, Canada.
4. With a snarl, the dog rose to his feet.

D Test-Proofreading

If a word is misspelled, fill in the oval by that word. If all the words are spelled correctly, fill in the oval by **no mistake**.

1. ● wisconson ○ decline ○ carton ○ no mistake
2. ○ soprano ● mygrant ○ combine ○ no mistake
3. ○ barrier ○ compartment ○ atomic ● no mistake
4. ○ gather ● glossery ○ parallel ○ no mistake
5. ● raskal ○ crisis ○ pride ○ no mistake
6. ○ caramel ● continint ○ aspire ○ no mistake
7. ○ fiery ○ compare ○ eyeing ● no mistake
8. ○ aisle ○ random ● cartliage ○ no mistake
9. ○ department ○ aware ● statick ○ no mistake
10. ○ borrow ● cardiack ○ bottom ○ no mistake
11. ● commurse ○ deposit ○ Colorado ○ no mistake
12. ○ embarrassed ○ college ● harty ○ no mistake

112

E **Test-Table** Name ____________________

If a word is misspelled, fill in the space on the grid.

airea	dart	geometrey	arobics
arizona	device	imply	narrow
compiel	dining	Indyana	Nevada
contact	convirsation	mammel	radar

Review

Lesson 18

F **Writing Assessment**

Imagine you are Heather or Tony. Write a letter to your Uncle Mark about the Piano Federation and how Heather performed.

____

____

____

____

____

____

____

____

Scripture
Psalm 43:4

113

A rubric for scoring is provided in Appendix B.

RAISE/RAZE are homophones with approximately opposite meanings.

1 Test-Table

Test mastery of words in this unit.

If a word is misspelled, fill in the space on the grid.

2 Writing Assessment

Assess student's spelling, grammar, and composition skills through personal writing.

- Who thought Heather should play for the judges at the Piano Federation (Miss Paula her piano teacher, Beth, Tony, and Grandma Miller.)
- Why do you think Heather decided to play at the Piano Federation? (Grandma Miller provided a piano to practice the duet on, bought a special dress for her to wear, and encouraged her to use her talents for the Lord.)
- What are some ways you can praise God with exceeding joy like Psalm 43:4 talks about? (Students may suggest: By what I say. By how I act. By developing and using my talents.)
- How do you think Heather will play for the Piano Federation judges?

1 Test-Sentences

Reinforce recognizing misspelled words.

Read each sentence carefully. Write the sentences on the lines in your Worktext, correcting each misspelled word, as well as all capitalization and punctuation errors.

Review Lesson 18

G Test-Sentences Name ______

Write the sentences on the lines below. Correct each misspelled word, as well as all capitalization and punctuation errors. Two words are misspelled in each sentence.

dad carried the gallin bucket to the composte pile

1. Dad carried the gallon bucket to the compost pile.

my uncle lives in a beautiful vallee in arkansaw

2. My uncle lives in a beautiful valley in Arkansas.

an arguemint can easily disturb the group harmoney

3. An argument can easily disturb the group harmony.

our family docter pointed to a charte on the wall

4. Our family doctor pointed to a chart on the wall.

H Test-Words

Write each spelling word on the line as your teacher says it.

1. decline
2. bottom
3. aware
4. comment
5. embarrassed
6. perhaps
7. concentrate
8. compare
9. prepare
10. borrow
11. deposit
12. department
13. gather
14. aisle
15. marriage
16. Colorado

114

2 Test-Words

Test for knowledge of the correct spellings of these words.

I will say the word once, use the word in a sentence, then say the word again. Write the word on the lines in your Worktext.

1. decline — Heather planned to **decline** the invitation to play at Federation.
2. bottom — "Let's talk and get to the **bottom** of those fears," Grandma Miller teased.
3. aware — Heather wasn't **aware** Mrs. Miller knew there was a problem.
4. comment — At first, Heather didn't want to **comment** on her feelings.
5. embarrassed — "I'd be **embarrassed** to wear the dress I have," she admitted.
6. perhaps — "Would you, **perhaps**, let me worry about the dress?" Grandma Miller asked.
7. concentrate — "That will allow you to **concentrate** on your piano piece."
8. compare — "My talents might not **compare** with the other students," said Heather.
9. prepare — "I can't **prepare** properly without a piano, either," she continued.
10. borrow — Since pianos are hard to **borrow**, Grandma Miller let Heather use hers.
11. deposit — "Just **deposit** your books on the table and start practicing!" she said.
12. department — Grandma Miller bought Heather a new outfit at a **department** store.
13. gather — Heather tried to **gather** her thoughts before going on stage.
14. aisle — She was glad to be in the front row and not have to walk down an **aisle**.
15. marriage — Heather was thankful for her parents' strong, happy **marriage**.
16. Colorado — Heather's dad had just returned from a run in his truck to **Colorado**.

I **Test-Editing** Name ____________

If a word is spelled correctly, fill in the oval under **Correct**. If the word is misspelled, fill in the oval under **Incorrect**, and spell the word correctly on the blank.

	Correct	Incorrect	
1. Alabama	●	○	
2. barrin	○	●	barren
3. combatt	○	●	combat
4. iceburg	○	●	iceberg
5. suvannah	○	●	savanna
6. valve	●	○	
7. demolish	●	○	
8. artiry	○	●	artery
9. partner	●	○	
10. bargin	○	●	bargain
11. narate	○	●	narrate
12. byseps	○	●	biceps
13. collinies	○	●	colonies
14. intise	○	●	entice
15. hikuu	○	●	haiku
16. scalopp	○	●	scallop
17. gallup	○	●	gallop
18. anartica	○	●	Antarctica
19. softwear	○	●	software
20. hardship	●	○	

Review Lesson 18

115

3 Test-Editing

Reinforce recognizing and correcting misspelled words.

4 Action Game

Reinforce spelling skills and provide motivation and interest.

Materials

- whiteboard or chalkboard
- markers or chalk
- word list on certificate at end of unit

PICTOSPELL

Divide the class into two teams. Have each team sit on the floor as far away from each other as possible, but where they can see the board. Call a player up from one team and show him or her a spelling word to be reviewed. When you say "go" the player begins drawing a picture of the word. That player's team must guess the word in one minute or the other team has a chance to guess. When a word is guessed, it must be spelled correctly by the team member who guessed it in order for that team to get a point. When that word has been guessed, a player from the other team will be given a word to draw. Continue to alternate between teams. The team with the most points wins!

Game

Reinforce spelling skills and provide motivation and interest.

Materials

- game page (from student text)
- colored pencils (1 per child)
- game word list

Game Word List

Check off each word lightly in pencil as it is used.

The Musicians

1. **Wisconsin**
2. **migrant**
3. **atomic**
4. **glossary**
5. **rascal**
6. **continent**
7. **fiery**
8. **cartilage**
9. **static**

The Audience

1. **cardiac**
2. **commerce**
3. **hearty**
4. **area**
5. **Arizona**
6. **compile**
7. **contact**
8. **device**
9. **dining**

The Judges

1. **Delaware**
2. **geometry**
3. **imply**
4. **Indiana**
5. **mammal**
6. **aerobics**
7. **narrow**
8. **Nevada**
9. **radar**

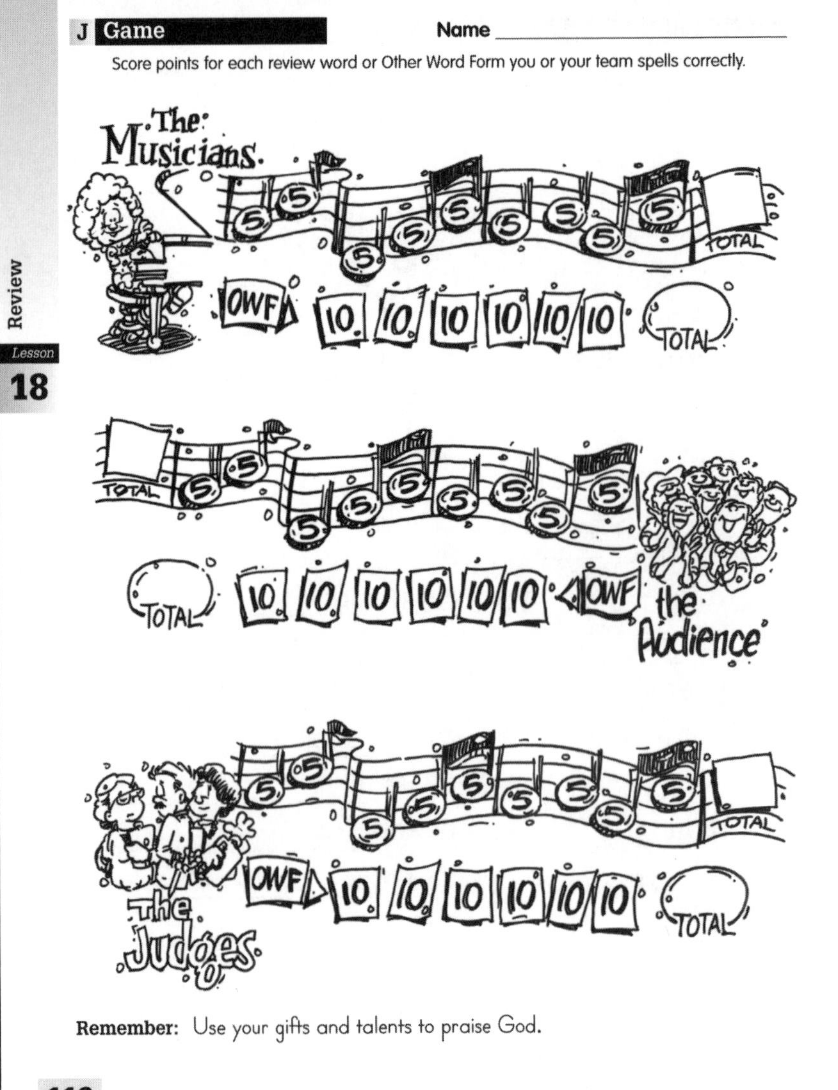

How to Play:

- Divide the class into three teams. Name one team **The Musicians**, one **The Audience**, and one **The Judges**. (Option: You may wish to seat students in groups of three, each student from a different team. They should share one game page.)
- Have a student from the first team go to the board.
- Say the spelling word.
- Have the student write the word on the board.
- If the word is spelled correctly, have each team member color a point symbol by his/her team name. If the word is misspelled, have him/her put an **X** through one point symbol. That word may not be given again.
- Repeat this process with the second team and then the third.
- When the words from all three lists have been used, the team with the most points is the winner.
- Play another round using Other Word Forms.

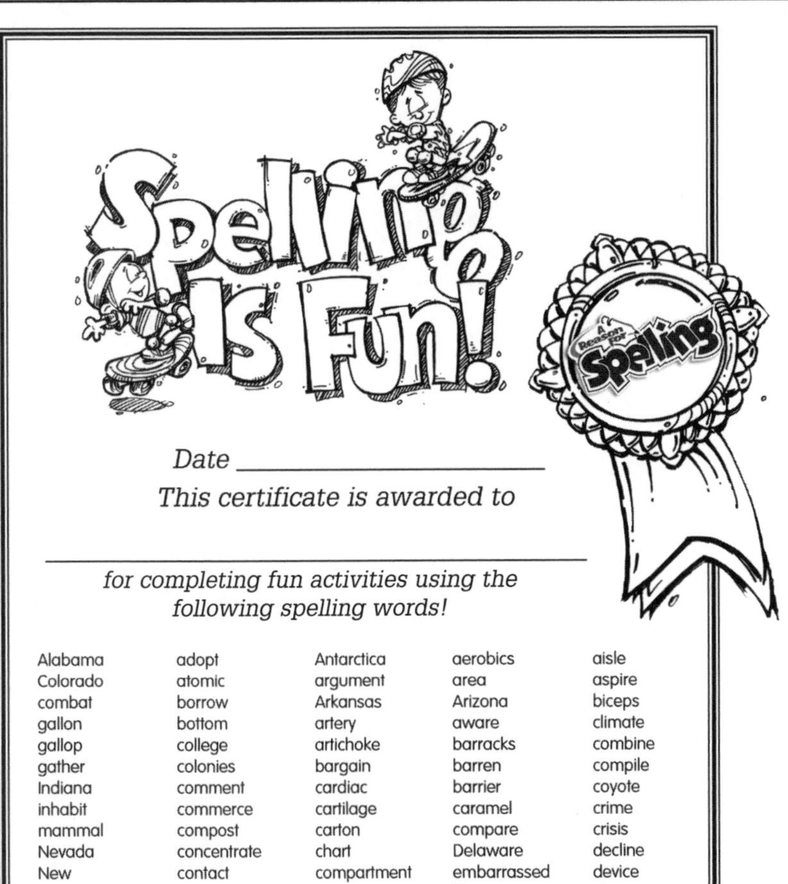

Date ____________________

This certificate is awarded to

____

for completing fun activities using the following spelling words!

Alabama	adopt	Antarctica	aerobics	aisle
Colorado	atomic	argument	area	aspire
combat	borrow	Arkansas	Arizona	biceps
gallon	bottom	artery	aware	climate
gallop	college	artichoke	barracks	combine
gather	colonies	bargain	barren	compile
Indiana	comment	cardiac	barrier	coyote
inhabit	commerce	cartilage	caramel	crime
mammal	compost	carton	compare	crisis
Nevada	concentrate	chart	Delaware	decline
New	contact	compartment	embarrassed	device
Hampshire	continent	dart	librarian	dining
perhaps	conversation	department	marriage	entice
random	crocodile	harbor	narrate	eyeing
rascal	demolish	hardship	narrow	fiery
savanna	deposit	harmony	Ontario	haiku
scallop	doctor	hearty	parakeet	iceberg
soprano	geometry	partner	parallel	imply
static	glossary	radar	prepare	migrant
valley	Wisconsin	snarl	software	pride
valve				

2 Certificate

Provide an opportunity for parents or guardians to encourage and assess their child's progress.

Fill in today's date and your name on your certificate.

Take a minute to memorize...

Psalm 43:4

3 Letter

Provide the parent or guardian with the spelling word lists for the next unit.

Give your parents or guardian this letter that lists your spelling words for the next unit. Put it where you will remember to practice the words together.

Dear Parent,

We are about to begin a new spelling unit containing five weekly lessons. A set of twenty words will be studied each week. All the words will be reviewed in the sixth week. Values based on the Scriptures listed below will be taught in each lesson.

Lesson 19	Lesson 20	Lesson 21	Lesson 22	Lesson 23
Africa	average	Alaska	Amazon	afternoon
autograph	badge	backup	blaze	basketball
difference	cringe	banquet	blizzard	broadcast
difficult	dungeon	chaos	bruise	brother-in-law
dolphin	gadget	chorus	citizen	candlestick
effort	heritage	earthquake	closet	driveway
fiber	hinges	echoes	design	evergreen
forecast	jacket	equal	desire	foolproof
forth	jaguar	equator	despise	footnote
fossil	jogging	inquire	enclose	grasshopper
funds	junior	Kentucky	freezing	grassland
hyphen	jury	liquid	graze	greenhouse
nephew	justice	Nebraska	horizon	greyhound
paragraph	legend	o'clock	Kansas	livestock
photos	manage	preschool	laser	newborn
phrase	merge	quality	Missouri	Newfoundland
sheriff	pledge	Quebec	plaza	old-fashioned
siphon	plunge	quicksand	raise	password
sphere	refuge	squall	stanza	peppermint
trophy	rigid	squid	surprise	runaway
Psalm 27:14	Psalm 66:8,9	Psalm 19:9,10	Psalm 25:4,5	Psalm 141:1

Extraordinary Adventure

Thorny goes cross-country skiing for the first time and has to be brave and wait patiently for help.

"A-h-h-h-h. Pristine air such as this is incredibly invigorating!" Thorny took a deep breath and exhaled, his breath forming a white cloud. "One might even call such an unpolluted atmosphere intoxicating."

"No one but you would." Tommy shook his head. "I don't know about the 'intoxicating' bit, but if you keep huffing and puffing like that you'll probably get light-headed before we even get started skiing."

"Ah, yes. The molecules are significantly more widely dispersed at higher altitudes." Thorny pulled a bulging day pack out of the trunk.

"What on earth have you got in that?" Tommy reached up to unload the cross-country skis from the roof rack. "You didn't bring a bunch of books like you did when we went canoeing, did you?"

"Of course not." Hubert Thornton Remington III looked down his nose at the shorter Tommy. "One must not endeavor to carry more than is reasonable, particularly when not accustomed to the extreme physical challenge provided by cross-country skiing. One of the first rules of safety for cross-country skiing is—'Know your own physical limits.'"

"I see." Tommy stuck a long, thin pair of skis upright in the snow. "You didn't bring a bunch of books 'cause you've already researched everything there is to know about cross-country skiing."

"And found it to be truly fascinating." Thorny dropped a pile of poles on the snow beside the skis. "The sport's origins can be traced back about 5,000 years to people in Scandinavia who strapped the bones of large animals to shoes with leather thongs."

"These beauties sure beat bones." Tommy ran his hand along the sleek blue skis.

Thorny laced his ski boots. "Along with the much-improved runners of fiberglass, wood, and plastics, these bindings that keep the heel free have revolutionized the sport of cross-country skiing."

"Well, then, let's see what all these improvements do for you." Tommy handed Thorny a pair of green skis with a fish-scale pattern on the bottom. "These are the ones Dad rented for you. They're waxless. The pattern on the bottom of the skis grabs the snow but also makes you glide faster." When Thorny had attached the skis, Tommy handed him poles. "I'm sure you know all about these, too."

"Of course." Thorny stood and shoved off with the poles. "I kno-o-o-o-o-o-O-O-O-W!" SPLAT! Thorny sat up and looked at Tommy, snow plastering his face. "Well, I do know—in theory, that is." He struggled around in the snow trying to get up, enlarging the hole in the drift. Finally Tommy stopped laughing long enough to give Thorny a hand.

"I know something else, too. The snow conditions are ideal for cross-country skiing today, with at least a two-foot base," Thorny announced, brushing the snow off his head. "I just checked it myself." Both boys laughed so hard they almost ended up back in the snow.

"You guys ready?" Mr. Rawson and Steve Simmons trudged through the snow from the ranger outpost.

"Looks like we'd better get these two on the trail before they get into any more trouble," Mr. Simmons teased as he swiped more snow off Thorny's backside.

Mr. Rawson clipped his skis on expertly. "We're going only about two and one-half miles to this warm-up shelter." He pointed to a spot on a small map with green, blue and black lines weaving around on it. He traced the routes with a gloved finger, "We'll stop for lunch there and decide if we want to take this longer loop back to the car or this shorter one. Remember, watch for the green trail blazes. We're sticking to those today since it's the first time out for some of us." He winked at Thorny. "I'll lead and Steve will bring up the rear. That way you boys will always be between us, so even if we get spread out we can keep track of you." He folded the map and stuck it in his windbreaker pocket. "Let's hit the trail!"

"YIPPEE!" Tommy yelled as he shoved off down the trail. "Come on, Thorny, I'll show you a few things you may not have learned in your research. This is the diagonal stride." Tommy demonstrated and Thorny tried. "No, no, no, no!" Tommy covered his eyes with his hand when Thorny took another dive into the snow.

But before long Thorny was getting the hang of it. He stopped for a break and wiped the sweat off his forehead, "Now I begin to comprehend why the articles I read indicated that one of the most common mistakes of novice cross-country skiers is to wear more clothing than they need."

"It's a workout!" Tommy swished to a stop beside his friend. "I bet we're almost to the warm-up shelter. I'm starved!" On cue his stomach growled loudly.

"If I should lose sight of you I'll simply follow the sound of your stomach." Thorny laughed.

A few minutes later the skiers gathered in the shelter and passed around sandwiches and hot cocoa. "M-mmm, I needed that." Tommy licked the chocolate off his lips."

Thorny helped himself to another sandwich, "At

800 calories an hour, we've burned a considerable number this morning."

Mr. Rawson stretched his arms above his head. "I can sure tell I've worked all the muscle groups in my body. Guess I need to get out here more often. Well, which way back to the car?"

They decided on the longer route. In the still afternoon the only sounds were the swish of the skis against the packed snow. Thorny considered what the right word would be to describe the experience. It was calming, peaceful, beautiful. Extraordinary. That was it!

"Hello!" A lone skier came toward them. Following the rules of cross-country skiing, they moved to the right of the trail. The man nodded as he passed, then stopped and asked Mr. Simmons a question.

"You all go on," Mr. Simmons called to the rest of the group, "I'm just going to show this guy where we are on the map; then I'll catch up."

Mr. Rawson waved his understanding and they headed up the rise. As they skied down the other side, Thorny felt something give on his left boot. He snowplowed to a stop and bent to tie the lace. By the time he was finished, Tommy and his dad were out of sight.

"A perfect opportunity to test my newly acquired skating skills," Thorny muttered to himself as he eyed the upward slope. "With proper weight shift, a skier can easily skate or scale even the steepest hill." He took a deep breath, "Here goes!"

After struggling up the hill, Thorny stopped to catch his breath. There was no sign of Tommy and his dad other than their tracks in the snow. "Perhaps I'll overtake them on this downhill stretch." Thorny started to shove off when he noticed the trail forked. The green trail blaze was on a tree between two sets of tracks—and it appeared there were a similar number of ski tracks going each way.

Thorny finally decided the blaze looked a little closer to one of the trails and headed that way. He watched carefully for green blazes, but didn't see any. Other ski tracks cut across the trail he was following several times, but he didn't pay any attention to them until he decided he was going the wrong way. When he tried to retrace his way back to the fork, those tracks were a real problem. He suddenly realized he didn't know which way he'd come!

"Perhaps the wisest course of action is to remain in this location." Thorny leaned on his poles and looked around. "It is highly likely that I'm becoming more disoriented with each turn I make. If I just stay still, the others will notice I'm missing and endeavor to locate me."

Thorny took off his skis and stood them beside the trail. Brushing the snow off a fallen log, he sat down to wait. And wait. When his teeth began to chatter from sitting still, he shrugged on another layer of clothes from his day pack.

He occupied himself with reviewing everything he'd researched about cross-country skiing—especially what to do in emergencies. Then he began repeating all the Scriptures he could remember learning since he'd come to live with the Simmons and attend Knowlton Elementary School. The most recent one, Psalm 27:14, seemed particularly fitting. "Don't be impatient. Wait for the Lord, and he will come and save you! Be brave, stouthearted and courageous. Yes, wait and he will help you."

Although it seemed like he'd been waiting on the frozen log forever, he kept telling himself it hadn't been all that long—until the sun started going down. Then he knew he'd been waiting for hours, and the panic started to rise in his throat. Shadows lengthened across the wooded valley around him. Moonlight on the snow made the shadows more obvious. Why hadn't they found him? He wanted to scream! He wanted to get up and ski out—but where?

"Get a grip, Thorny!" He spoke aloud in the silence. "You know what to do. Remember, be brave and courageous!" He clipped on his skis and began gathering twigs and small logs. Using one of the larger sticks, he cleared a small area of most of the snow and arranged the wood on it. From his day pack he took matches, toilet paper, an insulated blanket and a candy bar.

When his friends found him an hour after sundown, the fire was burning and the candy bar was gone!

"Well, what did you think of your first cross-country skiing trip?" Tommy joked in the car on the way home.

"Upon due consideration," Thorny answered thoughtfully, "I'd say it was… extraordinary!"

2 Discussion Time

Check understanding of the story and development of personal values.

- Had Thorny ever gone cross-country skiing before?
- What happened when Thorny first stood on his rented skis?
- Why did Mr. Rawson ski in front and Mr. Simmons in the back?
- What kind of trail markers were they following?
- How did Thorny become separated from the group?
- Why couldn't he find his way back to the original trail?
- How did Thorny keep from panicking as more and more time passed?
- What did Thorny do while he waited for someone to find him?

A Preview Name ____________

Write each word as your teacher says it.

1. autograph
2. paragraph
3. phrase
4. hyphen
5. difference
6. effort
7. difficult
8. nephew
9. forecast
10. sheriff
11. siphon
12. dolphin
13. funds
14. Africa
15. forth
16. sphere
17. fiber
18. fossil
19. trophy
20. photos

Words with /f/

Lesson 19

Scripture
Psalm 27:14

119

3 Preview

Test for knowledge of the correct spellings of these words.

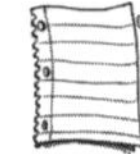

Customize Your List

On a separate sheet of paper, additional words of your choice may be tested.

I will say each word once, use the word in a sentence, then say the word again. Write the words on the lines in your Worktext.

Correct Immediately!

Let's correct our Preview. I will spell each word out loud. If you spelled a word incorrectly, rewrite it correctly.

Progress Chart

Students may record scores. (Reproducible master provided in Appendix B.)

1.	**autograph**	Tommy's skis had a famous skier's **autograph** along the bottom.
2.	**paragraph**	Thorny quoted an entire **paragraph** from a book he'd read.
3.	**phrase**	"Could you translate a **phrase** or two into layman's terms?" teased Tommy.
4.	**hyphen**	"Is there a **hyphen** anywhere in that long word you just used?" he queried.
5.	**difference**	They noticed a **difference** in their breathing in the higher altitude.
6.	**effort**	Thorny made every **effort** to stay upright on his skis.
7.	**difficult**	He found skiing a little more **difficult** than he'd expected.
8.	**nephew**	Mr. Simmons has a **nephew** that is an exceptionally good skier.
9.	**forecast**	"The **forecast** showed today as favorable for our outing," commented Thorny.
10.	**sheriff**	The county **sheriff** and his men patrol the mountain roads routinely.
11.	**siphon**	The sheriff helped one stranded man to **siphon** gas into his empty tank.
12.	**dolphin**	Thorny looked wistfully at the **dolphin** on the candy wrapper.
13.	**funds**	"Perhaps we will use our vacation **funds** to visit a warmer climate."
14.	**Africa**	"At the moment, **Africa** sounds incredibly appealing!" he shivered.
15.	**forth**	He reached in his pack and brought **forth** the necessary matches for a fire.
16.	**sphere**	"Forming a large **sphere** of snow will block the wind from this side."
17.	**fiber**	The **fiber** content of his blanket was wool, which would help him keep warm.
18.	**fossil**	To pass the time, Thorny examined surrounding rocks for a **fossil**.
19.	**trophy**	"You deserve a **trophy** for bravery," smiled Tommy.
20.	**photos**	After the trip, the boys enjoyed looking at the **photos** they had taken.

4 Word Shapes

Help students form a correct image of whole words.

Look at each word and think about its shape. Now, write the word in the correct word Shape Boxes. You may check off each word as you use it.

(In many words, the sound of **/f/** is spelled with **f**, **ff**, **gh**, or **ph**. The **ff** and **gh** spellings are never found at the beginning of a word.)

In the word shape boxes, fill in the boxes containing the letter or letters that spell the **/f/** sound in each word.

Take a minute to memorize...

Psalm 27:14

Words with /f/ — Lesson 19

B Word Shapes Name ______________________

Using the word bank below, write each word in the correct word shape boxes. Next, in the word shape boxes, fill in the boxes containing the letter or letters that spell the sound of **/f/** in each word.

1. difficult
2. phrase
3. trophy
4. difference
5. Africa
6. hyphen
7. autograph
8. sphere
9. paragraph
10. effort
11. forecast
12. fossil
13. fiber
14. nephew
15. funds
16. sheriff
17. forth
18. siphon
19. dolphin
20. photos

Word Bank

Africa	dolphin	forth	nephew	sheriff
autograph	effort	fossil	paragraph	siphon
difference	fiber	funds	photos	sphere
difficult	forecast	hyphen	phrase	trophy

120

Answers may vary for duplicate word shapes.

Be Prepared For Fun

Check these supply lists for **Fun Ways to Spell** - presented **Day 2**.
Purchase and/or gather these items ahead of time!

General
- Pencil
- Graph Paper (1 sheet per child)
- Spelling List

Auditory
- Voice Recorder
- Spelling List

Visual
- American Sign Language reproducible master (provided in Appendix B)
- Spelling List

Tactile
- Soccer Ball, Basketball, Tennis Ball, or 4-Square Ball
- Spelling List

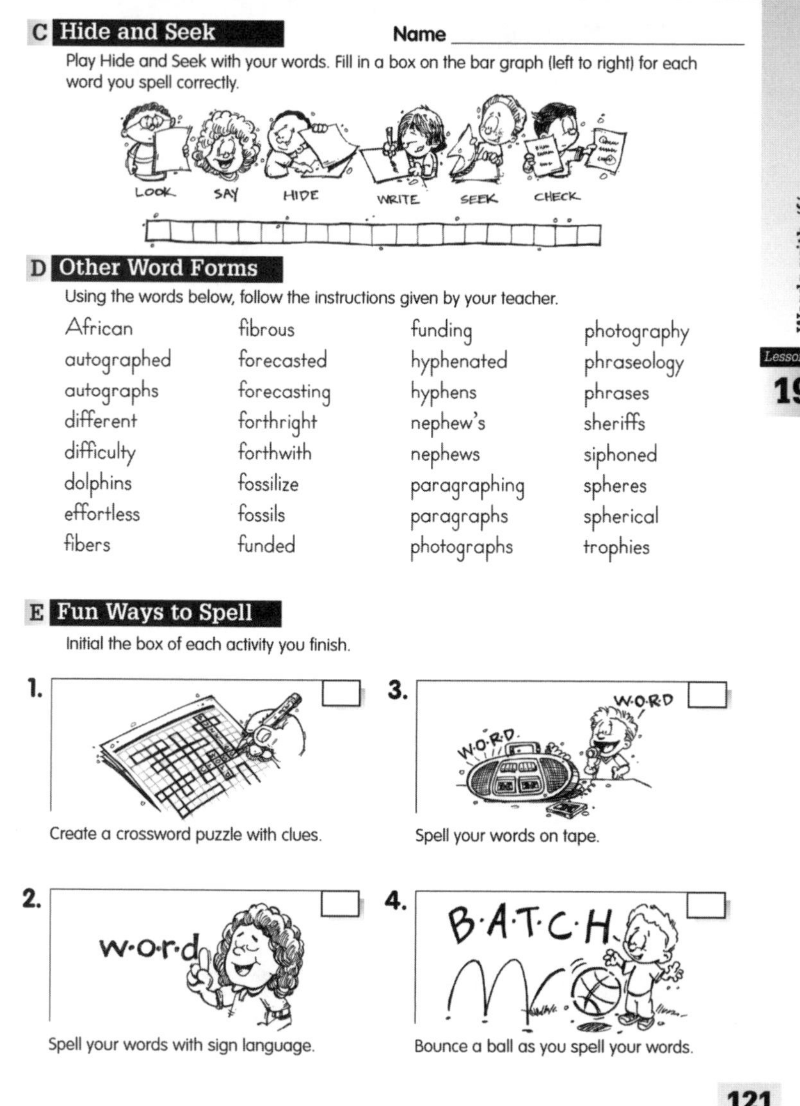

1 Hide and Seek

Reinforce spelling by using multiple styles of learning.

On a white board, Teacher writes each word — one at a time. **Have students:**

- **Look** at the word.
- **Say** the word out loud.
- **Spell** the word out loud.
- **Hide** (teacher erases word.)
- **Write** the word on paper.
- **Seek** (teacher rewrites word.)
- **Check** spelling. If incorrect, rewrite word correctly.

2 Other Word Forms

This activity is optional. Have students write original sentences using these Other Word Forms:

effortless
spherical
forecasted
funded

3 Fun Ways to Spell

Four activities are provided. Use one, two, three, or all of the activities. Have students initial the box for each activity they complete.

Options:

- assign activities to students according to their learning styles
- set up the activities in learning centers for the students to do throughout the day
- divide students into four groups and assign one activity per group
- do one activity per day

General

To create a crossword puzzle...
- Use a pencil to arrange your words on graph paper.
- Overlap words where letters are shared.
- Don't create any new words.
- Outline each word with a marker and number it.
- Write a clue for each word.
- Erase your words.
- Trade with a classmate and work each other's puzzles.

Auditory

To spell your words using a voice recorder...
- Record yourself as you say and spell each word on your spelling list.
- Listen to your recording and check your spelling.

Visual

To spell your words with sign language...
- Have a classmate read a spelling word to you from the list.
- Spell the word using the American Sign Language alphabet.
- Do this with each word on your list.

Tactile

To bounce a ball as you spell your words...
- Look at the first word on your list.
- Bounce the ball as you say each letter of the word aloud.
- Do this with each word on your list.

Working with Words

Familiarize students with word meaning and usage.

Secret Words

The boxed letters in the acrostic are a phrase from the Scripture verse for this week.

Use the clues to write the words in the puzzle. You may use a dictionary to help you. Then write the boxed letters on the lines below to find the secret words from this week's Scripture.

Take a minute to memorize...

Psalm 27:14

F Working with Words Name ______________________

Secret Words

Use the clues to write the words in the puzzle. Then write the boxed letters on the lines below to find the secret words from this week's Scripture.

1. nephew
2. paragraph
3. Africa
4. forth
5. forecast
6. siphon
7. funds
8. photos
9. sheriff
10. w
11. difference
12. dolphin
13. fossil
14. phrase
15. sphere
16. difficult
17. trophy
18. hyphen
19. effort
20. autograph

1. son of a brother or sister
2. passage
3. continent
4. forward
5. prediction
6. pump
7. money
8. snapshots
9. county police department
10. the letter before x
11. contrast
12. water mammal
13. petrified remains
14. saying
15. globe
16. hard
17. award
18. punctuation mark
19. attempt
20. signature

Write the secret phrase:

Wait and he will help you.

Word Bank

Africa	dolphin	forth	nephew	sheriff
autograph	effort	fossil	paragraph	siphon
difference	fiber	funds	photos	sphere
difficult	forecast	hyphen	phrase	trophy

G Dictation

Name ____________________

Write each sentence as your teacher dictates. Use correct punctuation.

1. It took some effort, but he was soon able to get up and begin skiing across the snow.
2. Thorny found it to be more difficult than he had thought.
3. He had read several paragraphs about the history of skiing and had listened to the weather forecast.

Words with /f/

Lesson 19

H Proofreading

If a word is misspelled, fill in the oval by that word. If all the words are spelled correctly, fill in the oval by **no mistake**.

1. ○ Africa ● autograff ○ imply ○ no mistake
2. ○ paragraph ● frase ○ biceps ○ no mistake
3. ● ephort ○ crisis ○ nephew ○ no mistake
4. ○ sphere ● diference ○ device ○ no mistake
5. ○ difficult ○ pride ○ migrant ● no mistake
6. ○ sheriff ○ coyote ● hyfen ○ no mistake
7. ○ fiber ● syphon ○ eyeing ○ no mistake
8. ○ crime ○ forth ○ entice ● no mistake
9. ○ photos ● dolfin ○ trophy ○ no mistake
10. ○ aisle ● fossel ○ compile ○ no mistake
11. ○ funds ○ iceberg ○ haiku ● no mistake
12. ○ forecast ○ combine ○ dining ● no mistake

123

1 Dictation

Reinforce correct spelling by using current and previous words in context.

Listen as I read each sentence and then write it in your Worktext. Remember to use correct capitalization and punctuation. (Slowly read each sentence twice. Sentences are found in the Student Worktext to the left.)

2 Proofreading

Familiarize students with standardized test format and reinforce recognition of misspelled words.

Look at each set of words. If a word is misspelled, fill in the oval by that word. If all the words are spelled correctly, fill in the oval by **no mistake**.

Day 4 | Lesson 19

3 Hide and Seek

Reinforce correct spelling of current spelling words. Repeat this activity from Day 2.

4 Vocabulary Extension

Have your students complete this activity to strengthen spelling ability and expand vocabulary. The reproducible master is provided in Appendix A as shown on the inset page to the right.

1 Posttest

Test mastery of the spelling words.

I will say the word once, use it in a sentence, then say it again. Write your words on a separate sheet of paper.

Progress Chart

Students may record scores. (Reproducible master in Appendix B.)

Personal Dictionary

Students may add any words they have misspelled to their personal dictionaries for reference when writing. (Cover in Appendix B.)

Vocabulary Extension | Lesson 19

Hide and Seek

Play Hide and Seek with your words. Fill in a bar graph (left to right) for each word you spell correctly.

Vocabulary Extension

Crossword Puzzle

Use the clues below to complete the puzzle.

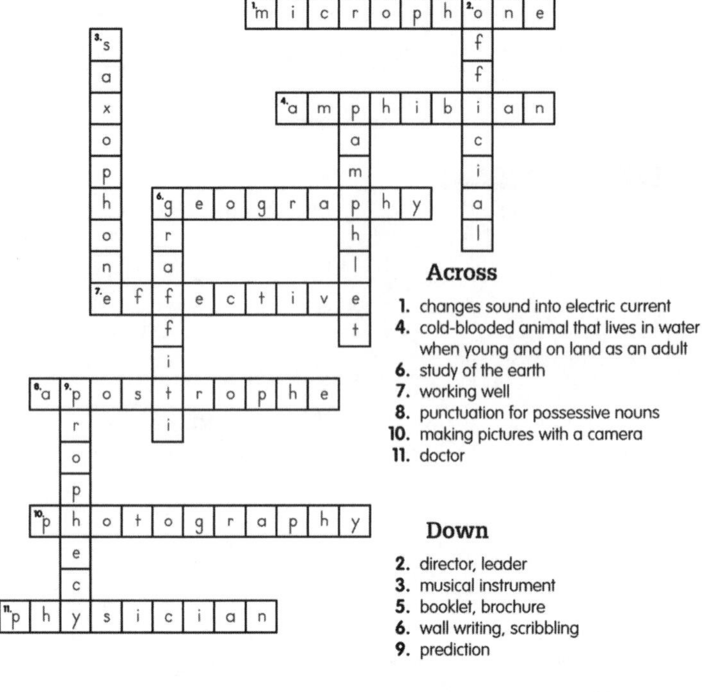

Across

1. changes sound into electric current
4. cold-blooded animal that lives in water when young and on land as an adult
6. study of the earth
7. working well
8. punctuation for possessive nouns
10. making pictures with a camera
11. doctor

Down

2. director, leader
3. musical instrument
5. booklet, brochure
6. wall writing, scribbling
9. prediction

Word Bank

amphibian	geography	official	physician
apostrophe	graffiti	pamphlet	prophecy
effective	microphone	photography	saxophone

340

1. **sheriff** — The **sheriff** and his deputies carry extra gasoline for stranded drivers.
2. **siphon** — The man was thankful the sheriff could **siphon** gas into his empty tank.
3. **paragraph** — Thorny effortlessly quoted a **paragraph** from a skiers guide book.
4. **hyphen** — "I believe there is a **hyphen** in that technical term," stated Thorny.
5. **phrase** — "Repeat that last **phrase** in English, please," teased Tommy.
6. **forecast** — "The **forecast** is most favorable for a cross–country ski trip!" Thorny reported.
7. **difficult** — He found skiing much more **difficult** than he'd expected.
8. **forth** — "An adequate amount of practice should bring **forth** the desired results!"
9. **nephew** — "Your foster dad's **nephew** is a professional skier, right?" asked Tommy.
10. **photos** — Tommy took several **photos** of Thorny sprawled in the snow.
11. **trophy** — "I expect I will not receive a **trophy** for my skiing skills today," joked Thorny.
12. **difference** — The setting sun made a **difference** in the appearance of his surroundings.
13. **sphere** — As the giant **sphere** dropped behind the hills, the temperature dropped.
14. **fossil** — To occupy his time, he tried to find a **fossil** in a nearby rock.
15. **dolphin** — The **dolphin** on the candy bar wrapper made him think of a tropical island.
16. **fiber** — He was thankful for the high wool **fiber** content of his blanket.
17. **funds** — "Perhaps our vacation **funds** would be better spent on a summer retreat."
18. **Africa** — "The climate in **Africa** sounds quite appealing to me at the moment!"
19. **effort** — "I made an **effort** to have courage, like the verse said to do!" said Thorny.
20. **autograph** — "Can I have your **autograph**, Thorny?" smiled Tommy.

Lesson 19 — Words with /f/

I Game Name ______________________

Ski down the slope with Thorny. Move one space for each word you or your team spells correctly.

Remember: Patiently watch for the help God will send.

J Journaling

Think about the Scriptures you've learned so far this year. In your journal, write how one of them has helped (or could help) you like Psalm 27:14 helped Thorny.

124

How to Play:

- Divide the class into two teams.
- Have each student place his/her game piece on Start.
- Have a student from team A go to the board.
- Say the spelling word.
- Have the student write the word on the board.
- If correct, instruct each member of team A to move his/her game piece forward one space.
- Alternate between teams A and B.
- The team to reach the bottom of the slope first is the winner.
- **Small Group Option**: Students may play this game without teacher direction in small groups of two or more.

2 Game

Reinforce spelling skills and provide motivation and interest.

Materials

- game page (from student text)
- game pieces (1 per child)
- game word list

Game Word List

1. **Africa**
2. **autograph**
3. **paragraph**
4. **phrase**
5. **effort**
6. **nephew**
7. **sphere**
8. **difference**
9. **difficult**
10. **sheriff**
11. **hyphen**
12. **fiber**
13. **siphon**
14. **forecast**
15. **forth**
16. **photos**
17. **trophy**
18. **dolphin**
19. **fossil**
20. **funds**

3 Journaling

Provide a meaningful reason for correct spelling through personal writing.

Review the story using discussion leads provided on the following page. Encourage students to apply the Scriptural value in their journaling.

Journaling (continued)

- Have you ever been cross-country skiing or down-hill skiing? (Allow time to share experiences.)
- Why didn't Thorny bring any books about skiing along on the trip? (He'd already read everything he could find about the subject.)
- What did Thorny say the first skis were made of? (Animal bones.)
- Did Thorny know how to ski because of all the research he'd done? (No. He had to try skiing to learn.)
- What wise choice did Thorny make when he realized he was lost? (He decided to stay put and wait for someone to come find him.)
- What did Thorny do to pass the time? (Repeated all the Scriptures he could remember learning since he'd come to live in the Simmons foster home.)
- How did that help him? (He remembered the verse that said to be patient, brave, and courageous, waiting for the Lord to save you.)
- Why do you think it was a good thing Thorny had done all that reading about cross-country skiing? (He had packed extra clothes, matches, toilet paper in a plastic bag, an insulated blanket, and a candy bar.)

E is the most frequently occurring letter in English as well as in French, Spanish, and German.

Word Wow!

Socially Acceptable

Daniel attends a fancy dinner party with his parents and has a hard choice to make.

"Well, how do I look, Milli?" Daniel struck a pose, hands held palm up to the side.

Milli, the DeVore's live-in maid, slowly circled the boy, eyeing him critically. Then she stopped in front of him, her hand tucked under her chin and her head cocked to one side. Finally, she winked. "Sure'n you be a-lookin' right smart tonight! 'Twould be surprisin' if you weren't the best lookin' lad attendin' that fancy shindig."

"Aw, Milli," Daniel grinned in embarrassment. "Of course that's not true, but you really think I look okay? I'm just so glad Dad and Mom want me to go tonight. They don't usually take me anywhere with them, and they've never taken me with them to anything like this. I want to be sure I do everything right!"

"Now that sounds a right-fine goal to be a-aimin' for, young Daniel." Milli straightened his tie a bit. "And you be a-lookin' more than okay."

"Milli! Send Daniel down, please," Mr. DeVore called from the bottom of the stairs. "We should be leaving for the Hopewell's right away."

Daniel wiped suddenly damp palms on his designer slacks. Milli grinned. "Now I can't be a-figurin' out any reason for you to be nervous, lad. You know more about which fork to be a-usin' first than most of us." She gave him a quick hug, then straightened his suit coat. "Just have a grand time, m'lad."

"See you later, Milli." Daniel offered a crooked grin and started down the broad, curved staircase.

"There you are." Mrs. DeVore looked her only son over with a critical eye. "By all means, stand up straight, Daniel. You hardly look impressive all hunched over like that. Now, remember to greet Mrs. Hopewell first, like I showed you, with a small bow over her hand. Then, greet Mr. Hopewell, but be sure to call him 'Sir.' After all, he's from England and that is his title. It simply wouldn't do for you to call him 'mister.' Now...."

The steady stream of instructions continued as the three DeVores took their places in the Cadillac. They kept coming as Mr. DeVore eased the luxurious sedan out onto Stoneridge Court and headed toward the Hopewell's home. When Mrs. DeVore finally fell silent, Mr. DeVore spoke up. "Are you sure you want to take Daniel with us, Sandra? You're just going to be worrying all evening about how he behaves."

"I will not!" Daniel's mother snapped. "You know very well that we have to take Daniel tonight to make a good impression on the Hopewells. They dote on their boy, Carson. Especially Cynthia. Why, she acts as if that child is absolutely perfect. They center their lives around him." She shook her perfectly groomed head. "They'd think us very strange if we didn't bring Daniel."

Daniel didn't hear the rest of the discussion. He stared out the window without seeing anything, but his thoughts were resentful. "It shouldn't surprise me, really. They've never cared enough about me to want to be with me. I don't know why I thought this was any different, but somehow I did. I thought they wanted to take me to this fancy party because they were proud of me. I'm such a stupid jerk, I never learn!"

The hurt inside Daniel churned up familiar feelings of helpless anger. Parents are supposed to love and care for their kids! Why couldn't his parents get the message?

When they arrived at the Hopewell's sprawling estate, Daniel performed perfectly. The introductions, the pre-dinner chitchat, the formal dinner with three forks and two spoons—Daniel dealt with each flawlessly. He even kept his cool when he tripped slightly on the edge of a thick Persian carpet and the Hopewell's "perfect" son, Carson, asked him when he learned to walk. But inside, his feelings continued to boil. After dinner, the adults drifted around in small groups visiting and gossiping. Daniel found an inconspicuous spot in a corner and flopped into a soft chair.

A boy about Daniel's own age spotted him. "Hey, aren't you the DeVore kid?"

Daniel nodded.

"Daniel, isn't it? Well, I'm Jonathan Hightower, but you can call me Rusty." The boy tugged a reddish brown curl and shrugged. "Hey, you guys, come here!" He motioned two other boys over to Daniel's corner. "This is Peter and that's Randall, Randy for short. We've got a plan. You want to hear it?"

Daniel shrugged. The three boys moved in closer. "It's like this," Rusty began. "It's that Carson Hopewell. We've got to do something about him."

"Why?" Daniel was confused.

"Haven't you met him?" Rusty demanded, as if that was enough of an explanation. When Daniel nodded, Rusty went on, "Then you know. His parents think he can't do anything wrong and he believes it! He thinks he's better than anyone else and treats everyone like dirt. When Peter's family arrived tonight Carson ignored him—looked through him like he wasn't even there. Randy said "Yo" instead of "Hello," and this Carson guy looked at Randy like he was insane and asked him why he didn't learn to speak proper English."

Judging from his flashing green eyes, Rusty

was working himself into quite a temper. "Why, I heard his mother telling someone he didn't want to eat with us, so she let him eat in a private dining room. Well, our dads are rich, too. Maybe they aren't 'Sirs,' but we're just as important as he is—and we've got a plan to show him just that!"

Daniel's own feelings of hurt and anger grew. Maybe he couldn't do anything about his own parents not thinking he was good enough for them to spend time with, but he could sure do something about this Carson character not thinking he was good enough! He leaned forward in the chair. "What's the plan?" The other three boys huddled around and explained.

"So," Rusty finished. "Are you in?"

Daniel started to reply, but another voice interrupted.

"What kind of drinks have you got there?" Peter had spotted a server passing through the hallway. The young woman, looking official in a black dress and crisp white apron, carried a silver tray of frosty crystal glasses.

"There be white grape juice, apple juice, strawberry-kiwi and raspberry lemonade, sir," she answered Peter's question respectfully.

Randy and Peter made their selections. Rusty frowned. "Don't you have any pop?"

"No, sir." The girl answered respectfully. "I can be a-checkin' in the kitchen if you be a-wishin' it."

"No, this is fine." Rusty took apple juice. Daniel picked up a glass, too, not even sure what he was getting. The girl didn't look anything like Milli, but she sounded so much like her!

Just hearing that lilting voice made Daniel think about Milli and their earlier conversation. "Milli is proud of me. Milli thinks I look better than okay—and she expects me to do what is right."

As the waitress walked away, Rusty repeated the question. "So, DeVore, are you in?"

Daniel shook his head and calmly said, "No."

"NO!?" The three echoed. "Why ever not?" Peter demanded.

Daniel rubbed the moisture off the outside of his glass. "Well, I want to, but I can't."

Randy looked puzzled. "What's the problem?"

"Well, even though he made fun of me and was a real jerk to you guys, it just wouldn't be right, that's all." Daniel took a sip of raspberry lemonade.

"Well, well." Rusty shook his head and stared at Daniel as if he had sprouted another head or something. "I'd heard you were a pretty tough guy, that you could handle yourself in things like this, that you'd even gotten into major trouble over some stuff you'd done. You must have changed." He turned away. "C'mon guys."

"Uh, see ya." Randy and Peter seemed embarrassed.

"Yeah, see you later." Peter half-waved and the two sauntered off.

Later that evening, Daniel told Milli all about it. "So, if that maid hadn't sounded so much like you, I probably would have gotten in big trouble. As it was, the other guys didn't follow through with their plan, and Carson Hopewell got away with his meanness." Daniel sighed and rested his chin on his hands where he sat at the kitchen work table watching Milli make up a tray for his parents, who'd gone straight to their room.

"That's where you be a-thinkin' wrong." Milli placed two fine china cups and saucers on the tray.

"Where?" Daniel rubbed the bridge of his nose, trying to ease the headache building behind his eyes.

"Everyone must be a-payin' for their actions sooner or later, lad. Carson Hopewell will be a-payin' for his as surely as you will pay for yours." Milli reached for the delicate sugar bowl and put it on the tray. "I be a-thinkin' your payments will be vastly different, though!" She winked. "Sure'n you have changed, m'lad, and I be a-praisin' God for a-holdin' you tight in His hand and a-keepin' your feet on the right path this night."

"Whether I wanted to stay there or not!" Daniel chuckled.

Milli walked over and shook her finger under Daniel's nose. "You made the choice, lad. The right choice." She squeezed his shoulder, then stepped back to study him, tucking one hand under her chin and cocking her head to one side in thought. Finally, she winked. "Sure'n you be a-lookin' right smart tonight!"

2 Discussion Time

Check understanding of the story and development of personal values.

- Where were Daniel's parents taking him?
- What did Daniel's mother say to him on the way?
- What did Rusty, Peter, and Randy ask Daniel to help them do?
- Why did the boys want to "do something" about Carson Hopewell?
- What happened just as Daniel was about to answer the boys?
- What choice did Daniel make?
- What did Milli say about the choice Daniel made?

A Preview Name ____________

Write each word as your teacher says it.

1. average
2. jacket
3. merge
4. cringe
5. jury
6. manage
7. heritage
8. badge
9. junior
10. legend
11. jaguar
12. dungeon
13. jogging
14. gadget
15. hinges
16. rigid
17. justice
18. plunge
19. refuge
20. pledge

Scripture
Psalm 66:8,9

Words with /j/ Lesson 20

125

3 Preview

Test for knowledge of the correct spellings of these words.

Customize Your List

On a separate sheet of paper, additional words of your choice may be tested.

I will say each word once, use the word in a sentence, then say the word again. Write the words on the lines in your Worktext.

Correct Immediately!

Let's correct our Preview. I will spell each word out loud. If you spelled a word incorrectly, rewrite it correctly.

Progress Chart

Students may record scores. (Reproducible master provided in Appendix B.)

Lesson 20 | Day 1

1. **average**	"You be lookin' a might above **average** tonight!" complimented Milli.
2. **jacket**	The **jacket** Daniel wore complimented his slacks and tie.
3. **merge**	Mr. DeVore began to carefully **merge** the expensive sedan into the next lane.
4. **cringe**	Daniel's mother's constant instructions made him **cringe** and feel more nervous.
5. **jury**	He felt as if he were standing before a judge and **jury**.
6. **manage**	"I do hope you can **manage** to do right!" worried Mrs. DeVore.
7. **heritage**	"The Hopewell family has a rich family **heritage**," she commented.
8. **badge**	"They wear their son Carson like a **badge** or something!" she sneered.
9. **junior**	"They act as if he's **junior** partner in the firm already!"
10. **legend**	"This is the only known copy of this ancient English **legend**," bragged Carson.
11. **jaguar**	Daniel thought the porcelain **jaguar** in the dining room looked fierce.
12. **dungeon**	"I'll bet there's a creepy **dungeon** under this huge house," joked Randy.
13. **jogging**	"Your dad goes **jogging** with Sir Hopewell, doesn't he?" asked Rusty.
14. **gadget**	While the boys talked in the kitchen, Daniel noticed many a fancy **gadget**.
15. **hinges**	The metal door to the kitchen had **hinges** that swung both ways.
16. **rigid**	At first Daniel felt **rigid** with anger and wanted to join the boys.
17. **justice**	"Let's serve a little **justice** on Conceited Carson!" laughed Rusty.
18. **plunge**	"Are you too scared to take the **plunge** with us?" Rusty mocked Daniel.
19. **refuge**	When he got home, he hurried to take **refuge** in the kitchen with Milli.
20. **pledge**	"I remembered my **pledge** to God to follow His path," he told her.

Lesson 20 | Day 1

4 Word Shapes

Help students form a correct image of whole words.

Look at each word and think about its shape. Now, write the word in the correct word Shape Boxes. You may check off each word as you use it.

(In many words, the sound of **/j/** is spelled with **j**, and it is often spelled this way when it is at the beginning of a word. The **/j/** sound can also be spelled with **g** when followed by **i**, **y**, or **e**. The spelling **dge** is used at the end of a word.)

In the word shape boxes, color the letter or letters that spell the sound of **/j/** in each word.

Take a minute to memorize...

Psalm 66:8,9

Words with /j/ — Lesson 20

B Word Shapes Name ____________

Using the word bank below, write each word in the correct word shape boxes. Next, in the word shape boxes, fill in the boxes containing the letter or letters that spell the sound of **/j/** in each word.

1.	gadget	11.	pledge
2.	heritage	12.	average
3.	merge	13.	cringe
4.	legend	14.	justice
5.	jaguar	15.	manage
6.	jury	16.	jogging
7.	rigid	17.	dungeon
8.	jacket	18.	junior
9.	refuge	19.	plunge
10.	badge	20.	hinges

Word Bank

average	gadget	jaguar	justice	pledge
badge	heritage	jogging	legend	plunge
cringe	hinges	junior	manage	refuge
dungeon	jacket	jury	merge	rigid

126

Answers may vary for duplicate word shapes.

Be Prepared For Fun

Check these supply lists for **Fun Ways to Spell** - presented **Day 2**.
Purchase and/or gather these items ahead of time!

General
- Pencil
- Notebook Paper
- Spelling List

Auditory
- Pencil
- Notebook Paper
- Dictionary
- Spelling List

Visual
- Pencil
- Notebook Paper
- Spelling List

Tactile
- Computer Keyboard
- Spelling List

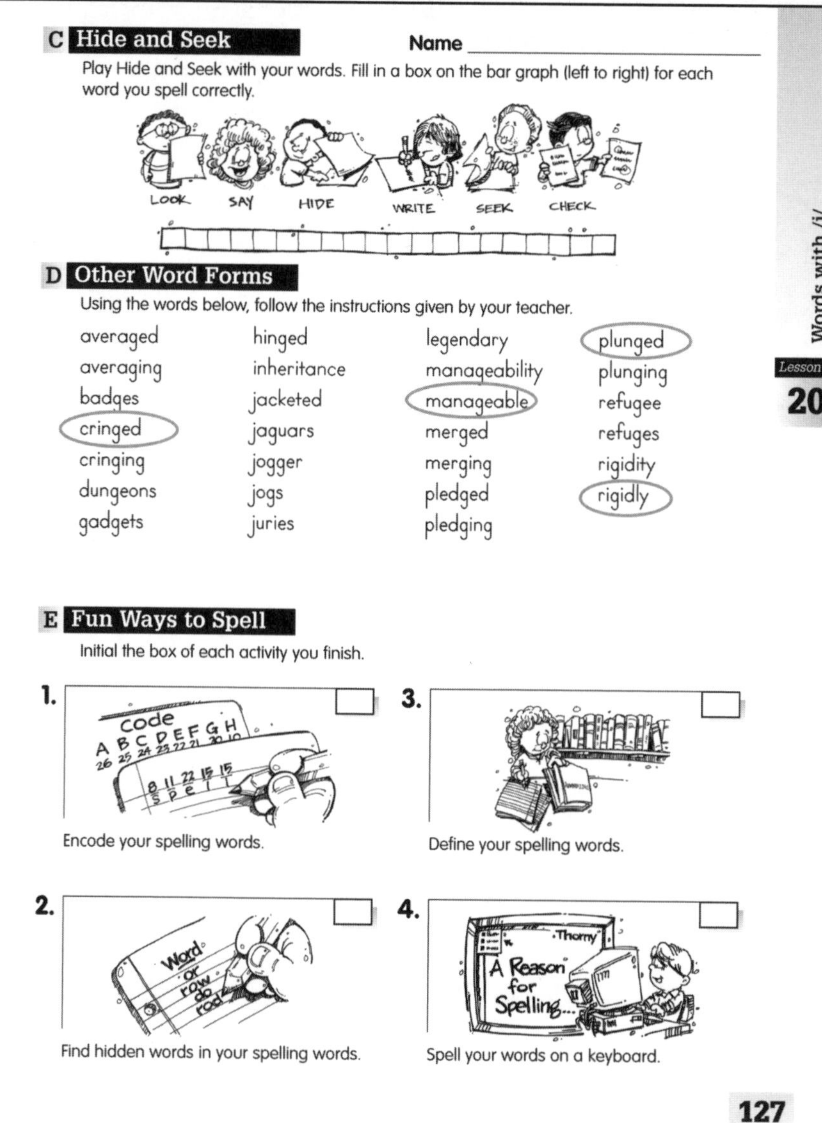

1 Hide and Seek

Reinforce spelling by using multiple styles of learning.

On a white board, Teacher writes each word — one at a time. **Have students:**

- **Look** at the word.
- **Say** the word out loud.
- **Spell** the word out loud.
- **Hide** (teacher erases word.)
- **Write** the word on paper.
- **Seek** (teacher rewrites word.)
- **Check** spelling. If incorrect, rewrite word correctly.

Day 2

Lesson 20

2 Other Word Forms

This activity is optional. Have students find and circle the Other Word Forms that are most nearly synonyms of the following:

recoiled
unyieldingly
doable
dived

3 Fun Ways to Spell

Four activities are provided. Use one, two, three, or all of the activities. Have students initial the box for each activity they complete.

Options:

- assign activities to students according to their learning styles
- set up the activities in learning centers for the students to do throughout the day
- divide students into four groups and assign one activity per group
- do one activity per day

General

To encode your spelling words...
- Write the alphabet on your paper.
- Write your own code for each letter underneath it.
- Write your spelling words in your code.
- Trade papers with a classmate and decode the words.
- Check to make sure your classmate spelled the words correctly.

Auditory

To define your spelling words...
- Ask a classmate to look up a word from your spelling list in the dictionary and read the definition to you, but not the spelling word.
- Decide which word on your list matches this definition and write the word.
- Ask your classmate to check your spelling.
- Switch and continue taking turns.

Visual

To find hidden words in your spelling words...
- Choose a word from your spelling list.
- Write it on your paper.
- Find and write as many smaller words as you can that are contained within your spelling word.
- Do this with each word.

Tactile

To spell your words on a keyboard...
- Type your spelling words on a keyboard.
- Check your spelling.

Lesson 20 | Day 3

1 Working with Words

Familiarize students with word meaning and usage.

Drawing Conclusions

Explain that to figure something out using logic is to draw a conclusion. On the board write:

You are riding a large, strong animal with hoofs. You are probably riding a ___________.

Have a volunteer supply the word **horse**.

Complete each conclusion by writing a word from the word bank. You may use a dictionary to help you.

Take a minute to memorize...

Psalm 66:8,9

Words with /j/ — Lesson 20

F Working with Words Name ______________________

Drawing Conclusions

Complete each conclusion by writing a word from the word bank.

1. The weather is chilly. You should probably wear a ___jacket___.
2. You are standing, facing the flag. You are about to say the ___pledge___.
3. The door squeaks when it is opened. It needs oil on the ___hinges___.
4. If something is usual and ordinary, it is said to be ___average___.
5. You are running at a slow, steady pace. You are ___jogging___.
6. A sheriff is wearing a silver star on his uniform. He is wearing a ___badge___.
7. You decided to jump off the high dive. You will ___plunge___ into the water.
8. Twelve men and women sit listening to the lawyers. They are probably the ___jury___.
9. The verdict sounds fair. ___Justice___ has been done.
10. The old castle has a room for prisoners. This room is called the ___dungeon___.
11. Mom has a small tool for slicing eggs. She says it is a new ___gadget___.
12. You have good self-control. You are able to ___manage___ yourself.
13. Dad needs to change lanes into a line of cars. He needs to ___merge___.
14. Our teacher is pretty strict. Her rules are very ___rigid___.
15. We needed to find shelter from the storm. We looked for a place of ___refuge___.
16. I am an American. Freedom is my ___heritage___.
17. I shrank in fear when I heard the thunder. It made me ___cringe___.
18. We read a story about a blue ox named Babe. The story is a ___legend___.
19. My brother will graduate next year. He is a ___junior___ in high school.
20. At the zoo, I saw a cat that looked like a big leopard. It must be a ___jaguar___.

Word Bank

average	gadget	jaguar	justice	pledge
badge	heritage	jogging	legend	plunge
cringe	hinges	junior	manage	refuge
dungeon	jacket	jury	merge	rigid

128

G Dictation

Name ______________________

Write each sentence as your teacher dictates. Use correct punctuation.

1. Daniel looked sharp in his new suit jacket, although he felt tense.
2. It made him cringe as he thought of the plan to get even.
3. Daniel managed to stay out of trouble, although his choice embarrassed the boys.

Words with /j/

Lesson 20

H Proofreading

If a word is misspelled, fill in the oval by that word. If all the words are spelled correctly, fill in the oval by **no mistake**.

1. ● avrige ○ badge ○ Africa ○ no mistake
2. ○ gadget ○ autograph ○ effort ● no mistake
3. ● jackit ○ paragraph ○ jaguar ○ no mistake
4. ○ sphere ● manige ○ pledge ○ no mistake
5. ○ forth ○ refuge ● legind ○ no mistake
6. ○ cringe ○ difference ○ sheriff ● no mistake
7. ○ dolphin ● junor ○ funds ○ no mistake
8. ○ justice ● merje ○ hyphen ○ no mistake
9. ○ hinges ○ rigid ○ fossil ● no mistake
10. ○ jogging ○ phrase ○ nephew ● no mistake
11. ● heritige ○ plunge ○ difficult ○ no mistake
12. ○ fiber ○ jury ● dunjon ○ no mistake

129

1 Dictation

Reinforce correct spelling by using current and previous words in context.

Listen as I read each sentence and then write it in your Worktext. Remember to use correct capitalization and punctuation. (Slowly read each sentence twice. Sentences are found in the Student Worktext to the left.)

Day 4

2 Proofreading

Familiarize students with standardized test format and reinforce recognition of misspelled words.

Lesson 20

Look at each set of words. If a word is misspelled, fill in the oval by that word. If all the words are spelled correctly, fill in the oval by **no mistake**.

Lesson 20 | Day 4 / Day 5

3 Hide and Seek

Reinforce correct spelling of current spelling words. Repeat this activity from Day 2.

4 Vocabulary Extension

Have your students complete this activity to strengthen spelling ability and expand vocabulary. The reproducible master is provided in Appendix A as shown on the inset page to the right.

1 Posttest

Test mastery of the spelling words.

I will say the word once, use it in a sentence, then say it again. Write your words on a separate sheet of paper.

Progress Chart

Students may record scores. (Reproducible master in Appendix B.)

Personal Dictionary

Students may add any words they have misspelled to their personal dictionaries for reference when writing. (Cover in Appendix B.)

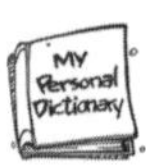

Hide and Seek

Play Hide and Seek with your words. Fill in a bar graph (left to right) for each word you spell correctly.

Vocabulary Extension

Trade-off

Choose a word from the word bank to replace the word(s) in parentheses. Write the word in the blank.

1. Dad bought Mom a corsage (small bouquet) to wear to church for Mothers' Day.
2. The hungry deer had to forage (search) for food during the harsh winter.
3. Medics are trained to act quickly and carefully in an emergency (crisis).
4. Michael forgot to put the milk back in the refrigerator (icebox), so it soured.
5. Measles, chicken pox, and the flu are all contagious (infectious) diseases that can spread to other people.
6. A generation (span of time) is said to be around 30 years between the births of parents and that of their children.
7. A sergeant (member of the armed forces) was waiting at the train station.
8. Mom and Dad had made an arrangement (agreement) for me to stay at a neighbor's house until they got home.
9. Getting used to his new school took some adjustment (adaptation), but he soon made new friends.
10. We say a pledge to our country's flag each day to show allegiance (loyalty) to the country we live in.
11. People train dogs with high intelligence (aptitude) to serve as police dogs and seeing-eye dogs.
12. The traffic accident occurred because of the negligence (carelessness) of the driver who ran the stop sign.

Word Bank

adjustment	contagious	forage	negligence
allegiance	corsage	generation	refrigerator
arrangement	emergency	intelligence	sergeant

Vocabulary Extension — Lesson 20 — 341

---

1. average — "This is no **average** party," Daniel told Milli.
2. badge — Sometimes people with lots of money wear their success like a **badge.**
3. jogging — Mrs. DeVore and Mrs. Hopewell go **jogging** together sometimes.
4. jacket — Milli dusted some lint off the back of Daniel's dinner **jacket.**
5. merge — Mr. DeVore began to slowly **merge** the sedan into the flow of traffic.
6. manage — "Can you **manage** to behave like a gentleman tonight?" asked his mother.
7. cringe — His mother's sharp remarks made Daniel **cringe.**
8. heritage — "The Hopewell's are extremely proud of their family **heritage,**" she continued.
9. junior — "Carson will be the **junior** partner in his father's firm one day," said Mrs. DeVore.
10. legend — An antique book of an ancient English **legend** sat on the table in the foyer.
11. jaguar — A large porcelain **jaguar** stood in the corner of the Hopewell's dining room.
12. hinges — The **hinges** on the kitchen door allowed it to swing freely both ways.
13. gadget — There was more than one fancy **gadget** in the huge kitchen.
14. dungeon — "Think there's a **dungeon** underneath this castle?" joked Randy.
15. justice — "Let's serve some **justice** on that old Carson Hopewell," suggested Rusty.
16. rigid — At first, the boys' comments made Daniel feel **rigid** with anger.
17. pledge — Daniel thought for a moment and said, "I made a **pledge** to follow the right path."
18. jury — "You're acting like a judge and **jury,** Daniel," mocked Rusty.
19. plunge — "We thought you were tough enough to take the **plunge,**" they sneered.
20. refuge — After he got home, Daniel took **refuge** in the kitchen with Milli.

Words with /j/ — Lesson 20

I Game Name ____________________

Complete the secret phrase by spelling the words from this week's word list.

Remember: God will give you strength to do right!

J Journaling

In your journal, write about a time you wanted to get even with someone. Tell why you were upset with them and what you chose to do about the situation. Remember to ask God to hold your feet on the right path.

130

2 Game

Reinforce spelling skills and provide motivation and interest.

Materials

- game page (from student text)
- pencils (1 per child)
- game word list

Game Word List

Team A	Team B
1. **average (O)**	1. **cringe (O)**
2. **badge (D)**	2. **hinges (D)**
3. **gadget (H)**	3. **rigid (H)**
4. **jacket (O)**	4. **jogging (O)**
5. **jaguar (L)**	5. **junior (L)**
6. **manage (D)**	6. **jury (D)**
7. **pledge (M)**	7. **merge (M)**
8. **legend (Y)**	8. **justice (Y)**
9. **refuge (E)**	9. **dungeon (E)**
10. **heritage (E)**	10. **plunge (E)**
11. **cringe (T)**	11. **average (T)**
12. **hinges (T)**	12. **badge (T)**
13. **rigid (O)**	13. **gadget (O)**
14. **jogging (T)**	14. **jacket (T)**
15. **junior (H)**	15. **jaguar (H)**
16. **jury (E)**	16. **manage (E)**
17. **merge (P)**	17. **pledge (P)**
18. **justice (A)**	18. **legend (A)**
19. **dungeon (T)**	19. **refuge (T)**
20. **plunge (H)**	20. **heritage (H)**

How to Play:

- Divide the class into two teams, and decide which team will go first.
- Have a student from team A choose a number from 1 to 20.
- Say the word that matches that number from the team's word list.
- Have the student write the word on the board.
- If correct, have each member of team A write the given letter in the matching space on his/her game page.
- Alternate between teams A and B having the students choose a number of a blank space.
- The team to complete the secret phrase first is the winner.

3 Journaling

Provide a meaningful reason for correct spelling through personal writing.

Review the story using discussion leads provided on the following page. Encourage students to apply the Scriptural value in their journaling.

Journaling (continued)

- Why was Daniel so happy that his parents were taking him to the fancy dinner party? (He wanted to be with them and thought that they were taking him because they were proud of him and wanted to be with him, too.)
- What made him realize that they weren't taking him because they wanted to? (His mother said they had to take him to make a good impression on the Hopewells.)
- How did Daniel react to knowing his parents didn't really want him with them? (He felt very angry and upset.)
- What was Carson Hopewell like? (He was a spoiled brat. His parents thought he couldn't do anything wrong, but he was selfish and mean to the other boys.)
- How did the serving girl stop Daniel from choosing to go along with the boys' plan to do something to Carson? (Her accent sounded like Milli's and thinking of Milli reminded Daniel to do what was right.)

The longest word with one vowel is STRENGTHS.

Over the Limit

Carlos learns how important it is to obey all laws – including traffic laws.

"Carlos, that sign says the speed limit is 40 miles an hour!" Rosa waved at the sign they'd just sped by. "You know, f-o-r-t-y, FORTY!"

"Yeah, yeah, yeah." Carlos flipped on the radio. "I'm only going a little over that. Relax already, would ya?" When he located a station he liked, he turned up the volume. Music throbbed through the yellow Honda and put a halt to any further discussion.

Soon Carlos braked to a stop in the Wrights' driveway. He spoke loudly to be heard over the radio. "See, little sister? Here you are, safe and sound. I'll be back to pick you up when basketball practice is over at 8:00."

Rosa gathered up her stuff and climbed out of the little car. She waved as her older brother backed out of the driveway and turned down Appleby Road. True to form, he didn't come to a stop at the corner—just a pause and then off down the road again.

"Hi, Rosa!" Kristin opened the front door. "Come on in. Burrrr. It's cold out there!"

The Wrights' house was warm and smelled delicious. "Mom's baking cinnamon rolls," Kristin informed her friend when she saw her sniffing the air. "They should be out in time for supper. Let's work in my room." She led the way to the room she shared with her younger sister, Cathy. "Did you bring everything?"

When Rosa upended her tote bag a variety of objects rolled out onto the carpet—Popsicle sticks, a Ziploc bag of hay, small pieces of wood, and a couple of metal pop-bottle lids.

"Dad said we could use this box." Kristin sank down Indian style on the floor and began adding her contributions to the pile, "Here are glue, paints, wire, cotton balls, and pipe cleaners." Kristin set the box on its side. "Well, let's get started."

Rosa picked up the wire and some Popsicle sticks. "I'll start the fence and you can paint the background, okay?"

Kristin jumped up, "Just a second. I'll get some plastic to put down so we don't mess up the carpet."

Gradually the diorama began to take shape. By the time Cathy came to call them to supper, she could tell that the scene was a horse barn and pasture.

After a yummy supper of vegetable soup and warm cinnamon rolls, the two friends went back to work. "Do you think this hay looks all right by the barn like this?" Rosa leaned back to study the effect.

"Uh-huh." Kristin placed a fluff of cotton on the background and glued the cloud in place. "Looks GREAT to me!" She stretched and looked at the mess around them. "What time is Carlos coming to get you?"

Rosa began picking up leftover bits and pieces. "He said basketball practice would be over at 8:00, so he'll probably get here two minutes after that." She shook her head. "He drives so fast!"

"Does his driving scare you?" Kristin held open a plastic bag and Rosa dropped the leftovers inside.

"No, not really." Rosa leaned back against the side of Cathy's bed. "He always says he's in control and that he doesn't go faster than is safe, but I say speed limits are posted for a reason and he should pay attention to them."

"What does your dad say about it?"

Rosa shrugged. "I haven't said anything to Dad about it. Carlos worked so hard to get the money to buy that car, and he's spent so much time and effort fixing it up. It's like a person to him. I'm pretty sure Dad wouldn't let him drive if he knew he was breaking some rules, so I've just been trying to get Carlos to slow down and stuff on my own." She sighed. "Maria just ignores the whole situation. She doesn't care how he drives as long as he'll take her places."

"Well, I think you should tell your dad." Kristin looked at her friend seriously.

"Carlos would never forgive me if I did that and Dad took away his car!" Rosa protested.

"Maybe not," Kristin admitted. "But like you said, those speed limits and stop signs are there for a reason. He'll get a ticket or, worse yet, have an accident if he keeps on ignoring them—and then your dad will find out for sure."

Rosa got up and changed the subject. "Since we're done with this project, let's do something fun till Carlos gets here. How about that new game you got for Christmas?"

Kristin plopped onto her stomach and helped Rosa set up the game on the floor. Kristin was winning when the doorbell chimed. She helped Rosa carry the diorama out and settle it safely in the back seat of the Honda. "Don't forget to bring it to school tomorrow!" she reminded as Rosa climbed in the front seat by her brother. "See you later, alligator!"

"After a while, crocodile!" Rosa waved as Carlos backed out of the driveway.

"That thing you guys made looks good, Rosita." Carlos slowed at the stop sign, and, after glancing around, accelerated again.

"Thanks, Carlos." Rosa gulped, then went on, "You didn't stop at that stop sign. Don't you think you should have?"

"Naaa!" Carlos changed his headlights to low beam as a car came toward them. "You could see as well as I could that there weren't any cars at the intersection! It was totally safe to keep going. What's

Story (continued)

the big deal?"

"Well, the sign said to stop. That's the law." Rosa took a deep breath. "What if you get so used to ignoring traffic signs that you ignore them when it isn't safe?"

"Give me a break, Rosa!" Carlos shifted into a higher gear. "I think I know a bit more about driving than you do. After all, I have a license and you don't!" The yellow car picked up speed rapidly.

"Carlos, you're going too fast!" Rosa insisted. "The speed limit here is 55!"

"Nag, nag, nag!" Carlos exploded. "You're always complaining and carrying on! Well, I'm a good driver! Besides, this is my car and I'll drive it the way I want! You just be quiet and be glad you have a ride! Just because I don't stop and wait an hour at every stop sign doesn't mean that...."

Suddenly, everything seemed to slide into slow motion. Carlos stomped on the brake pedal. The tires shrieked against the pavement, but couldn't cling to it. The road quietly curved around the bend as it always did—but the shiny yellow Honda didn't make the turn. Rosa screamed! The little car launched into space. There was the sound of an impact; everything went dark.

When Rosa woke up she hurt all over. It took a major effort to open her eyes. "Well, hello, young lady." A pleasant stranger leaned over her and peered into her eyes.

"Wh-what happened?" Rosa didn't recognize her own scratchy voice.

"What do you remember?" The woman began writing on a clipboard.

Slowly Rosa's thoughts became less muddled. She realized she was in a hospital room and this must be a nurse. "We," her voice squeaked. She cleared her throat and tried again. "We had a wreck. Is Carlos okay?"

"Yes, he'll be just fine." The woman checked the IV hanging by the bed. "He's been very anxious to see you." She smiled down at Rosa. "And your father and sister are here, too, along with several other people. They'll be very glad you decided to wake up!"

Rosa started to raise her head to look around the room. "OUCH!"

"Now, don't try to move, young lady." The woman rested a hand lightly on her forehead. "You're going to be pretty sore for a few days. The best thing is just to lie still and let your body mend itself."

"What's wrong with me?" The nurse could hear the fear in Rosa's voice.

"Nothing that won't heal up just fine," she reassured the injured girl. "You have three broken ribs, a punctured lung, and lots of scrapes and cuts, as well as a bump on the head. None of those injuries are fun, but you'll soon be as good as new. Now, are you ready to let your family—especially that brother of yours—in to see you before they break the door down?"

"Okay." Rosa smiled a little at the woman's exaggeration. She closed her eyes for a moment and listened to the voices in the hallway. When the door opened, her dad rushed in with Maria on his heels. Carlos hung back near the door.

Rosa could see tears in Dad's eyes when he leaned over the hospital bed and wordlessly stroked the hair off her forehead.

Maria circled around to the other side of the bed and pulled a chair close. "You look awful, but I'm sure glad you're in one piece! You should see your diorama—it's totally smashed! And Carlos' car will never be the same."

"Is Carlos really okay?" Rosa tried to look over by the door, but it hurt too much to turn her head.

"I'm fine." Carlos stood at the foot of the bed so she could see him. He had a couple of stitches on his chin and a long white bandage on one arm. "I'm sorry, Rosa." His voice broke and he paused and stared down at his hands, twisting them nervously. "Since it was all my fault, I wish I'd been the one hurt worse. I know I can't ever make this up to you, but I'll try." He took a deep breath. "Little sister, I promise I'll obey all the traffic laws from now on."

Rosa smiled up at her big brother, looking so worried and upset. "Maybe redoing my diorama would make it up to me!"

A big grin creased Carlos' face. "You got it, Rosa! You got it!"

2 Discussion Time

Check understanding of the story and development of personal values.

- Why was Rosa concerned about Carlos' driving?
- On what school project were Kristin and Rosa working?
- Why hadn't Rosa told her father about Carlos not obeying all the traffic rules?
- How did Carlos react when Rosa reminded him that he hadn't really stopped at the stop sign?
- What happened to the yellow Honda?
- How badly was Rosa hurt?
- How did Carlos feel about Rosa being hurt so badly?

A Preview Name ____________________

Write each word as your teacher says it.

1. squid
2. Quebec
3. equator
4. chorus
5. banquet
6. Nebraska
7. Alaska
8. Kentucky
9. squall
10. earthquake
11. equal
12. chaos
13. backup
14. o'clock
15. quicksand
16. echoes
17. preschool
18. inquire
19. liquid
20. quality

Words with /k/ or /kw/

Lesson 21

Scripture

Psalm 19:9,10

131

3 Preview

Test for knowledge of the correct spellings of these words.

Customize Your List

On a separate sheet of paper, additional words of your choice may be tested.

I will say each word once, use the word in a sentence, then say the word again. Write the words on the lines in your Worktext.

Correct Immediately!

Let's correct our Preview. I will spell each word out loud. If you spelled a word incorrectly, rewrite it correctly.

Progress Chart

Students may record scores. (Reproducible master provided in Appendix B.)

Lesson 21 | Day 1

1.	squid	"Have any of you ever seen a live **squid**?" Mr. Canfield asked.
2.	Quebec	"A fisherman from **Quebec** caught this one last year."
3.	equator	Mr. Canfield pointed to the **equator** on the large map.
4.	chorus	The class practiced a **chorus** for morning assembly.
5.	banquet	They also made plans for the spring **banquet**.
6.	Nebraska	The speed limit is clearly marked on the **Nebraska** interstate.
7.	Alaska	**Alaska** also requires all drivers to wear seatbelts.
8.	Kentucky	The **Kentucky** Highway Patrol enforces the speed limits.
9.	squall	Storm clouds in the distance forecasted a coming **squall**.
10.	earthquake	Rosa suddenly felt like she was in the middle of an **earthquake**.
11.	equal	She had never felt any pain to **equal** this.
12.	chaos	To the untrained eye, the busyness in the ER can look like **chaos**.
13.	backup	The nurse switched the machine to the **backup** oxygen supply.
14.	o'clock	Visiting hours at the hospital began at 4 **o'clock**.
15.	quicksand	Carlos' legs felt weak, like he was in the middle of **quicksand**.
16.	echoes	He could still hear **echoes** of the squeal of his brakes.
17.	preschool	Some of the children in the **preschool** sent Rosa pictures.
18.	inquire	Mr. Canfield called the hospital to **inquire** about Rosa.
19.	liquid	The **liquid** in the clear pack dripped slowly through the IV tube.
20.	quality	The **quality** of Rosa's handwriting will be poor till she fully recovers.

4 Word Shapes

Help students form a correct image of whole words.

Look at each word and think about its shape. Now, write the word in the correct word Shape Boxes. You may check off each word as you use it.

(In many words, the sound of **/k/** is spelled with **k**, and it is often spelled this way when it is at the beginning or middle of a word. The **/k/** sound can also be spelled with **c** when followed by **a**, **o**, or **u**. The spelling **ck** occurs in the middle or at the end of a word. The letter **q** is always followed by **u** and usually has the sound of **/kw/**.)

In the word shape boxes, color the letter or letters that spell the sound of **/k/** or **/kw/** in each word.

Take a minute to memorize...

Psalm 19:9,10

Words with /k/ or /kw/ — Lesson 21

B Word Shapes Name ____________________

Using the word bank below, write each word in the correct word shape boxes. Next, in the word shape boxes, fill in the boxes containing the letter or letters that spell the sound of **/k/** or **/kw/** in each word.

1. preschool
2. o'clock
3. squid
4. liquid
5. chorus
6. earthquake
7. quality
8. Quebec
9. equal
10. backup
11. squall
12. Kentucky
13. Alaska
14. Nebraska
15. echoes
16. chaos
17. equator
18. inquire
19. quicksand
20. banquet

Word Bank

Alaska	chorus	equator	Nebraska	Quebec
backup	earthquake	inquire	o'clock	quicksand
banquet	echoes	Kentucky	preschool	squall
chaos	equal	liquid	quality	squid

132

Answers may vary for duplicate word shapes.

Be Prepared For Fun

Check these supply lists for **Fun Ways to Spell** - presented **Day 2**.
Purchase and/or gather these items ahead of time!

General
- Pencil
- 3 X 5 Cards cut in half (20 per child)
- Spelling List

Auditory
- Spelling List

Visual
- Pencil
- Notebook Paper
- Spelling List

Tactile
- Blackboard and Chalk
  -OR-
- White Board and Marker
- Spelling List

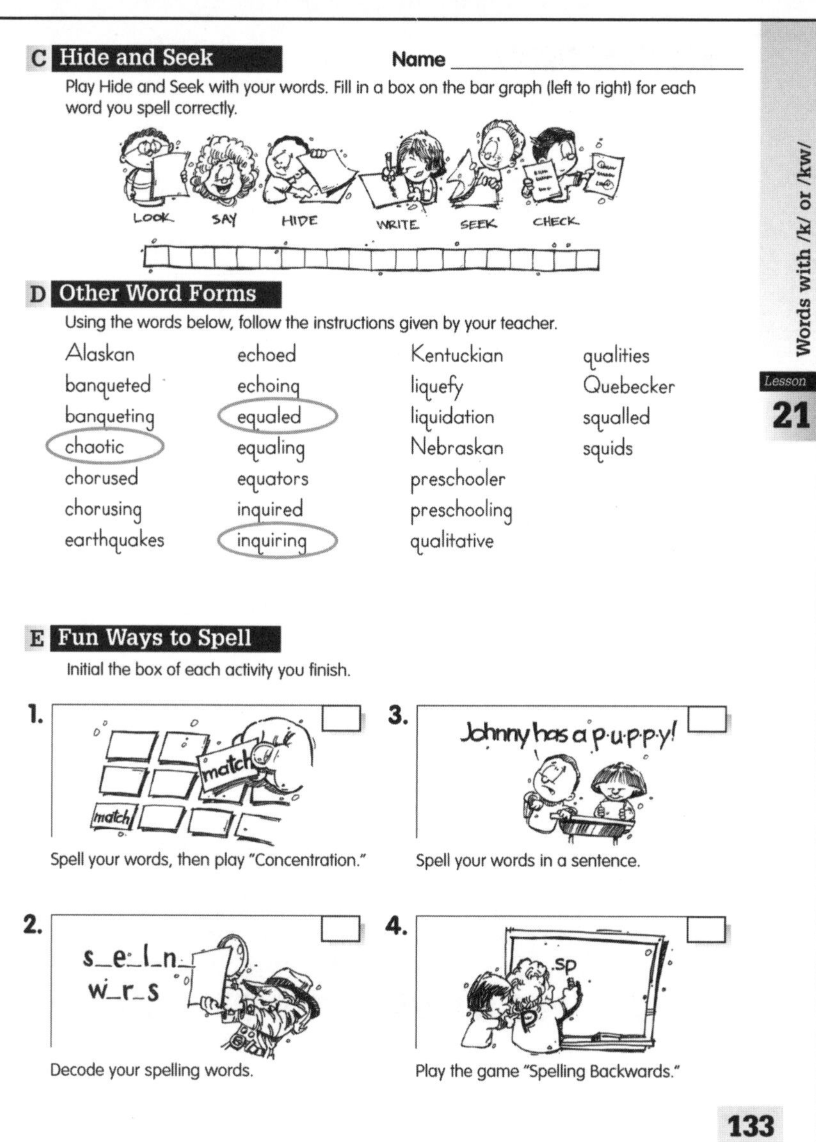

C Hide and Seek

Name ______________________

Play Hide and Seek with your words. Fill in a box on the bar graph (left to right) for each word you spell correctly.

D Other Word Forms

Using the words below, follow the instructions given by your teacher.

Alaskan	echoed	Kentuckian	qualities
banqueted	echoing	liquefy	Quebecker
banqueting	equaled	liquidation	squalled
chaotic	equaling	Nebraskan	squids
chorused	equators	preschooler	
chorusing	inquired	preschooling	
earthquakes	inquiring	qualitative	

E Fun Ways to Spell

Initial the box of each activity you finish.

1.
Spell your words, then play "Concentration."

2.
Decode your spelling words.

3.
Spell your words in a sentence.

4.
Play the game "Spelling Backwards."

Words with /k/ or /kw/

Lesson 21

133

1 Hide and Seek

Reinforce spelling by using multiple styles of learning.

On a white board, Teacher writes each word — one at a time. **Have students:**

- **Look** at the word.
- **Say** the word out loud.
- **Spell** the word out loud.
- **Hide** (teacher erases word.)
- **Write** the word on paper.
- **Seek** (teacher rewrites word.)
- **Check** spelling. If incorrect, rewrite word correctly.

Day 2

Lesson 21

2 Other Word Forms

This activity is optional. Have students find and circle the Other Word Forms that are most nearly antonyms of the following:

differed
orderly
reporting

3 Fun Ways to Spell

Four activities are provided. Use one, two, three, or all of the activities. Have students initial the box for each activity they complete.

Options:

- assign activities to students according to their learning styles
- set up the activities in learning centers for the students to do throughout the day
- divide students into four groups and assign one activity per group
- do one activity per day

General

Spell your words; then play "Concentration"...
- Write each spelling word on a card. Mix your cards and a classmate's cards together. Arrange them face down in five rows of eight. Pick up two cards. If the cards match, play again. If the cards do not match, turn them back over. It is your classmate's turn. Continue taking turns until all the cards are matched. The player with the most cards wins!

Auditory

To spell your words in a sentence...
- Ask a classmate to read a spelling word to you from the list.
- Spell the word aloud and use it in a sentence.
- Ask your classmate to check your spelling.
- Each correctly spelled word that is used properly in a sentence counts as one point.
- Switch and continue taking turns.

Visual

To decode your spelling words...
- Look at the first word on your list.
- Write every other letter of the word on your paper, putting a blank where each missing letter belongs.
- Trade papers with a classmate and fill in the missing letters.
- Check your spelling.

Tactile

To play the game "Spelling Backwards"...
- Ask a classmate to stand behind you and draw the letters to spell a word from your list on your back.
- Write the spelling word on the board as your classmate traces the letters on your back.
- Ask your classmate to check your spelling.
- Trade places and take turns until you have each spelled all the words.

1 Working with Words

Familiarize students with word meaning and usage.

Rhyming Clues

Write the words **girlfriend**, **surrender**, **pretend**, and **endurance** on the board. Have a volunteer underline the two words that rhyme (**girlfriend**, **pretend**). Tell students that, for this exercise, words need to rhyme on at least the last syllable to be considered rhyming words. Explain that students will be matching some of their spelling words to a rhyming word.

Write the spelling word that rhymes with each word below.

The K's and KW's Have It

Each spelling word in this lesson has the **/k/** or **/kw/** sound. Answer each question with a word from the word bank. You may use a dictionary to help you. Write the word in the blank.

Take a minute to memorize...

Psalm 19:9,10

F Working with Words Name ______________

Similar Sounds

Write the spelling word that rhymes with the last syllable of each word below.

1. cheesecake earthquake
2. moonlit banquet
3. wall squall
4. watchband quicksand
5. unlucky Kentucky
6. padlock o'clock
7. wrap-up backup
8. grid squid
9. forbid liquid
10. emboss chaos
11. paycheck Quebec
12. frivolity quality
13. perspire inquire
14. translator equator
15. sequel equal
16. porous chorus
17. compose echoes
18. whirlpool preschool

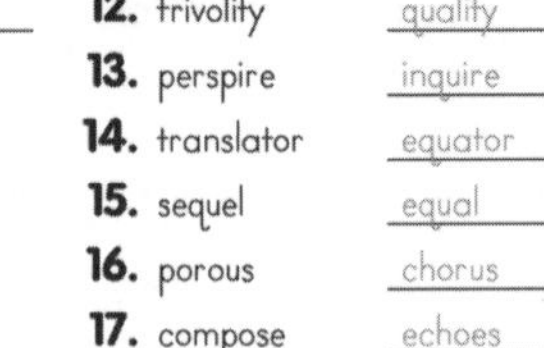

The K's and KW's Have It

Answer each question with a **/k/** or **/kw/** word from the word bank. Write the word in the blank.

1. What **/kw/** word means degree of excellence? quality
2. What **/k/** word is a state in the Great Plains? Nebraska
3. What **/kw/** word means to ask about? inquire
4. What **/k/** word relates to a child's life from infancy to the age of five or six? preschool
5. What **/k/** word means one that serves as a substitute or alternative? backup
6. What **/kw/** word is a province of eastern Canada? Québec
7. What **/kw/** word is a long-bodied sea mollusk with eight arms? squid
8. What **/kw/** word means a deep mass of loose sand mixed with water? quicksand
9. What **/k/** word means complete disorder, confusion, and disarray? chaos
10. What **/k/** word was explored by Daniel Boone? Kentucky

Word Bank

Alaska	chorus	equator	Nebraska	Quebec
backup	earthquake	inquire	o'clock	quicksand
banquet	echoes	Kentucky	preschool	squall
chaos	equal	liquid	quality	squid

134

G Dictation Name ______________________

Write each sentence as your teacher dictates. Use correct punctuation.

1. The girls did good quality work on their farm scene.
2. Carlos said he would pick up his sister at eight o'clock.
3. After the crash, everything was in chaos.

Words with /k/ or /kw/

Lesson 21

H Proofreading

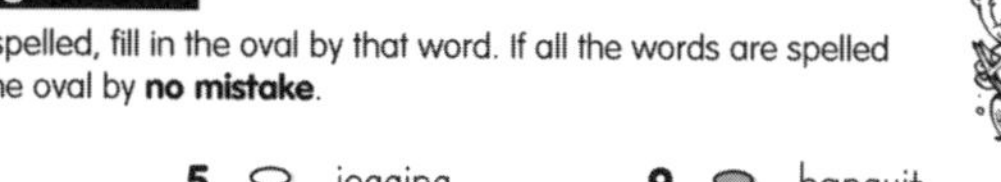

If a word is misspelled, fill in the oval by that word. If all the words are spelled correctly, fill in the oval by **no mistake**.

1. ○ backup ○ average ● kaoss ○ no mistake
2. ○ rigid ● korus ○ echoes ○ no mistake
3. ○ Kentucky ● oclock ○ preschool ○ no mistake
4. ○ legend ○ heritage ○ Alaska ● no mistake
5. ○ jogging ○ junior ○ Nebraska ● no mistake
6. ○ jury ● erthquake ○ pledge ○ no mistake
7. ○ equal ○ jaguar ● equater ○ no mistake
8. ○ refuge ○ inquire ○ liquid ● no mistake
9. ● banquit ○ hinges ○ quality ○ no mistake
10. ● Kwebec ○ quicksand ○ dungeon ○ no mistake
11. ○ jacket ● squal ○ plunge ○ no mistake
12. ○ cringe ○ gadget ○ squid ● no mistake

135

1 Dictation

Reinforce correct spelling by using current and previous words in context.

Listen as I read each sentence and then write it in your Worktext. Remember to use correct capitalization and punctuation. (Slowly read each sentence twice. Sentences are found in the Student Worktext to the left.)

2 Proofreading

Familiarize students with standardized test format and reinforce recognition of misspelled words.

Look at each set of words. If a word is misspelled, fill in the oval by that word. If all the words are spelled correctly, fill in the oval by **no mistake**.

Hide and Seek

Reinforce correct spelling of current spelling words. Repeat this activity from Day 2.

Vocabulary Extension

Have your students complete this activity to strengthen spelling ability and expand vocabulary. The reproducible master is provided in Appendix A as shown on the inset page to the right.

Vocabulary Extension — Lesson 21

Hide and Seek

Play Hide and Seek with your words. Fill in a bar graph (left to right) for each word you spell correctly.

Vocabulary Extension

Multiple Choice

Fill in the oval by the word(s) with the same or nearly the same meaning as the word in bold type.

1. **comedian**
   - ○ process of catching fire and burning
   - ○ punctuation used to split a sentence
   - ○ booklet with cartoon stories
   - ● entertainer who tells funny stories
2. **custodian**
   - ● person who cleans a large building
   - ○ dessert made of milk, eggs, and sugar
   - ○ something you do regularly
   - ○ arrested by the police
3. **reflection**
   - ○ automatic action such as blinking
   - ● an image on a shiny surface
   - ○ shelter from danger or trouble
   - ○ to happen again
4. **confidence**
   - ○ organize something and carry it out
   - ○ to ask someone's advice
   - ● strong belief in your own abilities
   - ○ say that something is definitely true
5. **circumference**
   - ● distance around something
   - ○ cautious or careful
   - ○ conditions of an event
   - ○ move in a circle or pattern
6. **conference**
   - ○ a famous Chinese philosopher
   - ○ mistake one thing for another
   - ○ doing what the law requires
   - ● meeting for discussing ideas
7. **creature**
   - ● living thing
   - ○ something that has been made
   - ○ using your imagination
   - ○ model of the baby Jesus
8. **culture**
   - ○ guilty of doing wrong
   - ○ to develop by studying
   - ● way of life, ideas, customs, traditions
   - ○ used to make sofas more comfortable
9. **sculpture**
   - ○ confused and disorderly fight
   - ● figure made of wood, metal, or stone
   - ○ to examine something closely
   - ○ strong feelings about right and wrong
10. **accuracy**
    - ○ performs gymnastic acts
    - ○ skin condition from clogged pores
    - ○ to admit something
    - ● precision, exactness

342

Posttest

Test mastery of the spelling words.

I will say the word once, use it in a sentence, then say it again. Write your words on a separate sheet of paper.

Progress Chart

Students may record scores. (Reproducible master in Appendix B.)

Personal Dictionary

Students may add any words they have misspelled to their personal dictionaries for reference when writing. (Cover in Appendix B.)

1. inquire — "Could I **inquire** about your speed?" Rosa asked worriedly.
2. preschool — "I'm not in **preschool**, you know!" Carlos snapped back.
3. quality — He knew the **quality** of his safety habits was questionable.
4. chaos — There was instant **chaos** as Carlos slammed on his brakes.
5. earthquake — Everything around them blurred as if they were in an **earthquake.**
6. echoes — The **echoes** of the accident would haunt Carlos for a long time.
7. Kentucky — **Kentucky** is proud of its clean and safe highways and interstates.
8. backup — The **backup** surgeon came quickly to the hospital.
9. Alaska — The speed limit laws are no less strict in **Alaska.**
10. Nebraska — The **Nebraska** Highway Patrol enforces safe driving.
11. o'clock — Visiting hours at the hospital end at 7 **o'clock** sharp.
12. liquid — Rosa awoke to see a nurse replacing the IV **liquid** pack.
13. equal — She could not remember feeling any pain **equal** to this!
14. quicksand — Even though she was not standing, Rosa felt as if there were **quicksand** beneath her feet.
15. squall — Right before the accident, Rosa remembered seeing signs of a **squall** to the north.
16. equator — Kristin listed the continents north of the **equator.**
17. Quebec — She loaned Rosa her notes from social studies about the province of **Quebec.**
18. squid — She sketched a **squid** in her science notes so Rosa could understand the lesson better.
19. banquet — "I hope Rosa will be able to come to the Spring **banquet,**" Kristin said.
20. chorus — The class recorded more than one funny **chorus** to send to Rosa.

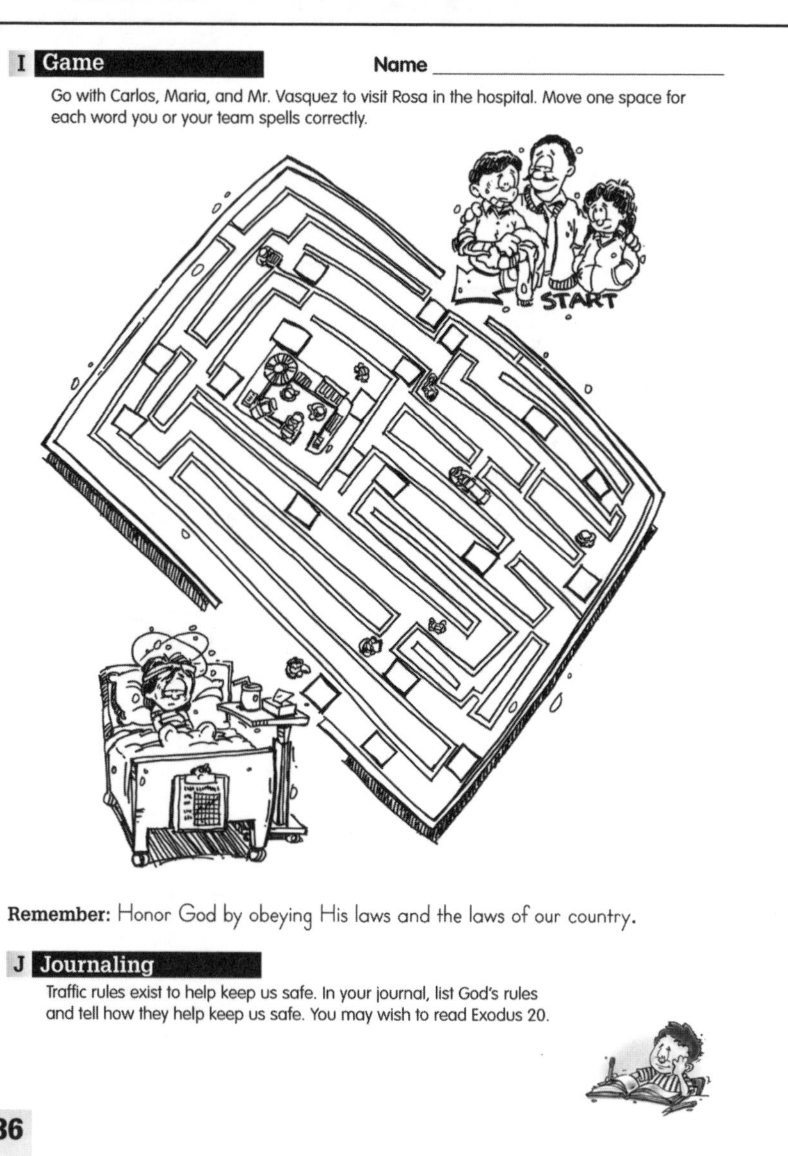

Words with /k/ or /kw/

Lesson 21

I Game Name ____________________

Go with Carlos, Maria, and Mr. Vasquez to visit Rosa in the hospital. Move one space for each word you or your team spells correctly.

Remember: Honor God by obeying His laws and the laws of our country.

J Journaling

Traffic rules exist to help keep us safe. In your journal, list God's rules and tell how they help keep us safe. You may wish to read Exodus 20.

136

2 Game

Reinforce spelling skills and provide motivation and interest.

Materials

- game page (from student text)
- game pieces (1 per child)
- game word list

Game Word List

1. **backup**
2. **chaos**
3. **chorus**
4. **echoes**
5. **Kentucky**
6. **o'clock**
7. **preschool**
8. **Alaska**
9. **Nebraska**
10. **banquet**
11. **earthquake**
12. **equal**
13. **equator**
14. **inquire**
15. **liquid**
16. **quality**
17. **Quebec**
18. **quicksand**
19. **squall**
20. **squid**

How to Play:

- Divide the class into two teams.
- Have each student place his/her game piece on Start.
- Have a student from team A go to the board.
- Say the spelling word.
- Have the student write the word on the board.
- If correct, instruct each member of team A to move his/her game piece forward one space.
- Alternate between teams A and B.
- The team to reach Rosa first is the winner.
- **Small Group Option**: Students may play this game without teacher direction in small groups of two or more.

3 Journaling

Provide a meaningful reason for correct spelling through personal writing.

Review the story using discussion leads provided on the following page. Encourage students to apply the Scriptural value in their journaling.

Journaling (continued)

- Why did Rosa need a ride to Kristin's house? (The two girls were supposed to work together on a school project, a diorama of a horse barn and pasture.)
- Why was Carlos so proud of his car? (He'd worked very hard to earn the money to buy it and spent a lot of time and effort fixing it up.)
- What did Kristin advise Rosa to do about Carlos' poor driving habits? (To tell her dad.)
- What caused the wreck? (Carlos got angry when Rosa said something about him not stopping at the stop sign and he sped up too fast to make the turn.)
- Where did Rosa wake up? (In the hospital.)
- What injuries did Rosa and Carlos have? (Rosa had three broken ribs, a punctured lung, and lots of scrapes and cuts along with a bump on the head. Carlos had a cut on his chin and a gash on one arm.)
- Do you think Carlos learned something from the accident? Why or why not? (Yes. He realized he'd caused the wreck by going too fast and was very sorry. He wished he'd been the one hurt worse instead of Rosa. He promised to obey traffic rules in the future.)

SUPERCALIFRAGILISTICEXPIALIDOCIOUS from the movie Mary Poppins is not the longest word in English, although many people believe it is. Floccinaucinihilipilification isn't either with 28 letters and meaning "the estimation of something as valueless!" It is enough to give you hippopotomonstrosesquipedaliophobia or a "fear of long words."

1 **Literature Connection**
Topic: Discerning God's will
Theme Text: Psalm 25:4, 5

Way to Go!

Rachel and her family contemplate moving.

"Come on, Rache. Father wants all of us in the living room. It's family council time."

Rachel Jacobson groaned, "I wonder what we need to decide now?"

"Who knows? I just hope democracy works fast tonight. I have a math test I need to study for." Rebecca lead the way downstairs.

Helen Jacobson was already in the living room designing a huge zoo with the brightly colored Duplo blocks. The 18-month-old twins were "helping" her. Leah held up a white polar bear, "He needs cold."

"That's right, Leah. Polar bears live where it's cold. Benj, help Mommy find some white blocks to build an icy home for this ferocious bear." Helen smiled as she watched the toddlers search through the pile for white blocks.

Vanessa came into the living room and joined the construction crew on the floor. "I think this seal and her pup need a place to swim." The seventh grader nudged a black seal with her toe and started collecting blue blocks.

"Me hep." Benjamin handed his sister a handful of blocks.

"Just the blue ones, Benj," eight-year-old Natalie instructed as she peered down from her perch on the edge of the couch.

"Now that we're all here...." David Jacobson looked up and smiled at Rachel and Rebecca as they walked into the room. "Your mother and I have something we'd like to discuss with you."

Vanessa stopped building. Rachel and Rebecca exchanged a quick glance, then gave David Jacobson their undivided attention.

"I got a call yesterday from a fellow I went to law school with, an old friend named Tyler. He lives in a remote area out west. He's started a program at Shadow Creek Ranch for troubled kids. The program's been up and running for a few years, and it's doing quite well. To get right to the point, he needs help running the ranch. The program is growing, and they'd like to be able to accommodate more kids—which means more help. And that's where we come in." Mr. Jacobson paused and made eye contact with each of his girls. Even the twins stopped building and watched him intently.

Rachel was the first to find her voice, "They want us to—like move out there? We just moved here from Dallas."

"It's been over three years, Rache," Rebecca corrected.

"What would you do?...Where out west?...When would we have to leave?...Can we finish school?...Do we sell our house first?...Would we home school?...Is there electricity?...What about running water?" The girls paused in their questioning when Father raised his hand.

"Hold on. One at a time. Shadow Creek Ranch is in Montana. They would like us in the spring or early summer. You would have to be home-schooled because school buses can't always make it out to the ranch through all the snow. There is electricity, running water and indoor plumbing. Because of her teaching background, your mom would help with the home school for all the staff children. Since I grew up on a ranch, I'd be involved with general upkeep of the place and also teach the guests who come basic ranching skills." Father leaned back in his chair and folded his arms across his broad chest.

"It sounds like you've already made up your mind." Vanessa frowned.

"On the contrary, I'm very happy here—just as all of you seem to be. I don't miss Dallas at all and I'm not anxious to leave. But I have been praying recently for God to show me how I can effectively share His love. I've also asked to be open to His will—and willing to do whatever that is. Frankly, I'm not sure what He has in mind here. I don't know if this is God's invitation or not. I'd simply like each of you to pray and ask the Lord to lead our family." Father uncrossed his arms and leaned back in his chair.

The room was absolutely quiet. Even the twins did not resume playing with the Duplo blocks.

"Let's pray," Mrs. Jacobson suggested.

Mr. Jacobson smiled at his wife and motioned with his arms for his family to gather in a prayer circle. He picked up Benjamin, and the little boy snuggled against his father's neck and gave him a damp kiss on the cheek. "Lord, help us as we make this decision. Show us the path where we should go. Lead us. Teach us. Enable us to understand Your will for our lives. Give us the courage to follow no matter where You lead. In your name, Amen."

Rachel followed her older sister back up to the bedroom they shared. Rebecca sat down at her desk and took out her math book, but she had a hard time concentrating. "How do you figure out God's will, Rache? How do you know what God wants?"

Rachel looked up from the book she'd been staring at. "I don't remember a lot about our mommy. I was only four when she died. But I do remember her pulling me into her lap on one of her good days sometime in that last year she was alive. It's like a framed picture in my mind. She had on a green baseball cap because her hair had all fallen out from the chemo. She cupped my face between her hands and looked me right in the eye. She said, 'Rache, you can always talk to Jesus

Story (continued)

about any problem, any time. He's always willing to help you.' You know, I don't even remember why she thought I needed to talk to Jesus—just that I could and should. I guess that's the best way to figure it out. What I don't get is—how does He talk to us?"

Rebecca leaned back in her chair. "The Bible?...Parents, teachers, Christian friends?... Nature?..." She looked her sister in the eye and said slowly, "Those answers we've heard in Bible class don't seem very realistic tonight. I guess I don't know how He'll speak to us."

"The Bible isn't going to say, 'The Jacobsons should move to Shadow Creek Ranch next spring!' And I'm sure my friend Laney Ausherman won't tell me to go. Father just said he wasn't sure, and how in the world is Mr. Canfield supposed to know if we should leave?" Rachel picked up her Bible, closed her eyes, and then opened it in her lap. With her eyes still closed, she pointed to a verse on the left page, then opened her eyes. "'Be still and know that I am God,'" she read. "There's our answer. 'Be still' it says. We can't go anywhere if we're still."

Rebecca laughed at her sister's suggestion. "Yeah, but what about the text that says, 'Do unto others as you would have them do unto you'? If you were a kid in trouble, wouldn't you want someone to take you out to a ranch and teach you about God's love?"

Rachel stood up and headed out the door. "That's not the one that I read." She smiled, "My texts says 'Be still.'"

Rebecca looked up at her younger sister. "I think what Mommy said so long ago makes sense. Let's just pray. Maybe He'll surprise us with an answer!"

The next morning when Rachel went out to the garage to feed the cat, she met Vanessa coming in the garage door carrying her new navy wool sweater. It was covered with frost. "Vanessa, what are you doing with that? Did you leave it outside?"

The younger girl nodded. "I was putting out a fleece, like Gideon. I didn't have a sheepskin, but this sweater is wool." She smiled sheepishly, "I asked God to make the sweater dry if we should go, and have the ground wet, just like Gideon in the Bible. I forgot about it being winter. That complicates things. The ground is frozen and the sweater is dry now. I guess when this frost melts, it'll be wet then; but I don't know if that counts. Maybe I should pray for the sweater to be wet. That would be hard to do in the middle of winter. Maybe the ground should be wet and the sweater dry." Vanessa headed on into the house muttering to herself.

Rachel stared at Vanessa's back, then finished giving the yellow cat its breakfast. She paused for a moment and prayed, "Lord, I think our family's a little mixed up right now. Please hurry up and point us in the right direction, Amen."

(to be continued. . .)

2 Discussion Time

Check understanding of the story and development of personal values.

- How do you figure out what God wants you to do?
- What were the Jacobson family's two choices?
- How do you feel about Rachel's way of finding God's will in the Bible?
- How did Vanessa try to discover what God wanted them to do?
- What did Rachel's father suggest the children do while they "contemplate this invitation?"
- What would you do?
- Do you think the Jacobsons will move? (You may want to take a vote. Remind your students how they voted before you find out the answer in lesson 25.)

3 Preview

Test for knowledge of the correct spellings of these words.

Customize Your List

On a separate sheet of paper, additional words of your choice may be tested.

I will say each word once, use the word in a sentence, then say the word again. Write the words on the lines in your Worktext.

Correct Immediately!

Let's correct our Preview. I will spell each word out loud. If you spelled a word incorrectly, rewrite it correctly.

Progress Chart

Students may record scores. (Reproducible master provided in Appendix B.)

1.	**plaza**	Dad drove home from his office on the downtown **plaza.**
2.	**bruise**	Benjamin had a **bruise** on his forehead from a recent tumble.
3.	**enclose**	His mom helped him build a block fence to **enclose** his zoo animals.
4.	**laser**	"I need to finish reading an article about **laser** surgery," Vanessa told her dad.
5.	**surprise**	The announcement came as a **surprise** to the entire family.
6.	**Missouri**	"Did you say **Missouri** or Montana, Dad?" asked Rebecca.
7.	**raise**	"I knew this announcement would **raise** a lot of questions," chuckled Dad.
8.	**despise**	Rachel felt sure she would **despise** living out west.
9.	**Amazon**	"We might as well move to the **Amazon,**" she muttered.
10.	**graze**	"I don't want to live where cattle **graze** in your front yard," she continued.
11.	**citizen**	"Will I still be considered an American **citizen**?" she asked sarcastically.
12.	**blizzard**	"Don't they have a **blizzard** or two every winter?" she asked.
13.	**Kansas**	Rachel thought Montana might look like **Kansas.**
14.	**blaze**	"I wish God would just **blaze** the answer across the sky!" said Rachel.
15.	**stanza**	A **stanza** of an old hymn ran through Vanessa's mind.
16.	**closet**	Vanessa pulled her navy blue sweater from her **closet.**
17.	**desire**	She had a real **desire** to know God's will for their family.
18.	**freezing**	She laid her sweater on the **freezing** ground.
19.	**design**	Rachel doodled a **design** on her prayer journal.
20.	**horizon**	There was too much potential change on the **horizon** for her liking.

Lesson 22 Day 1

4 Word Shapes

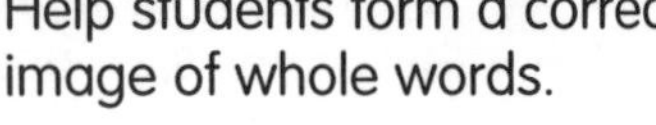

Help students form a correct image of whole words.

Say: Look at each word and think about its shape. Now, write the word in the correct word Shape Boxes. You may check off each word as you use it.

(The sound of **/z/** can be spelled with **s**, **z**, or **zz**. The **/z/** sound can also be spelled **ss** in the middle of a word.)

Say: In the word shape boxes, color the letter or letters that spell the sound of **/z/** in each word.

Take a minute to memorize...
Psalm 25:4,5

Lesson 22 — Words with /z/

B Word Shapes Name ____________________

Using the word bank below, write each word in the correct word shape boxes. Next, in the word shape boxes, fill in the boxes containing the letter or letters that spell the sound of **/z/** in each word.

1. laser
2. blaze
3. raise
4. plaza
5. design
6. stanza
7. graze
8. Amazon
9. Missouri
10. Kansas
11. despise
12. horizon
13. enclose
14. freezing
15. blizzard
16. citizen
17. bruise
18. desire
19. surprise
20. closet

Word Bank

Amazon	citizen	despise	horizon	plaza
blaze	closet	enclose	Kansas	raise
blizzard	design	freezing	laser	stanza
bruise	desire	graze	Missouri	surprise

138

Answers may vary for duplicate word shapes.

Be Prepared For Fun

Check these supply lists for **Fun Ways to Spell** - presented **Day 2**.
Purchase and/or gather these items ahead of time!

General
- Pencil
- Notebook Paper
- Spelling List

Auditory
- Pencil
- 3 X 5 Cards Cut in half lengthwise (20 per child)
- Spelling List

Visual
- Colored Pencils
- Graph Paper (2 sheets per child)
- Spelling List

Tactile
- Clay
- Spelling List

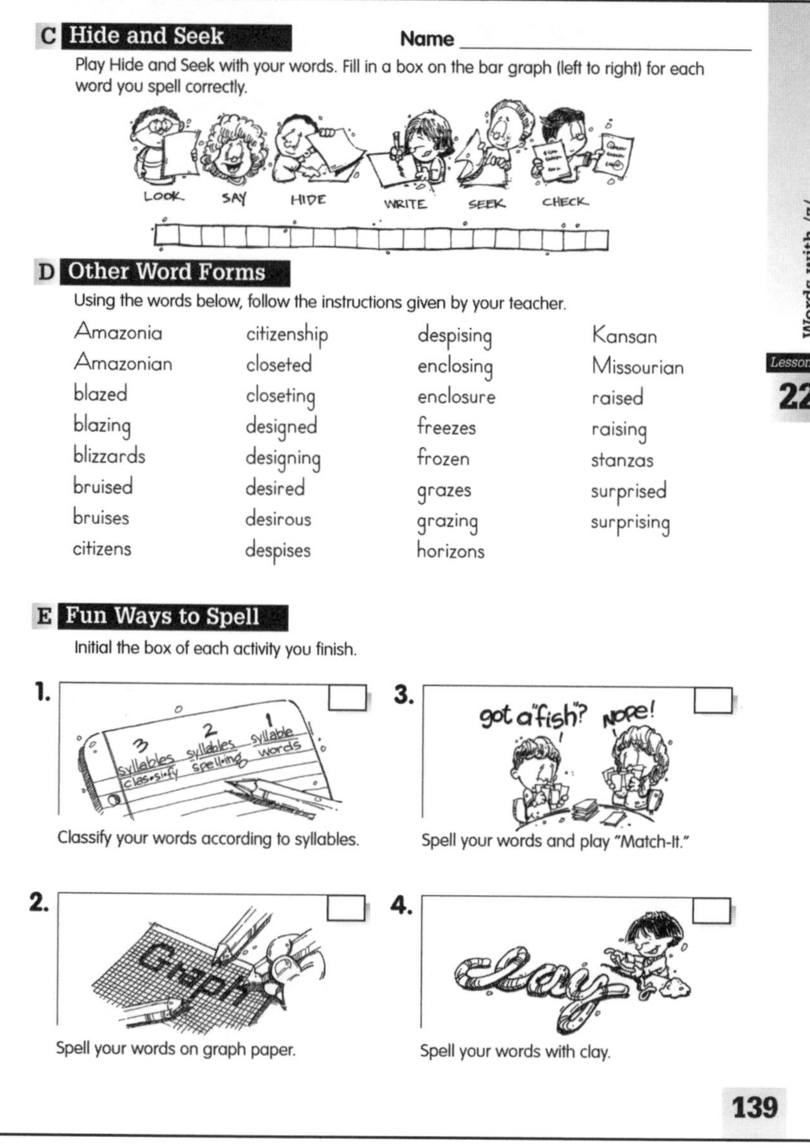

C Hide and Seek Name ____________

Play Hide and Seek with your words. Fill in a box on the bar graph (left to right) for each word you spell correctly.

D Other Word Forms

Using the words below, follow the instructions given by your teacher.

Amazonia	citizenship	despising	Kansan
Amazonian	closeted	enclosing	Missourian
blazed	closeting	enclosure	raised
blazing	designed	freezes	raising
blizzards	designing	frozen	stanzas
bruised	desired	grazes	surprised
bruises	desirous	grazing	surprising
citizens	despises	horizons	

E Fun Ways to Spell

Initial the box of each activity you finish.

1. Classify your words according to syllables.

2. Spell your words on graph paper.

3. Spell your words and play "Match-It."

4. Spell your words with clay.

Words with /z/

Lesson 22

139

1 Hide and Seek

Reinforce spelling by using multiple styles of learning.

On a white board, Teacher writes each word — one at a time. **Have students:**

- **Look** at the word.
- **Say** the word out loud.
- **Spell** the word out loud.
- **Hide** (teacher erases word.)
- **Write** the word on paper.
- **Seek** (teacher rewrites word.)
- **Check** spelling. If incorrect, rewrite word correctly.

Day 2 | Lesson 22

2 Other Word Forms

This activity is optional. Have students write original sentences using these Other Word Forms:

blazing
citizens
enclosure
blizzards

3 Fun Ways to Spell

Four activities are provided. Use one, two, three, or all of the activities. Have students initial the box for each activity they complete.

Options:

- assign activities to students according to their learning styles
- set up the activities in learning centers for the students to do throughout the day
- divide students into four groups and assign one activity per group
- do one activity per day

General

To classify your words according to syllables...
- Write three headings on your paper: One-syllable, Two-syllable, and Three-syllable.
- Write the first word on your list under the proper heading.
- Draw a line through the word to divide it into syllables.
- Do this with each word.

Auditory

To spell your words and play "Match-It"...
- Write each word on a card. Mix your word-cards and a classmate's together. Deal six cards to each player; the rest face down between you. Ask your classmate for a word-card. If the word-card matches, take it and play again. If not, draw from the stack, and it is your classmate's turn. Take turns until all cards are matched.

Visual

To spell your words on graph paper...
- Look at the first word on your list.
- Shade in squares to form the letters of each word.
- Check your spelling.
- Do this with each word.

Tactile

To spell your words with clay...
- Roll pieces of clay into ropes.
- Use the ropes to make the letters of each word.
- Put them in the right order to spell each word.
- Check your spelling.

Lesson 22 Day 3

Working with Words

Familiarize students with word meaning and usage.

Scrambled Words

Write the letters **abneqtu** on the board. Have a student unscramble the letters to make the word **banquet**.

Unscramble each spelling word. Write the word correctly on the line. Remember to use capital letters where they are needed.

Word Clues

Use your word bank to help you match the spelling words to the clues. Some of the clues are synonyms, words that have the same meaning as the spelling word. You may use a dictionary or thesaurus to help you.

Take a minute to memorize...

Psalm 25:4,5

Words with /z/ Lesson 22

F **Working with Words** Name ____________________

Scrambled Words

Unscramble each word. Write the unscrambled word on the line. Use capital letters where they are needed.

1. aeirs raise
2. deeirs desire
3. eefignrz freezing
4. abdilrzz blizzard
5. aalpz plaza
6. aaknss Kansas
7. abelz blaze
8. beirsu bruise
9. degins design
10. ceelnos enclose
11. hinoorz horizon
12. aamnoz Amazon
13. aanstz stanza
14. iimorssu Missouri
15. ceiintz citizen
16. deeipss despise
17. eiprrssu surprise
18. aelrs laser
19. celost closet
20. aegrz graze

Word Clues

Match the spelling words to the clues. You may use a dictionary or thesaurus to help you.

1. inhabitant of a city citizen
2. public square plaza
3. wardrobe, locker closet
4. 2nd longest river in the world Amazon
5. arrangement, plan design
6. verse, refrain stanza
7. long for, crave desire
8. central state whose capitol is Topeka Kansas
9. hate, scorn despise
10. flame, burn blaze
11. central state whose capitol is Jefferson City Missouri
12. astonishment, shock surprise
13. brush against graze
14. surround, encircle enclose
15. light beam laser
16. frigid, icy freezing
17. elevate, lift raise

Word Bank

Amazon	citizen	despise	horizon	plaza
blaze	closet	enclose	Kansas	raise
blizzard	design	freezing	laser	stanza
bruise	desire	graze	Missouri	surprise

140

G Dictation

Name ______________________

Write each sentence as your teacher dictates. Use correct punctuation.

1. After breakfast, the whole family helped to design Antarctica.
2. Some of Dad's comments about the ranch surprised the family.
3. Vanessa had a desire to know God's will, but was not sure how to find it.

Words with /z/

Lesson 22

H Proofreading

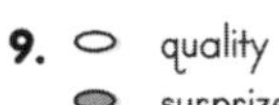

If a word is misspelled, fill in the oval by that word. If all the words are spelled correctly, fill in the oval by **no mistake**.

1. ● plazza ○ equator ○ earthquake ○ no mistake	**5.** ● Amozon ○ raise ○ echoes ○ no mistake	**9.** ○ quality ● surprize ○ Nebraska ○ no mistake	
2. ○ stanza ● Misouri ○ backup ○ no mistake	**6.** ○ citizen ○ Alaska ● clozit ○ no mistake	**10.** ○ enclose ○ Quebec ● bruse ○ no mistake	
3. ○ chaos ○ blaze ○ graze ● no mistake	**7.** ● dezine ○ desire ○ banquet ○ no mistake	**11.** ○ freezing ○ horizon ○ equal ● no mistake	
4. ● lazer ○ o'clock ○ squall ○ no mistake	**8.** ● Kansus ○ liquid ○ despise ○ no mistake	**12.** ○ inquire ● blizard ○ chorus ○ no mistake	

141

1 Dictation

Reinforce correct spelling by using current and previous words in context.

Listen as I read each sentence and then write it in your Worktext. Remember to use correct capitalization and punctuation. (Slowly read each sentence twice. Sentences are found in the Student Worktext to the left.)

Day 4

2 Proofreading

Familiarize students with standardized test format and reinforce recognition of misspelled words.

Look at each set of words. If a word is misspelled, fill in the oval by that word. If all the words are spelled correctly, fill in the oval by **no mistake**.

Lesson 22

3 Hide and Seek

Reinforce correct spelling of current spelling words. Repeat this activity from Day 2.

4 Vocabulary Extension

Have your students complete this activity to strengthen spelling ability and expand vocabulary. The reproducible master is provided in Appendix A as shown on the inset page to the right.

1 Posttest

Test mastery of the spelling words.

I will say the word once, use it in a sentence, then say it again. Write your words on a separate sheet of paper.

Progress Chart
Students may record scores. (Reproducible master in Appendix B.)

Personal Dictionary
Students may add any words they have misspelled to their personal dictionaries for reference when writing. (Cover in Appendix B.)

Hide and Seek

Play Hide and Seek with your words. Fill in a bar graph (left to right) for each word you spell correctly.

Vocabulary Extension

Cause and Effect

Write a word from the word bank to complete each sentence.

1. If you are using a piece of clear, triangular glass that breaks light up into colors, you are looking through a prism.
2. If you want to measure something very precisely, you want it to be exact.
3. If you are reading the book of the Bible that comes before Daniel, you are reading the book of Ezekial.
4. If you exaggerate, you try to make something seem bigger, better, or more important than it really is.
5. If you are reading a booklet that has news, articles, photographs, and advertisements, you are reading a magazine.
6. If you are a detective , you will examine the evidence carefully.
7. If a company makes, sells or provides a service, it is known as a business.
8. If you have painted some pictures that you want to show to the public, you would set up an exhibit.
9. If were reading Paul's letter to the people who lived in Ephesus, you would be reading the Bible book of Ephesians.
10. If you were living in a war zone and heard the sounds of guns and bombings, you would be hearing explosions.
11. If you are about to dive into a lake that you know is cold, you may pause or hesitate before jumping in.
12. If you live in a neighborhood, you are considered a resident.

Word Bank

business	exaggerate	explosion	magazine
Ephesians	examine	Ezekiel	prism
exact	exhibit	hesitate	resident

Vocabulary Extension — Lesson 22 — 343

1. **laser**	"I just need to finish that article on **laser** surgery," said Vanessa.
2. **bruise**	She kissed a little **bruise** on her baby brother's head.
3. **enclose**	She helped Benjamin and Leah **enclose** their Duplo zoo with a block fence.
4. **surprise**	The whole family listened in **surprise** to their dad's announcement.
5. **plaza**	"Don't you like your new office on the **plaza** downtown, Dad?" queried Rebecca.
6. **desire**	"Yes, but I **desire** to go where the Lord needs me," he replied.
7. **raise**	"I know this will **raise** a lot of questions in your minds," Dad continued.
8. **blaze**	"God may not **blaze** the answer across the sky, but He will show us somehow!" Dad said.
9. **Amazon**	"Montana! It might as well be the **Amazon**!" cried Rebecca.
10. **Kansas**	"I'd rather move to a shanty in the middle of **Kansas**," she groaned.
11. **Missouri**	"Did I misunderstand? Did you really say **Missouri**?" she asked.
12. **graze**	"Yuk! I don't want cows to **graze** in my front yard!" muttered Rachel.
13. **citizen**	"Can I still be an American **citizen**?" she said grouchily.
14. **blizzard**	"I can do without a **blizzard** every winter!" continued Rachel.
15. **closet**	Vanessa went quietly to her **closet** to get her wool sweater.
16. **freezing**	She tiptoed outside and laid it on the **freezing** ground.
17. **stanza**	She hummed a **stanza** of a hymn that encouraged her to trust God.
18. **design**	She was excited about the **design** God had in mind for their future.
19. **despise**	Rachel, on the other hand, knew she would **despise** having to move.
20. **horizon**	She was not keen on the idea of so much change on the **horizon**.

Words with /z/

Lesson 22

I Game Name ____________________

Record points for each word you or your team spells correctly. Earn bonus points for each row in which all four words are spelled correctly.

	1	2	3	4	Row Totals
Row A					
Row B					
Row C					
Row D					
Row E					
				TOTAL	
				BONUS	
				GRAND	

Remember: Ask God to show you the way, and He will!

J Journaling

In your journal, write how you think the Jacobsons will determine God's will about moving to Montana.

142

How to Play:

- Divide the class into two teams.
- Have a student from team A choose a square on the grid by indicating the row letter and number.
- Say the word that matches that row letter and number from the team's word list.
- Have the student write the word on the board.
- If correct, have each member of that team record the awarded points (in parentheses by the word) in the circle in that box. If the word is misspelled, have him/her put an **X** in that circle. That square may not be chosen again.
- Repeat this process with the second team.
- When all the words have been spelled by both teams, have each team tally its score. Award a bonus of 5 points for each row in which all four words were spelled correctly.
- Have the teams record their grand totals. The team with the highest score is the winner.

2 Game

Reinforce spelling skills and provide motivation and interest.

Materials

- game page (from student text)
- pencils (1 per child)
- game word list

Game Word List

Team A		Team B
E4	**plaza (1)**	A1
E3	**Amazon (4)**	A2
E2	**Kansas (3)**	A3
E1	**stanza (2)**	A4
D4	**Missouri (1)**	B1
D3	**blaze (4)**	B2
D2	**graze (2)**	B3
D1	**laser (3)**	B4
C4	**raise (4)**	C1
C3	**bruise (2)**	C2
C2	**citizen (3)**	C3
C1	**closet (1)**	C4
B4	**design (2)**	D1
B3	**desire (3)**	D2
B2	**despise (4)**	D3
B1	**surprise (1)**	D4
A4	**enclose (4)**	E1
A3	**freezing (3)**	E2
A2	**horizon (1)**	E3
A1	**blizzard (2)**	E4

Day 5

Lesson 22

3 Journaling

Provide a meaningful reason for correct spelling through personal writing.

Review the story using discussion leads provided on the following page. Encourage students to apply the Scriptural value in their journaling.

Journaling (continued)

- Why did Mr. Jacobson call a family council? (He wanted to tell them about a job offer he had. He asked them to pray about the invitation to move.)
- How did Rachel feel about moving? (She didn't want to go.)
- How did Vanessa feel about moving? (She wanted to stay.)
- Before she died what had Rachel's mommy told her about problem solving? ("You can always talk to Jesus about any problem, any time. He's always willing to help you.")
- How did Rachel's older sister Rebecca think God might talk to them? (Through teachers, Christian friends, parents, Bible, nature.)
- Tell about a time God helped you make a decision.

SMILES is supposed to be the longest word in the dictionary because "there's a mile between the two S's."

1

Literature Connection

Topic: Dealing with a sick parent
Theme Text: Psalm 141:1

Tired of Sleeping

Katelynn prays for a quick resolution to her mom's constant fatigue.

Katelynn unhooked the safety chain on the front door to let her mother in. "Hi Mom," the dark-haired girl smiled in greeting. "I'm almost done with the list of stuff you left for me to do. I just need to finish vacuuming my room. You'll never guess what I did on the spelling preview today. I got all 20 right! Let me finish vacuuming and then I'll show you."

Katelynn stopped chattering and started down the hall toward her room. She paused when she remembered the phone call. "Someone from the church called—Lin Chow." Katelynn saw a shadow fall across her mother's face. "I know I'm not supposed to answer the phone when I'm home by myself." She hurried to explain, "The message is on the answering machine. It sounded important." Mrs. Hatasaki just nodded and headed toward the answering machine on the kitchen counter.

Katelynn finished vacuuming her room. She returned the vacuum cleaner to its place in the hall closet, then hurried back to her room for the spelling paper. She looked at the bright sticker and the red 100% at the top of the page and smiled in anticipation. Doing well in school was important to both her parents. She knew her mom would be proud of her high score, especially on a preview.

"See, check this out!" Katelynn said as she walked into the kitchen. When there was no response, the girl realized she was alone. "I wonder where Mom went?" she murmured.

Katelynn stopped short in the doorway of her parents' bedroom. "Asleep again," she muttered. She glanced at the form of her mother curled under a quilt on the queen-sized bed. A book lay unopened beside the sleeping woman. Katelynn noticed the red bookmark was near the beginning of the book.

"She's tired all the time."

Katelynn jumped at the sound of her older sister's voice. "When did you get home?"

"Just now," the older girl whispered.

"Why isn't Dad home?" Katelynn moved back down the hall toward the kitchen.

"He said he'd be late today—remember?" Jennifer sat down on a high stool and scooted up to the counter. "He needed to go by the bank."

"He usually comes home early on Tuesdays." Katelynn looked out the window by the front door.

"That was when Mom was playing racquetball with Mrs. Hill. She doesn't do that any more."

"Yeah, she doesn't do a lot of things anymore. I think something's wrong with her. Nothing used to keep her from racquetball night."

"I know," the older girl agreed. "Why don't we make tacos and let her sleep? She might feel better when she wakes up."

But Mrs. Hatasaki didn't wake up for the meal; in fact, she slept the entire evening. She got up for a few minutes to wish the girls good night, then went back into the bedroom. Her husband came in a few minutes later with the phone in his hand.

He held the phone out to his wife, "It's for you, My Sweet."

"Ask if I can call them back or just take a message," she whispered.

Mr. Hatasaki nodded and said, "Janette, can I take a message or have her call you tomorrow? She's already in bed." He walked back into the kitchen while he continued to talk to his wife's friend. "I'll tell her. She loves to go to the spring craft fairs. I don't think she'll want to miss it. I'll have her call. Bye now." After Mr. Hatasaki hung up the phone, he went back to the bedroom to talk to his wife. But he found her asleep—again.

Early the next morning, as he watched her prepare for work, he told his wife about Janette Hill's invitation. "You should go. You'd have fun, My Sweet."

"I don't really feel like it," the petite woman responded in a dull voice. "I'll call her on my first break this morning and let her know."

Greg Hatasaki looked back down at the open Bible in his lap and sent a quick prayer heavenward before he responded to his wife's lack of enthusiasm.

"You love craft fairs, My Sweet. I'll come home early and be here for Katelynn so she won't be alone until 5:00. Or maybe she could go over to a friend's house or something. You always go to the craft fairs. Why don't you want to go this year?"

Soo Ling Hatasaki shrugged, picked up her ID card, and shoved it into the pocket of her white pants. "I'm just too tired. I don't have the energy to wander around craft fairs all day Friday. We need to save all the money we can, anyway."

She walked out of the room before her husband had time to add anything to the conversation.

"Lord, help her," he prayed. "She's been to the doctor and there doesn't seem to be anything physically wrong with her. But she's losing weight and interest in life itself. She's so tired all the time. She moves in slow motion and just isn't the same person she was six months ago. Help me know what to do, Lord. Amen."

Katelynn's head jerked up when Mr. Decker walked into her classroom later that morning

Story (continued)

and called her name. She couldn't imagine what the principal of Knowlton Elementary would want with her. As soon as they were in the hall, her eyebrows shot up and furrows appeared in her forehead. "Is my mother all right?"

Mr. Decker turned around and looked into Katelynn's dark eyes. "Your mother is fine, as far as I know. I just called you out for the testing your parent's requested at the last parent/teacher conference. They want to know exactly where your weak areas in math are. Your mother plans to work with you at home but needs to pinpoint what you need help with. It's really no big deal." The principal headed toward his office and motioned for her to follow.

"It would be a miracle if Mom kept her eyes open for an evening," the girl muttered.

"Excuse me?" The principal turned and looked at Katelynn again.

"Nothing important. Where am I going to take the test and how long will it take?"

"Right in my office." Mr. Decker continued down the hall, adding, "It will take you about half an hour today. You'll be coming every day this week in order to complete the test. Some sections will take more time than others." Mr. Decker paused to answer a question for the school secretary.

Katelynn groaned. "I'm going to miss PE. It's not fair. Mom will probably never help me anyway. She isn't even keeping up with all the stuff she used to do for us. She hasn't been cooking or washing as often—and now she isn't even making the evening meal anymore." Katelynn was so engrossed in her melancholy thoughts she didn't hear the principal invite her into his office.

"Katelynn," Mr. Decker repeated.

When Katelynn just stood in front of Mrs. Bentley's desk staring out the window, the principal noticed the clouded look on the girl's face and gently touched her shoulder. "Katelynn, you look a thousand miles away. Are you okay?"

Katelynn nodded and followed Mr. Decker into his spacious office.

Friday morning Katelynn and Beth were headed out the door for morning recess.

"What's that verse we need to know for spelling this week? Our test is right after we come back in." Beth returned to her desk and took out her spelling worktext.

Katelynn waited impatiently. "I think this is only the second recess I've had this week because of those stupid tests Mr. Decker is making me take. It's a stupid, stupid, stupid waste of time. Mom doesn't even notice when we're out of groceries any more. She just sleeps all the time. I don't know how she'll stay awake long enough to help me with math...."

Beth ignored her friend's complaints and read from the spelling worktext. "'Quick, Lord, answer me—for I have prayed. Listen when I cry to you for help! Psalm 141:1'" Beth shut the book and headed back out the door. "Quick, Lord, answer me!" Beth chanted.

"No, you answer me!" Katelynn interrupted.

Beth turned to look at her friend and noticed for the first time the look of desperation in her eyes. "How long has your mom been acting this way? Has she been working weekends or an extra shift or something?"

"No, but I'd say more than a month now. It started before parent/teacher conferences. But it wasn't so bad then. She isn't even going to the craft fairs with your mom today."

"I know. Mom said something about it this morning."

"She's been to Dr. Weaver, our family doctor. He says she's fine; but I say she isn't. I could've been the one who wrote our Scripture this week instead of David. 'Quick, Lord, answer me—for I have prayed. Listen when I cry to you for help!'"

"Well, you don't need to study the verse anymore. You know it—but don't forget to do it."

Katelynn wrinkled her brow. "Do what?"

Beth looked intently at her friend. "Pray for help. The Lord knows what's wrong with your mom."

"I have." Katelynn scuffed the toe of her shoe on the gray carpet. "I feel like the guy who wrote that Psalm. I wish the Lord would be quicker with His answers. I'm tired of Mom being tired."

Beth tossed Katelynn her glove. "Quick! Let's play ball while you can. You may have to take another math test this afternoon."

Katelynn caught the glove and smiled in spite of herself as she followed Beth to the ball diamond.

2 Discussion Time

Check understanding of the story and development of personal values.

- How does Katelynn feel when her mom walks in the door?
- Why is she excited?
- When does Mrs. Hatasaki take a nap?
- How long does she sleep?
- What are some of the things Katelynn's mom has quit doing?
- What would you do if your mom started acting like Katelynn's mom?

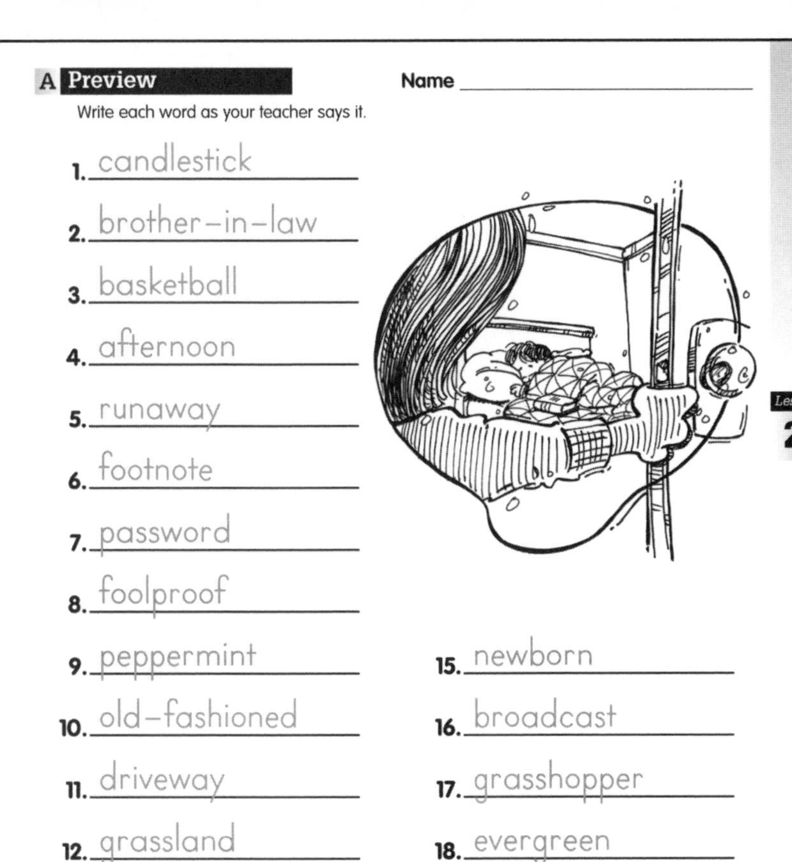

A Preview Name ____________________

Write each word as your teacher says it.

1. candlestick
2. brother-in-law
3. basketball
4. afternoon
5. runaway
6. footnote
7. password
8. foolproof
9. peppermint
10. old-fashioned
11. driveway
12. grassland
13. greenhouse
14. greyhound
15. newborn
16. broadcast
17. grasshopper
18. evergreen
19. livestock
20. Newfoundland

Compound Words

Lesson 23

Scripture

Psalm 141:1

143

3 Preview

Test for knowledge of the correct spellings of these words.

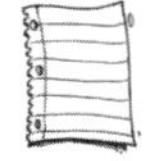

Customize Your List

On a separate sheet of paper, additional words of your choice may be tested.

I will say each word once, use the word in a sentence, then say the word again. Write the words on the lines in your Worktext.

Correct Immediately!

Let's correct our Preview. I will spell each word out loud. If you spelled a word incorrectly, rewrite it correctly.

Progress Chart

Students may record scores. (Reproducible master provided in Appendix B.)

1.	**candlestick**	Katelynn put the **candlestick** back on the shelf after she dusted.
2.	**brother-in-law**	"Mr. Canfield's **brother-in-law** may come to our class," she said.
3.	**basketball**	"He has played professional **basketball** for six years!" she continued.
4.	**afternoon**	Mrs. Hatasaki seemed not to hear and went to take her **afternoon** nap.
5.	**runaway**	She noticed a **runaway** ball rolling down the sidewalk.
6.	**footnote**	Katelynn felt like everything she said was no more important than a **footnote.**
7.	**password**	She wondered wryly if she needed a **password** to talk to her mom.
8.	**foolproof**	There seemed to be no **foolproof** way to keep her mom awake lately.
9.	**peppermint**	Katelynn planned to buy a **peppermint** plant for her mom.
10.	**old-fashioned**	Katelynn missed her mom's **old-fashioned** chocolate cake.
11.	**driveway**	A short **driveway** leads to the apartment parking lot.
12.	**grassland**	Katelynn read over a paragraph in her geography book about **grassland.**
13.	**greenhouse**	From her window, she could see through the roof of the nearby **greenhouse.**
14.	**greyhound**	She watched a man walk by with a **greyhound** on a leash.
15.	**newborn**	She heard the small cry of the neighbor's **newborn** in the next apartment.
16.	**broadcast**	She did not want to **broadcast** their family problems to Beth.
17.	**grasshopper**	Katelynn didn't even smile at the antics of a nearby **grasshopper.**
18.	**evergreen**	Katelynn braided three needles together from the **evergreen** tree on the playground.
19.	**livestock**	No one keeps **livestock** in the city; it's against city ordinance.
20.	**Newfoundland**	Mr. Canfield read an interesting article about the people of **Newfoundland.**

4 Word Shapes

Help students form a correct image of whole words.

Look at each word and think about its shape. Now, write the word in the correct word Shape Boxes. You may check off each word as you use it.

(Compound words are words that are made up of two or more words. In some words, a hyphen separates the words.)

In the word shape boxes, circle each word in the compound words.

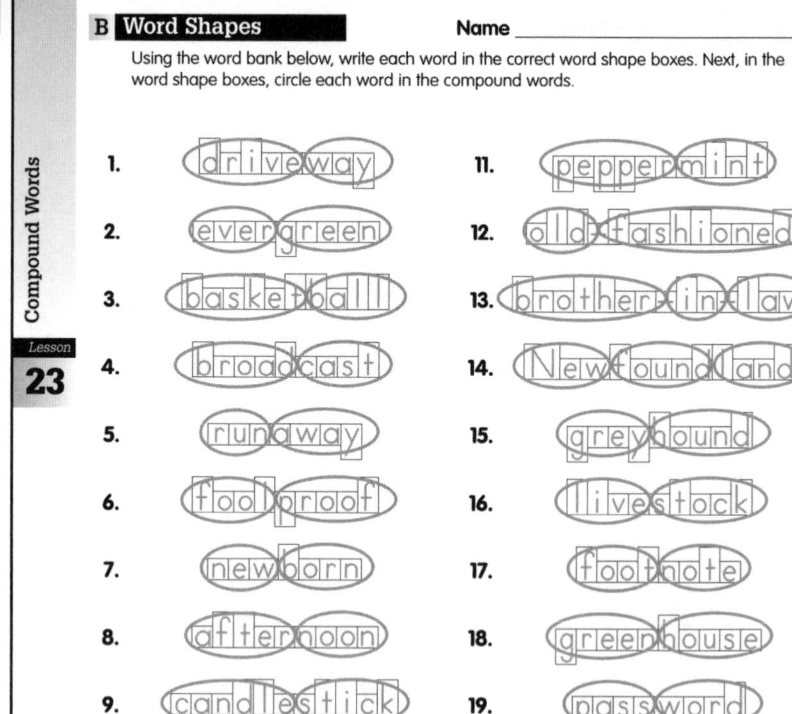

Compound Words — Lesson 23

B Word Shapes Name ____________

Using the word bank below, write each word in the correct word shape boxes. Next, in the word shape boxes, circle each word in the compound words.

1. driveway
2. evergreen
3. basketball
4. broadcast
5. runaway
6. foolproof
7. newborn
8. afternoon
9. candlestick
10. grassland
11. peppermint
12. old-fashioned
13. brother-in-law
14. Newfoundland
15. greyhound
16. livestock
17. footnote
18. greenhouse
19. password
20. grasshopper

Word Bank

afternoon	candlestick	footnote	greyhound	old-fashioned
basketball	driveway	grasshopper	livestock	password
broadcast	evergreen	grassland	newborn	peppermint
brother-in-law	foolproof	greenhouse	Newfoundland	runaway

144

Answers may vary for duplicate word shapes.

Take a minute to memorize...

Psalm 141:1

Be Prepared For Fun

Check these supply lists for **Fun Ways to Spell** - presented **Day 2**. Purchase and/or gather these items ahead of time!

General
- Pencil
- Graph Paper (1 sheet per child)
- Spelling List

Auditory
- Pencil
- Notebook Paper
- Spelling List

Visual
- Colored Pencils
- Alphabet Stencils
- Paper

Tactile
- Uncooked Rice
- Art Paper (1 sheet per child)
- Glue
- Spelling List

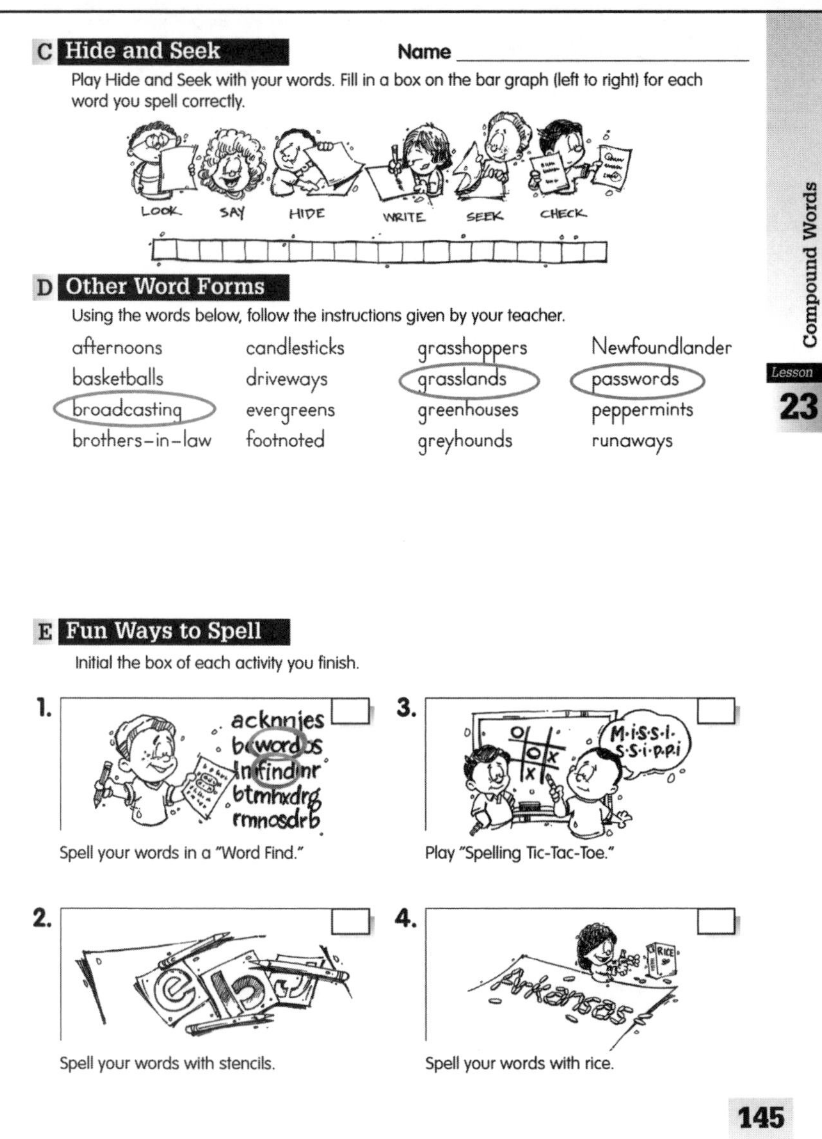

C Hide and Seek Name ____________________

Play Hide and Seek with your words. Fill in a box on the bar graph (left to right) for each word you spell correctly.

D Other Word Forms

Using the words below, follow the instructions given by your teacher.

afternoons	candlesticks	grasshoppers	Newfoundlander
basketballs	driveways	grasslands	passwords
broadcasting	evergreens	greenhouses	peppermints
brothers-in-law	footnoted	greyhounds	runaways

E Fun Ways to Spell

Initial the box of each activity you finish.

1. Spell your words in a "Word Find."

3. Play "Spelling Tic-Tac-Toe."

2. Spell your words with stencils.

4. Spell your words with rice.

Compound Words

Lesson 23

145

1 Hide and Seek

Reinforce spelling by using multiple styles of learning.

On a white board, Teacher writes each word — one at a time. **Have students:**

- **Look** at the word.
- **Say** the word out loud.
- **Spell** the word out loud.
- **Hide** (teacher erases word.)
- **Write** the word on paper.
- **Seek** (teacher rewrites word.)
- **Check** spelling. If incorrect, rewrite word correctly.

Day 2

Lesson 23

2 Other Word Forms

This activity is optional. Have students find and circle the Other Word Forms that are most nearly synonyms of the following:

keys
announcing
prairies

3 Fun Ways to Spell

Four activities are provided. Use one, two, three, or all of the activities. Have students initial the box for each activity they complete.

Options:

- assign activities to students according to their learning styles
- set up the activities in learning centers for the students to do throughout the day
- divide students into four groups and assign one activity per group
- do one activity per day

General

To spell your words in a "Word Find"...

- Arrange your words on a piece of graph paper.
- Put one letter of each word in a square.
- Words may be written backwards, forwards, or diagonally.
- Outline your puzzle.
- Hide your words by filling in all the spaces inside the puzzle with random letters.
- Trade grids with a classmate and find the hidden words.

Auditory

To play "Spelling Tic-Tac-Toe"...

- Draw a Tic-Tac-Toe grid.
- Ask a classmate to read a word from the list.
- Spell the word aloud.
- If the word is spelled correctly, place your mark on the grid.
- Take turns with your classmate.

Visual

To spell your words with stencils...

- Look at the first letter of a word on your list.
- Place the stencil for the proper letter over your paper.
- Shade inside the stencil.
- Choose the proper stencil for the next letter of the word and shade it in next to the first letter.
- Finish the word in this way.
- Do this with each word.

Tactile

To spell your words with rice...

- Choose a word from your spelling list.
- Shape the letters of your word with rice.
- Glue the rice to art paper.
- Do this for each word on your list.

Working with Words

Familiarize students with word meaning and usage.

Hidden Words

Explain that the spelling words for this week are hidden in the puzzle. After finding each word, the student should write the word under the correct heading.

Use the word bank to help you find each of the words in the puzzle. Words may go across, down, or diagonally. Circle, then write the words.

Take a minute to memorize...

Psalm 141:1

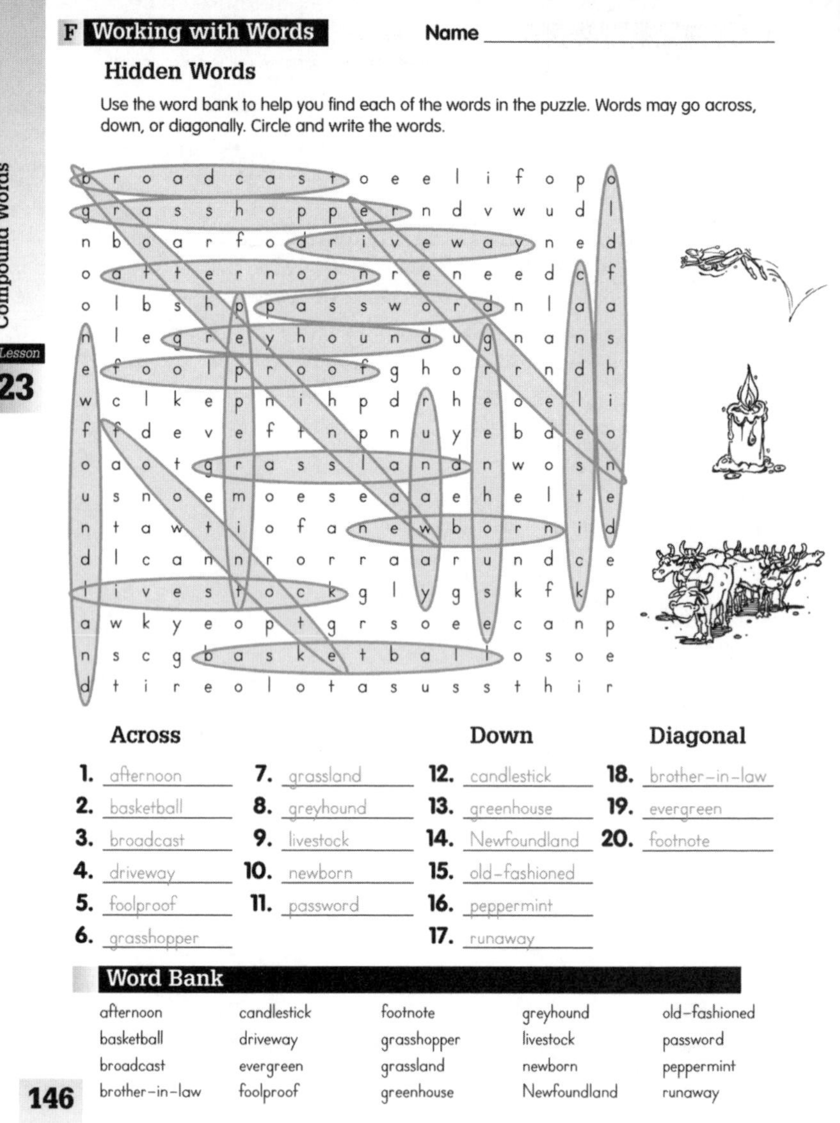

Compound Words

Lesson 23

F Working with Words Name ____________

Hidden Words

Use the word bank to help you find each of the words in the puzzle. Words may go across, down, or diagonally. Circle and write the words.

b r o a d c a s t o e e l i f o p o
g r a s s h o p p e r n d v w u d l
n b o a r f o d r i v e w a y n e d
o a f t e r n o o n r e n e e d c f
o l b s h p p a s s w o r d n l a a
n l e g r e y h o u n d u g n a n s
e f o o l p r o o f g h o r r n d h
w c l k e p n i h p d r h e o e l i
f f d e v e f t n p n u y e b d e o
o a o t g r a s s l a n d n w o s n
u s n o e m o e s e a a e h e l t e
n t a w t i o f a n e w b o r n i d
d l c a n n r o r r a a r u n d c e
l i v e s t o c k g l y g s k f k p
a w k y e o p t g r s o e e c a n p
n s c g b a s k e t b a l l o s o e
d t i r e o l o t a s u s s t h i r

Across		Down	Diagonal
1. afternoon	7. grassland	12. candlestick	18. brother-in-law
2. basketball	8. greyhound	13. greenhouse	19. evergreen
3. broadcast	9. livestock	14. Newfoundland	20. footnote
4. driveway	10. newborn	15. old-fashioned	
5. foolproof	11. password	16. peppermint	
6. grasshopper		17. runaway	

Word Bank

afternoon	candlestick	footnote	greyhound	old-fashioned
basketball	driveway	grasshopper	livestock	password
broadcast	evergreen	grassland	newborn	peppermint
brother-in-law	foolproof	greenhouse	Newfoundland	runaway

146

G Dictation

Name ______________________

Write each sentence as your teacher dictates. Use correct punctuation.

1. Mrs. Hatasaki was asleep all afternoon.

2. Katelynn noticed the neighbor playing basketball in his driveway.

3. My brother-in-law saw a broadcast about how someone built a greenhouse.

Compound Words

Lesson 23

H Proofreading

If a word is misspelled, fill in the oval by that word. If all the words are spelled correctly, fill in the oval by **no mistake**.

1. ○ afternoon ○ plaza ● basketbal ○ no mistake
2. ○ broadcast ● brother in law ○ Missouri ○ no mistake
3. ● candelstick ○ driveway ○ laser ○ no mistake
4. ○ foolproof ○ enclose ○ citizen ● no mistake
5. ○ footnote ● grashopper ○ despise ○ no mistake
6. ○ grassland ● greenhous ○ surprise ○ no mistake
7. ○ evergreen ○ Amazon ○ Kansas ● no mistake
8. ● grayhound ○ stanza ○ livestock ○ no mistake
9. ○ horizon ● newborne ○ graze ○ no mistake
10. ● oldfashioned ○ blaze ○ password ○ no mistake
11. ● newfoundland ○ closet ○ design ○ no mistake
12. ○ peppermint ○ desire ○ runaway ● no mistake

147

1 Dictation

Reinforce correct spelling by using current and previous words in context.

Listen as I read each sentence and then write it in your Worktext. Remember to use correct capitalization and punctuation. (Slowly read each sentence twice. Sentences are found in the Student Worktext to the left.)

2 Proofreading

Familiarize students with standardized test format and reinforce recognition of misspelled words.

Look at each set of words. If a word is misspelled, fill in the oval by that word. If all the words are spelled correctly, fill in the oval by **no mistake**.

3 Hide and Seek

Reinforce correct spelling of current spelling words. Repeat this activity from Day 2.

4 Vocabulary Extension

Have your students complete this activity to strengthen spelling ability and expand vocabulary. The reproducible master is provided in Appendix A as shown on the inset page to the right.

1 Posttest

Test mastery of the spelling words.

I will say the word once, use it in a sentence, then say it again. Write your words on a separate sheet of paper.

Progress Chart

Students may record scores. (Reproducible master in Appendix B.)

Personal Dictionary

Students may add any words they have misspelled to their personal dictionaries for reference when writing. (Cover in Appendix B.)

Vocabulary Extension

Lesson 23

Hide and Seek

Play Hide and Seek with your words. Fill in a bar graph (left to right) for each word you spell correctly.

Vocabulary Extension

Fill in the Blanks

Choose a word from the word bank that best fits each sentence clue.

1. Someone who is attractive in appearance is said to be handsome.
2. This book of the Bible, Song of Solomon, comes just before the book of Isaiah.
3. This pancake recipe calls for three teaspoons of baking powder. This is the same as one tablespoon.
4. A beautiful flower is blooming in the garden. Dad took a close-up shot of it to get all the details.
5. The sauce didn't taste quite right so Mom added a teaspoon of salt.
6. When the factory workers went on strike, many people formed a picket line to keep anyone from entering the building.
7. My older brothers both married, so I have two sisters-in-law.
8. The team captain organized his teammates for the ice hockey game.
9. We have a computer class at school. We are learning to type faster on the keyboard.
10. The new boy in our class likes to draw pictures of airplanes and spacecraft.
11. One of my favorite classes is physical education. We are learning how to play volleyball.
12. We are going camping when school gets out on Friday. It will be a great weekend.

Word Bank

close-up	picket line	spacecraft	teaspoon
handsome	sisters-in-law	tablespoon	volleyball
keyboard	Song of Solomon	teammates	weekend

344

1.	brother-in-law	Mr. Canfield said his **brother-in-law** was coming the next day.
2.	basketball	They all were looking forward to a professional **basketball** player visiting their class.
3.	afternoon	Katelynn was eager to tell her mom about it that **afternoon**.
4.	old-fashioned	She thought she might make her mom an **old-fashioned** chocolate cake.
5.	newborn	She heard the tiny cry of the **newborn** baby in the apartment next door.
6.	runaway	She noticed a **runaway** baseball rolling down the sidewalk.
7.	greyhound	A **greyhound** on a leash seemed to be leading his master.
8.	greenhouse	Katelynn liked looking through the nearby **greenhouse** roof.
9.	driveway	She saw Mom turn the car into the short **driveway** and into a parking space.
10.	Newfoundland	"**Newfoundland** was the easiest word on our preview," she told her mom.
11.	peppermint	Mrs. Hatasaki absently unwrapped a **peppermint**, then laid it on the counter.
12.	candlestick	She didn't even straighten the candle in the **candlestick** on the hall shelf.
13.	password	"Is there a special **password** to get your attention?" Katelynn muttered.
14.	evergreen	Katelynn pulled several more needles from the nearby **evergreen** tree.
15.	foolproof	"There's no **foolproof** way to take care of this," she told Beth.
16.	broadcast	"I feel silly having **broadcast** my family's problems to you," she admitted.
17.	footnote	"I just don't like feeling like an insignificant **footnote** in my mom's life."
18.	grasshopper	She scooped up a **grasshopper** sunning on the sidewalk.
19.	grassland	"Find which animals inhabit the American **grassland**, or prairie," said Mr. Canfield.
20.	livestock	No **livestock** are allowed within the city limits.

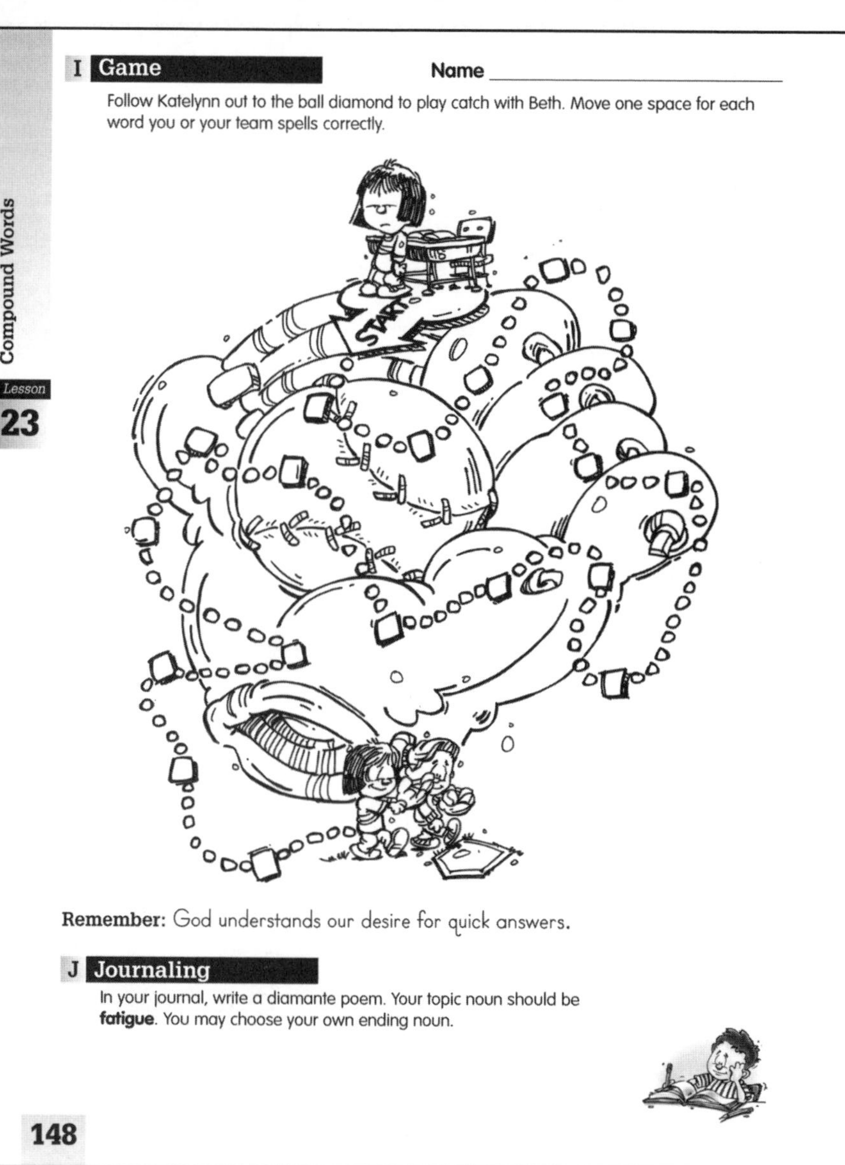

Compound Words

Lesson 23

I Game

Name ______________________

Follow Katelynn out to the ball diamond to play catch with Beth. Move one space for each word you or your team spells correctly.

Remember: God understands our desire for quick answers.

J Journaling

In your journal, write a diamante poem. Your topic noun should be **fatigue**. You may choose your own ending noun.

148

How to Play:

- Divide the class into two teams.
- Have each student place his/her game piece on Start.
- Have a student from team A go to the board.
- Say the spelling word.
- Have the student write the word on the board.
- If correct, instruct each member of team A to move his/her game piece forward one space.
- Alternate between teams A and B.
- The team to reach Beth first is the winner.
- **Small Group Option**: Students may play this game without teacher direction in small groups of two or more.

2 Game

Reinforce spelling skills and provide motivation and interest.

Materials

- game page (from student text)
- game pieces (1 per child)
- game word list

Game Word List

1. **afternoon**
2. **basketball**
3. **broadcast**
4. **brother-in-law**
5. **candlestick**
6. **driveway**
7. **evergreen**
8. **foolproof**
9. **footnote**
10. **grasshopper**
11. **grassland**
12. **greenhouse**
13. **greyhound**
14. **livestock**
15. **newborn**
16. **Newfoundland**
17. **old-fashioned**
18. **password**
19. **peppermint**
20. **runaway**

3 Journaling

Provide a meaningful reason for correct spelling through personal writing.

Review the story using discussion leads provided on the following page. Encourage students to apply the Scriptural value in their journaling.

Journaling (continued)

- Why did Mr. Decker want Katelynn? (To give her some math tests.)
- How did Katelynn feel about taking the tests? (She thought it would be a waste of time because her mom couldn't even keep up with what she was doing.)
- What did Beth want to check before she went out to recess? (She wanted to look at the Scripture in spelling.)
- What did Beth say Katelynn should do? (Pray for help like the Scripture said.)
- Diamante is the Italian word for diamond. A diamante poem is written in the shape of a diamond. Diamantes don't rhyme but there is a formula for writing each of the seven lines.

China
Asian, distant
Creating, writing, biking
Ancient, wise—Young, boisterous
Mechanizing, typing, driving
Multicultural, near
United States

1. First you choose a topic noun (first line): **China**
2. Then pick an antonym (for the last line): **United States**
3. Next select two describing words for the topic noun (second line): **Asian, distant**
4. Then select two describing words for the antonym (sixth line): **Multicultural, near**
5. Think of three action words ("ing" words) for the topic noun (third line): **Creating, writing, biking**
6. Think of three action words ("ing" words) for the antonym too (fifth line): **Mechanizing, typing, driving**
7. Last decide on four words—two for the topic noun and two that go with the ending noun (fourth line): **Ancient, wise—Young, boisterous**

The longest place name is TAUMATAWHAKATANGIHAN-GAKOAUAUTAMATEATURIPU-KAKAPIKIMAUNGAHORONUK-UPOKAIWHENUAKITANATAHU in New Zealand. Now, it is usually called Taumata.

1 **Literature Connection**
Topic: Trust in God
Theme Text: Psalm 125:1

What a Pain!

Rosa faces more health problems and becomes discouraged.

"Hello? Oh, hi, Kristin." Rosa Vasquez lowered herself gingerly onto the couch, careful not to jostle her mending ribs. "Yeah, thanks for sending it. Maria brought it home with all my schoolwork from today. It looks like a really good book, but I haven't read any of it yet." She rested her head against the back of the overstuffed sofa and listened to her best friend's chatter.

"Really? What a great field trip that'll be! Next Wednesday, huh? Well, I hope I'll be back by then." Rosa closed her eyes for a moment. "I have another checkup with Dr. Harrington tomorrow afternoon. Maybe she'll say I'm ready to go back to school." She scratched under Chipper's chin when the red squirrel crawled up her jeans and settled in her lap. "What? Yes, I'm okay. I don't hurt so much anymore. I guess it's just that I'm really tired or something." The dark-haired girl sighed. "So, tell me everything that's going on. It seems like I've been away forever!"

"Rosa? Rosa!" She awoke with a start a while later when her older sister, Maria, plopped down on the couch beside her. "Oops, sorry," Maria grimaced. "Did I hurt you?"

"No." Rosa rubbed her eyes. "What time is it, anyway?"

"Nearly 5:00." Maria's forehead wrinkled with concern as she peered into her sister's face. "Are you all right? You've been asleep ever since you got off the phone."

"I'm fine." Rosa shoved the hair out of her face and sat up carefully.

"Well, okay." Maria didn't look convinced. "Dad and Carlos are working outside and I'm going to plant some pansies. You want to come out with us?"

"Sure." Rosa relocated the snoozing Chipper to a throw pillow and got up. "What's Dad doing?"

"I don't know." Maria fastened her hair into a ponytail as she led the way to the front porch. "He's messing around with the mower. You know how he works it over every spring as soon the grass starts to turn green." She pulled a pair of gardening gloves out of her back jeans pocket. "Should I mix up all three colors or separate them in groups?" She pointed at the flats of delicate purple, yellow, and white pansies lined up along the edge of the porch.

But Rosa was too tired to care how Maria arranged the pansies.

Carlos was working in the shade of the huge oak tree, busily repainting the wooden swing that usually hung on the front porch. He waved his paintbrush in the air and called, "Rosa! Just a sec and I'll fetch you a lawn chair to sit in!"

"That's okay. I don't need...." Rosa shrugged as Carlos jogged into the garage. He reappeared moments later and set up the chair with a flourish.

"From here you can boss all of us around, m'lady." He bowed low, holding one arm out toward the chair like a royal servant. "Hey, are you okay? You don't look too good." Carlos dropped his banter and knelt on one paint-splattered knee in front of the lawn chair. "Are you feeling worse?"

"Everyone keeps asking that! I'm FINE!" Rosa rolled her eyes. "You better finish painting the swing before all the paint on you dries and you can't move."

"Yeah, yeah, yeah," Carlos groaned. "Everyone's a critic. Just wait, it will be a perfect job when I'm finished painting."

"What? You or the swing?" Maria dodged the acorn Carlos tossed her way as he returned to his painting. She took a deep breath, filling her lungs with the fresh air. "I just love spring, don't you, Rosa? Take a look at all the wildflowers in that field across the road. Then there are the daffodils, the wild plum thickets, the dogwood blossoms, all the tiny new green leaves." She turned in a circle as she spoke. "Everything is just bursting out in this warm spring weather! Doesn't the air smell wonderful?"

Rosa nodded and breathed in, but she couldn't seem to get enough air, couldn't breathe deeply at all. And it sure didn't feel like "warm spring weather" to her! She shivered. "Are you sure it's not too early to plant flowers, Maria?"

"Not at all." Maria bent and picked up a pansy with velvety purple blossoms. "We shouldn't have any more freezing weather, but even if we did, these guys could handle it." She gently patted the soil down around the transplanted pansy.

"Well, not me, I guess." Rosa's stood up and wrapped her arms around herself. "I'm freezing! I guess I'll go back inside and read that book Kristin sent."

A couple of hours later Carlos went in search of her. "Rosa, where are you? Time to eat! Dad's got supper ready, so come and get it." He paused in the doorway of her bedroom. "Rosa, are you in here?" He flipped on the light.

"Uh-huh." Rosa groaned from beneath a pile of covers topped with a heavy quilt. "B-but I d-don't th-think I'm all right anymore." She shook with chills, and her teeth chattered so hard she could barely speak. "I'm s-so c-c-cold." She tugged the blankets tighter around her flushed face. She coughed and winced at the pain ripping through her chest.

"I'll get Dad!" Carlos darted out of the room and was back in a flash with Dad and Maria. Over the phone, Dr. Harrington

Story Continued

listened carefully to Mr. Vasquez's description of Rosa's condition. The evening meal was abandoned on the table when the doctor advised him to bring Rosa to the hospital right away.

"Well, young lady, it seems you were awfully anxious to see me again," Dr. Harrington teased when she checked Rosa over in the emergency room. "Couldn't even wait till tomorrow, could you?" The doctor monitored Rosa's symptoms as she spoke. "It looks like you'll be spending some more time with us here in the hospital." After completing her examination, she turned to Mr. Vasquez. "Your daughter's developed pneumonia. She'll need to be admitted to the hospital for…"

Rosa broke into a fit of painful coughing. When it was over, she struggled to catch her breath. Dad gripped her hand tightly and leaned over to drop a kiss on her forehead. "It'll be better soon, Rosita. I'm going to get you checked into the hospital right now and they'll give you something to help real soon. Hang in there, little one."

By the next afternoon Rosa imagined she felt a tiny bit better. The antibiotics dripping through the IV tube were beginning to take effect. The oxygen tube in her nose certainly made it easier to breath. But Rosa was discouraged. She stared unseeingly at the images flickering on the wall-mounted television, a fierce expression on her face. Back in the hospital again! Following the accident, she'd been hospitalized for a couple of weeks. Doctors had inserted a chest tube and reinflated her punctured lung, as well as caring for her other injuries. Even after being released to go home, she'd been bedfast for several more days. And now, here she was again, right when everything was supposed to be healed! Was she ever going to be well again?

"Hi, Rosa!" Maria breezed through the door, followed by Carlos.

"Shhhh. Dad's asleep," Rosa whispered. Mr. Vasquez was draped on the vinyl visitor's chair in the most uncomfortable-looking position imaginable, head back, mouth open in sleep.

"Was asleep." Mr. Vasquez stretched and yawned. He checked his watch. "4:30 already! Well, how are you doing, Rosita?" He got up stiffly and walked over to the bed.

"Okay, I guess." Rosa mumbled.

"Come on, Dad." Carlos took his dad's arm. "Let's walk down to the snack bar and get a cold drink. You look like you could use a break."

Dad hesitated. "Well…"

"You go on; I'll stay with Rosa," Maria insisted as she wheeled the bedside table closer to her sister. "I brought a bunch of stuff from school to show her." Maria punched a button on the side of Rosa's bed that turned the TV off and another one to move the hospital bed into an upright position. Rosa started to protest, but couldn't seem to find the energy. "Just wait till you see what's in here!" Maria reached into the bag and pulled out a bunch of cards and pictures. "Everyone made get-well cards for you. See?" She fanned them out in front of Rosa. "Want me to put them up on the wall like I did last time?"

"No." Rosa leaned her head back on the pillow.

Maria laid the cards on the table and reached into the bag again. "And we brought you this. TA DA!" She pulled out a pot with three blooming pansy plants. "Since you're stuck in here, we thought we'd bring spring inside to you!" Maria turned toward the window. "I'll put them right here in the windowsill so they can grow and you can still see them."

While Maria gave the flowers a drink, Rosa picked up the top card without much enthusiasm. A large yellow smiley face was drawn on the front of the card. Inside the card, the smiley face was drawn broken in two—but STILL smiling. Beneath the picture the card read, "'Those who trust in the Lord are steady as Mount Zion, unmoved by any circumstance.' Psalm 125:1. In your circumstances, aren't you glad you can trust in Him? Your friend, Kristin."

Rosa felt tears prick her eyelids. She'd forgotten. True, she'd had a rough time lately with the accident—and now pneumonia—but she didn't have to let it discourage her. Her dad had spent the night by her bedside. Her friends were sending her encouraging messages. Her brother and sister did everything they could think of for her. But most of all, she had God on her side.

"Hey, are you okay?" Maria looked worried. "Should I call the nurse?"

"I'm fine." Rosa grinned through the tears. "I really am fine."

2 Discussion Time

Check understanding of the story and development of personal values.

- How did Rosa get her assignments while she was at home recovering from the accident?
- What were Maria, Carlos, and Mr. Vasquez doing outside?
- What question did everyone keep asking Rosa?
- Why did Mr. Vasquez have to take Rosa back to the hospital that evening?
- What did Dr. Harrington say was wrong with Rosa?
- What did Maria bring Rosa from her classmates the next day?
- Describe the card that Kristin made.

A Test-Words Name ____________

Write each spelling word on the line as your teacher says it.

1.	photos	9.	jacket
2.	o'clock	10.	afternoon
3.	forecast	11.	manage
4.	desire	12.	cringe
5.	effort	13.	hinges
6.	jogging	14.	difficult
7.	grasshopper	15.	raise
8.	freezing	16.	echoes

Review Lesson 24

B Test-Sentences

Write the sentences on the lines below, correcting each misspelled word, as well as all capitalization and punctuation errors. Two words are misspelled in each sentence.

the baskitbal game was brodcast on the radio:

1. The basketball game was broadcast on the radio.

The Sheriff gave him a trophey for his act of bravery

2. The sheriff gave him a trophy for his act of bravery.

my parents are going to a banquitt in Kintuckey

3. My parents are going to a banquet in Kentucky.

in the brush the jagaur took reffuge from the hunter

4. In the brush, the jaguar took refuge from the hunter.

149

4 Test-Sentences

Reinforce recognizing misspelled words.

Read each sentence carefully. Write the sentences on the lines in your Worktext. There are two misspelled words in each sentence. Correct each misspelled word, as well as all capitalization and punctuation errors.

Take a minute to memorize...

Psalm 125:1

Day 1 | Review 24

3 Test-Words

Test for knowledge of the correct spellings of these words.

I will say each word once, use the word in a sentence, then say the word again. Write the words on the lines in your Worktext.

1.	photos	She aimlessly looked at some **photos** while she rested on the couch.
2.	o'clock	"It's five **o'clock**; want to come outside with us?" Maria asked Rosa.
3.	forecast	"The **forecast** says SPRING!" quipped Maria cheerfully.
4.	desire	"Does the lady **desire** a chair? I shall be happy to get her one!" said Carlos.
5.	effort	Rosa made an **effort** to smile at Carlos although she did not feel well.
6.	jogging	Carlos went **jogging** into the garage for a lawn chair for Rosa.
7.	grasshopper	She smiled weakly as a **grasshopper** landed right in Carlos' fresh paint job.
8.	freezing	"I'm **freezing**," Rosa told Maria with a shiver.
9.	jacket	"Do you want a **jacket**?" Maria asked.
10.	afternoon	"I didn't read any of that book this **afternoon**," she replied.
11.	manage	"If I can **manage** to stay awake, I'll read that for a while," she continued.
12.	cringe	Rosa tried not to **cringe** as she stood up to go inside.
13.	hinges	Even the **hinges** on the front screen door seemed to squeak much more loudly.
14.	difficult	Rosa found it **difficult** to breathe, and very painful, too!
15.	raise	She tried to **raise** up on her elbow when Carlos called, but she could not.
16.	echoes	"Every noise **echoes** in my head," Rosa told her dad.

Day 2 | Review 24

1 Test-Dictation

Reinforce correct spelling by using current and previous words in context.

Listen as I read each sentence, then write it in your worktext. Remember to use correct capitalization and punctuation. (Slowly read each sentence twice. Sentences are found in the student text to the right. The words **blaze**, **candlestick**, **quicksand**, and **Amazon** are found in this unit.)

2 Test-Proofreading

Familiarize students with standardized test format and reinforce recognizing misspelled words.

Look at each set of words. If a word is misspelled, fill in the oval by that word. If all the words are spelled correctly, fill in the oval by **no mistake**.

Review Lesson 24

C Test-Dictation

Name ______________________

Write each sentence as your teacher dictates. Use correct punctuation.

1. The blaze swept quickly across the plain.
2. The boy put a candlestick in the front window.
3. He threw a rope to the man in the quicksand!
4. There are a few towns on the Amazon River.

D Test-Proofreading

If a word is misspelled, fill in the oval by that word. If all the words are spelled correctly, fill in the oval by **no mistake**.

1. ○ forecast ● mirge ○ photos ○ no mistake
2. ● autograff ○ funds ○ effort ○ no mistake
3. ○ desire ● syphon ○ jogging ○ no mistake
4. ○ squall ○ grasshopper ○ freezing ● no mistake
5. ● cittizen ○ jacket ○ afternoon ○ no mistake
6. ○ grassland ○ cringe ○ manage ● no mistake
7. ○ o'clock ● fosill ○ hinges ○ no mistake
8. ○ echoes ○ difficult ● old fashioned ○ no mistake
9. ○ raise ○ inquire ● pre-school ○ no mistake
10. ● inclose ○ closet ○ newborn ○ no mistake
11. ○ driveway ● Misourri ○ plaza ○ no mistake
12. ○ heritage ○ surprise ○ average ● no mistake

150

E Test-Table Name ______________________

If a word is misspelled, fill in the space on the grid.

Kansis	pasword	dispise	quality
phraze	junior	Nufounland	equator
sphear	chaos	gadgit	badge
stanza	earthquake	livestock	Quibec

Review Lesson 24

F Writing Assessment

Write about a time when you were very sick or hurt. What was wrong? How old were you? What happened? How did you feel?

Scripture

Psalm 125:1

151

A rubric for scoring is provided in Appendix B.

The most common word in the King James Bible is THE.

Test-Table

Test mastery of words in this unit.

If a word is misspelled, fill in the space on the grid.

Writing Assessment

Assess student's spelling, grammar, and composition skills through personal writing.

- Have you ever been very sick or had to stay in the hospital? (Allow time to share experiences.)
- Why was Rosa anxious to get back to school? (She'd been in the hospital and then at home for several weeks.)
- Why do you think Rosa got tired of people asking her if she was okay? (She'd been asked that so much since the accident.)
- What did Rosa do after she talked on the phone with Kristin? (She fell asleep on the couch.)
- Why didn't Rosa stay outside with the rest of her family? (She was too cold.)
- Where was Rosa when Carlos went to tell her supper was ready? (She was huddled beneath a pile of covers on her bed.)
- Why was Rosa discouraged about getting pneumonia? (She felt horrible and had to stay in the hospital again.)
- What did Maria bring Rosa from home? (Pansies like the ones planted in the front yard.)
- How did Kristin's card help Rosa feel better? (It reminded her to trust in God even in circumstances like this.)

1 Test-Sentences

Reinforce recognizing misspelled words.

Read each sentence carefully. Write the sentences on the lines in your Worktext, correcting each misspelled word, as well as all capitalization and punctuation errors.

Review Lesson 24

G Test-Sentences Name ______________________

Write the sentences on the lines below. Correct each misspelled word, as well as all capitalization and punctuation errors. Two words are misspelled in each sentence.

her brother in law has plants in his greanhuose

1. Her brother-in-law has plants in his greenhouse.

on the horrizon angry clouds foretold a blizard

2. On the horizon, angry clouds foretold a blizzard.

Write a paragraff about the dolfin's habitat

3. Write a paragraph about the dolphin's habitat.

the lawyer pleaded with the jurrey to choose justise

4. The lawyer pleaded with the jury to choose justice.

H Test-Words

Write each spelling word on the line as your teacher says it.

1. inquire
2. closet
3. newborn
4. driveway
5. plaza
6. surprise
7. average
8. bruise
9. difference
10. forth
11. liquid
12. peppermint
13. Africa
14. funds
15. chorus
16. pledge

152

2 Test-Words

Test for knowledge of the correct spellings of these words.

I will say the word once, use the word in a sentence, then say the word again. Write the word on the lines in your Worktext.

1.	inquire	Mr. Vasquez called the doctor to **inquire** about what to do for Rosa.
2.	closet	Maria grabbed Rosa's back-pack from the **closet.**
3.	newborn	Mr. Vasquez carried Rosa as gently as if she were a **newborn.**
4.	driveway	He quickly backed the jeep out of the garage and into the **driveway.**
5.	plaza	Maria and Carlos waited in the beautiful hospital **plaza.**
6.	surprise	"It's a **surprise** to find a miniature park inside a building," commented Maria.
7.	average	"Are you're feeling a little below **average**, Rosa?" smiled Dr. Harrington.
8.	bruise	"That **bruise** and scrape on your head have healed nicely though," she noted.
9.	difference	"The **difference** in your energy level is caused by pneumonia," she continued.
10.	forth	The nurse came back and **forth** in to Rosa's room to check on her.
11.	liquid	She administered a **liquid** antibiotic through the IV.
12.	peppermint	Kristin sent a small bag of soft **peppermint** candies for Rosa.
13.	Africa	Thorny sent Rosa a very interesting article about animals in **Africa.**
14.	funds	Sometimes Rosa worried if her dad had the **funds** for all the doctor bills.
15.	chorus	God brought a **chorus** to Rosa's mind that encouraged her.
16.	pledge	God has given us His **pledge**, or promise, to help us through everything!

I **Test-Editing** Name ______________________

If a word is spelled correctly, fill in the oval under **Correct**. If the word is misspelled, fill in the oval under **Incorrect**, and spell the word correctly on the blank.

	Correct	Incorrect	
1. dungeon	●	○	______
2. design	●	○	______
3. legind	○	●	legend
4. equall	○	●	equal
5. back-up	○	●	backup
6. grayhound	○	●	greyhound
7. nephew	●	○	______
8. hyphen	●	○	______
9. fiber	●	○	______
10. rijid	○	●	rigid
11. footnote	●	○	______
12. plunge	●	○	______
13. Allaska	○	●	Alaska
14. evergreen	●	○	______
15. Nebraska	●	○	______
16. squid	●	○	______
17. graze	●	○	______
18. lazer	○	●	laser
19. foolproof	●	○	______
20. runaway	●	○	______

Review Lesson 24

153

3 Test-Editing

Reinforce recognizing and correcting misspelled words.

4 Action Game

Reinforce spelling skills and provide motivation and interest.

Materials

- music
- beanbag
- word list on certificate at end of unit

BEANBAG SPELLING

Seat students in a large circle. As music is played, the students toss a beanbag randomly around or across the circle. When the music stops, whoever has the beanbag is given a spelling word to be reviewed. If the student misspells the word he or she passes the beanbag to the right and that student must spell the word. If the student spells the word correctly the music starts again and the game continues.

1 Game

Reinforce spelling skills and provide motivation and interest.

Materials

- game page (from student text)
- colored pencils (1 per child)
- game word list

Game Word List

Check off each word lightly in pencil as it is used.

The Nurses

1. **merge**
2. **autograph**
3. **siphon**
4. **citizen**
5. **grassland**
6. **fossil**
7. **old-fashioned**
8. **preschool**
9. **enclose**

The Doctors

1. **Missouri**
2. **heritage**
3. **Kansas**
4. **phrase**
5. **sphere**
6. **stanza**
7. **password**
8. **junior**
9. **earthquake**

The Lab Techs

1. **despise**
2. **chaos**
3. **Newfoundland**
4. **gadget**
5. **livestock**
6. **quality**
7. **equator**
8. **liquid**
9. **Quebec**

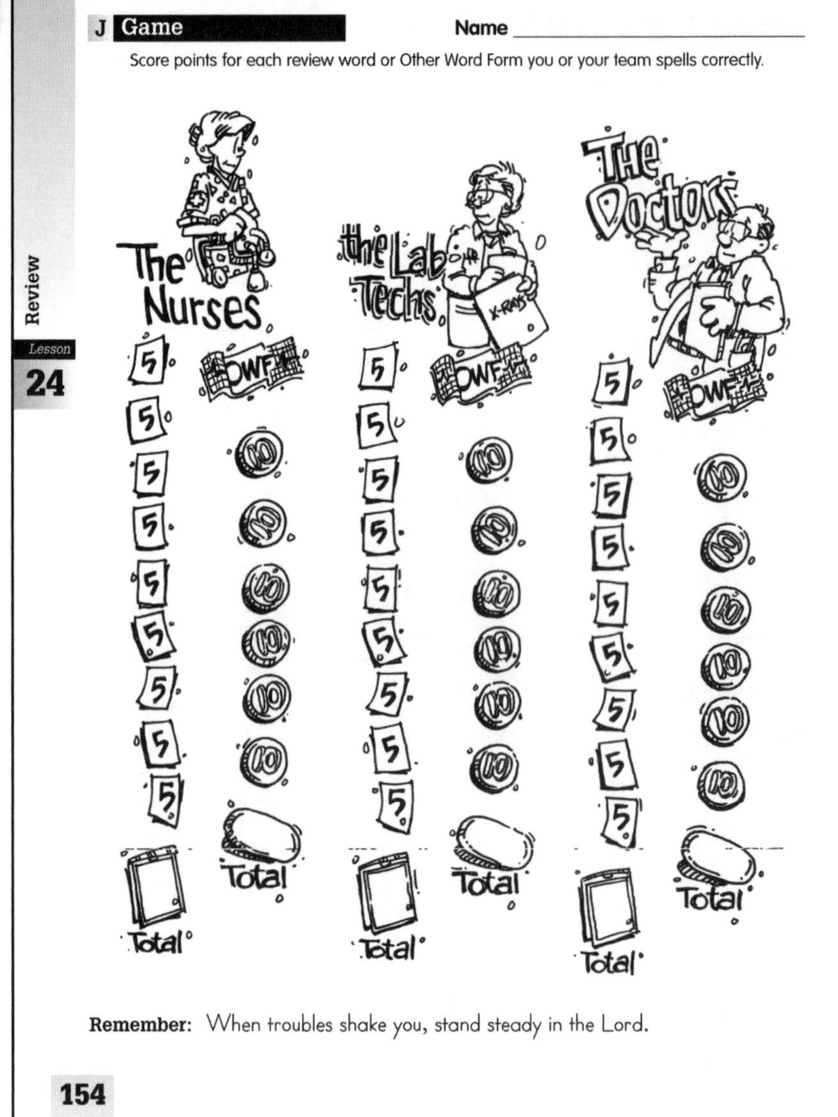

How to Play:

- Divide the class into three teams. Name one team **The Nurses**, one **The Doctors**, and one **The Lab Techs**. (Option: You may wish to seat students in groups of three, each student from a different team. They should share one game page.)
- Have a student from the first team go to the board.
- Say the spelling word.
- Have the student write the word on the board.
- If the word is spelled correctly, have each team member color a point symbol by his/her team name. If the word is misspelled, have him/her put an **X** through one point symbol. That word may not be given again.
- Repeat this process with the second team and then the third.
- When the words from all three lists have been used, the team with the most points is the winner.
- Play another round using Other Word Forms.

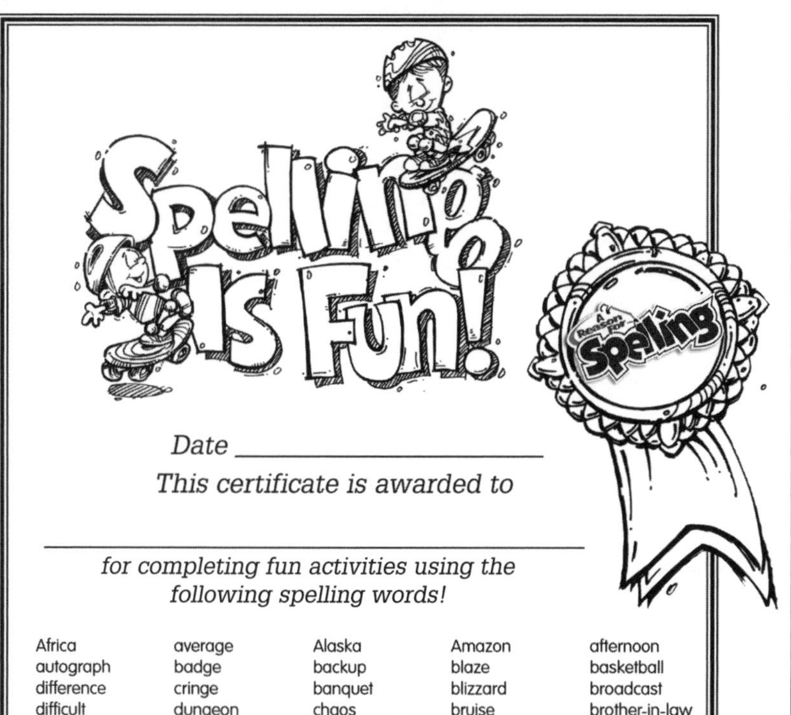

Date ______________________

This certificate is awarded to

____

for completing fun activities using the following spelling words!

Africa	average	Alaska	Amazon	afternoon
autograph	badge	backup	blaze	basketball
difference	cringe	banquet	blizzard	broadcast
difficult	dungeon	chaos	bruise	brother-in-law
dolphin	gadget	chorus	citizen	candlestick
effort	heritage	earthquake	closet	driveway
fiber	hinges	echoes	design	evergreen
forecast	jacket	equal	desire	foolproof
forth	jaguar	equator	despise	footnote
fossil	jogging	inquire	enclose	grasshopper
funds	junior	Kentucky	freezing	grassland
hyphen	jury	liquid	graze	greenhouse
nephew	justice	Nebraska	horizon	greyhound
paragraph	legend	o'clock	Kansas	livestock
photos	manage	preschool	laser	newborn
phrase	merge	quality	Missouri	Newfoundland
sheriff	pledge	Quebec	plaza	old-fashioned
siphon	plunge	quicksand	raise	password
sphere	refuge	squall	stanza	peppermint
trophy	rigid	squid	surprise	runaway

2 Certificate

Provide an opportunity for parents or guardians to encourage and assess their child's progress.

Fill in today's date and your name on your certificate.

Take a minute to memorize...

Psalm 125:1

3 Letter

Provide the parent or guardian with the spelling word lists for the next unit.

Give your parents or guardian this letter that lists your spelling words for the next unit. Put it where you will remember to practice the words together.

Dear Parent,

We are about to begin a new spelling unit containing five weekly lessons. A set of twenty words will be studied each week. All the words will be reviewed in the sixth week. Values based on the Scriptures listed below will be taught in each lesson.

Lesson 25	Lesson 26	Lesson 27	Lesson 28	Lesson 29
angle	adverb	aimless	border	account
bundle	anchor	cirrus	cornea	announcer
burial	burden	citrus	cornerstone	boundary
central	chapter	closeness	corridor	browse
crumple	charter	congress	dinosaur	clout
crystal	clerk	cumulus	dormitory	compound
decimal	clever	fungus	Florida	counterfeit
double	courage	interest	forehead	coward
dribble	deliver	mollusk	foreign	crouch
entitle	desert	nucleus	format	drought
example	deserve	obvious	formula	foul
fragile	energy	octopus	Georgia	mountains
humble	error	radius	horror	pronounce
mingle	journey	reckless	New York	scoundrel
miracle	major	restless	normal	scowl
missile	molar	services	North Carolina	snout
multiple	New Jersey	stillness	North Dakota	South Carolina
mumble	solar	virus	orbit	South Dakota
particle	version	walrus	ordeal	whereabouts
riddle	West Virginia	witness	Oregon	willpower
Psalm 25:14	Psalm 37:3	Psalm 59:16	Psalm 121:5-7	Psalm 47:1,2

1 Literature Connection
Topic: Knowing God's will
Theme: Psalm 25:14

Moving Right Along

Rachel and her family try to determine if it is God's plan for them to move.

Laney put her hands on her waist and looked intently at her friend. "Well I say you shouldn't!"

"But what if God wants our family to move to Montana?" Rachel picked up the bright yellow tennis ball Wicker was nudging toward her feet and threw it for the dog.

"How can you possibly hear God telling you what to do? I think that's what He gave us brains for. If your family is happy here, why should you move to some ranch in the middle of nowhere?" Laney watched her Gordon Setter drop the tennis ball at her best friend's feet again; then she looked up into her eyes. "You do like it here—don't you?"

Rachel frowned, deliberately teasing her friend. "Sometimes I miss Dallas. But I suppose I'm getting used to this small-town life." When she saw Laney's shocked reaction, she couldn't keep the sparkle out of her eyes. "Of course I like it here, silly."

"Then why would you move? We moved here from New York because my mom married Coach Larkin. But your dad barely knows that family out there in Montana. How do you know you'll even like them?"

"We don't. And we haven't decided to move. My dad explained how he's been praying for God to open his eyes and show him how to share the love of Jesus. He also asked God to help him be willing to do whatever His will is. Then out of nowhere he gets this phone call from someone he went to school with! All Father wants us to do is pray. We haven't decided to go yet."

When Elisa Larkin came out on the back porch and called the girls in for supper, they hurried to put Wicker back in his kennel. "Laney tells me your family is thinking of moving," Laney's mom said as the girls followed her into the house.

Rachel nodded. "I can't see why God would want us to leave. Nothing has happened since our father told us about the idea a few weeks ago to make me think we should go."

Laney didn't think about her conversation with Rachel until she was in bed that night. "How would God let the Jacobsons know what to do?" She pondered until she drifted off to sleep.

David Jacobson sat on the couch beside his wife. The house was quiet. It wasn't that way very often—not with six energetic children. He turned to Helen. "Are they all asleep?"

She leaned her head against his shoulder. "In bed, but not asleep. Natalie should be calling for a drink about now."

"Mom. Mom?"

David Jacobson smiled at his wife. "How did you know?"

"Because I know Natalie. I think she needs an extra kiss more than the drink." Helen shifted and started to get up. "She wants reassurance. The thought of moving and leaving everything that's familiar makes her feel insecure. She probably doesn't remember much about living in the apartment with just me and Vanessa. This is the only home she knows."

Mr. Jacobson put a hand on his wife's knee. "I'll get it for her, Love. But don't go away. I want to talk to you."

David Jacobson returned to the couch and pulled his wife close. "Well, Natalie should feel loved and secure now. And now I want to share an idea with you. What would you think about putting our house up for sale?" He paused to let the words sink in. "I've been doing a little figuring, and I don't see how we could possibly afford to move without selling this place. We'd need to build in Montana, and that won't be cheap because of the remote location."

He squeezed his wife's shoulder as he continued, "If the house doesn't sell before Tyler needs an answer, maybe that's a way to determine God's will in this situation. Moving so far will cost a lot of money. We haven't saved much since we got married four years ago and moved here. With four girls in a private school and you staying home with the twins, we go through what I earn pretty quickly. I don't make the money I made in Dallas, either. Of course, I have time to spend with my family—and a lot less stress—but money is not something we have a surplus of."

The dark-haired man smiled down at his wife. "How does this idea sound to you?"

Helen didn't say anything for a while. "I love this home. It's our first." She reached for her husband's hand. "We brought the twins here from the hospital after they were born. I enjoy our church, and Knowlton Elementary has been such a blessing for the girls. But your idea is good. Do we have to put a sign in the front yard, or can we just let the Lord send a buyer?"

David laughed. "Now you sound like Vanessa and her wool sweater. You really want to make it hard for the Lord, don't you?"

Helen frowned. "I just want to make sure God wants us to move, because I'm not sure I do. It would be nice to visit Shadow Creek; I think that might help us make a decision."

"Let's just keep praying. I think the Lord will share His plan for us in His own time." Mr. Jacobson gave his wife a squeeze, and the two headed toward the master bedroom for some much-needed rest.

Lesson 25 | Day 1

Story (continued)

The next evening David Jacobson took his place at the head of the table. All conversations ceased as he scooted his chair in. Even the twins were too engrossed in the Cheerios they were eating off the trays of their highchairs to chatter.

Father glanced around the table and cleared his throat. "Since we're all together, I want to tell you about something that happened today at work. One of the owners of the design studio next to my law office stopped by for a few minutes. He mentioned how much they're growing because of curriculum development and designing they're doing for local Christian publishers."

He paused a moment to let the drama build before continuing, "The bottom line is they'd like to buy my office. Todd said they need room for more workstations. They'd like to hire a couple more graphic designers, but just don't have the space to set them up with computers. They'd rather not relocate."

Mr. Jacobson studied the faces around the table. "Last night your mother and I discussed putting the house up for sale, but we haven't discussed selling the office. If our house would sell quickly, we'd be free to move to Montana. Real estate is not moving very fast right now, which is one reason I'd be hesitant to move without selling."

Rebecca asked the first question. "Aren't we at least going to go look at the ranch and meet the people? What if we sell everything and don't like Montana at all?"

"That's a good point, Rebecca." Father picked up his napkin and spread it across his lap. "Which brings me to the next thing I want to discuss. How would you four older girls like to fly out with your mother and me to visit the ranch? Mrs. Hill has offered to watch the twins for us. I called the ranch today and Tyler says the end of this week will work well for them. I made reservations today."

Everyone started talking at once. Rachel didn't think she ever wanted to move. Natalie agreed wholeheartedly. Rebecca, as the oldest, tried to be mature and said she wanted to see the place first. Vanessa didn't say much as she rubbed the wool of the navy sweater she was wearing. "Maybe the house won't sell," she finally added. Helen caught the eye of her husband at the far end of the table, smiled, and shrugged her shoulders.

The next weekend, the Jacobson family stopped on the steps as they were leaving church to chat with the Larkin family.

Coach pulled Mr. Jacobson aside. "So how was the trip, David?" he asked.

The dark-haired man got right to the point. "We're moving. We decided on the plane coming home."

"How do your kids feel?" Coach glanced over at the women and girls.

"They all agree."

"Amazing! Your house sell, too?"

"We have an offer. Someone called about buying my law practice and came to look at both it and the house before we flew out Thursday morning. My head's still spinning. God has opened every door. We believe He wants us to move."

"What convinced the girls?"

"Tyler Hansan and his family. They were wonderful. The girls immediately saw how they could be a part of God's work. They'll miss their friends here, but they can't help but see the needs out West as well as God's guidance in this move."

"Well, isn't that what God promises?" Coach Larkin slapped his friend on the back. "'Trust in the Lord with all your heart; and lean not unto your own understanding. In all your ways acknowledge Him, and He will direct your paths.'"

David Jacobson smiled. "That's quite a promise, Edward! But so true. When we reverence the Lord, He shares the secrets of His promises. But hold on tight—you never know what'll happen!"

2 Discussion Time

Check understanding of the story and development of personal values.

- Tell about a friend of yours who has moved away.
- What are some ways you can still keep in touch with your distant friend?
- How do you feel about it?
- How did Laney feel about her friend Rachel moving?
- How did the Jacobsons decide God's will was for them to move?
- How do you think Laney will feel when Rachel tells her they are moving?
- Is it always hard to follow God's will?

A Preview

Name ______________________

Write each word as your teacher says it.

1. crystal
2. dribble
3. missile
4. angle
5. miracle
6. riddle
7. fragile
8. mingle
9. burial
10. humble
11. mumble
12. particle
13. decimal
14. crumple
15. example
16. multiple
17. entitle
18. double
19. bundle
20. central

Words with /əl/

Lesson 25

Scripture

Psalm 25:14

157

3 Preview

Test for knowledge of the correct spellings of these words.

Customize Your List

On a separate sheet of paper, additional words of your choice may be tested.

Say: I will say each word once, use the word in a sentence, then say the word again. Write the words on the lines in your Worktext.

Correct Immediately!

Let's correct our Preview.

Say: I will spell each word out loud. If you spelled a word incorrectly, rewrite it correctly.

Progress Chart

Students may record scores. (Reproducible master provided in Appendix B.)

Lesson 25 | Day 1

1.	crystal	Mrs. Larkin served the girls juice in **crystal** punch cups.
2.	dribble	When Rachel would **dribble** the ball, Wicker would bark loudly.
3.	missile	Wicker tossed his head and the ball flew like a **missile.**
4.	angle	He could jump and catch the ball at any **angle.**
5.	miracle	"It will be a **miracle** if God makes me want to move," exclaimed Rachel.
6.	riddle	God's will sometimes seems like a **riddle** to us.
7.	fragile	We like feeling strong, not **fragile** and helpless.
8.	mingle	Rachel felt a little excitement begin to **mingle** with her worries.
9.	burial	"Dad says there is an ancient Indian **burial** ground near the ranch."
10.	humble	"Dad also says we need to **humble** ourselves and listen to the Holy Spirit."
11.	mumble	"Why does God's will mean my best friend has to move?" she heard Laney **mumble.**
12.	particle	"Not one **particle** of my being will be happy if you leave!" Laney said dramatically.
13.	decimal	Getting the **decimal** in the right place really frustrated her today!
14.	crumple	She felt the urge to **crumple** her worksheet up and toss it into the trash.
15.	example	She looked absently at the **example** at the top of her worksheet.
16.	multiple	She could think of **multiple** reasons why Rachel shouldn't move.
17.	entitle	"Doesn't being your best friend **entitle** me to be upset?" Laney exclaimed.
18.	double	Helen packed **double** of everything for the twins' stay at the Hills.
19.	bundle	Leah and Benjamin are a **bundle** of energy and then some!
20.	central	In the **central** part of the airport, the Jacobsons looked at their itinerary.

Lesson 25 | Day 1

4 Word Shapes

Help students form a correct image of whole words.

Look at each word and think about its shape. Now, write the word in the correct word Shape Boxes. You may check off each word as you use it.

(In many words, the sound of **/əl/** is spelled with **le**, **al**, **el**, or **il**. Because spellers cannot rely on a phonetic way of remembering the various spellings, this sound is often difficult.)

In the word shape boxes, fill in the boxes containing the letters that spell the sound of **/əl/** in each word.

Take a minute to memorize...

Psalm 25:14

Words with /əl/ — Lesson 25

B Word Shapes Name ______________________

Using the word bank below, write each word in the correct word shape boxes. Next, in the word shape boxes, fill in the boxes containing the letter or letters that spell the sound of **/əl/** in each word.

1.	decimal	11.	mingle
2.	particle	12.	double
3.	bundle	13.	riddle
4.	central	14.	humble
5.	angle	15.	crystal
6.	fragile	16.	example
7.	crumple	17.	multiple
8.	entitle	18.	burial
9.	missile	19.	dribble
10.	mumble	20.	miracle

Word Bank

angle	crumple	dribble	humble	multiple
bundle	crystal	entitle	mingle	mumble
burial	decimal	example	miracle	particle
central	double	fragile	missile	riddle

158

Answers may vary for duplicate word shapes.

Be Prepared For Fun

Check these supply lists for **Fun Ways to Spell** - presented **Day 2**. Purchase and/or gather these items ahead of time!

General
- Pencil
- Graph Paper (1 sheet per child)
- Spelling List

Auditory
- Voice Recorder
- Spelling List

Visual
- American Sign Language reproducible master (provided in Appendix B)
- Spelling List

Tactile
- Soccer Ball, Basketball, Tennis Ball, or 4-Square Ball
- Spelling List

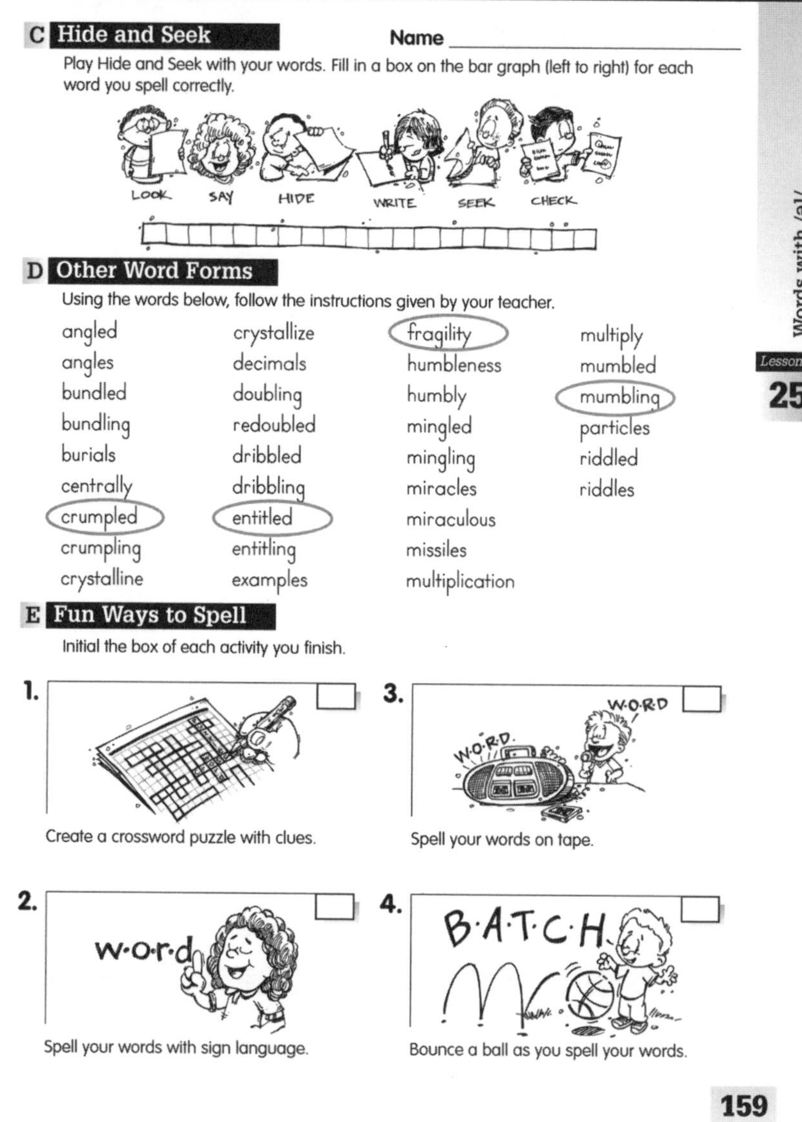

1 Hide and Seek

Reinforce spelling by using multiple styles of learning.

On a white board, Teacher writes each word — one at a time. **Have students:**

- **Look** at the word.
- **Say** the word out loud.
- **Spell** the word out loud.
- **Hide** (teacher erases word.)
- **Write** the word on paper.
- **Seek** (teacher rewrites word.)
- **Check** spelling. If incorrect, rewrite word correctly.

Day 2

Lesson 25

2 Other Word Forms

This activity is optional. Have students find and circle the Other Word Forms that are most nearly antonyms of the following:

articulating
unauthorized
strength
smoothed

3 Fun Ways to Spell

Four activities are provided. Use one, two, three, or all of the activities. Have students initial the box for each activity they complete.

Options:

- assign activities to students according to their learning styles
- set up the activities in learning centers for the students to do throughout the day
- divide students into four groups and assign one activity per group
- do one activity per day

General

To create a crossword puzzle...
- Use a pencil to arrange your words on graph paper.
- Overlap words where letters are shared.
- Don't create any new words.
- Outline each word with a marker and number it.
- Write a clue for each word.
- Erase your words.
- Trade with a classmate and work each other's puzzles.

Auditory

To spell your words using a voice recorder...
- Record yourself as you say and spell each word on your spelling list.
- Listen to your recording and check your spelling.

Visual

To spell your words with sign language...
- Have a classmate read a spelling word to you from the list.
- Spell the word using the American Sign Language alphabet.
- Do this with each word on your list.

Tactile

To bounce a ball as you spell your words...
- Look at the first word on your list.
- Bounce the ball as you say each letter of the word aloud.
- Do this with each word on your list.

Lesson 25 | Day 3

1 Working with Words

Familiarize students with word meaning and usage.

Clues

Write this incomplete sentence on the board:

The upper surface inside a room is called a ________.

Guide the students in choosing the word **ceiling**.

Read each sentence and choose a spelling word for each definition. You may use a dictionary to help you. Write the word in the blank.

Take a minute to memorize...

Psalm 25:14

Words with /əl/ — Lesson 25

F Working with Words

Name ______________________

Clues

Write a spelling word for each clue.

1. Central means situated at, in, or near the middle.
2. An object or weapon that is fired or thrown at a target is a missile.
3. The dot between dollars and cents is called a decimal point.
4. Something that is easily broken, damaged, or destroyed is fragile.
5. A number divided by another number with no remainder is a multiple.
6. To double means to make twice as much in size, strength, or amount.
7. To move a ball or puck with repeated light bounces or kicks is to dribble it.
8. A particle is a very small piece or part; a tiny portion or speck.
9. Something wrapped or tied up for carrying is called a bundle.
10. To mumble is to talk indistinctly by lowering the voice.
11. To mix or bring together in combination, usually without loss of individual characteristics, is to mingle.
12. The figure formed by two lines diverging from a common point is called an angle.
13. A miracle is an event that appears unexplained. by the laws of nature and so is held to be an act of God.
14. To crush together or press into wrinkles is to crumple.
15. The act of placing something in a grave or a tomb is a burial.
16. A riddle is a question or statement requiring thought to understand.
17. To be humble is to be meek or modest in behavior and attitude.
18. A crystal is a glass-like mineral, especially a transparent form of quartz.
19. One thing that is representative of a group as a whole is an example.
20. To furnish with a right or claim to something is to entitle.

Word Bank

angle	crumple	dribble	humble	multiple
bundle	crystal	entitle	mingle	mumble
burial	decimal	example	miracle	particle
central	double	fragile	missile	riddle

160

G Dictation Name ______________________

Write each sentence as your teacher dictates. Use correct punctuation.

1. Selling the house and the law practice was like a double miracle.
2. The girls saw examples of how they could be part of God's work.
3. She mumbled as she swept up multiple particles of crystal from the broken glass.

Words with /əl/ Lesson 25

H Proofreading

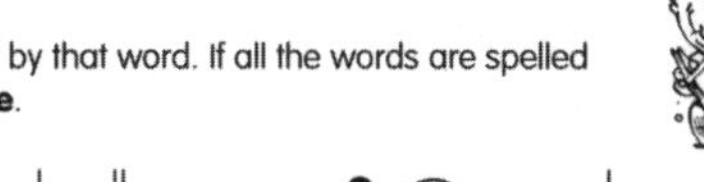

If a word is misspelled, fill in the oval by that word. If all the words are spelled correctly, fill in the oval by **no mistake**.

1. ● dribbel ○ double ○ afternoon ○ no mistake
2. ○ humble ○ brother-in-law ○ basketball ● no mistake
3. ○ mumble ● particel ○ driveway ○ no mistake
4. ○ miracle ○ candlestick ○ evergreen ● no mistake
5. ○ bundle ○ riddle ○ grasshopper ● no mistake
6. ○ fragile ○ foolproof ● missill ○ no mistake
7. ● angul ○ grassland ○ greenhouse ○ no mistake
8. ● mingel ○ broadcast ○ footnote ○ no mistake
9. ○ crumple ○ old-fashioned ● decimel ○ no mistake
10. ○ example ○ multiple ○ peppermint ● no mistake
11. ● buriul ○ entitle ○ password ○ no mistake
12. ○ crystal ● centrel ○ newborn ○ no mistake

161

1 Dictation

Reinforce correct spelling by using current and previous words in context.

Listen as I read each sentence and then write it in your Worktext. Remember to use correct capitalization and punctuation. (Slowly read each sentence twice. Sentences are found in the Student Worktext to the left.)

2 Proofreading

Familiarize students with standardized test format and reinforce recognition of misspelled words.

Look at each set of words. If a word is misspelled, fill in the oval by that word. If all the words are spelled correctly, fill in the oval by **no mistake**.

3 Hide and Seek

Reinforce correct spelling of current spelling words. Repeat this activity from Day 2.

4 Vocabulary Extension

Have your students complete this activity to strengthen spelling ability and expand vocabulary. The reproducible master is provided in Appendix A as shown on the inset page to the right.

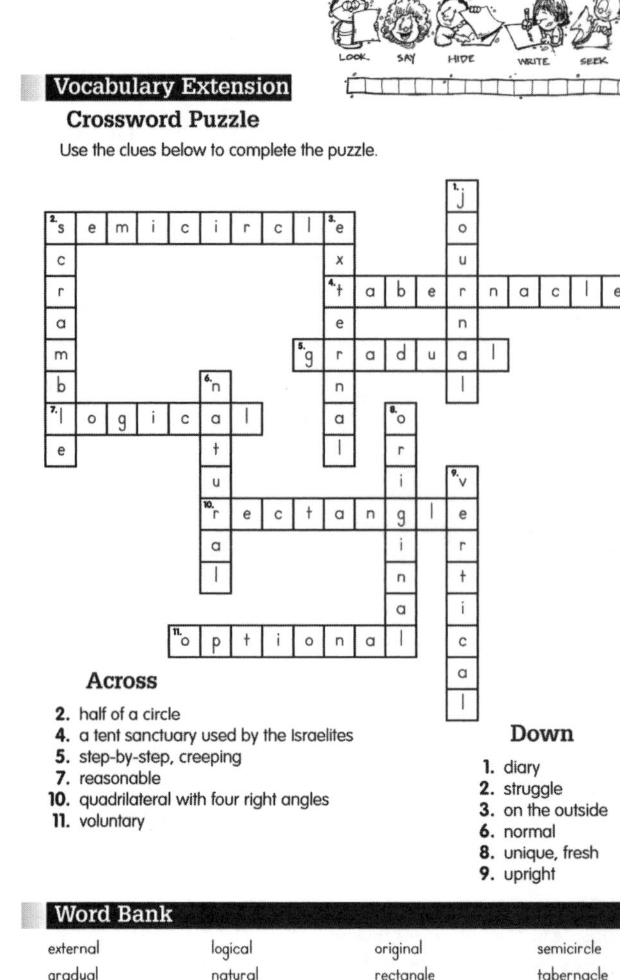

Hide and Seek

Play Hide and Seek with your words. Fill in a bar graph (left to right) for each word you spell correctly.

Vocabulary Extension

Crossword Puzzle

Use the clues below to complete the puzzle.

Across

2. half of a circle
4. a tent sanctuary used by the Israelites
5. step-by-step, creeping
7. reasonable
10. quadrilateral with four right angles
11. voluntary

Down

1. diary
2. struggle
3. on the outside
6. normal
8. unique, fresh
9. upright

Word Bank

external	logical	original	semicircle
gradual	natural	rectangle	tabernacle
journal	optional	scramble	vertical

1 Posttest

Test mastery of the spelling words.

I will say the word once, use it in a sentence, then say it again. Write your words on a separate sheet of paper.

Progress Chart

Students may record scores. (Reproducible master in Appendix B.)

Personal Dictionary

Students may add any words they have misspelled to their personal dictionaries for reference when writing. (Cover in Appendix B.)

1. **dribble** "If you **dribble** the ball, Wicker goes absolutely nuts!" laughed Laney.
2. **angle** "Watch him; Wicker can catch this tennis ball from any **angle**," Laney said.
3. **missile** Wicker lunged through the air like a **missile** to catch the tennis ball.
4. **double** "When we mix up the cookies, let's make a **double** batch," said Laney.
5. **particle** The girls scraped the last **particle** of cookie dough from the bowl.
6. **crystal** They thought it was fun to drink out of **crystal** cups at dinner time.
7. **mumble** "I know it's wrong to **mumble** and grumble," confessed Laney.
8. **example** "You've been a good **example** to me and a great friend!" Laney said.
9. **entitle** "Doesn't that **entitle** me to feel upset that you're leaving?" she questioned.
10. **humble** "I'm learning to **humble** myself—more listening, less talking," Rachel told her.
11. **mingle** "I actually feel some excitement starting to **mingle** with my anxiousness."
12. **burial** "Dad says there's an Indian **burial** ground near the ranch," she told Laney.
13. **fragile** "I don't really enjoy feeling **fragile** and not in control," confessed Rachel.
14. **decimal** Laney couldn't concentrate enough to put the **decimal** in the right place.
15. **crumple** She wanted to **crumple** up her math homework and throw it away!
16. **multiple** It was easy to think of **multiple** reasons Rachel should stay.
17. **bundle** "Here's another **bundle** of diapers for the twins," said Mrs. Jacobson.
18. **central** "Let's stay in a **central** location till they call our flight number," said Dad.
19. **riddle** God does not want His will for us to be a giant **riddle**.
20. **miracle** "I know it's a **miracle**, but I want to move now," said Rachel amazed.

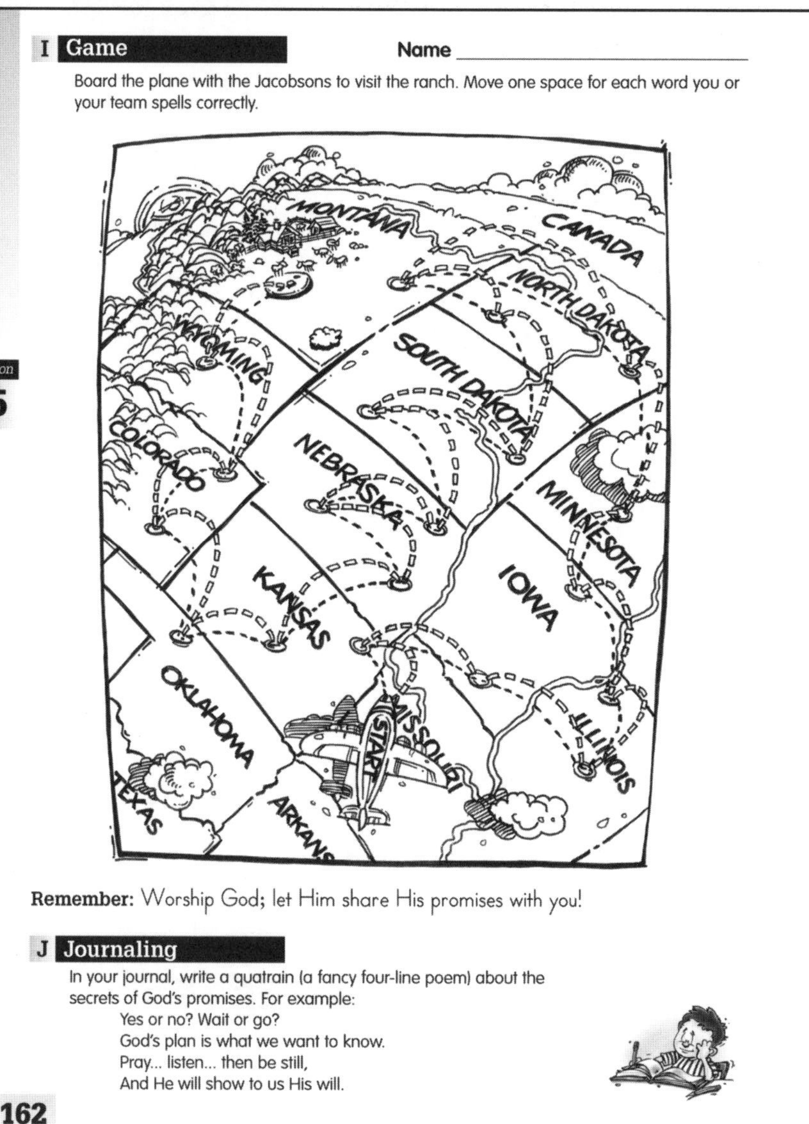

Words with /əl/

Lesson 25

I **Game** Name ____________________

Board the plane with the Jacobsons to visit the ranch. Move one space for each word you or your team spells correctly.

Remember: Worship God; let Him share His promises with you!

J **Journaling**

In your journal, write a quatrain (a fancy four-line poem) about the secrets of God's promises. For example:

Yes or no? Wait or go?
God's plan is what we want to know.
Pray... listen... then be still,
And He will show to us His will.

162

2 Game

Reinforce spelling skills and provide motivation and interest.

Materials

- game page (from student text)
- game pieces (1 per child)
- game word list

Game Word List

1. **double**
2. **dribble**
3. **humble**
4. **mumble**
5. **particle**
6. **miracle**
7. **bundle**
8. **riddle**
9. **fragile**
10. **missile**
11. **angle**
12. **mingle**
13. **decimal**
14. **crumple**
15. **example**
16. **multiple**
17. **burial**
18. **entitle**
19. **central**
20. **crystal**

How to Play:

- Divide the class into two teams.
- Have each student place his/her game piece on Start.
- Have a student from team A go to the board.
- Say the spelling word.
- Have the student write the word on the board.
- If correct, instruct each member of team A to move his/her game piece forward one space.
- Alternate between teams A and B.
- The team to reach the ranch first is the winner.
- **Small Group Option**: Students may play this game without teacher direction in small groups of two or more.

3 Journaling

Provide a meaningful reason for correct spelling through personal writing.

Review the story using discussion leads provided on the following page. Encourage students to apply the Scriptural value in their journaling.

Journaling (continued)

- What are ways God reveals His will to us? (Brainstorm. You may want to write students' ideas on the board. The Bible, parents, teachers, nature…Christian friends could be included.)
- What did the Jacobsons do to prepare themselves for God's answer? (Prayed together and individually)
- How did God reveal the "secret of his promises" to the Jacobson family? (The business and house have a buyer. The whole family loved Shadow Creek Ranch. All the girls saw how they could be a part of God's work and agreed the family should move.)
- Does God always quickly and clearly reveal His will for your life?
- Tell about a time you asked God to help you make a decision.
- There are four quarters in a dollar. There are four cups in a quart. A quadrangle has four angles. What do you think a quatrain is? A quatrain is a four-line poem—rhymed or unrhymed. Like a triplet, it can have a lot of different rhyming patterns. All four lines can rhyme (aaaa). The first two lines can rhyme and then the last two (aabb). Sometimes the first line rhymes with the third and the second with the fourth (abab). The second and fourth lines may be the only ones that rhyme (abac). Quatrains are a common form of poetry.
- When you write a quatrain, you may choose whatever rhyming pattern you like best.

Here are a few words named for people.

BEGONIA	***Michel Bégon***
BOYSENBERRY	***Rudolph Boysen***
MAVERICK	***Samuel A. Maverick***
SANDWICH	***John Montagu, the Fourth Earl of Sandwich***
DUNCE	***John Duns Scotus (who was actually very smart)***
SAXOPHONE	***Antoine Joseph Sax***
SIDEBURNS	***Gen. Ambrose Everett Burnside***
TEDDY BEAR	***Theodore Roosevelt***

Word Wow!

1 **Literature Connection**
Topic: Being good to others
Theme Text: Psalm 37:3

Home Plans and Helping

Just when Setsuko's family has saved enough to build a home of their own, the Johansen's car won't run anymore. What will the Nomas do?

"Okasan! Come here please!" Setsuko sat on her bedroom floor surrounded by various-sized wooden boxes.

"What happened here, Hurricane Suzy-Q?" Mrs. Noma stopped in the doorway, wiping her hands on a kitchen towel.

Setsuko held up one of the wooden boxes. "I can't find anywhere to put these. My dresser's full, my closet's full, even the storage boxes under my bed are full! What am I going to do with all these boxes? They've got to go someplace safe, but every place was already crammed before Grandmother sent me these beautiful Hina Matsuri (hi nä mä tsū ri) dolls!"

Mrs. Noma stepped carefully over the boxes to open the closet. "Hmmm. I see what you mean." She tried unsuccessfully to rearrange the shelf and gain more space.

"Maybe I should just leave the display up all year." Setsuko removed the ornate empress doll from her box. The doll was dressed in an elaborate imperial silk wedding kimono, complete with a phoenix coronet and flowering tassels of coral beads. "When they were all in the dining room I didn't have to worry about storing them."

"That would never do!" Mrs. Noma lifted the edge of the bedspread and searched in vain for storage space under the bed. "Who knows what might happen to you if we left them displayed after March 3."

"What do you mean, something might happen to me?"

"Well, you know that Hina Matsuri dolls are made for Girls' Day, which is March 3. It's a spring celebration for girls, just when the ornamental peach trees are in bloom." Mrs. Noma sat down on Setsuko's bed and picked up one of the wooden boxes. "Traditionally, the dolls are given to a girl on her first Girls' Day by relatives and close friends. They're often passed from mother to daughter as family heirlooms."

"I know all that." Setsuko smoothed the empress's shiny silk kimono. "What does that have to do with something happening to me?"

"It has to do with timing, Setsuko. About 10 days before the festival, a seven-tiered stand—seven is thought to be a lucky number—is set up in the best room of the house. It's draped with red, which also stands for good luck. The 15 special dolls are carefully unwrapped and arranged on the stand, with the emperor and empress on the top."

"We did all that—so what does it have to do with me?" Setsuko replaced the empress in her box.

"On Girls' Day, girls eat hishimochi (hi shi mō chi - a lozenge shaped rice cake) and Hinaarare (hi nä ä rä re - assorted rice crackers)." Mrs. Noma stroked the emperor's smooth black lacquered hat and continued, "Although people display these dolls from the middle of February, it is necessary to put them away on the day of the festival, March 3. The tradition is that while the set of dolls is displayed, evil is transferred from girls to the dolls. So you have to put them away as soon as the festival is over. Otherwise evil may come back to girls and they may be doomed."

"Doomed!" Setsuko squeaked in alarm.

"Of course the real reason we took the display down on the third was that I needed the space in the dining room." Mrs. Noma laughed as she put the lid back on the emperor's box. "Now if we just had a place to store them." She stood up and moved toward the door. "Why don't you stack the boxes in that corner for now."

Setsuko stacked the boxes carefully, remembering that dolls like this could cost between $1000 and $10,000. Surely she wouldn't be doomed just because the doll boxes weren't really put away. After all, they weren't being displayed!

Setsuko wandered into the small duplex kitchen where her mother was fixing supper. "Okasan, where did this come from?" She picked up a Home Plan Ideas magazine from the counter.

"I picked that up when I went to the store yesterday." Mrs. Noma turned to her daughter with a sparkle in her eye, "We have enough money saved to start looking for land and choosing the house we want to build."

"ALL RIGHT!" Setsuko twirled herself completely around on the stool three times. "YES!" Then she opened the magazine and began to flip through it, studying each floor plan.

"I like the way this one looks outside with the porch all across the front, but it's not brick. And I like the way this one has a huge utility room near the back door—a great place to keep Chimi's stuff and boots and snowsuits and everything." She turned pages in silence for a few moments.

"I found it! Look, Okasan, it's perfect!" Mrs. Noma leaned over the counter while Setsuko pointed out the merits of the Open Country plan. "See, it's brick with a big porch and lots of windows. It's got a big utility room by the back door and a workshop area in the garage." Her index finger pointed out each item on the floor plan as she spoke. "And look here—this bedroom has a bay window and a huge walk-in closet! I'd have plenty room for the Hina Matsuri dolls and all my other stuff if we built this house!"

"Which house, Suzy-Q?" Mr. Noma came

Story (continued)

through the door from the carport.

"Otosan!" Setsuko launched herself at her father. "Can we really start looking for a place to build our house? Are you sure we have enough money? When can we look? How long will it take to build? Can I choose all the paint and carpet and stuff for my room?"

"Let's see now," Mr. Noma held up fingers as he counted off answers to Setsuko's questions, "Yes. I think so. Maybe this weekend. I don't know. Probably."

Mrs. Noma laughed, "If you don't want all the answers at once, Setsuko-chan, don't ask all the questions at once!" She nudged the house plan magazine across the counter towards her husband as the phone rang. "I do like that Open Country plan Setsuko found. See what you think while I get the phone."

Setsuko perched beside her father and waited for him to look over the house plan.

Mrs. Noma squeezed the phone between her shoulder and ear as she stirred something on the stove. "Oh, hi, Paula....Hmmm....Yes, I see....Certainly. I'd be glad to and it's no problem at all....I'm sure.... Right....7:30 tomorrow morning will be fine. Don't worry, Paula. I'm glad you called me. After all, what are friends for?...Okay, bye."

Mrs. Noma put the lid back on the pot and returned the cordless phone to its cradle on the wall. "I do like this floor plan." Mr. Noma thumped the page in front of him. "It's really nice the way the kitchen is so open to the family room. The whole design appears to be well thought out, don't you think, Sweetheart?"

"Mmm-hmm, I do." Mrs. Noma joined her husband and daughter at the bar, but seemed preoccupied. "That was Paula Johansen on the phone. You know how hard she's been trying to turn her life around—working two jobs now, going to AA and parenting meetings to get help in controlling her drinking and to be a better mother. Well, apparently her old car quit and the mechanics say it's no use to try fixing it anymore. She called to ask for a ride to get the girls to school and her to work tomorrow."

Later, as the three Nomas sat around the supper table, Mr. Noma put down his fork. "You know, I keep thinking we ought to do something about Paula's car."

"You too?" Mrs. Noma smiled at her husband. "That thought keeps crossing my mind as well. It just seems like the right thing to do, doesn't it?"

"What do you think, Suzy-Q?" Both parents turned to Setsuko. "We wouldn't be able to go ahead with building a house for a while longer if we get a car for Mrs. Johansen. How would you feel about that?"

The half-chewed bite in Setsuko's mouth suddenly seemed like sawdust. "Uh, um. Well, we've, uh, been waiting so long already to get a real house..." Setsuko paused. She'd been going to say that it wasn't fair to have to wait any longer, but deep inside she knew what Jesus would do and wasn't she supposed to follow His example? She swallowed hard. "...so I guess since we've waited this long it won't hurt to wait a while longer." She even managed a small smile.

Mrs. Noma reached over and squeezed her hand. Mr. Noma grinned. "So it's settled. I'll talk to Judy tomorrow. She's one of my assistants at the hospital, and her husband repairs wrecked cars that are practically new otherwise, then sells them for a reasonable price." He picked up his fork, but paused before taking another bite. "Keep that Open Country plan handy, though. Sooner or later, we'll be ready to build."

After she'd crawled into bed that night Setsuko looked around her tiny room. She was disappointed about not getting a big new house right away, but she felt good about helping Sarah's mom. She noticed the Hina Matsuri doll boxes stacked in the corner and grinned sleepily. She didn't need to worry about being doomed because of some dolls. All she had to do was love God and try to do what He would do. She could trust Him to take care of everything—including when the Noma family got their new house.

2 Discussion Time

Check understanding of the story and development of personal values.

- Why was Setsuko having trouble putting the Hina Matsuri dolls away?
- Where had she gotten the dolls?
- The dolls were a part of the celebration of what special Japanese holiday?
- Why had Mrs. Noma bought the Home Plan Idea magazine?
- What kind of room did Setsuko want?
- Who called and asked for a ride?
- What did the Noma family decide to do to help Paula Johansen?
- Do you think they made a good choice? Why or why not?

A Preview Name ____________

Write each word as your teacher says it.

1. anchor
2. clerk
3. solar
4. energy
5. clever
6. West Virginia
7. New Jersey
8. version
9. deliver
10. charter
11. journey
12. major
13. burden
14. error
15. desert
16. deserve
17. molar
18. chapter
19. courage
20. adverb

Words with /ər/ or /ûr/

Lesson 26

Scripture
Psalm 37:3

163

3 Preview

Test for knowledge of the correct spellings of these words.

Customize Your List
On a separate sheet of paper, additional words of your choice may be tested.

I will say each word once, use the word in a sentence, then say the word again. Write the words on the lines in your Worktext.

Correct Immediately!

Let's correct our Preview. I will spell each word out loud. If you spelled a word incorrectly, rewrite it correctly.

Progress Chart
Students may record scores. (Reproducible master provided in Appendix B.)

Day 1 | Lesson 26

1. anchor	She thoughtfully traced the **anchor** embroidered on her sleeve.
2. clerk	The **clerk** pointed Mrs. Noma to the house plan books.
3. solar	Many of the house plans made use of **solar** power.
4. energy	The natural **energy** of the sun could heat and cool an entire house.
5. clever	"What a **clever** design for a kitchen," her mom told Mr. Noma.
6. West Virginia	Mrs. Noma was eager to receive a plan she'd ordered from **West Virginia.**
7. New Jersey	Mrs. Noma had also ordered a book from a **New Jersey** company.
8. version	Dad really liked their **version** of a combination toolshed/workshop.
9. deliver	"I hope the mail carrier will **deliver** it today," Mrs. Noma said.
10. charter	"They were a **charter** company in energy–efficient house plans," he said.
11. journey	"This **journey** to build a house is taking too long," complained Setsuko.
12. major	"A car is a **major** expense, especially for the Johansens," reminded her mom.
13. burden	"Why do their car problems have to be our **burden**?" she muttered.
14. error	"Don't you think there is an **error** in your thinking?" her mom questioned.
15. desert	"They're in the middle of a **desert,** so to speak, and we have the water they need."
16. deserve	"We have been blessed with a lot we don't **deserve,**" said her dad.
17. molar	Setsuko ran her tongue over her new **molar** and tender gum.
18. chapter	She read a **chapter** in her Bible and asked God for help with her attitude.
19. courage	"Give me the **courage** to do right even when I don't feel like it," she prayed.
20. adverb	She marked the last **adverb,** then put her grammar book in her backpack.

Word Shapes

Help students form a correct image of whole words.

Look at each word and think about its shape. Now, write the word in the correct word Shape Boxes. You may check off each word as you use it.

(The sound of **/ər/** or **/ûr/** can be spelled with **ar**, **er**, **ir**, **or**, **ur**, or **ure**. Because spellers cannot rely on a phonetic way of remembering the various spellings, this sound is often difficult.)

In the word shape boxes, fill in the boxes containing the letters that spell the sound of **/ər/** or **/ûr/** in each word.

Take a minute to memorize...

Psalm 37:3

Lesson 26 | Day 1

B Word Shapes Name ______________________

Words with /ər/ or /ûr/ — Lesson 26

Using the word bank below, write each word in the correct word shape boxes. Next, in the word shape boxes, fill in the boxes containing the letter or letters that spell the sound of **/ər/** or **/ûr/** in each word.

1. solar
2. courage
3. major
4. clerk
5. anchor
6. charter
7. molar
8. desert
9. chapter
10. deliver
11. journey
12. burden
13. energy
14. version
15. West Virginia
16. clever
17. New Jersey
18. deserve
19. adverb
20. error

Word Bank

adverb	charter	deliver	error	New Jersey
anchor	clerk	desert	journey	solar
burden	clever	deserve	major	version
chapter	courage	energy	molar	West Virginia

164

Answers may vary for duplicate word shapes.

Be Prepared For Fun

Check these supply lists for **Fun Ways to Spell** - presented **Day 2**.
Purchase and/or gather these items ahead of time!

General
- Pencil
- Notebook Paper
- Spelling List

Auditory
- Pencil
- Notebook Paper
- Dictionary
- Spelling List

Visual
- Pencil
- Notebook Paper
- Spelling List

Tactile
- Computer Keyboard
- Spelling List

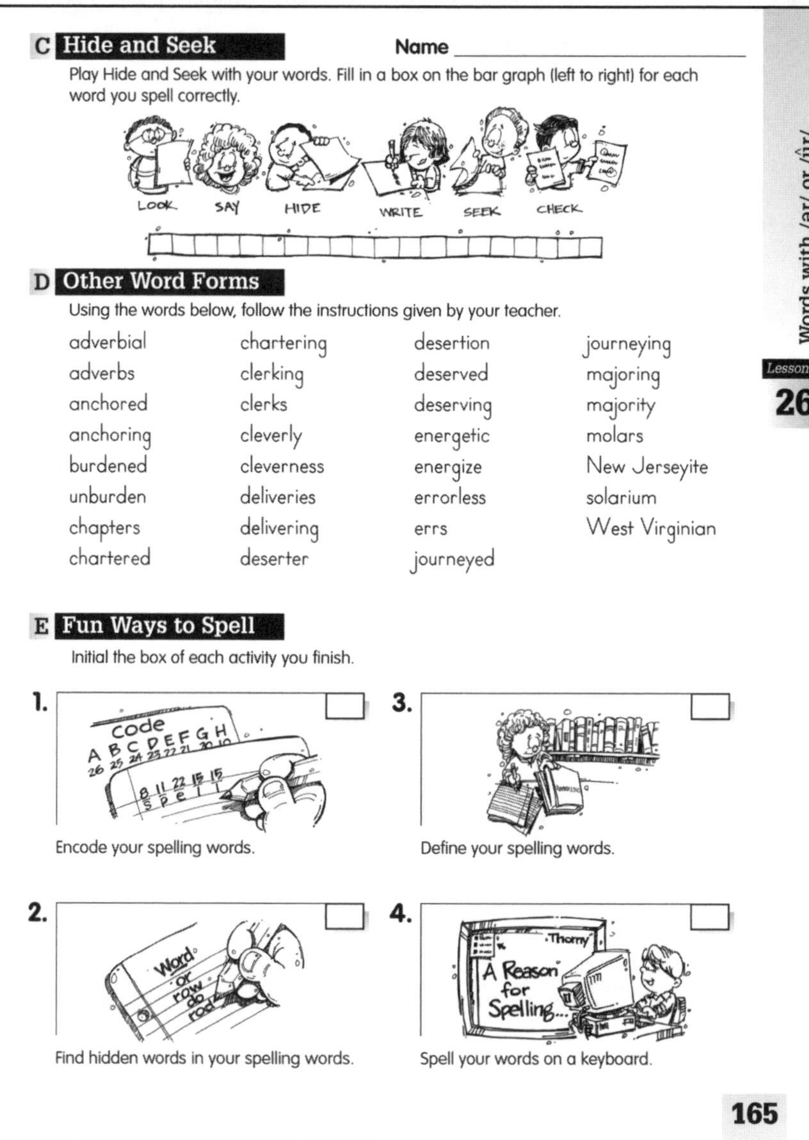

C Hide and Seek Name ______________________

Play Hide and Seek with your words. Fill in a box on the bar graph (left to right) for each word you spell correctly.

D Other Word Forms

Using the words below, follow the instructions given by your teacher.

adverbial	chartering	desertion	journeying
adverbs	clerking	deserved	majoring
anchored	clerks	deserving	majority
anchoring	cleverly	energetic	molars
burdened	cleverness	energize	New Jerseyite
unburden	deliveries	errorless	solarium
chapters	delivering	errs	West Virginian
chartered	deserter	journeyed	

E Fun Ways to Spell

Initial the box of each activity you finish.

1. Encode your spelling words.

2. Find hidden words in your spelling words.

3. Define your spelling words.

4. Spell your words on a keyboard.

Words with /ər/ or /ûr/

Lesson 26

165

1 Hide and Seek

Reinforce spelling by using multiple styles of learning.

On a white board, Teacher writes each word — one at a time. **Have students:**

- **Look** at the word.
- **Say** the word out loud.
- **Spell** the word out loud.
- **Hide** (teacher erases word.)
- **Write** the word on paper.
- **Seek** (teacher rewrites word.)
- **Check** spelling. If incorrect, rewrite word correctly.

2 Other Word Forms

This activity is optional. Have students write original sentences using these Other Word Forms:

anchored
molars
deserving
cleverly

3 Fun Ways to Spell

Four activities are provided. Use one, two, three, or all of the activities. Have students initial the box for each activity they complete.

Options:

- assign activities to students according to their learning styles
- set up the activities in learning centers for the students to do throughout the day
- divide students into four groups and assign one activity per group
- do one activity per day

General

To encode your spelling words...
- Write the alphabet on your paper.
- Write your own code for each letter underneath it.
- Write your spelling words in your code.
- Trade papers with a classmate and decode the words.
- Check to make sure your classmate spelled the words correctly.

Auditory

To define your spelling words...
- Ask a classmate to look up a word from your spelling list in the dictionary and read the definition to you, but not the spelling word.
- Decide which word on your list matches this definition and write the word.
- Ask your classmate to check your spelling.
- Switch and continue taking turns.

Visual

To find hidden words in your spelling words...
- Choose a word from your spelling list.
- Write it on your paper.
- Find and write as many smaller words as you can that are contained within your spelling word.
- Do this with each word.

Tactile

To spell your words on a keyboard...
- Type your spelling words on a keyboard.
- Check your spelling.

Working with Words

Familiarize students with word meaning and usage.

Secret Words

The boxed letters in the acrostic are a phrase from the Scripture verse for this week.

Use the clues to write the words in the puzzle. You may use a dictionary to help you. Then write the boxed letters on the lines below to find the secret words from this week's Scripture.

Take a minute to memorize...

Psalm 37:3

Words with /ər/ or /ûr/ — Lesson 26

F Working with Words Name ____________________

Secret Words

Use the clues to write the words in the puzzle. Then write the boxed letters on the lines below to find the secret words from this week's Scripture.

1. burden
2. deserve
3. clerk
4. West Virginia
5. energy
6. adverb
7. solar
8. anchor
9. desert
10. courage
11. error
12. journey
13. deliver
14. chapter
15. molar
16. major
17. t
18. charter
19. clever
20. New Jersey
21. version

1. hardship, affliction
2. be worthy of
3. salesperson
4. Charleston is the capitol
5. power, force
6. modifies a verb
7. relating to the sun
8. weight for mooring a ship
9. wasteland, sand
10. bravery
11. mistake, blunder
12. expedition, trip
13. rescue from danger
14. division of a book
15. tooth for grinding food
16. dominant, primary
17. letter before **u**
18. founding, original
19. quick-witted, intelligent
20. Trenton is the capitol
21. account, report

Write the secret phrase:

Be kind and good to others.

Word Bank

adverb	charter	deliver	error	New Jersey
anchor	clerk	desert	journey	solar
burden	clever	deserve	major	version
chapter	courage	energy	molar	West Virginia

166

G Dictation

Name ____________________

Write each sentence as your teacher dictates. Use correct punctuation.

1. Mrs. Noma told her daughter a short version of the Girls' Day festival.
2. In the next chapter we will learn about adverbs.
3. The clerk will make plans to deliver the package.

Words with /ər/ or /ûr/

Lesson 26

H Proofreading

If a word is misspelled, fill in the oval by that word. If all the words are spelled correctly, fill in the oval by **no mistake**.

1.
● burdin
○ missile
○ crumple
○ no mistake

2.
○ angle
● ancher
○ particle
○ no mistake

3.
○ miracle
○ riddle
● clirk
○ no mistake

4.
○ courage
○ decimal
● sollar
○ no mistake

5.
○ chapter
● mollar
○ mumble
○ no mistake

6.
● new jersey
○ deserve
○ fragile
○ no mistake

7.
○ multiple
○ version
● journie
○ no mistake

8.
○ dribble
● majer
○ humble
○ no mistake

9.
○ energy
○ mingle
● eror
○ no mistake

10.
● desertt
○ charter
○ example
○ no mistake

11.
○ bundle
● West Virginya
○ double
○ no mistake

12.
○ adverb
○ clever
● delivr
○ no mistake

167

Dictation

Reinforce correct spelling by using current and previous words in context.

Listen as I read each sentence and then write it in your Worktext. Remember to use correct capitalization and punctuation. (Slowly read each sentence twice. Sentences are found in the Student Worktext to the left.)

Day 4

2 Proofreading

Familiarize students with standardized test format and reinforce recognition of misspelled words.

Look at each set of words. If a word is misspelled, fill in the oval by that word. If all the words are spelled correctly, fill in the oval by **no mistake**.

Lesson 26

Lesson 26 Day 4 / Day 5

3 Hide and Seek

Reinforce correct spelling of current spelling words. Repeat this activity from Day 2.

4 Vocabulary Extension

Have your students complete this activity to strengthen spelling ability and expand vocabulary. The reproducible master is provided in Appendix A as shown on the inset page to the right.

1 Posttest

Test mastery of the spelling words.

I will say the word once, use it in a sentence, then say it again. Write your words on a separate sheet of paper.

Progress Chart

Students may record scores. (Reproducible master in Appendix B.)

Personal Dictionary

Students may add any words they have misspelled to their personal dictionaries for reference when writing. (Cover in Appendix B.)

Hide and Seek

Play Hide and Seek with your words. Fill in a bar graph (left to right) for each word you spell correctly.

Vocabulary Extension

Vocabulary Extension — Lesson 26

Trade-off

Choose a word from the word bank to replace the word(s) in parentheses. Write the word in the blank.

1. Several ways to preserve (keep) food include drying, salting, freezing, and canning.
2. Each graduate left a short interval (pause) before starting down the aisle.
3. The boys have been forbidden (prohibited) to climb on the steep, jagged cliffs.
4. The primary (main) reason for this meeting is to nominate a mayor for our town.
5. The intense basketball game caused the players to perspire (sweat) profusely.
6. Our trip to the mountains turned in to an exciting adventure (experience).
7. Fog lay low over the valleys due to so much moisture (dampness) in the air.
8. After you fill out the form, please place your signature (written name) at the bottom.
9. Autumn gives me a lot of pleasure (enjoyment) with its crisp air, colorful leaves, and hayrides at Grandpa's farm.
10. I thought the dog leash was secure (fastened), but when I came home, Rover was gone.
11. There are several countries in Europe (this continent) I would like to visit, such as Germany, Spain, France, and Italy.
12. Failure (neglecting) to do your homework will result in bad grades.

Word Bank

adventure	forbidden	perspire	primary
Europe	interval	pleasure	secure
failure	moisture	preserve	signature

346

1. clerk	The hardware store **clerk** showed Mrs. Noma the house plan books.
2. solar	Mrs. Noma liked the innovative use of **solar** power in many of the plans.
3. energy	She wanted their new home to be **energy**–efficient.
4. West Virginia	She hoped to receive the plan she'd ordered from **West Virginia.**
5. clever	"This is a **clever** kitchen design, don't you think?" she asked her husband.
6. New Jersey	"Did you request the plan book from that **New Jersey** company?" he asked.
7. charter	"They were a **charter** company in the move to energy–efficient house plans."
8. deliver	"I expect the carrier to **deliver** it with today's mail," his wife replied.
9. version	"I really liked that one **version** of a detached workshop," said Mr. Noma.
10. anchor	Setsuko fiddled with the **anchor** embroidered on her sleeve.
11. molar	A new **molar** breaking through made her gum sore.
12. journey	"Planning to build a house seems like an endless **journey,**" she moaned.
13. major	"The Johansens' need for a car is **major,**" Mrs. Noma said with concern.
14. burden	"Do we have to bear that **burden** for them?" Setsuko asked sullenly.
15. courage	"We must have the **courage** and selflessness to give to others," replied her dad.
16. error	She knew in her heart that her feelings were in **error.**
17. desert	"They're in a **desert,** sort of, and need water; we've got just that!" said her dad.
18. chapter	After reading a **chapter** in her Bible, she prayed for help with her attitude.
19. deserve	"God, thank you for all I have that I don't even **deserve,**" she prayed.
20. adverb	Before closing her grammar book, she marked one more **adverb** she saw.

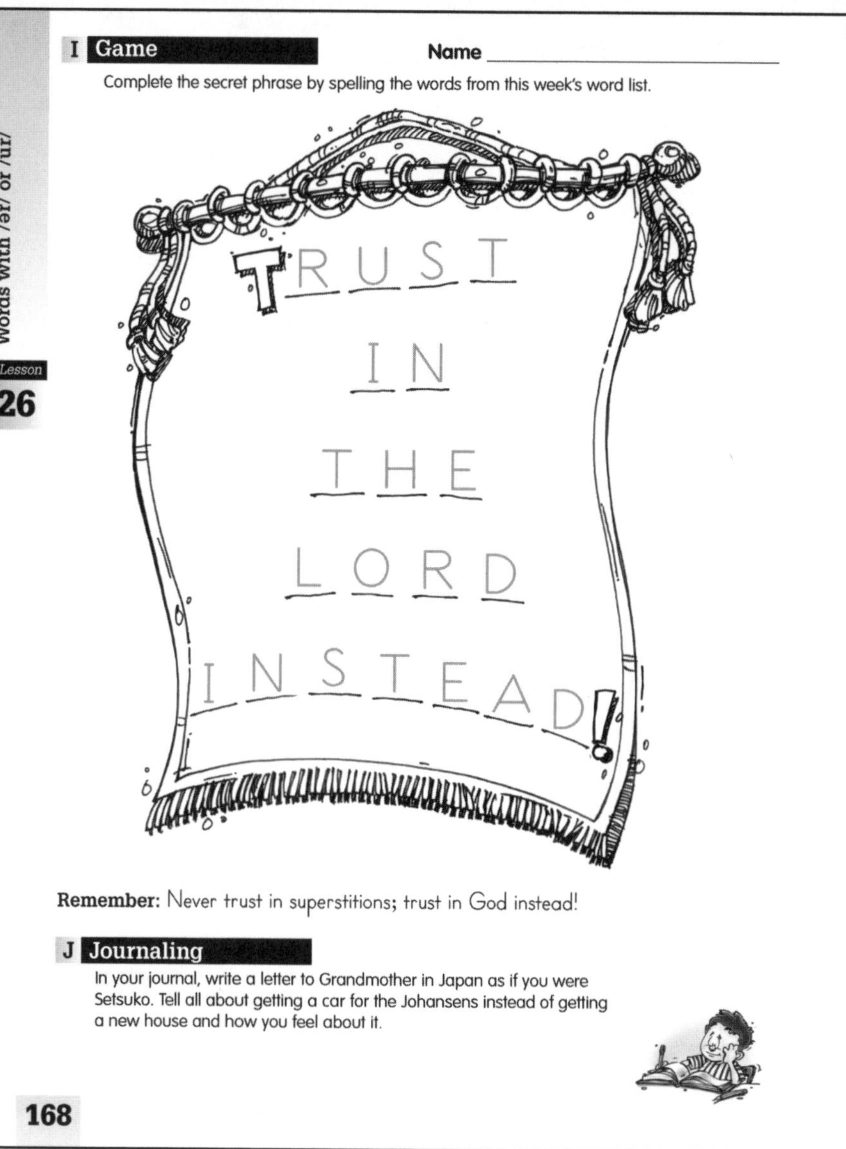

Words with /ər/ or /ûr/

Lesson 26

I Game Name ____________________

Complete the secret phrase by spelling the words from this week's word list.

Remember: Never trust in superstitions; trust in God instead!

J Journaling

In your journal, write a letter to Grandmother in Japan as if you were Setsuko. Tell all about getting a car for the Johansens instead of getting a new house and how you feel about it.

168

How to Play:

- Divide the class into two teams, and decide which team will go first.
- Have a student from team A choose a number from 1 to 20.
- Say the word that matches that number from the team's word list.
- Have the student write the word on the board.
- If correct, have each member of team A write the given letter in the matching space on his/her game page.
- Alternate between teams A and B having the students choose a number of a blank space.
- The team to complete the secret phrase first is the winner.

2 Game

Reinforce spelling skills and provide motivation and interest.

Materials

- game page (from student text)
- pencils (1 per child)
- game word list

Game Word List

	Team A		Team B
1.	**burden (R)**	1.	**clever (A)**
2.	**anchor (U)**	2.	**deliver (D)**
3.	**clerk (S)**	3.	**major (R)**
4.	**courage (T)**	4.	**energy (U)**
5.	**solar (I)**	5.	**error (S)**
6.	**molar (N)**	6.	**desert (T)**
7.	**West Virginia**	7.	**deserve (I)**
8.	**(T)**	8.	**charter (N)**
9.	**New Jersey**	9.	**chapter (T)**
10.	**(H)**	10.	**adverb (H)**
11.	**version (E)**	11.	**clever (E)**
12.	**journey (L)**	12.	**deliver (L)**
13.	**major (O)**	13.	**burden (O)**
14.	**energy (R)**	14.	**anchor (R)**
15.	**error (D)**	15.	**clerk (D)**
16.	**desert (I)**	16.	**courage (I)**
17.	**deserve (N)**	17.	**solar (N)**
18.	**charter (S)**	18.	**molar (S)**
19.	**chapter (T)**	19.	**West Virginia**
20.	**adverb (E)**	20.	**(T)**

3 Journaling

Provide a meaningful reason for correct spelling through personal writing.

Review the story using discussion leads provided on the following page. Encourage students to apply the Scriptural value in their journaling.

Journaling (continued)

- Why couldn't Setsuko find a place to put the dolls in her bedroom? (Her bedroom was small and what space there was had already been filled with other things.)
- What are Hina Matsuri dolls? (Elaborate Japanese dolls, including an emperor and an empress, that are displayed in the best room of the house for a few weeks before Girls' Day, when they are taken down.)
- Why did traditional superstition dictate that they had to be put away on Girls' Day? (The superstition was that the girls of the house would be doomed if the dolls were not put away on March 3.)
- Do you think the Nomas believed the superstition? Why or why not? (No. They believed in God.)
- Why were Setsuko and her parents waiting to look for a place to build a new house? (They were saving the money they would need.)
- What kind of car did the Nomas plan to get for Paula Johansen? (A car that had been wrecked when it was fairly new and then repaired so it would be a little less expensive but still dependable.)
- How did getting the car for the Johansens affect their plans for a house of their own? (They would have to wait and save some more money.)

Homophones have one pronunciation and more than one spelling.

6-way homophone

air are heir ere err e'er

(This pronunciation of "are" is for 100 square meters, i.e. 1/100 hectare. E'er is a contraction of ever. And of course there is also Jane Eyre.)

4-way homophone

right Wright rite write

3-way homophones

aisle isle I'll
do dew due
for four fore

Table-Top Refuge

A flood on Mason Creek puts Heather and her family in danger.

"Come on, Heather! I can't hear with you practicing so loud." Collin grabbed sofa pillows and made himself comfortable in front of the TV. He added a few blocks to the tower the Jensen children had been building earlier. A boom of thunder competed with the keyboard, but Heather continued playing without missing a note.

Collin threw a pillow at his sister, just missing the back of her head. The ten-year-old girl was concentrating on the music and didn't even notice. Collin sighed and placed a few more blocks on the tower.

When she finished the song, Heather Starks gazed out the window at the glow of the streetlight. Curtains of rain rippled in windy gusts. She checked her watch. "It's raining again," she announced. "And it's time for the movie Mom said we could watch. Where's the remote?"

Collin laughed, "Welcome back to planet earth!"

"Here, let me see the remote. That's not the right channel," Heather directed.

Collin held the remote high. "I don't think so! I remember almost missing that home run because you were surfing the channels too long during commercials."

"But you didn't, did you?" Heather smiled.

"Mom!" Heather yelled as she grabbed for the remote held just out of her reach. "It's time for the movie to start—and he won't go to the right channel."

Mrs. Starks walked in with a huge bowl of popcorn. "I may take it away from both of you if it's such a bone of contention." Mom held out her hand for the remote. She punched in the right channel before she set the remote on the floor and dipped out bowls of popcorn. The movie theme music drew their attention to the screen, and no more thought was given to the remote—or the rain.

Halfway through the movie a flood watch started scrolling across the bottom of the screen in red letters.

"When does dad get back?" Collin asked as a commercial began.

"Tomorrow." Mom picked out the last kernels of popcorn from her bowl.

Collin looked out the window. "What if it keeps raining? Will Mason Creek flood?"

"I'm sure it could with all this rain," Mrs. Starks answered.

"How high do you think it'll get?"

"It depends. The longer it rains the more saturated the ground becomes. Then the water starts running off and filling up all the storm drains, creeks, and rivers. When they get full, things start backing up. I hope this weather system will move through quickly." Mom refilled her popcorn bowl.

"Shhhhh!" Heather interrupted. "The commercials are over!"

Collin was still looking at his mom. "It's not forecasted to."

Mom wiped her buttery fingers on a napkin. "It would take a lot of water to put this town in any kind of danger! I don't think we have anything to worry about, but Dad has to drive through...."

"Shhhh!" Heather interrupted again. "It's starting."

"Heather, aren't you worried about Dad?"

Moments later the movie disappeared from the screen. "We interrupt this program to bring you the latest report from the National Weather Service. Sebastian and Cole counties are under a flood watch throughout the night. Heavy rains are forecasted to continue. The Illinois River is expected to be out of its banks by late tomorrow morning. Please do not drive or walk into flowing water. If your car is stranded in water, do not stay in it! If you become trapped in your home, remain there until help arrives. Keep a flashlight and cell phone ready for emergency use. I repeat—get out of stranded cars, but remain in your homes. Stay tuned to this station for the latest updates."

Later Mom came into Heather's room to tuck her in for the night. She sat on the edge of the bed and smoothed back her daughter's red hair. Rain still slashed against the window and lightning occasionally lit up the room.

"Are you worried about the creek flooding?" Heather asked.

"Not really. This house has been around for many years, and it's never been flooded before. God can keep us safe even if the river floods. Remember that Scripture verse you were practicing on the way home from school today?" Heather nodded.

Mom tucked the covers under her daughter's chin and kissed her nose. "I don't think we have anything to worry about. Here's your flashlight if you need it in the night."

Heather sat up in bed, not knowing how long she'd been asleep or what had awakened her. She rubbed her eyes and tried to shake the fog from her mind. It was still dark. She glanced at the clock beside the bed, but the hands weren't moving. She reached for her flashlight.

Heather was jolted to alertness when her toes felt icy dampness instead of warm carpet. The rain had stopped slashing against the window—but there was an ominous new sound.

Heather headed for the living room when she saw her mom standing at the front window. She aimed her flashlight across the living room floor. Water was seeping under the door, and a little rivulet was running

Story (continued)

across the wooden floor toward the block tower. She picked up the remote just before the water reached it. Mom waved her toward the window. Their streetlight illuminated a rushing river of brown water. She gazed wide-eyed as objects bobbed through the pool of light and on downstream. They watched in stunned silence until the streetlight went out.

Heather ran to the side window, relieved to see their car still parked on the gravel driveway.

Mrs. Starks took a final look at the rising water before going to the telephone and dialing her sister's number. "Maria! Maria!" she blurted as soon as her sister answered. "Yes. Our carpet is already wet. Has creek water reached your house yet?…Maria?… Maria!" she cried as the connection was broken. She hurriedly redialed the number—but the phone line was dead.

Mrs. Starks joined her daughter at the back door. Collin followed, rubbing sleep from his eyes. The three stepped out onto the patio in time to see the eastern sky turning pink. "Will the water get any higher?" Heather asked.

"Probably. Even though the rain has stopped here, the smaller streams will keep draining into the river. And it might still be raining upstream. We need to get out of here, but I'm not sure how or where to go. The electricity is off…the radio in the car doesn't work… and the phone is dead." She paused. "Let's move stuff out of the water before we leave."

"The TV weatherman said we're supposed to stay in our house and out of our cars!" Heather reminded them.

"This wasn't supposed to happen," Collin mumbled.

"Where will we go? How will Dad find us?" Heather prayed as tears rolled down her cheeks, "Lord help us."

The water was now ankle deep—and rising. Mom finally came up with a plan. "I want you both to get dressed. Put on your wool sweaters—they'll be warm even if they get wet. Then let's pick everything up off this wet floor."

Heather was the first to return to the living room. She felt better with something purposeful to do. She picked up the blocks and put them on the dining room table. Mom looped the end of the drapes over the curtain rods. Collin brought in some cement blocks from the garage and the three of them lifted the couch out of the rising water. Just as they finished, a surge of muddy water pushed the back door open and lapped at the couch fabric. Heather watched the remote float off the coffee table and disappear into the murky water. Something in the water hit her leg, and she screamed. She sloshed to the dining room and climbed up beside the building blocks.

Mom and Collin soon realized the hopelessness of the situation and joined her. They watched numbly as the swirling brown water continued to rise. Heather spoke first. "I wonder why nobody warned us? Are all our neighbors gone?"

Mrs. Starks shrugged. "They're probably as surprised and unprepared as we are. I think the Rozells are out of town. Who knows where the Gunters are?"

"Do you think we should get up on the roof so someone will see us?" Collin finally said.

Mom wasn't sure what to do. "I'm thinking and praying," she finally explained. Heather added a silent prayer to her mom's. She watched as Collin began to build a tower with the blocks. As it got higher, her anxiety began to drain away. She started to hum the tune of a new praise song Mr. Canfield had been teaching them. Mom hopped down from the table and waded over to try the phone again. Heather added a few blocks to Collin's tower. She thought she heard a car engine but realized it was impossible with the street covered with water. Everyone jumped when the front door crashed open and a familiar voice boomed, "What's for breakfast?"

"Dad!" Heather yelled. "You're home early. Where's your rig?"

"I'm a boat driver now, Heather, and I think we'd better eat out this morning!" Dad smiled as he surveyed his children sitting on the dining room table. He sloshed over and turned around so Heather could hop on his back.

"I'm glad you came, Dad." Heather tightened her arms around him. "Our table seems to be shrinking, and this tower won't keep us out of the muddy water. And I couldn't figure out how God was going to get us out of here. I think sending you in a boat was a good idea."

Dad smiled and patted the arms that clung to his neck. "He's a powerful God, Heather. A powerful God."

2 Discussion Time

Check understanding of the story and development of personal values.

- Talk about a flood you have seen or been in.
- Where is a safe place to be in a flood?
- How did Heather feel when something hit her leg in the swirling brown water?
- Where did Heather and Collin go as the water started to rise?
- Whom did Heather silently ask to help her?
- How did she begin to feel after praying?
- How can you tell her feelings were changing?
- Who came to rescue the Stark family?

A Preview

Name ______________________

Write each word as your teacher says it.

1. nucleus
2. obvious
3. radius
4. interest
5. fungus
6. cirrus
7. cumulus
8. octopus
9. mollusk
10. restless
11. stillness
12. witness
13. citrus
14. virus
15. congress
16. walrus
17. services
18. aimless
19. closeness
20. reckless

Words with /es/ or /is/

Lesson 27

Scripture
Psalm 59:16

169

3 Preview

Test for knowledge of the correct spellings of these words.

Customize Your List

On a separate sheet of paper, additional words of your choice may be tested.

I will say each word once, use the word in a sentence, then say the word again. Write the words on the lines in your Worktext.

Correct Immediately!

Let's correct our Preview. I will spell each word out loud. If you spelled a word incorrectly, rewrite it correctly.

Progress Chart

Students may record scores. (Reproducible master provided in Appendix B.)

1.	nucleus	The **nucleus** of the storm shimmered in green on the weather map.
2.	obvious	It was **obvious** that this storm was potentially dangerous.
3.	radius	The map showed the **radius** of the storm was increasing.
4.	interest	Their **interest** in the weather bulletins grew as the clouds darkened.
5.	fungus	"Wet carpet smells like some kind of **fungus**!" grimaced Heather.
6.	cirrus	"Those aren't **cirrus** clouds," said Collin importantly.
7.	cumulus	"They aren't **cumulus** clouds either," he said knowingly.
8.	octopus	"It felt like an **octopus** just touched my leg," squealed Heather.
9.	mollusk	"Maybe it was just a **mollusk**," Collin joked.
10.	restless	As the storm grew worse, Heather and Collin grew **restless**.
11.	stillness	In the **stillness**, the lapping of the water against the house seemed loud.
12.	witness	"I've never had any desire to **witness** a flood firsthand," he said.
13.	citrus	"Our little **citrus** tree is all under water now," noticed Heather.
14.	virus	"This would be perfect weather to come down with a **virus**," Heather mused.
15.	congress	"We should have a **congress** on the dining room table," directed Mom.
16.	walrus	"I'm sure I look like a **walrus** on a rock," she said.
17.	services	"We could use the **services** of a rescue party anytime now!" they agreed.
18.	aimless	"Our prayers are not **aimless**!" encouraged Mom.
19.	closeness	She thanked God for His **closeness** and asked for His help.
20.	reckless	Now was not the time for **reckless** abandon.

Word Shapes

Help students form a correct image of whole words.

Look at each word and think about its shape. Now, write the word in the correct word Shape Boxes. You may check off each word as you use it.

(The sound of **/əs/** can be spelled with **as**, **us**, or **ous**. The sound of **/is/** can be spelled with **es**, **ess**, or **ice**. Because spellers cannot rely on a phonetic way of remembering the various spellings, this sound is often difficult.)

In the word shape boxes, fill in the boxes containing the letters that spell the sound of **/əs/** or **/is/** in each word.

Take a minute to memorize...

Psalm 59:16

Words with /əs/ or /is/ — Lesson 27

B Word Shapes Name ______________________

Using the word bank below, write each word in the correct word shape boxes. Next, in the word shape boxes, fill in the boxes containing the letter or letters that spell the sound of **/əs/** or **/is/** in each word.

1. reckless
2. aimless
3. radius
4. congress
5. restless
6. fungus
7. cumulus
8. walrus
9. nucleus
10. cirrus
11. obvious
12. citrus
13. mollusk
14. witness
15. closeness
16. stillness
17. interest
18. virus
19. octopus
20. services

Word Bank

aimless	congress	mollusk	radius	stillness
cirrus	cumulus	nucleus	reckless	virus
citrus	fungus	obvious	restless	walrus
closeness	interest	octopus	services	witness

170

Answers may vary for duplicate word shapes.

Be Prepared For Fun

Check these supply lists for **Fun Ways to Spell** - presented **Day 2**. Purchase and/or gather these items ahead of time!

General
- Pencil
- 3 X 5 Cards cut in half (20 per child)
- Spelling List

Auditory
- Spelling List

Visual
- Pencil
- Notebook Paper
- Spelling List

Tactile
- Blackboard and Chalk
  -OR-
- White Board and Marker
- Spelling List

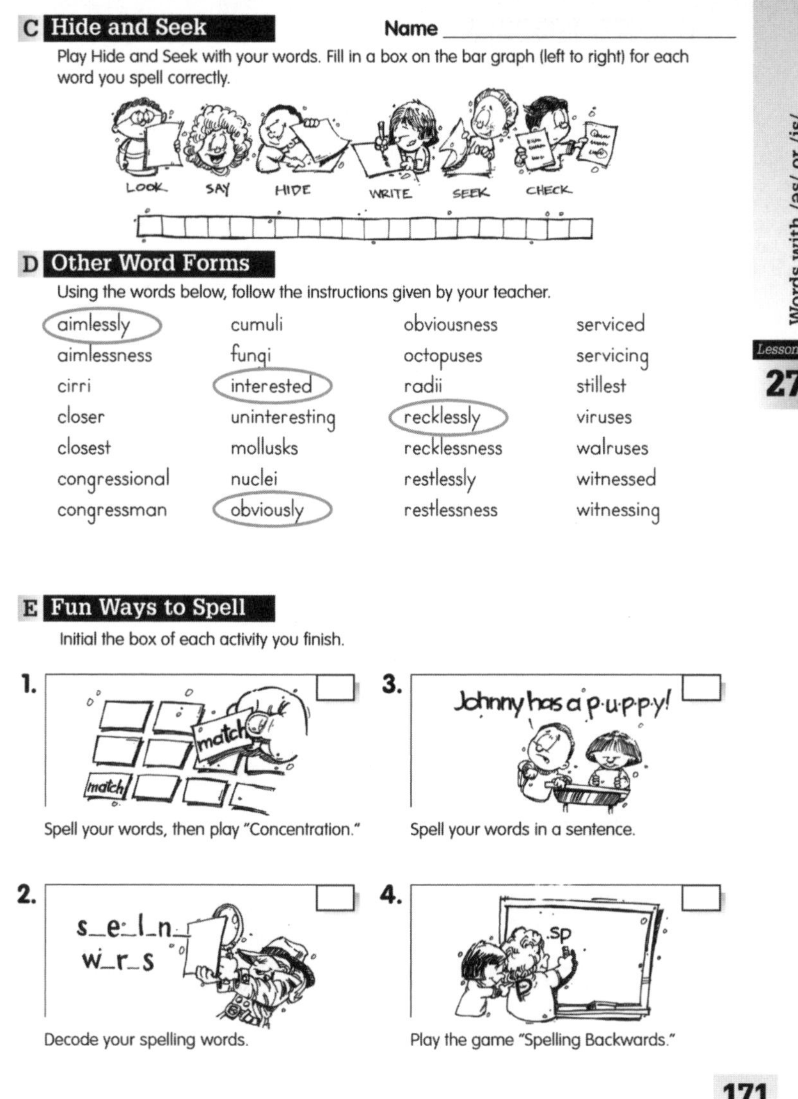

C Hide and Seek Name ____________

Play Hide and Seek with your words. Fill in a box on the bar graph (left to right) for each word you spell correctly.

D Other Word Forms

Using the words below, follow the instructions given by your teacher.

aimlessly	cumuli	obviousness	serviced
aimlessness	fungi	octopuses	servicing
cirri	interested	radii	stillest
closer	uninteresting	recklessly	viruses
closest	mollusks	recklessness	walruses
congressional	nuclei	restlessly	witnessed
congressman	obviously	restlessness	witnessing

E Fun Ways to Spell

Initial the box of each activity you finish.

1.
Spell your words, then play "Concentration."

2.
Decode your spelling words.

3.
Spell your words in a sentence.

4.
Play the game "Spelling Backwards."

Words with /əs/ or /is/ — Lesson 27

171

Day 2 — Lesson 27

1 Hide and Seek

Reinforce spelling by using multiple styles of learning.

On a white board, Teacher writes each word — one at a time. **Have students:**

- **Look** at the word.
- **Say** the word out loud.
- **Spell** the word out loud.
- **Hide** (teacher erases word.)
- **Write** the word on paper.
- **Seek** (teacher rewrites word.)
- **Check** spelling. If incorrect, rewrite word correctly.

2 Other Word Forms

This activity is optional. Have students find and circle the Other Word Forms that are antonyms of the following:

purposefully
carefully
not apparently
inattentive

3 Fun Ways to Spell

Four activities are provided. Use one, two, three, or all of the activities. Have students initial the box for each activity they complete.

Options:

- assign activities to students according to their learning styles
- set up the activities in learning centers for the students to do throughout the day
- divide students into four groups and assign one activity per group
- do one activity per day

General

Spell your words; then play "Concentration"...
- Write each spelling word on a card. Mix your cards and a classmate's cards together. Arrange them face down in five rows of eight. Pick up two cards. If the cards match, play again. If the cards do not match, turn them back over. It is your classmate's turn. Continue taking turns until all the cards are matched. The player with the most cards wins!

Auditory

To spell your words in a sentence...
- Ask a classmate to read a spelling word to you from the list.
- Spell the word aloud and use it in a sentence.
- Ask your classmate to check your spelling.
- Each correctly spelled word that is used properly in a sentence counts as one point.
- Switch and continue taking turns.

Visual

To decode your spelling words...
- Look at the first word on your list.
- Write every other letter of the word on your paper, putting a blank where each missing letter belongs.
- Trade papers with a classmate and fill in the missing letters.
- Check your spelling.

Tactile

To play the game "Spelling Backwards"...
- Ask a classmate to stand behind you and draw the letters to spell a word from your list on your back.
- Write the spelling word on the board as your classmate traces the letters on your back.
- Ask your classmate to check your spelling.
- Trade places and take turns until you have each spelled all the words.

Working with Words

Familiarize students with word meaning and usage.

Drawing Conclusions

Explain that to figure something out using logic is to draw a conclusion. On the board write:

You are learning the art of Japanese paper folding. You are learning ________.

Have a volunteer supply the word **origami**.

Complete each conclusion by writing a word from the word bank. You may use a dictionary to help you.

Take a minute to memorize...

Psalm 59:16

F Working with Words Name ______________________

Drawing Conclusions

Complete each conclusion by writing a word from the word bank.

1. You are studying snails and clams. You are learning about mollusk s.
2. The night is calm and quiet. Sitting on the porch, you enjoy the stillness .
3. You see a high-altitude cloud of thin, white patches. It is a cirrus cloud.
4. You feel affection towards your parents. You feel a closeness to them.
5. You feel like you are getting the flu. You may have caught a virus .
6. You see dense, fluffy clouds that are rounded on top. These are cumulus clouds.
7. You are learning about yeasts, molds, and mushrooms. A yeast is a fungus .
8. Draw a line from the center of a circle to the edge. You have drawn the radius .
9. A doctor, lawyer, dentist, and repairman have something in common. They all provide services for people.
10. Your savings account is earning money in the bank. It earns interest .
11. You are learning about DNA. You study about a cell's nucleus .
12. You easily understand a joke. The answer is obvious .
13. You go to the mall without money. Your trip is probably aimless .
14. You are buying oranges and lemons. You are buying citrus fruit.
15. This mollusk has a soft body with eight tentacles. It may be an octopus .
16. You ride your bike very carelessly. You are being reckless .
17. You cannot relax or sit still. You are feeling restless .
18. You see a large marine mammal with long tusks. It is a walrus .
19. The national legislative body is meeting. It is a meeting of congress .
20. You saw an accident happen. You are a witness .

Word Bank

aimless	congress	mollusk	radius	stillness
cirrus	cumulus	nucleus	reckless	virus
citrus	fungus	obvious	restless	walrus
closeness	interest	octopus	services	witness

G Dictation

Name ____________________

Write each sentence as your teacher dictates. Use correct punctuation.

1. It soon became obvious that they could not leave the house.
2. Heather saw the nucleus of the huge storm on the screen.
3. In science class we learned the meanings of cumulus and cirrus.

Words with /es/ or /is/

Lesson 27

H Proofreading

If a word is misspelled, fill in the oval by that word. If all the words are spelled correctly, fill in the oval by **no mistake**.

1. ○ chapter ● nuckleus ○ obvious ○ no mistake
2. ○ congress ○ New Jersey ○ fungus ● no mistake
3. ○ deserve ○ energy ● aimliss ○ no mistake
4. ○ cumulus ○ adverb ● molusk ○ no mistake
5. ● reckliss ○ restless ○ anchor ○ no mistake
6. ● cloesness ○ clerk ○ stillness ○ no mistake
7. ○ desert ○ witness ● octoppus ○ no mistake
8. ○ solar ○ cirrus ○ error ● no mistake
9. ○ interest ○ journey ○ major ● no mistake
10. ○ West Virginia ● vyrus ○ version ○ no mistake
11. ● wallrus ○ courage ○ services ○ no mistake
12. ○ citrus ● raddius ○ burden ○ no mistake

173

1 Dictation

Reinforce correct spelling by using current and previous words in context.

Listen as I read each sentence and then write it in your Worktext. Remember to use correct capitalization and punctuation. (Slowly read each sentence twice. Sentences are found in the Student Worktext to the left.)

2 Proofreading

Familiarize students with standardized test format and reinforce recognition of misspelled words.

Look at each set of words. If a word is misspelled, fill in the oval by that word. If all the words are spelled correctly, fill in the oval by **no mistake**.

Lesson 27 | Day 4

3 Hide and Seek

Reinforce correct spelling of current spelling words. Repeat this activity from Day 2.

4 Vocabulary Extension

Have your students complete this activity to strengthen spelling ability and expand vocabulary. The reproducible master is provided in Appendix A as shown on the inset page to the right.

1 Posttest

Test mastery of the spelling words.

I will say the word once, use it in a sentence, then say it again. Write your words on a separate sheet of paper.

Progress Chart

Students may record scores. (Reproducible master in Appendix B.)

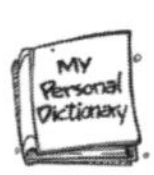

Personal Dictionary

Students may add any words they have misspelled to their personal dictionaries for reference when writing. (Cover in Appendix B.)

Hide and Seek

Play Hide and Seek with your words. Fill in a bar graph (left to right) for each word you spell correctly.

Vocabulary Extension

Multiple Choice

Fill in the oval by the word(s) with the same or nearly the same meaning as the word in bold type.

1. **conscious**
   - ● mentally awake or alert
   - ○ thoughtful, attentive
   - ○ showing self–importance
   - ○ taking into account
2. **delicious**
   - ○ easily damaged
   - ○ ready–to–eat food products
   - ● pleasing to the taste
   - ○ harmful, poisonous
3. **dangerous**
   - ○ hang loosely with a swinging motion
   - ● likely to inflict injury
   - ○ small missile used in a game
   - ○ sharp pointed knife for stabbing
4. **generous**
   - ○ unusually intelligent person
   - ○ the origin or beginning of something
   - ○ bend the knee in worship
   - ● free in giving or sharing
5. **precious**
   - ● of great value
   - ○ undue hastiness
   - ○ highly accurate
   - ○ water that falls to earth
6. **Celsius**
   - ○ thin transparent wrapping material
   - ● scale for measuring temperature
   - ○ relating to the sky
   - ○ condemning sternly
7. **emptiness**
   - ○ eternal, everlasting
   - ○ threatened with extinction
   - ○ wife of an emperor
   - ● vacancy, void, hollow
8. **loneliness**
   - ○ length of life
   - ● isolation, lacking company
   - ○ to hang around idly
   - ○ not rigidly fastened
9. **readiness**
   - ○ to understand written language
   - ○ already made up for sale
   - ○ information printed be a computer
   - ● preparedness
10. **ugliness**
    - ○ last in a progression
    - ● disagreeableness, repulsiveness
    - ○ an open sore that festers
    - ○ resentment, taking offense

Vocabulary Extension — Lesson 27 — 347

1. virus — "Collin, sometimes you're like an annoying **virus**," teased Heather.
2. restless — Heather felt **restless** as they watched the weather bulletin.
3. radius — The weather map showed the **radius** of the storm.
4. nucleus — The **nucleus** of the storm was highlighted in green.
5. interest — Their **interest** in the news grew as the storm worsened.
6. fungus — The smell of the wet carpet reminded Heather of **fungus.**
7. cumulus — "There aren't any **cumulus** clouds up there," Collin said knowingly.
8. aimless — They were not **aimless** in their efforts to keep the couch dry.
9. reckless — Now was not the time to be **reckless**!
10. closeness — No one enjoyed the **closeness** of the cold, muddy water.
11. witness — "I'd really rather not **witness** a flood firsthand," said Collin.
12. octopus — "An **octopus** would like it in here, but I don't!" he exclaimed.
13. mollusk — "Hey, I think I see a **mollusk** down there," he said, trying to be funny.
14. cirrus — There were no **cirrus** clouds to be seen in this severe thunderstorm.
15. citrus — The little **citrus** tree in their backyard was soon covered with water.
16. congress — "Let's have a little **congress** on the dining table," smiled Mom.
17. obvious — It was **obvious** that things were serious now.
18. walrus — "I feel like a **walrus** perched on a rock," joked Heather nervously.
19. stillness — In the **stillness**, Heather's mom asked the Lord to send help.
20. services — "Lord, we could use the **services** of a rescue team!" prayed Heather.

Words with /əs/ or /is/

Lesson 27

I Game Name ____________________

Follow along with Heather's dad as he rescues his family. Move one space for each word you or your team spells correctly.

Remember: Let God be your place of safety.

J Journaling

Summarize in your journal how **Docked in the Dining Room** illustrates this week's Scripture verse.

174

Game

Reinforce spelling skills and provide motivation and interest.

Materials

- game page (from student text)
- game pieces (1 per child)
- game word list

Game Word List

1. **New Jersey (E)**
2. **version (A)**
3. **journey (D)**
4. **nucleus**
5. **obvious**
6. **radius**
7. **congress**
8. **fungus**
9. **aimless**
10. **cumulus**
11. **mollusk**
12. **reckless**
13. **restless**
14. **closeness**
15. **stillness**
16. **witness**
17. **octopus**
18. **cirrus**
19. **citrus**
20. **interest**

How to Play:

- Divide the class into two teams.
- Have each student place his/her game piece on Start.
- Have a student from team A go to the board.
- Say the spelling word.
- Have the student write the word on the board.
- If correct, instruct each member of team A to move his/her game piece forward one space.
- Alternate between teams A and B.
- The team to reach Heather and family first is the winner.
- **Small Group Option**: Students may play this game without teacher direction in small groups of two or more.

3 Journaling

Provide a meaningful reason for correct spelling through personal writing.

Review the story using discussion leads provided on the following page. Encourage students to apply the Scriptural value in their journaling.

Journaling (continued)

- What is our Scripture this week? (Psalm 59:16)
- Why would King David (who wrote this Psalm) say a high tower was a safe place to be when he's distressed? (He was a soldier. Higher ground is preferred by soldiers because they can see the enemy better and it usually gives them an advantage.)
- Where did Heather go when muddy water pushed open the back door and swirled into the living room? (Up on top of the dining room table.)
- Where did Collin think they should go as the water continued to rise? (To the roof)
- What did Heather and Mom do while they waited for help to come? (Mom thought and prayed. Heather prayed and hummed a praise song while she helped Collin build a block tower.)
- How did Dad get to the house in the rising water? (In a boat)
- What did David sing about each morning? (God's power and mercy.)
- What did Dad say about God? ("He's a powerful God, Heather. A powerful God.")

Dusting a cake with sugar means putting dust on it. Dusting the furniture means taking dust off it.

Literature Connection

Topic: God's protecting presence
Theme Text: Psalm 121:5-7

A Life Preserver

When a stranger's car is washed off the road by floodwaters, the Wright family has to act fast.

"Dozens of rivers and creeks in northwestern areas of the state overflowed their banks Friday and Saturday, forcing hundreds of people in four counties to flee their homes, with more flooding possible Sunday."

"Shhh, everybody!" Mr. Wright quieted the rest of his family. "Here's an update on the flooding." He reached over to turn up the volume on the station wagon's radio.

"Officials estimate that 900 people have been forced from their homes. National Guard troops were called out Saturday and are still on the job helping people evacuate from low-lying areas."

"Governor Williams toured the flooded areas on Saturday. He declared a state of emergency for Fulbright, Cole, and Sedgewick counties. The Illinois River cut off access to the town of Winrock and was still rising Sunday as workers filled sandbags."

"According to Joy Moser, State Emergency Management spokeswoman, Aurora was hardest hit as water flowed over a 35-foot levee protecting the town from the Whitewater and Walnut rivers. Seven feet of water covered downtown streets Friday, but the level had fallen to three feet by Saturday afternoon as the river receded."

"About 300 homes and 30 businesses were inundated in Aurora. It will probably be Wednesday or Thursday before the waters recede enough for residents to return home. Officially, 8 inches of rain fell in Aurora by Friday night, but many locations across the area reported as much as 11 inches of rain."

"The flooding was spawned by a slow-moving storm system that hit late Thursday. Flooding elsewhere in the region has forced hundreds from their homes and caused millions of dollars in damage."

"One person has died; the body of 19-year-old Kate Tucker was found hours after water washed the car she and her mother were in off a road. Her mother was rescued and is hospitalized in stable condition. More after this."

Mr. Wright punched the "off" button and silenced the commercial blaring something about rushing over to Jerry's Fine Furniture for the deal of a lifetime.

Cory broke the lengthening silence in the car, "Dad, what if our house is full of water?"

"Yeah, maybe we should have stayed at Granny and Gramp's house." Christopher wriggled around to get a better view at the water-logged scenery.

Dad focused on his youngest son's question. "You know I have to get back to work, Cory. But I don't think our house will be flooded because Appleby Road is on pretty high ground."

Mom reached over and ruffled Cory's hair, "Don't worry about it, pumpkin. We'll deal with whatever we find when we get there."

"It won't be long now." Kristin pointed to a green highway sign, "Just 12 miles to go. Dad, could we stop by Rosa's house to see how she's doing? It's really not out of the way if we get off the highway sooner and take back roads."

Dad flipped on the right-turn blinker. "This exit, isn't it? We'll try, Kristin, but if the roads are covered with water we'll have to turn around. It's not smart to try to drive through flooded areas."

"Wow, look at that grass stuck so high up in the trees!" Cory pointed out the front window as the car traveled more slowly down the rural road. "Is that how high the water was?"

"Yeah. Just think, Cory, we'd be totally under water if it was still flooded!" Cathy leaned over Christopher to get a better look.

"It is still flooded." Kristin gazed out the window on her side of the car. "The ditches on both sides of the road are totally full of rushing water. It's like we're right between two creeks."

"Uh, oh." Dad stopped the car. "Looks like your two creeks come together into a river up ahead. I just hope we can find a good place to turn around or we'll have to back up quite a way."

"Charles!" Mrs. Wright exclaimed, "that car in front of us is driving into the water!" The six Wrights stared as the small white car they'd been following crawled forward into the water rushing across the roadway. The water inched up the sides of the car as it drove ever deeper.

"Whew!" Christopher let out a relieved breath a minute or two later. "Look, she's giving up and is backing out."

But suddenly the white car lurched to the side. The family watched in horror as the current shoved the car off the roadway. They were close enough to see the terror on the woman's face as her car was swept away from the road into the rough waters beyond.

"Call 911!" Mr. Wright was out of the car before Mrs. Wright could grab her cell phone. He rushed along the edge of the swollen waters, splashing through the mud, heedless of his good clothes and leather dress shoes.

The children were silent while their mother gave the necessary information to the 911 operator. "That's right. As far as we could tell, the driver appeared to be the only passenger.…Oh, I see.… Well, thank you." Mother pushed the button to end the call.

"How long till they get here, Mom?" Kristin twisted a lock of hair around her finger.

"All rescue units are out

right now so it may be a little while. Maybe too long." She rushed away to let Dad know. "You children stay in the car. Do you understand?"

"Is that woman going to drown?" Cory unbuckled his seat belt and turned around on his knees to face his brother and sisters in the back seat.

Christopher shrugged, "I don't know. Sometimes people do die in situations like this. Remember that news report we heard earlier?"

Kristin frowned across at her twin. "But she might be fine, Cory. Dad and Mom will do everything they can to help."

"We can, too." Cathy tickled her younger brother's tummy. "Let's pray." The children bowed their heads and Cathy began. Cory was just finishing his prayer when Mom and Dad came back to the car. "So dear God, please take care of that woman. Amen."

Mom opened Kristin's door. "Christopher, Kristin, come here, please, and help us undo the rope that's holding everything on top of the station wagon. Cory, you and Cathy may get out, too, but don't go near the water."

"We're going to try to rescue them," Dad explained as he frantically tugged at the knots securing the family's luggage under the plastic tarp.

"THEM?" Kristin dropped the end of the rope she was working on.

"Yes, there's a small child as well as the driver." Mother struggled with yet another wet and stubborn knot. "For now the car is stuck on its side against a couple of small trees."

"But if we don't get them out of there soon, it may be too late." Dad pulled another section of the rope loose. "The current is strong and may knock the car away. There, that's it." He began to wind the long rope in loops. "We'll tie this securely around a large tree on the bank and around my waist. Then I can safely wade out to the car. You kids can help Mom pull the rope if I need help getting back to the shore. Okay? Let's go!"

Kristin's skin crawled when they got to the bank. The car was tilted on one side and most of it was hidden by the rushing brown water. The woman seemed to be standing with her feet against the driver's side window. Her face looked chalky through the window; she was clutching the child in her arms.

Mr. Wright secured the rope to a sturdy oak and handed his wallet and watch to Cory for safekeeping. After tying the rope around his own waist, he stepped into the torrent of water. Mom held the rope taut, ready to pull Dad back to safety in an instant. Minute by agonizing minute crawled by as Dad worked his way through the flood waters, careful to maintain his footing and balance. Finally he reached the car.

Mom sucked in her breath when the car rocked slightly as Dad helped the woman out the window. Kristin looked away. If the car should come loose, the strong current was sure to hurl it away, along with its passengers—and probably Dad. The rope could never hope to stop that. "Oh, dear God, protect them. Take care of Dad."

She didn't even realize she'd spoken aloud until she heard Mom say, "Amen."

When Kristin got the courage to look up again, Mr. Wright was torturously picking his way back toward the bank. The woman was riding piggy-back; he held the child against his chest. The muscles stood out along his neck. His face looked exhausted and strained as he concentrated on keeping his balance and finding firm footing. Kristin whispered her prayer over and over again.

Dad was out of the deepest water when he slipped! Cathy screamed. Even there, the current immediately swept the three downstream. "PULL!" Mom shouted, tugging at the rope. The children added their combined energy born of fear for Dad.

Finally, the raging waters lost and the three struggled onto the bank. Mom threw her arms around Dad, laughing and crying at the same time. Kristin was surprised to find tears running down her own face.

"Thank you. Thank you. Thank you." The bedraggled woman sat in the mud, holding her small daughter tightly. A sudden sharp crack caught the attention of everyone on the bank. One of the small trees holding the car had given way. In slow motion the white car turned in the water, then jerked loose and moved downstream.

"Oh, thank you." The mother repeated, "How will I ever thank you?"

The Wrights gathered in a family hug. Kristin squeezed her dad and smiled over at the little girl and her mother on the bank. "Thank you, God."

2 Discussion Time

Check understanding of the story and development of personal values.

- Where had the Wright family been when the flooding began?
- Why didn't Dad think they would find their house flooded when they got home?
- What happened to the white car the Wrights were following?
- Why couldn't an emergency rescue unit respond to the call right away?
- How many people were in the car?
- How did Mr. Wright help them?
- What did Kristin do while Mr. Wright was in the flood waters?
- What happened to the car after the people were safe on the bank?

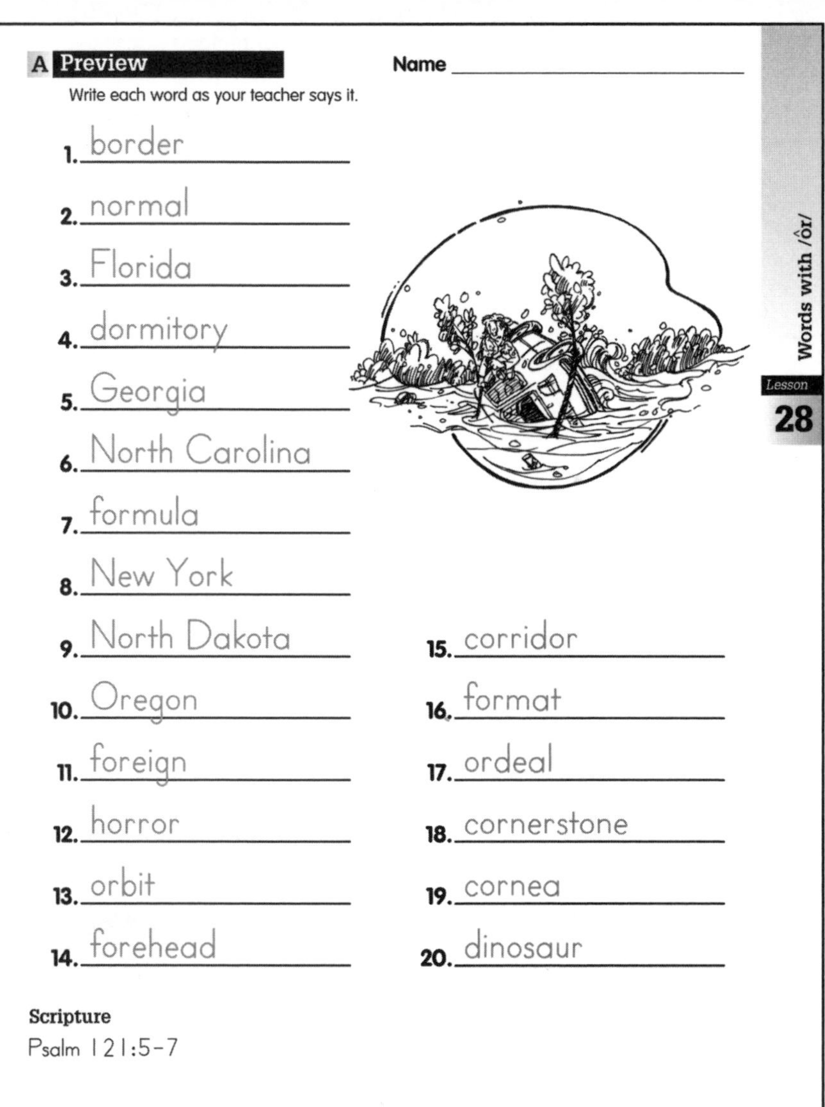

3 Preview

Test for knowledge of the correct spellings of these words.

Customize Your List

On a separate sheet of paper, additional words of your choice may be tested.

I will say each word once, use the word in a sentence, then say the word again. Write the words on the lines in your Worktext.

Correct Immediately!

Let's correct our Preview. I will spell each word out loud. If you spelled a word incorrectly, rewrite it correctly.

Progress Chart

Students may record scores. (Reproducible master provided in Appendix B.)

1.	border	"The state that shares our southern **border** was also hit hard," Dad said.
2.	normal	Rainfall was far above **normal** for this time of year.
3.	Florida	The **Florida** Red Cross was very helpful throughout this disaster.
4.	dormitory	They set up a cafeteria and first aid center in a **dormitory**.
5.	Georgia	The volunteers that came in from **Georgia** were a great help.
6.	North Carolina	**North Carolina** was unable to spare even one crew.
7.	formula	They did send a huge supply of baby **formula** to distribute to mothers.
8.	New York	The flood victims greatly appreciated the donations from **New York**.
9.	North Dakota	**North Dakota** sent two choppers and a huge supply of blankets.
10.	Oregon	An extra disaster relief crew from **Oregon** came in on Monday.
11.	foreign	The little white car was a **foreign** make.
12.	horror	They looked on in **horror** as the car floated through the water.
13.	orbit	Kristin's mind went into momentary **orbit** with fear.
14.	forehead	She could see the veins in Dad's **forehead** as he struggled through the water.
15.	corridor	Kristin wished the water would open into a **corridor** for Dad.
16.	format	Kristin did not worry about the **format** of her prayers!
17.	ordeal	She just begged God to help them through this **ordeal** safely.
18.	cornerstone	She knew God was the **cornerstone** on which she could trust.
19.	cornea	Mom felt sure the little girl had a scratched **cornea**.
20.	dinosaur	Cory handed the little girl his stuffed **dinosaur**.

4 Word Shapes

Help students form a correct image of whole words.

Look at each word and think about its shape. Now, write the word in the correct word Shape Boxes. You may check off each word as you use it.

(In many words, the sound of **/ôr/** is spelled with **or** or **ore**. In a few words the sound of **/ôr/** is spelled **our** or **aur** when it is at the end of a word or comes before a final consonant sound.)

In the word shape boxes, color the letters that spell the sound of **/ôr/** in each word.

Take a minute to memorize...

Psalm 121:5-7

Words with /ôr/ — Lesson 28

B Word Shapes Name ______________

Using the word bank below, write each word in the correct word shape boxes. Next, in the word shape boxes, fill in the boxes containing the letter or letters that spell the sound of **/ôr/** in each word.

1.	forehead	11.	ordeal
2.	North Carolina	12.	orbit
3.	Georgia	13.	corridor
4.	border	14.	dinosaur
5.	horror	15.	Oregon
6.	foreign	16.	format
7.	normal	17.	New York
8.	formula	18.	cornea
9.	cornerstone	19.	North Dakota
10.	Florida	20.	dormitory

Word Bank

border	dinosaur	foreign	horror	North Dakota
cornea	dormitory	format	New York	orbit
cornerstone	Florida	formula	normal	ordeal
corridor	forehead	Georgia	North Carolina	Oregon

176

Answers may vary for duplicate word shapes.

Be Prepared For Fun

Check these supply lists for **Fun Ways to Spell** - presented **Day 2**.
Purchase and/or gather these items ahead of time!

General
- Pencil
- Notebook Paper
- Spelling List

Auditory
- Pencil
- 3 X 5 Cards Cut in half lengthwise (20 per child)
- Spelling List

Visual
- Colored Pencils
- Graph Paper (2 sheets per child)
- Spelling List

Tactile
- Clay
- Spelling List

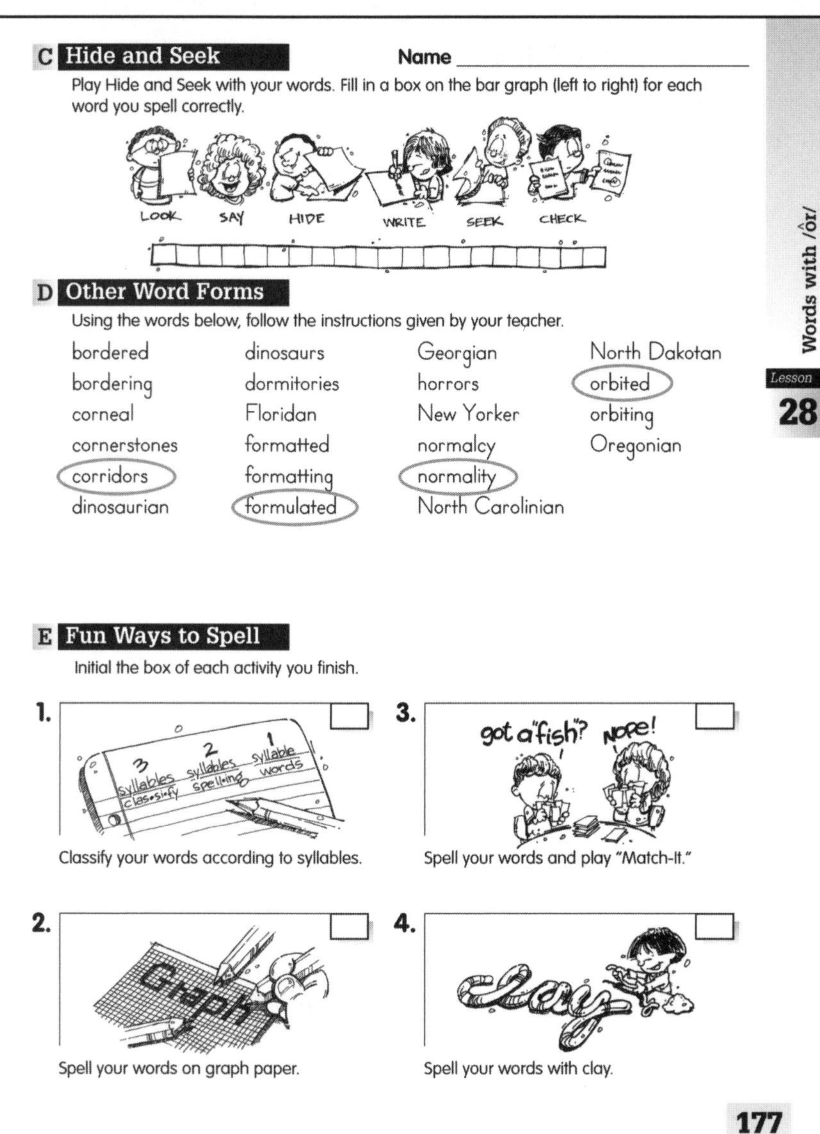

C Hide and Seek Name ____________________

Play Hide and Seek with your words. Fill in a box on the bar graph (left to right) for each word you spell correctly.

D Other Word Forms

Using the words below, follow the instructions given by your teacher.

bordered, bordering, corneal, cornerstones, corridors, dinosaurian, dinosaurs, dormitories, Floridan, formatted, formatting, formulated, Georgian, horrors, New Yorker, normalcy, normality, North Carolinian, North Dakotan, orbited, orbiting, Oregonian

E Fun Ways to Spell

Initial the box of each activity you finish.

1. Classify your words according to syllables.

2. Spell your words on graph paper.

3. Spell your words and play "Match-It."

4. Spell your words with clay.

Words with /ôr/

Lesson 28

177

1 Hide and Seek

Reinforce spelling by using multiple styles of learning.

On a white board, Teacher writes each word — one at a time. **Have students:**

- **Look** at the word.
- **Say** the word out loud.
- **Spell** the word out loud.
- **Hide** (teacher erases word.)
- **Write** the word on paper.
- **Seek** (teacher rewrites word.)
- **Check** spelling. If incorrect, rewrite word correctly.

2 Other Word Forms

This activity is optional. Have students find and circle the Other Word Forms that are most nearly synonyms of the following:

expressed concisely
commonplaceness
circled
hallways

3 Fun Ways to Spell

Four activities are provided. Use one, two, three, or all of the activities. Have students initial the box for each activity they complete.

Options:

- assign activities to students according to their learning styles
- set up the activities in learning centers for the students to do throughout the day
- divide students into four groups and assign one activity per group
- do one activity per day

General

To classify your words according to syllables...
- Write three headings on your paper: One-syllable, Two-syllable, and Three-syllable.
- Write the first word on your list under the proper heading.
- Draw a line through the word to divide it into syllables.
- Do this with each word.

Auditory

To spell your words and play "Match-It"...
- Write each word on a card. Mix your word-cards and a classmate's together. Deal six cards to each player; the rest face down between you. Ask your classmate for a word-card. If the word-card matches, take it and play again. If not, draw from the stack, and it is your classmate's turn. Take turns until all cards are matched.

Visual

To spell your words on graph paper...
- Look at the first word on your list.
- Shade in squares to form the letters of each word.
- Check your spelling.
- Do this with each word.

Tactile

To spell your words with clay...
- Roll pieces of clay into ropes.
- Use the ropes to make the letters of each word.
- Put them in the right order to spell each word.
- Check your spelling.

Lesson 28 | Day 3

Working with Words

Familiarize students with word meaning and usage.

Rhyming Clues

Write the words **climber**, **climb**, **I'm**, and **china** on the board. Have a volunteer underline the two words that rhyme (**climb**, **I'm**). Tell students that, for this exercise, words need to rhyme on at least the last syllable to be considered rhyming words. Explain that students will be matching some of their spelling words to a rhyming word.

Write the spelling word that rhymes with each word below.

The OR's Have It

Each spelling word in this lesson has the **/ôr/** sound. Answer each question with a word from the word bank. You may use a dictionary to help you. Write the word in the blank.

Take a minute to memorize...

Psalm 121:5-7

Words with /ôr/ — Lesson 28

F Working with Words Name ____________

Similar Sounds

Write the spelling word that rhymes with the last syllable of each word below.

1. recorder ___border___
2. horrid ___forehead___
3. formal ___normal___
4. pulpit ___orbit___
5. unreal ___ordeal___
6. stegosaur ___dinosaur or corridor___
7. stork ___New York___
8. explorer ___horror___
9. saxophone ___cornerstone___
10. anymore ___corridor or dinosaur___
11. category ___dormitory___
12. doormat ___format___
13. stepson ___Oregon___
14. South Carolina ___North Carolina___
15. Minnesota ___North Dakota___

The OR's Have It

Answer each question with an **/ôr/** word from the word bank. Write the word in the blank.

1. What /ôr/ word means the arrangement and layout of a publication? ___format___
2. What /ôr/ word is a state which has Raleigh as its capitol? ___North Carolina___
3. What /ôr/ word indicates an intense dislike and abhorrence? ___horror___
4. What /ôr/ word means the part that forms the outer edge of something? ___border___
5. What /ôr/ word is the part of the head between the eyebrows and the hairline? ___forehead___
6. What /ôr/ word is a narrow hallway, often with rooms opening onto it? ___corridor___
7. What /ôr/ word means from another country? ___foreign___
8. What /ôr/ word is the path of a celestial body as it revolves around another body? ___orbit___
9. What /ôr/ word is a state which has Atlanta as its capitol? ___Georgia___

Word Bank

border	dinosaur	foreign	horror	North Dakota
cornea	dormitory	format	New York	orbit
cornerstone	Florida	formula	normal	ordeal
corridor	forehead	Georgia	North Carolina	Oregon

178

G Dictation

Name ______________________

Write each sentence as your teacher dictates. Use correct punctuation.

1. Many people had the horror of cleaning up after the storm.
2. It would take a long time for things to get back to normal.
3. He walked down the corridor of the dormitory where his family had found refuge.

Words with /ôr/

Lesson 28

H Proofreading

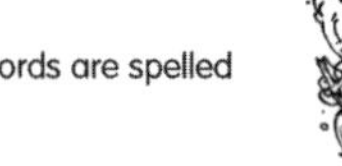

If a word is misspelled, fill in the oval by that word. If all the words are spelled correctly, fill in the oval by **no mistake**.

1. ○ border ● ordeel ○ obvious ○ no mistake
2. ● corneea ○ aimless ○ cirrus ○ no mistake
3. ○ congress ● cornerstoan ○ corridor ○ no mistake
4. ○ dormitory ○ cumulus ● orbitt ○ no mistake
5. ● forhead ○ witness ○ foreign ○ no mistake
6. ● formatt ○ formula ○ closeness ○ no mistake
7. ● Floorida ○ interest ○ virus ○ no mistake
8. ○ radius ● Gorgia ○ fungus ○ no mistake
9. ● horor ○ restless ○ mollusk ○ no mistake
10. ○ normal ○ octopus ● North Carrolina ○ no mistake
11. ● North Dakoata ○ Oregon ○ stillness ○ no mistake
12. ● dinosor ○ New York ○ nucleus ○ no mistake

179

1 Dictation

Reinforce correct spelling by using current and previous words in context.

Listen as I read each sentence and then write it in your Worktext. Remember to use correct capitalization and punctuation. (Slowly read each sentence twice. Sentences are found in the Student Worktext to the left.)

Day 4

2 Proofreading

Familiarize students with standardized test format and reinforce recognition of misspelled words.

Look at each set of words. If a word is misspelled, fill in the oval by that word. If all the words are spelled correctly, fill in the oval by **no mistake**.

3 Hide and Seek

Reinforce correct spelling of current spelling words. Repeat this activity from Day 2.

4 Vocabulary Extension

Have your students complete this activity to strengthen spelling ability and expand vocabulary. The reproducible master is provided in Appendix A as shown on the inset page to the right.

Hide and Seek

Play Hide and Seek with your words. Fill in a bar graph (left to right) for each word you spell correctly.

Vocabulary Extension

Cause and Effect

Write a word from the word bank to complete each sentence.

1. If you are always talking, your parents say that you are forever talking.
2. If you give up winning a race to help someone who has been hurt, you may forfeit the trophy.
3. If you see something that is extremely large, you might call it enormous.
4. If you help a friend dress up for a skit, and she looks completely different, you have helped to transform her.
5. If you visit the zoo and see a giant turtle that lives on land, you are watching a tortoise.
6. If you are learning the art of Japanese paper folding, you are learning origami.
7. If you are lying down instead of standing up, you are horizontal instead of vertical.
8. If a submarine sends out an underwater missile that explodes when it hits a target, it is sending out a torpedo.
9. If nothing unusual happens today, I would consider it an ordinary day.
10. If a violent, whirling column of air appears as a dark, funnel-shaped cloud, it is called a tornado.
11. If we are making small decorations to hang on a Christmas tree, we are making ornaments.
12. If you have won a prize for your science display, you have won an award.

Word Bank

award	forfeit	origami	torpedo
enormous	horizontal	ornament	tortoise
forever	ordinary	tornado	transform

Vocabulary Extension — Lesson 28 — 348

1 Posttest

Test mastery of the spelling words.

I will say the word once, use it in a sentence, then say it again. Write your words on a separate sheet of paper.

Progress Chart
Students may record scores. (Reproducible master in Appendix B.)

Personal Dictionary
Students may add any words they have misspelled to their personal dictionaries for reference when writing. (Cover in Appendix B.)

1. normal	This much rain was not **normal** for this time of year.
2. border	"Even the states that **border** ours have been affected," Dad told them.
3. North Dakota	"Can it be snowing in **North Dakota** and raining here?" wondered Cory.
4. dormitory	The Red Cross set up a relief station in a nearby college **dormitory**.
5. Florida	The **Florida** Red Cross volunteered some of its people to aid in the crisis.
6. Georgia	The state of **Georgia** also sent in volunteers.
7. North Carolina	All the **North Carolina** volunteers were already in the field.
8. Oregon	**Oregon** was able to send one of its disaster relief crews and a chopper.
9. New York	The city of **New York** sent several semitrucks with food items.
10. foreign	The white car in front of them was a small **foreign** car.
11. corridor	It seemed like they had walked through a **corridor** in time.
12. horror	They watched in **horror** as the car lurched and slipped off the road.
13. forehead	Kristin could see the veins bulging on her dad's **forehead**.
14. orbit	Kristin felt her mind go into momentary **orbit** with fear.
15. formula	There seemed to be no sure **formula** for success in this situation.
16. format	Kristin didn't worry about the perfect **format**; she just prayed.
17. cornerstone	Jesus is a solid **cornerstone** on which we can place our trust.
18. cornea	The little girl seemed to have a scratched **cornea**.
19. ordeal	She had had quite an **ordeal** and was very frightened!
20. dinosaur	Cory let her hold his stuffed **dinosaur**.

2 Game

Reinforce spelling skills and provide motivation and interest.

Materials

- game page (from student text)
- pencils (1 per child)
- game word list

Game Word List

Team A		Team B
E4	**virus**	A1
E3	**walrus**	A2
E2	**services**	A3
E1	**border (3)**	A4
D4	**cornea (1)**	B1
D3	**cornerstone (2)**	B2
D2	**corridor (4)**	B3
D1	**dormitory (3)**	B4
C4	**forehead (4)**	C1
C3	**foreign (2)**	C2
C2	**format (1)**	C3
C1	**formula (2)**	C4
B4	**Florida (3)**	D1
B3	**Georgia (1)**	D2
B2	**horror (4)**	D3
B1	**normal (2)**	D4
A4	**North Carolina (1)**	E1
A3	**North Dakota (4)**	E2
A2	**Oregon (3)**	E3
A1	**orbit (3)**	E4

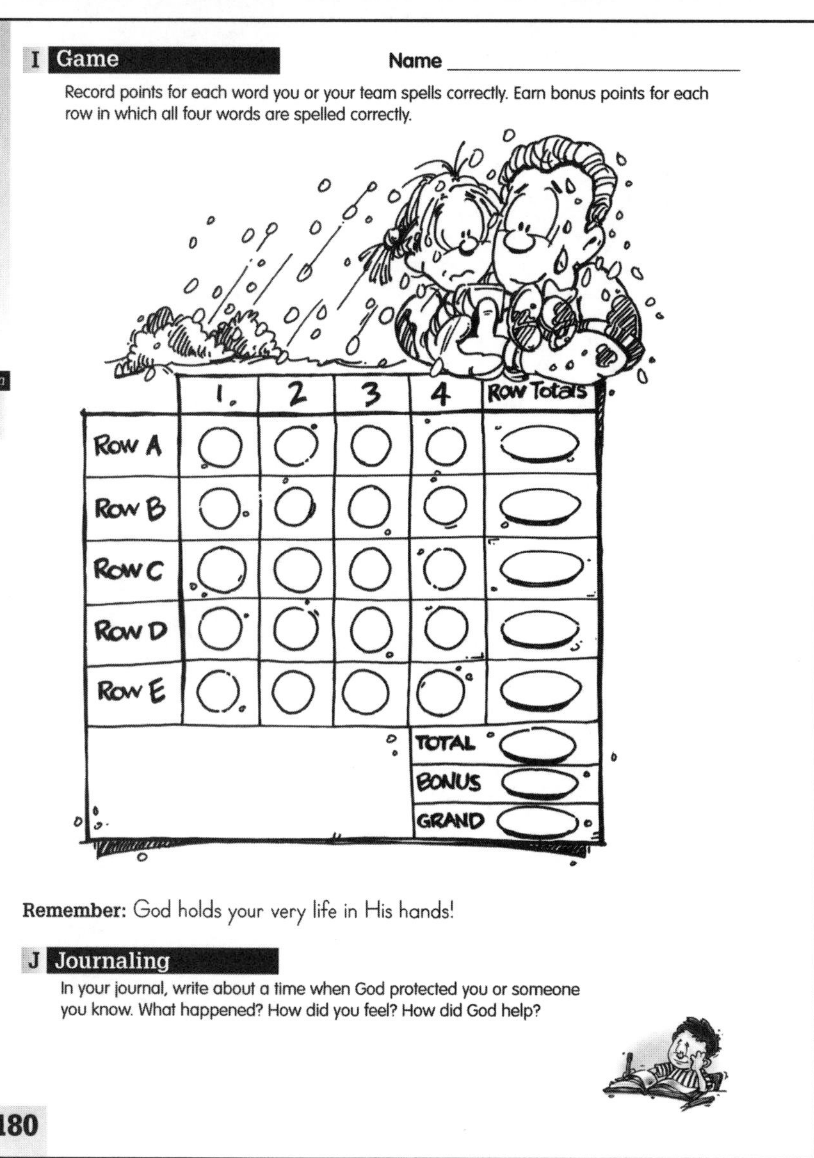

Words with /ôr/ — Lesson 28

I Game Name ____________________

Record points for each word you or your team spells correctly. Earn bonus points for each row in which all four words are spelled correctly.

	1	2	3	4	Row Totals
Row A					
Row B					
Row C					
Row D					
Row E					
				TOTAL	
				BONUS	
				GRAND	

Remember: God holds your very life in His hands!

J Journaling

In your journal, write about a time when God protected you or someone you know. What happened? How did you feel? How did God help?

180

How to Play:

- Divide the class into two teams.
- Have a student from team A choose a square on the grid by indicating the row letter and number.
- Say the word that matches that row letter and number from the team's word list.
- Have the student write the word on the board.
- If correct, have each member of that team record the awarded points (in parentheses by the word) in the circle in that box. If the word is misspelled, have him/her put an **X** in that circle. That square may not be chosen again.
- Repeat this process with the second team.
- When all the words have been spelled by both teams, have each team tally its score. Award a bonus of 5 points for each row in which all four words were spelled correctly.
- Have the teams record their grand totals. The team with the highest score is the winner.

3 Journaling

Provide a meaningful reason for correct spelling through personal writing.

Review the story using discussion leads provided on the following page. Encourage students to apply the Scriptural value in their journaling.

Journaling (continued)

- Has it ever flooded in the community where you live? (Allow time to share experiences.)
- Why did the Wright family turn off the highway on their way home? (They decided to go home the back way in order to go by Rosa's house and see how she was doing.)
- Why did they have to turn around? (The flood waters were across the road.)
- Should you ever drive through flood water crossing a road? (No. It is NEVER safe as it is hard to tell how deep and swift the water is.)
- Where did the Wrights get the rope to tie around Dad's waist? (They used the rope that was holding the plastic cover over the luggage on the top of their station wagon.)
- Why didn't the Wrights wait for a rescue unit to come? (They were afraid the small trees the car was resting against wouldn't hold and the car would be swept away with the people still inside it.)
- Do you think God helped Mr. Wright save the woman and her child? Why or why not? (Yes. Because Kristin and the others were asking God for help and He has promised to help us whenever we ask.)

A good palindrome for a time of drought: Niagara, O roar again!

1 **Literature Connection**
Topic: God is awesome
Theme Text: Psalm 47:12

In a Bug's Eye

When his class studies insects, Tommy understands a bit better how awesome God really is.

"You're making a what?" Tommy Rawson stared suspiciously at the lumpy mass of soggy newspaper on the Simmonses' kitchen table.

"A model of the compound eye," Hubert Thornton Remington III repeated patiently. "Admittedly, it is a somewhat complex project, but well worth the effort. To begin with, I cut up 10 egg cartons into individual 'eyes.' Next, I inverted this large mixing bowl for a mold and covered it with two layers of newspaper. Then, using a glue gun, I attached the individual eyes to each other and to the newspaper covering the bowl. Naturally, the closer together the eyes fit, the better."

"Naturally," Tommy echoed, looking confused.

"Now I'm ripping newspaper into thin strips to be dipped in paper mâche paste. Application of these strips fills in and smoothes out the spaces between the individual eyes." Thorny carefully wove the dripping strip between the egg carton bumps and patted it into place.

"Since drying time may take several days, it's vital to complete this stage of the project today. Otherwise it would not be possible to finish the entire project in a timely fashion before our science project due date." Thorny applied another strip with precision.

"Uh, this stage, huh?" Tommy scooted down in the chair and rested his head on its back.

Thorny dipped another strip in the paste bowl. "After it's completely dry, I'll remove the compound eye from the bowl and apply a layer of paper mâche to the inside, again smoothing out and filling in spaces between the individual eyes. Once it's completely dry, I'll cover both surfaces with metallic blue paint. The finishing touch will be hot-gluing 120 mirrors on the concave side of the compound eye, one to the bottom of each individual eye. By looking into the compound eye, one can get a small indication of what an insect might see, although dragonflies have as many as 30,000 such lenses in each eye."

"Sounds good." Tommy picked up a stack of one-inch-round mirrors. "I wish our projects didn't have to be about insects, though. I can't think of anything to do. Insects are just so boring. If we were studying animals, or magnetism, or the ocean, or the human body, or anything else, it would be more fun!"

"What's black and red, hairy, with six legs and a long stinger?" Thorny paused to look across the table at his friend.

Tommy shrugged, "I don't know—what is it?"

Thorny shrugged too. "I don't know either, but there's one crawling on your shoulder."

"What? Where?" Tommy jumped up and craned his neck, trying to see his own shoulders.

"Gotcha!" Thorny chuckled and applied another strip of newspaper. "Then there's the one about the centipede complaining to his physician: 'Doc, when my feet hurt, I hurt all over.'"

"Awww." Tommy dropped back into the chair he'd vacated so swiftly. "No fair. Besides, you can't convince me that insects are interesting with a joke about a centipede. Even I know that real insects have six legs."

"Touché!" Thorny scratched his face with his thumb, leaving a blob of paper mâche paste on his chin. "How about 'Time flies like an arrow, but fruit flies like a banana.'"

Tommy groaned and clutched at his belly as if he were sick.

"Well, do you know what has four wheels and flies?" Thorny persevered.

"No, no! I don't know and I don't think I want to know, either."

"As you wish." Thorny shrugged and proceeded in silence for a few seconds till Tommy couldn't stand it anymore.

"All right, I've gotta know. Tell me." Tommy braced himself against the table with his hands as if he were about to receive a blow.

"A garbage truck, naturally." Thorny laughed as Tommy flung his head back as if he'd been punched.

"AWWW! I should have seen that one coming."

"Seriously, there are things about the insect world that are fascinating." Thorny took a step back to look for uneven places on his project.

"Fascinating to you or to someone like me?" Tommy propped one elbow on the table and rested his chin in that hand.

"Well, do you find it fascinating that mosquitoes of genus Malaya steal honeydew from the jaws of worker ants? Or that comparative studies show that humans have 792 distinct muscles, whereas grasshoppers have 900, and caterpillars may have as many as 4,000? Did you know an average man can pull about 0.86 times his own weight, but a leaf beetle (Donacia) can pull 42.7 times its own weight?"

Thorny kept peppering Tommy with facts. "There are more than a million species of insects—90,000 in North America. Insects outnumber all other animals four to one. Or what about the fact that 12 states have chosen the honeybee for the official state insect?"

Thorny paused for breath and Tommy just stared at him. "Or have you ever wondered how far insects can fly? Painted ladies migrating from Africa to England travel more than 3,000 miles. Perhaps it might interest you that the longest insect is

Story (continued)

13 inches long, a tropical stick insect; the heaviest is the goliath beetle in Africa, weighing in at one-quarter pound, and the largest butterfly is the Queen Alexandra's birdwing from New Guinea (an endangered species), with a wingspan of 11 inches. Truly remarkable is the owlet moth of tropical America, with a wingspan of 18 inches; the smallest butterfly is the blue from Africa, which has only a one-half inch wingspan. Would you care to hear more?"

Tommy grinned sheepishly, "Uh, sure. I guess these guys are pretty interesting. So what's the tiniest insect?"

"Well, the smallest insects are fairy flies, which are insects that parasitize or lay their eggs inside other insects' eggs. Fairy flies are only one-fifth of a millimeter long." Thorny began cleaning up the mess on the table.

"So, tell me more," Tommy prompted after a moment of silence.

Thorny held his hands out, a gesture of innocence. "Just remember, you asked for it! Tabanid flies, related to horse flies, have been clocked at 90 miles per hour. Honeybees fly at about seven miles per hour, and have to beat their wings 190 times per second to do it. But that's nothing. The 'no-see-ums,' or very tiny midges, beat their hairy wings 1,046 times per second. Cockroaches are the fastest runners—almost a foot per second, or a little more than one mile per hour. Fleas jump 200 times their body length. In human terms, that would be like a human clearing a 70-story building. And finally, one of my personal favorites, the queen of a termite colony may lay 6,000 to 7,000 eggs per day, and may live 15 to 50 years. Does that baffle the mind or what?"

"Awesome." Tommy leaned back in his chair, one hand to his head. "So maybe this field trip to the Bug Bowl will be pretty interesting after all."

A few days later Tommy discovered that "interesting" was only one of many words that would apply to the Bug Bowl. "Revolting" came to mind when he saw the Chinese- and Cajun-style fried mealworms, and "gag" seemed appropriate when he spotted the Grasshopper Fritters. Tommy took one look, and promptly decided that if he wanted to eat something crunchy, he'd stick to carrot sticks!

By making learning fun, kids discovered facts about insects and their value to people and the environment. The students got to hold three-inch-long Madagascar hissing cockroaches and three-horned rhinoceros beetles the size of hamsters. Displays showed the commercial uses for bugs, including an array of products based on honey and beeswax. The class saw red worms worth $17 a pound to be used for composting—which with worms can be done indoors in small containers—and fish bait. Cricket-spitting contests and building their own butterfly hats were also fun.

But the cockroach races were the greatest. Huge two-tone Madagascar hissing roaches took an average of 35 seconds to complete one lap around a coffee-table-sized plastic track. However, the American cockroaches proved to be winners, and as crowds of children cheered for their favorites, the speedsters routinely raced around the track in 15 seconds.

By the end of the afternoon, the whole class was excited about insects and eager to complete their projects.

The day they turned their projects in to Mr. Canfield, the students went around the room admiring each one. Everybody wanted to get the bug's eye view with Thorny's compound eye. And they were amazed at the results of Tommy's project.

"Wow, Tommy I had no idea the Scriptures mentioned bugs so much!" Tony leaned over the counter where Tommy's project was displayed. "Hey, Laney!" he called, "can you believe grasshoppers are mentioned in the Scriptures 10 times and locusts 28 times?"

Thorny admired the listing of insects mentioned in the Scriptures that Tommy had designed. "So, Tommy, you did come up with a project about insects. An impressive one at that."

"Thanks." Tommy grinned. "But you gave me the idea."

"Excuse me?" Thorny's eyebrows shot up under his sandy-colored bangs.

"When I thought about all those incredible insect facts you were spouting the other day, I thought about what an awesome God designed them all. I decided to see what the Scriptures said about them." Tommy hadn't noticed Mr. Canfield standing behind him till the teacher spoke.

"Well, boys, of all these excellent projects, both of yours are designed to help us see things from a little different perspective." He turned to walk away and spoke back over his shoulder. "See what I mean? Think about it!"

2 Discussion Time

Check understanding of the story and development of personal values.

- What was Thorny making for his science project?
- Can you remember any of the interesting facts Thorny told Tommy about insects?
- Where did the class go on their field trip?
- What kinds of races were held at the Bug Bowl?
- What other types of things did the students do at the Bug Bowl?
- What project did Tommy end up doing?

A Preview

Name ____________________

Write each word as your teacher says it.

1. compound
2. account
3. crouch
4. snout
5. scowl
6. browse
7. whereabouts
8. announcer
9. boundary
10. counterfeit
11. coward
12. willpower
13. clout
14. drought
15. foul
16. mountains
17. pronounce
18. South Carolina
19. South Dakota
20. scoundrel

Welcome to the BUG BOWL!

Words with /ou/

Lesson 29

Scripture

Psalm 47:1,2

3 Preview

Test for knowledge of the correct spellings of these words.

Customize Your List
On a separate sheet of paper, additional words of your choice may be tested.

I will say each word once, use the word in a sentence, then say the word again. Write the words on the lines in your Worktext.

Correct Immediately!
Let's correct our Preview. I will spell each word out loud. If you spelled a word incorrectly, rewrite it correctly.

Progress Chart
Students may record scores. (Reproducible master provided in Appendix B.)

1.	compound	"Your project of the **compound** eye of an insect is awesome!" said Tommy.
2.	account	Thorny was careful to take into **account** every detail in his design.
3.	crouch	Thorny started to **crouch** down and add another strip of paper mache.
4.	snout	"Hey, you've got more paste on your **snout** than the bug's eye," teased Tommy.
5.	scowl	Thorny stood back up with a pretend **scowl** and wiped his face.
6.	browse	Mr. Canfield encouraged his students to **browse** through the Bug Bowl.
7.	whereabouts	"Do you know the **whereabouts** of the butterfly exhibits?" he asked.
8.	announcer	The event **announcer** pointed to the south side of the convention hall.
9.	boundary	The clear plastic walls provided a **boundary** or barrier for the racing roaches.
10.	counterfeit	It would be impossible to **counterfeit** God's creation.
11.	coward	"Don't be a **coward**, have a fried grasshopper," encouraged Daniel.
12.	willpower	"I'll have to summon all my **willpower**, but I believe I'll pass," smiled Setsuko.
13.	clout	One of the three-horned rhinoceros beetles delivered a swift **clout** to another.
14.	drought	"Wow! This bug can survive a long **drought**," marveled the boys.
15.	foul	"What is that **foul** stench?" questioned Thorny.
16.	mountains	"A toasted worm from the **mountains** of Colorado," noted Tommy.
17.	pronounce	"I can't even begin to **pronounce** its name though," he said.
18.	South Carolina	"Tommy, did you see this cool insect from the **South Carolina** forest?"
19.	South Dakota	"Here's a neat one from **South Dakota**, too," continued Christopher.
20.	scoundrel	"This big guy is an ugly **scoundrel**," commented Laney.

Lesson 29 | Day 1

4 Word Shapes

Help students form a correct image of whole words.

Look at each word and think about its shape. Now, write the word in the correct word Shape Boxes. You may check off each word as you use it.

(The diphthong **/ou/** is spelled **ow** or **ou**.)

In the word shape boxes, color the letters that spell the sound of **/ou/** in each word.

Lesson 29 — Words with /ou/

B Word Shapes Name ______________

Using the word bank below, write each word in the correct word shape boxes. Next, in the word shape boxes, fill in the boxes containing the letter or letters that spell the sound of **/ou/** in each word.

1. crouch
2. snout
3. account
4. browse
5. foul
6. pronounce
7. boundary
8. drought
9. South Carolina
10. clout
11. compound
12. scowl
13. mountains
14. announcer
15. whereabouts
16. coward
17. willpower
18. South Dakota
19. counterfeit
20. scoundrel

Word Bank

account	clout	crouch	pronounce	South Carolina
announcer	compound	drought	scoundrel	South Dakota
boundary	counterfeit	foul	scowl	whereabouts
browse	coward	mountains	snout	willpower

182

Answers may vary for duplicate word shapes.

Take a minute to memorize...

Psalm 47:1,2

Be Prepared For Fun

Check these supply lists for **Fun Ways to Spell** - presented **Day 2**. Purchase and/or gather these items ahead of time!

General
- Pencil
- Graph Paper (1 sheet per child)
- Spelling List

Auditory
- Pencil
- Notebook Paper
- Spelling List

Visual
- Colored Pencils
- Alphabet Stencils
- Paper

Tactile
- Uncooked Rice
- Art Paper (1 sheet per child)
- Glue
- Spelling List

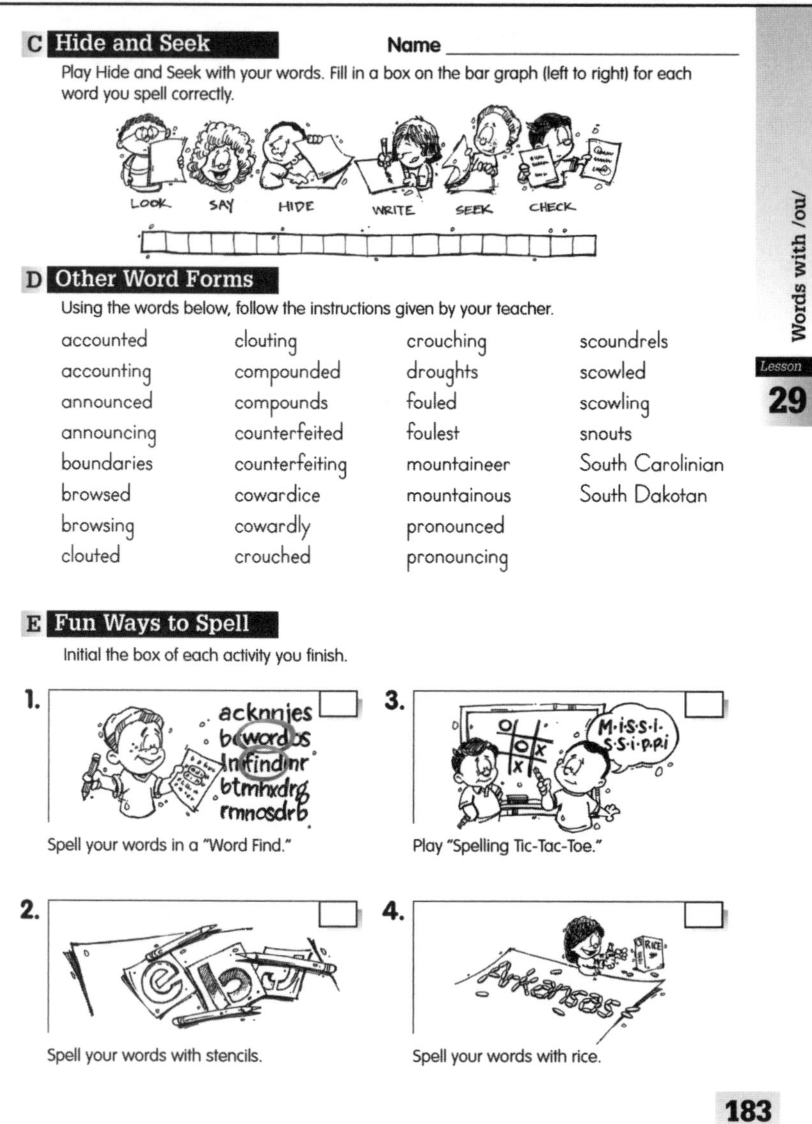

C Hide and Seek Name ______________________

Play Hide and Seek with your words. Fill in a box on the bar graph (left to right) for each word you spell correctly.

D Other Word Forms

Using the words below, follow the instructions given by your teacher.

accounted	clouting	crouching	scoundrels
accounting	compounded	droughts	scowled
announced	compounds	fouled	scowling
announcing	counterfeited	foulest	snouts
boundaries	counterfeiting	mountaineer	South Carolinian
browsed	cowardice	mountainous	South Dakotan
browsing	cowardly	pronounced	
clouted	crouched	pronouncing	

E Fun Ways to Spell

Initial the box of each activity you finish.

1.

Spell your words in a "Word Find."

2.

Spell your words with stencils.

3.

Play "Spelling Tic-Tac-Toe."

4.

Spell your words with rice.

Words with /ou/

Lesson 29

183

1 Hide and Seek

Reinforce spelling by using multiple styles of learning.

On a white board, Teacher writes each word — one at a time. **Have students:**

- **Look** at the word.
- **Say** the word out loud.
- **Spell** the word out loud.
- **Hide** (teacher erases word.)
- **Write** the word on paper.
- **Seek** (teacher rewrites word.)
- **Check** spelling. If incorrect, rewrite word correctly.

2 Other Word Forms

This activity is optional. Have students write original sentences using these Other Word Forms:

accounted
cowardly
clouting
scowled

3 Fun Ways to Spell

Four activities are provided. Use one, two, three, or all of the activities. Have students initial the box for each activity they complete.

Options:

- assign activities to students according to their learning styles
- set up the activities in learning centers for the students to do throughout the day
- divide students into four groups and assign one activity per group
- do one activity per day

General

To spell your words in a "Word Find"...

- Arrange your words on a piece of graph paper.
- Put one letter of each word in a square.
- Words may be written backwards, forwards, or diagonally.
- Outline your puzzle.
- Hide your words by filling in all the spaces inside the puzzle with random letters.
- Trade grids with a classmate and find the hidden words.

Auditory

To play "Spelling Tic-Tac-Toe"...

- Draw a Tic-Tac-Toe grid.
- Ask a classmate to read a word from the list.
- Spell the word aloud.
- If the word is spelled correctly, place your mark on the grid.
- Take turns with your classmate.

Visual

To spell your words with stencils...

- Look at the first letter of a word on your list.
- Place the stencil for the proper letter over your paper.
- Shade inside the stencil.
- Choose the proper stencil for the next letter of the word and shade it in next to the first letter.
- Finish the word in this way.
- Do this with each word.

Tactile

To spell your words with rice...

- Choose a word from your spelling list.
- Shape the letters of your word with rice.
- Glue the rice to art paper.
- Do this for each word on your list.

Working with Words

Familiarize students with word meaning and usage.

Scrambled Words

Write the letters **adeefhor** on the board. Have a student unscramble the letters to make the word **forehead**.

Unscramble each spelling word. Write the word correctly on the line. Remember to use capital letters where they are needed.

Word Clues

Use your word bank to help you match the spelling words to the clues. Some of the clues are synonyms, words that have the same meaning as the spelling word. You may use a dictionary or thesaurus to help you.

Take a minute to memorize...

Psalm 47:1,2

Lesson 29 | Day 3

Words with /ou/ — Lesson 29

F Working with Words Name ____________

Scrambled Words

Unscramble each word. Write the unscrambled word on the line. Use capital letters and spaces where they are needed.

1. abdnoruy boundary
2. acdorw coward
3. acennnoru announcer
4. beorsw browse
5. cacnout account
6. cchoru crouch
7. cdmnoopu compound
8. ceefinorttu counterfeit
9. dghortu drought
10. tolcu clout
11. tosuh alaricon South Carolina
12. husot atodka South Dakota
13. abeehorstuw whereabouts
14. aimnnostu mountains
15. cdelnorsu scoundrel
16. cennoopru pronounce
17. closw scowl
18. eilloprww willpower
19. flou foul
20. nostu snout

Word Clues

Match the spelling words to the clues. You may use a dictionary or thesaurus to help you.

1. strength of will willpower
2. location, site whereabouts
3. nose, proboscis snout
4. frown, grimace scowl
5. rascal, rogue scoundrel
6. enunciate, say pronounce
7. disgusting, offensive foul
8. stoop, bend crouch
9. high country mountains
10. a fearful person coward
11. false, fraudulent counterfeit
12. mixture, blend compound
13. influence, pull clout
14. leaf through, glance browse
15. border, confines boundary
16. commentator, reporter announcer
17. lack of moisture drought

Word Bank

account	clout	crouch	pronounce	South Carolina
announcer	compound	drought	scoundrel	South Dakota
boundary	counterfeit	foul	scowl	whereabouts
browse	coward	mountains	snout	willpower

G Dictation

Name ______________________

Write each sentence as your teacher dictates. Use correct punctuation.

1. Tommy scowled as he thought about his science homework.
2. Thorny gave an account of creepy crawly details as he worked on the compound eye.
3. The announcer told about the drought in the mountains.

Words with /ou/

Lesson 29

H Proofreading

If a word is misspelled, fill in the oval by that word. If all the words are spelled correctly, fill in the oval by **no mistake**.

1. ● wherabouts ○ formula ○ Florida ○ no mistake
2. ○ forehead ○ foreign ● browze ○ no mistake
3. ○ cornea ● boundery ○ cornerstone ○ no mistake
4. ● acount ○ corridor ○ dormitory ○ no mistake
5. ● counterfit ○ orbit ○ New York ○ no mistake
6. ○ South Dakota ○ border ● cowerd ○ no mistake
7. ○ drought ● fouwl ○ North Carolina ○ no mistake
8. ○ South Carolina ● mountins ○ horror ○ no mistake
9. ● anouncer ○ pronounce ○ Georgia ○ no mistake
10. ○ compound ● wilpower ○ normal ○ no mistake
11. ● scoundril ○ crouch ○ format ○ no mistake
12. ○ scowl ○ snout ● cloutt ○ no mistake

185

Dictation

Reinforce correct spelling by using current and previous words in context.

Listen as I read each sentence and then write it in your Worktext. Remember to use correct capitalization and punctuation. (Slowly read each sentence twice. Sentences are found in the Student Worktext to the left.)

2

Proofreading

Familiarize students with standardized test format and reinforce recognition of misspelled words.

Look at each set of words. If a word is misspelled, fill in the oval by that word. If all the words are spelled correctly, fill in the oval by **no mistake**.

Day 4

Lesson 29

3 Hide and Seek

Reinforce correct spelling of current spelling words. Repeat this activity from Day 2.

4 Vocabulary Extension

Have your students complete this activity to strengthen spelling ability and expand vocabulary. The reproducible master is provided in Appendix A as shown on the inset page to the right.

1 Posttest

Test mastery of the spelling words.

I will say the word once, use it in a sentence, then say it again. Write your words on a separate sheet of paper.

Progress Chart

Students may record scores. (Reproducible master in Appendix B.)

Personal Dictionary

Students may add any words they have misspelled to their personal dictionaries for reference when writing. (Cover in Appendix B.)

Hide and Seek

Play Hide and Seek with your words. Fill in a bar graph (left to right) for each word you spell correctly.

Vocabulary Extension

Fill in the Blanks

Choose a word from the word bank that best fits each sentence clue.

1. There are more girls in class than boys; girls outnumber boys two to one.
2. My parents give me some money each week. This is my allowance.
3. After the farmer cut his hay, countless birds flocked from all around to get hay seeds.
4. We bought our winter clothes on sale. Mom was glad to get a discount on them.
5. I love the huge hills around us. I always wanted to live in a mountainous area.
6. When Julie learned to play the clarinet, she was taught how to hold her mouth on the mouthpiece to get a clear tone.
7. I know you are upset, but you do not need to make such an outburst in the middle of class.
8. Before we write our three-point paragraph, we have to make an outline of the points we will cover.
9. When Heather writes a story, she uses so many pronouns that nobody can tell who is doing what.
10. We drove home by a different route because men were working on a culvert under one of the roads.
11. Jesus traveled to many outlying villages and towns, preaching and healing the people.
12. His mom says embarrassing things in public. She is much too outspoken.

Word Bank

allowance	mountainous	outline	outspoken
countless	mouthpiece	outlying	pronoun
discount	outburst	outnumber	route

Vocabulary Extension — Lesson 29 — 349

1. compound — "I am making a **compound** eye," explained Thorny.
2. snout — "Hey, you've got paste on your **snout**," he laughed.
3. scowl — Thorny gave Tommy a pretend **scowl**.
4. account — Thorny's attention to detail would **account** for his terrific project!
5. whereabouts — Thorny was interested to find the **whereabouts** of the hissing roaches.
6. boundary — "It seems the creativity of the Creator knew no **boundary**!" he commented.
7. browse — It was exciting and interesting to **browse** through the Bug Bowl.
8. counterfeit — No one can **counterfeit** God's magnificent handiwork.
9. crouch — A flea is so small you can't see it **crouch** down before it hops.
10. clout — "Can this insect deliver a fierce **clout** with its hind legs?" wondered Tommy.
11. South Carolina — "Tommy, this insect inhabits the forests of **South Carolina**."
12. drought — "This amazing insect can survive a long **drought**," he noted.
13. foul — "What is that **foul** smell?" asked Tommy.
14. mountains — "A delectable stir-fried worm! This one is found in the **mountains**."
15. South Dakota — "Yeah, it says here that they live mainly in **South Dakota**!" said Tommy.
16. pronounce — Daniel got tickled as he tried to **pronounce** one of the names.
17. coward — "Don't be a **coward**; munch on a meal worm," teased Tommy.
18. willpower — "I'll exercise **willpower** and skip the meal worms," joked Tony.
19. scoundrel — "This three-horned rhinoceros beetle looks like a **scoundrel**," said Beth.
20. announcer — An **announcer** called for everyone to gather around the platform.

Words with /ou/

Lesson 29

I Game Name ______________________________

Walk along with Tommy and observe some amazing insects. Move one space for each word you or your team spells correctly.

Remember: The Lord is God of all and King of everything!

J Journaling

In your journal, make a list of as many different kinds of insects as you can think of, then write riddles for some of them to share with your classmates.

186

2 Game

Reinforce spelling skills and provide motivation and interest.

Materials

- game page (from student text)
- game pieces (1 per child)
- game word list

Game Word List

1. **ordeal (4)**
2. **dinosaur (2)**
3. **New York (1)**
4. **whereabouts**
5. **browse**
6. **boundary**
7. **account**
8. **counterfeit**
9. **coward**
10. **crouch**
11. **clout**
12. **drought**
13. **foul**
14. **mountains**
15. **announcer**
16. **pronounce**
17. **compound**
18. **willpower**
19. **South Carolina**
20. **South Dakota**

How to Play:

- Divide the class into two teams.
- Have each student place his/her game piece on Start.
- Have a student from team A go to the board.
- Say the spelling word.
- Have the student write the word on the board.
- If correct, instruct each member of team A to move his/her game piece forward one space.
- Alternate between teams A and B.
- The team to reach the exit of the Bug Bowl first is the winner.
- **Small Group Option**: Students may play this game without teacher direction in small groups of two or more.

3 Journaling

Provide a meaningful reason for correct spelling through personal writing.

Review the story using discussion leads provided on the following page. Encourage students to apply the Scriptural value in their journaling.

Journaling (continued)

- What was Thorny using to make his model of the compound eye? (Ten egg cartons cut apart, newspaper, paper mache, and mirrors.)
- Why was Tommy having a hard time thinking of a science project to do? (The projects had to be about insects and Tommy thought insects were boring.)
- How did Tommy get the idea for the project he did? (From listening to Thorny talk about so many interesting facts about insects.)
- Have you been to an insect fair of some kind similar to the Bug Bowl which Tommy's class attended?
- Of the insect facts that Thorny told Tommy, which did you find most interesting? (Allow time for discussion.)
- How many insect species are there? (Over a million.)
- Imagine trying to create a million different kinds of insects—besides all the animals, plants, fish, birds, and other things God made? Isn't He an awesome God?
- Can you solve this riddle? While a colony is my home, Sometimes far away from it I roam, With other insects of my kind, I search for any food that I can find, My strong jaws lift loads others can't, Have you guessed by now that I'm an _____?
- You will write some riddles of your own in your journal today.

Add-on!

en
sent
resent
present
presentation
representation
representational
nonrepresentational
nonrepresentationalism

1 Literature Connection

Topic: Dishonesty and lying
Psalm 24:3, 4

No Luck for Liars

Katelynn lies about having her homework completed.

Katelynn turned the dead bolt in the red door and slid the safety chain into place before she headed toward the kitchen counter to check the list.

"He adds more to this list every day!" The dark-haired girl marched over to the window by the front door and yanked the blinds closed. The sunlit room darkened to match her mood.

She read the words at the top of the list her father had written. "Monday—Vacuum bedrooms. Empty dishwasher. Read for at least 20 minutes. Do homework. Write thank-you letter to grandparents."

Katelynn carried the list back to her bedroom and set it on the dresser. Her lucky money packet leaning against the mirror caught her attention. She picked it up and sat down on the edge of her bed. Her mother had given it to her at Chinese New Year. Katelynn fingered the gold characters on the red envelope that wished her good luck in the New Year. She took out the four crisp five-dollar bills from the envelope. "Yee (ee), uhr (arr), sahn (san), suh (zee)," she counted.

She remembered her mom's excitement and anticipation about the holiday of her homeland. February seemed like such a long time ago. Mom had been feeling good then. She'd prepared for weeks beforehand. First she cleaned the apartment from top to bottom. Then she'd decorated by stringing red firecrackers around the front window and hanging red good-luck banners on the front door. She bought special holiday foods, such as tangerines. She even purchased new clothes for everyone in the family.

"It's much more important than the New Year here," Mom had explained on one of their shopping trips. "In China it's the biggest celebration of the year and lasts 15 days. It's the beginning of spring—time for a fresh start. The color red is used everywhere to symbolize joy and happiness. There's a spectacular procession in the heart of the city. It was my favorite holiday when I was a little girl growing up in Hong Kong. Hong Kong was a British Colony then, you know," Mom had smiled, remembering. She didn't do that much any more.

A smile now spread across Katelynn's face as she thought of how delighted Mom had been when she found a kumquat tree. The fruit looked like a miniature orange but tasted a little sour. Mom had explained that its Chinese name is a play on the word lucky.

Mom had fixed a sumptuous feast for New Year's Day. The meal began with tea. It included a vegetable pancake dish called Fu Young and Lin Guo, a sticky rice cake, which was Katelynn's favorite. The family had practiced using chopsticks and everyone laughed a lot. Mom was the only one who could get much rice to her mouth.

Even though Dad was Asian and Hatasaki was a name from the Orient, he wasn't sure from where or when his ancestors had immigrated. He'd grown up in California and had never left the continental United States. He was the worst with chopsticks. Big hunks of sticky rice kept landing in his lap. He'd finally asked for a fork. The meal had ended with tea. Mom was the only one that really liked tea, but they all drank it. Mom had been so happy.

The celebration had ended with the Festival of Lights. Mom's parents had come from their home in Burtonsville, Maryland, to be with them. "It all seems so long ago," thought Katelynn.

She returned the red envelope to her dresser and picked up the list. "I'd better get started. Mom will be home soon." She emptied the dishwasher and got the vacuuming done before she started to work on the thank-you letter. She'd just sat down at the kitchen table with her stationary when she heard her mom come to the door. She got up to unfasten the chain.

"Ni Hao ma (nee HOW mah)?" Mom shut the door and walked over to the kitchen counter.

Katelynn looked over at her mother without answering. "Mom rarely speaks the Mandarin language she learned in Hong Kong, along with English. She must really be tired," she thought.

Katelynn finally spoke. "How am I? Fine, I guess." She went back to her letter writing.

"Have you done your reading and finished your homework?" Mom asked as she walked back toward the bedroom. She didn't even look at her daughter.

Katelynn didn't answer. She wanted to scream what she was thinking, "I've emptied the dishwasher. I've vacuumed the bedrooms. I'm writing a thank-you letter—but did you notice any of that? No! You'll probably go back to your room and sleep until Dad gets home and starts supper. You might come help then, Mom, but I doubt it," Katelynn sputtered to herself.

"Did you finish everything on the list?" Dad asked when he came in later.

Katelynn felt the anger rising in her again as she thought about what he'd said. "No 'Thank-you for emptying the dishwasher,' or, 'The apartment looks nice—thanks for vacuuming,' or maybe, 'I'm glad you got that letter written. I'll mail it tomorrow. Supper smells good.'"

Katelynn busied herself taking the muffins out of the oven and just nodded her head. She wasn't done with her homework. She still had her reading to do too; but somehow she didn't care. She didn't care

Story Continued

about the lie she had just told her father. She didn't care that her dad was tired. She was angry that her mom couldn't get herself together to fix supper and act like a normal mother. Katelynn shut the door to her bedroom. She felt guilty about the lies she'd just told, but her feelings of anger were stronger. She didn't come out of her room until her sister called her to supper.

Father continued to leave a list of things for Katelynn to do every day, and Katelynn got in the habit of doing only the things he could easily check up on. He asked now and then if she had homework or what she'd done at school. It got easier to shake her head no when he asked about the homework—even if it was a lie. She didn't tell him much about the unit on electricity they were working on at school, either. Whether she was reading or not didn't come up again until one night when she was in her room working a jigsaw puzzle on the floor.

"So what book have you been reading, Katelynn?" Dad knelt down beside her and picked up a puzzle piece. "Is it something about electricity? You seem to be enjoying that unit at school."

Katelynn shook her head no, hoping he'd drop the subject or leave her room.

Dad looked at the lid of the puzzle box, then studied the piece he held in his hand. "So what's it about?"

"What's what about?" To avoid her father's eyes, Katelynn looked at the picture of Thomas Edison on the box.

"The book, Katelynn. The one you read every day when you get home. What's the name of it?" Dad tapped a puzzle piece into place.

Katelynn tried to put her puzzle piece in a couple of different places, but she was distracted and tried to put the silver piece in her hand on the brown hair of Thomas Edison.

Dad gently took the puzzle piece from her fingers and put it in the correct spot for her. "Katelynn, what's wrong? Why don't you want to talk about the book you've been reading. You usually love to read."

Katelynn looked down at the puzzle, hoping the water forming in her eyes wouldn't roll down her cheeks. When the pieces blurred, she knew it was hopeless. "Dad, I'm not reading any book. I didn't do my homework, either. I'm sorry I've been lying to you. It's just that I'm at school all day and then you leave me all this stuff to do when I get home. Mom doesn't fix lunches for us anymore or wash clothes. Jennifer's even been doing the ironing."

Dad found a place for a couple more puzzle pieces before he said anything. "Katelynn, I'm glad you've decided to tell me the truth, but being truthful is a constant action, not a one-time event. I have a feeling you've been lying about this for a while. Haven't you?"

Katelynn just nodded. Dad continued, "Trust is the reward for being truthful. I can't trust you now. Whenever you tell me something, I'll wonder if it's really true or if you're lying again."

Dad put his arm around his daughter. "I'm sorry about your mom. I'm worried about her, too. She's been talking to some people at work, and she's made an appointment to see a counselor. Maybe he'll be able to help her. I feel bad you've had so much to do lately. You can skip the reading for a while, but you do need to keep up with your homework. What are you doing in math now?"

Katelynn got her math book from her backpack. She looked her dad in the eye as she handed him the book. "It's the last chapter." He took the book, sat back down on the floor, and leaned against the bed.

When he got up to leave, he paused at the door and set the math book on her dresser. He picked up the lucky money envelope and turned it over slowly in his hands. He rubbed the gold Chinese characters with his thumb. "I like the Chinese New Year, but there's a lot more to a new start than luck, Katelynn. It has more to do with the choices you make. You don't have to wait until the new year for a fresh start. Shall we ask the Lord to give you a new, truthful start—beginning right now?"

2 Discussion Time

Check understanding of the story and development of personal values.

- What was Katelynn supposed to do when she got home from school every day?
- What jobs are you responsible for at home?
- How did Katelynn feel about all the jobs she had to do?
- What did Katelynn's mom do when she got home?
- What did Katelynn's dad ask her when he arrived?
- What did Katelynn want her parents to notice?
- Why did Katelynn lie to her dad?
- What did Katelynn's dad tell her when he finally caught her lying?

A Test-Words Name ______________________

Write each spelling word on the line as your teacher says it.

1. aimless
2. interest
3. normal
4. virus
5. burden
6. clerk
7. clever
8. forehead
9. energy
10. deliver
11. scowl
12. decimal
13. crumple
14. entitle
15. browse
16. compound

Review Lesson 30

B Test-Sentences

Write the sentences on the lines below, correcting each misspelled word, as well as all capitalization and punctuation errors. Two words are misspelled in each sentence.

wherebouts in orregon do you live she asked

1. "Whereabouts in Oregon do you live?" she asked.

down the museum coriddor he saw a huge dinosuar

2. Down the museum corridor, he saw a huge dinosaur.

in the state of florrida cittrus groves are numerous

3. In the state of Florida, citrus groves are numerous.

they had a bundel of crisp green counterfit bills

4. They had a bundle of crisp, green counterfeit bills.

187

4 Test-Sentences

Reinforce recognizing misspelled words.

Read each sentence carefully. Write the sentences on the lines in your Worktext. There are two misspelled words in each sentence. Correct each misspelled word, as well as all capitalization and punctuation errors.

Take a minute to memorize...

Psalm 24:3,4

3 Test-Words

Test for knowledge of the correct spellings of these words.

Say: I will say each word once, use the word in a sentence, then say the word again. Write the words on the lines in your Worktext.

1. aimless — Katelynn's mom was not cheerful and energetic, but **aimless** and tired.
2. interest — She seemed to have lost **interest** in life in general.
3. normal — "What's wrong with mom? She isn't acting **normal**," Katelynn thought.
4. virus — "Does she have a **virus** or something?" wondered Katelynn.
5. burden — Everything seemed like a huge **burden** to her mother these days.
6. clerk — At the grocery, Mrs. Hatasaki didn't even speak to or smile at the **clerk**.
7. clever — She usually had a **clever** wit and great sense of humor.
8. forehead — Mrs. Hatasaki just rubbed her **forehead** and headed for her bedroom.
9. energy — "I just don't have any **energy**," she mumbled as she lay down.
10. delivery — She didn't even get up to open the package when a special **delivery** came.
11. scowl — Katelynn looked down at her math homework with a dark **scowl**.
12. decimal — She didn't care where the **decimal** needed to go!
13. crumple — She wanted to **crumple** up the page and throw it in the trash.
14. entitle — "Being tired does not **entitle** Mom to ignore all of us!" she said angrily.
15. browse — Mrs. Hatasaki used to really like to **browse** at the craft fairs.
16. compound — Instead of helping her, more sleep seemed to **compound** the problem.

1 Test-Dictation

Reinforce correct spelling by using current and previous words in context.

Listen as I read each sentence, then write it in your worktext. Remember to use correct capitalization and punctuation. (Slowly read each sentence twice. Sentences are found in the student text to the right. The words **courage**, **snout**, **cornea**, and **octopus** are found in this unit.)

2 Test-Proofreading

Familiarize students with standardized test format and reinforce recognizing misspelled words.

Look at each set of words. If a word is misspelled, fill in the oval by that word. If all the words are spelled correctly, fill in the oval by **no mistake**.

Review Lesson 30

C Test-Dictation

Name ______________________

Write each sentence as your teacher dictates. Use correct punctuation.

1. The beautiful horse showed spirit and courage.
2. The dog pushed his snout deep into the grass.
3. The cornea of your eye should not be scratched.
4. An octopus, when afraid, can move very quickly.

D Test-Proofreading

If a word is misspelled, fill in the oval by that word. If all the words are spelled correctly, fill in the oval by **no mistake**.

1. ● fungis ○ aimless ○ interest ○ no mistake
2. ○ normal ○ virus ● boundery ○ no mistake
3. ○ burden ○ clerk ● misille ○ no mistake
4. ● nuclues ○ clever ○ forehead ○ no mistake
5. ○ energy ○ deliver ● forren ○ no mistake
6. ○ scowl ○ decimal ○ radius ● no mistake
7. ● wittness ○ crumple ○ formula ○ no mistake
8. ○ West Virginia ○ entitle ○ browse ● no mistake
9. ○ congress ○ fragile ○ crystal ● no mistake
10. ● cloute ○ double ○ ordeal ○ no mistake
11. ○ molar ○ compound ○ closeness ● no mistake
12. ○ mumble ● horrer ○ chapter ○ no mistake

188

E Test-Table Name ____________________

If a word is misspelled, fill in the space on the grid.

crouch	multiple	restliss	sollar
New Jersey	adverb	services	cirus
centrall	Newyork	South Dekota	North Dekota
forrmat	North Carolina	coward	charter

Review

Lesson 30

F Writing Assessment

Make a list of things your parents do for you every day. Make another list of things they do on a weekly basis. Start a third list for things they do once or twice a year for you. You may add things to the list as you think of them. Make three more lists of things you do for your parents—daily, weekly, and yearly.

Scripture

Psalm 24:3,4

189

A rubric for scoring is provided in Appendix B.

An ambigram is a word or words that can be read in more than one way or from more than a single vantage point. The classic ambigram is a 180-degree symmetric rotation, which means it reads the same upside down and right side up: MOM=WOW, NO=ON

Test-Table

Test mastery of words in this unit.

If a word is misspelled, fill in the space on the grid.

2

Writing Assessment

Assess student's spelling, grammar, and composition skills through personal writing.

- How do you feel when it's hard to tell the truth but you choose to do it?
- Why did Katelynn lie to her dad? (She was angry about all the work he was asking her to do around the house and hurt that he didn't thank her.)
- What could Katelynn's parents have done to help her feel better even though she was working hard? (Acknowledged and thanked her for all the work she was doing so well.)
- Tell about the jobs you do at home.
- Do you think Katelynn did more jobs than you are required to do?
- Do you think it was okay for Katelynn to lie since her parents were insensitive to her needs because of their own problems? (Talk about Exodus 20:16. Does the ninth commandment make any exceptions?)

Day 3

Review 30

1 Test-Sentences

Reinforce recognizing misspelled words.

Read each sentence carefully. Write the sentences on the lines in your Worktext, correcting each misspelled word, as well as all capitalization and punctuation errors.

Review Lesson 30

G Test-Sentences Name ______________

Write the sentences on the lines below. Correct each misspelled word, as well as all capitalization and punctuation errors. Two words are misspelled in each sentence.

while on vacation in south caralina I saw a wallrus

1. While on vacation in South Carolina, I saw a walrus.

Jesus taught us by exampel, how to be humbel.

2. Jesus taught us, by example, how to be humble.

the decaying molusk on the beach had a fuol smell

3. The decaying mollusk on the beach had a foul smell.

a journy through the deserrt can cost you your life!

4. A journey through the desert can cost you your life!

H Test-Words

Write each spelling word on the line as your teacher says it.

1. formula
2. fragile
3. crystal
4. double
5. ordeal
6. closeness
7. mumble
8. chapter
9. border
10. obvious
11. error
12. major
13. version
14. miracle
15. mountains
16. willpower

190

2 Test-Words

Test for knowledge of the correct spellings of these words.

I will say the word once, use the word in a sentence, then say the word again. Write the word on the lines in your Worktext.

1. formula	"I wish there was magic **formula** to get Mom back to normal!" said Katelynn.
2. fragile	She picked up a **fragile** bowl out of the dish drain.
3. crystal	She was so mad she didn't care if she broke her mom's nice **crystal** bowl.
4. double	"We'll just have to **double** up on chores till she's better," Jennifer said.
5. ordeal	"I hate this whole **ordeal**!" Katelynn complained to herself.
6. closeness	She missed the **closeness** she usually had with her mom.
7. mumble	When her dad asked about her homework, Katelynn would **mumble** a reply.
8. chapter	"Which **chapter** are you reading in your book about castles?" he asked.
9. border	Katelynn looked guilty as she fiddled with the **border** of the puzzle.
10. obvious	By the look on her face, it was **obvious** to her dad that she had been lying.
11. error	Katelynn knew lying was not just an **error** in judgment; it was a sin!
12. major	"I consider your lying a **major** breach of trust," said Mr. Hatasaki.
13. version	"I don't want your **version** of the truth; I want the truth!"
14. miracle	"We need the Lord to work a **miracle** for Mom," Dad said.
15. mountains	"He can move **mountains** and help you and Mom, too!" he encouraged.
16. willpower	Don't trust in your own **willpower**; trust in God for help!

I Test-Editing

Name ______________________

If a word is spelled correctly, fill in the oval under **Correct**. If the word is misspelled, fill in the oval under **Incorrect**, and spell the word correctly on the blank.

	Correct	Incorrect	
1. Goergia	○	●	Georgia
2. dormitory	●	○	
3. particle	●	○	
4. scoundrel	●	○	
5. acount	○	●	account
6. reckliss	○	●	reckless
7. dribble	●	○	
8. burial	●	○	
9. angle	●	○	
10. mingel	○	●	mingle
11. stillness	●	○	
12. drought	●	○	
13. riddle	●	○	
14. pronownce	○	●	pronounce
15. anchor	●	○	
16. deserve	●	○	
17. cornerstone	●	○	
18. anouncer	○	●	announcer
19. cummulus	○	●	cumulus
20. orbitt	○	●	orbit

Review Lesson 30

191

3 Test-Editing

Reinforce recognizing and correcting misspelled words.

4 Action Game

Reinforce spelling skills and provide motivation and interest.

Materials

- two balls
- word list on certificate at end of unit

SPELLING ZIGZAG

Divide the class into two teams. Each team forms two lines which stand about eight feet apart facing each other. Choose a student to monitor each team. The first player on each team holds a ball. Call out the first spelling word to be reviewed. The first player on each team says the first letter of the word and tosses the ball to the player across from him. That player says the second letter of the word and tosses the ball to the player next in line on the other side. The pattern continues until the word has been spelled, the monitor for each team checking the team's spelling. The team to spell the word correctly first gets a point. The team with the most points wins!

1 Game

Reinforce spelling skills and provide motivation and interest.

Materials

- game page (from student text)
- colored pencils (1 per child)
- game word list

Game Word List

Check off each word lightly in pencil as it is used.

The Dragons

1. **scoundrel**
2. **scowl**
3. **snout**
4. **fungus**
5. **boundary**
6. **missile**
7. **nucleus**
8. **foreign**
9. **radius**

The Firecrackers

1. **witness**
2. **West Virginia**
3. **congress**
4. **clout**
5. **molar**
6. **horror**
7. **crouch**
8. **New Jersey**
9. **central**

The Chinese Lanterns

1. **format**
2. **multiple**
3. **adverb**
4. **New York**
5. **North Carolina**
6. **restless**
7. **services**
8. **South Dakota**
9. **coward**

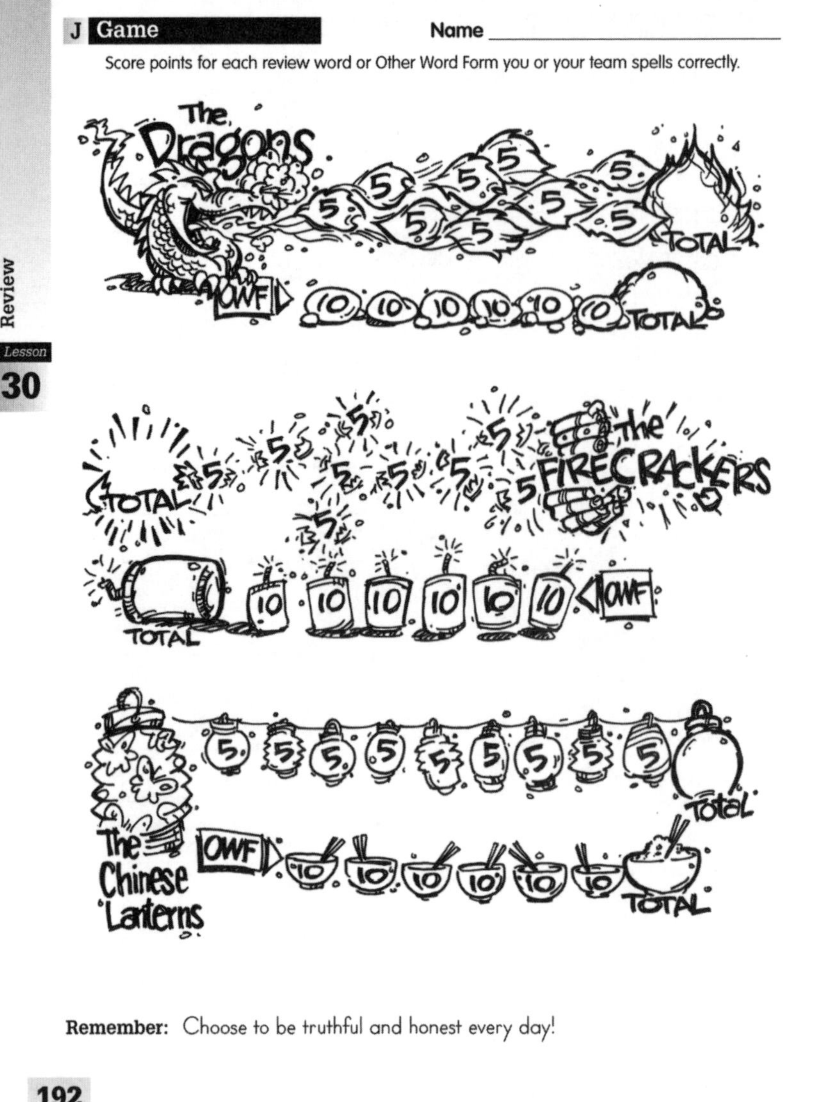

Review Lesson 30

J Game Name ____________________

Score points for each review word or Other Word Form you or your team spells correctly.

Remember: Choose to be truthful and honest every day!

192

How to Play:

- Divide the class into three teams. Name one team **The Dragons**, one **The Firecrackers**, and one **The Chinese Lanterns**. (Option: You may wish to seat students in groups of three, each student from a different team. They should share one game page.)
- Have a student from the first team go to the board.
- Say the spelling word.
- Have the student write the word on the board.
- If the word is spelled correctly, have each team member color a point symbol by his/her team name. If the word is misspelled, have him/her put an **X** through one point symbol. That word may not be given again.
- Repeat this process with the second team and then the third.
- When the words from all three lists have been used, the team with the most points is the winner.
- Play another round using Other Word Forms.

Date ____________________

This certificate is awarded to

____

for completing fun activities using the following spelling words!

angle	adverb	aimless	border	account
bundle	anchor	cirrus	cornea	announcer
burial	burden	citrus	cornerstone	boundary
central	chapter	closeness	corridor	browse
crumple	charter	congress	dinosaur	clout
crystal	clerk	cumulus	dormitory	compound
decimal	clever	fungus	Florida	counterfeit
double	courage	interest	forehead	coward
dribble	deliver	mollusk	foreign	crouch
entitle	desert	nucleus	format	drought
example	deserve	obvious	formula	foul
fragile	energy	octopus	Georgia	mountains
humble	error	radius	horror	pronounce
mingle	journey	reckless	New York	scoundrel
miracle	major	restless	normal	scowl
missile	molar	services	North Carolina	snout
multiple	New Jersey	stillness	North Dakota	South Carolina
mumble	solar	virus	orbit	South Dakota
particle	version	walrus	ordeal	whereabouts
riddle	West Virginia	witness	Oregon	willpower

2 Certificate

Provide an opportunity for parents or guardians to encourage and assess their child's progress.

Fill in today's date and your name on your certificate.

Take a minute to memorize...

Psalm 24:3,4

3 Letter

Provide the parent or guardian with the spelling word lists for the next unit.

Give your parents or guardian this letter that lists your spelling words for the next unit. Put it where you will remember to practice the words together.

Dear Parent,

We are about to begin the last spelling unit of the year containing only one lesson. A set of twenty words will be studied next week. All the words will be reviewed the following week. Values based on the Scripture listed below will be taught.

Lesson 31

Connecticut	knock
doorknob	knuckle
flight	nighttime
highland	plight
Illinois	Rhode Island
khaki	rhyme
knack	sigh
kneel	slight
knitting	wharves
knives	wreck

Psalm 33:4,5

Trivia and Trust

Laney questions why God would want Rachel to move.

Rachel tore open her yellow bag of M&M®'s and looked down at the magazine in her lap. "True or false? 'Names for Crayola® crayon colors come from official government books.'" Rachel turned to Laney and dumped some of the brightly colored candy in her friend's open hand.

"False," Beth guessed. "I don't think Razzmatazz comes from a book the government wrote."

Rachel swallowed the chocolate morsels in her mouth before she pronounced judgment. "That's right!" She beamed as she surveyed her classmates' faces. "Okay, 'How many crayons are made in the Crayola® factory every day?'"

A thick cloud suddenly hid the sun. Laney picked the last orange M&M® from her hand and popped it into her mouth. There weren't ever enough M&M®s to satisfy her! She stood up to leave the group still sitting around the lone pine tree on the playground. She shivered as she put her jacket back on. It was cold now that the sun's warming rays had disappeared.

"One-hundred thousand," guessed Rosa.

"A million," Heather took a bite of her chocolate cupcake.

"Guess again. No one's close." Rachel rubbed her hands together in anticipation.

"On a normal production day I'd say somewhere in the proximity of five million, which is about one for each human being in Chicago, Houston and Seattle combined, or roughly two billion a year." Thorny looked very serious as he joined the game. "Hypothetically speaking, in two years enough are made that when laid end to end they'd reach the moon. Of course the possibilities of proving that hypothesis other than mathematically are remote. There is the problem of gravity in our atmosphere and the lack of it in space to consider...." Thorny's voice trailed off as he started pondering his own thoughts.

Laney raised her eyebrows and frowned as she looked at her best friend, Rachel.

"He's right—about the five million part at least," Rachel announced with a happy face. "How did you know that?" Thorny didn't respond, so Rachel continued. "You must've read this. Okay. Here's the next one."

"'According to Crayola® surveys, what is the all-time favorite crayon color?'"

"I say Tickle-Me-Pink or Macaroni-and-Cheese." Kristin guessed.

"Very good, Kristin. Those are Crayola® color names, but not the ones we are looking for! Do I have another guess?" Rachel finished the juice in her box with a noisy slurp.

Thorny was still considering the possibilities of a trail of crayons to the moon and didn't attempt to answer.

"Blue!" Beth yelled out her favorite color.

Rosa tried hers, "Red!"

"Blue it is! Beth is right! With two correct answers, you are a winner!" Rachel picked up the magazine again. "One final question. 'How many shades of wrappers are Crayola® crayons wrapped in?'"

Laney ran her fingers through her short hair and rolled her eyes. "Who cares?" She picked up her lunch bag and headed toward the trash can by the back door of the school.

"National Geographic World® magazine reported 18!" Thorny announced as Laney passed him. "And did you know that in three months there are enough Crayola® crayons made to circle the earth at the equator about one and one-eighth times?"

"Are you sure?" Laney taunted.

Rachel stood and pointed toward Thorny. "Who agrees with this gentleman in the blue T-shirt?" Everyone raised their hands. Hubert Thorton Remington III was always right.

"If your hand is raised you are..." Rachel paused for effect, "...right! And that concludes round one of Knowlton Knows Trivia Game! Beth and Thorny are tied with two correct answers each!"

Laney turned and looked over her shoulder at her friend's animated face. She watched her show the cover of World magazine to Thorny. She was too far away now to hear what Rachel was saying, but she could see Thorny laugh and open the magazine. Everyone else gathered around to look at the pictures.

"I'm going to miss Rachel," Laney thought as she hurried on toward the trash can. "Montana is so far away the Jacobsons might as well be moving to the other side of the earth—or the moon for that matter. I can't believe she's leaving in just three weeks. But it's true!"

Laney walked slowly to the other side of the playground and leaned against the warm bricks of the school. She wiped her eyes with the back of her hand. Sometimes she wanted to spend every waking moment with Rachel—making sure they did as many things together as they could before she moved. Other times she just wished the Jacobson family would hurry up and get out of town so the hurt in her heart could begin to heal. "How could they know God wanted them at Shadow Creek Ranch in Montana?" She thought.

"What's wrong?" Rachel joined Laney against the sun-warmed wall a few minutes later. "Why'd you leave?"

Story (continued)

"You're the one who's leaving," Laney snapped. "And you don't seem too unhappy about it."

"I will really miss all the people here, Laney—especially you. But I think God wants our family in Montana. I'm not exactly sure what it will be like living out there, but God loves us and I guess I trust Him to plan only good things."

"What about me? You said we'd be best friends forever. If I can't trust you, how I can trust God?"

"God sent someone to buy Father's business and our house, and I've told you how much they need us at Shadow Creek Ranch. With more guests coming, they need me to help with the horses. It's a lot of work keeping a barn clean and 10 horses groomed."

"But I need you right here."

"Do you believe five million Crayola® crayons are made every day?"

"Yeah, that's what Thorny said. But what do five million crayons have to do with you leaving?"

"Don't you think the Bible is more reliable than World magazine?" Rachel handed Laney three orange M&M®s.

"What do you mean?"

"I mean that if you trust Thorny when he tells us World magazine says five million crayons are made every day, you should trust God when He says He loves you and will take care of you."

The bell rang. The two girls lined up at the door with the rest of Mr. Canfield's class. Laney ate the orange M&M®s in silence. The sun peaked out from behind the gigantic cloud and the bright rays began warming the playground again. She took the magazine from Rachel's hand and thumbed her way through it, looking for the Crayola® article.

"'When was the first box of colored wax crayons in the Untied States made, and how much did they cost?'" Laney smiled.

Rachel rapidly replied, "1903. A nickel for a box of eight."

"You're right! And you are a winner with two correct answers in the ongoing Knowlton Knows Trivia Game." Rachel laughed and felt the tension leaving her body.

"You're right about God, too, Rache," Laney said quietly. "And I'm glad you're my best friend even if you're moving. Now, 'What retired colors are placed in the Crayola® Hall of Fame?'"

2 Discussion Time

Check understanding of the story and development of personal values.

- Talk about a best friend you have had who no longer lives near you.
- How did it feel when you could no longer see him or her on a regular basis?
- How does Laney feel about her best friend Rachel moving to Montana?
- What game is Rachel leading out in during lunch hour?
- Who are some of the kids participating in the game?
- Why doesn't Laney play?
- What does Rachel tell Laney about trusting and relying on God?

A Preview Name ____________

Write each word as your teacher says it.

1. Connecticut
2. flight
3. nighttime
4. sigh
5. plight
6. Illinois
7. wharves
8. slight
9. Rhode Island
10. khaki
11. doorknob
12. kneel
13. knock
14. knives
15. knuckle
16. rhyme
17. knack
18. knitting
19. wreck
20. highland

Scripture
Psalm 33:4,5

Silent Letters — Lesson 31

195

3 Preview

Test for knowledge of the correct spellings of these words.

Customize Your List

On a separate sheet of paper, additional words of your choice may be tested.

I will say each word once, use the word in a sentence, then say the word again. Write the words on the lines in your Worktext.

Correct Immediately!

Let's correct our Preview. I will spell each word out loud. If you spelled a word incorrectly, rewrite it correctly.

Progress Chart

Students may record scores. (Reproducible master provided in Appendix B.)

Lesson 31 | Day 1

1.	Connecticut	**Connecticut** borders Laney's home state of New York.
2.	flight	She remembered the **flight** she made with her mom to visit Knowlton Elementary.
3.	nighttime	"It was **nighttime** when we arrived," she reflected.
4.	sigh	She let out a **sigh** as she remembered how nervous she was.
5.	plight	Laney felt God did not understand her **plight** of losing her best friend.
6.	Illinois	"Isn't there a ranch in **Illinois**? That's a lot closer!" she pleaded.
7.	wharves	Laney enjoyed looking at a painting of New England **wharves.**
8.	slight	She liked the look of a **slight** storm brewing in the sky.
9.	Rhode Island	Her mom had purchased the painting at a gallery in **Rhode Island.**
10.	khaki	She put on her **khaki** walking shorts and went out to play with Wicker.
11.	doorknob	Wicker bounded toward her when he heard her hand on the **doorknob.**
12.	kneel	She didn't want to **kneel** in the grass, so she sat on the lawn chair.
13.	knock	Mr. Canfield gave a quick **knock** on the podium to get the class's attention.
14.	knives	"Who can bring spreading **knives** to our class party?" he asked.
15.	knuckle	Rachel hit her **knuckle** on her desk as she tried to raise her hand.
16.	rhyme	"I want each of you to write a short, humorous **rhyme** to share at the party."
17.	knack	"You have real **knack** for cheering me up," Laney told Rachel.
18.	knitting	"I guess I can to take up **knitting** if you move," she told her.
19.	wreck	"I'm sure you won't be the **wreck** you think you will," said Rachel.
20.	highland	"The **highland** areas on and around the ranch are gorgeous," said Rachel.

Word Shapes

Help students form a correct image of whole words.

Say: Look at each word and think about its shape. Now, write the word in the correct word Shape Boxes. You may check off each word as you use it.

(A silent letter occurs when two letters spell the sound of only one letter or when one or two letters stand for a completely silent sound.)

Say: In the word shape boxes, fill in the boxes containing the silent consonant or consonants in each word.

Take a minute to memorize...

Psalm 33:4,5

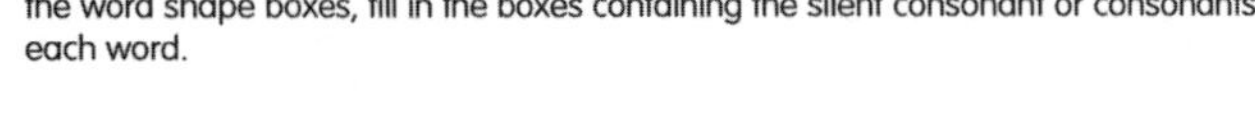

B Word Shapes Name ______________________

Using the word bank below, write each word in the correct word shape boxes. Next, in the word shape boxes, fill in the boxes containing the silent consonant or consonants in each word.

Silent Letters — Lesson 31

1. khaki
2. kneel
3. knock
4. plight
5. rhyme
6. Illinois
7. slight
8. wharves
9. flight
10. wreck
11. knack
12. knitting
13. knives
14. highland
15.  Rhode Island
16. knuckle
17. doorknob
18. sigh
19. Connecticut
20. nighttime

Word Bank

Connecticut	Illinois	knitting	nighttime	sigh
doorknob	khaki	knives	plight	slight
flight	knack	knock	Rhode Island	wharves
highland	kneel	knuckle	rhyme	wreck

196

Answers may vary for duplicate word shapes.

Be Prepared For Fun

Check these supply lists for **Fun Ways to Spell** - presented **Day 2**. Purchase and/or gather these items ahead of time!

General
- Pencil
- Graph Paper (1 sheet per child)
- Spelling List

Auditory
- Voice Recorder
- Spelling List

Visual
- American Sign Language reproducible master (provided in Appendix B)
- Spelling List

Tactile
- Soccer Ball, Basketball, Tennis Ball, or 4-Square Ball
- Spelling List

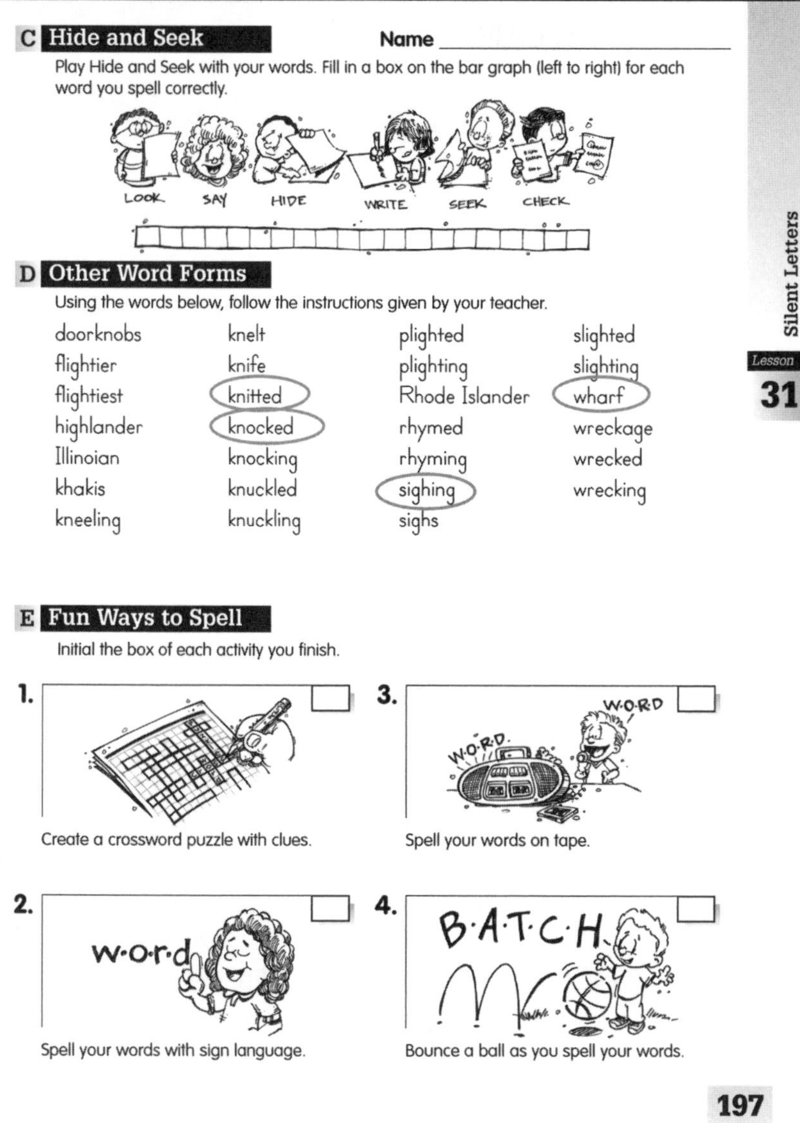

C Hide and Seek Name ____________

Play Hide and Seek with your words. Fill in a box on the bar graph (left to right) for each word you spell correctly.

D Other Word Forms

Using the words below, follow the instructions given by your teacher.

doorknobs	knelt	plighted	slighted
flightier	knife	plighting	slighting
flightiest	knitted	Rhode Islander	wharf
highlander	knocked	rhymed	wreckage
Illinoian	knocking	rhyming	wrecked
khakis	knuckled	sighing	wrecking
kneeling	knuckling	sighs	

E Fun Ways to Spell

Initial the box of each activity you finish.

1. Create a crossword puzzle with clues.

3. Spell your words on tape.

2. Spell your words with sign language.

4. Bounce a ball as you spell your words.

Silent Letters

Lesson 31

197

Day 2 Lesson 31

1 Hide and Seek

Reinforce spelling by using multiple styles of learning.

On a white board, Teacher writes each word — one at a time. **Have students:**

- **Look** at the word.
- **Say** the word out loud.
- **Spell** the word out loud.
- **Hide** (teacher erases word.)
- **Write** the word on paper.
- **Seek** (teacher rewrites word.)
- **Check** spelling. If incorrect, rewrite word correctly.

2 Other Word Forms

This activity is optional. Have students find and circle the Other Word Forms that are most nearly synonyms of the following:

pier
rapped
intertwined
sighing

3 Fun Ways to Spell

Four activities are provided. Use one, two, three, or all of the activities. Have students initial the box for each activity they complete.

Options:

- assign activities to students according to their learning styles
- set up the activities in learning centers for the students to do throughout the day
- divide students into four groups and assign one activity per group
- do one activity per day

General

To create a crossword puzzle...
- Use a pencil to arrange your words on graph paper.
- Overlap words where letters are shared.
- Don't create any new words.
- Outline each word with a marker and number it.
- Write a clue for each word.
- Erase your words.
- Trade with a classmate and work each other's puzzles.

Auditory

To spell your words using a voice recorder...
- Record yourself as you say and spell each word on your spelling list.
- Listen to your recording and check your spelling.

Visual

To spell your words with sign language...
- Have a classmate read a spelling word to you from the list.
- Spell the word using the American Sign Language alphabet.
- Do this with each word on your list.

Tactile

To bounce a ball as you spell your words...
- Look at the first word on your list.
- Bounce the ball as you say each letter of the word aloud.
- Do this with each word on your list.

Working with Words

Familiarize students with word meaning and usage.

Hidden Words

Explain that the spelling words for this week are hidden in the puzzle. After finding each word, the student should write the word under the correct heading.

Use the word bank to help you find each of the words in the puzzle. Words may go across, down, or diagonally. Circle, then write the words.

Take a minute to memorize...

Psalm 33:4,5

F Working with Words Name ______________________

Hidden Words

Use the word bank to help you find each of the words in the puzzle. Words may go across, down, or diagonally. Circle and write the words.

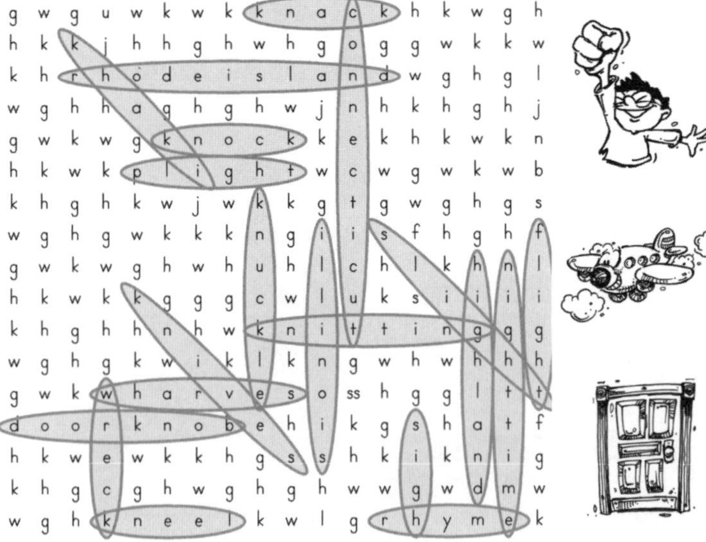

Across

1. doorknob
2. knack
3. kneel
4. knitting
5. knock
6. plight
7. Rhode Island
8. rhyme
9. wharves

Down

10. Connecticut
11. flight
12. highland
13. Illinois
14. knuckle
15. nighttime
16. sigh
17. wreck

Diagonal

18. khaki
19. knives
20. slight

Word Bank

Connecticut	Illinois	knitting	nighttime	sigh
doorknob	khaki	knives	plight	slight
flight	knack	knock	Rhode Island	wharves
highland	kneel	knuckle	rhyme	wreck

G Dictation Name ______

Write each sentence as your teacher dictates. Use correct punctuation.

1. Laney felt lonely as she let out a huge sigh.

2. Thorny cut his knuckle with one of the knives he was playing with.

3. She caught her khaki pants on the chair when she tried to kneel.

Silent Letters

Lesson 31

H Proofreading

If a word is misspelled, fill in the oval by that word. If all the words are spelled correctly, fill in the oval by **no mistake**.

1. ○ wreck ● Conneticut ○ foul ○ no mistake
2. ○ scowl ○ flight ○ crouch ● no mistake
3. ○ highland ○ boundary ● nightime ○ no mistake
4. ○ plight ○ sigh ○ mountains ● no mistake
5. ○ slight ● kaki ○ clout ○ no mistake
6. ● rhime ○ Rhode Island ○ browse ○ no mistake
7. ○ doorknob ○ knack ○ snout ● no mistake
8. ○ South Dakota ○ kneel ○ coward ● no mistake
9. ● kniting ○ knives ○ willpower ○ no mistake
10. ○ knock ○ knuckle ○ compound ● no mistake
11. ○ announcer ● Ilinois ○ drought ○ no mistake
12. ● warves ○ whereabouts ○ pronounce ○ no mistake

199

1 Dictation

Reinforce correct spelling by using current and previous words in context.

Say: Listen as I read each sentence and then write it in your Worktext. Remember to use correct capitalization and punctuation. (Slowly read each sentence twice. Sentences are found in the Student Worktext to the left.)

Day 4

Lesson 31

2 Proofreading

Familiarize students with standardized test format and reinforce recognition of misspelled words.

Say: Look at each set of words. If a word is misspelled, fill in the oval by that word. If all the words are spelled correctly, fill in the oval by **no mistake**.

Day 4 / Day 5

Lesson 31

3 Hide and Seek

Reinforce correct spelling of current spelling words. Repeat this activity from Day 2.

4 Vocabulary Extension

Have your students complete this activity to strengthen spelling ability and expand vocabulary. The reproducible master is provided in Appendix A as shown on the inset page to the right.

1 Posttest

Test mastery of the spelling words.

I will say the word once, use it in a sentence, then say it again. Write your words on a separate sheet of paper.

Progress Chart

Students may record scores. (Reproducible master in Appendix B.)

Personal Dictionary

Students may add any words they have misspelled to their personal dictionaries for reference when writing. (Cover in Appendix B.)

Vocabulary Extension

Lesson 31

Hide and Seek

Play Hide and Seek with your words. Fill in a bar graph (left to right) for each word you spell correctly.

Vocabulary Extension

Crossword Puzzle

Use the clues below to complete the puzzle.

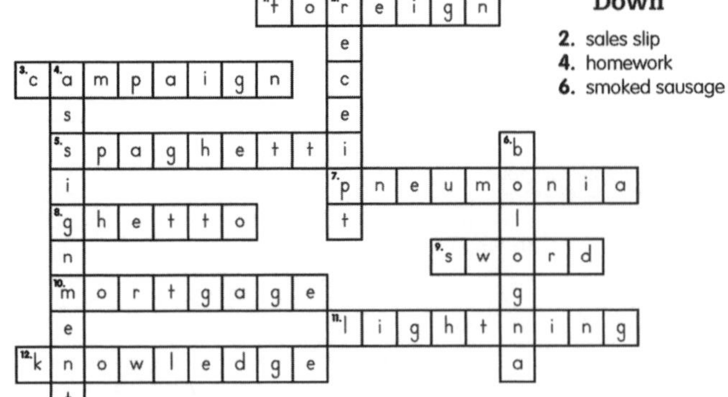

Down

2. sales slip
4. homework
6. smoked sausage

Across

1. from another country
3. run for office
5. pasta
7. serious disease of the lungs
8. slum
9. sharp edged metal blade
10. debt on a house
11. streak of electricity
12. understanding

Word Bank

assignment	foreign	lightning	receipt
bologna	ghetto	mortgage	spaghetti
campaign	knowledge	pneumonia	sword

350

1. Connecticut	Laneys' home state of New York borders **Connecticut.**
2. highland	"Dad showed us some of the beautiful **highland** areas on the ranch," she said.
3. flight	She recalled the **flight** that brought her and her mom here.
4. nighttime	"It was **nighttime,** and I couldn't tell a thing about the town," she remembered.
5. sigh	"Now I have a good friend here and she's going to move!" she said with a **sigh.**
6. knitting	"Maybe I can take up **knitting** in my spare time," she thought mournfully.
7. plight	"God, do you even care about my **plight**?" she asked.
8. slight	"I feel a **slight** bit annoyed and grumpy about all of this!"
9. Illinois	"Why Montana, Lord? Why not **Illinois** or someplace close like that?"
10. khaki	After putting on **khaki** walking shorts, she went to see Wicker.
11. doorknob	Hearing the **doorknob** turn, Wicker bounded toward the patio.
12. kneel	Not wanting to **kneel** on the wet grass, she sat in a lawn chair.
13. knuckle	"Want me to throw you a **knuckle** ball, Wicker?" she asked.
14. knack	"You have a **knack** for making me feel better," she told the dog.
15. Rhode Island	Laney showed Rachel a painting her mom had purchased in **Rhode Island.**
16. wharves	"I love the colors of the sky and all the goods being unloading on the **wharves.**"
17. knock	A **knock** on the podium by Mr. Canfield got the class's attention quickly.
18. knives	"Who will volunteer to bring spreading **knives** to the class party?" he asked.
19. rhyme	"Write a funny **rhyme** or two to share with the class at our party," he said.
20. wreck	"Lord, help me not to be a total **wreck** when Rachel moves!" Laney exclaimed.

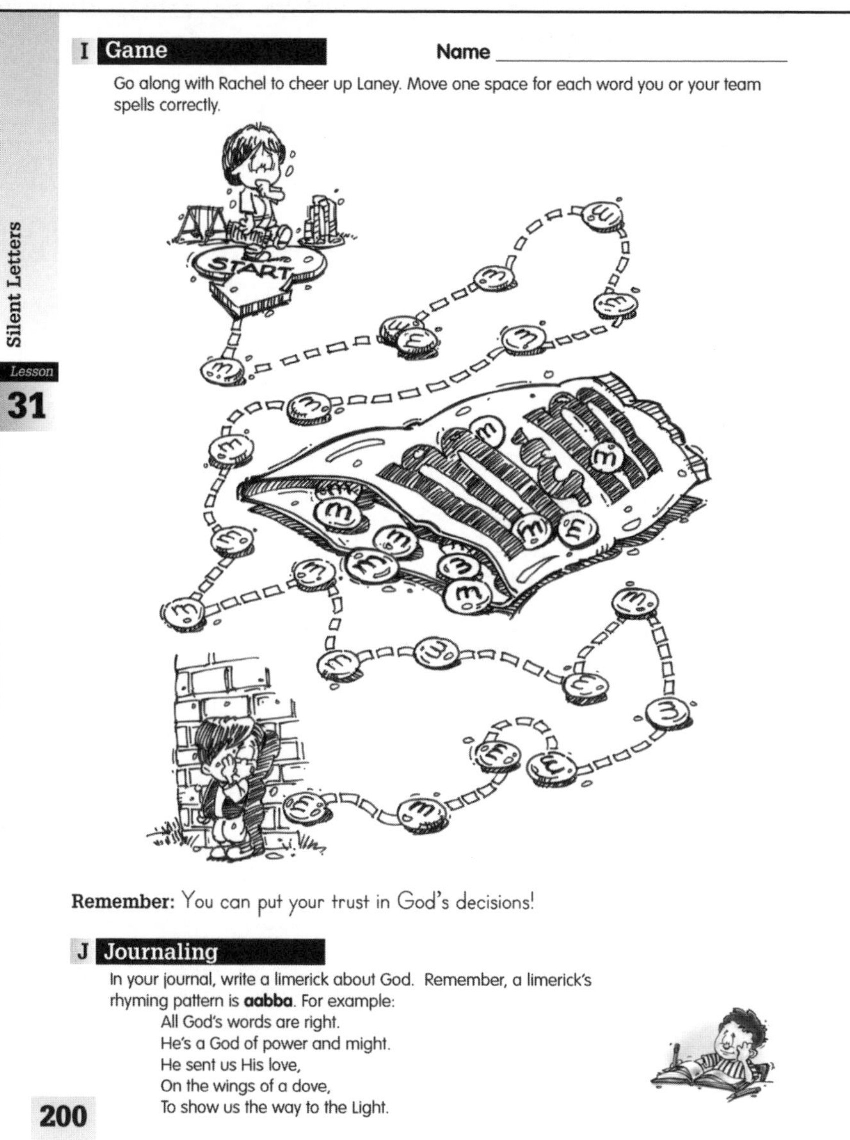

I Game Name ______________________

Go along with Rachel to cheer up Laney. Move one space for each word you or your team spells correctly.

Remember: You can put your trust in God's decisions!

J Journaling

In your journal, write a limerick about God. Remember, a limerick's rhyming pattern is **aabba**. For example:

All God's words are right.
He's a God of power and might.
He sent us His love,
On the wings of a dove,
To show us the way to the Light.

Silent Letters | Lesson 31 | 200

How to Play:

- Divide the class into two teams.
- Have each student place his/her game piece on Start.
- Have a student from team A go to the board.
- Say the spelling word.
- Have the student write the word on the board.
- If correct, instruct each member of team A to move his/her game piece forward one space.
- Alternate between teams A and B.
- The team to reach Laney first is the winner.
- **Small Group Option**: Students may play this game without teacher direction in small groups of two or more.

2 Game

Reinforce spelling skills and provide motivation and interest.

Materials

- game page (from student text)
- game pieces (1 per child)
- game word list

Game Word List

1. **solar**
2. **cirrus**
3. **charter**
4. **Connecticut**
5. **flight**
6. **highland**
7. **nighttime**
8. **plight**
9. **sigh**
10. **slight**
11. **khaki**
12. **Rhode Island**
13. **rhyme**
14. **doorknob**
15. **knack**
16. **kneel**
17. **knitting**
18. **knives**
19. **knock**
20. **knuckle**

3 Journaling

Provide a meaningful reason for correct spelling through personal writing.

Review the story using discussion leads provided on the following page. Encourage students to apply the Scriptural value in their journaling.

Journaling (continued)

- How many crayons did Thorny say the Crayola company made every day? (Five million or about one for each human being in Chicago, Houston and Seattle combined....or roughly two billion a year.)
- How many shades of wrappers are Crayola crayons wrapped in? (18)
- Who said there were 18 shades of wrappers when Rachel asked her classmates that question? (Thorny)
- Where did Thorny get his information? (National Geographic World magazine.)
- Why did Rachel ask Laney, "Don't you think the Bible is more reliable than World magazine?" (She wanted Laney to understand that if you trust Thorny when he tells us facts from World magazine you should trust God when he says he loves you and will take care of you.)
- No one knows exactly where limericks came from; but Edward Lear wrote some that everyone liked in the early 1800's. Two examples of his limericks are:

A flea and a fly in a flue
Didn't know quite what to do
Said the flea, "Let us fly."
Said the fly, "Let us flee."
So they flew through a flaw in the flue.

There was an Old Man with a beard,
Who said, "It is just as I feared!
Two Owls and a Hen,
Four Larks and Wren.
Have all built their nest in my beard."

- The rhyming pattern of a limerick is always aabba. Lines 3 and 4 are often shorter too.

The plastic things on the ends of shoelaces are called aglets.

Word Wow!

Good Times, Bad Times

Tommy gets a chance at a major role in a school play. When his grandmother dies, he loses the part — or was there another reason.

"Guess what, Mom?" Tommy bounded into the house when Mrs. Simmons dropped him off after school.

"Let's see, it probably has something to do with the baseball season coming up." Mrs. Rawson neatly folded an undershirt and reached into the drier for another. "I know! You found out which team you've been drafted by in the city Little League!"

"No, not yet." Tommy put his math book down on the washing machine. "Our school is having an end-of-the-year program and our class is doing a play. Guess who got a really big part?"

Somehow Mrs. Rawson kept a straight face as she guessed, "Daniel?"

"Aw, Mom." Tommy gently knocked his forehead against the door-jamb he was leaning against.

"So what part did you get?" Mom picked up a stack of neatly folded laundry and headed upstairs.

Tommy grabbed his math book and followed. "Well, see, it's about several inventor guys and how they never gave up and stuff—and I'm Thomas Edison."

"How fitting, Tommy Edison," Mom teased. "I'm impressed." She put a pile of clean clothes in the proper drawer in her bedroom. "That sounds like quite a responsibility. Do you have a lot of lines to memorize?"

"I've got it right here." Tommy pulled out several sheets of folded paper out of the math book. "I guess it's about five pages, but I'm not the one talking all the time."

Mom took the sheets and looked them over. "That's true, Tommy, but you have to know when to say your lines and that's almost as hard as remembering what to say. There's really quite a bit here. When is this play?"

"Next week right at the end of school." Tommy refolded the papers and stuck them back in his book. "Mr. Canfield is having two people learn each part in case someone gets sick or something, but I'm Thomas Edison. Tony is my understudy like in a real production."

"I hope Grandma's doing better by then." A worried frown crossed Mrs. Rawson's face. "Lately she's gotten extremely agitated—sometimes even violent—if I'm not right here, even though she doesn't know who I am." She rubbed the back of her neck and smiled. "We'll work something out, though, because I can't miss Tommy Edison, actor."

Tommy gave his mom a hug. "Where is Grandma, anyway?"

"She's asleep downstairs in her room." Mom rested her chin on the top of Tommy's head. "She's been sleeping a lot and seems to have a harder time walking and talking." Tommy felt her sigh ruffle his hair softly. "I just don't know how much longer I'll be able to keep her even though I know it's better for her to be here with her family."

Tommy gave his mom a tight squeeze. He knew she worked awfully hard taking care of Grandma, and now that Grandma had to wear adult diapers it was even worse. "Want me to finish the laundry?" He offered.

"Why, thank you, kind sir." Mom dropped a kiss on the top of his head. "You betcha I do. I'll go ahead and get started on supper." Arms looped around each other they marched back downstairs in step.

After supper, Tommy fetched his math book. By the time his homework was done he decided he was just too tired of using his brain to practice his Edison lines that night.

The next afternoon was one of those near-perfect days when it seems almost a crime to stay indoors. Tommy got out his pitch-return backstop and began sharpening up his baseball skills.

"Tommy the Terror!" Lisa called out the back door, "Mom said to remind you to practice your lines tonight. You've only got four more days to learn it all!"

"Okay!" Tommy called back over his shoulder. "I'll practice 'em in a little while." But it was a soft, beautiful spring evening and the ball felt good when it thunked into his glove. Tommy stayed outside till supper time, then he had to finish his homework and do his chores.

As soon as Tommy walked in the door the next afternoon, Mrs. Rawson insisted that he sit down and work on memorizing his lines. And he did, for a little while. Then the phone rang and it was Daniel telling him all about a multi-sport camp his parents were sending him to that summer. Somehow Tommy didn't get back to rehearsing his part. When he went to bed that night it hit him. Three days. Three days to know it all by heart. He HAD to get busy and spend time memorizing those lines!

But school was almost over for another year and the days were busy. Tommy was embarrassed when they practiced the play at school the next day and he only knew the first page by memory. "At least no one else knows every bit of their parts perfectly yet either," Tommy consoled himself even though he realized everyone else knew much more than he did.

He practiced well that evening—until a baseball special came on TV and he got sidetracked again. Lying in bed that night staring at the dark ceiling, Tommy promised himself that he'd drop everything

Story Continued

the next day and LEARN THAT PART.

Sometime in the night Tommy stirred. Voices, he thought sleepily, Mom and Dad's voices. It wasn't uncommon now for Grandma to get up and attempt major house cleaning in the middle of the night. Mom and Dad would handle it. Tommy rolled over and drifted into a deep sleep again.

The next morning, Tommy read through his lines as he felt his way foot-by-foot down the steps to the kitchen. "…so there must be an answer and I will find it!" he read in his best Thomas Edison voice. He stopped abruptly in the kitchen door when he looked up and saw the serious looks on Mom's and Dad's faces. "Was I that bad?"

Dad smiled a little. "Not quite, son. Come join us." Tommy took his chair at the round table between Lisa and his mom. Dad reached over and took Mom's hand. "Grandma fell last night and broke her hip. We took her to the hospital, but I'm afraid the trauma was just too much for her in her condition." He swallowed. "She died this morning about 5:00."

It was quiet for several seconds until Lisa choked back a cry and, jumping up from the table, ran upstairs to her room. Tommy wished tears would come. Instead he felt this awful, hot, choking thing in his throat and his eyes burned dry and bright. Mom started to get up, but Dad put a hand on her shoulder. "I'll go to her." He stood slowly. "Tommy, are you all right?" He leaned over his son. Tommy nodded stiffly. He couldn't get a sound past that horrid thing in his throat.

The play rehearsal at school later that morning was a disaster for Tommy. He couldn't even remember the few lines he did know. Mr. Canfield took him to one side and kindly let him know that Tony would be taking his place as Thomas Edison. No one made fun of Tommy. Everyone thought it was just because of his grandmother, but deep inside Tommy knew there was more to it than that.

That evening the Rawson family gathered in the living room. "So, we'll have a small memorial service day after tomorrow, then." Dad held a small pad of paper on his knee and jotted down notes. "Say 7:00 at the church?"

Mrs. Rawson nodded from her favorite chair. "That will work out well since the school program is tomorrow evening. I'm sorry this happened right before your program, son. I was really looking forward to seeing my son, the actor."

Tommy squirmed. "I didn't lose the part just 'cause Grandma died." He ran his fingernail along the jeans seam at the side of his leg as he admitted the truth. "I didn't take time to practice enough. I just wasn't ready. It seemed like time passed so quickly."

"Time does, son." Dad made little squiggles down the side of the pad. "It seems like just yesterday that I was your age and Grandma was making me eat my green beans!"

"Ugh!" Tommy grinned. "Remember when Grandma lived in that house with all the roses? She always had this huge garden every summer. I loved to stuff myself with corn-on-the-cob and tomatoes and stuff, but she always grew row after row of green beans, too!"

"Mmmmm." Lisa rolled over on her back on the carpet and rubbed her tummy. "I remember Grandma's strawberry pie. I've never tasted anything better."

"Grandma certainly had a green thumb, all right." Mom tucked her feet up under her. "She grew the best strawberries for miles around, not to mention everything else. And did she ever know her way around the kitchen!" Mom smiled across the room at Dad, "With all your mother's good cooking, it's a wonder you didn't weigh 300 pounds when I met you."

"I would've if she hadn't worked me so hard," Dad chuckled. "Grandma always was a stickler for keeping things neat and clean." His smile slowly faded. "I guess that's why she kept trying to clean house at odd hours after the Alzheimer's changed her so."

"I miss her so much." Lisa sniffed.

"Me, too." Tommy moved across the couch and leaned against his dad. "Why couldn't everything just stay the way it used to be before Grandma got sick?"

"Time doesn't slow down for anyone, kids." Dad laid the pad and pen down on the table beside the couch. "None of us has much time on this old earth. Your Grandma had a full and fulfilling life. We'll miss her, but we can remember all the good times we had with her and remember to live wisely and well in the time we have.

2 Discussion Time

Check understanding of the story and development of personal values.

- What part did Tommy get in the school play his class was presenting?
- Why was Mrs. Rawson worried about Grandma?
- How come Tommy didn't learn his part well?
- What happened to Grandma during the night?
- Why did Tommy lose the part of Thomas Edison?
- What did Tommy's grandmother like to do before she got sick with Alzheimer's?
- Why is it important to use your time wisely?

A Test-Editing Name ____________

If a word is spelled correctly, fill in the oval under **Correct**. If the word is misspelled, fill in the oval under **Incorrect**, and spell the word correctly on the blank.

	Correct	Incorrect	
1. highlind	○	●	highland
2. flight	●	○	
3. plite	○	●	plight
4. kakki	○	●	khaki
5. slight	●	○	
6. Rhode Island	●	○	
7. Conetticut	○	●	Connecticut
8. rhyme	●	○	
9. doorknob	●	○	
10. nock	○	●	knock
11. warves	○	●	wharves
12. nightime	○	●	nighttime
13. knack	●	○	
14. kneel	●	○	
15. sigh	●	○	
16. kniting	○	●	knitting
17. knives	●	○	
18. knuckle	●	○	
19. Ilinios	○	●	Illinois
20. reck	○	●	wreck

Review Lesson 32

201

Take a minute to memorize...

Psalm 90:12

Day 1

Review 32

3 Test-Editing

Reinforce recognizing and correcting misspelled words.

1 Game

Reinforce spelling skills and provide motivation and interest.

Materials

- game page (from student text)
- game pieces (1 per child)
- game word list

Game Word List

1. **Illinois**
2. **wharves**
3. **wreck**
4. **Connecticut**
5. **flight**
6. **highland**
7. **nighttime**
8. **plight**
9. **sigh**
10. **slight**
11. **khaki**
12. **Rhode Island**
13. **rhyme**
14. **doorknob**
15. **knack**
16. **kneel**
17. **knitting**
18. **knives**
19. **knock**
20. **knuckle**

How to Play:

- Divide the class into two teams.
- Have each student place his/her game piece on Start.
- Have a student from team A go to the board.
- Say the spelling word.
- Have the student write the word on the board.
- If correct, instruct each member of team A to move his/her game piece forward one space.
- Alternate between teams A and B.
- The team to reach the stage first is the winner.
- **Small Group Option**: Students may play this game without teacher direction in small groups of two or more.

Name ______________________________

Review

Lesson 32

Remember: Ask God to help you spend your time wisely!

A rubric for scoring is provided in Appendix B.

1 Writing Assessment

Assess student's spelling, grammar, and composition skills through personal writing.

- Have you ever had a special part in a play or program? (Allow time to share experiences.)
- What did Mrs. Rawson say was almost as hard as remembering what to say? (Remembering when to say your lines in a play.)
- What are some of the things Tommy did when he should have been focused on learning his lines? (Practiced his pitching, talked to Daniel on the phone, and watched a baseball special on TV.)
- How did Tommy feel when Dad told him Grandma had died early that morning? (Very sad. He wished he could cry, but just felt an awful, hot, choking thing in his throat and burning, dry eyes.)
- Why did Tommy's classmates think he wasn't doing the part of Thomas Edison anymore? (Because his grandma had died.)
- Was that the only reason Tony got the part instead of Tommy? Why? (No. He lost the part because he hadn't learned the lines.)
- What lesson do you think Tommy learned? (That time passes very quickly and we need to use every bit of it wisely.)

Review | Lesson 32

C Writing Assessment Name ____________________

Write a short story about someone using their time wisely or unwisely. Don't forget to identify your characters, the setting, the plot or conflict, and the resolution.

____
____
____
____
____
____
____
____
____
____
____
____
____

Scripture
Psalm 90:12

204

The right side of a boat was called the starboard side due to the fact that the astro navigators used to stand out on the plank (which was on the right side) to get an unobstructed view of the stars. The left side was called the port side because that was the side you put in on at the port. This was so that they didn't knock off the starboard!

D Proofing Name ____________________

To better prepare for his role in the play, Tommy wrote a brief character sketch of Thomas Edison. Use the proofreading marks to show the errors in his report. Write the misspelled words correctly on the lines.

◯	word is misspelled	^	word or words missing
≡	capitalize letter	⊙	comma is missing
⊙	period is missing	↩	take out word
/	letter should be lower case	∨	apostrophe is missing

Review Lesson 32

Thomas edison, a famous inventor was born well over a sentury ago in Milan Ohio. Even as a little boy, Thomas very intelligent and extremely curious. A laboratory in his parents cellar allowed him to conduct dificult experiments and desine and cunstruct various divices.

When Edison became an udult, he continued with his experimenting and inventing. Two character traits that Were apparent in his work were patience and diligence When an experiment failed, he did not panik, become embarrased or give up. he would work all day long even when he was exausted. Sometimes he worked late into the Night seeking the correct formyela.

Not everyone did supported Edison in his pursuits. a good many people did not rispect or udmire his metheds, but thought he was the crazy and foolesh. Only a few Men stood by Edison and asisted him in perfecting his ingenious inventions. They partnired with him, pledgeing to devote their inergy to gethering information and combineing their knowledge Together they uspired to invent quolity products and Then presented them to a skeptical public.

1. century	9. exhausted	16. partnered
2. difficult	10. formula	17. pledging
3. design	11. respect	18. energy
4. contruct	12. admire	19. gathering
5. devices	13. methods	20. combining
6. adult	14. foolish	21. aspired
7. panic	15. assisted	22. quality
8. embarrassed		

205

3 Proofing

Reinforce recognizing capitalization, punctuation, and spelling errors.

Write this sentence on the board: **tommy did not lern up his lines for the plae.** Have volunteers come to the board to insert the proofer's marks needed for a misspelled word, letter to capitalize, and unnecessary word.

You will be using these and other proofer's marks to show the errors in Tommy's report about Edison. Read his report, then use the proofer's marks to show the errors. Write the misspelled words correctly on the lines.

Day 4 | Review 32

2 Action Game

Reinforce spelling skills and provide motivation and interest.

Materials

- masking tape
- four square ball
- word list on certificate at end of unit

BOUNCE BACK

Use tape to mark a two-square game grid on the classroom floor. Divide the class into two teams. Line up the two teams on opposite sides of the two-square court. The first player from each team steps into the court, one player holding a ball. Call out the first spelling word to be reviewed. The player with the ball says the first letter of the word as he or she hits the ball into the opposite square. The player in that square says the second letter of the word as he or she hits the ball back. This continues until the word has been spelled. If a player misspells a word by saying an incorrect letter, play stops and the other team gets a point. If the word is spelled correctly, both teams get a point. Give a new word to the next two players and continue in this pattern. The team with the most points wins!

Review 32 | Day 5

Word Find

Familiarize students with word meaning and usage.

Write the letters **lleps** on the board. Ask the students to read the letters backwards to spell the word **spell**. Write the letters **sdrawkcab** on the board. Allow time for the students to decide that the letters spell the word **backwards**. The students will be challenged with some words that are hidden backwards in this puzzle.

Read each of the sentences below. Find the bold words in the puzzle and circle them. Words may go down, across, forwards, or backwards.

Review
Lesson 32

E Word Find

Name ______________________

Find each of the bold words in the sentences below and circle them in the puzzle. Words may go down, across, diagonal, forwards, or backwards.

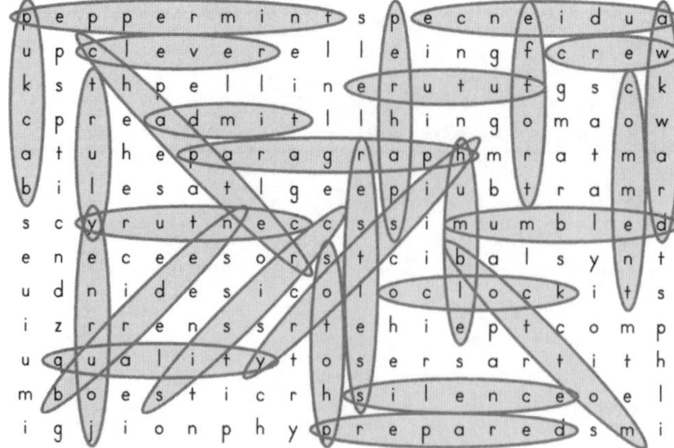

1. Tommy read a **chapter** on the **clever** Edison.
2. He wrote a **paragraph** or two about the inventor.
3. Dad told Lisa and Tommy about the **crisis** in the night.
4. Grandma's life was a **journey** that covered nearly a **century**.
5. She had grown very **restless** near the end.
6. Her care was not a **burden** to those who loved her.
7. Some of Grandma's old **photos** smelled of **peppermint**.
8. The memorial service was at seven **o'clock**.
9. There was an **awkward silence** when Tommy **mumbled** a line incorrectly.
10. Tommy felt **truly** foolish and felt sick in the **bottom** of his stomach.
11. He had to **humble** himself and **admit** he was not **prepared**.
12. **Perhaps** in the **future** he will make a real **effort**.
13. Tony was Tommy's **backup**, or understudy.
14. Some students are part of the stage **crew**.
15. Mr. Canfield did not **comment** on the **quality** of Tommy's acting.
16. The **audience** will enjoy seeing events from **history**.

206

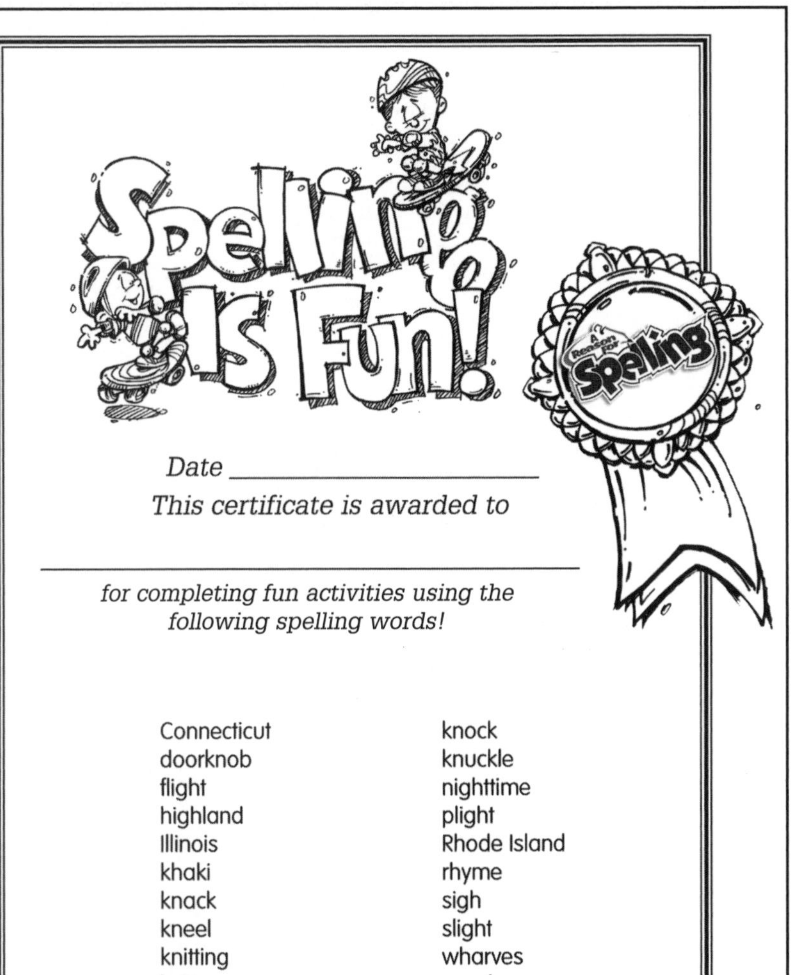

Date ____________________

This certificate is awarded to

____

for completing fun activities using the following spelling words!

Connecticut	knock
doorknob	knuckle
flight	nighttime
highland	plight
Illinois	Rhode Island
khaki	rhyme
knack	sigh
kneel	slight
knitting	wharves
knives	wreck

2 Certificate

Provide an opportunity for parents or guardians to encourage and assess their child's progress.

Fill in today's date and your name on your certificate.

Take a minute to memorize...

Psalm 90:12

The End

PLEASE PHOTOCOPY!*

The following pages contain Black Line Masters for use with the ***A Reason For Spelling®*** Student Worktext.

*Photocopy privileges extend only to the material in this section, and permission is granted only for those classrooms or homeschools using ***A Reason For Spelling®*** Student Worktexts. Any other use of this material is expressly forbidden and all copyright laws apply.

Hide and Seek

Play Hide and Seek with your words. Fill in a bar graph (left to right) for each word you spell correctly.

Vocabulary Extension

Crossword Puzzle

Use the clues below to complete the puzzle.

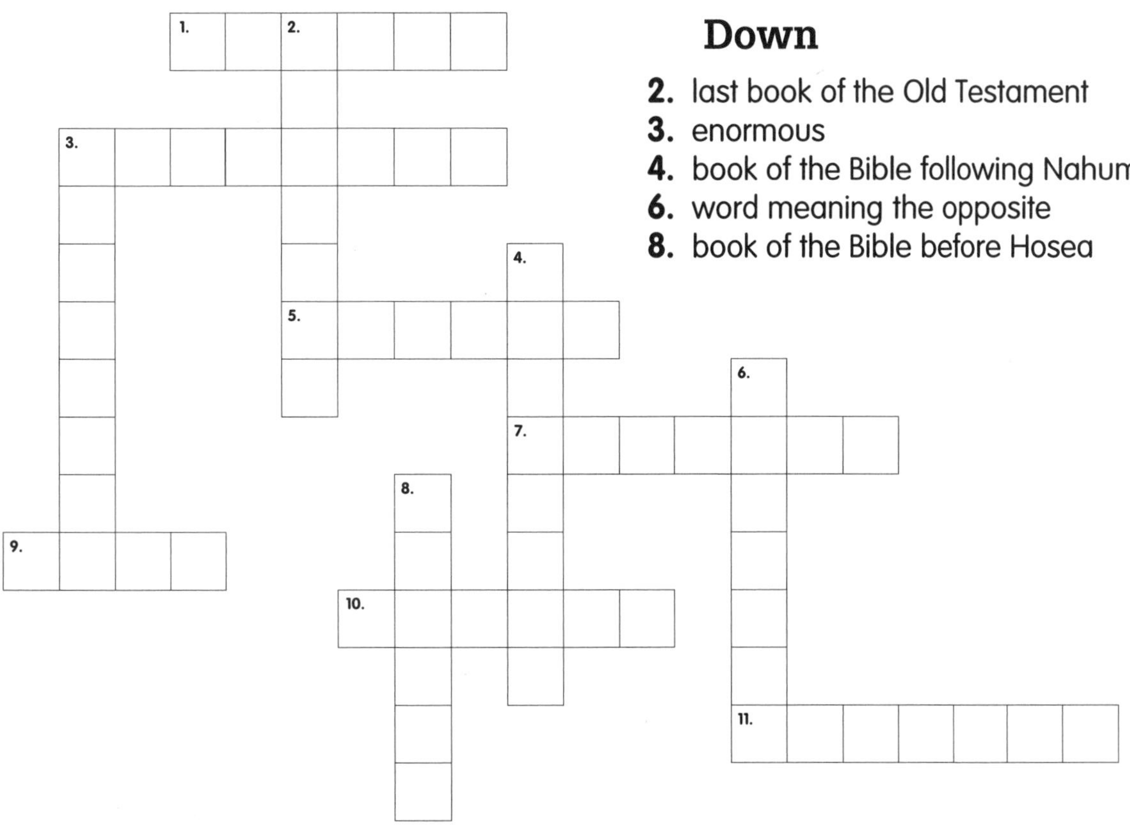

Down

2. last book of the Old Testament
3. enormous
4. book of the Bible following Nahum
6. word meaning the opposite
8. book of the Bible before Hosea

Across

1. book of the Bible that follows Ruth
3. motor fuel
5. book of the Bible between Zephaniah and Zechariah
7. move forward
9. fifth book of the New Testament
10. occurring every year
11. one of the four gospels

Word Bank

Acts	antonym	gigantic	Malachi
advance	Daniel	Habakkuk	Matthew
annual	gasoline	Haggai	Samuel

Hide and Seek

Play Hide and Seek with your words. Fill in a bar graph (left to right) for each word you spell correctly.

Vocabulary Extension

Trade-off

Choose a word from the word bank to replace the word(s) in parentheses. Write the word in the blank.

1. _______________ (book of the Bible meaning beginning) tells sacred history from the first day of creation to the death of Joseph.
2. I don't _______________ (suggest) that you wait very long to begin your science project.
3. I have only a vague _______________ (recollection) of when I was very little.
4. It is _______________ (important) for you to understand how to work these math problems.
5. King Artaxerxes sent _______________ (a priest) to set up civil and religious laws in Jerusalem.
6. Moses led the Israelites from Egypt in a grand _______________ (departure) after they had been held in slavery for a long time.
7. The king sent a _______________ (courier) to tell the other armies the news of the battle.
8. There is an _______________ (index) at the end of the book that tells the definitions of your words.
9. This beautiful woman, _______________, (Mordecai's cousin) became the Queen of Persia.
10. This table looks so old, I am sure it must be a _______________ (authentic) antique.
11. We like to visit the _______________ (graveyard) to read the names and dates on the tombstones.
12. You can record this music on a _______________ (tape) to listen to in your car.

Word Bank

appendix	essential	Ezra	memory
cassette	Esther	Genesis	messenger
cemetery	Exodus	genuine	recommend

Hide and Seek

Play Hide and Seek with your words. Fill in a bar graph (left to right) for each word you spell correctly.

Vocabulary Extension

Multiple Choice

Fill in the oval by the word(s) with the same or nearly the same meaning as the word in bold type.

1. consider
- ⬭ ponder
- ⬭ babble
- ⬭ thoughtless
- ⬭ balance

2. Timothy
- ⬭ Old Testament book
- ⬭ companion of Paul
- ⬭ first king of Israel
- ⬭ town in western Judah

3. convince
- ⬭ chosen one
- ⬭ lenses for your eyes
- ⬭ prisoner
- ⬭ persuade

4. Corinthians
- ⬭ friends of Isaiah
- ⬭ Old Testament book
- ⬭ people who lived in Corinth
- ⬭ Abraham's nephew

5. initials
- ⬭ beginning letters of a name
- ⬭ first book of the Bible
- ⬭ important document
- ⬭ good judgment

6. political
- ⬭ ethical
- ⬭ governmental
- ⬭ noticeable
- ⬭ license

7. friction
- ⬭ smoothness
- ⬭ disagreement
- ⬭ roll carefully
- ⬭ flattering

8. grimace
- ⬭ expression
- ⬭ enemy
- ⬭ lonely
- ⬭ frightening

9. minimum
- ⬭ receive
- ⬭ administer
- ⬭ smallest
- ⬭ record

10. Kings
- ⬭ to take an oath
- ⬭ to persuade
- ⬭ prophet of Israel
- ⬭ Old Testament books

Hide and Seek

Play Hide and Seek with your words. Fill in a bar graph (left to right) for each word you spell correctly.

Vocabulary Extension

Cause and Effect

Write a word from the word bank to complete each sentence.

1. If you are reading the fifth book of the Bible, you are reading ________________.
2. If a machine runs by mechanical or computerized means, it is an ________________ device.
3. If you are reading a collection of sacred hymns from the Bible, you are reading the ________________.
4. If someone brings something to completion, they were able to ________________ it.
5. If someone pretends to be very good but is not, he is guilty of ________________.
6. If something is too small to see without using a special magnifying lens, it is ________________.
7. If you are reading a poetical book of essays and practical statements, you are reading ________________.
8. If you live where there is government rule by the people, you live in a ________________.
9. If you want to learn about the reign of King David, you may read the books of ________________.
10. If you wanted to read about Jesus' cousin, you would read about ________________ the Baptist.
11. If you wanted to read a letter written by Paul, you could read the book of ________________.
12. If you wanted to learn more about the man who led the Israelites after Moses, you would learn about ________________.

Word Bank

accomplish	democracy	hypocrisy	microscopic
Chronicles	Deuteronomy	John	Proverbs
Colossians	electronic	Joshua	Psalms

Hide and Seek

Play Hide and Seek with your words. Fill in a bar graph (left to right) for each word you spell correctly.

Vocabulary Extension

Fill in the Blanks

Choose a word from the word bank that best fits each sentence clue.

1. If you want the cookies to turn out well, you must follow the ________________.
2. The seventh book of the Bible, ________________, is named for the way Israel was ruled during this time.
3. I had to ________________ to get the saddle on the huge horse, but I finally was successful.
4. ________________, the fourth book of the Bible, begins with a census taken at Sinai.
5. The art class I want to sign up for allows a ________________ of twenty students.
6. When our sink developed a leak underneath, we called a ________________.
7. It felt absolutely ________________ to go swimming in the middle of the hot day.
8. Someday she would like to travel to several other ________________ for a visit.
9. The stray cat soon became a ________________ visitor to our dog's bowl on the back porch.
10. The motel where we stayed provided ________________ service to the nearby shopping malls.
11. Several ________________ sent me their catalogs of outdoor gear when I subscribed to a ski magazine.
12. Mom is looking forward to the ________________ of a long soak in the whirlpool.

Word Bank

companies	Judges	Numbers	shuttle
countries	luxury	plumber	struggle
instructions	maximum	regular	wonderful

Hide and Seek

Play Hide and Seek with your words. Fill in a bar graph (left to right) for each word you spell correctly.

Vocabulary Extension

Crossword Puzzle

Use the clues below to complete the puzzle.

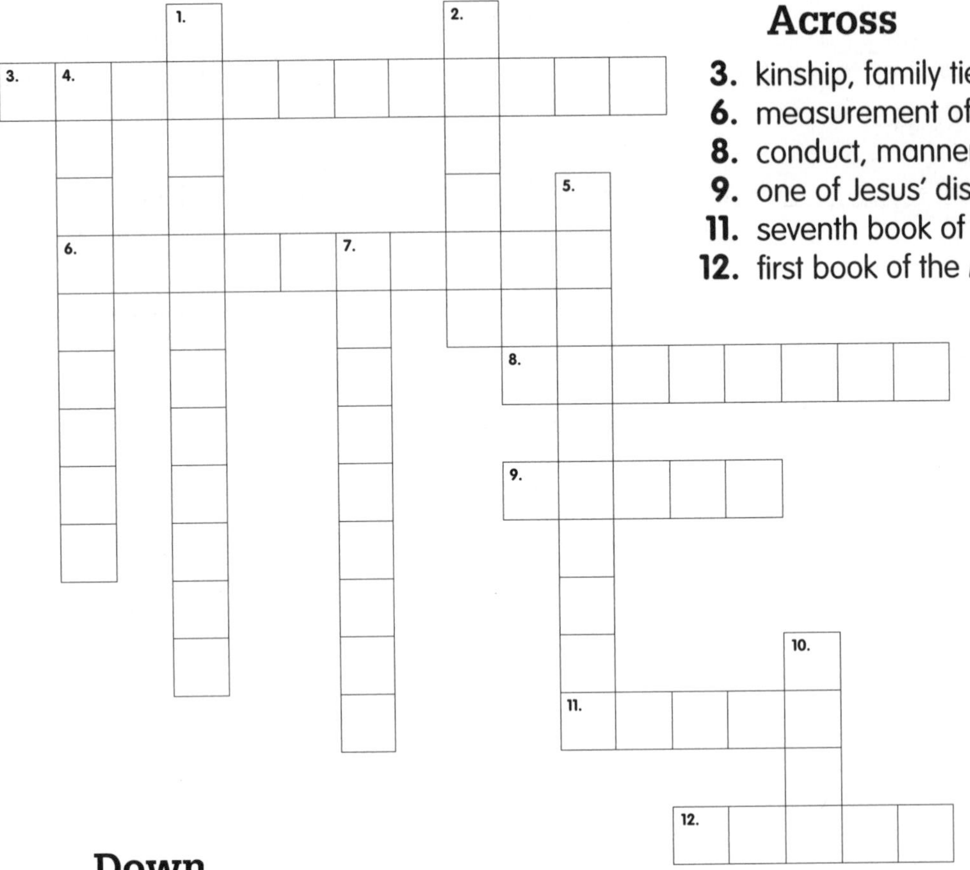

Across

3. kinship, family tie
6. measurement of temperature
8. conduct, manners
9. one of Jesus' disciples
11. seventh book of the Minor Prophets
12. first book of the Minor Prophets

Down

1. Old Testament book following Jeremiah
2. Old Testament book before Jeremiah
4. instruction, schooling
5. last book of the Bible
7. letter written by Paul
10. third book of the Minor Prophets

Word Bank

Amos	education	Isaiah	Nahum
behavior	Galatians	James	relationship
centigrade	Hosea	Lamentations	Revelation

Hide and Seek

Play Hide and Seek with your words. Fill in a bar graph (left to right) for each word you spell correctly.

Vocabulary Extension

Trade-off

Choose a word from the word bank to replace the word(s) in parentheses. Write the word in the blank.

1. Descendants of Jacob became known as ________________ (Israelites).
2. Levers, screws, pulleys, and gears are all simple ________________(devices).
3. Anne has always done very well. She will ________________(triumph) now.
4. Dad ________________ (surrendered) to the other car so we would not have an accident.
5. When we go out in the ________________ (excessive) cold, we dress in many layers of clothes.
6. Paul wrote a letter to ________________ (Onesimus' master) asking him to treat the slave as a brother in Christ.
7. Brushing your teeth after every meal is an example of good ________________ (health habits).
8. ________________(Simon) was an eager, earnest, and courageous disciple of Jesus Christ.
9. We quickly called the police and hoped they would catch the ________________ (burglars) who had robbed us.
10. I am teaching my dog how to ________________ (fetch) a stick when I throw it for him.
11. ________________ (Old Testament book) was written by King Solomon and tells his view of life.
12. She has the gift of ________________ (administration), so she is the yearbook editor.

Word Bank

Ecclesiastes	hygiene	Peter	succeed
extreme	leadership	Philemon	thieves
Hebrews	machines	retrieve	yielded

Hide and Seek

Play Hide and Seek with your words. Fill in a bar graph (left to right) for each word you spell correctly.

Vocabulary Extension

Multiple Choice

Fill in the oval by the word(s) with the same or nearly the same meaning as the word in bold type.

1. Obadiah
- ⬭ New Testament prophet
- ⬭ son of Ruth and Boaz
- ⬭ the shortest book in the Old Testament
- ⬭ the longest book in the Old Testament

2. sacrifice
- ⬭ to commandeer an airplane
- ⬭ an offering
- ⬭ to communicate
- ⬭ resemblance

3. satellite
- ⬭ to soak thoroughly
- ⬭ uncivilized
- ⬭ an object that orbits a heavenly body
- ⬭ sixth planet from the sun

4. Nehemiah
- ⬭ Old Testament book before Esther
- ⬭ Old Testament book after Esther
- ⬭ New Testament book after Ezra
- ⬭ follower of Jesus who called Peter

5. Jeremiah
- ⬭ important city in the Jordan Valley
- ⬭ city where the temple stood
- ⬭ first king of Israel
- ⬭ the "weeping prophet"

6. Micah
- ⬭ an archangel
- ⬭ a town near Bethel
- ⬭ book of the minor prophets
- ⬭ last Old Testament book

7. Zephaniah
- ⬭ prophet in the days of King Josiah
- ⬭ ninth book of the Bible
- ⬭ last book of the Old Testament
- ⬭ son of Zilpah

8. Zechariah
- ⬭ next to the last book of the Bible
- ⬭ Old Testament book following Haggai
- ⬭ a man who climbed a tree to see Jesus
- ⬭ a town in Shephelah in Judah

9. variety
- ⬭ undue pride in oneself
- ⬭ an animal considered a pest
- ⬭ assortment of different things
- ⬭ fine particles floating in the air

10. Titus
- ⬭ the 10th part of one's increase
- ⬭ letter written by Peter
- ⬭ a covenant
- ⬭ New Testament book before Philemon

Hide and Seek

Play Hide and Seek with your words. Fill in a bar graph (left to right) for each word you spell correctly.

Vocabulary Extension

Cause and Effect

Write a word from the word bank to complete each sentence.

1. If you wanted to ________________ someone, you would go up and talk to them.
2. If a family had lived in the city of Thessalonica, they would be known as ________________.
3. If you want to look at something that is very small, you would use a ________________.
4. If you want to read the book of the Bible between Hosea and Amos, you would read the book of ________________.
5. If you wanted to describe the brilliance that radiates from a heavenly angel, you might use the word ________________.
6. If a carpenter wanted to hold up the roof of a porch, he might use pillars to ________________ it.
7. If you wanted to describe someone who had suffered a lot, you might compare them to a man in the Bible named ________________.
8. If you want to go into a cave to discover what it is like, you will ________________ it.
9. If you were telling a story about a man who had been swallowed by a large fish, you would be telling the story of ________________.
10. If you had written a letter to a friend and needed to mail it, you would write the address on an ________________.
11. If you challenged a friend to a game of tennis, you would play at a tennis ________________.
12. If your family were citizens of Rome, they would be known as ________________.

Word Bank

approach	explore	Joel	Romans
court	glory	Jonah	support
envelope	Job	microscope	Thessalonians

Hide and Seek

Play Hide and Seek with your words. Fill in a bar graph (left to right) for each word you spell correctly.

Vocabulary Extension

Fill in the Blanks

Choose a word from the word bank that best fits each sentence clue.

1. When I saw my brother playing with my yo-yo, I had to ______________ that he had taken it.
2. We did not mean to ______________ you; we accidentally left you out of the game.
3. Grandma always smells like a rose garden. I like the ______________ she wears.
4. When my sister broke her leg, lots of people sent flowers to her. Their kindness was abundant and ______________.
5. I am memorizing a verse in the 26th book of the New Testament. I am learning a verse in the book of ______________.
6. My grandfather thinks I look very young. He comments on how ______________ I seem.
7. I have good opinions and feelings about school. I have a positive ______________.
8. My mother-in-law's name was Naomi. I was kind to her. I later married Boaz. My name was ______________.
9. The round black part of your eye that lets light travel through it is called the ______________.
10. I was a doctor and wrote the third gospel. I also traveled with Paul. My name was ______________.
11. The earth, the planets, the stars and everything in space make up the ______________.
12. My brother likes to make funny little drawings. He likes to draw ______________s.

Word Bank

attitude	exclude	perfume	Ruth
cartoon	Jude	profuse	universe
conclude	Luke	pupil	youthful

Hide and Seek

Play Hide and Seek with your words. Fill in a bar graph (left to right) for each word you spell correctly.

Vocabulary Extension

Crossword Puzzle

Use the clues below to complete the puzzle.

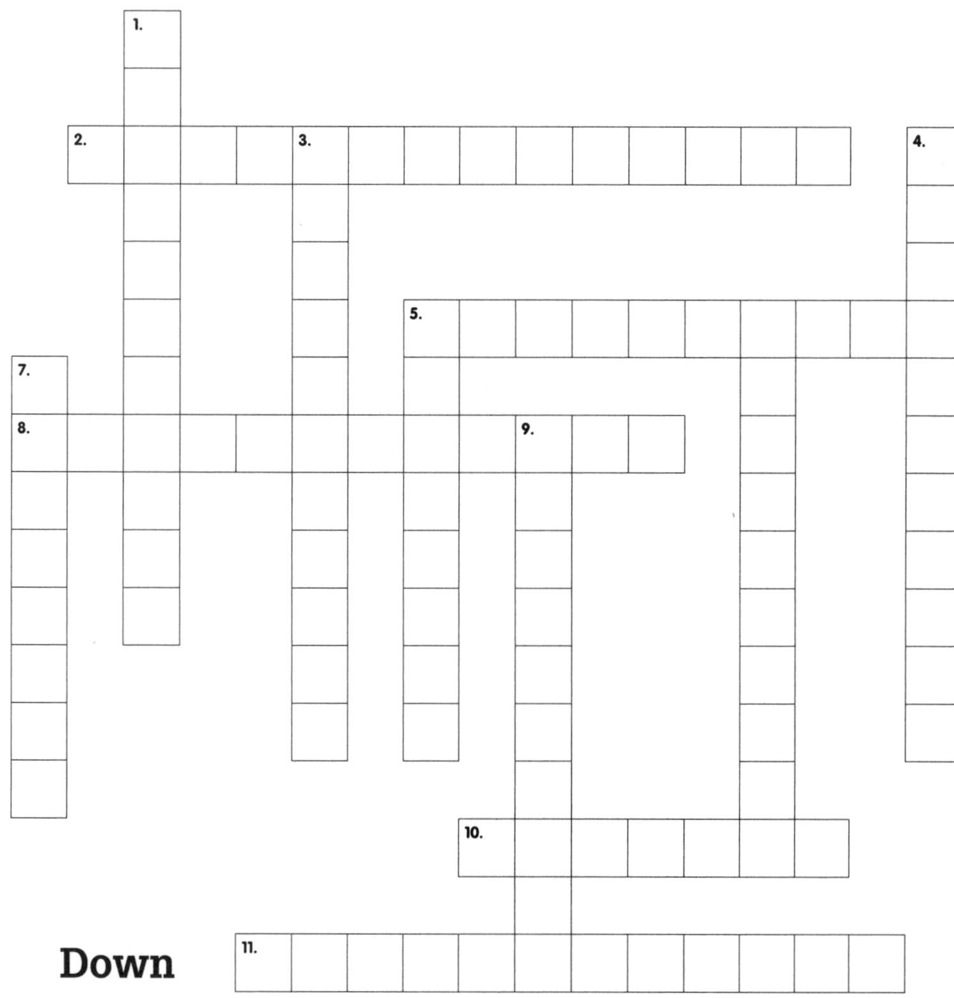

Down

1. questionnaire, test
3. pass blood into a vein of someone
4. done with extraordinary skill
5. catastrophe, misfortune
6. tenderness, mercy
7. six-pointed star
9. insufficient, imperfect

Across

2. writing or printing in uppercase letters
5. immature, juvenile
8. contentment, happiness
10. display, show
11. scarf, tissue

Word Bank

accident	capitalization	handkerchief	pageant
adolescent	compassion	inadequate	satisfaction
asterisk	examination	masterpiece	transfusion

Hide and Seek

Play Hide and Seek with your words. Fill in a bar graph (left to right) for each word you spell correctly.

Vocabulary Extension

Trade-off

Choose a word from the word bank to replace the word(s) in parentheses. Write the word in the blank.

1. My teacher said that the ________________ (essay) I wrote was really good.
2. There was a lot of ________________ (conflict) to the plans for the new gymnasium.
3. The lawyer for the ________________ (accuser) had plenty of evidence to convict the thief.
4. She was so upset that her arguments became very ________________ (unreasonable).
5. The boys finally gave up on the go-cart they were trying to build. They decided it was ________________ (hopeless).
6. The laws in our country that state the rights of the people and the powers of the government are known as the ________________ (written laws).
7. The fraction 13/7 is an ________________ (incorrect) fraction because the numerator is greater than its denominator.
8. I love to look at the ________________ (pattern of stars) Orion in the sky on a dark night.
9. Jeans are the most ________________ (most common) kind of clothes in my closet.
10. We need to be ________________ (accepting) of others by showing respect for their customs, beliefs, or opinions.
11. I want to protect valuable things such as forests, wildlife, and natural resources. I believe in ________________ (preservation).
12. If you have a ________________ (discourse) with someone, you talk to them for a while.

Word Bank

composition	constitution	illogical	opposition
conservation	conversation	impossible	prosecution
constellation	dominant	improper	tolerant

Hide and Seek

Play Hide and Seek with your words. Fill in a bar graph (left to right) for each word you spell correctly.

Vocabulary Extension

Multiple Choice

Fill in the oval by the word(s) with the same or nearly the same meaning as the word in bold type.

1. pharmacist
- ⬭ large, brightly colored bird
- ⬭ person who prepares and sells medicines
- ⬭ one who grows crops
- ⬭ machine that reproduces sounds

2. carpenter
- ⬭ thick floor covering made of fabric
- ⬭ vehicle pulled by horses
- ⬭ part of the engine in a car
- ⬭ someone who works with wood

3. bargain
- ⬭ discuss the price of something
- ⬭ to trade food for other goods
- ⬭ land where crops will not grow
- ⬭ common cereal plant

4. margin
- ⬭ something made of stone or cement
- ⬭ dark reddish brown color
- ⬭ place where people buy and sell food
- ⬭ blank space down the edge of a page

5. article
- ⬭ disease the makes people's joints swell
- ⬭ false, not real or natural
- ⬭ piece of writing published in a newspaper
- ⬭ conceited and proud

6. charming
- ⬭ enchanting and appealing
- ⬭ document that states the rights of people
- ⬭ raising money to help people in need
- ⬭ deep crack in the surface of the earth

7. regard
- ⬭ in spite of everything
- ⬭ opinion; esteem
- ⬭ to give money back to someone
- ⬭ person who is forced to leave their home

8. darkened
- ⬭ room with photography equipment
- ⬭ someone who is dearly loved
- ⬭ unpleasantly wet and damp
- ⬭ caused something to be without light

9. enlarged
- ⬭ made bigger or increased
- ⬭ gave something all your attention
- ⬭ mystery or puzzle
- ⬭ made something better or greater

10. guardian
- ⬭ person who is dirty or sloppy
- ⬭ musical instrument with strings
- ⬭ person legally responsible for a child
- ⬭ direction or supervision

Hide and Seek

Play Hide and Seek with your words. Fill in a bar graph (left to right) for each word you spell correctly.

Vocabulary Extension

Cause and Effect

Write a word from the word bank to complete each sentence.

1. If you promise that something will work, you ________________ it.
2. If you study about the tubes that carry blood throughout your body, you are learning about arteries, veins, and ________________.
3. If you want to write a letter to someone, you may write on some pretty ________________.
4. If you do not know what a word means, you can look it up in a ________________.
5. If you are riding an exercise bike, it does not take you anywhere because it is ________________.
6. If you are sent to teach people about Jesus, you are being a ________________.
7. If you recite the details of something that has happened, you are being a ________________.
8. If you have a glass tank in which you keep fish, you have an ________________.
9. If your mom says you must clean your room, it is ________________ for you to do it.
10. If a country has a group of soldiers in the navy, air force, or army, they are known as a country's ________________.
11. If you are hired to handle records, mail, and routine work for another person, you are their ________________.
12. If you own a store that sells tools, bolts, nails, knobs, and other such things, you own a ________________ store.

Word Bank

aquarium	guarantee	missionary	secretary
capillaries	hardware	narrator	stationary
dictionary	military	necessary	stationery

Hide and Seek

Play Hide and Seek with your words. Fill in a bar graph (left to right) for each word you spell correctly.

Vocabulary Extension

Fill in the Blanks

Choose a word from the word bank that best fits each sentence clue.

1. I spoke to my mom in a rude manner. I'm afraid I was being ________________.

2. I have learned to ride my mountain bike well. I am a good ________________.

3. My dad had to get new glasses that have two sections in the lenses. He can see up close and far away with his new ________________.

4. We had to change the plans for our tree house; however, we only needed to ________________ them a little.

5. We visited a ________________, a factory where raw materials are purified and made into finished products.

6. Your body needs foods that give you energy. Eat plenty of ________________, such as bread, pasta, and potatoes.

7. We needed lightweight foods to take on our backpack trip, so Mom helped us ________________ some in the food dryer.

8. Uncle Paul sure can eat a lot. He has a huge ________________ because he works so hard.

9. My nephews play in the community orchestra. They are both good ________________s.

10. I like to study about nature and the physical world. I really enjoy ________________ experiments.

11. Some drivers travel too fast. This is a ________________ of the speed limit laws.

12. We watched a play in which the story was told through gestures, body movements, and facial expressions instead of words. It was called a ________________.

Word Bank

appetite	carbohydrates	modify	scientific
bicyclist	dehydrate	pantomime	violation
bifocals	impolite	refinery	violinist

Hide and Seek

Play Hide and Seek with your words. Fill in a bar graph (left to right) for each word you spell correctly.

Vocabulary Extension

Crossword Puzzle

Use the clues below to complete the puzzle.

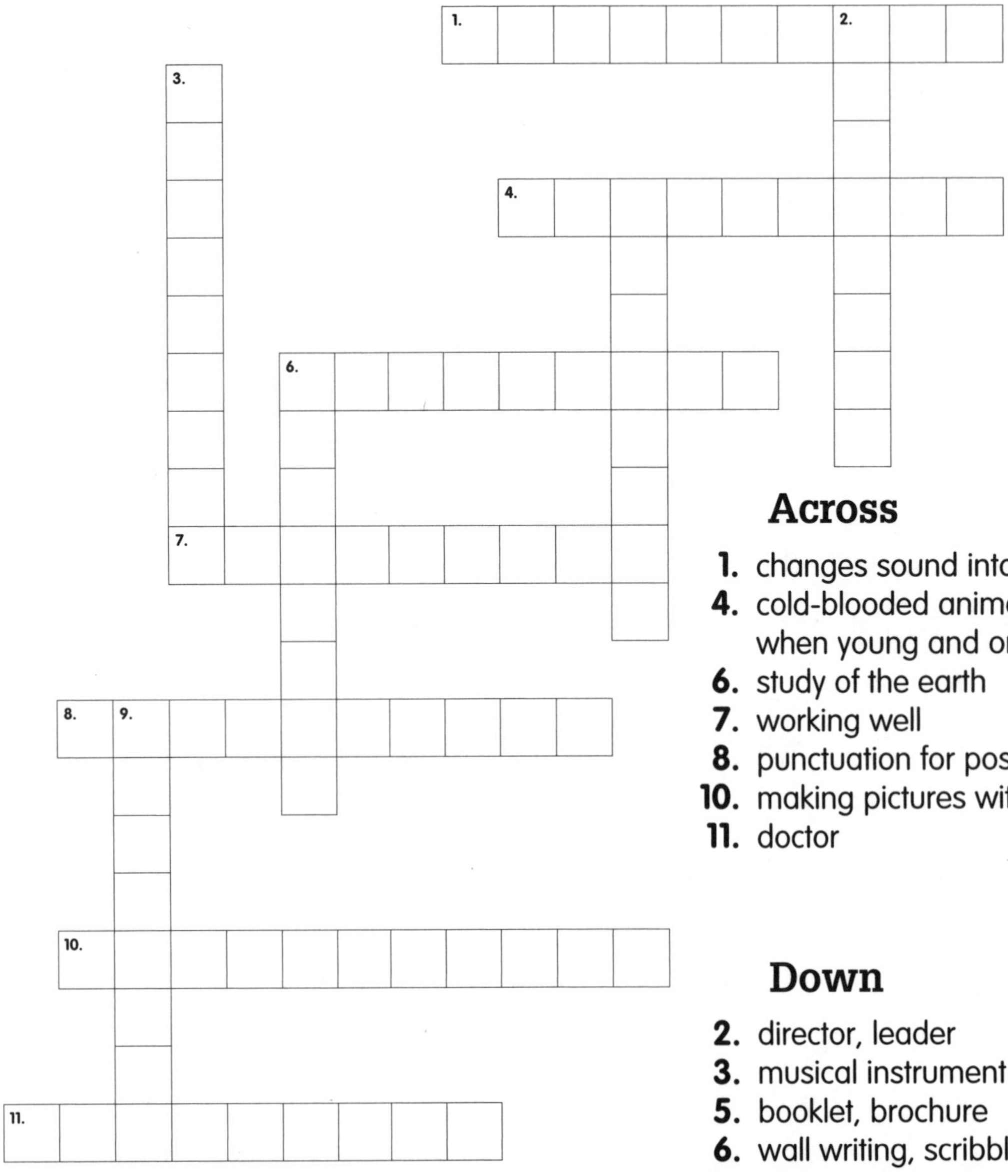

Across

1. changes sound into electric current
4. cold-blooded animal that lives in water when young and on land as an adult
6. study of the earth
7. working well
8. punctuation for possessive nouns
10. making pictures with a camera
11. doctor

Down

2. director, leader
3. musical instrument
5. booklet, brochure
6. wall writing, scribbling
9. prediction

Word Bank

amphibian	geography	official	physician
apostrophe	graffiti	pamphlet	prophecy
effective	microphone	photography	saxophone

Hide and Seek

Play Hide and Seek with your words. Fill in a bar graph (left to right) for each word you spell correctly.

Vocabulary Extension

Trade-off

Choose a word from the word bank to replace the word(s) in parentheses. Write the word in the blank.

1. Dad bought Mom a ________________ (small bouquet) to wear to church for Mother's Day.
2. The hungry deer had to ________________ (search) for food during the harsh winter.
3. Medics are trained to act quickly and carefully in an ________________ (crisis).
4. Michael forgot to put the milk back in the ________________(icebox), so it soured.
5. Measles, chicken pox, and the flu are all ________________ (infectious) diseases that can spread to other people.
6. A ________________ (span of time) is said to be around 30 years between the births of parents and that of their children.
7. A ________________ (member of the armed forces) was waiting at the train station.
8. Mom and Dad had made an ________________ (agreement) for me to stay at a neighbor's house until they got home.
9. Getting used to his new school took some ________________ (adaptation), but he soon made new friends.
10. We say a pledge to our country's flag each day to show ________________ (loyalty) to the country we live in.
11. People train dogs with high ________________(aptitude) to serve as police dogs and seeing–eye dogs.
12. The traffic accident occurred because of the ________________(carelessness) of the driver who ran the stop sign.

Word Bank

adjustment	contagious	forage	negligence
allegiance	corsage	generation	refrigerator
arrangement	emergency	intelligence	sergeant

Vocabulary Extension Lesson 20

Hide and Seek

Play Hide and Seek with your words. Fill in a bar graph (left to right) for each word you spell correctly.

Vocabulary Extension

Multiple Choice

Fill in the oval by the word(s) with the same or nearly the same meaning as the word in bold type.

1. comedian
- ○ process of catching fire and burning
- ○ punctuation used to split a sentence
- ○ booklet with cartoon stories
- ○ entertainer who tells funny stories

2. custodian
- ○ person who cleans a large building
- ○ dessert made of milk, eggs, and sugar
- ○ something you do regularly
- ○ arrested by the police

3. reflection
- ○ automatic action such as blinking
- ○ an image on a shiny surface
- ○ shelter from danger or trouble
- ○ to happen again

4. confidence
- ○ organize something and carry it out
- ○ to ask someone's advice
- ○ strong belief in your own abilities
- ○ say that something is definitely true

5. circumference
- ○ distance around something
- ○ cautious or careful
- ○ conditions of an event
- ○ move in a circle or pattern

6. conference
- ○ a famous Chinese philosopher
- ○ mistake one thing for another
- ○ doing what the law requires
- ○ meeting for discussing ideas

7. creature
- ○ living thing
- ○ something that has been made
- ○ using your imagination
- ○ model of the baby Jesus

8. culture
- ○ guilty of doing wrong
- ○ to develop by studying
- ○ way of life, ideas, customs, traditions
- ○ used to make sofas more comfortable

9. sculpture
- ○ confused and disorderly fight
- ○ figure made of wood, metal, or stone
- ○ to examine something closely
- ○ strong feelings about right and wrong

10. accuracy
- ○ performs gymnastic acts
- ○ skin condition from clogged pores
- ○ to admit something
- ○ precision, exactness

Hide and Seek

Play Hide and Seek with your words. Fill in a bar graph (left to right) for each word you spell correctly.

Vocabulary Extension

Cause and Effect

Write a word from the word bank to complete each sentence.

1. If you are using a piece of clear, triangular glass that breaks light up into colors, you are looking through a ________________.
2. If you want to measure something very precisely, you want it to be ________________.
3. If you are reading the book of the Bible that comes before Daniel, you are reading the book of ________________.
4. If you ________________, you try to make something seem bigger, better, or more important than it really is.
5. If you are reading a booklet that has news, articles, photographs, and advertisements, you are reading a ________________.
6. If you are a detective , you will ________________ the evidence carefully.
7. If a company makes, sells or provides a service, it is known as a ________________.
8. If you have painted some pictures that you want to show to the public, you would set up an ________________.
9. If were reading Paul's letter to the people who lived in Ephesus, you would be reading the Bible book of ________________.
10. If you were living in a war zone and heard the sounds of guns and bombings, you would be hearing ________________s.
11. If you are about to dive into a lake that you know is cold, you may pause or ________________ before jumping in.
12. If you live in a neighborhood, you are considered a ________________.

Word Bank

business	exaggerate	explosion	magazine
Ephesians	examine	Ezekiel	prism
exact	exhibit	hesitate	resident

Hide and Seek

Play Hide and Seek with your words. Fill in a bar graph (left to right) for each word you spell correctly.

Vocabulary Extension

Fill in the Blanks

Choose a word from the word bank that best fits each sentence clue.

1. Someone who is attractive in appearance is said to be ________________.
2. This book of the Bible, ________________, comes just before the book of Isaiah.
3. This pancake recipe calls for three teaspoons of baking powder. This is the same as one ________________.
4. A beautiful flower is blooming in the garden. Dad took a ________________ shot of it to get all the details.
5. The sauce didn't taste quite right so Mom added a ________________ of salt.
6. When the factory workers went on strike, many people formed a ________________ to keep anyone from entering the building.
7. My older brothers both married, so I have two ________________.
8. The team captain organized his ________________ for the ice hockey game.
9. We have a computer class at school. We are learning to type faster on the ________________.
10. The new boy in our class likes to draw pictures of airplanes and ________________.
11. One of my favorite classes is physical education. We are learning how to play ________________.
12. We are going camping when school gets out on Friday. It will be a great ________________.

Word Bank

close-up	picket line	spacecraft	teaspoon
handsome	sisters-in-law	tablespoon	volleyball
keyboard	Song of Solomon	teammates	weekend

Hide and Seek

Play Hide and Seek with your words. Fill in a bar graph (left to right) for each word you spell correctly.

Vocabulary Extension

Crossword Puzzle

Use the clues below to complete the puzzle.

Across

2. half of a circle
4. a tent sanctuary used by the Israelites
5. step-by-step, creeping
7. reasonable
10. quadrilateral with four right angles
11. voluntary

Down

1. diary
2. struggle
3. on the outside
6. normal
8. unique, fresh
9. upright

Word Bank

external	logical	original	semicircle
gradual	natural	rectangle	tabernacle
journal	optional	scramble	vertical

Hide and Seek

Play Hide and Seek with your words. Fill in a bar graph (left to right) for each word you spell correctly.

Vocabulary Extension

Trade-off

Choose a word from the word bank to replace the word(s) in parentheses. Write the word in the blank.

1. Several ways to ________________(keep) food include drying, salting, freezing, and canning.
2. Each graduate left a short ________________(pause) before starting down the aisle.
3. The boys have been ________________(prohibited) to climb on the steep, jagged cliffs.
4. The ________________ (main) reason for this meeting is to nominate a mayor for our town.
5. The intense basketball game caused the players to ________________ (sweat) profusely.
6. Our trip to the mountains turned into an exciting ________________ (experience).
7. Fog lay low over the valleys due to so much ________________ (dampness) in the air.
8. After you fill out the form, please place your ________________ (written name) at the bottom.
9. Autumn gives me a lot of ________________ (enjoyment) with its crisp air, colorful leaves, and hayrides at Grandpa's farm.
10. I thought the dog leash was ________________ (fastened), but when I came home, Rover was gone.
11. There are several countries in ________________ (this continent) I would like to visit, such as Germany, Spain, France, and Italy.
12. ________________ (neglecting) to do your homework will result in bad grades.

Word Bank

adventure	forbidden	perspire	primary
Europe	interval	pleasure	secure
failure	moisture	preserve	signature

Hide and Seek

Play Hide and Seek with your words. Fill in a bar graph (left to right) for each word you spell correctly.

Vocabulary Extension

Multiple Choice

Fill in the oval by the word(s) with the same or nearly the same meaning as the word in bold type.

1. conscious
- ⬭ mentally awake or alert
- ⬭ thoughtful, attentive
- ⬭ showing self–importance
- ⬭ taking into account

2. delicious
- ⬭ easily damaged
- ⬭ ready–to–eat food products
- ⬭ pleasing to the taste
- ⬭ harmful, poisonous

3. dangerous
- ⬭ hang loosely with a swinging motion
- ⬭ likely to inflict injury
- ⬭ small missile used in a game
- ⬭ sharp pointed knife for stabbing

4. generous
- ⬭ unusually intelligent person
- ⬭ the origin or beginning of something
- ⬭ bend the knee in worship
- ⬭ free in giving or sharing

5. precious
- ⬭ of great value
- ⬭ undue hastiness
- ⬭ highly accurate
- ⬭ water that falls to earth

6. Celsius
- ⬭ thin transparent wrapping material
- ⬭ scale for measuring temperature
- ⬭ relating to the sky
- ⬭ condemning sternly

7. emptiness
- ⬭ eternal, everlasting
- ⬭ threatened with extinction
- ⬭ wife of an emperor
- ⬭ vacancy, void, hollow

8. loneliness
- ⬭ length of life
- ⬭ isolation, lacking company
- ⬭ to hang around idly
- ⬭ not rigidly fastened

9. readiness
- ⬭ to understand written language
- ⬭ already made up for sale
- ⬭ information printed by a computer
- ⬭ preparedness

10. ugliness
- ⬭ last in a progression
- ⬭ disagreeableness, repulsiveness
- ⬭ an open sore that festers
- ⬭ resentment, taking offense

Hide and Seek

Play Hide and Seek with your words. Fill in a bar graph (left to right) for each word you spell correctly.

Vocabulary Extension

Cause and Effect

Write a word from the word bank to complete each sentence.

1. If you are always talking, your parents say that you are ________________ talking.
2. If you give up winning a race to help someone who has been hurt, you may ________________ the trophy.
3. If you see something that is extremely large, you might call it ________________.
4. If you help a friend dress up for a skit, and she looks completely different, you have helped to ________________ her.
5. If you visit the zoo and see a giant turtle that lives on land, you are watching a ________________.
6. If you are learning the art of Japanese paper folding, you are learning ________________.
7. If you are lying down instead of standing up, you are ________________ instead of vertical.
8. If a submarine sends out an underwater missile that explodes when it hits a target, it is sending out a ________________.
9. If nothing unusual happens today, I would consider it an ________________ day.
10. If a violent, whirling column of air appears as a dark, funnel-shaped cloud, it is called a ________________.
11. If we are making small decorations to hang on a Christmas tree, we are making ________________s.
12. If you have won a prize for your science display, you have won an ________________.

Word Bank

award	forfeit	origami	torpedo
enormous	horizontal	ornament	tortoise
forever	ordinary	tornado	transform

Hide and Seek

Play Hide and Seek with your words. Fill in a bar graph (left to right) for each word you spell correctly.

Vocabulary Extension

Fill in the Blanks

Choose a word from the word bank that best fits each sentence clue.

1. There are more girls in class than boys; girls ________________ boys two to one.
2. My parents give me some money each week. This is my ________________.
3. After the farmer cut his hay, ________________ birds flocked from all around to get hay seeds.
4. We bought our winter clothes on sale. Mom was glad to get a ________________ on them.
5. I love the huge hills around us. I always wanted to live in a ________________ area.
6. When Julie learned to play the clarinet, she was taught how to hold her mouth on the ________________ to get a clear tone.
7. I know you are upset, but you do not need to make such an ________________ in the middle of class.
8. Before we write our three-point paragraph, we have to make an ________________ of the points we will cover.
9. When Heather writes a story, she uses so many ________________s that nobody can tell who is doing what.
10. We drove home by a different ________________ because men were working on a culvert under one of the roads.
11. Jesus traveled to many ________________ villages and towns, preaching and healing the people.
12. His mom says embarrassing things in public. She is much too ________________.

Word Bank

allowance	mountainous	outline	outspoken
countless	mouthpiece	outlying	pronoun
discount	outburst	outnumber	route

Hide and Seek

Play Hide and Seek with your words. Fill in a bar graph (left to right) for each word you spell correctly.

Vocabulary Extension

Crossword Puzzle

Use the clues below to complete the puzzle.

Down

2. sales slip
4. homework
6. smoked sausage

Across

1. from another country
3. run for office
5. pasta
7. serious disease of the lungs
8. slum
9. sharp edged metal blade
10. debt on a house
11. streak of electricity
12. understanding

Word Bank

assignment	foreign	lightning	receipt
bologna	ghetto	mortgage	spaghetti
campaign	knowledge	pneumonia	sword

PLEASE PHOTOCOPY!*

The following pages contain Black Line Masters for use with the ***A Reason For Spelling®*** Student Worktext.

*Photocopy privileges extend only to the material in this section, and permission is granted only for those classrooms or homeschools using ***A Reason For Spelling®*** Student Worktexts. Any other use of this material is expressly forbidden and all copyright laws apply.

Spelling Progress Chart

Fill in the five lesson numbers for the unit in the first row of blocks. Use the first half of the column under each block to record the score for the Preview, and the second half of the column for the Posttest. To record the score, begin at the bottom of the column and color the blanks to show the number of words spelled correctly. Use one color for Preview and another for Postest.

Words Spelled Correctly	Lesson Numbers									
	Preview	Posttest	Preview	Posttest	Preview	Posttest	Preview	Posttest	Preview	Posttest
20.										
19.										
18.										
17.										
16.										
15.										
14.										
13.										
12.										
11.										
10.										
9.										
8.										
7.										
6.										
5.										
4.										
3.										
2.										
1.										

Rubric for Scoring

You may wish to use this rubric at the end of each unit to track student progress.

	Standard	Usually	Sometimes	Not Yet
1.	Writes all letters correctly and legibly (upper and lower case)			
2.	Uses correct spelling on words from current and previous lessons			
3.	Writes a paragraph in response to a prompt			
4.	Uses appropriate punctuation			
5.	Uses capital letters correctly			
6.	Writes complete, coherent, and organized sentences			
7.	Includes descriptive language			
8.	Forms plurals correctly			
9.	Subjects and verbs agree			
10.	Uses a logical sequence of events			

my dictionary
bulb:(n)
bulge:(a)
bulldoz
bulletin:(n)

my journal
March 16

American Sign Language

The American Sign Language alphabet is widely used in communicating with the hearing impaired.

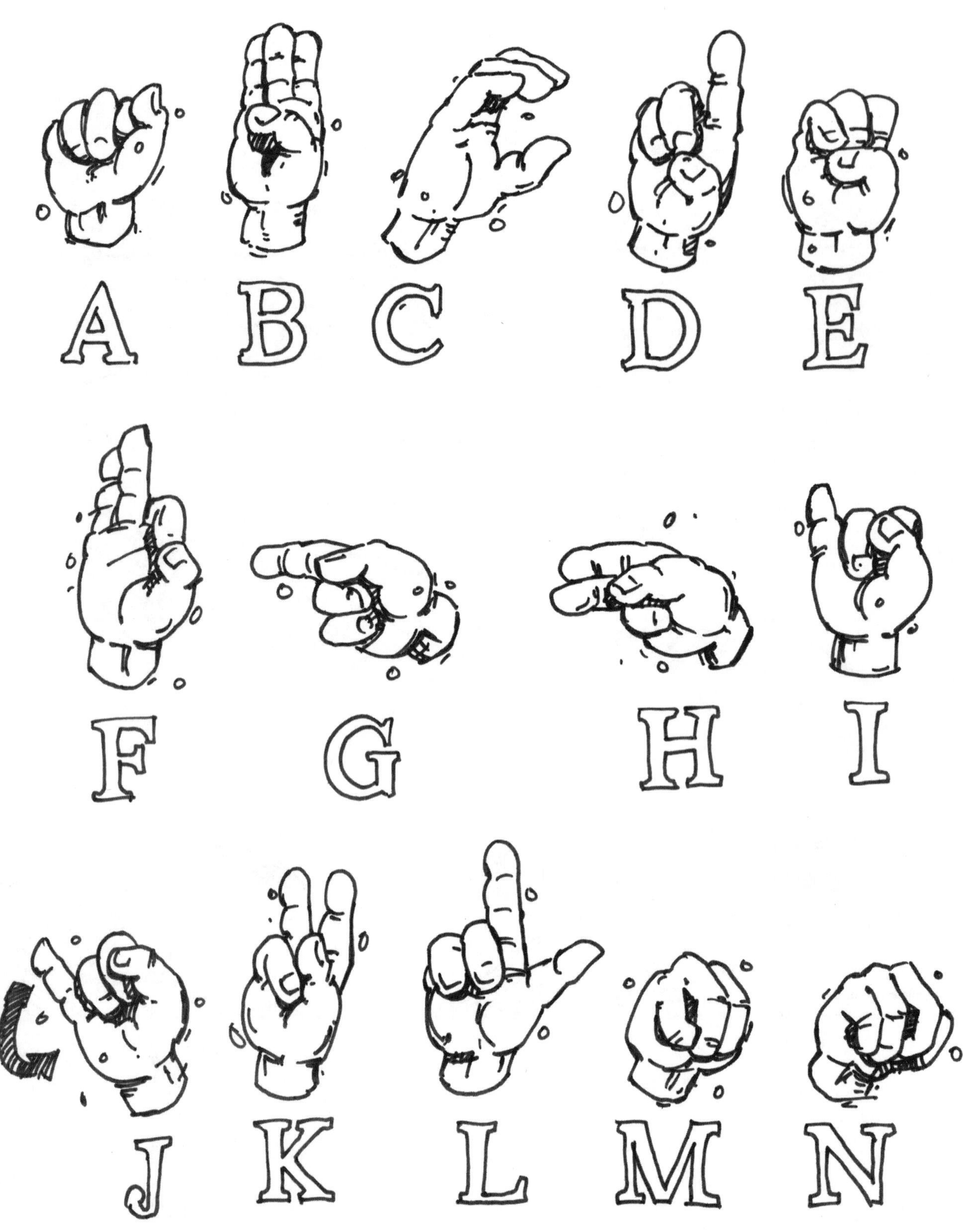

American Sign Language

The American Sign Language alphabet is widely used in communicating with the hearing impaired.

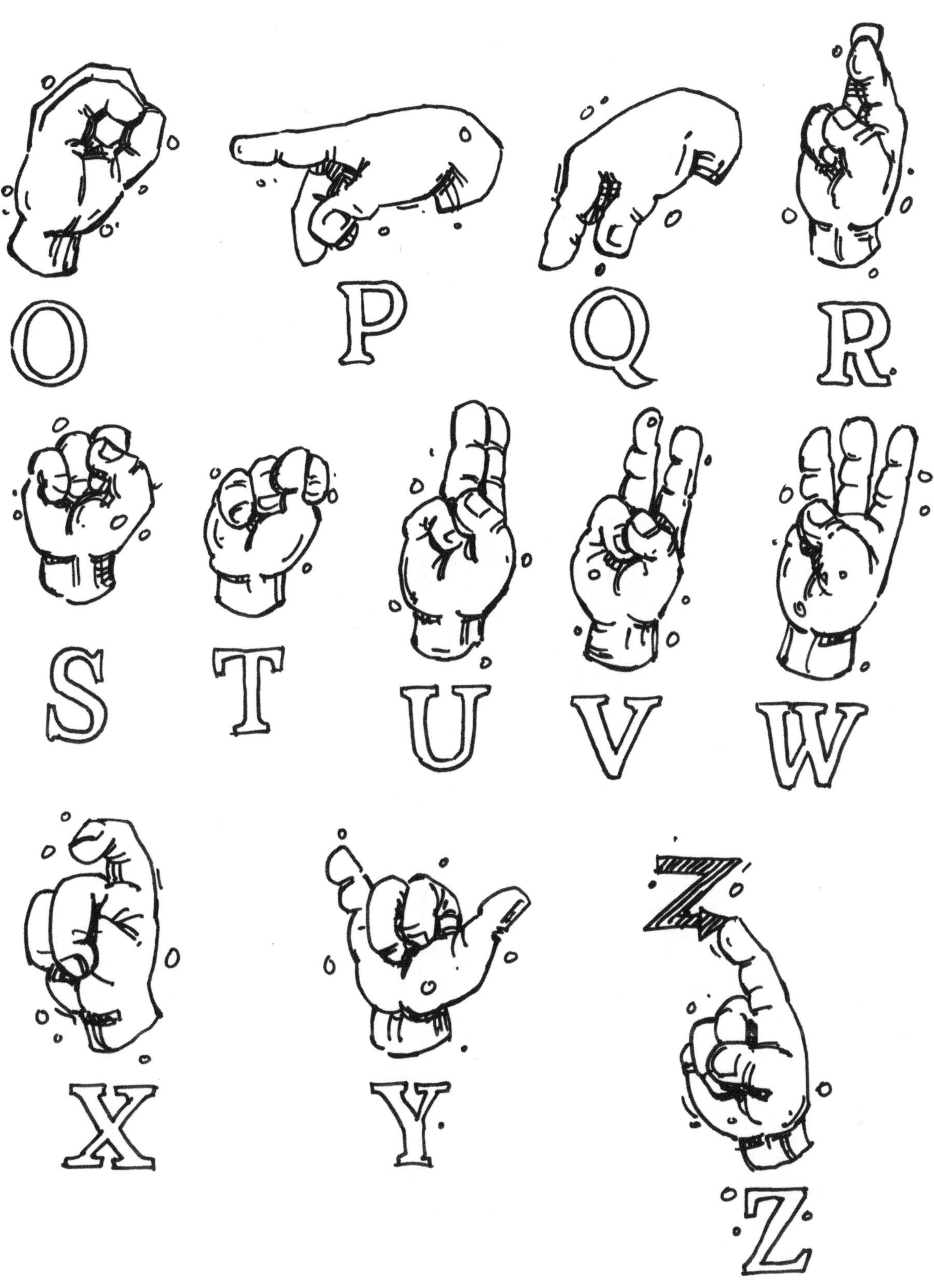

The End